ISBN 978-1-5280-8128-3
PIBN 10927390

This book is a reproduction of an important historical work. Forgotten Books uses state-of-the-art technology to digitally reconstruct the work, preserving the original format whilst repairing imperfections present in the aged copy. In rare cases, an imperfection in the original, such as a blemish or missing page, may be replicated in our edition. We do, however, repair the vast majority of imperfections successfully; any imperfections that remain are intentionally left to preserve the state of such historical works.

# 1 MONTH OF
# FREE
# READING

at

## www.ForgottenBooks.com

By purchasing this book you are eligible for one month membership to ForgottenBooks.com, giving you unlimited access to our entire collection of over 1,000,000 titles via our web site and mobile apps.

To claim your free month visit:

www.forgottenbooks.com/free927390

English
Français
Deutsche
Italiano
Español
Português

# www.forgottenbooks.com

**Mythology** Photography **Fiction**
Fishing Christianity **Art** Cooking
Essays Buddhism Freemasonry
Medicine **Biology** Music **Ancient
Egypt** Evolution Carpentry Physics
Dance Geology **Mathematics** Fitness
Shakespeare **Folklore** Yoga Marketing
**Confidence** Immortality Biographies
Poetry **Psychology** Witchcraft
Electronics Chemistry History **Law**
Accounting **Philosophy** Anthropology
Alchemy Drama Quantum Mechanics
Atheism Sexual Health **Ancient History**
**Entrepreneurship** Languages Sport
Paleontology Needlework Islam
**Metaphysics** Investment Archaeology
Parenting Statistics Criminology
**Motivational**

ALBERT LEONARD—See page 8

RICHARD G. BOONE—1893-1899                    CHARLES McKENNY—1896-1900

ELMER A LYMAN—1899

DWIGHT B. WALDO—1899                    CHARLES T. GRAWN—1900

# SIXTY-THIRD ANNUAL REPORT

OF THE

# SUPERINTENDENT OF PUBLIC INSTRUCTION

OF THE

# STATE OF MICHIGAN

WITH

## ACCOMPANYING DOCUMENTS

FOR

THE YEAR 1899

## BY AUTHORITY

LANSING
ROBERT SMITH PRINTING CO., STATE PRINTERS AND BINDERS
1900

# LETTER OF TRANSMITTAL.

STATE OF MICHIGAN,
DEPARTMENT OF PUBLIC INSTRUCTION.
*Lansing, December 31, 1899.*

To His Excellency, HAZEN S. PINGREE,
      *Governor of the State of Michigan:*

SIR—In compliance with the provisions of law, I have the honor herewith to transmit through you to the Legislature, the annual report of the Superintendent of Public Instruction, together with the accompanying documents for the year 1899.

Very respectfully,

Your obedient servant,

JASON E. HAMMOND,
*Superintendent of Public Instruction.*

# TABLE OF CONTENTS.

# SUPERINTENDENT'S REPORT.

The year 1899 has been a busy one in educational affairs in Michigan. All the departments of education, from the university to the common schools, have felt the influence of returning business life and activity. Although the schools were the last of the numerous interests to suffer from the business depression, they have by no means been the last to feel the enthusiasm and encouragement that comes with the return of business prosperity.

In this report it is my desire to comment upon those features of educational work with which the department has had more or less to do within the calendar year, and my remarks and suggestions are classified under appropriate headings.

### REDUCTION IN SIZE OF DEPARTMENT REPORT.

For several years there has been a strong sentiment in the legislature and among people generally, that there was being printed at public expense, a large number of worthless books and documents, to be scattered broadcast over the state and eventually find their way into waste baskets and furnaces of county buildings. This feeling took definite form in the passage of Act No. 44, Laws of 1899, the purpose of which was to reduce expense in the publication of said reports, documents, pamphlets, etc.

We have no reason to complain of the treatment received from the legislature, as compared with the other state departments; but this department did not escape the general pruning. The result is that our annual report, which had gradually grown till it contained six or seven hundred pages, has been reduced to one of three hundred pages, inclusive of contents and index; and our ingenuity has been somewhat taxed to know what to omit and what to retain. Several changes in the ordinary form have been necessary, and we present this report in its new form, with the foregoing explanation.

### DISTRIBUTION OF STATE MANUAL.

I am very glad to state, however, that in reducing our report the legislature has, on the other hand, been very generous indeed with the schools in re-enacting the resolution of 1897, giving to every school district of the state a copy of the valuable State Manual (Red Book). This act of the legislature has been hailed with satisfaction by all the friends of our schools; and while we suffered in one respect, we feel ourselves great gainers in the other.

I would also state in this connection that the number of volumes of our report has been increased so that there may now be a sufficient number to furnish a copy to every school library in the state and one copy "to each Superintendent of Public Instruction, State University and State Normal School in the United States; each living ex-Superintendent and Deputy Superintendent of Public Instruction in this state; each member of county boards of examiners; each city superintendent of schools; two hundred copies for deposit with the Secretary of State for future distribution, and such number of additional copies as the Superintendent of Public Instruction may, in his discretion, deem necessary, not exceeding three hundred copies." By these provisions the number of copies has been doubled, with the size of the same decreased one-half.

## EDUCATIONAL AND CHARITABLE INSTITUTIONS.

As is well-known, each of the educational and charitable institutions incorporated under the laws of the state, has its separate board of control which semi-annually or biennially makes a somewhat detailed report to the governor and legislature, thus rendering it unnecessary for the department of public instruction to enter into all the details. But in accordance with Section 4803 of the Compiled Laws, a report must be made to this department by every such institution; and in Tables xxiv and xxv of our report may be found certain statistics regarding them, showing the valuation of property, amount of legislative appropriation, income for support, number of students enrolled, number of graduates, and other information of general interest. Elsewhere in this volume is also a brief write-up of all the educational and charitable institutions that are on record in the Secretary of State's office, the number being fifty-seven. By noting the headings it will be seen that a new and more systematic classification of them has been made.

## TEACHERS' INSTITUTES.

The arrangement and management of the state teachers' institute is probably the most important and perplexing question with which the Superintendent of Public Instruction has to deal. No other duty devolving upon him causes so much care and anxiety, such a sense of responsibility, as the planning and conducting of teachers' institutes. The conditions that apply to one portion of the state, do not always fit in other portions; and the general policy formulated in the department office must of necessity be so often modified and changed to meet varying conditions that the more the question is studied, the more perplexing it becomes.

I shall not, in this last year of my administration, attempt to advise future superintendents concerning the improvement of our present institute law. The plain truth is, I do not myself know what would be best along this line. I am certain, however, that the institute law of Michigan enacted in 1877, should be radically changed and strengthened. More money should be raised in some way. Our institutes should not be shorter; they should be longer. The compensation paid should not be diminished; it should be increased. This is one feature of the situation so difficult to handle. Our neighbor states are able to pay more than we. I believe Michigan's institutes have improved every year under our present law, but it seems to me the time is ripe for the adoption of some strong measures to meet the demand of new times and new conditions. Traveling expenses are greater in Michigan than in states geographically more compact in form. There is likewise greater difference in educational conditions than are found in such states as Iowa, Indiana, or Illinois. Therefore, I would earnestly urge that committees of the State Teachers' Association and of the Upper Peninsula Association, give this question very careful and thorough consideration at their next meetings, to the end that the legislature of 1901 may be induced to give more substantial support to teachers' institutes.

### STATE TEACHERS' READING CIRCLE.

I refer in this report to an educational agency that, if properly handled, may be productive of great good to the common school interests of the state. In former reports my comments concerning this work in Michigan, have not been as favorable as was desired by managers of the circle; but, during the past year, I have devoted some careful and conscientious attention to the subject, with a view to giving all possible aid to those persons who were laboring to increase the efficiency of the work. It has been my desire that the managers themselves should evolve such plans as might prove of greatest good to the circle. A year or more ago the commissioners' section of the State Teachers' Association appointed a committee to investigate this matter and advise with the Reading Circle Board concerning advisable amendments to the rules and regulations under which the board had heretofore transacted its business. This committee saw fit to make the Superintendent of Public Instruction ex-officio member of the Reading Circle Board; and in December, 1899, I entered upon my new duties with an earnest desire to make the department as helpful to the commissioners and teachers of the state as might be possible through the agency of the Teachers' Reading Circle.

The books used during the school year of 1899-1900 have been, so far as I can learn, popular books, suited to the majority of those who have purchased and studied them. The work has been carried on with a greater degree of success than during the one or two years immediately perceding, and the outlook for the ensuing year is most promising.

### STATE TEACHERS' ASSOCIATION.

Under this heading I wish to call attention to the necessity for the executive committee to inaugurate some plan whereby all those attending this association shall become members, thereby contributing to its success. Year after year the attendance is several hundred persons, presumably eight or nine hundred, and less than half that number become members of the association or assist in bearing its expense. It seems to me that some plan might be devised similar to the one employed by the National Educational Association, whereby membership tickets are sold at the same time railroad tickets are purchased, and thus the amount of money in the treasury greatly increased. We hear many complaints that teachers come to the association and slip away without contributing their share toward expenses, but very probably the fault lies largely with the management.

I would especially call attention to this important matter, since the action of the legislature now makes it necessary for the Superintendent of Public Instruction to omit the proceedings of the association from his annual report, thus compelling the association itself to bear the entire expense of their publication.

## UPPER PENINSULA TEACHERS' ASSOCIATION.

I am pleased to note that an association has been formed in the Upper Peninsula of Michigan, whereby those too remote from the meeting place of the State Association to attend it, can yet keep in touch with the educational problems of the day.

The last meeting of the Upper Peninsula Teachers' Association was one of the most successful and attractive educational gatherings ever held in Michigan. A more scholarly and better appearing body of teachers than the one recently gathered at Ironwood, very seldom convenes in any portion of our country. The business management of this organization is, in my opinion, in good hands; and the success of the association, both from a business and educational standpoint, is already assured. I feel it my duty, however, to call attention to one feature of the management which may, in future, cause some criticism; namely, the influence of outside parties in determining the policy of this association.

## STATE LIBRARY COMMISSION.

Brief reference is here made to Act No. 115, Laws of 1899, which is an act to promote the establishment and efficiency of free public libraries throughout the state. This act provides for the appointment of four commissioners who, with the State Librarian, shall constitute the board. The present membership of this board is as follows: Ex-Governor Cyrus G. Luce, Coldwater; Hon. Peter White, Marquette; Hon. Henry M. Loud, Oscoda; Hon. John M. C. Smith, Charlotte; Mary C. Spencer, State Librarian, Lansing. The latter is secretary of the board; and those interested in the establishment of free public libraries, will do well to communicate with her for such assistance and encouragement as the library commission may be able to give.

## TEXT-BOOKS.

The legislature of 1899 had under consideration every kind of text-book scheme imaginable. The agitation that followed the passage of the Graham-Forsyth law of 1897, was of great benefit to the state. The more the question was studied in all its details, the more the people were convinced that unformity of text-books by state law was neither desirable nor practicable. One of the first acts of the legislature, therefore, was to repeal, by almost unanimous consent, the entire law of 1897, the same being the much talked-of uniform text-book law with its free text-book *alternative*.

An industrious lobby was present in the Lansing hotels for the promotion of other text-book measures which proposed all manner of plans for the furnishing of text-books to the children of the state. It is needless to add that these bills were evidently not drafted in the interests of the people of the state, but for the furtherance of the business interests of publishers and lobbyists. It is not my intention to comment further in this report upon the merits or demerits of these proposed laws. It is, however, matter of great congratulation that all of them were defeated with such emphasis as to make it a safe prediction that no legislation of any kind looking toward a uniform series of text-books, either by adoption or state publication, will be seriously considered in the near future.

This department was anxious to secure such changes in the free text-book law of 1889 as would simplify the present method of furnishing text-books to such districts as desire to take advantage of its provisions. With this object in mind, the bill known as the "Gillam bill" was prepared in this office—a bill practically the same as the present law with the exception that, under its provisions, it became the duty of all school districts to submit the question of free text-books at each annual school meeting. The other changes made were merely for the purpose of correcting the grammatical and rhetorical mistakes that now exist in the present bungling law on our statute books. So far as I am aware, there were no dangerous nor suspicious clauses or sentences in the entire bill; it was drafted purely with a desire to simplify the law and make it easier of observance. But there seemed to be a feeling among all members of the legislature that all text-book measures of whatever kind should be summarily dealt with. Therefore the Gillam bill met the same fate as the others, and the legislature adjourned with the text-book laws of the state practically the same as before the Graham-Forsyth law was passed in 1897.

I would earnestly recommend that the next legislature pass a law whereby the present free text-book law may more easily be carried into effect. Beyond this the legislature should let text-book laws severely alone. I am more and more convinced that any effort made to enact laws for uniformity or state publication, should be looked upon with suspicion.

### DAY SCHOOLS FOR THE DEAF.

Act No. 176, Laws of 1899, provides that $150 for each pupil shall be paid out of the general fund for the purpose of maintaining day schools for the deaf in the cities of the state. This law may be found on page 105 of the general school laws of 1899, and a careful perusal will give the principle, or theory, upon which these schools have been established in the cities of Detroit and Grand Rapids. There are in each of these schools two teachers and about fifteen pupils. But one room is provided, both teachers working in the same room and doing individual work with the pupils. I have visited both these schools twice; and though not claiming to know much concerning the instruction of the deaf, the apparent results were gratifying; but it is yet too soon to comment specifically concerning the success of the experiment now being tried of giving oral instruction to deaf children. Those interested in securing more definite information concerning these schools, can do so by writing to Supt. W. C. Martindale of Detroit or Supt. F. R. Hathaway of Grand Rapids.

The authority to establish these schools and to fix rules and regulations for their general conduct, was given to the Superintendent of Public Instruction; and we give below the regulations formulated in this office to be accepted by boards of education whenever permission is granted for the establishment of a school under the provisions of this law:

Department of Public Instruction,
Lansing, Mich., Oct. 3, 1899.

To the Board of Education, Grand Rapids, Mich.:

Your request for the establishment of a day school for deaf children in your city is at hand. The act of the legislature of 1899 (No. 176), which gives the superintendent of Public Instruction authority to grant his permission in such cases, has been carefully examined, and it has seemed advisable, in view of certain laws and conditions which exist, to prescribe certain rules or regulations as a uniform system for the entire State.

The law is brief and need not be quoted fully in this communication. We wish briefly to state that, in fixing conditions under which permission will be granted, there is no disposition to evade the law or to impose requirements that are unreasonable or unlawful. We desire simply to harmonize this law with other existing laws, and provide other requirements that the law seems to contemplate.

1. *Boards of Education must advance the funds.* This becomes necessary for one reason, at least. By section 1205 of the compiled laws—which see—a system of accounting to the Auditor General of the state is required, involving more labor than either the Auditor General or the treasurer of a Board of Education will be willing to undertake.

2. *Reports of this Department.* Immediately after the close of the school year and previous to June 30, a complete report, on blanks furnished by this office, must be made by the Board of Education showing—

(a) Name, experience, special qualifications, etc., of each teacher employed, with salary paid.

(b) Name, age, sex, parent or guardian's name, place of residence—street and number—of each pupil in attendance, together with a complete record of attendance at school, days present and days absent. Holidays should be counted as days taught.

(c) The aggregate attendance of all pupils enrolled.

3. *Number of pupils necessary to the establishment of a school.* The law provides that there shall be an average attendance of at least three pupils. No Board of Education shall ask for the establishment of a school unless there are six pupils in the school district eligible to attend such school, and whose parents or guardians agree to send such children to the school.

4. *Non-resident pupils.* No non-resident pupils should be admitted. The State has an institution for the deaf, and day schools should not compete to the extent of receiving non-residents.

5. *Length of the school year.* This is fixed by law at nine months. This department rules that 180 days of attendance (holidays included) shall be the basis on which vouchers for the maximum of $150 per pupil will be allowed.

6. *Qualifications of teachers.* Teachers employed must have had special training in the teaching of the deaf, and one year's experience as a teacher in a school for the deaf. Information as to an applicant's qualification should be furnished this department previous to the making of a contract.

7. *Salaries paid to teachers.* Boards of Education should be as careful in the expenditure of State funds as with the funds of the district, and it is suggested that all teachers in schools for the deaf be employed at a definite salary, and that such salaries be not greater than 25 per cent more than the average salary paid to the other teachers of their schools. For the present year salaries ranging from $600 to $900 should be considered liberal. $100 per month should be the limit under present conditions.

8. *School appliances.* The Board of Education should furnish building or rooms, heating facilities, desks, tables, chairs, black-boards, and such other appliances or apparatus as are usually furnished to the regular public schools. The only appliances paid for out of the State funds should be such as are mentioned in the following list: text-books, pencils, tables, slates, writing material, toys, and apparatus used in schools for the deaf not used in the public schools.

9. *Vouchers.* The vouchers for use in the disbursement of funds from the State will be prepared by the Auditor General. These vouchers should be made up in triplicate each month for the salaries of the month and for any appliances purchased during the month. All vouchers for salaries should state the time covered by the payment and the rate of salary per school year. Those paying for appliances should state the article, the price per unit, number of units, and total for each purchase. These vouchers should be receipted as provided, and the date of payment by the treasurer of the school board should be inserted in the receipt. The Board of Education will preserve one voucher and the other two should be forwarded to this office. We will preserve one and file the other in the office of the Auditor General.

10. *Time and manner of payment.* The aggregate number of days attendance in the school year should be divided by 180 to determine the number of years of attendance, and this quotient multiplied by 150 to find the maximum amount to be audited by the Auditor General. Immediately on receiving the report in June, the Superintendent of Public Instruction will advise the Auditor General as to the maximum amount to be allowed to a Board of Education maintaining a school for the deaf under the provisions of the law. The Auditor General will then examine the vouchers filed in his office and draw his warrant on the State Treasurer for the full amount of the vouchers allowed by him, such amount not to exceed $150 for each 180 days of actual attendance.

Before granting permission for the establishment of a day school for the deaf, I most respectfully request your board to take formal action agreeing to comply with the above requirements.

Yours very truly,
JASON E. HAMMOND.

## MANUAL TRAINING IN THE PUBLIC SCHOOLS.

An examination of the reports published by this department in years past, shows that this question has been under discussion in various forms for the past ten or fifteen years. The more progressive educators of the state, have, during the years when our school courses were being extended by the addition of various branches, quietly and thoroughly studied the necessity for the education of the hand and eye, along with the head. The results in Michigan are just beginning to be manifest. Great progress has been made in neighboring states, but Michigan is just feeling the awakening.

In my report for 1900 this subject will be fully discussed, and the result of investigations to be made by this department will be published in considerable detail. These investigations, which are now in progress, will also be reported in circular form to the commissioners and superintendents throughout the state. This report will therefore contain only brief reference to this question, since, as above stated, it will be exhaustively discussed in the report for 1900.

### THE NORMAL SCHOOLS.

In the following pages are given sketches of the president and principals of the normal schools of the state, together with a brief description of the normal school system as at present organized with Dr. Albert Leonard, late of Syracuse, N. Y., as its official head. (Portraits of these educators appear as the frontispiece of this volume.) Under Dr Leonard's direct charge are the State Normal College at Ypsilanti, the Central State Normal School at Mt. Pleasant, and the Northern State Normal School at Marquette. The State Board of Education will also delegate to Dr. Leonard the visitation of all Michigan colleges having a course in pedagogy, and will place the state teachers' examination in his charge.

Nearly all those who give this report careful perusal, are sufficiently familiar with conditions in Michigan to know that a very small percentage of the teachers employed in the state have had special training for their work. Facts and figures along this line are easily obtainable in the statistical tables of this and previous reports, and therefore such information is not here repeated. Though in 1899 Michigan made a great stride in the matter of furnishing facilities for the professional preparation of teachers, there is still much to be accomplished before she does for her teachers what her neighbor states are doing. Provision should at once be made for the training of teachers who will, in the near future, be called upon to teach the manual, or industrial arts, in the public schools. A new normal, known as the Western State Normal School, should be created; and I venture the suggestion that the wealthy and public spirited citizens of the enterprising city of Muskegon, could easily be persuaded to interest themselves in the establishment of a normal school in that city, and, by some arrangement of mutual profit to city and state, make the magnificent Hackley Manual Training School a prominent part of the institution. I also believe that there is a strong impression on the part of the educators of the state that a manual training department s be added to the State Normal College.

Before leaving this subject, I wish to recommend amendments to the ill-advised law of 1897 (Act No. 175), by the provisions of which only short term certificates may be granted by the authorities of the Central State Normal School. The law creating the Northern State Normal School places the latter institution under the same provision; and this law, if not repealed altogether, should be so amended as to authorize the granting of life certificates and diplomas from every normal school in the state.

---

## THE NORMAL SCHOOL SYSTEM OF MICHIGAN.

---

### DR. ALBERT LEONARD, YPSILANTI, PRESIDENT.

#### *Biographical.*

The recently elected head of Michigan's normal school system is in life's prime, being but forty-two years old.

Dr. Leonard completed his elementary education in his native state of Ohio and entered Ohio University, where, in connection with the regular classical course, he took a. four years' course in pedagogy.

From 1889 to 1893 he was principal of the high school at Dunkirk, N. Y., after which he so successfully filled the principalship of the central high school at Binghampton, N. Y., that in June, 1897, he was made professor of pedagogy in Syracuse University and Dean of the faculty of the College of Liberal Arts.

His work as editor of the widely known *Journal of Pedagogy*, published at Syracuse, has still farther extended his reputation as an educator.

Dean Leonard comes to his new field of labor well qualified, both by education and experience, for the responsible position he has accepted.

---

The legislative act of 1849 that established our first normal school, also created the State Board of Education,—a body that has watched and guided the evolution of our normal work until, with the addition of two new schools, there has grown up a symmetrical system whose crowning feature is the Normal College at Ypsilanti.

The first code of rules adopted placed the internal affairs of the normal in the hands of the teaching body, with the principal as executive officer; and, with the passing years, the management remained practically unchanged, save that the principal was given some judicial authority, with an advisory "Normal Council" which should make certain recommendations to the board and advise with the principal on such matters as he should submit to them.

At first the school was conducted more like a continuous teachers' institute, but soon a more definite course of study was laid out which, by discussion and experimentation, gradually widened to meet the needs of the school, until at last many of the *special* courses were merged in one prescribed course with optional electives, and the different courses have now crystallized into the following:

1. The general degree course of two years.
2. The specializing degree course of two years.

3. The general diploma course of four years.

4. A four year specializing course.

5. Course of one year for college graduates.

(Partial courses not leading to diploma or certificate, may be taken by permission.)

It was in 1897, after the organization of the Central Normal School at Mt. Pleasant, that the legislature passed "An act to fix the relations of the existing normal schools of the state," its intent being "to maintain substantial uniformity and reciprocity" in the courses of the two normal schools; to provide for the renewal of two and three year certificates by the State Board of Education and the granting of five-year and life certificates by the Ypsilanti Normal. And in 1899 the latter institution was dignified by the legislature's bestowing upon it the title of Michigan State Normal College.

In the spring of 1899 State Superintendent Hammond became so impressed with the desire on the part of progressive school superintendents working in the smaller towns of the state, to avail themselves during summer vacations of the advantages offered by the Normal College, that he presented the following resolution to the Board of Education, the same being unanimously adopted:

*Resolved*, that the Normal College work be reorganized upon the basis of four terms, or quarters, of twelve weeks each, in the year; that three-quarters—any three-quarters—constitute the academic year, or the unit of employment for members of the faculty; that the several quarters begin on the first Tuesday of January, April, July, and October; that the entrance fee be three ($3.00) dollars for each quarter; and that the corps of teachers be so engaged that each teacher may, at his discretion, be absent one quarter each calendar year, without prejudice to his position—substitutions in case of absence to be made satisfactory to the President and State Board of Education.

Though the above policy has been inaugurated only at Ypsilanti, it will doubtless become a feature of the entire system that will greatly extend the usefulness of our normal schools.

When the Northern Normal School was established at Marquette, the need of still farther unifying the normal work and guarding against possible rivalry, led the Board of Education to make other modifications of the system, and the general policy adopted made some changes in the internal management of the Normal College, as will be seen from the following resolutions advocated by E. F. Johnson and F. A. Platt, and unanimously adopted June 23, 1899:

Whereas, in the judgment of the State Board of Education, by reason of the rapid growth of the Normal School interests in this State, it has become necessary to unite all the Normal Schools of the State and to place them under one general control, or supervision, in order that they may be more efficient in their work, to increase their influence upon the educational interests and welfare of the State, and to bring them into a closer relation with each other, to the end that the various departments of work in the various schools may be co-ordinated and subordinated and that the work may be duplicated as little as desirable; therefore, be it

*Resolved* by the State Board of Education:

1st. That there be elected a man whose official title shall be that of "President of the Normal Schools of Michigan," who shall have general supervisory control of the educational welfare and of all the State Normal Schools of the State of Michigan, and who shall have power, subject to the approval of the State Board of Education and together with the advice and counsel of the principal of said school, to prescribe courses of instruction for said system of schools, to recommend men and women for the various positions of instruction, and to dismiss the same when their services cease to be efficient for the best interests of the State or for any other just and reasonable cause.

2d. That there shall be elected by the said Board of Education a person for each of the State Normal Schools whose official title shall be "Principal of the .......... ...... School," and who shall, subject to the co-operation of the "President of the ....mal Schools of Michigan," have supervisory control of the particular school f has been elected, during the absence of the said president.

3d. That it shall be the duty of the "President of the Normal Schools to give one or more courses of instruction in each of the said schools v

the general subjects of philosophy, theory and art of teaching, and the history of education, which courses shall constitute a part of the course of instruction in the particular
school.

4th. That the "President of the Normal Schools of Michigan" shall be paid a salary
and necessary expenses incurred in the management of the said schools, which salary
shall be paid out of the funds of the various schools in proportion to the appropriation
for current expenses for the particular term:

(a) $............ out of the funds of the State Normal College.
(b) $............ out of the funds of the Central State Normal School.
(c) $............ out of the funds of the Northern State Normal School.

5th. That it shall be the duty of the president to keep the State Board of Education
informed at all times, upon request, concerning the courses of instruction, professors
and teachers, number of students, receipts and disbursements, and general needs of the
schools, etc., and shall annually, at the close of each school year, make a detailed report
to the State Board of Education concerning the general welfare and needs of each of the
various schools, which reports shall be spread upon the records of said board.

6th. That it shall be the duty of the president, with the approval of the Board of
Education, together with the advice and counsel of said principal, to so arrange, subordinate, and co-ordinate the courses of instruction in each of the various Normal
Schools of the State, that there shall be an interchange of credits between all of the
said schools.

From these prefatory remarks regarding the general policy and management of the system, we will pass to a more specific account of each school.

---

## STATE NORMAL SCHOOL (COLLEGE).

---

### *Biographical.*

#### RICHARD G. BOONE, PRINCIPAL (PRESIDENT), 1893-1899.

Dr. Boone, being of Quaker parentage, received his early education at the Friend's
Academy, Spiceland, Ind., and began teaching in the rural schools at the early age of
seventeen.

From 1871 to 1876 he had charge of graded and high schools in his native state, and then
became superintendent of schools at Frankfort, Ind. Being next invited to organize the
Department of Pedagogy in Indiana University, he was for a year head of that department, and was also acting professor of philosophy in the University, after which he was
granted a year's absence for philosophical study at Johns Hopkins University, and shortly
afterward became professor of pedagogy at Bloomington, Ill.

In 1893 he was chosen as head of the Normal School at Ypsilanti, retaining this position
for six years and then accepting the superintendency of the Cincinnati public schools.

His six years' administration at Ypsilanti was an energetic one, his broad knowledge
of educational interests enabling him to infuse new life into the school and gain such a
grasp of affairs as tended to modernize the methods and unify the work. The policy
outlined and inaugurated by Dr. Boone has proven itself of great value. His recognition
of intellectual differences among students and the offering of electives and options,
encouraged the fitting for definite lines of work; during his administration there was
a ten per cent increase in enrollment and a twenty-four per cent increase in attendance.

In the midst of a busy life Dr. Boone has found time to publish his well-known "Education in the United States," and another book entitled "History of Education in Indiana."
For the past twenty-five years he has also been prominent as institute director in many
states, and as member of various educational bodies. He deservedly ranks as one of the
foremost educators in the United States.

#### ELMER A. LYMAN, PRINCIPAL, 1899.

The present principal of the Normal College was born at Manchester, Vt., July 27, 1861.
Moving to Indiana in 1869, he lived the life of a farmer lad till seventeen years old, then
entered the Kendallville public school to prepare for college.

In 1886 he graduated from Ann Arbor with the degree of A. B., and for the next four years engaged in teaching, first as assistant superintendent at Paola, Kansas, then as high school principal at Troy, Ohio.

In 1890 he returned to the Michigan University as instructor in mathematics, and for several years also did graduate work in mathematics and astronomy, besides acting from '93 to '96 as chairman of the University Summer School.

In connection with Prof. Goddard of the University, he has prepared a work on higher algebra, a trigonometry, and a set of computation tables.

In 1896 he was made professor of mathematics in the State Normal College, and in 1899, when the new normal system went into effect, was elected as principal of the Normal College and continued as professor of mathematics. Thus a new and most promising era in the history of the Normal College begins with another experienced and able man in charge of the work.

———

Michigan has the distinction of having organized the fourth normal school in the United States; for on October 5, 1852, occurred the dedicatory exercises of the first normal building erected at Ypsilanti. This building costing $20,296.64, was burned in 1859, with all its contents save a little chemical and physical apparatus; but the work of restoration was pushed with such vigor that a new and improved building was ready for the spring term of 1860.

As early as 1859 efforts were made to secure a gymnasium; and the legislature failing to respond, a somewhat primitive building was finally erected by means of funds that the State Board managed to save from the regular appropriation. But again a fiery disaster occurred, and in August, 1873, the "old gym." went up in smoke. Though for years intermittent efforts were made to secure a new gymnasium, it was not till 1893 that they were crowned with success, at which time an appropriation of $20,000 was secured for the model building wherein is now taught that physical culture which helps to secure "a sound mind in a sound body."

It is worthy of note that the public spirited citizens of Ypsilanti voluntarily came to the assistance of the Board with funds for the purchase of a suitable site for this building, the original grounds not being sufficiently large. And the Lecture Association of the school faculty contributed $500 towards the same purpose, besides over $1,000 for necessary apparatus.

In 1865 there was begun on the Normal School grounds, through the joint efforts of the State Board of Agriculture and the citizens of Ypsilanti, a building to be known as the "Normal Museum." But numerous delays and obstacles intervening, the Agricultural Society became discouraged; and in 1868, after an expenditure of $3,250, all claims to said building were assigned to the State Board of Education, the legislature subsequently allowing $7,500 for its completion and also reimbursing the Board of Agriculture for the amount originally expended. Thus the completed edifice was christened the "New Normal Building," and up to 1882 was devoted to the use of the training school, being since then known as the "Conservatory of Music."

In 1874 the need for more room became so evident that the legislature was asked for $30,000, though the amount was not secured until 1877. Then the original building was so enlarged and remodeled as to ( l an expense of $43,347.18, the amount exceeding the appropriation ing taken from an accumulated current expense fund, while some ~e $2,000 was contributed by generous Ypsilantians.

The continued growth of the school induced the legislature of 1881 to make another appropriation, this time of $25,000; and a large rear addition was made to the main building. In 1883, $7,700 was granted for a third addition, while in 1886 the legislature yielded to urgent requests for an appropriation of $60,000, with which large wings having connecting corridors, were erected on the north and south sides of the old center building, a separate boiler house being put up and equipped with heating apparatus. In 1892 two smaller additions were made for lavatories and closets; and so, by successive degrees, the unpretentious building of 1852 has grown into the commodious and imposing main building of today.

The legislature of 1895 granted $25,000 for the erection of a separate training school building, and again the citizens of Ypsilanti showed their public spirit by purchasing and donating a most desirable site adjoining the old campus, paying therefor $8,500. The plans at first adopted for this building being found to call for more than the amount appropriated, it was completed under reduced plans and within the appropriation in such a way as to accommodate a large part of the training school, with the expectation of enlarging it at some future time along the lines of the original plans.

In 1897 an appropriation of $15,000 was granted for a new boiler house, while in 1899 $15,000 more was given to complete the training school building.

Starkweather Hall, the beautiful home of the Student's Christian Association, is the outcome of a mass meeting held in 1892, at which $960 was pledged toward an Association Hall. Gradually interest in the project grew and the funds increased until, in 1895, the gift of $10,000 made the fulfilment of their dreams possible, and the building was named in grateful remembrance of the generous donor, Mrs. Mary Starkweather of Ypsilanti.

So has this institution grown from small beginnings, until today Michigan may well be proud of her finely equipped Normal College, with its beautiful campus, spacious buildings, and able faculty. It is the largest institution of its kind in the country, the enrollment for 1899 passing the thousand mark.

---

## CENTRAL MICHIGAN NORMAL SCHOOL.

---

*Biographical.*

### CHAS. McKENNY, PRINCIPAL, 1896-1900.

Charles McKenny, who has recently been called to the presidency of the Milwaukee State Normal School, was born Sept. 5, 1860, in a log house in Eaton county, Michigan. His boyhood was mostly spent upon a farm, and his early education was gained in the district school.

At seventeen years of age he entered Agricultural College, like many of the students teaching school during the winter months. Graduating in 1881, he taught for three years in the eighth grade of the Charlotte schools, going from there to Vermontville, where he was for two years in charge of the public schools. While here he was elected member of the Eaton County Board of School Examiners, holding this position for eleven years.

Entering Olivet College in 1887, he completed the classical course in 1889 and was for seven years a teacher in the college, finally holding the Chair of History, which was created for him. On the death of Joseph Estabrook, he became head of the Normal Department.

Since 1889 he has also been a popular institute worker, and in 1896 was a prominent candidate for Superintendent of Public Instruction, but withdrew to accept the principalship of the Central State Normal School, which then enrolled only 84 students and now numbers over 400. To this institution Mr. McKenny has for nearly four years devoted his best talents and efforts. He possesses great personal magnetism, and has succeeded in so imbuing the entire student body with his own enthusiasm for learning that the school has come to be noted for the earnest, helpful spirit of co-operation existing between teachers and students.

In addition to his educational duties, Mr. McKenny has been an active religious worker, having preached almost continually from 1890 to 1897, in 1892 being regularly ordained to the ministry by the Congregational body.

He enters upon his new duties in April, 1900, and numerous friends rejoice in his deserved promotion, while regretting his departure from Michigan. The State of Wisconsin has great cause for congratulation over securing the services of so able an educator.

## CHAS. T. GRAWN, PRINCIPAL, 1900.

The parents of Charles T. Grawn came from Sweden in 1855, and settled on a farm in Washtenaw county, Michigan, where in 1857 the subject of this sketch was born. Gaining a common school education in the district school and the Newaygo high school, he entered the Normal School at Ypsilanti and graduated from the classical course in 1880. For the next four years he was in charge of the schools at Plymouth, in 1884 going thence to Traverse City, where he labored for five years, becoming known as one of Michigan's most efficient city superintendents.

In June. 1899, he was made superintendent of the Normal College training school, remaining until February, 1900, when he accepted an appointment to succeed Principal McKenny at the Central Normal School.

---

The idea of establishing a normal school at Mt. Pleasant first originated in the mind of Hon. S. W. Hopkins, a prominent resident of that city, who in 1891 gained the co-operation of eleven leading business men and formed the Mt. Pleasant Improvement Company, with the avowed object of establishing another normal school. Fifty-two acres of land adjoining the city was bought, and the land platted as the Normal School Addition. A fine campus of ten acres, with a beautiful grove of native trees, was reserved as the site of the proposed building; and the rest was divided into 224 residence lots, most of which found ready sale at $110 each, the remainder selling later for $150. This fund was increased by 143 citizens becoming shareholders in the Improvement Company at $25 per share, and preparations were soon made for the erection of a building whose corner stone was laid November 15, 1892.

Meantime, Prof. C. F. R. Bellows of Ypsilanti, who had already contemplated a Normal School movement for Northern Michigan, was interested in the scheme and engaged as principal of the new school which, pending the completion of the building, was opened in rooms fitted up over one of the business blocks. On June 21, 1893, the closing exercises of the first school year were held in the new building in connection with the dedicatory exercises, with a class of twenty graduates.

The next year a Kindergarten Department was added; the third year the Commercial Department was discontinued, and a "Model District School Department" was organized for observation work and practice.

During the legislative session of 1893, Mr. Hopkins labored untiringly to secure state adoption of the school, though the bill failed to pass the House. Hard times coming on, the future of the school trembled in the balance; but the untiring citizens supplemented the receipts by purchasing scholarships at $25 each and so kept the school running until in 1895 when a bill was successfully carried through both House and Senate, the former by Hon. Robt. Brown of Isabella County, the latter by Hon. E. O. Shaw of Newaygo, each asking the acceptance by the state of the buildings and grounds for normal school purposes. However, this bill contained no provisions for the maintenance of the school; and the people of Mt. Pleasant were once more obliged to pledge the amount, over and above tuition, necessary to carry it on. In this connection the services of Judge Peter F. Dodds were invaluable in soliciting and collecting this amount, and at last the State Board of Education assumed control of the work, the school opening under state auspices on September 11, 1895.

In September, 1896, Prof. Chas. McKenny of Olivet College was installed as principal with ten assistant faculty members and six teachers in the training school. A "Graded School Course" was organized, and arrangement made for ten-week classes in the "Rural School Course," for review purposes of more advanced students. A Musical Course was also arranged. In 1897 the legislature showed its faith in the school by granting an appropriation of $24,000.

The three years of Mr. McKenny's administration were successful ones during which there was steady growth in enrollment and faculty; and in 1899 the legislature expressed increasing confidence by appropriating $90,000 for running expenses and $43,000 for building purposes, thus enabling the Central Normal School to keep pace with its increasing needs. The enrollment for 1899 was 410.

## NORTHERN STATE NORMAL SCHOOL.

*Biographical.*

### DWIGHT B. WALDO, PRINCIPAL, 1900.

Principal Waldo of the new Normal School was born at Arcade, Wyoming county, N. Y., in 1864. Moving with his parents to Plainwell, Michigan, in 1873, he graduated from the public school there in 1879.

He was a student of the Michigan Agricultural College from 1881 to 1883, after which he took a four year course at Albion College, paying special attention to history and civics. After graduation he taught history and German in the preparatory department of the college.

In January, 1890, he entered the graduate department of Harvard University for special work in American history and economics, and the following year accepted a call to become instructor in these two branches at Beloit College, Wisconsin.

In 1892 he was elected to the chair of political science and economics at Albion, where he remained until his recent call to the principalship of the Northern Normal. Mr. Waldo has entered with great zeal into the numerous details incident to starting a new educational institution, his tact and ability gaining him many friends and awakening much enthusiastic interest in the new enterprise.

It was in 1893, after various unavailing attempts, that a strong effort was made to bring the advantages of a normal school within the reach of Upper Peninsula teachers, at which time Hon. F. C. Chamberlain introduced a bill for that purpose which failed of passage by only a few votes. Again, in the sessions of both '95 and '97, Mr. Chamberlain labored in vain for his Normal School bill; but in 1899 his efforts, aided by those of John R. Gordon and others, were finally rewarded with success, and the Northern Normal School was located at Marquette.

The Marquette Land and Improvement Company joined with Hon. J. M. Longyear in donating a fine building site of twenty acres, the city also giving $5,000 towards beautifying the grounds. The legislature appropriated $10,000 for running expenses, and $25,000 for a suitable building which is now in process of construction. The full plan adopted, contemplates a structure costing not less than $125,000, and the part this year erected will eventually become a wing of the main building.

Temporary quarters having been fitted up in the City Hall, the first term of the new normal opened most auspiciously, September 19, 1899, with an enrollment the first week of 55, or ten more than was the attendance at the great Milwaukee Normal during its first year. By the holidays this number had increased to 75, and the Northern Normal is already on the high road to success.

(We here insert a short history of the persistent struggle made by Upper Peninsula people to secure this Normal School. It was written by the Hon. Peter White of Marquette, who is the senator referred to in this article.)

"We believe that the initial point, the time when the idea was first advanced that the Upper Peninsula should or ought to have a State Normal, was at the Legislative session of 1875. The Upper Peninsula Senator from the thirty-second senatorial district on the twelfth of March, 1875, introduced a bill in the State Senate 'To establish a branch of the State Normal School in the Upper Peninsula to be known as the Upper Peninsula State Normal School.' This bill made no appropriation of money, and by its terms it would appear that the State was not expected at any time to appropriate anything out of the state treasury for its support or maintenance. The second section provided that three commissioners were to be appointed, two of whom should reside in the Upper Peninsula, and this board was given power "to receive donations of lands, money, or building materials, and to establish a site. The fifth section provided for an appropriation of 'thirty sections of land to be taken from the school lands of the Upper Peninsula,' the interest only of the fund created by the sale of these school lands to be used to construct the necessary buildings and carry on the school. If donations of money should be received, of course that would increase the fund and the probable chances of its beggarly existence. The tenth section provided that when the buildings were ready for pupils, thenceforth it should be under the care, management, and control of the State Board of Education, and it should form a branch of the State Normal School at Ypsilanti; and the principal of that school was to deliver a course of lectures twice in each year to the Upper Peninsula branch, his expenses to be paid by said branch. As we look at the matter now in 1900, it would have required some years to acquire the money necessary to build the Normal School buildings and at the same time have enough to maintain and carry on the educational work. One would have thought such a bill would not encounter any opposition; but no, it passed the Senate by only a fair majority, and within two days brought to Lansing the principal of the Ypsilanti Normal and all his professors, two or three influential professors of the State University accompanying them to kill the bill before it could pass the House of Representatives. And they succeeded. The Normal School principal went before the Committee on Education and talked long and eloquently to the effect that 'another normal in the state would weaken the one we had, and in the end ruin would come to both.' As these lobbyists were experienced educators, no argument could combat their expert judgment; and the bill was killed and no other bill was ever introduced on the same lines.

Numerous bills were introduced in subsequent legislatures, notably in 1893 and 1895. Vigorous push was made by friends of the Upper Peninsula to secure the prize; but the efforts of Mt. Pleasant and other places defeated us, and in 1895 Mt. Pleasant secured the passage of the bill providing for the second normal school in the State. No sooner was the second one established than everybody, both in the Upper and Lower Peninsula, educators and citizens generally, conceded that there should be a normal in the Upper Peninsula.

The Northern Normal owes much for its existence to the Upper Peninsula Educational Association. Its annual sessions were attended by Superintendent of Public Instruction Hammond, Acting-President Hutchins of the University, Professor Hinsdale of Ann Arbor, Dr. Boone, principal of the Ypsilanti Normal, and many teachers and friends of education of the Northern Peninsula, in the years 1898 and 1899. At both of these meetings the subject was discussed at great length, resolutions favoring and demanding were adopted, and all present at each session pledged their efforts to do all that could be done to accomplish the object; so, after prodigious efforts by almost everybody at the legislative session of 1899, it became an accomplished fact."

### DEPARTMENT OF PEDAGOGY AT UNIVERSITY OF MICHIGAN.

Act No. 144, Laws of 1891, authorizes the faculty of the Department of Literature, Science, and the Arts, in Michigan University, to grant a teachers' certificate, good anywhere in the state, to every person receiving a bachelor's, master's, or doctor's degree, who shall also complete a certain prescribed course in the science and art of teaching.

Though not properly a part of the normal school system, this law deserves mention in this connection as being one agency whereby teachers' ranks are filled.

### DEPARTMENT OF PEDAGOGY IN DENOMINATIONAL COLLEGES.

Act No. 136, Laws of 1893, confers upon the State Board of Education power to grant a teacher's certificate to graduates recommended by the faculty of any Michigan college having a course of study of not less than four years (in addition to the work necessary for admission to the University), and in addition thereto a course in the science and art of teaching approved by the State Board and requiring at least one college year of five and one-half hours each week.

Under this law 332 college certificates have been granted, distributed among graduates from different colleges as follows: Adrian, 47; Albion, 67; Alma, 14; Benzonia, 4; Hillsdale, 60; Kalamazoo, 30; Olivet, 110.

### GRANTING OF CERTIFICATES BY STATE BOARD OF EDUCATION.

Since 1867 the Board of Education has granted state certificates under certain regulations that have, from time to time, varied somewhat, the total number granted to July 1, 1899, being 384.

The law at present giving this authority is known as "An act to revise and consolidate the laws relative to the State Board of Education," the same being Act No. 194, Laws of 1889. Examinations are held in August and December, and the following extract from a circular sent out twice each year by the State Board of Education, will show the requirements for these certificates:

State certificates will be granted to teachers of approved qualifications, in accordance with section 1826 of the Compiled Laws, which reads as follows:
"The State Board of Education shall hold at least two meetings each year, at which they shall examine teachers and shall grant certificates to such as have taught in the schools of the State at least two years, and who shall, upon a thorough and critical examination in every study required for such certificate, be found to possess eminent scholarship, ability, and good moral character. Such certificate shall be signed by the members of said board and be impressed with its seal, and shall entitle the holder to teach in any of the public schools of this State without further examination, and shall be valid for life unless revoked by said board. No certificate shall be granted except upon the examination herein prescribed:
"*Provided*, That graduates of the literary and scientific departments of the University and of incorporated colleges of the State, shall not be required to teach as preliminary to taking such examination and certificate."
The State Board of Education, in order to carry into effect the provisions of this law, will require of each applicant for a certificate:
1. Written testimonials from responsible persons as to the moral character of the applicant.
2. Testimonials from present or former employers as to success in teaching.
3. A statement by the applicant of the length of time taught.
4. Each applicant to pass a satisfactory examination in orthography, reading, penmanship, arithmetic, algebra, geometry, grammar, geography, United States history, general history, civil government, theory and art of teaching, physics, physiology and hygiene, botany, zoology, geology, chemistry, rhetoric, general literature, and the school law of Michigan.

### INDORSEMENT OF CERTIFICATES AND DIPLOMAS GRANTED IN OTHER STATES.

The law providing for the granting of state certificates on examination, also provides that the State Board may, in its discretion, endorse state certificates or normal school diplomas granted in other states, if it be shown to the satisfaction of such board that the examinations required or courses of study pursued are fully equal to the requirements of Michigan. Fifty-seven such indorsements have been given, and the states with which reciprocal relations now exist are the following: Minnesota, New York, New Jersey, North and South Dakota, Oregon, Pennsylvania, Washington, Wisconsin.

## EDUCATIONAL FUNDS.

### PRIMARY SCHOOL FUNDS.

*Seven per cent fund:*

| | | |
|---|---:|---:|
| Amount on which State pays interest, June 30, 1899 | 3,947,232 11 | |
| Due from perchasers of lands, June 30, 1899...... | 107,612 09 | |
| Total seven per cent fund, June 30, 1899...... | | $4,054,844 20 |

*Five per cent fund:*

| | | |
|---|---:|---:|
| Amount on which State pays interest, June 30, 1899........... | | 846,778 52 |
| Total school funds, June 30, 1899........................ | | $4,901,622 72 |

### INCOME ON PRIMARY SCHOOL INTEREST FUND.

| | | |
|---|---:|---:|
| Interest paid by State on 7 per cent fund during year ending June 30, 1899.............................. | $271,549 39 | |
| Interest and penalty paid by holders of lands on 7 per cent fund during year ending June 30, 1899........ | 9,564 38 | |
| Interest paid by State on 5 per cent fund............. | 41,818 52 | |
| Total income from both funds............................ | | $322,932 29 |
| Surplus of specific taxes transferred................. | $648,857 11 | |
| Paid by trespassers on school land................... | 627 25 | |
| Total ............................. ..................... | | 649,484 36 |
| Total income for year ending June 30, 1899...................... | | $972,416 65 |

### UNIVERSITY FUND.

| | | |
|---|---:|---:|
| Amount on which State pays interest June 30, 1899.... | $533,904 00 | |
| Interest paid by State ......................................... | | $37,303 08 |
| Interest and penalty paid by holders of lands..................... | | 1,187 12 |
| Total income for year ending June 30, 1899............... | | $38,490 20 |

### AGRICULTURAL COLLEGE FUND.

| | | |
|---|---:|---:|
| Amount on which State pays interest June 30, 1899.... | $725,843 81 | |
| Interest paid by State......................................... | | $46,315 76 |
| Interest and penalty paid by holders of lands...................... | | 5,870 98 |
| Paid by trespassers on lands................................... | | 369 87 |
| Received from United States government....................... | | 24,000 00 |
| Total income for year ending June 30, 1899................ | | $76,556 61 |

### NORMAL SCHOOL FUND.

| | | |
|---|---:|---:|
| Amount on which State pays interest June 30, 1899.... | $66,245 12 | |
| Interest paid by State......................................... | | $3,969 92 |
| Interest and penalty paid by holders of lands..................... | | 224 88 |
| Total income for year ending June 30, 1899............... | | $4,194 80 |

JASON E. HAMMOND,
*Superintendent of Public Instruction.*

## HISTORY OF THE ORIGIN OF EDUCATIONAL FUNDS OF MICHIGAN.

DR. DANIEL PUTNAM, YPSILANTI.

### I.

At the close of the War of the Revolution the territory west of Pennsylvania and north of the Ohio River was claimed by the states of Virginia, Connecticut, and Massachusetts, by virtue of original grants, charters, and purchase. Even before the close of the war the most far-sighted statesmen of that day reached the conclusion that it would be greatly to the advantage of the country as a whole, if the individual states would cede this western territory to the Congress of the Confederacy, to be disposed of for the benefit of all the states alike.

In 1780 Congress invited the states having claims upon these lands to make such cession. After considerable negotiation Virginia finally ceded her claims in 1784, Massachusetts in 1785, and Connecticut in 1786. Virginia retained a small portion of her lands; this portion was known as the "Military Reservation." Connecticut retained the ownership of the "Western Reserve," so-called, consisting of the territory between Lake Erie and the forty-first parallel of latitude, and extending westward one hundred twenty miles from the western boundary of Pennsylvania.

### II.

The question of the disposition of these lands caused much discussion in Congress, and propositions of various kinds were introduced and considered. We are here concerned only with the propositions which in some way had relation to education.

The first proposition to appropriate, or set apart, lands for educational purposes was made in 1783; but no action was taken upon the proposition at that time. This proposition was introduced by a motion of Colonel Bland, a delegate from Virginia, and had reference to the founding of "Seminaries," or higher institutions of learning, and not to the support of common schools.

Various circumstances induced Congress to adopt an ordinance, in the early months of the year 1785, which contained the following clause, "There shall be reserved from sale the lot numbered 16 of every township, for the maintenance of public schools within the said township."

The adoption of this clause of the ordinance was the beginning of a policy, which has since been uniformly followed, of setting apart one section in every township, or one thirty-sixth of the land, for the support of public or common schools. This date deserves to be remembered as the opening of a new epoch in the educational affairs of our country. We find in this action of Congress the origin of our primary, or common school fund. Henceforth the sixteenth section of every township was held sacred for the support of the education of the common people.

## III.

*Ordinance of 1787:* The Ordinance of 1787 is so well known that the history of its enactment need not be repeated. We are concerned only with the provisions which relate to the education in what was then the great Northwest Territory. Judge Campbell regards this famous ordinance, not as a statute subject to repeal, but rather as a constitution of the whole Northwest, not subject in its most important provisions to alteration. In some particulars, he says, "It was meant to operate as a permanent compact between the United States and the people of the Territory." Of the six articles forming the compact, only the third related to the subject of education. This article declares, "Religion, morality, and knowledge being necessary to good government and the happiness of mankind, schools and the means of education shall forever be encouraged."

By these articles the government of the Confederation expressed, in the most deliberate and emphatic manner, its desire and purpose that education and schools should be fostered and supported by the coming states of the great Northwest.

Soon after the adoption of the Ordinance of 1787 Congress provided for the sale of a large tract of land in southeastern Ohio, to the New England Ohio Company. In this sale important reservations were made for educational purposes. Section 16 in every township was reserved for the support of schools within the township; section 29 in every township was to be given for the purposes of religion; sections 8, 11, and 26 in every township were reserved for the future disposal of Congress; two entire townships of land were given for the support of a university. This last reservation of the two townships is to be noted as the beginning of the policy of giving land for higher education. In the policy then adopted by Congress we find the origin of our university fund.

A little later in the year a contract was made with John Cleves Symmes for the sale of lands lying between the Great and Little Miami rivers, with the same reservations as in the previous sale and with the gift of one township for higher education. Under the Confederacy these three townships were to be devoted to the purposes of higher learning. Before any further land grants were made, the constitution was adopted and the Union took up the work begun by the Confederation.

## IV.

*Act for disposing of the public lands in the territory of Indiana in 1804:* In the year 1800 the Northwest Territory was divided, a portion of it being organized into the Territory of Indiana. This new territory embraced what is now the State of Michigan. By the act of 1804 Section 16 of every township was reserved for the support of schools, and three entire townships were set apart for the support of "Seminaries of Learning." One of these townships was to be located in each of the districts afterwards forming Michigan, Indiana, and Illinois. We have here "the germ of the primary school fund and the university fund."

## V.

*Organization of Michigan Territory:* The territory of Michigan was organized by an act of Congress in 1805. By this act the provisions of the Ordinance of 1787 were recognized as in force in the new territory. Section 16 of every township and the entire township previously mentioned, were thus renewedly set apart for the support of schools.

## VI.

In September, 1817, a treaty was made at Fort Meigs, by Generals Cass and McArthur on behalf of the United States, with the Indian Tribes of the Northwest. By this treaty "The Chippewas, Ottawas, and Potta-wattamies, in view of their attachment to the church and their desire to have their children educated, gave to St. Anne's Church, Detroit, and to the College of Detroit, each an undivided half of six sections reserved to these nations by Hull's treaty of 1807,—three of the sections being on the Macon Reserve on the River Raisin, and the remainder to be selected thereafter."

Our interest in this treaty arises from the fact that the three sections reserved for the College of Detroit, were subsequently transferred to the endowment fund of the University of Michigan.

## VII.

In 1826 Congress gave to the Territory of Michigan two full townships of land, seventy-two sections, for the support of a "Seminary of Learning," with the provisions that "the land might be located in detached parcels." One of these townships was to take the place of the township donated in 1804, which had never been selected and located. The university fund has been derived from the sale of these two townships and the three sections donated by the Indians,—in all seventy-five sections.

Up to this time it had been impossible to locate the townships, as the acts granting them required that they should be located as wholes. The permission to select lands in detached portions made it possible to locate the townships to great advantage.

## VIII.

Michigan was fully admitted into the Union in January, 1837. In the final act of admission the provisions in relation to education were the following:

First. "That section numbered sixteen in every township of the public lands, and where such section has been sold or otherwise disposed of, other lands equivalent thereto, and as contiguous as may be, shall be *granted to the state* for the use of schools." This grant gave to the state, for the benefit of primary schools, more than a million acres of land. (The estimated amount was 1,148,000 acres). The larger part of the present primary school fund has been derived from the sale of this land, the proceeds being paid into the treasury of the state and held by the state as a "trust fund." The constitution of 1835 provided that "The proceeds of all lands that have been or hereafter may be granted by the United States to this state for the support of schools, which shall hereafter be sold or disposed of, shall be and remain a perpetual fund; the interest of which, together with the rents of all such unsold lands, shall be inviolably appropriated to the support of schools throughout the state."

The state pays seven per cent interest on the fund derived from the sale of the sixteenth sections; hence this part of the primary school fund is sometimes called the "seven per cent fund." The amount of this fund on June 30, 1897, was $3,953,223.52. The amount June 30, 1899, is $3,947.232.11. The remainder of the primary school fund has been derived from the sale of "swamp lands." The state pays five per cent interest on this part of the fund; hence it is frequently called the "five per cent fund."

The history of the "swamp lands" is peculiarly interesting to the inhabitants of our state. In 1812 Congress passed an act setting apart two million acres of land in the then Territory of Michigan, as bounty land for soldiers who might enlist in the war just breaking out between the United States and Great Britain. As soon as circumstances permitted, the Surveyor-General, Mr. Tiffin, sent agents to locate these lands. The report of these agents was such as to induce him to recommend the transfer of the locations of the bounty lands to some other part of the country. The result was that the lands were finally located in Illinois and Missouri. The surveyors "described the country as an unbroken series of tamarack swamps, bogs, and sand-barrens, with not more than one acre in a hundred and probably not one in a thousand, fit for cultivation."

It is difficult to account for the report of the surveyors, but it gave Michigan the reputation of being a great swamp, or at least of having a large quantity of swamp lands. In subsequent surveys the swampy sections were marked as "swamp" and were reserved from sale. In 1850 Congress donated these lands to the state. The number of acres of swamp land patented to the state has been stated to be 5,838,775. The proceeds of the sale of these lands, as far as necessary, were to be used for drainage and for other purposes connected with the preparation of the lands for the market and for use. After this application of moneys there still remained a large fund to be used for other purposes.

In 1858 the legislature enacted as follows: "All moneys heretofore received and all moneys hereafter received from the sale of said swamp lands donated by the aforesaid act of Congress, after deducting the expenses of sales, fifty per cent shall be denominated a primary school fund, and the interest thereof, at five per centum per annum, shall be appropriated and distributed in like manner as the primary school [interest] fund of the state.

The amount of money received from this source up to June 30, 1897, was $829,069.38. The amount received to June 30, 1899, is $846,778.52 This fund is usually called the "five per cent fund."

The total amount of the primary school fund on June 30, 1897, was

| | |
|---|---|
| 7 per cent fund | $3,953,223 52 |
| 5 per cent fund | 829,069 38 |
| Total | $4,646,240 13 |

The interest on these funds is called the primary school interest fund, and is distributed semi-annually to the various school districts in proportion to the number of children of school age.

The primary school interest fund for the year ending June 30, 1897, was as follows:

| | |
|---|---|
| Interest on 7 per cent fund | $288,461 69 |
| Interest on penalty paid by holders of lands | 10,563 26 |
| Interest on 5 per cent fund | 44,737 06 |
| Total income from both funds | $343,762 01 |

| | |
|---|---|
| Surplus of specific taxes transferred | $673,647 49 |
| Rent of land | 1 00 |
| Paid by trespassers on schools lands | 461 48 |
| Total | $674,109 97 |
| Total income distributed | $1,017,871 98 |

## IX.

The second provision as to education in the admission of Michigan into the Union was the following: "That the seventy-two sections of land set apart and reserved for the support of a University by an act of Congress approved on the twentieth of May, 1826, are hereby granted and conveyed to the State, to be appropriated solely to the use and support of such University, in such manner as the Legislature may prescribe." The seventy-two sections and the three reserved by the treaty of Fort Meigs have been the source of the university fund. The amount of this fund on June 30, 1897, was $529,621.59. The income from the fund for the year just mentioned was $38,507.81.

## X.

By the same act Congress donated to the state "salt spring lands" to an amount not exceeding seventy-two sections. These lands were not donated or reserved for educational purposes; but the state legislature subsequently devoted a small portion, twenty-five sections, to be sold for the purpose of creating a fund for the normal school. This fund on the thirtieth of June, 1897, was $65,945.12; and the income of the fund was $4,203.66.

## XI.

The Agricultural College of Michigan was established several years before the grant of land was made by Congress. The constitution of 1850 required the establishment of an agricultural school as soon as practicable, and gave permission for the appropriation of twenty-two sections of salt-spring lands for the maintenance of such an institution. An act establishing the college was passed in 1855. This act appropriated the twenty-two sections of salt-spring lands for the purchase of a site and the erection of buildings. With the proceeds of the sale of these lands and an appropriation from the legislature of $40,000, the college was organized. Nearly seven thousand acres of swamp lands, situated in the four townships adjoining the college, were given by the legislature to the college. From the sale of these lands $42,396.87 were derived. The institution was supported entirely by legislative appropriations until the Congressional land grant was made.

In the year 1862 an act was passed by Congress donating to the several states and territories thirty thousand acres of the public lands for each one of their senators and representatives in Congress, to provide for the endowment of colleges of agriculture and the mechanical arts. This act gave to Michigan two hundred forty thousand acres. The selection and disposal of these lands was placed in the hands of a board called the Agricultural Land Grant Board, and the lands were located to a large extent in Northern Michigan. The lands are not yet all sold; but the fund derived from the portion sold amounted, on June 30, 1897, to $569,951.82. The college will have a very large endowment fund when the lands are all disposed of and the proceeds placed to the credit of the institution.

The income of the college, aside from legislative appropriations, for the year ending June 30, 1897, was as follows:

| | |
|---|---:|
| Interest paid by the State............................................ | $39,009 66 |
| Interest paid by holders of lands.................................... | 4,520 85 |
| Penalty on college fund.............................................. | 296 15 |
| Paid by trespassers on lands......................................... | 54 09 |
| Received from United States government.............................. | 22,000 00 |
| Total ................................................. | $65,880 75 |

. Summary of Educational Funds as reported June 30, 1897.

Primary School Funds:

| | |
|---|---:|
| 7 per cent fund.............................................. | $3,953.223 52 |
| 5 per cent fund.............................................. | 829,069 38 |
| Total ................................................. | $4,646,240 13 |
| University fund ............................................. | 529,621 59 |
| Agricultural College fund ................................... | 569,951 82 |
| Normal School fund ......................................... | 65,945 12 |
| Total ................................................. | $5,811,758 66 |

# UNIVERSITY OF MICHIGAN.

## THE TREASURER'S REPORT FOR THE FISCAL YEAR ENDING JUNE 30, 1899.

To the Finance Committee, Board of Regents, University of Michigan,

Gentlemen—Herewith I submit my annual report for the fiscal year ending June 30, 1899:

Respectfully,

H. SOULE, Treasurer.

### RECEIPTS.

| | |
|---|---:|
| From State Treasurer, account one-sixth Mill Tax...... | $147,346 67 |
| "  State Treasurer, account University Interest........ | 38,529 91 |
| "  State Treasurer, account Special Appropriations.... | 9,000 00 |
| "  State Treasurer, account Special Accumulation one-sixth mill ...................... .................. | 88,364 40 |
| "  earnings and miscellaneous sources .............. | 228,605 62 |
| "  Balance overdrawn, June 30, 1899............... | 18,764 53 |
| | $530,611 13 |

### DISBURSEMENTS.

| | |
|---|---:|
| Balance overdrawn, July 1, 1898........................ | $9,799 52 |
| Special fund accounts, legislative appropriations........ | 10,718 27 |
| Special from accumulation one-sixth mill................ | 81,188 05 |
| General fund, account of general expenses............... | 428,905 29 |
| | $530,611 13 |

### GENERAL FUND.

#### RECEIPTS TO THE GENERAL FUND.

| | |
|---|---:|
| From State Treasurer, account University Interest........ | $38,529 91 |
| "  State Treasurer, account one-sixth mill tax........ | 147,346 67 |
| "  interest on deposits............................. | 582 02 |
| "  University hospital earnings..................... | 28,387 01 |
| "  Homœopathic hospital earnings.................... | 9,014 46 |
| "  dental college operating room earnings........... | 4,411 03 |
| "  mechanical laboratory (earnings in shops)......... | 197 43 |
| "  miscellaneous sources ........................... | 1,597 19 |
| "  general library (sale of duplicate books)........... | 3 45 |
| | $230,069 17 |

| From Students' Fees:— | |
|---|---:|
| Literary department ........................ | $49,070 00 |
| Literary department summer school.......... | 8,890 00 |
| Engineering department...................... | 10,505 00 |
| Medical department.......................... | 19,170 00 |
| Law department ............................ | 35,887 50 |

| | | | |
|---|---|---|---|
| Law department summer school .............. | $1,802 00 | | |
| Dental department ........................... | 11,040 00 | | |
| Homœopathic department..................... | 2,475 00 | | |
| Pharmacy department........................ | 3,530 00 | | |
| Chemical laboratory ......................... | 13,149 64 | | |
| Hygienic laboratory ......................... | 2,732 39 | | |
| Botanical laboratory ......................... | 705 00 | | |
| Zoological laboratory ......................... | 347 00 | | |
| Physiological laboratory ...................... | 87 00 | | |
| Pathological laboratory ...................... | 1,550 00 | | |
| Histological laboratory ....................... | 1,372 00 | | |
| Anatomical laboratory ....................... | 2,365 00 | | |
| Mechanical laboratory ....................... | 1,805 00 | | |
| Dental laboratory ........................... | 627 00 | | |
| Pharmacological laboratory .................. | 45 00 | | |
| Electrotherapeutical laboratory ............. | 792 00 | | |
| Medical demonstrations ..................... | 5,150 00 | | |
| Key deposits ................................ | 215 00 | | |
| Electrical engineering (physics)............... | 517 00 | | |
| Drawing boards ............................. | 171 00 | | |
| Waterman gymnasium lockers ................ | 2,384 00 | | |
| Women's Gymnasium lockers................. | 558 00 | | |
| Diplomas .......................... | 7,320 00 | $184,261 53 | $184,261 53 |
| | | | |
| Fees Total .......................... | $184,261 53 | | |
| Fees Refunded ...................... | 6,009 23 | | |
| | | | |
| Net ................................. | $178,252 30 | | |
| Balance overdrawn, June 30, 1898............ | | | 20,823 25 |
| | | | |
| | | | $435,153 95 |

### DISBURSEMENTS FROM THE GENERAL FUND.

| | | |
|---|---|---|
| Balance overdrawn, July 1, 1898 .............. | | $6,248 66 |
| General pay roll ............................ | $147,798 95 | |
| General pay roll summer school .............. | 4,551 75 | $152,350 70 |
| Current expenses summer school ............. | | 607 91 |
| Engineering department pay roll ............. | 30,630 58 | 30,630 58 |
| Engineering department expenses ............ | | 302 92 |
| Law department pay roll ..................... | 32,985 04 | |
| Law department pay roll summer school...... | 731 23 | 33,716 27 |
| Law department expenses summer school .... | | 108 40 |
| Law department expenses.................... | | 596 12 |
| Law department books ...................... | | 1,578 50 |
| Medical department pay roll ................. | 36,715 10 | 36,715 10 |
| Medical department expenses ................ | | 552 27 |
| Medical department books ................... | | 1,777 73 |
| School of pharmacy and chemical department pay roll ............................... | 22,879 64 | 22,879 64 |
| School of pharmacy and chemical department expenses ......................... ....... | | 8,745 64 |
| Homœopathic college pay roll................ | 3,500 00 | 3,500 00 |
| Homœopathic college expenses.............. | | 135 80 |
| Homœopathic college books.................. | | 223 65 |
| University hospital pay roll .................. | 6,309 54 | 6,309 54 |
| University hospital expenses ................. | | 16,180 75 |
| Homœopathic hospital pay roll.............. | 2,639 38 | 2,639 38 |
| Homœopathic hospital expenses............. | | 10,749 80 |
| Dental college pay roll...................... | 11,512 42 | 11,512 42 |
| Dental college expenses..................... | | 5,581 53 |
| Dental college books ....................... | | 123 27 |

Amount of salaries paid from general fund $300,253 63

| | | |
|---|---|---|
| Contingent account | $5,164 | 61 |
| Repairs | 11,412 | 63 |
| Fuel | 14,070 | 83 |
| Light | 2,341 | 98 |
| Books for general library | 9,384 | 26 |
| Current expenses for general library | 519 | 87 |
| Bindery | 2,237 | 69 |
| Postage | 2,353 | 94 |
| Advertising and printing | 2,408 | 61 |
| Theory and practice of medicine | 133 | 92 |
| Materia medica | 223 | 92 |
| Museum | 708 | 85 |
| Mineralogy | 2 | 00 |
| Histology | 703 | 01 |
| Hygiene | 1,894 | 73 |
| Botanical gardens | 99 | 64 |
| Botany | 861 | 42 |
| Zoology | 858 | 84 |
| Engineering Shops | 679 | 90 |
| Civil engineering | 398 | 19 |
| Astronomical observatory | 324 | 17 |
| School inspection | 605 | 63 |
| Practical anatomy | 1,984 | 52 |
| Electrical engineering (physics) | 1,482 | 41 |
| Physiology | 760 | 62 |
| Pathology | 980 | 89 |
| Electrotherapeutics | 440 | 17 |
| Nervous Diseases | 82 | 10 |
| Student's fees refunded | 6,009 | 23 |
| Hospital lighting plant | 101 | 48 |
| Waterman gymnasium | 176 | 78 |
| Hospital dormitory | 765 | 71 |
| Teams | 1,116 | 55 |
| News letter | 104 | 21 |
| Carpenter shop | 374 | 81 |
| Alumni association | 600 | 00 |
| Women's gymnasium | 621 | 45 |
| Diplomas | 1,140 | 40 |
| Geology | 226 | 17 |
| Surgical demonstrations | 211 | 65 |
| Surgical clinic | 312 | 73 |
| Latin | 255 | 90 |
| Gynæcology | 273 | 31 |
| Ophthalmology | 39 | 45 |
| Philology | 13 | 92 |
| General chemistry | 848 | 95 |
| Dermatology | 5 | 05 |
| Diseases of women and children | 1 | 05 |
| Psychology | 69 | 56 |
| Philosophy | 300 | 45 |
| German | 54 | 08 |
| General catalogue | 409 | 15 |
| Electric supplies | 1,085 | 96 |
| Engineering laboratory | 504 | 34 |
| Greek | 452 | 65 |
| Music | 181 | 95 |
| Water supply | 1,689 | 86 |
| Commencement expenses | 819 | 73 |

$428,905 29

$435,153 95

## SPECIAL FUND ACCOUNTS.

### HOMOEOPATHIC COLLEGE.

*Receipts.*

| | | |
|---|---|---|
| Balance in Treasury, July 1, 1898 ..................... | $1,600 00 | |
| From State Treasurer ............................... | 6,000 00 | |
| | | $7,600 00 |

*Disbursements.*

| | | |
|---|---|---|
| Salaries .......................................... | $7,500 00 | |
| General Expenses .................................. | 90 52 | |
| Balance in Treasury, June 30, 1899.................... | 9 48 | |
| | | $7,600 00 |

### ELECTRIC LIGHT PLANT.

*Receipts.*

| | | |
|---|---|---|
| Material sold .............. .................... | $151 50 | |
| Balance overdrawn, June 30, 1899.................... | 381 93 | |
| | | $533 43 |

*Disbursements.*

| | | |
|---|---|---|
| Balance overdrawn, July 1, 1898..................... | $405 68 | |
| Vouchers .......................................... | 127 75 | |
| | | $533 43 |

### SUMMER HOSPITALS.

*Receipts.*

| | | |
|---|---|---|
| From State Treasurer................................ | $3,000 00 | $3,000 00 |

*Disbursements.*

| | | |
|---|---|---|
| Vouchers ............. ........................... | $3,000 00 | $3,000 00 |

### ACCUMULATION OF SAVINGS, LAW BUILDING.

*Receipts.*

| | | |
|---|---|---|
| From State Treasurer................................ | $49,000 00 | $49,000 00 |

*Disbursements.*

| | | |
|---|---|---|
| Balance overdrawn, July 1, 1898...................... | $4,745 18 | |
| Vouchers .......................................... | 43,756 43 | |
| Balance in Treasury, June 30, 1899.................... | 498 39 | |
| | | $49,000 00 |

### ACCUMULATION OF SAVINGS, EXTENSION TO FOUNDRY.

*Receipts.*

| | | |
|---|---|---|
| From State Treasurer ............................... | $1,500 00 | $1,500 00 |

*Disbursements.*

| | | |
|---|---|---|
| Vouchers .......................................... | $1,457 45 | |
| Balance in Treasury, June 30, 1899.................... | 42 55 | |
| | | $1,500 00 |

### ACCUMULATION OF SAVINGS, EXTENSION TO CHEMICAL LABORATORY.

*Receipts.*

From State Treasurer ............................... $1,571 14     $1,571 14

*Disbursements.*

Vouchers ........................................... $1,571 14     $1,571 14

### ACCUMULATION OF SAVINGS, REPAIRS ON UNIVERSITY HOSPITAL.

*Receipts.*

From State Treasurer ............................... $2,000 00     $2,000 00

*Disbursements.*

Vouchers ........................................... $1,701 00

Balance in Treasury, June 30, 1899.................... 299 00

                                                     $2,000 00

### ACCUMULATION OF SAVINGS, ADDITION TO GENERAL LIBRARY.

*Receipts.*

From State Treasurer ............................... 15,000 00     $15,000 00

*Disbursements.*

Vouchers ........................................... $14,011 27

Balance in Treasury, June 30, 1899.................... 988 73

                                                     $15,000 00

### ACCUMULATION OF SAVINGS, ADDITION TO HOMOEOPATHIC HOSPITAL.

*Receipts.*

From State Treasurer ............................... $1,500 00     $1,500 00

*Disbursements.*

Vouchers ........................................... $948 64

Balance in Treasury, June 30, 1899.................... 551 36

                                                     $1,500 00

### ACCUMULATION OF SAVINGS, ADDITION TO HEATING PLANT.

*Receipts.*

From State Treasurer ............................... $1,250 00     $1,250 00

*Disbursements.*

Vouchers ........................................... $1,231 52

Balance in Treasury, June 30, 1899.................... 18 48

                                                     $1,250 00

### ACCUMULATION OF SAVINGS, ROOF ON MAIN BUILDING.

*Receipts.*

From State Treasurer ............................... $13,664 26     $13,664 26

*Disbursements.*

Vouchers ........................................... $13,664 26     $13,664 26

## ACCUMULATION OF SAVINGS, UNIVERSITY HOSPITAL LAUNDRY.

### Receipts.

| | | |
|---|---|---|
| From State Treasurer | $2,879 00 | $2,879 00 |

### Disbursements.

| | | |
|---|---|---|
| Vouchers | $2,846 34 | |
| Balance in Treasury, June 30, 1899 | 32 66 | |
| | | $2,879 00 |

## SUMMARY OF BALANCES, JUNE 30, 1899.

### Overdrafts.

| | | |
|---|---|---|
| General fund | | $20,823 25 |
| Electric light plant | | 381 93 |
| | | $21,205 18 |

### Balances in Treasury.

| | | |
|---|---|---|
| Homœopathic college | $9 48 | |
| Law building | 498 39 | |
| Extension to foundry | 42 55 | |
| Repairs on University hospital | 299 00 | |
| Addition to general library | 988 73 | |
| Addition to Homoeopathic hospital | 551 36 | |
| Addition to heating plant | 18 48 | |
| University hospital laundry | 32 66 | 2,440 65 |
| Net overdraft, as previously stated | | $18,764 53 |

## GIFTS AND TRUST FUNDS.

Under this head are included gifts and other funds which the Regents have received from time to time from benefactors for special purposes. The new accounts which have been opened by your Treasurer during the year are as follows: Special Latin Fund; United States Pharmacopœia Fund; Good Government Club Fund; Peter White Fellowship Fund; '99 Law Class Scholarship Fund; Biological Laboratory Fund; Woman's Professorship Fund; Bates Professorship Fund; all of which are fully detailed below.

### PHILO PARSONS FUND.

#### Receipts.

| | | |
|---|---|---|
| Balance in Treasury, July 1, 1898 | $96 21 | |
| Interest | 2 93 | |
| | | $99 14 |

#### Disbursements.

| | | |
|---|---|---|
| Balance in Treasury, June 30, 1899 | $99 14 | $99 14 |

### GOETHE FUND.

#### Receipts.

| | | |
|---|---|---|
| Balance in Treasury, July 1, 1898 | $204 45 | |
| Interest | 6 23 | |
| | | $210 68 |

#### Disbursements.

| | | |
|---|---|---|
| Vouchers | $7 58 | |
| Balance in Treasury, June 30, 1899 | 203 10 | |
| | | $210 68 |

## ELISHA JONES CLASSICAL FELLOWSHIP FUND.

### Receipts.

| | | |
|---|---|---|
| Balance in Treasury, July 1, 1898...................... | $8 07 | |
| Interest .............................................. | 22 | |
| | | $8 29 |

### Disbursements.

| | | |
|---|---|---|
| Balance in Treasury, June 30, 1899.................... | $8 29 | $8 29 |

## WOMEN'S GYMNASIUM.

### Receipts.

| | | |
|---|---|---|
| Balance in Treasury, July 1, 1898...................... | $330 65 | |
| John Canfield, Manistee ............................. | 5,000 00 | |
| Interest .............................................. | 140 37 | |
| | | $5,471 02 |

### Disbursements.

| | | |
|---|---|---|
| Vouchers .............................................. | $1,100 48 | |
| Balance in Treasury, June 30, 1899.................... | 4,370 54 | |
| | | $5,471 02 |

## COYL COLLECTION.

### Receipts.

| | | |
|---|---|---|
| Balance in Treasury, July 1, 1898...................... | $10,990 92 | |
| Interest .............................................. | 531 65 | |
| | | $11,522 57 |

### Disbursements.

| | | |
|---|---|---|
| Vouchers .............................................. | $335 33 | |
| Balance in Treasury, June 30, 1899.................... | 11,187 24 | |
| | | $11,522 57 |

## BUHL LAW LIBRARY.

### Receipts.

| | | |
|---|---|---|
| Balance in Treasury, July 1, 1898...................... | $2,262 53 | |
| Interest .............................................. | 63 39 | |
| | | $2,325 92 |

### Disbursements.

| | | |
|---|---|---|
| Vouchers .............................................. | $744 50 | |
| Balance in Treasury, June 30, 1899.................... | 1,581 42 | |
| | | $2,325 92 |

## SETH HARRISON SCHOLARSHIP FUND.

### Receipts.

| | | |
|---|---|---|
| Balance in Treasury, June 30, 1898.................... | $26,163 59 | |
| Interest .............................................. | 1,580 87 | |
| | | $27,750 46 |

### Disbursements.

| | | |
|---|---|---|
| Vouchers .............................................. | $705 50 | |
| Balance in Treasury, June 30, 1899.................... | 27,044 96 | |
| | | $27,750 46 |

## CLASS OF NINETY-FOUR SCHOLARSHIP FUND.

### Receipts.

| | | |
|---|---:|---:|
| Balance in Treasury, July 1, 1898...................... | $932 70 | |
| Interest ............................................... | 28 02 | |
| Subscriptions paid ..................................... | 268 40 | |
| | | $1,229 12 |

### Disbursements.

| | | |
|---|---:|---:|
| Balance in Treasury, June 30, 1899..................... | $1,229 12 | $1,229 12 |

## FORD-MESSER FUND.

### Receipts.

| | | |
|---|---:|---:|
| Balance in Treasury, July 1, 1898...................... | $15,001 28 | |
| Bryant Walker, administrator of Estate Corydon L. Ford | 6,400 00 | |
| Interest ............................................ | 1,598 85 | |
| | | $23,000 13 |

### Disbursements.

| | | |
|---|---:|---:|
| Vouchers ................................................ | $374 10 | |
| Balance in Treasury, June 30, 1899..................... | 22,626 03 | |
| | | $23,000 13 |

## THE PHILLIPS SCHOLARSHIPS FUND.

### Receipts.

| | | |
|---|---:|---:|
| Balance in Treasury, July 1, 1898...................... | $162 77 | |
| Fram Samuel Fox & Co., for the estate.................. | 214 03 | |
| Interest ............................................. | 7 75 | |
| | | $384 55 |

### Disbursements

| | | |
|---|---:|---:|
| Balance in Treasury, June 30, 1899..................... | $384 55 | $384 55 |

## MUSIC HALL FUND.

### Receipts.

| | | |
|---|---:|---:|
| Balance in Treasury, July 1, 1898...................... | $1,084 97 | |
| Interest ........... ......... ...................... | 8 23 | |
| Contributions ......................................... | 100 00 | |
| | | $1,193 20 |

### Disbursements.

| | | |
|---|---:|---:|
| Balance in Treasury, June 30, 1899..................... | $1,193 20 | $1,193 20 |

## CLASS OF NINETY-SIX MEMORIAL.

### Receipts.

| | | |
|---|---:|---:|
| Balance in Treasury, July 1, 1898...................... | $19 00 | |
| Subscriptions ......................................... | 6 00 | |
| Interest .............................................. | 12 | |
| | | $25 12 |

### Disbursements.

| | | |
|---|---:|---:|
| Vouchers ............................................... | $19 00 | |
| Balance in Treasury, June 30, 1899..................... | 6 12 | |
| | | $25 12 |

## CLASS OF NINETY-SEVEN SCHOLARSHIP FUND.

### *Receipts.*

| | | |
|---|---|---|
| Balance in Treasury, July 1, 1898....................... | $138 43 | |
| Interest ............................................. | 3 48 | |
| | | $141 91 |

### *Disbursements.*

| | | |
|---|---|---|
| Balance in Treasury, June 30, 1899..................... | $141 91 | $141 91 |

## CLASS OF NINETY-EIGHT SCHOLARSHIP FUND.

### *Receipts.*

| | | |
|---|---|---|
| Balance in Treasury, July 1, 1898..................... | $253 30 | |
| Subscriptions ......................................... | 4 00 | |
| Interest ............................................. | 5 55 | |
| | | $262 85 |

### *Disbursements.*

| | | |
|---|---|---|
| Balance in Treasury, June 30, 1899..................... | $262 85 | $262 85 |

## PARKE, DAVIS & CO. FUND.

### *Receipts.*

| | | |
|---|---|---|
| Balance in Treasury, July 1, 1898...................... | $10 00 | |
| Parke, Davis & Co..................................... | 500 00 | |
| Interest ............................................. | 2 12 | |
| | | $512 12 |

### *Disbursements.*

| | | |
|---|---|---|
| Vouchers ............................................. | $500 00 | |
| Balance in Treasury, June 30, 1890.................... | 12 12 | |
| | | $512 12 |

## STEARNS PHARMACY FELLOWSHIP FUND.

### *Receipts.*

| | | |
|---|---|---|
| Balance in Treasury, July 1, 1898..................... | $0 78 | |
| Stearns & Co.......................................... | 350 00 | |
| | | $350 78 |

### *Disbursements.*

| | | |
|---|---|---|
| Vouchers ............................................. | $350 00 | |
| Balance in Treasury, June 30, 1899.................... | 78 | |
| | | $350 78 |

## LIBRARY OF EARLY CHRISTIAN LITERATURE FUND.

### *Receipts.*

| | | |
|---|---|---|
| Balance in Treasury, July 1, 1898...................... | $6 50 | |
| Transfer from Special Latin Fund...................... | 71 | |
| Transfer from James E. Scripps Library Fund........... | 15 | |
| | | $7 36 |

### *Disbursements.*

| | | |
|---|---|---|
| Vouchers ............................................. | $7 36 | $7 36 |

5

### JAMES E. SCRIPPS LIBRARY FUND.

*Receipts.*

| | | |
|---|---|---|
| Balance in Treasury, July 1, 1898...................... | $0 15 | $0 15 |

*Disbursements.*

| | | |
|---|---|---|
| Transfer to Library of Early Christian Literature Fund.. | $0 15 | $0 15 |

### FRIEZE MEMORIAL FUND.

*Receipts.*

| | | |
|---|---|---|
| Balance in Treasury, July 1, 1898...................... | $396 66 | |
| Collection to the Fund................................. | 703 37 | |
| | | $1,100 03 |

*Disbursements.*

| | | |
|---|---|---|
| Vouchers ............................................. | $742 90 | |
| Balance in Treasury, June 30, 1899.................... | 357 13 | |
| | | $1,100 03 |

### UNITED STATES PHARMACOPOEIA FUND.

*Receipts.*

| | | |
|---|---|---|
| Appropriation by Committee on Publication.............. | $815 00 | $815 00 |

*Disbursements.*

| | | |
|---|---|---|
| Vouchers ............................................. | $765 00 | |
| Balance in Treasury, June 30, 1899.................... | 50 00 | |
| | | $815 00 |

### SPECIAL LATIN FUND.

*Receipts.*

| | | |
|---|---|---|
| From Contributor to the fund ......................... | $200 00 | $200 00 |

*Disbursements.*

| | | |
|---|---|---|
| Vouchers ............................................. | $48 78 | |
| Transfer to Library of Early Christian Literature Fund.... | 71 | |
| Balance in Treasury, June 30, 1899.................... | 150 51 | |
| | | $200 00 |

### GOOD GOVERNMENT CLUB.

*Receipts.*

| | | |
|---|---|---|
| From Contributor to the fund......................... | $500 00 | $500 00 |

*Disbursements.*

| | | |
|---|---|---|
| Balance in Treasury, June 30, 1899................... | $500 00 | $500 00 |

### PETER WHITE FELLOWSHIP.

*Receipts.*

| | | |
|---|---|---|
| From Peter White .................................... | $400 00 | $400 00 |

*Disbursements.*

| | | |
|---|---|---|
| Balance in Treasury, June 30, 1899.................... | $400 00 | $400 00 |

## WOMAN'S PROFESSORSHIP FUND.

*Receipts.*

| | | |
|---|---|---|
| From the Donor | $10,000 00 | $10,000 00 |

*Disbursements.*

| | | |
|---|---|---|
| Balance in Treasury, June 30, 1899 | $10,000 00 | $10,000 00 |

## NINETY-NINE LAW CLASS SCHOLARSHIP FUND.

*Receipts.*

| | | |
|---|---|---|
| From Subscriptions | $25 00 | $25 00 |

*Disbursements.*

| | | |
|---|---|---|
| Balance in Treasury, June 30, 1899 | $25 00 | $25 00 |

## BIOLOGICAL LABORATORY FUND.

*Receipts.*

| | | |
|---|---|---|
| From the Donor, D. M. Ferry | $50 00 | $50 00 |

*Disbursements.*

| | | |
|---|---|---|
| Vouchers | $50 00 | $50 00 |

## WILLIAMS PROFESSORSHIP FUND—PROPERTY.

The property fund of this account was by order of the Board of Regents under date July 21, 1898, placed in the hands of Hon. Levi. L. Barbour, of Detroit, and for this I hold his acknowledgment as follows:

| | | |
|---|---|---|
| Mortgage securities, value | $7,077 44 | |
| Other property | 3,153 68 | |
| | | $10.231 12 |

The same being in his hands for future management.

## WILLIAMS PROFESSORSHIP FUND—CASH.

| | | |
|---|---|---|
| Balance in Treasury, July 1, 1898 | $4,727 23 | |
| Subscription (H. B. Hutchins) | 50 00 | |
| Interest | 151 35 | |
| | | $4,928 58 |

*Disbursements.*

| | | |
|---|---|---|
| Vouchers | $29 20 | |
| Balance in Treasury, June 30, 1899 | 4,899 38 | |
| | | $4,928 58 |

## MORRIS ALUMNI FUND.

| | | |
|---|---|---|
| Balance in Treasury, July 1, 1898, securities | $1,150 00 | |
| Balance in Treasury, July 1, 1898, cash | 1,095 83 | |
| Interest | 131 18 | |
| | | $2,377 01 |

*Disbursements.*

| | | |
|---|---|---|
| Balance in Treasury, June 30, 1899 | $2,377 01 | $2,377 01 |

## BATES PROFESSORSHIP.

*Receipts.*

| | | |
|---|---|---|
| Balance overdrawn, June 30, 1899 | $1,177 10 | $1,177 10 |

*Disbursements.*

| | | |
|---|---|---|
| Vouchers | $1,177 10 | $1,177 10 |

## D. M. FERRY BOTANICAL FUND.

*Receipts.*

Balance in Treasury, July 1, 1898........................ $50 00     $50 00

*Disbursements.*

Vouchers .............................................. $50 00     $50 00

## SUMMARY OF GIFT FUND BALANCES.

| | Cash. | Loaned. | Total. |
|---|---|---|---|
| Philo Parsons fund.......................... | $99 14 | | $99 14 |
| Goethe fund ................................ | 203 10 | | 203 10 |
| Elisha Jones classical fellowship fund........ | 8 29 | | 8 29 |
| Women's gymnasium fund .................. | 4,370 54 | | 4,370 54 |
| Coyl collection fund....................... | 1,187 24 | $10,000 00 | 11,187 24 |
| Buhl law library fund....................... | 1,581 42 | | 1,581 42 |
| Seth Harrison scholarship fund.............. | 5,544 96 | 21,500 00 | 27,044 96 |
| '94 scholarship fund ....................... | 1,229 12 | | 1,229 12 |
| Ford-Messer library fund .................. | 15,876 03 | 6,750 00 | 22,626 03 |
| Phillips scholarships fund .................... | 384 55 | | 384 55 |
| Music hall fund ........................... | 193 20 | 1,000 00 | 1,193 20 |
| '96 class memorial fund ..................... | 6 12 | | 6 12 |
| '97 class scholarship fund................... | 1 91 | 140 00 | 141 91 |
| '98 class scholarship fund................... | 262 85 | | 262 85 |
| Parke, Davis & Co. fund.................... | 12 12 | | 12 12 |
| Stearns pharmacy fellowship fund........... | 78 | | 78 |
| Frieze memorial fund ..................... | 357 13 | | 357 13 |
| U. S. pharmacopœia fund................... | 50 00 | | 50 00 |
| Special Latin fund ......................... | 150 51 | | 150 51 |
| Good government club fund ................ | 500 00 | | 500 00 |
| Peter White fellowship fund................ | 400 00 | | 400 00 |
| Woman's professorship fund ............... | | 10,000 00 | 10,000 00 |
| '99 law class scholarship fund............... | | 25 00 | 25 00 |
| Williams fund ............................ | 4,899 38 | | 4,899 38 |
| Morris alumni fund........................ | 1,227 01 | 1,150 00 | 2,377 01 |
| | $38,545 40 | $50,565 00 | $89,110 40 |

Bates professorship fund overdrawn ........     1,177 10

Net balance in gift funds..............     $87,933 30

# QUESTIONS FOR EXAMINATION

FOR

# STATE AND COUNTY CERTIFICATES

---

# STATE EXAMINATIONS.

---

I. QUESTIONS PREPARED BY STATE BOARD OF EDUCATION FOR EXAMINATIONS HELD AT LANSING, CADILLAC, AND MARQUETTE, AUGUST, 1899.

## ALGEBRA.

1. Define algebra, term, factor, exponent, surd, ratio, logarithm, equation.
2. Find the highest common factor of $x^4+3x^3+12x-16$ and $x^3-13x+12$.
3. Find the L. C. M. of $x^3+6x^2+11x+6$ and $x^3-7x+6$.
4. Solve: $\dfrac{8}{x} - \dfrac{9}{y} = 1$ and $\dfrac{10}{x} + \dfrac{6}{y} = 7$.
5. A takes 3 hours longer than B to walk 30 miles, but if he doubles his pace he takes two hours less than B; find their rates of walking.
6. Prove that any quantity with zero index is equal to 1.
7. What are the two parts of 20 whose product is equal to 24 times their difference?
8. Show that if $x$ is real, the expression $\dfrac{x^2-15}{2x-8}$ cannot lie between 3 and 5.
9. Thirteen persons take their places at a round table. Show that it is 5 to 1 against two particular persons sitting together.
10. Expand $(1-2y)^5$.

## ARITHMETIC.

1. Discuss the relative values of the Grube and Speer methods in arithmetic.
2. Distinguish between number as ratio and number as number; between discrete and continuous number. Define unit and number.
3. How do you teach fractions? Give reasons.
4. How do you teach long division?
5. Illustrate the application of the spiral plan in the teaching of arithmetic.
6. How is arrested development said to result from the teaching of arithmetic?
7. What do you do with definitions and rules? Give reasons.
8. Find the G. C. D. of 247 and 221 by division. Give analysis and proof of process.
9. Distinguish between arithmetic and algebra.
10. Name ten important and ten unimportant topics in arithmetic.

## BOTANY.

*Directions*—(1) Be sure you understand the question. (2) Take time enough and pains enough to answer it in the way you wish it to be understood and graded. (3) Number your answers to correspond with the number of the question or its several subdivisions. (4) Write plainly and legibly.

1. Give some of the distinguishing characteristics of the following groups of plants and arrange the groups in their natural order: liverworts, algae, mosses, fungi, gymnosperms, dicotyledons, monocotyledons, ferns.
2. Give the chief characteristics of three families of flowering plants, and name three plants in each family, using illustrations familiar to this region.
3. Name the principal, parts or members, of one of the higher plants, and tell in few words the function of each part.
4. Name six modifications of plant organs, illustrating in each case from horticultural, or garden plants, and telling for what use to the plant the modification is made.
5. Describe the location, structure, and function of the wood and bark in higher plants, and tell what uses are made of these parts in manufacture.
6. Describe the manufacture of sugar and starch by plants.
7. Describe and contrast the processes of carbon-assimilation and of respiration in plants.
8. What factors go to make a fertile soil, and what substances do plants take from the soil?
9. What means known to you do plants possess for non-sexual propagation? What means do horticulturists use for the same purpose?
10. Describe the process of sexual reproduction in flowering plants.

*Note*—State what training and experience you have had in the science of botany.

## CHEMISTRY.

*Directions*—(1) Be sure you understand the question. (2) Take time enough and pains enough to answer it in the way you wish it to be understood and graded. (3) Number your answers to correspond with the number of the question or its several subdivisions. (4) Write plainly and legibly.

1. Define and give example:
   (a) Heat of combustion; (b) indirect oxidizing agent; (c) basic salt; (d) hydrocarbon; (e) osmotic pressure.
2. Discuss chlorine in respect to preparation, and physical and chemical properties.
3. What experiments are necessary to teach the pupil the essentials concerning the composition of water?
4. Describe a method for determining accurately, the composition of air by volume.
   (b) Write out the formula commonly applied in reducing the volume of a gas to standard conditions.
5. (a) Describe fully the Marsh test for the detection of arsenic.
   (b) How can arsenic be distinguished from antimony?
6. (a) Name and briefly describe the three allotropic modifications of carbon.
   (b) Make a diagram of the ordinary gas flame.
   (c) How may a non-luminous flame be made luminous? How may a luminous flame be made non-luminous?
7. (a) Outline the chemical work necessary to determine the atomic weight of oxygen.
   (b) Describe briefly the specific heat method of determining atomic weights.
8. (a) Briefly describe a test for sulphuric acid and carbonic acid, writing the equation for reaction.
   (b) How is a chloride detected in the presence of a bromide?
9. (a) Give brief description of a method for the separation and identification of lead, silver, and mercurosum.
   (b) For the separation and identification of iron.
10. What chemical preparation should the student possess before being admitted to qualitative analysis?

*Note*—State fully what work you have done in chemistry.

## COMPOSITION—RHETORIC.

*Directions*—(1) Be sure you understand the question. (2) Take time enough and pains enough to answer it in the way you wish it to be understood and graded. (3) Number your answers to correspond with the number of the question or its several subdivisions. (4) Write plainly and legibly.

1. Give in narrative form a short account of your preparation in rhetoric and composition, as follows: (1) State the school (or schools) you attended; (2) the time spent upon these studies; (3) the number of compositions written; (4) the text-books used; (5) any exercises or methods of instruction that seem to you to have been particularly profitable or unprofitable.

2. Prepare an outline for an essay of about 1,000 words on one of the following topics, indicating the divisions and sub-divisions with such definiteness that the course of the thought from point to point can easily be traced:
   (a) Resources of the State of Michigan.
   (b) Origin of the War with Spain.
   (c) Influence of a Circulating Library.

N. B.—Do not write an essay.

3. Having examined the following essay written by a pupil in the 9th grade, state (1) what you regard as the prevailing faults; (2) what advice you would give the writer to assist him in overcoming his defects of composition:

   While I was spending my summer vacation in the country we had quite a bad runaway. While out driving one afternoon, myself and a friend, we had a very spirited span of horses, and we were going by a bicycle when the horses took fright and started to run away. Of course I was so frightened, never being in a runaway before, that I really did not know what to do. So I jumped out over the wheel, spraining my ankle. The driver soon got the horses under control and came back to where I was and took me home, which place I did not leave for three weeks, and you may be sure when I did I didn't go out riding, and after it I was so timid I would not go again.

N. B.—Write what you would actually say to the pupil, if you were talking with him about his essay.

4. State three important rhetorical principles with which pupils in the 8th grade should, in your opinion, be familiar.

5. Analyze the following paragraph, indicating (a) the leading thought, (b) the office of each sentence in the development of this thought: (Sentences are numbered for convenience of reference).

   (1) I would save the Union. (2) I would save it in the shortest way under the Constitution. (3) The sooner the national authority can be restored, the nearer the Union will be "The Union as it was." (4) If there be those who would not save the Union unless they could at the same time destroy slavery, I do not agree with them. (5) My paramount object in this struggle is to save the Union and is not either to save or destroy slavery. (6) If I could save the Union without freeing any slave, I would do it, and if I could do it by freeing some and leaving others alone, I would also do that. (7) What I do about slavery and the colored race, I do because it helps to save this Union; and what I forbear, I forbear because I do not believe it would help to save the Union. (8) I shall do less, whenever I shall believe what I am doing hurts the cause; and I shall do more, whenever I shall believe doing more will help the cause. (9) I shall try to correct errors when shown to be errors, and I shall adopt new views so fast as they shall appear to be true views. (10) I have here stated my purpose according to my view of official duty, and I intend no modification of my oft-expressed personal wish that all men, everywhere, could be free.

6. Make a list of all the words which can be used to supply the omission in the following sentence, indicating the word which, in your opinion, is most fitting for this purpose, and giving reasons for your choice:
   "After the concert the people often waited outside to accompany him to his hotel. Paganini seemed delighted with this kind of homage and would go out at such seasons and mix freely with them; but he was often quite ———, and bent upon absolute seclusion."

6

## CIVIL GOVERNMENT.

1. (a) Give a synonym for equity.
   (b) Define "good citizenship."
2. Show how the town government of New England grew out of parish government in Old England.
3. What first created two great political parties in America, and who were the leaders?
4. Give some of the most important safe-guards of our government?
5. Name five prohibitions on Congress.
6. (a) What are "representatives at large?"
   (b) What is a "pocket veto," and what president first made use of it?
7. Name the four ordinary functions of the governor of a state.
8. (a) Of what value is the president's annual message?
   (b) What president first issued a written message to Congress?
9. What are the duties of the United States Attorney General?
10. (a) What is an Administrative Board?
    (b) Name several of the more important ones.

## GENERAL HISTORY.

1. State the causes and results of the Peloponnesian War. What part did Alcibiades take in this war?
2. Enumerate the steps by which Philip of Macedon gained the controlling influence in Greece.
3. Briefly contrast Greece and Italy in regard to manner of growth and influence.
4. What changes were made in the Roman constitution by the rivalry between the patricians and plebeians?
5. (a) Through what means did the church gain temporal power?
   (b) Briefly characterize the reign of Constantine.
6. What brought about the Revolution of 1688? State the main features of the Bill of Rights.
7. Account for the interest taken by the United States in the Venezuelan question.
8. How does the Clayton-Bulwer treaty affect the construction by the United States of a Nicaraguan canal?
9. State in full the cause of the Transvaal trouble.
10. What has the Peace Congress accomplished?

## GEOGRAPHY.

1. Mention some sciences which are connected with geography. Show the relation.
2. Quote the Committee of Twelve on the commercial side of farm products.
3. What is the importance of the Trans-Siberian railway?
4. Of what value are topographical names? Illustrate.
5. (a) What do you understand by mathematical geography?
   (b) At what stage of school work would you introduce it?
6. Distinguish between springs, artesian wells, hot springs, and geysers.
7. What should be the aim of map drawing?
8. In what part of the United States is most of the manufacturing carried on? Give reasons.
9. Explain the formation of a natural bridge, and locate one.
10. For what purposes do you consider the use of the map superior to that of the globe, and vice versa? Give reasons for your answer.

## GEOLOGY.

1. Explain how plants and animals have contributed to the formation of rocks.
2. *Describe the rocks in the lower Silurian era.*

3. What is the composition of quartz? Give three characteristics by which quartz is known.
4. State the difference between talc and soapstone.
5. Make a drawing showing how water is forced to the surface in artesian wells.
6. What is the composition of each of the following: granite, limestone, lime, feldspar, and mica?
7. How does soil differ from subsoil in regard to composition, depth, and use?
8. Define fossil, delta, peat, dip, and erosion.
9. (a) Distinguish between a stalactite and a stalagmite.
   (b) What chemical change takes place when limestone is changed to lime?
10. How much geology can be profitably taught in the grades?

## GEOMETRY.

1. (a) Define geometry, point, line, theorem. (b) Distinguish between proof and demonstration, axiom and postulate, lemma and corollary.
2. Give two postulates and three axioms.
3. Give an outline of the process of demonstration of the rule for finding the volume of a sphere. The same for the arcs of a triangle.
4. Demonstrate the Pythagorean proposition.
5. Divide a given line into mean and extreme ratio, and prove your work.
6. The radius of a circle is one; what is the side of an inscribed equilateral triangle, square, pentagon, and hexagon?
7. Discuss the relative educational value of an original and a committed demonstration.
8. Discuss the place that mensuration should occupy in geometry.
9. What are some of the methods of modern geometry?
10. Compare the German and American methods of teaching geometry.

## GRAMMAR.

1. Give an example of a simple, a compound, and a complex sentence. Analyze each according to your model of analysis.
2. Define factitive. Illustrate by examples and diagram.
3. "They are never alone who are accompanied by their dog." Diagram by at least two methods and give the relative values of each.
4. Parse each word according to your model:
   "The tender grace of a day that is dead,
   Will never come back to me."
5. Make sentences containing the following words properly used: sit, lie, him, whom, and they. Parse the words and diagram the sentences.
6. Give a general outline of your method of teaching grammar.
7. Does grammar have any relation to composition or reading? Discuss.
8. Discuss the value of learning rules and definitions in grammar.
9. Give examples illustrating the technical grammatical use of words, and the use of the same words in general.
10. Discuss the end to be attained by the teaching of formal grammar.

## LITERATURE.

1. Define and give examples of epic, lyric, and dramatic poetry.
2. (a) Give the approximate date of the introduction of the sonnet into English poetry.
   (b) Mention some of the most perfect English sonnets.
3. (a) What is the meter of "Hiawatha?" of "Paradise Lost?" Of "Snow Bound?"
   (b) Name five English and American poets noted for the music of their verse.
4. Name three of our best American historians, briefly stating the historical ground covered by each.
5. Mention several text-books on literature which you would recommend for high school use, with reasons for choice.

6. (a) Who is the poet laureate of England, and who preceded him?
   (b) Briefly characterize the work of each.
7. Give your opinion of the literary value of the works of George Eliot. (Discuss quite fully.)
8. (a) What is the plot of Julius Caesar?"
   (b) In your opinion was the chief motive of Cassius jealousy or patriotism?
9. Discuss some of the literary merits of the above named play.
10. If obliged to teach the "History of English Literature" in twenty weeks, what authors would you ask your pupils to read in class?

## ORTHOGRAPHY.

1. (a) What is your opinion of reformed spelling?
   (b) Name several words that are now quite commonly spelled by the reform method.
2. Give words to illustrate five of the six substitutes for *sh*.
3. Indicate pronunciation of the following: chamois, busy, colonel, extol, verge, greasy, victuals, formidable, decade, pyramidal.
4. Write sentences containing homonyms for the following: be, stile, blue, him, rain.
5. Give correct spelling for the names of ten vegetables.

## PENMANSHIP.

Write a paragraph of not less than fifty words, descriptive of that position in writing which you deem hygienically the best, stating some of the reasons for your belief.

What three ends do you seek to obtain in teaching penmanship?

## PHYSICS.

1. What concept characterizes the largest number of topics in physics? Show the truth of this.
2. What must be the displacement of a balloon filled with hydrogen, to have a lifting buoyancy of one ton, calling hydrogen $\frac{1}{14}$ the weight of air?
3. Engine No. 999, N. Y. C. R. R., ran one mile in 32 seconds. From what height would it have to fall to attain this speed?
4. The weight of engine No. 999 is 110 tons; what energy does it possess by virtue of its motion when going at the rate of a mile in 32 seconds?
5. At what rate must a one-pound mass move to possess a foot-pound of energy?
6. Discuss the relative values of the text-book method, lecture method, and the laboratory method of teaching physics, showing the limitations of each.
7. How would you teach the physics of the rainbow?
8. Illustrate and describe the simplest form of the ordinary steam engine.
9. Define the electrical units.
10. (a) What are some recent advances in physical science? (b) Name six books upon the subject of physics.

## PHYSIOLOGY.

1. (a) What is the composition of bone?
   (b) Explain as to a class how stooping causes "round shoulders."
2. (a) Discuss the muscular system—including tendons—as to structure and use.
   (b) How is strabismus cured?
3. (a) Explain oxidation as applied to digestion.
   (b) How does nature compensate for the lack of teeth in birds?
4. (a) Define food and classify as to composition and use.

(b) What three purposes do foods serve?

5. Give the scientific explanation of the fact that alcohol lowers the temperature of the body.
6. Explain respiration under the following heads:  (a) purpose; (b) organs—structure and function; (c) breathing.
7. Discuss the relation between respiration and repair.
8. Describe the nervous system. (20 credits.)
9. Describe the ear, illustrating by drawings.

## SCHOOL LAW.

*Directions*—(1) Be sure you understand the question. (2) Take time enough and pains enough to answer it in the way you wish it to be understood and graded. (3) Number your answers to correspond with the number of the question or its several subdivisions. (4) Write plainly and legibly.

1. (a) With whom should a contract to teach in the common schools be made?
   (b) Is it neccessary to have this contract in writing?
2. Under the laws of Michigan, who may teach in the common schools?  Explain fully.
3. Who may grant teachers' certificates in this State?
4. May non-resident pupils attend the common schools without paying tuition?
5. (a) May a teacher in this State inflict corporal punishment?
   (b) What control has the teacher over his pupils on their way to and from school?
6. Who decides what text-books shall be used in a particular common school in this State?
7. Give general duties of the county commissioner of schools.
8. Can parents be compelled to send their children to school in this State?  Explain fully.
9. (a) What is the source of the money with which the teacher is paid?
   (b) Who fixes the amount of the school fund in the State as well as in a particular district?
10. What have you read upon the subject of "School Law"?

## THEORY AND ART OF TEACHING.

1. Name four great educational writers of the past whose teachings you best know, and describe the theory of each. (25 credits.)
2. What is the difference between the science and the art of teaching?  In your own experience which came first?  (6 credits.)
3. What steps are included in the preparation of a lesson by a teacher?  (8 credits.)
4. "Spare the rod and spoil the child."  Give your own reasons for and against the soundness of this as a principle of teaching.  (5 credits.)
5. What do you understand to be the purpose of a "Course of Study"?  Why not allow each teacher to follow any chance order of lessons?  (8 credits.)
6. (a) Distinguish between remembering and recollecting;  (b) between judging and reasoning;  (c) between feeling and thinking.  (10 credits.)
7. In what sense is the following statement true:  "I know, but I can't tell"?  In what sense untrue?  (10 credits.)
8. What defects in teaching arise from a lack of scholarship on the part of the teacher?  (10 credits.)
9. What defects arise from a lack of professional knowledge?  (10 credits.)
10. What are the qualities of a teacher who is "strong in government"?  (8 credits.)

## UNITED STATES HISTORY.

1. How was American colonization affected by the defeat of the Spanish Armada?  State reasons for your answer.
2. (a) What were the five so-called "Intolerable Acts of Parliament?"

(b) What were the Townshend Acts?
3. Briefly describe the financial condition of the country at the beginning of Washington's administration. What financial measures were adopted?
4. State the purpose and political results of the Hartford convention.
5. Mention five charges made against George III in the Declaration of Independence.
6. Show the relation between Jackson's policy toward the United States banks and the panic of 1837.
7. What was the Webster-Ashburton treaty?
8. Briefly state the sectional feeling in regard to the "tariff of abominations," and tell why so-called.
9. What was the National Bank Act of 1863? What was its special purpose? State its effect upon state banks.
10. Give a brief history of slavery in the United States, including effects and ultimate result.

## ZOOLOGY.

1. Define the following terms: cell, embryology, fauna, zoölogy, comparative anatomy.
2. Describe the amoeba.
3. (a) How does the sponge obtain its food, and how reproduce itself?
   (b) From what waters are the sponges of commerce taken?
4. (a) What is the main difference between the sea anemone and coral?
   (b) Describe the growth of a coral reef.
5. (a) Why is the ground often covered with worms after a heavy rain?
   (b) In what way does the earth worm benefit man?
6. Describe the breathing apparatus of a beetle.
7. Describe the metamorphosis of a tomato worm, and tell what moth it produces.
8. Cite some facts to show that ants possess considerable intelligence.
9. Mention some feature to show that nature has adapted each of the following to its manner of life: woodpecker, duck, hawk, pelican, snipe.
10. Contrast the general characteristics of mollusks with those of vertebrates.

## II. QUESTIONS PREPARED BY THE STATE BOARD OF EDUCATION FOR EXAMINATION HELD AT LANSING, DECEMBER, 1899.

### ALGEBRA.

1. Solve: $3x^2 - 6x + 1 = 0$

2. Simplify: (a) $\dfrac{1}{2x-1} - \dfrac{2x - \dfrac{1}{2x}}{4x^2-1}$,    (b) $\left[ x^3 - \dfrac{1}{x^3} - 3\left(x - \dfrac{1}{x}\right)\right] \div \left(x - \dfrac{1}{x}\right)$

3. Factor completely: $x^6 - 4096$, $a^2 - b^2 + a - b$, $x^2 + a^2 + 2ax - y^2$.

4. Simplify and express with positive indices: $\sqrt[3]{(a+b)^5} \times (a+b)^{-\frac{2}{3}}$, $\left(\dfrac{a^{-\frac{2}{3}}x^{\frac{1}{2}}}{ax^{-1}}\right)^2 \div \sqrt[3]{\dfrac{a^{-1}}{x^{-2}}}$

5. Solve without clearing of fractions: $\begin{cases} \dfrac{1}{4x} + \dfrac{1}{3y} - 2 = 0 \\ \dfrac{1}{y} - \dfrac{1}{2x} - 1 = 0 \end{cases}$

6. What is the property of a person whose income is $1,140, when one-twelfth of it is invested at 2%, one-half at 3%, one-third at 4½%, and the remainder pays no dividend?

. Solve: $x - 12 : y + 3 = 2x - 19 : 5y - 13 = 5 : 14.$

8. Solve: $\begin{cases} x^3 + y^3 = \frac{341}{8} \\ x + y = \frac{1}{4} . \end{cases}$

9. The perimeter of one square exceeds that of another by 100 feet, and the area of the larger square exceeds three times the area of the smaller by 325 sq. ft.; find the length of their sides.

10. Express the condition that the roots of $ax^2 + bx + c = 0$ may both be (a) real and equal; (b) real and unequal; (c) imaginary; (d) equal in magnitude but opposite in sign.

## AMERICAN HISTORY.

1. What did William Pitt have to do with the French and Indian war?
2. What laws of Congress provoked the passage of the Virginia and Kentucky Resolutions, who wrote the resolutions, what was their purport and effect?
3. What were the political effects of the war of 1812?
4. What bearing does the Monroe doctrine have on our occupancy of Cuba and control of the Philippines?
5. Over what question did the struggle for the right of petition occur? Who was the champion for the right of petition, and who was the leading man against it?
6. Trace briefly the history of Nullification in the North and South from the adoption of the constitution to 1832.
7. Upon what principles was the Whig party organized, and who were its two greatest leaders?
8. How can the present so-called "expansion" policy of the United States be justified; or, if not to be justified, why condemned?
9. Give some account of the resumption of specie payment after the close of the civil war.
10. What was the New England Confederacy; how long did it last; why was it not permanent?

## ARITHMETIC.

1. What is the educational value of checks in arithmetical work? To what extent should answers be given to pupils?
2. In extracting square root, why separate the number into periods of two figures each? Consider 761.4. Explain what is meant by the trial divisor; by the complete divisor.
3. What is the weight of air in a room 5m. long, 3m. wide, and 4m. high, if one c. dm. of air weighs .0018kg?
4. The perimeters of a square, a circle, and an equilateral triangle are each 17 ft. in length. Find by how much the area of the circle exceeds the area of the other two figures.
5. Buffalo is 78° 57' 48" W. and San Francisco is 122° 26' 12" W. long. When it is 20 min. after 6 a. m., standard time, at San Francisco, what time is it at Buffalo? What time is it at a place 186° 30' W. long.?
6. Prove that a number is divisible by 9 if the sum of its digits is divisible by 9. State the check for divisibility by casting out the 9s.
7. The list price of an article is $150. If trade discounts of 25%, 10%, and 2% are allowed, what is the net price?
8. A note for $1,500, dated April 14, 1894, with interest at 5%, bears the following indorsements: June 8, 1894, $450; Sept. 1, 1894, $10; Oct. 29, 1894, $740. What is due April 14, 1895?
9. Write a 60 day note, signed by John Smith and payable to the order of Thomas Jones, bearing the legal rate of interest. What is the contract rate of interest in Michigan? What is the penalty for usury?
10. A ladder 78 ft. long stands perpendicularly against a building. How far must it be pulled out at the foot that the top may be lowered 6 ft.?

## BOTANY.

*Directions*—(1) Be sure you understand the question. (2) Take time enough and pains enough to answer it in the way you wish it understood and graded. (3) Number your answers to correspond with the number of the uestion or its several subdivisions. (4) Write plainly and legibly. Do not be in a hurry.q

N. B.—Write as carefully and fully as possible on any ten of the following questions.

1. Describe in correct botanical language any flowering plant with which you are familiar.
2. Give a detailed account of the vegetable cell, including structure, modifications of form, and adaptation to different functions.
3. Describe the microscopic structure of the most important cell-contents, as starch, aleurone, etc., and discuss their behavior with various micro-chemical reagents.
4. Discuss the morphology of stems.
5. Describe (with diagram) a typical flower, and discuss deviations from the type.
6. Give in detail the life history of any fungus with which you are familiar.
7. Describe in the same way and in full, any species of algae.
8. Give an account of the various means by which pollination is accomplished.
9. Describe the process of fertilization as it takes place in flowering plants.
10. Give an account of the germination of seeds and the conditions under which it takes place.
11. Figure and describe a simple form of apparatus for demonstrating the *respiration* of plants.
12. Describe the most important processes in the nutrition of green plants.
13. Describe the changes undergone by the nucleus during the process of cell-formation.
14. Discuss the adaptation of plants to their environment.
15. Define *species, genus, variety*. What was Darwin's view as to the origin of species?
16. Define "alternation of generations," and illustrate by the cycle of development of mosses and ferns.
17. Write the scientific and also the common name of five families of flowering plants, and give their distinguishing characteristics.
18. Write a classification of fruits, giving the principle on which it is based.
19. Name half a dozen important botanical works or periodicals.
20. Give a brief working plan for a half year's course in botany in a high school.

NOTE.—State where you studied botany, the length of time, text-books (if any), nature and extent of laboratory or other practical work.

## CHEMISTRY.

*Directions*—(1) Be sure you understand the question. (2) Take time enough and pains enough to answer it in the way you wish it to be understood and graded. (3) Number your answers to correspond with the number of the question or its several subdivisions. (4) Write plainly and legibly. Do not be in a hurry.

1. What text-books have you studied and what laboratory work have you done in: (a) General chemistry; (b) qualitative analysis; (c) organic chemistry? Define and give example: (a) base; (b) acid; (c) normal salt; (d) primary salt; (e) carbohydrate.
2. Fully discuss sulphur dioxide in respect to (a) methods of preparation; (b) physical properties; (c) chemical properties.
3. What experiments are necessary to teach the student the essentials concerning the composition of ammonia?
4. (a) Describe the preparation of hydrogen sulphide from iron, sulphur, and hydrochloric acid. (Write equation for each reaction.) (b) What use is made of hydrogen sulphide in the separation of metals?
5. Are nitrogen and oxygen mixed or chemically combined in the atmosphere? What are the proofs?
6. How are sulphuric, oxalic, and orthophosphoric acids separated in solution? *Write* all equations.

7.  Outline a method for the separation of barium, calcium, and strontium.
8.  State Avogadro's Law, give its physical basis, and explain its application to the determination of molecular weights.
9.  Write the formulae of cane sugar, grape sugar, alcohol, and acetic acid; discuss the chemical relationship between these substances.
10. What chemical preparation should the student have before beginning the study of qualitative analysis?

## CIVIL GOVERNMENT.

1.  Name the principal forms of government, and give leading features of each.
2.  Discuss the methods of electing president of the United States.
3.  How are national banks organized?
4.  (a) What is meant by the fifty-sixth congress? (b) Long session? (c) Short session? (d) Special session?
5.  (a) What is meant by jurisdiction as applied to a court? (b) Explain the terms original, appellate, exclusive, and concurrent jurisdiction. (20 credits.)
6.  (a) By what authority is a village charter granted? (b) Name the governing body. (c) Who determines rate of taxation in your township?
7.  (a) When and by what governor were several state officers removed? (b) What was the cause of their removal?
8.  (a) In what court would you sue a man for a debt of fifty dollars? Ten thousand dollars? (b) In what court would a person accused of murder be tried? A boy accused of disorderly conduct?
9.  Give five arguments in favor of the election of United States senators by direct vote of the people.

## GENERAL HISTORY.

1.  What permanent good resulted from the conquests of Alexander?
2.  What were the results to Greece, of the Persian invasions of Grecian territory?
3.  Give an account of Pompey's career before the Triumvirate which he joined.
4.  In what way was it brought about that Christianity became the religion of the Roman empire? At what time?
5.  Who was Richelieu and what did he accomplish?
6.  Give a brief account of the struggle between Charles the First and the English Parliament.
7.  Give somewhat in detail the causes and results of the French Revolution.
8.  How did England get control of Egypt and on what conditions? What is the present status of affairs in Egypt?
9.  How are Russia and England rivals? Where do their interests conflict?
10. What was Bismark's policy for the unification of Germany and how was it carried out?

## GEOMETRY.

1.  Demonstrate: If the bisector of the vertical angle of a triangle also bisects the base, the triangle is isosceles.
2.  How many sides has a polygon the sum of whose interior angles is 48 right angles?
3.  The base of a pyramid is a square whose sides are each 10 inches in length; the faces are equilateral triangles. Find the volume.
4.  Define spherical excess. What is the area of a spherical triangle whose angles are 90°, 100°, and 110°?
5.  What are the essentials of a good unit of measure? How is an inscribed angle measured? Show that your answers to these two questions are consistent.
6.  Construct the triangle ABC; given the angle A, the side opposite the angle A, and the altitude on the side opposite the angle A.

7. Under what conditions are triangles similar? Under what conditions are they congruent (equal)? In general, how many conditions determine similarity? How many determine congruence?
8. In the same circle, or in equal circles, the less of two unequal chords is at the greater distance from the center. State and prove the converse of this proposition.
9. Demonstrate: The area of the surface of a sphere is equal to the area of four great circles.
10. Demonstrate: In any right triangle the line drawn from the vertex of the right angle to the middle of the hypotenuse is equal to one-half of the hypotenuse.

NOTE.—Name three good text-books in geometry, and tell why you consider them good books.

## GEOGRAPHY.

1. Tell how you teach the relation existing between geography, geology, and mineralogy.
2. Compare the advantages of the farm and city for the study of geography.
3. Locate accurately Jerusalem, Waterloo, Sevastopol, Ladysmith, and Trafalgar.
4. State what you understand by a "production" map and tell how you would make one.
5. Show the influence of latitude, altitude, land, and water upon temperature.
6. Explain the importance of the situation of the Hawaiian Islands?
7. Briefly speak on the work of the winds.
8. Name and locate a great delta formation in each of the following: North America, Asia, Africa, and South America.
9. Distinguish between astronomical and physical climate, telling upon what each depends.
10. (a) What is the cause of tides?
   (b) Illustrate by diagram the production of tidal waves.

## GEOLOGY.

1. In what ways are mountains formed? Illustrate by diagrams the structure of the different kinds of mountains.
2. (a) How are springs formed and where would you expect to find them?
   (b) How are caves formed and where would you expect to find them?
   (c) Name the conditions favorable for artesian wells?
3. What are geysers? Describe the phenomena and cause of eruption?
4. Define and illustrate by drawings, cleavage, dip, strike, dike, and drift?
5. In what period does man first appear? What are the evidences of his early existence?
6. What is the difference between slate and shale? Between marble, chalk, and lime-stone?
7. Account for the metamorphic rocks?
8. Give a full account of the Nebular Hypothesis.
9. What is the difference between historical, structural, and dynamical geology?
10. When would you begin the teaching of geology and with what subjects would you correlate it?

## GRAMMAR.

1. Analyze, or diagram according to Reed and Kellogg's system, the following:
   But whether I put the present numbers too high or too low is a matter of little moment......Whilst we are discussing any given magnitude, they are grown to it......I put this consideration of the present and the growing numbers in the front of our deliberation, because, Sir, this consideration will make it evident to a blunter discernment than yours, that no partial, narrow,

contracted, pinched, occasional system will be at all suitable to such an object.—Burke on Conciliation with the Colonies.

In question 1, what is the difference between the formation and meaning of the verb-phrases, "are discussing" and "are grown?"

Analyze, or diagram as above, the following:

Lake Leman lies by Chillon's walls:

...........................

A double dungeon wall and wave
Have made—and *like* a living *grave*
Below the surface of the lake
The dark vault lies *wherein* we lay,
We heard it *ripple* night and *day;*
Sounding o'er our heads it knocked;
And I have felt the winter's *spray*
*Wash* through the bars when winds were high
And wanton in the happy sky.
—Byron's "The Prisoner of Chillon."

Give grammatical construction of italicized words.

3. Correct errors in the following, and give your reasons:
   1. One or the other have erred in their statement.
   2. He don't like it.
   3. Who did he refer to, he or I?
   4. Him being a stranger, they easily misled him.
   5. I only laugh when I feel like it.
4. Write a sentence containing a transitive verb, a direct and an indirect object. Change the sentence to the passive voice, and point out changes in construction.
5. Write a full declension of the following words: him, wolf, piano, whosoever, folly.
6. What do you understand by comparison? Compare two adjectives, one regular and the other irregular; also two adverbs, one regular, the other irregular.
7. Write a synopsis in the first person, singular number, active and passive, of the verb *smite*. Write also all infinitives and participles of this verb.
8. Illustrate by sentences the difference in use between participles and infinitives. Explain fully.
9. Write a *single* page, giving brief account of your journey to this place, or a description of your home, or the narrative of some recent event in your neighborhood.
10. Name at least three distinct objects you have in view in instruction in grammar.

## LITERATURE.

1. Name 12 great English authors between Chaucer and Tennyson, giving one or two of the chief works of each. Mention 8 great American authors with two works of each.
2. Name the author of each of the following works, and mention another work by each author: Areopagitica, Annus Mirabilis, The Tale of a Tub, English Bards and Scotch Reviewers, Lay of the Last Minstrel, Rasselas, Essays of Elia, Sketch Book, Marble Faun, American Flag, Evangeline, Biglow Papers, The Task, The Rivals, Tam O'Shanter, Marmion, The Giaour.
3. Sketch briefly the plan of the Canterbury Tales. Name other English or American poems written on the same general plan.
4. When and by whom were the following books written: Robinson Crusoe, Gulliver's Travels, Pickwick Papers, Faery Queen, In Memoriam? Briefly outline one of them.
5. Give an account of the life of the greatest Scotch poet, and mention two of his poems.
6. (a) Who were the so-called "Lake School" poets? Mention an important poem by each.
   (b) Mention three leading English historians and two American historians of the nineteenth century; also the leading work of each.

7. Locate in literature and write a brief character sketch of one of the following: Cassius, Iago, Shylock, Hamlet, Lady Macbeth.
8. Explain and locate the following: Gulliver, Micawber, Rip Van Winkle, Little Nell, Geoffrey Crayon, Wizard of the North, Old Manse, Will Carleton, Biglow Papers, Bard of Avon.
9. Compare the poetry of Tennyson with that of Browning.
10. Write a brief essay on the poetry of Whittier.

## ORTHOGRAPHY.

1. What is the value, if any, of oral spelling? Why use a spelling book in spelling exercises.
2. Illustrate all the vowel sounds.
    (a) Abbreviate: the same, that is, take notice, next month, for example.
    (b) Give meaning of the prefixes un, bi, intro, col, de.
    Indicate pronunciation: debris, mirage, decadence, vehement, menu, finale, won't, easel, gladiolus, Himalaya.
4. What is word analysis? Analyze immigration.

## PHYSIOLOGY.

1. Speak briefly of cellular growth.
2. (a) What use of the microscope do you make in class work?
    (b) Give directions for preparing a solid specimen for the microscope in such a manner that all parts will remain intact.
3. (a) Account for the fact that sugar is fattening.
    (b) State the function of the liver.
4. (a) What is the effect of alcohol upon the tissues of the body?
    (b) Is pure alcohol or a solution of the same used to preserve specimens of animal or vegetable matter? Why?
5. (a) What is meant by "fatty" heart and palpitation of the heart?
    (b) Give the physiological explanation of fainting.
6. Describe digestion and tell where most of the food is digested.
7. Tell what is meant by asphyxia and give directions for restoring one suffering from the same.
8. What is the purpose of the vaso-motor nerves? Illustrate.
9. Why should the schoolroom be especially well ventilated? Give some approved methods of ventilation.
10. Show the relation between bacteria and disease.

## PHYSICS.

1. (a) What force acting for 10 sec. will give 150 g. of matter a velocity of 50 cm?
    (b) How much energy will the same body have by virtue of its velocity?
    (c) Define the units in which the results in (a) and (b) are given.
2. (a) When a barometer reads 29.34 in., what is the pressure per square inch?
3. (a) What is meant by "latent heat of steam?"
    (b) How would you find it experimentally?
    (c) If a metal rod at 40° C. is 20 ft. long and at 75° C. 20.014 ft., what is its coefficient of expansion?
4. (a) By what simple means can electro-static charges be produced?
    (b) What apparatus should first be constructed, or purchased, for use in electro-statics?
5. (a) What current strength will eight cells produce through a coil of 50 ohms, when each cell has an E. M. F. of 1.4 volts and a resistance of 1.15 ohms (1) arranged in series, and (2) in parallel?
6. (a) Diagram and describe an ordinary electric bell.
    (b) An electro-magnet.
7. (a) Describe the induction coil and state some of its uses.
    (b) State the laws underlying its action.

8. (a) Construct the path of a ray of light through water, assuming the angle of incidence to be 30° and the index of refraction ⅘.
9. (a) State fully how a converging lens disposes of light.
    (b) Diagram a compound microscope and show its action upon light.
    (c) What is a "real" image? Give examples.
10. (a) What is resonance? Example.
    (b) If a string 4 ft. long vibrates 225 times per second when its tension is 25 pounds, what will be its vibration number when its length is three feet and its tension 9 lbs.?

## RHETORIC AND COMPOSITION.

*Directions*—(1) Be sure you understand the question. (2) Take time enough and pains enough to answer it in the way you wish it understood and graded. (3) Number your answers to correspond with the number of the question or its several subdivisions. (4) Write plainly and legibly. Do not be in a hurry.

1. Give a brief account of your preparation for this part of the examination. Include (a) the school or schools in which you have studied rhetoric and composition; (b) the places in which you have taught the subject; (c) the books upon it that you have studied or read. Throw the account into the form of a letter to a friend.
2. The following essay subjects were assigned by a teacher of composition to pupils in the second year of the high school course. Criticize them and propose any modification that seems desirable: 1. Chivalry. 2. The Philippines. 3. Shakespeare's Art. 4. The Dangers of Imperialism.
3. Name and illustrate three common errors in the use of words. Give the correct forms.
4. What is the chief rhetorical excellence of the following passage?
    "Herein, I think, lies the chief attraction of railway travel. The speed is so easy and the train disturbs so little the scenes through which it takes us, that our heart becomes full of the placidity and stillness of the country; and while the body is borne forward in the flying chain of carriages the thoughts alight, as the humor moves them, at unfrequented stations; they make haste up the poplar alley that leads towards the town; they are left behind with the signal man as, shading his eyes with his hand, he watches the long train sweep away into the golden distance."
5. Supply the missing portion in the following passage. Show that the words supplied are logically called for by the course of the thought:
    "Some races of men seem moulded in wax, soft and melting, at once plastic and feeble. Some races, like some metals, combine the greatest flexibility with the greatest strength. But the Indian is hewn out of a rock. You can rarely change the form without destruction of the substance. Races of inferior energy have possessed a power of expansion and assimilation to which he is a stranger; and • • • • • • • He will not learn the arts of civilization, and he and his forest must perish together. The stern unchanging features of his mind excite an admiration from their very immutability; and we look with deep interest on the fate of this irreclaimable son of the wilderness, the child who will not be weaned from the breast of his rugged mother."
6. Discriminate the meanings of the following pairs of words. Write sentences in which they are used correctly:
    1 { adduce / educe    2 { exceptional / exceptionable    3 { credible / creditable
7. (a) What is the rhetorical value of the figures in the following passage? (b) Rewrite the passage, changing the figures to plain statements:
    "A perfectly healthy sentence, it is true, is extremely rare. For the most part we miss the hue and fragrance of the thought; as if we could be satisfied with the dews of the morning or evening without their colors, or the heavens without their azure. The most attractive sentences are, perhaps, not the wisest, but the surest and roundest."
8. What is the difference between description and narration?
9. State the essential principles of good narration?
10. Criticize the following composition written by a pupil eleven years of age:

## ALCOHOL.

Alcohol is a kind of fluid. It is found in different liquors. It is taken from these liquors by distillation. It is this that makes such liquors as brandy, rum and whisky intoxicating, if you take too much of these liquors.

Alcohol when pure will cause death if it is taken. Alcohol will burn like a lamp and has a pale bluish flame. It gives out no smoke.

If the cork is left out of a bottle of alcohol the alcohol will evaporate very fast.

## SCHOOL LAW.

*Directions*—(1) Be sure you understand the question. (2) Take time enough and pains enough to answer it in the way you wish it understood and graded. (3) Number your answers to correspond with the number of the question or its several subdivisions. (4) Write plainly and legibly. Do not be in a hurry.

1. How many months of school must be maintained during a school year to entitle a district to its share of the primary school money?
2. (a) who has the power to locate a school site: (b) to establish a district library?
3. (a) What is the general extent of a teacher's authority over the pupil. (b) What control has the teacher over the pupil beyond the school premises?
4. Who fixes the standard of examination for teachers in the rural schools?
5. Are the holders of diplomas from the various private colleges in this state qualified to teach without taking the regular teacher's examination? Explain fully.
6. State briefly your understanding of the compulsory school law in this state. What is the duty of the teacher in respect to such law?
7. How may a new school district be organized in Michigan?
8. State fully the duties and powers of the "county commissioner of schools."
9. State fully the rights of a teacher to collect salary who has not been granted a certificate to teach.
10. Give the time when the different constitutions of Michigan were adopted.

## THEORY AND ART.

*Directions*—(1) Be sure you understand the question. (2) Take time enough and pains enough to answer it in the way you wish it understood and graded. (3) Number your answers to correspond with the number of the question or its several subdivisions. (4) Write plainly and legibly. Do not be in a hurry.

1. (a) State fully what, in your judgment, is the value of the study of the history of education. (b) What histories of education have you read.
2. What may a teacher do in the school for the development of the moral character of his pupils?
3. (a) Discuss the value of good literature in the education of the child. (b) When should the reading of good literature begin. (c) Explain fully the reasons for your last answer.
4. State fully what you consider to be the chief requisites of a good teacher.
5. What may the teacher do, and what means do you employ to cultivate a taste for good literature on the part of your students?
6. (a) Give your general method of teaching United States history. (b) What criticism have you to offer upon the methods employed by other teachers whom you know, in teaching this subject?
7. (a) Give three advantages, or benefits, which a teacher gains in attending educational meetings for teachers. (b) What educational meetings have you attended during the past year?
8. In prescribing a course of reading for your pupils, do you permit the existing conditions in society in the particular community to govern you? Explain fully.
9. (a) What may a teacher do to induce his patrons to assist him in promoting the general welfare of the school? (b) What have you done along these lines? Explain fully.
10. Give the chief facts in the life of Horace Mann.

## ZOÖLOGY.

1. Describe the simplest forms of animal life.
2. What is comparative anatomy and of what value?
3. (a) What points of difference are there between the oyster and the fresh water mussel?
   (b) How are pearls produced?
4. To what family does the so-called "grasshopper" belong, and what are the names of several of its relatives?
5. Give an account of the genus aphis, and of its value to other insect life.
6. Give brief description of the growth of a hive of bees
7. (a) Describe the nervous system of the fish.
   (b) What can you say of the salmon of the Pacific?
8. What is the typical batrachian, and what metamorphosis does it undergo?
9. Give the general characteristics of the subkingdom vertebrata, class *aves*.
10. (a) Name the higher mammals. (b) Describe the manner of life of the mammal from which the whale-bone of commerce comes.

# COUNTY EXAMINATIONS.

## RULES GOVERNING EXAMINATIONS.

[Note to examiners and applicants—Read No. 11 carefully.]

1. The package containing the question shall be opened by the commissioner and he shall direct their distribution.

2. The questions upon a given subject shall be distributed at the same time to all applicants and no recess be allowed until the subject is finished.

3. Applicants, when absent at its opening, shall not be admitted to the examination except by the unanimous consent of the board of examiners.

4. No candidate shall leave the room or communicate with any other candidate or any visitor during the examination, except by permission of the commissioner.

5. All papers must be written on legal cap paper, unless the commissioner prescribes or permits some other size.

6. The commissioner shall be the custodian of the completed examination papers, and they *shall be kept on file at his office at least six months* after the examination.

7. In arithmetic a knowledge of principles and general accuracy in method, shall be considered not less than three times as important as obtaining a correct answer.

8. In grammar allowance shall be made for different authorities.

9. A candidate's handwriting shall be judged from the answers to the questions in penmanship.

10. Applicants for third grade certificates shall be examined in writing, orthography, reading, grammar, arithmetic, geography, United States history, civil government, theory and art of teaching, school law, physiology and hygiene with special reference to the effect upon the human system of alcoholic drinks, stimulants, and narcotics. Applicants for second grade certificates shall, in addition to the third grade branches, be required to write on two additional ones which they may select from the lists furnished in general history, botany, physics and algebra. Applicants for first grade certificates shall, in addition to third grade branches, be required to pass an examination in general history, botany, physics, algebra, and geometry.

11. Third grade certificates of class B are valid in ALL districts of the county in which they are granted. Third grade certificates of class A should be issued ONLY to those who teach in primary departments (first four grades) of graded schools. Holding a certificate of class A does not legally qualify a teacher for any other school. Boards of examiners must not grant certificates of class B to applicants who have done only the work required for a certificate of class A. Each printed list is plainly marked and no mistake should be made. (See Sec. 6, Act 147, Public Acts of 1893; also compiler's Section 131, School Law of 1897.)

12. Follow carefully the program given below, and do not vary to accommodate candidates who are tardy or who do not appear until the second half day.

| FIRST DAY. | SECOND DAY. |
|---|---|
| a. m. | a. m. |
| Orthography. | Reading. |
| Penmanship. | Civil Government. |
| Geography. | Grammar. |
| General History. | Physiology. |
| p. m. | p. m. |
| Arithmetic (oral and written). | Algebra. |
| U. S. History. | Botany. |
| School Law. | Physics (second grade). |
| Theory and Art. | |

Third Day (for first grade applicants only) Physics and Geometry.

JASON E. HAMMOND,
*Superintendent of Public Instruction.*

## ALGEBRA.

### First Grade.

1. General excellence, including neatness, will count for this number.
2. (a) How would you lead a class of beginners to understand elimination?
   (b) Why are the roots of an affected quadratic equation generally numerically unequal? When may they be equal?
3. Factor, showing the principle involved in each:—
   (a) $2x^2 + 6x - 8$.  (b) $1 - 14x^2y + 49x^4y^2$.  (c) $a^4 + a^2b^2 + b^4$.
4. Simplify $\dfrac{x+y}{x-y} + \dfrac{x-y}{x+y} + \dfrac{x+y}{x-y}$.
5. Find two numbers such that their product is equal to their sum, and their sum added to the sum of their squares equal to 12.
6. If $a : b :: c : d$, show that $b : a+b :: d : c+d$, giving reason for all changes.
7. A and B began to play together with equal sums of money; A first won $20, but afterwards lost half of all he then had, when his money was half as much as B's. How much had each at first? (Why can this be solved with one unknown quantity?)
8. (a) What is a surd, and what factor will always rationalize a monomial surd?
   (b) Find the square root of $14 + 6\sqrt{5}$.
9. Explain how to simplify the following by application of formulas, without actual multiplication: $(x+\dfrac{1}{x})(x^2 + \dfrac{1}{x^2})(x - \dfrac{1}{x})$.
10. A boy rode ten miles on his bicycle, when it broke down and he was compelled to return on foot. He found that it took one hour and fifteen minutes longer to walk back than to ride out. How fast did he ride, if he walked four miles less per hour than he rode?

### SECOND GRADE.

1. General excellence, including neatness, will count for this number.
2. (a) Explain why changing the signs of the subtrahend diminishes the result.
   (b) Why does every pure quadratic equation have two roots numerically equal, but with opposite signs?
3. Factor and give principles involved:
   (a) $4a^2 - 20ax + 25x^2$.  (b) $a^2b^2 - 1$.  (c) $x^2 + 8x + 15$.
4. When $a$ is added to the greater of two quantities, it is one-half the less; but if $b$ is added to the less, it is one-half the greater. Find the quantities.
5. Solve the following:
   (a) $\dfrac{1}{4}(3x + \dfrac{11}{3}) - \dfrac{1}{6}(4x - 2\dfrac{2}{3}) = \dfrac{1}{2}(5x - \dfrac{11}{6})$.

   (b) $(a + x)(b + x) = a(b + c) + \dfrac{a^2c}{b} + x^2$.

8

6. Find H. C. D. $\begin{cases} 3x^3 - 3x^2y + xy^2 - y^3. \\ 4x^2y - 5xy^2 + y^3. \end{cases}$

7. A certain fraction becomes one-half, if 6 is added to its denominator; it becomes one-fourth, if 5 is subtracted from its numerator. Find the fraction.

8. Find the number whose double diminished by 24, exceeds 80 by as much as the number itself is less than 100.

9. A can row a skiff 6 miles per hour with the current and 3 miles per hour against it; how far can he go down stream and yet return to the starting point in 8 hours?

10. (a) Find the square root of the completed square of which $x^2 - 4x$ are two terms.

   (b) Solve $\dfrac{x-2}{5} - \dfrac{8}{3x-4} - \dfrac{7}{5}$.

## ARITHMETIC.

### First and Second Grades.

1. A and B can do a piece of work in 12 days. A can do ¾ as much as B. How long will it take each to do the work?

2. At 20 cts. of sq. ft. what will be the cost of a close-fitting cover to a circular cistern 10 ft. deep, and holding 100 bbls?

3. Stock paying a 12% dividend nets investors 8% on their money. What is the market value?

4. What will be the face of a 60-day draft costing $450, if the rate of exchange is ⅛% premium and the rate of discount is 6%?

5. Find the contents of a globe having the same diameter as a 250 gallon cylinder whose length is six feet.

### THIRD GRADE, CLASS B.

1. Multiply 126⅔ by 36½ without reducing to improper fractions. (Let your work indicate in full what you would require of pupils in solving this class of examples.)

2. How many acres in a rectangular field ½ mile long and ⅓ mile broad?

3. What will it cost to dig a cellar 38 ft. long, 30 ft. wide, and 8 ft. deep, at 45 cts. per cu. yd.?

4. What is the face of a 90-day note that, discounted at 6%, yields $150?

5. A man sold 2 farms at $1,200 each. Ou one he gained 20%; on the other he lost ¼ of this gain. What is the ratio of his loss per cent to his gain per cent?

### CLASS A.

1. Multiply 126⅔ by 36½ without reducing to improper fractions. (Let your work indicate in full what you would require of pupils in solving this class of examples.)

2. How many acres in a rectangular field ½ mile long and ⅓ mile broad?

3. What will it cost to dig a cellar 38 ft. long, 30 ft. wide, and 8 ft. deep, at 45 cts. per cu. yd.?

4. What number diminished by 33⅓% of its 60% leaves 24?

5. Outline a term of second grade number work as given in the State Manual and Course of Study.

## MENTAL ARITHMETIC.

### All Grades.

NOTE.—A member of the Examining Board will examine candidates in classes of twenty-five or less, testing quickness to grasp the salient features of a problem, accuracy and rapidity of work, clearness and simplicity of analysis. In the right hand margin applicants will write *as many answers to the first twenty questions as possible in fifteen minutes*: one half per cent for each answer and one per cent additional for each *correct* one, is given in this part of the examination.

1. If a man buys a 10-cent cigar each day, what will he spend in a year?
2. Bought 10 lbs. of beef at $12\frac{1}{2}$ cents, 2 cans of oysters at 25 cents, 3 lbs. of sausage at 9 cents. I gave the shopkeeper a \$5 bill. Make the change.
3. Find the sum of 12 times 24 and 18 times 24.

   How many times 24?
4. John can earn as much in 3 days as Henry in 5 days. When John receives 60 cents, how much should Henry receive?
5. James earned \$$2\frac{3}{8}$, \$$5\frac{5}{8}$, \$$3\frac{1}{4}$, and spent $\frac{3}{4}$ of it. How much had he left?
6. Multiply 75 by $66\frac{2}{3}$.
7. Multiply $12\frac{1}{2}$ by 88.
8. Divide 75 by $\frac{1}{3}$.
9. Divide 2,500 by $12\frac{1}{2}$.
10. Multiply the quotient of 1,600 divided by 8,000, by 2,500.
11. If $2\frac{1}{2}$ lbs. of butter cost 28 cents, what will $12\frac{1}{2}$ lbs. cost?
12. A, B, and C worked together; A earned $\frac{2}{3}$ of \$1,000, B $\frac{5}{3}$ of \$1,000, and C $2\frac{2}{3}$ times \$1,000. How many thirds of \$1,000 did they together earn?
13. When 3 tons of coal cost as much as 10 cords of wood, how much is wood worth a cord, if coal is \$6 a ton?
14. How many cords of stove-wood in a pile 12 ft. long and 6 ft. high?
15. Jan. 1, 1899, fell on Sunday; on what day of the week was March 1?
16. A collector who charges 5% for collecting, paid me \$380. How much did he collect?
17. What fraction of a year is 5 mo. 18 days?
18. What is the bank discount on \$360 for 60 days at 6%?
19. A and B earned \$60, A earning $\frac{2}{3}$ as much as B. How much did each earn?
20. Find the length of that cube whose entire surface contains 1 sq. ft. 6 sq. in.

(From the remaining problems, second and third grade applicants write the full analysis of *four* selected by the examiner. First grade applicants must write the *last four*. Examiners should give ample time on this work.)

21. The rare metal gallium sells at the rate of \$25 for $1\frac{1}{2}$ grs. How much will a pwt. cost?
22. A seamstress can make a dress in 5 days; but with the assistance of her sister, she can make it in 2 days. How long will it take her sister to make the dress?
23. The sum of two numbers is 20 and their difference is 4. What are the numbers?
24. I sent a man \$240 out of which he was to take his commission of 20% for buying goods with the remainder. What was his commission?
25. 5 lbs. of lard are worth 2 lbs. of butter. How much should be paid for $3\frac{1}{3}$ lbs. of lard, if butter is 25 cents a pound?
26. A sold B a watch and gained $\frac{1}{6}$ of its cost. If he had received \$5 more he would have gained $\frac{1}{4}$ of the cost. Required the cost.
27. Which is better and how much per cent; to sell 100 oranges at the rate of 5 for 8 cents, or to divide them into two lots of 50 each and sell one lot at the rate of 2 for 3 cents, and the other at the rate of 3 for 5 cents?
28. A can plow a field in 6 days and B in 4 days. How long for both to plow the field, if A works only $\frac{1}{2}$ the time?
29. A two-inch pipe fills a cistern in 18 hrs. If a three-inch pipe is added, how long will it take both together to fill it?

## BOTANY.

### First Grade.

1. (a) What are the chief controlling agents in the geographical distribution of plants?
   (b) Give some illustrations of the adaptation of plants to their habitat.
2. How does the growth of root and stem differ?
3. (a) What sort of plants require most light?
   (b) Name some that flourish best in the shade.
4. (a) What gives to the stalk of grains their necessary stiffness?
   (b) What is the "smut" found on wheat?
5. What kind of plant study does the Committee of Twelve say should take the the place of the old-fashionèd "grinding out of Latin names by an analytical key? (If you have not been fortunate enough to obtain a copy of their report, give your own ideas on this question).
6. Give full description of the corolla of the larkspur.
7. Give general directions for the making of an herbarium.
8. What can you say of the axillary buds on a plant having a well developed terminal bud?
9. Name as many agencies as you can for the distribution of seeds.
10. Make a drawing of the plant radicle.

### SECOND GRADE.

1. (a) What is a plant cell?
   (b) How are new cells formed?
2. How does the growth of root and stem differ?
3. Distinguish between close and cross fertilization, and name a plant whose flowers are adapted to each.
4. (a) Give the origin and structure of root hairs.
   (b) What is their function?
5. What kind of plant study does the Committee of Twelve say should take the place of the old-fashioned "grinding out of Latin names by an analytica key?" (If you have not been fortunate enough to obtain a copy of their report give your own ideas on this question.)
6. (a) Name a plant that has a root stock, and one that has tubers.
   (b) Name a plant whose flower is a raceme; an umbel; a spike.
7. Give general directions for the making of an herbarium. (20 credits.)
8. Define peduncle, panicle, cotyledon, ovary, plumule.
9. Make a drawing of the plant radicle.

## CIVIL GOVERNMENT.

### First and Second Grades.

1. General excellence, including neatness, will count for this number.
2. How and by whom was the Constitution ratified.
3. What is the new method of taxing railroads now under discussion by the Michigan Legislature?
4. In case of non-election by votes of electors, why should the House rather than the Senate choose a president?
5. Why make the judges permanent office-holders and pay them larger salaries than congressmen?
6. What difference between a direct and an indirect tax? Give two examples of each.
7. Name five divisions of Michigan civil government as given in Institute Outline.
8. What is interstate commerce? Why not left to the state?
9. Give a distinction between freedom and license. Illustrate by example.
10. How is the study of civil government preceding the eighth grade treated in the State Manual and Course of Study?

THIRD GRADE, CLASS B.

1. General excellence, including neatness, will count for this number.
2. In what grade in the State Manual and Course of Study is the subject of civil government introduced?
3. How long must an alien live in the United States before becoming eligible to the Senate?
4. Why is it incorrect to speak of the president pro tempore of the Senate as vice-president?
5. What is a joint resolution of Congress? How does it differ from a bill?
6. What steps must be taken in order to move the county seat from one part of the county to another?
7. What are the duties of the judge of probate? For how long a term of office is he elected?
8. What is the dead letter office?
9. What is a copyright. How long do copyrights continue in force?
10. What is a patent? Name five important patented inventions.

CLASS A.

1. General excellence, including neatness, will count for this number.
2. In what grade in the State Manual and Course of Study is the subject of civil government introduced?
3. Why do we have a national judiciary?
4. Name four ends set forth in the preamble of the Constitution.
5. Why should senators hold office longer than representatives?
6. What steps must be taken in order to move the county seat from one part of the county to another?
7. What are the duties of judge of probate? For how long a term of office is he elected?
8. What is the dead letter office?
9. What is a copyright? How long do copyrights continue in force?
10. What is a patent? Name five important patented inventions.

GENERAL HISTORY.

First Grade.

1. (a) Mention at least five characters in mythology, telling what they represent and of what educational value they are.
2. How did the repeal of the Edict of Nantes affect France?
3. (a) In what country are the Jewish people much persecuted?
   (b) What movement is on foot among the more favored Jews to free them from these persecutions?
4. Write a brief description of the movement in which Garibaldi was interested.
5. Give the approximate date of the fall of Constantinople and state the effect upon learning.
6. What effect had the partition of Poland upon Russia?
7. What is the disarmament plan, by whom advanced, and how is it regarded by the nations of the world?
8. State some interesting fact in connection with each of the following: Don Carlos, Kitchener, Emperor Francis Joseph, Pope Leo XIII, Depew.
9. Briefly trace the growth of papacy.
10. Contrast modern with medieval history.

SECOND GRADE.

1. Briefly describe the work of Alexander, including the influence upon civilization.
2. State cause, result, and effect of the Revolution of 1688.
3. (a) Trace the changes in government of France from the time of Louis XVI to the present.
   (b) What case has recently brought France before the public?

4.  State the effect of the Norman conquest upon England.
5.  Write fifteen lines on any one of the following: Von Moltke, Bismarck, William II, Prince of Wales, Salisbury, Aguinaldo, Gen. Miles.
6.  Give an account of the contest which the names Gladstone and Parnell suggest.
7.  Briefly characterize some important personage in ancient history.
8.  State in full the causes of the fall of the Roman Empire.
9.  Mention at least two names that have become famous within the last century in connection with each of the following: geographical discoveries, science, invention, philosophy, literature, music.
10. Briefly trace the rise and growth of Prussia.

## GEOGRAPHY.

### First and Second Grades.

1.  General excellence, including neatness, will count for this number.
2   Give the names of any geographers whose physical or political maps you consider of value.
3.  Locate the Samoan Islands and tell in what connection they have recently been brought before the public.
4.  To what physical conditions do you attribute the commercial traits of the English and the high perfection of art and literature in ancient Athens?
5.  What can you say of the formation of flood-plains and deltas?
6.  Give directions for making transfer or stencil maps.
7.  Account for differences in aridity along the western coast of South America.
8.  Name and locate the leading industries now carried on in the limits of the Louisiana Purchase.
9.  Sketch a rude map showing ocean currents of the eastern hemisphere, indicating direction by arrows.
10. Name some books or articles on geography which you consider beneficial, giving reasons for choice.

#### THIRD GRADE, CLASS B.

1.  General excellence, including neatness, will count for this number.
2.  (a) What do you understand by the term *weathering* of rocks?
    (b) State the effect of the process.
3.  Should a direct cable be laid between Germany and the United States, in what waters would it be placed?
4.  Briefly state how you would teach a class:—
    (a) Reasons for change of seasons.
    (b) Existence of mountains and valleys.
5.  What is your method for interesting pupils in supplementary reading in geography work?
6.  Locate the Canaries, telling to whom they belong and their value to the mother country.
7.  Name and locate ten of the most prosperous cities in the United States, giving reasons for their growth.
8 and 9.  Give an outline for a careful study of South America.
10. Are places along shore warmer or colder in summer than in the interior? Why? In winter? Why?

#### CLASS A.

1.  General excellence, including neatness, will count for this number.
2.  (a) What do you understand by a relief map? A progressive map?
    (b) Tell what stress you place upon map reading.
3.  Should a direct cable be laid between Germany and the United States, in what waters would it be placed?
4.  (a) Name some apparatus which you find of valuable assistance in your geography work.
    (b) How do you interest pupils in contributing to this work?

5. Name ten commercial routes.
6. Locate the Canaries, telling to whom they belong and their value to the mother country.
7. Name and locate ten of the most prosperous cities in the United States, giving reasons for their growth.
8. Draw a rude map of Michigan, indicating the occupations of the people.
9. Designate five rivers of historic significance, briefly indicating their importance.
10. What practical methods do you use to interest pupils in manufactures?

## GEOMETRY.

### First Grade.

1. Draw three straight lines and make a triangle with sides respectively equal to them.
2. Inscribe a circle in a given triangle. Explain.
3. What is the measure of the angles made by the following lines:
   (a) Two secants?
   (b) Two chords within a circle?
   (c) A tangent and a secant?
   (d) Two tangents?
   Demonstrate one of your answers.
4. Prove that the areas of the regular inscribed hexagon and triangle are as 2:1.
5. Prove that if four quantities are in proportion, they are in proportion by composition.
6. Prove that the diagonals of a parallelogram mutually bisect each other.
7. Construct an isosceles triangle of a given altitude, whose sides pass through two given points, and whose vertex is in a given straight line.
8. A man wishes to ascertain the width of an impassable river. Explain how it can be done, using the necessary drawings.
9. Prove that the area of a regular inscribed dodecagon is equal to three times the square of the radius.
10. From a point two tangents are drawn to a circle. If the tangents are 30 ft. long and intersect at an angle of 60 degrees, what is the area of the circle?

## GRAMMAR.

### First and Second Grades.

NOTE—Capitalization, punctuation, paragraphing, diction, and grammatical construction should all be carefully noted by the examiner in marking the final question of each grade, as it counts for thirty credits.

1. General excellence of paper, arrangement of headings and subheadings, separation and classification of answers, will count for this number.
2. The Institute Outline calls attention to some of the different names given by different authorities to the *same* case. Give several of them.
3. If one possessive is in apposition with another, should the sign be annexed to the principal or the explanatory term? Illustrate.
4. Classify clauses and explain connectives in the following:—
   "Thus we see the discipline by which the young child is so successfully taught to regulate its movement, is also the discipline by which the great mass of adults are kept in order and more or less improved."
5. Of what value is the elliptical sentence, and when would you make use of it?
6. In the sentence, "He came *to work*," dispose of the italicised words according to two differing authorities to the *same* case, citing authority for each.
7. Discuss the error found in the following:—"Even a four weeks' institute does not always help the teachers as they should."
   Give another sentence to illustrate the same error.
8. In a discussion of not less than 150, nor more than 250 words, give *one* of the two following:—
   (a) Your ideas as to the necessity for professional training of teachers.
   (b) The sources from which you have obtained aid in teaching, with some idea of the nature of the help received.

## THIRD GRADE, CLASS B.

1. General excellence of paper, arrangement of headings and subheadings, separation and classification of answers, will count for this number.
2. The Institute Outline calls attention to some of the different names given by different authorities to the *same case.* Give several of them.
3. Define grammar and state its relation to composition and language lessons.
4. The story of "Hero Hobson" is a good one to stimulate bravery. Give a set of questions calculated to aid sixth graders in writing a composition about it.
5. What is the purpose of fourth grade language work as given in the State Manual and Course of Study?
6. (a) Name an adverb of affirmation, of negation, of time, of manner, and of degree.
   (b) Where should the adverb be placed in a sentence?
7. Correct and give reason for changes:—
   (a) The work can be done easier.
   (b) Can I take your book?
   (c) I do not not like him appearing so bold.
   (d) Try and remember what I tell you.
   (e) He told we girls to go.
8. Write a letter to some pupil recommending five standard authors to be studied for literary culture, specifying some particular good to be derived from each. (Be careful about date, address, signature, etc.)

## CLASS A.

1. General excellence of paper, arrangement of headings and sub-headings, separation and classification of answers, will count for this number.
2. How would you help the child to a ready use of a larger vocabulary than he already possesses?
3. (a) Write appropriate masculine or feminine forms of the following:—niece, lad, spinster, negro, actress.
   (b) Give plural of money, canto, ally, beau, cactus.
4. Illustrate the meaning of the following words by using in sentences: want—need; lazy—idle; discover—invent; between—among; like—love.
5. What is the purpose of the fourth grade language work as given in the State Manual and Course of Study?
6. By sentences illustrate the use of the present perfect and past tenses of *sit, set, fly, begin, ring.*
7. Correct and give reason for changes:—
   (a) The work can be done easier.
   (b) Can I take your book?
   (c) I do not like him appearing so bold.
   (d) Try and remember what I tell you.
   (e) He told we girls to go.
8. Write a letter to some pupil recommending five standard authors to be studied for literary culture, specifying some particular good to be derived from each. (Be careful about date, address, signature, etc.)

## ORTHOGRAPHY.

### First and Second Grades.

NOTE.—These questions count 50 per cent and the list of words 50 per cent.

1. Write the abbreviation of each of the following—post-office, ounce, California, junior, Florida, assistant, secretary, preposition, right reverend, department.
2. Form the present participle and give rules for spelling of bet, die, ply, bite, prefer.
3. What sound of the letters is called for by the following diacritical markings:— wọlf, g̃em, ûnite, mọve, pîque.
4. (a) Give meaning and example of dieresis.
   (b) Distinguish between diphthong and digraph.

5. Accent, syllabify, and mark diacritically the following:—typographer, sugar, sacrilegious, chivalrous, docile, extant, vehement, financier, chirography, indicatory.

### THIRD GRADE, BOTH CLASSES.

1. Define and give examples of labials. palatals, dentals, nasals, and linguals.
2. Write two rules helpful in spelling and give words to illustrate.
3. Give at least two drills for articulation.
4. What is your method of teaching elementary sounds?
5. Indicate the pronunciation of the following:—orthoepy, indisputable, hymeneal, debris, jugular. acclimate, felicities, aspirant, lachrymose, obligatory.

### LIST OF WORDS.

#### All Grades.

bureau
pharynx
Beethoven
crystallize
ventilate
adjacent
hygiene
participle
surgeon
cylinder
anticipating
preference
circuitous

amateur
vaccinate
recommend
Missouri
dairy
aisle (passageway)
deign
Hindoo
alimentary
Eustachian
judgment
traveling

### PENMANSHIP.

#### All Grades.

NOTE.—This must be written with pen. Handwriting is marked upon the entire paper. 30 credits for answers. 70 for handwriting.

1. (a) What are the standard systems of penmanship?
   (b) Give your preference and reasons for the same.
2. Give three conditions necessary to successful teaching of writing.
3. What are the essential differences in the teaching of writing with pen and with pencil?

### PHYSICS.

#### First Grade.

1. (a) Distinguish between force and momentum
   (b) Give examples of action and reaction.
2. (a) What is a dyne?
   (b) Explain why the weight of a body is not always a perfect measure of its mass.
3. (a) What is meant by the term horse-power?
   (b) If a 2 horse-power engine can throw 1056 lbs. of water to the top of a steeple in 2 minutes, how high is the steeple?
4. (a) Give the laws of falling bodies.
   (b) What is the acceleration during the fourth second?
   (c) Illustrate some of these laws by drawings, as to a class.
5. A ship is moving east at the rate of 11¼ miles an hour; a passenger walks directly north across the deck at the rate of 5½ ft. per second. Draw the diagonal which represents his direction, and find his rate per second.
6. Explain why a body is lighter in water than in air.

9

7.  What is the "mechanical equivalent" of heat?  Define "radiant energy."
8.  Illustrate the different kinds of ordinary lenses, and explain the action of each.
9.  Explain the action of the Leyden jar.
10. (a) Define ampere, volt, watt.
    (b) Explain any one of the following: a gas meter; an electric meter; a galvanometer.

## PHYSIOLOGY.

### First and Second Grades.

1.  General excellence, including neatness, will count for this number.
2.  Name the kinds of joints found in the body and give examples to illustrate.
3.  Distinguish between sprains and dislocations; if possible, mention a treatment for each.
4.  (a) How do bacteria enter the body?
    (b) How is bacteria destroyed outside of the body?
5.  Give the meaning of the following terms:—euemia, digestion, jaundice, rickets, congestion.
6.  Where does animal heat originate?  Give the chemical action from which it results.
7.  Explain the physiology of sight.
8.  Tell what you understand by the peristaltic movements of the stomach, and state the result of these movements.
9.  Why are blows upon the abdomen dangerous?
10. Write an outline for the study of the brain.

### THIRD GRADE, CLASS B.

1.  General excellence, including neatness, will count for this number.
2.  What dangers attend the following:—(a) Boxing the ear?  (b) Abcess in the ear?  Why?
3.  The "Suggestive Oral Lessons" in the State Manual and Course of Study contain questions regarding the lungs.  Give five of them.
4.  State the cause of fainting and name some restoratives.
5.  Give five important cautions to be observed in the care of either the ear or eye.
6.  Distinguish between narcotics and stimulants, giving examples to illustrate.
7.  (a) Why is a mixed diet best for man?
    (b) Which is more easily digested—warm or cold bread?  Justify your answer.
8.  (a) State the use of muscles.  (b) Name the various kinds, giving an example of each.
9.  What is meant by the sympathetic nervous system, and why so-called?
10. The State Board of Health mentions restrictions for the spread of scarlet and typhoid fevers.  Give at least two of them.

### CLASS A.

1.  General excellence, including neatness, will count for this number.
2.  (a) What is the danger attendant upon boxing the ear?
    (b) How does a sore throat often affect the ear?
3.  The "Suggestive Oral Lessons" in the State Manual and Course of Study contain some questions regarding the lungs.  Give five of them.
4.  State the cause of fainting and mention some restoratives.
5.  What points would you emphasize in teaching children the effects of eating candy and drinking ice water?
6.  Distinguish between narcotics and stimulants, giving examples to illustrate.
7.  State some rules of hygiene that should be observed with reference to wearing apparel.
8.  What is the function of saliva; of bile?
9.  Write fifteen lines on the form and amount of exercise required to keep the body in health.
10. The State Board of Health mentions restrictions for the spread of scarlet and typhoid fevers.  Give at least two of them.

## READING.

### All Grades.

1. How does reading compare with other common school branches in importance?
2. Why do children repeat poetry in a sing-song style? How would you correct the habit?
3. Define modulation and give your idea of its importance.
4. What are some of the greatest difficulties to be surmounted in teaching reading?

### I.

The value of time has passed into a proverb;—"Time is money." It is so because its employment brings money. But it is more; it is knowledge. Still more, it is virtue. Nor is it creditable to the world that the proverb has
4   taken this material and mercenary complexion, as if money were the highest good and the strongest recommendation.

Time is more than money. It brings what money cannot purchase. It has in its lap all the learning of the past, the spoils of antiquity, the priceless
8   treasures of knowledge. Who would barter these for gold or silver? But knowledge is a means only, and not an end. It is valuable because it promotes the welfare, the development, and the progress of man. And the highest value of time is not even in knowledge, but in the opportunity of
12   doing good.

                           —*Charles Sumner.*

### II.

Breathes there a man with soul so dead,
Who never to himself hath said,
  This is my own, my native land?
4   Whose heart hath ne'er within him burned,
As home his footsteps he hath turned
  From wandering on a foreign strand?
If such there breathe, go, mark him well!
8   For him no minstrel raptures swell;
High though his titles, proud his name,
Boundless his wealth as wish can claim,—
Despite those titles, power, and pelf,
12   The wretch, concentered all in self,
Living, shall forfeit fair renown;
And, doubly dying, shall go down
To the vile dust from which he sprung,
16   Unwept, unhonored, and unsung.

                        - -*Sir Walter Scott.*

To EXAMINER.—The following questions on the last extract, may help to expedite the oral reading test:

1. Line 4—why is *ne'er* abbreviated?
2. Line 6—define *strand*.
3. Line 8—what is meant by "minstrel raptures"?
4. Line 10—whose *wealth* is boundless?
5. Line 11—define *despite* and *pelf*.
6. What is the strongest expression here used to express the ignominy of a man devoid of patriotism?
7. Is there any figurative language used in the above lines?
8. Name some other of Scott's writings.
9. Tell something of the poet.

## SCHOOL LAW.

### All Grades.

1. Name four duties of the township clerk in relation to education.
2. Give two ways in which sites for school houses may be established.
3. How may appeals from any action of the board of school inspectors be taken?
4. Give two ways mentioned in the School Law whereby money for district libraries may be obtained.
5. Name five kinds of certificates authorized to be issued by the county board of school examiners and the county commissioner of schools, and the legal conditions governing their issue.

## THEORY AND ART OF TEACHING.

### All Grades.

1. What does the State Manual and Course of Study say about opening exercises? What value do you attach to opening exercises?
2. Give several good reasons for committing to memory gems of literature.
3. (a) Explain the part attention plays in education.
   (b) What kind of attention should be developed?
4. Name and support your idea of the object of education.
5. (a) How is habit related to education; (b) work; (c) play; (d) method?

## UNITED STATES HISTORY.

### First and Second Grades.

1. General excellence, including neatness, will count for this number.
2. What acts of European explorers who first visited America led to the development of hostile feelings among the Indian tribes?
3. Tell about the discoveries and explorations of the Spaniards in America. What influence have they had on our history?
4. Tell of the part played by John Hancock in the Revolutionary War.
5. Write briefly of five men who were foremost in the preparation of the constitution.
6. Give both the immediate and remote results of "Nullification."
7. What use of maps is recommended by the State Manual and Course of Study in teaching United States history?
8. What have been the chief measures advocated during McKinley's administration?
9. What do you consider the greatest benefit to our nation growing out of the Spanish-American war?
10. Make a statement about any five of the following:—

    | | |
    |---|---|
    | Nelson Dingley, Jr. | Nicaragua Canal. |
    | The Treaty of Paris. | Joseph H. Choate. |
    | General E. S. Otis. | Agoncillo. |
    | Expansion Policy. | Ex-Attorney-General A. H. Garland. |
    | President Faure. | Booker T. Washington. |

### THIRD GRADE, CLASS B.

1. General excellence, including neatness, will count for this number.
2. Write briefly of the influence of commerce upon the discovery of America.
3. Describe the settlement of Virginia, contrasting it with the settlement of Pennsylvania.
4. Write briefly of the French Alliance with the Americans in the War of Independence.
5. What were some of the great compromises in the Constitutional Convention of 1787 that made a national government possible?

6. Write briefly about the conflicting claims of the Northwest Territory.
7. What use of maps is recommended by the State Manual and Course of Study in teaching United States History?
8. Give at least four important facts connected with the administration of General Cass as Governor of Michigan.
9. What do you consider the greatest benefit to our nation growing out of the Spanish-American War?
10. Make a statement about any five of the following:—

| | |
|---|---|
| Nelson Dingley, Jr. | Nicaragua Canal. |
| The Treaty of Paris. | Joseph H. Choate. |
| General E. S. Otis. | Agoncillo. |
| Expansion Policy. | Ex-Attorney-General A. H. Garland. |
| President Faure. | Booker T. Washington. |

### CLASS A.

1. General excellence, including neatness, will count for this number.
2. Of what use are maps and pictures in teaching history to beginners?
3. Describe the settlement of Virginia, contrasting it with the settlement of Pennsylvania.
4. What colonies made education a prominent feature of colonial life?
5. Compare the social life of our country in 1798 with the present.
6. Tell the story of Perry's victory on Lake Erie.
7. What use of maps is recommended by the State Manual and Course of Study in teaching United States history?
8. Compare the Old South with the New South.
9. Tell the story about the writing of "The Star Spangled Banner."
10. Make a statement about any five of the following:—

| | |
|---|---|
| Nelson Dingley, Jr. | Nicaragua Canal. |
| The Treaty of Paris. | Joseph H. Choate. |
| General E. S. Otis. | Agoncillo. |
| Expansion Policy. | Ex-Attorney-General A. H. Garland. |
| President Faure. | Booker T. Washington. |

## IV. QUESTIONS PREPARED BY THE SUPERINTENDENT OF PUBLIC INSTRUCTION FOR THE REGULAR EXAMINATION, JUNE, 1899.

### ALGEBRA.

#### Second Grade.

1. General excellence, including neatness, will count for this number.
2. What are the principal "transformations" used in algebra?
3. Evaluate the following: If $a=0$, $b=1$, $c=3$, $d=5$:—

$$\frac{(a+c)^c+(a+b^2+d)^2 - 4cd+b}{ac+ab+dc}.$$

4. Factor: $y^3+3y^2+1+3y$; $\dfrac{x^2}{y^2} + \dfrac{2x}{y} - 3$; $4a^2 - 16ab + 15b^2$.

5. Simplify: $\dfrac{a - \dfrac{ab}{a+b}}{a^2+\dfrac{a^2b^2}{a^2-b^2}} \times \dfrac{\dfrac{1}{a^2} - \dfrac{1}{b^2}}{\dfrac{1}{a} - \dfrac{1}{b}}$.

6. (a) Express without fractional or negative exponents: $\dfrac{2x^{\frac{1}{2}}}{y^{-\frac{1}{2}}}$.

   (b) Simplify: $\dfrac{b}{a}\sqrt[4]{\dfrac{a^2}{b^2}}$.

7. Find the square root of $25a^4+10a^3c-4b^3c+4b^4-20a^2b^2+c^2$.

8. The difference of the squares of two consecutive numbers is $h$. Find an expression for each number.

9. (a) $\sqrt{6+\sqrt{-13}} \times \sqrt{6-\sqrt{-13}} = ?$

(b) $\sqrt{x+3} = 1+\sqrt{x}$. Find value of $x$.

10. $5x - 23 + \frac{4}{x} = 7 - \frac{41}{x}$. Solve and tell why the answer should not take the sign $\pm$.

## ARITHMETIC.

### Second Grade.

1. Show that both the following problems can be explained by the same principle:
   (a) If 2½ tons of hay cost $30, what will one ton cost?
   (b) 1,200 is 25% of what number?
2. A man gave his son ⅝ of his estate and divided the rest equally between his wife and daughter, each receiving $500 less than ½ as much as the son. What was the value of the estate?
3. A sold his farm, costing $8,000, at a reduction of 16⅔ per cent from the asking price and yet gained 12½%. What was the asking price?
4. If a man every 5 months spends what he earns in 2 months, and earns $530 every 2½ months, how much does he save in a year?
5. How much lumber in the squared timber that can be sawed from a log 30 in. in diameter and 16 ft. long?

### THIRD GRADE, CLASS B.

1. (a) Given the minuend and difference, to find the subtrahend.
   (b) Given the subtrahend and difference, to find the minuend.
   (c) The dividend is 1864, the quotient 66, and the remainder 12 less than the divisor. What is the divisor?
2. A man gave to his two sons ⅓ of his farm, giving to the younger ⅘ as much as to the elder. What part of the farm had each?
3. Reduce ⅞ of a cubic yard to lower denominations, explaining each step in the process.
4. A man paid $25.50 for having his house insured for ¾ its value, at 1¼%. What was the value of the house?
5. Prepare a test exercise of five questions for any grade above the fourth, stating the grade.

### CLASS A.

1. (a) Given the minuend and difference, to find the subtrahend.
   (b) Given the subtrahend and difference, to find the minuend.
   (c) The dividend is 1864, the quotient 66, and the remainder 12 less than the divisor. What is the divisor?
2. A man gave to his two sons ⅓ of his farm, giving to the younger ⅘ as much as to the elder. What part of the farm had each?
3. Explain as to a class the following:
   (a) Inverting the divisor.
   (b) Pointing off in division of decimals.
4. If ⅞ of a load of hay is worth $8¾, what is 7½ loads worth?
   (Work by cancellation, and explain the application.)
5. Prepare a test exercise of five questions for any grade below the fifth, stating the grade.

## MENTAL ARITHMETIC.

### All Grades.

NOTE—A member of the Examining Board will examine candidates in classes of twenty-five or less, testing quickness to grasp the salient features of a problem, accuracy and rapidity of work, clearness and simplicity of analysis. In the right hand margin applicants will write *as many answers to the first twenty questions as possible in fifteen minutes*; one-half per cent for each answer and one per cent additional for each *correct* one, is given in this part of the examination.

1. What is the sum of 8, 9, 7, 6, 5, 9, 8, 7, 8, 7, 9, 8, 5?
2. Add 2, $2\frac{1}{4}$, $5\frac{3}{8}$, $8\frac{3}{4}$, $7\frac{1}{10}$, $1\frac{3}{10}$.
3. The divisor is $4\frac{3}{8}$, the quotient $4\frac{5}{8}$, the remainder 5. What is the dividend?
4. Find the product of the sum and difference of $\frac{1}{2}$ and $\frac{1}{3}$.
5. What cost 45 cows at $45 each?
6. How many horses at $75 each can be bought for $2,100?
7. What cost 960 lbs. of hay at $10 a ton?
8. What will 75 books cost, if 15 cost $12?
9. What cost 40 spoons at $3 a dozen?
10. At $\frac{3}{8}$ each, how many apples can be bought for 2c?
11. What is the area of a cube containing 27 cu. ft?
12. A lady has $40 with which to purchase a shawl at $25 and dress goods at $.62$\frac{1}{2}$ a yd. How many yards can she buy?
13. How must I sell an article costing 5c to gain 40%?
14. 3 pints is what per cent of a gallon?
15. What is the bank discount on $240 for 60 days at 6%?
16. How many feet in a timber 8 in. by 6 in., and 30 ft. long?
17. What is the cube root of the square of 2x4?
18. If a circular saw weighs 100 lbs., what will one of the same thickness with a circumference three times as great, weigh?
19. What is the diagonal of a rectangular field 30 rds. wide and 40 rds. long?
20. At 8c a dozen, how many cabbage plants can be bought for 40c?

(Of the remaining examples, third grade applicants write the full analysis of *four* selected by the examiner; the second grade applicants write the *last* four).

21. I buy hats at $2, mark them at an advance of 20%, and discount this so that I lose 40% on each hat. What is the rate per cent of discount?
22. If A can build a wall in 6 days and B in 8 days, how long will it take both together?
23. Find distance around a square field whose area is 10 acres.
24. What number added to its $\frac{1}{4}$ gives 24?
25. A mows $\frac{1}{4}$ an acre of grass in 2 hrs.; B mows an acre in 10 hrs. How long for them together to mow an acre?
26. What time is it when the time past noon is $\frac{3}{5}$ of the time past midnight?
27. A child is absent $\frac{1}{2}$ a day each week; what is his per cent of attendance?
28. A man sold a piece of property for $100, and another costing twice as much for $160. On the first he lost 20%; what per cent did he lose on the second?
29. A sold a house to B, and B to C, each gaining 20%. B's profit was $40 more than A's. What was A's profit?
30. A farm was sold at a profit of 20%, then at a profit of 20%, then at a loss of 25%, and finally sold at a profit of 50%. What per cent of the first selling price was the last selling price?

## BOTANY.

### Second Grade.

1. (a) Name the organs of vegetation. (b) Of reproduction.
2. When are leaves said to be palmately net-veined? Cite example.
3. Define corm, stigma, calyx, plumule, fascicle.
4. Define determinate and indeterminate inflorescence.
5. Classify the following as to composition and texture: raspberry, strawberry, cherry, almond, apple.
6. What are blight, mildew, rust, etc?
7. (a) To what family, or order, do the cereals belong?
   (b) What two cereals rank first in importance and why?

8. Name the following:
   (a) A medicinal plant.
   (b) A food plant.
   (c) A fibrous plant.
   (d) A timber plant.
   (e) An oil-yielding plant.
9. How is opium obtained?
10. Mention some things in nature study, for the month of June, suggested by the State Manual and Course of Study.

## CIVIL GOVERNMENT.

### Second Grade.

1. General excellence, including neatness, will count for this number.
2. (a) What are the requirements fixed by Congress for naturalization?
   (b) When does an alien become a voter in this State?
3. Give two ways whereby the elective franchise may be lost.
4. What is the purpose of the Australian ballot and its advantage to the voter?
5. Name some of the checks to legislation and tell why they are necessary.
6. Outline the steps whereby a bill becomes a law.
7. State two ways of making constitutional amendments.
8. How often does Congress meet, and for how long a time?
9. Give your ideas regarding the taxation of railroads.
10. Name the five subdivisions of government made in the outline on "Good Citizenship" found in the State Manual and Course of Study.

### THIRD GRADE, CLASS B.

1. General excellence, including neatness, will count for this number.
2. Name several powers belonging to the governor of a state.
3. How may the perpetrator of a crime be brought to trial?
4. What is meant by the term militia in its broadest sense? In its narrowest?
5. What are government lands and how are they secured?
6. (a) Who appoints the committee on equalization in a county?
   (b) What is the duty of this committee?
7. (a) Tell briefly how property is assessed.
   (b) What officer assesses property in a township?
8. Describe the steps necessary to raise money for the support of schools, commencing at the first step and ending with the money in the district treasury.
10. The State Manual and Course of Study suggests certain points to be emphasized in elementary civics. Name some of them.

### CLASS A.

1. General excellence, including neatness, will count for this number.
2. Name several powers belonging to the governor of a State.
3. What are the usual elective officers of a village?
4. Name two duties of the County Superintendent of the Poor. How is he chosen?
5. What are government lands and how are they secured?
6. Explain as to a child what is meant by a limited monarchy, giving example.
7. (a) Tell briefly how property is assessed.
   (b) What officer assesses property in a township?
9. Describe the steps necessary to raise money for the support of schools, commencing at the first step and ending with the money in the district treasury.
10. The State Manual and Course of Study suggests certain points to be emphasized in elementary civics. Name some of them.

## GENERAL HISTORY.

### Second Grade.

1. In what respect was the civilization of the Greeks superior to that of the Persians?
2. Briefly connect each of the following names with Roman history: Hannibal, Augustus, Constantine, Marius, Antony.
3. Give an account of the origin and development of feudalism in England.
4. Speak briefly of the troubles between Elizabeth and Mary, Queen of Scots.
5. What issues were involved in-the war of the Austrian Succession, and how were they adjusted.
6. What struggle aided the union of the German states?
7. Connect the Monroe Doctrine with the Holy Alliance.
8. Characterize France under Louis XV.
9. Who were the Chartists, and what was accomplished through their efforts?
10. What foreign countries occupy possessions in China? What is the probable fate of China?

## GEOGRAPHY.

### Second Grade.

1. General excellence, including neatness, will count for this number.
2. By a diagram show the meaning of the terms river-basins and divides.
3. Mention some modifications of climate.
4. Compare the occupations of the people in the eastern and central states, giving reasons for difference.
5. In what way is map-reading an aid to the pupil?
6. What enterprise is likely to open up Central Africa, and what Englishman is prominently connected therewith?
7. (a) What countries are included in Eurasia?
   (b) What archipelago lies between Australia and Asia? Between North and South America?
8. State your method for interesting pupils in supplemental work, and name two books suitable for such purpose.
9. Name five exports of the United States, telling from what states sent.
10. Mention some aids to commerce, and give five noted commercial centers.

#### THIRD GRADE, CLASS B.

1. General excellence, including neatness, will count for this number.
2. What is the purpose of meridians and parallels?
3. What must be considered in selecting a town site?
4. If the choice of a trip abroad were offered you, what would be your preference and why?
5. Name some collections for geography work which you encourage pupils to make.
6. What cargo would a steamer from the West Indies presumably bring to New York ?
7. Mention five of our most noted national institutions of learning, locating each.
8. What can you say of the salt production in Michigan?
9. Write at least seventy-five words about modern commerce.
10. Locate Tacoma. Ishpeming, St. Louis, Poughkeepsie, Denver, Atlanta, Newport.

#### CLASS A.

1. General excellence, including neatness, will count for this number.
2. Name five plants of commerce and tell where each is grown.
3. What must be considered in selecting a town-site?
4. State your method for teaching children direction on the map.

10

5. Name some collections for geography work which you encourage pupils to make.
6. What cargo would a steamer from the West Indies presumably bring to New York?
7. Mention five of our most noted national institutions of learning, locating each.
8. What can you say of the salt production in Michigan?
9. Briefly give some experiment for teaching children the cause of dew and rain.
10. Locate Tacoma, Ishpeming, St. Louis, Poughkeepsie, Denver, Atlanta, Newport.

## GRAMMAR.

### Second Grade.

NOTE.—Capitalization, punctuation, paragraphing, diction, and grammatical construction, should all be carefully noted by the examiner in marking the final question of each grade, as it counts for thirty credits.

1. General excellence, including neatness, will count for this number.
2. Give the chief reason why grammar often proves such an unprofitable subject in school work, and suggest a remedy.
3. (a) Name the principal copulative verbs, and tell what is the only pure copula.
(b) Why is it so necessary to distinguish copulative verbs from others?
4. Write sentences to show the use of copulative, disjunctive, and correlative conjunctions.
5. (a) How many properties of the verb belong to the participle?
(b) Why does the participle not have tense?
6. Justify the punctuation of the following: "If thine enemy hunger, feed him; if he thirst, give him drink: for in so doing, thou shalt heap coals of fire on his head."
7. Analyze or diagram: "Like the tiger, that seldom desists from pursuing man after having once preyed upon human flesh, the reader who has once gratified his appetite with calumny, makes ever after the most agreeable feast upon murdered reputation."
8. Write not less than 150, nor more than 250 words, on any one of the following subjects:

Childhood days.                Value of Arbor Day.
The Peace Congress.            Description of a Landscape.
Effect of Mountains upon Climate and People.

### THIRD GRADE, CLASS B.

1. General excellence, including neatness, will count for this number.
2. What is the foundation of good language, and when does the child begin to lay it?
3. (a) In what grade does the State Manual and Course of Study place the first language book?
(b) What material does this course suggest for written work in the 6th grade?
4. (a) Write three nouns that have no singular.
(b) Three nouns having irregular plurals.
5. How would you lead a class to see the difference between an adverb and an adjective? Illustrate with sentences.
6. What is the synopsis of a verb? Illustrate with the verb *fly*.
7. Make necessary corrections, giving reasons for all changes:
(a) The present state of affairs demand consideration.
(b) I will tell you as nearly as I can.
(c) If I was you, I would not go.
(d) He denied that the earth was round.
(e) This stone is rounder than that.
8. Write not less than 150, nor more than 250 words, on any one of the following subjects:

Childhood days.                Value of Arbor Day.
The Peace Congress.            Description of a Landscape.
Effect of Mountains upon Climate and People.

## CLASS A.

1. General excellence, including neatness, will count for this number.
2. What is the foundation of good language, and when does the child begin to lay it?
3. Write sentences to show the correct use of bad and badly; taller and tallest; close and closely.
4. Pluralize the following: analysis, appendix, syllabus, phenomenon, piano.
5. Write a short letter to some firm, ordering a list of books such as might aid in primary work.
6. What is the synopsis of a verb? Illustrate with the verb *fly*.
7. Make necessary corrections, giving reasons for all changes:
   (a) The present state of affairs demand consideration.
   (b) I will tell you as nearly as I can.
   (c) If I was you, I would not go.
   (d) He denied that the earth was round.
   (e) This stone is rounder than that.
8. Write not less than 150, nor more than 250 words, on any one of the following subjects:

| | |
|---|---|
| Childhood days. | Value of Arbor Day. |
| The Peace Congress. | Description of a Landscape. |

Effect of Mountains upon Climate and People.

## ORTHOGRAPHY.

### Second Grade.

NOTE.—These questions count 50 per cent and the list of words 50 per cent.

1. Give two rules for spelling with examples to illustrate.
2. Write words to illustrate use of the following sounds: â, ä, ê, ê, ô.
3. Give several short exercises in articulation.
4. Mark the following diacritically: acclimate, tryst, circuitous, tutor, culinary, disputable, lichen, salve, reconnoissance, hospitable.
5. Name five English or Latin prefixes and give meaning.

### THIRD GRADE, BOTH CLASSES.

1. Distinguish between orthography and orthoepy.
2. Name and illustrate five diacritical marks.
3. Give an example of each of the following: linguals, dentals, sibilants, gutterals, labials.
4. Mention at least one plan for conducting an interesting spelling lesson.
5. Indicate the pronunciation of the following: Phillippine, enervate, tomato, program, museum, advertisement, horrid, inquiry, exquisite, sacrifice.

### LIST OF WORDS.

#### All Grades.

| | |
|---|---|
| arrangement | initiate |
| February | controlled |
| sympathize | humorist |
| Adirondack | alien |
| ambulance | esophagus |
| invincible | paralysis |
| courageous | Kalkaska |
| inflammation | appreciate |
| Manistique | obedience |
| pitiable | contagious |
| cocaine | librarian |
| occurrence | gracious |

almonds

## PENMANSHIP.

### All Grades.

(NOTE.—This must be written in ink. 30 credits for answers and 70 for handwriting.)

1. Name three common faults in teaching writing.
2. In what grades would you have pupils use pens? Give reasons for answer.
3. Is rapid and legible penmanship any less necessary today than in the past? Give reasons for answer.

## PHYSICS.

### Second Grade.

1. Mention five cases to show the advantage of elasticity.
2. Give five practical uses of adhesion.
3. (a) Why do we not feel the weight of the atmosphere?
   (b) How can we feel it?
4. Mention three metals that will float in mercury. Explain why.
5. Which is the warmer, tight-fitting clothing or loose clothing? Why!
6. Why does one stamp the feet to throw off mud? Explain fully.
7. Which is the heavier, moist air or dry air? Give three phenomena based upon the truth of your answer.
8. During the past winter a Fahrenheit thermometer stood at 28 degrees below zero. Where did the Centigrade stand at the same time? Give full explanation.
9. (a) What is the velocity of light?
   (b) Explain the action of a convex lens.
   (c) What kind of lens should a near-sighted person wear?
10. (a) In what two ways does electrical energy manifest itself?
    (b) What is positive electricity? Negative electricity?

## PHYSIOLOGY.

### Second Grade.

1. General excellence, including neatness, will count for this number.
2. What can you say of the cellular growth of the body?
3. Where are the muscular and osseous tissues found?
4. State in full the importance of a healthy action of the liver.
5. Where is the greater part of the food digested?
6. Explain what is meant by "catching cold."
7. Describe the results arising from the use of the several forms of tobacco.
8. How does the nutriment of the food reach the blood?
9. Fully describe the ear.
10. What is the function of the following nerves: olfactory, optic, facial, auditory, and pneumeo-gastric.

### THIRD GRADE, CLASS B.

1. General excellence, including neatness, will count for this number.
2. Give reasons for the cartilaginous cushions between the vertebrae.
3. What food elements are contained in eggs? Why are they not a perfect food for man?
4. State the cause of the unnatural thirst following the use of alcoholics.
5. Name the organs of respiration.
6. Explain why the hearing is often affected by colds.
7. Why should there be an entire change of clothing at night?
8. (a) Locate two muscles and give the function of each.
   (b) Name some exercises for muscular development.
9. Mention some poisons and their antidotes.
10. What are the functions of the spinal cord?

## CLASS A.

1. General excellence, including neatness, will count for this number.
2. When a child seems inattentive in class work, what physiological examination would you deem wise?
3. What food elements are contained in eggs? Why are they not a perfect food for man?
4. State the cause of the unnatural thirst following the use of alcoholics.
5. Give a few rules to be observed in bathing.
6. Explain why the hearing is often affected by colds.
7. Why should there be an entire change of clothing at night?
8. Speak briefly of breathing through the mouth.
9. Mention some poisons and their antidotes.
10. Define stimulant and narcotic, giving examples of each.

## READING.

### All Grades.

(Answers to these four questions should be written and count for forty credits, sixty being given on the oral test.)

1. What is diction, and how does good diction prove a factor in the teacher's success?
2. What is "sight reading," and to what extent should it be used in school?
3. Mention five books you would suggest as good reading for children under fifteen years of age.
5. Define inflection, and give three rules for its use.

*Reading Extracts.*

i.

Here I have 'scaped the city's stifling heat,
　　Its horrid sounds and its polluted air;
3　And, where the season's milder fervors beat,
　　And gales, that sweep the forest border, bear
　　The song of bird and sound of running stream,
6　　　Am come awhile to wander and to dream.
Ay, flame thy fiercest, Sun! thou canst not wake,
　　In this pure air, the plague that walks unseen.
9　The maize leaf and the maple bough but take,
　　From thy fierce heats, a deeper, glossier green;
　　The mountain wind, that faints not in thy ray,
12　　　Sweeps the blue streams of pestilence away.
The mountain wind! most spiritual of all
　　The wide earth knows; when in the sultry time
15　He stoops him from his vast cerulean hall,
　　He seems the breath of a celestial clime;
　　As if from heaven's wide-open gates did flow
18　　　Health and refreshment on the world below.
　　　　　　　　　　*William Cullen Bryant.*

II.

Has the gentleman done? Has he completely done? He was unparliamentary from the beginning to the end of his speech. There was scarce a word he uttered that was not a violation of the privileges of the House.
4　But I did not call him to order,—why? Because the limited talents of some men render it impossible for them to be too severe without being unparliamentary. But before I sit down, I shall show him how to be severe and parliamentary at the same time.

8    The right honorable gentleman has called me "an unimpeached traitor."
I ask why not "traitor," unqualified by any epithet? I will tell him; it
was because he durst not. It was the act of a coward, who raises his arm
to strike, but has not courage to give the blow. I will not call him
12    villain, because it is unparliamentary, and he is a privy counsellor. I will
not call him fool, because he happens to be chancellor of the exchequer.
But I say he is one who has abused the privilege of parliament and the
freedom of debate, by uttering language which, if spoken out of the House, I
16    should answer only with a blow. I care not how high his situation, how
low his character, how contemptible his speech, whether a privy counsellor
or a parasite—my answer would be a *blow.*—*From Grattan's Reply to Mr.
Corry.*

## SCHOOL LAW.

### All Grades.

1. Name four school offices to which women are eligible.
2. Name five items of business that may be properly brought before the annual
   school meeting.
3. What are special school meetings, and how may such meetings be called?
4. (a) Name at least five items of school expense that must be provided for.
   (b) Where does the money come from?
5. What may the district do with buildings and grounds no longer in use?

## THEORY AND ART.

### All Grades.

1. (a) Give the educational value of vocal music.
   (b) To what extent is it practical to teach vocal music in rural schools?
2. How would you overcome inattention of pupils during recitation?
3. How may intermissions be profitably used upon stormy days?
4. Name four different methods of teaching primary reading. Describe the one
   you prefer, and give reasons for choice.
5. What would guide you in making a daily recitation program for a large
   rural school?

## UNITED STATES HISTORY.

### Second Grade.

1. General excellence, including neatness, will count for this number.
2. What invention in the time of Columbus made possible a voyage across the
   Atlantic Ocean?
3. What were the predominating influences that dictated the colonization of
   America by Spain, France, England, and Holland, respectively?
4. Briefly speak of the Massachusetts Bay Colony. Point out the difference
   between Pilgrims and Puritans.
5. (a) What effect did the American Revolution have upon French politics?
   (b) How were American politics affected by the French revolution?
6. Discuss the different constructions of the Constitution which led to the
   organization of two great parties.
7. Give brief history of Mormonism, telling how, where, and when it originated.
8. What states were at first represented in the confederate government? What
   other states subsequently joined it?
9. Briefly speak of the growth and development of the United States since the
   civil war.
10. Make a definite statement regarding any five of the following:

| | |
|---|---|
| Dewey Day. | Cecil Rhodes. |
| Capt. Coghlan's Speech. | C. P. Huntington. |
| Gen. Luna. | The Cruiser Raleigh. |
| The Quay Trial. | The Spanish Indemnity. |
| The Grant Monument. | The Samoan Difficulty. |

### THIRD GRADE, CLASS B.

1. General excellence, including neatness, will count for this number.
2. What is the attitude of the typical Indian towards manual labor?
3. Speak of Amerigo Vespucci, his work and voyages.
4. What good reasons may be given for so many failures to establish colonies in America?
5. What was the chief end accomplished by the league known as "The United Colonies of New England?"
6. Briefly speak of Lafayette, Baron de Kalb, Pulaski, and Baron Steuben, and their assistance to America in the Revolutionary struggle.
7. Point out why the Articles of Confederation were not suited to the needs of the American Government.
8. What trouble arose between this country and Spain at close of the War of 1812? How was it settled?
9. Name ten of the pivotal dates given in the State Manual and Course of Study.
10. Make a definite statement regarding any five of the following:

Dewey Day.            Cecil Rhodes.
Capt. Coghlan's Speech.       C. P. Huntington.
Gen. Luna.             The Cruiser Raleigh.
The Quay Trial.         The Spanish Indemnity.
The Grant Monument.       The Samoan Difficulty.

### CLASS A.

1. General excellence, including neatness, will count for this number.
2. What was the attitude of the typical Indian towards manual labor?
3. Speak of Amerigo Vespucci, his work and voyages.
4. What good reasons may be given for so many failures to establish colonies in America?
5. Speak of Washington as a boy, an officer in the French and Indian War, a general in the Revolution, President of the United States, and "first citizen" of the new republic.
6. Give an outline suitable for pupils to follow in studying the life and work of Benjamin Franklin.
7. Briefly speak of Henry Clay's work in connection with slavery.
8. Give an account of Abraham Lincoln's boyhood, and his efforts to obtain an education.
9. Name ten of the "pivotal dates" given in the State Manual and Course of Study.
10. Make a definite statement regarding any five of the following:

Dewey Day.            Cecil Rhodes.
Capt. Coghlan's Speech.       C. P. Huntington.
Gen. Luna.             The Cruiser Raleigh.
The Quay Trial.         The Spanish Indemnity.
The Grant Monument.       The Samoan Difficulty.

---

## V. QUESTIONS PREPARED BY THE SUPERINTENDENT OF PUBLIC INSTRUCTION FOR THE REGULAR EXAMINATION, AUGUST, 1899.

### ALGEBRA.

#### First Grade.

1. General excellence, including neatness, will count for this number.
2. Make and solve an original problem requiring the use of two unknown quantities.
3. A courier traveling $p$ miles in $q$ hours is followed at an interval of $m$ hours by another traveling $r$ miles in $s$ hours. In how many hours will the first courier be overtaken?

4. If I divide a certain number by the sum of its two digits, the quotient is 6, the remainder 3. If I reverse the order of digits and divide the resulting number by the sum of the digits, the quotient is 4, the remainder 9. Find the number.

5. (a) What is the formula whereby one may recall the rule for extracting cube root, in case it is forgotten?
   (b) What is the sign of an odd root of a negative quantity? Of an even root? Explain.

6. $\dfrac{x}{(x-2)(x-3)} + \dfrac{2(x-2)}{(3-x)(x-1)} - \dfrac{x-3}{(x-1)(2-x)} = ?$

7. A rectangular piece of land 84 rods by 52 rods, has a ditch of uniform breadth running entirely around the land. Within the ditch the area is 26 acres, 73 sq. rds. Find width of ditch. (Explain which of the two roots of the equation should be taken as the answer and why.)

8. $\dfrac{1}{y+\sqrt{y^2-1}} + \dfrac{1}{y-\sqrt{y^2-1}} = 12.$ Solve.

9. Find value of unknown quantities. $\begin{cases} x^2 + xy = 10 \\ xy - y^2 = -3 \end{cases}$

10. Find value of $x$ in the equation $x^4 - 1 = 0$.

### Second Grade.

1. General excellence, including neatness, will count for this number.

2. (a) $-\tfrac{1}{4} b^2 - \overline{(b^2-2} - b^2) \cdot \} - \left[ b^2 - \tfrac{1}{4} - (b^2 - 6) \right\} \right] = ?$

   (b) $\dfrac{60 \ x^{\frac{2}{3}} y^{-5} z^m - 2}{40 \ x^{\frac{3}{2}} y^{-7} z^{x \cdot n}} = ?$

3. A certain hall is four times as long as wide. If its length be increased by 2 ft. and its width decreased by the same amount, its area would be decreased by 52 sq. ft. Find length and breadth.

4. Factor $\begin{cases} x^2 - 14ax + 45a^2 \\ a^2 - b^2 + a - b \end{cases}$

5. Find H. C. D. of $12x^3 + 14x - 6$ and $12x^2 + 16x - 3$.

6. A rectangular field whose area is 363 sq. rds. has a perimeter of 88 sq. rds. Find its length and breadth.

7. Illustrate the following:
   (a) A literal equation of the third degree.
   (b) A pure quadratic equation.
   (c) A quadratic surd.
   (d) A mean proportional.
   (e) An imaginary quantity.

8. How do zero and negative exponents arise? Illustrate.

9. Find a fourth proportional to $\dfrac{a-b}{a+b}, \dfrac{(a-b)^2}{(a+b)^2}, \dfrac{a}{b}$.

10. Solve: $\sqrt{x} + \sqrt{4a+x} = 2\sqrt{b+x}$.

### BOTANY.

#### First Grade.

1. Fully describe the growth of the embryo.
2. How can you distinguish between the peduncle and plant-stem in case of solitary inflorescence?
3. (a) Make a drawing to show five kinds of leaf margin, and mention example of each.
   (b) Show that the shape and office of leaves are frequently determined by circumstances.

4. What terms designate a typical, or pattern flower?
5. When is a plant said to be dioecious? When monoecious? Give example of each.
6. Describe the process of cleft-grafting.
7. (a) In what portion of the plant is protoplasm most abundant?
   (b) What gives the green color to protoplasm in leaves?
8. What relation exists between the fauna and flora of a country?
10. What do you understand by "intercellular spaces," and what plants furnish opportunity for observing them?

### Second Grade.

1. Name and describe the parts of a leaf.
2. (a) Give the two general divisions of stems.
   (b) Do twining stems always twine in the same direction?
3. (a) From what three sources does the plant world derive food?
   (b) What exception is there to the rule?
4. What is included in the term bud?
5. Describe an umbel and give an example of one.
6. What agencies are active in promoting cross-fertilization of plants?
7. Describe and give example of three classes of simple fruits.
8. (a) What proof is there that ocean currents act as seed-distributing agencies?
   (b) What other agencies are employed?
9. (a) How does a forest increase the moisture of a district?
   (b) By what process is water carried upward from the root of a plant?
10. Give three reasons why a boy should study plant life. (Committee of Twelve.) If you have not seen the report, give your own ideas.

### CIVIL GOVERNMENT.

#### First and Second Grades.

1. General excellence, including neatness, will count for this number.
2. (a) What is the electoral college and how is it constituted?
   (b) What was its original design and in what respect has it departed from that design?
3. When may the federal government order troops into a state without the consent of the governor or legislature thereof?
4. (a) Under what conditions may a case be appealed to the supreme court?
   (b) What is the method of procedure in case of appeal?
5. For what purpose does the legislature resolve itself into a committee of the whole?
6. (a) On what grounds may impeachment be made?
   (b) In what branch of congress must impeachment begin, and before what body are the proceedings heard?
7. What are the necessary proceedings to an amendment of the constitution?
8. Do the first ten amendments to the constitution restrict the state government or general government, or both. Justify your answer.
9. Name three important bills that were before the last Michigan legislature. Give the main provisions of one.
10. Name the chief duties of the following administrative boards:
    (a) State Board of Health.
    (b) State Board of Equalization.
    (c) State Board of Immigration.

#### THIRD GRADE, CLASS B.

1. General excellence, including neatness, will count for this number.
2. Over what lands does congress exercise exclusive control.
3. State two rights, or immunities, given by the constitution to senators and representatives, and suggest the reason therefor.
4. Why was it deemed advisable to place the management of post-offices with the general government?
5. Explain how and when short and long sessions of congress occur.

11

6. State the process by which a territory becomes a state.
7. What are the "high seas?"
8. What is an indictment? A grand jury?
9. Name some of the prohibitions imposed on the states by the constitution.
10. What importance does the State Manual and Course of Study attach to the study of civics?

### CLASS A.

1. General excellence, including neatness, will count for this number.
2. Over what lands does congress exercise exclusive control?
3. What officers preserve peace in a county? In a village?
4. Why was it deemed advisable to place the management of post-offices with the general government?
5. Name two elements of good citizenship that the school should inculcate.
6. State the process by which a territory becomes a state.
7. Briefly give the steps that must be taken to convict a criminal and place him in prison.
8. Name the highest judicial officer of the township, and define his duties.
9. What is a capital crime?
10. What importance does the State Manual and Course of Study attach to the study of civics?

## GENERAL HISTORY.

### First Grade.

1. Explain what is meant by Assyria and Egypt being the birthplaces of material civilization, and the Phoenicians its missionaries?
2. What economic conditions led to the reforms of the Gracchi?
3. How did the new route to India affect the Italian cities?
4. What was the mission of Napoleon?
5. (a) In what war was the "Charge of the Light Brigade" made?
   (b) State the result of this war.
6. Tell why it seems important that the Graeco-Persian wars should have resulted as they did.
7. Give the cause, result, and effect of the Franco-Prussian War.
8. State in full the result of the divorce of Henry VIII from Catherine.
9. What can you say of the Anglo-Russian Agreement?
10. What plausible reason can you assign for the partition of China?

### SECOND GRADE.

1. Briefly give cause, result, and effect of the movement in which Scipio was interested.
2. Mention five prominent names in ancient history, giving some interesting fact in connection with each.
3. Characterize the Age of Pericles.
4. In what period of history did the French and German nations come into existence?
5. State the effect of feudalism upon English history.
6. What was the object of the Congress of Vienna?
7. Mention some of the events which marked the beginning of modern history.
8. Under what circumstances was Calais lost to England?
9. Mention two decisive battles of the world, briefly giving the effect of each.
10. What two prominent European statesmen have died during the last year, and with what question was each prominently connected?

## GEOGRAPHY.

### First and Second Grades.

1. General excellence, including neatness, will count for this number.
2. State the advantage of the topical method of study.

3. (a) What do you understand by the "reading hour" in school work?
   (b) During the "reading hour" in geography work do you or the pupils read to the class? Give reasons for your choice.
4. What is the importance of the prospective cable between Germany and the United States?
5. (a) What conditions are favorable to weathering of rocks?
   (b) State the result of such action.
6. Write a brief topical outline on commerce.
7. What factors determine the adaptability of a country to civilization? Illustrate.
8. Write fifteen lines on the fishing industries of the United States.
9. What is your opinion of map drawing?
10. Mention ten cities of the world which you consider valuable topics for class work, briefly giving reasons.

### THIRD GRADE, CLASS B.

1. General excellence, including neatness, will count for this number.
2. What agencies affect climate?
3. Mention five noted buildings in the world, locating each.
4. Explain how a telegram dated at Boston might be received in San Francisco at an earlier hour than that in which it was sent.
5. Mention five principal cities in Michigan, and tell what favored the growth of each.
6. How do beginners gain correct ideas of geographical forms?
7. What stress do you place upon progressive map drawing? Give reasons for your answer?
8. Locate the important manufacturing regions of North America, and mention some of the leading articles.
9. Locate the following, mentioning one point of interest in connection with each: White mountains, Cambridge, St. Louis, Leipsic, Edinburgh, Liverpool, Hong Kong, Annapolis, Cleveland, New Orleans.
10. Mention five commercial plants, telling their use and where found.

### CLASS A.

1. General excellence, including neatness, will count for this number.
2. Briefly discuss child life in Japan.
3. Mention five noted buildings in the world, locating each.
4. Explain how a telegram dated at Boston might be received in San Francisco at an earlier hour than it was sent.
5. Mention five principal cities in Michigan, and tell what favored the growth of each.
6. Name the principal races of man, giving nativity of each.
7. Mention some objects you would encourage pupils to bring to illustrate lessons on South America.
8. Locate the important manufacturing regions of North America, and mention some of the leading articles.
9. Why is spring water considered specially wholesome?
10. Draw an outline map of Africa, indicating location of the English and the Boers.

## GRAMMAR.

### First and Second Grades.

NOTE.—Capitalization, punctuation, paragraphing, diction, and grammatical construction, should all be carefully noted by the examiner in marking the final question of each grade, as it counts for thirty credits.

1. General excellence, including neatness, will count for this number.
2. "*It* is to the Union *that* we owe our safety at home, and our consideration and dignity abroad. Every year of its duration has teemed with fresh proof of its utility and its blessings; *and*, although our territory has stretched out wider and wider, *and* our population spread farther and farther, they have not *outrun* its protection or its benefits."
   (a) Classify the clauses in above, telling what each subordinate clause modifies.
   (b) Point out the subject of the first verb.
   (c) Specify the use of italicised words.

3. (a) Explain difference in meaning of the two phrases—"A bust of Cicero;" "A bust of Cicero's."
   (b) Which of these phrases is an idiom and why?
4. Distinguish between the two uses of italicised word:
   (a) That horse *running* away is mine.
   (b) He owns a *running* horse.
5. Write out analysis of the following, taking care to put it in just the form you would require of a pupil:
   "I hold this thing to be grandly true—
   That a noble deed is a step toward God."
6. "If he should injure you, I would punish him." Abridge the preceding in two ways:
   (a) By use of verbal noun.
   (b) By use of an abstract noun.
7. (a) What do you understand by a "noun nominative absolute by inscription?"
   (b) In your opinion is a first grade applicant excusable for failure to give any answer to such a question as the preceding, on the grounds that he "has never seen it in a grammar?"
8. Write not less than 150, nor more than 250 words, on one of the following topics:
   Recent Inventions.
   Gomez, the Cuban Patriot.
   The Philippine Problem.
   The Education of Travel.
   Is an Anglo-American Alliance desirable?

*N. B.—Take care that your essay reaches the required limit by the expression of thought, not by the addition of superfluous words.*

### THIRD GRADE, CLASS B.

1. General excellence, including neatness, will count for this number.
2. What do you understand from the statement that technical grammar is to the linguist what the carpenter's square is to the builder?
3. (a) What is the antecedent of an interrogative pronoun usually called? Why?
   (b) What is another name for the nominative absolute?
4. Name four expressions that may be used as nouns.
5. Give a collective noun, an ordinal numeral, a conjunctive adverb, an inseparable phrase, and a verbal.
6. In the sentence, "He was the Napoleon of his age," would it be proper to call Napoleon a common noun? Justify your answer.
7. Analyze without diagram: "Idleness and vice go hand in hand; that the parent, this the child."
8. Write not less than 150, nor more than 250 words, on any one of the following topics:
   Recent Inventions.
   Gomez, the Cuban Patriot.
   The Philippine Problem.
   The Education of Travel.
   Is an Anglo-American Alliance desirable?
   *(See note at close of first grade questions.)*

### CLASS A.

1. General excellence, including neatness, will count for this number.
2. What do you understand from the statement that technical grammar is to the linguist what the carpenter's square is to the builder?
3. Give the principal parts of cut, catch, slew, smitten, set, lost, risen, burst, fall.
4. Name four expressions that may be used as nouns.
5. Illustrate the correct order for I, you, and he, when used as subjects of the same verb. Give reasons for your arrangement.
6. What is the purpose of language work in the first three grades?
7. What directions does the State Manual and Course of Study give for drilling on the correct use of *who, whom,* and *which*?

8. Write not less than 150, nor more than 250 words, on any one of the following topics:

    Recent Inventions.

    Gomez, the Cuban Patriot.

    The Philippine Problem.

    The Education of Travel.

    Is an Anglo-American Alliance desirable?

        *(See note at close of first grade questions.)*

## ORTHOGRAPHY.

### First and Second Grades.

NOTE.—These questions count 50 per cent and the list of words 50 per cent.

1. Give words to illustrate the following sounds: short broad *a*, long *oo*, circumflex *a*, long *y*, foreign *e*.
2. Mention five Latin prefixes, giving the meaning of each.
3. Indicate the pronunciation of the following: acclimated, financiers, lamentably, incomparable, almond, inquiry, apparatus, vehement, irrevocable, clematis.
4. Distinguish between specie, species; canvass, canvas; frank, franc; fawn, faun; guild, gild.
5. Give examples of gutterals, liquids, palatals, lingua-dentals, labials.

### THIRD GRADE, BOTH CLASSES.

1. (a) What is the purpose of teaching diacritical marks?
   (b) Illustrate five diacritical marks used by Webster.
2. Expand the following abbreviations: incog., U. S. N., Ph. D., Wyo., Mme.
3. Indicate the pronunciation of the following: recess, quay, preface, newspaper, exhort.
4. Distinguish between suite, sweet; serge, surge; statue, statute; sale, sail; stationary, stationery.
5. Give two rules for spelling, with words to illustrate.

### LIST OF WORDS.

#### All Grades.

| | | |
|---|---|---|
| potential | compete | courteous |
| librarian | besiege | genuine |
| Fahrenheit | abdomen | executor |
| committee | peninsula | column |
| appreciate | controlled | Beethoven |
| Thames | argument | advertise |
| gracious | February | electrical |
| pioneer | preferred | Adirondack |
| Massachusetts | | |

## PENMANSHIP.

### All Grades.

NOTE.—This must be written with a pen. 30 credits for answers, 70 for handwriting.

1. What are the natural requisites for a good penman?
2. (a) How would you proceed to overcome a trembling hand?
   (b) An inaccurate eye?
   (c) Heedlessness?
3. In your teaching experience or your school experience, if you have never taught, what three faults have been most difficult to correct?

## PHYSICS.

### First Grade.

1. Before ascension the barometer in a balloon stood at 30 in.; at the highest point it stood at 20 in. Give approximate height of ascension?
2. A gold ring in water weighs 1½ pwt. How much gold does it contain?
3. Explain the magnified and diminished real image of a double convex lens, with drawing to illustrate.
4. (a) What is the unit of measurement of light?
   (b) Compare the intensity of sunlight with artificial light.
   (c) Describe a photometer.
5. Discuss mirrors with reference to the following:    (a) reflection;   (b)   real images;   (c) virtual images.
6. Discuss the solar spectrum.
7. (a) Define a musical sound.
   (b) Discuss the ratios of vibrations in the diatonic scale.
   (c) Explain a discord in music.
8. (a) What is heat?
   (b) Explain why combustion produces heat.
9. When a Fahrenheit thermometer stands at 28° above zero, how do the Reaumur and the Centigrade stand?
10. Explain:  (a) two kinds of electrification; (b) induction; (c) electrical potential.

## PHYSIOLOGY.

### First and Second Grades.

1. General excellence, including neatness, will count for this number.
2. Briefly explain the absorption of food.
3. Name the fluids of the body, briefly noting the function of each.
4. What do you understand by the term dialysis?  Illustrate.
5. Give directions for preparing a specimen for the microscope.
6. What is meant by accommodation of the eye?
7. Write an outline for the study of the heart.
8. Mention several metallic poisons, giving an antidote for one of them.
9. Briefly state the function of each division of the ear.
10. Name and describe the three kinds of motor impulses.

#### THIRD GRADE, CLASS B.

1. General excellence, including neatness, will count for this number.
2. Mention some of the most dangerous narcotics and the effects of two of them.
3. Tell what purpose the blood serves and by what means it is circulated through the body.
4. Show the relation between throat disease and deafness.
5. Give directions for ventilating a sick room.
6. What is the effect of alcohol upon the heart?
7. What means would you use to check the flow of blood from a wound?
8. How does the action of the skin affect the kidneys?
9. Give reasons for the separate bones and shape of the spinal column.
10. What are the following:  pleura, pylorus, retina, pharynx, aorta?

#### CLASS A.

1. General excellence, including neatness, will count for this number.
2. Mention some of the most dangerous narcotics and the effects of two of them.
3. Explain why dashing cold water upon the face will revive a fainting person.
4. Show the relation between throat disease and deafness.
5. Give directions for ventilating a sick room.
6. Why are coffee and tea considered specially injurious to children?
7. What means would you use to check the flow of blood from a wound?
8. How does the action of the skin affect the kidneys?
9. Give reasons for the separate bones and shape of the spinal column.
10. (a) What are the signs of sunstroke?
    (b) What would you do to relieve one suffering from sunstroke?

## READING.

### All Grades.

(Answers to these four questions should be written and count for forty credits, sixty being given on the oral test.)

1. What is classic literature? Mention some examples.
2. The natural movements in reading are three—rapid, moderate, and slow. Give some quotation or sentence to illustrate each.
3. Mention some points to be considered in the selection of school readers.
4. Tell what slides of the voice are necessary to interpret the thought of the following, and show on what words they should fall: "I am here to act, not talk."

### Questions to assist in the Oral Test.

#### I.

Line 4.  What are the "Jerseys?"
" Define *gorge*. Is this a literal or figurative use of the word?
" What can you say of this king?
" Define militant. Give some other word built on the same stem.
"  5.  Distinguish between the meaning of could, would, and should.
"  18.  Who was Watts?
What can you say of Bret Harte?
Which of the above stanzas requires the greatest variety of inflection?

#### II.

Line 2.  What is the "glory of arms?" Name some men who have recently experienced it.
"  8.  What is "the art of benevolence?"
What mistakes of articulation are commonly made in the pronunciation of *judgment, influence, transcendent*.
Who was Charles Sumner?

#### III.

Point out three figures of speech in this paragraph.
Where are "the shades of Vernon?"
Who was Edward Everett?

### Reading Extracts.

#### I.

     .................Stay, one moment; you've heard
Of Caldwell, the parson, who once preached the Word
3.  Down at Springfield? What! no? Come, that's bad! Why, he had
All the Jerseys aflame; and they gave him the name
Of "the rebel high-priest." He stuck in their gorge,
6.  For he loved the Lord God, and he hated King George!
  *   *   *   *   *   *   *   *   *   *   *

Did he preach—did he pray? Think of him as you stand
By the old church today; think of him and that band
9.  Of militant ploughboys! See the smoke and the heat
Of that reckless advance, of that straggling retreat!
Keep the ghost of that wife, foully slain, in your view—
12.  And what could you, what should you, what would *you* do?

Why, just what *he* did! They were left in the lurch
For want of more wadding. He ran to the church,
15.  Broke the door, stripped the pews, and dashed out in the road
With his arms full of hymn-books, and threw down his load
At their feet! Then above all the shouting and shots
18.  Rang his voice—"Put Watts into 'em! Boys, give 'em Watts!"

And they did. That is all. Grasses spring, flowers blow,
Pretty much as they did ninety-three years ago.
21.  You may dig anywhere and you'll turn up a ball,
But not always a hero like this—and that's all.

          *Bret Harte.*

## II.

Whatever may be the judgment of poets, of moralists, of satirists, or even of soldiers, it is certain that the glory of arms still exercises no mean influence over the minds of men. The art of war, which has been happily
4. térmed by a French divine, the baleful art by which men learn to exterminate one another, is yet held, even among Christians, to be an honorable pursuit; and the animal courage which it stimulates and develops, is prized as a transcendent virtue. It will be for another age and a higher civilization
8. to appreciate the more exalted character of the art of benevolence—the art of extending happiness and all good influences, by word or deed, to the largest number of mankind, which in blessed contrast with the misery, the degradation, the wickedness of war, shall shine resplendent—the true gran-
12. deur of peace. All then will be willing to join with the early poet in saying, at least,

> "Though louder fame attend the martial rage,
> 'Tis greater glory to reform the age."

*Chas. Sumner.*

## III.

To be cold and breathless—to feel not and speak not—this is not the end of existence to the men who have breathed their spirits into the institutions of their country, who have stamped their characters on the pillars of the
4. age, who have poured their heart's blood into the channels of the public prosperity! Tell me, ye who tread the sods of yon sacred height, is Warren dead? Can you not see him—not pale and prostrate, the blood of his gallant heart pouring out of his ghastly wound, but moving resplendent over the
8. field of honor, with the rose of heaven upon his cheek and the fire of liberty in his eye? Tell me, ye who make your pious pilgrimage to the shades of Vernon, is Washington indeed shut up in that narrow house? That which made these men and men like these, cannot die! The hand that traced the
12. charter of Independence is, indeed, motionless; the eloquent lips that sustained it are hushed; but the lofty spirits that conceived, resolved, and maintained it, and which alone to such men "make it life to live"—these cannot expire.

*Edward Everett.*

## SCHOOL LAW.

### All Grades.

1. What is the source of the teachers' institute fund? Have you derived any benefit therefrom?
2. Give the steps necessary to change the boundary lines of a fractional district.
3. What is the power of the district board in regard to changing the length of school year as voted at the annual meeting?
4. State exactly the conditions by which a teacher can obtain a legal contract.
5. Name and locate the Michigan Normal Schools for which the law now provides.

## THEORY AND ART.

### All Grades.

1. State five good reasons for making the primary school room neat, cheerful, and beautiful.
2. How may the teaching of reading be made helpful in character building?
3. Give some means whereby the primary school may cultivate the child's powers of rapid, accurate observation.
4. What are the essential points to note in preparing to teach a lesson?
5. (a) State the value of a good district school library.
   (b) How does the State Manual and Course of Study assist teachers in securing a library?

# UNITED STATES HISTORY.

### First and Second Grades.

1. General excellence, including neatness, will count for this number.
2. What discoveries are associated with these names: Cabot, Balboa, De Soto, Cartier, Magellan?
3. Contrast the conflicting opinions held by Hamilton and Jefferson.
4. (a) What rights were secured to the United States by Jay's treaty? (b) In what respect was it unsatisfactory?
5. Give cause for each of the following colonial wars: King William's, Queen Anne's, King George's.
6. Discuss five lines of development that have characterized the western portion of our country within the past generation.
7. (a) Name the so-called "border states" of the Civil War. (b) On which side did the following generals fight: Johnston, Sherman, Hooker, Jackson, McClellan?
8. What two great obstacles stood in the way of a true reconstruction of the South, and how are they being overcome?
9. Discuss the responsibilities coming to us as an outgrowth of the Spanish-American War.
10. Make a definite statement about any five of the following:

| | |
|---|---|
| General Lawton. | Rear-Admiral Kautz. |
| Justice Field. | The Peace Congress. |
| Finnish Immigration. | The Mazet Committee. |
| The Samoan Ambush. | The German Meat Bill. |
| Jamaican Imports. | Disputed Alaskan Boundary. |

#### THIRD GRADE, CLASS B.

1. General excellence, including neatness, will count for this number.
2. Tell something of the various substitutes for money used in colonial times.
3. Why were the Spanish unsuccessful in their attempts to colonize North America?
4. When and how was slavery introduced into the English colonies in America?
5. Name the extent of the Louisiana Territory, the President who promoted its purchase, and the states carved from it.
6. Describe the greatest battle of the Civil War.
7. What does the State Manual and Course of Study say in regard to teaching political questions in history?
8. What leading political issues have divided the people since the Civil War, and what new issues are now being discussed?
9. State the terms of peace concluding the late Spanish-American War.
10. Make a definite statement about any five of the following:

| | |
|---|---|
| General Lawton. | Rear-Admiral Kautz. |
| Justice Field. | The Peace Congress. |
| Finnish Immigration. | The Mazet Committee. |
| The Samoan Ambush. | The German Meat Bill. |
| Jamaican Imports. | Disputed Alaskan Boundary. |

#### CLASS A.

1. General excellence, including neatness, will count for this number.
2. Tell something of the various substitutes for money used in colonial times?
3. Why are history stories preferable to text-books in teaching beginners?
4. When and how was slavery introduced into the English colonies in America?
5. Of what value in history teaching is Longfellow's *Evangeline?*
6. Mention some historic fact previous to the revolution, connected with the life of George Washington, Benjamin Franklin, Marquis de La Fayette.
7. Name the presidents who died in office.
8. What does the State Manual and Course of Study say in regard to teaching political questions in history?
9. State the terms of peace concluding the late Spanish-American War.

12

10. Make a definite statement about any five of the following:

General Lawton.
Justice Field.
Finnish Immigration.
The Samoan Ambush.
Jamaican Imports.

Rear-Admiral Kautz.
The Peace Congress.
The Mazet Committee.
The German Meat Bill.
Disputed Alaskan Boundary.

### WRITTEN ARITHMETIC.

#### First and Second Grades.

1. Construct a problem in interest which can be solved by the following statement: $\dfrac{1200 \times 6 \times 36}{360}$.

2. Compute the length of a degree of longitude at the equator.

3. A man loaned two equal amounts of money, one at 4% and the other at 4½%, receiving $8.50 interest per month. How much did he loan?

4. The last State legislature raised the university mill tax from $\frac{1}{8}$ mill to $\frac{1}{4}$ mill. The state valuation is $1,105,100,000. How much additional revenue will the university receive?

5. A man dug a well 6 ft. across and 30 ft. deep. He then "stoned up" the well, leaving a circular opening 2 ft. in diameter. How many cords of stone did it take?

#### THIRD GRADE, CLASS B.

1. Explain as to a class:
   (a) Simple and local value of figures.
   (b) Use of horizontal vinculum.

2. $\dfrac{\frac{1}{2}+\frac{1}{2}\times\frac{1}{2}+\frac{1}{2}\times\frac{6}{7}}{\frac{2+3\times4}{7}} = ?$

3. It is noon in Paris, 5 hrs. 10 min. before noon in Philadelphia. The longitude of Philadelphia is 75° 10′ W. What is the longitude of Paris?

4. A man buys goods 20, 10, and 5 off. He sells them at a profit of 25%. What per cent of the list price is his asking price?

5. Draw a note for $1,200, for 2 yrs., at 6%, with $240 indorsed in 3 mos., $160 in 6 mos., $400 in 13 mos., and find amount due at maturity.

#### CLASS A.

1. Explain as to a class the following:
   (a) Simple and local value of figures.
   (b) Use of the signs of aggregation found in arithmetic.

2. $\dfrac{\frac{1}{2}+\frac{1}{2}\times\frac{1}{2}+\frac{1}{2}\times\frac{1}{2}}{\frac{2+3\times4}{7}} = ?$

3. Explain as to a class:
   (a) $\frac{1}{2}=\frac{3}{6}$; (b) $\frac{6}{8}=\frac{3}{4}$; (c) $\frac{1}{2}+\frac{1}{4}=\frac{5}{4}$; (d) $3+\frac{1}{3}=4$.

4. Work the following by *comparison*:
   (a) If 2½ lbs. of sugar cost 7¾ cts., what will 7½ lbs. cost?
   (b) At $3¼ for 4 books, what will 10 books cost?
   (c) If 12½ acres of land cost $50, what will 37½ acres cost?

5. Prepare a table of fractional equivalents such as you would have a class in percentage commit to memory.

## MENTAL ARITHMETIC.

### All Grades.

NOTE.—A member of the Examining Board will examine candidates in classes of twenty-five or less, testing quickness to grasp the salient features of a problem, accuracy and rapidity of work, clearness and simplicity of analysis. In the right hand margin applicants will write as many answers to the first twenty questions as possible in fifteen minutes; one-half per cent for each answer and one per cent additional for each correct one is given in this part of the examination.

1. What cost 75 horses at $75 each?
2. At $66 an acre, how many acres of land can be bought for $2,200?
3. At two shillings each, how many books can I buy for $20?
4. How many packages of berries, each containing 2⅜ quarts, at 2½ cts. a quart, must be given for 3 8-lb. jars of butter at 20 cts. a pound?
5. What is the cost of 9½ bu. of oats at 9½c a bu?
6. Divide 24 into parts to each other as 2, 3, and 7.
7. How many tons of coal at $6¼ a ton can be bought for $37.50?
8. At $150 a cord, what cost a pile of wood 12 ft. long and 6 ft. high?
9. Two-thirds of $45 is ⅜ of twice the cost of my watch. Required the cost.
10. 12 is how many sixths of 18?
11. Sold a ball for 60 cts., which was ⅓ less than cost. Required the cost.
12. 18 is ⅔ of ¾ of what number?
13. What cost 600 eggs at 13 cts. a dozen?
14. At 10 cts. a doz., how many apples can I buy for 25 cts.?
15. What part of ⅘ is ⅔?
16. 50% of 6 is 25% of what?
17. What is the bank discount on $120 for 60 days at 6%?
18. What number increased by its 20% equals 600?
19. How many ft. of lumber in six boards each 14 ft. long and 8 in. wide?
20. What time of day is it when the time past noon equals the time to midnight?
21. In a certain school of 50 pupils there are 3 boys to every 2 girls. How many boys must leave school that there may be 3 girls to every 2 boys?
22. Five-sixths of 30 is how many twelfths of 10?
23. A man twice increased his capital by 50%, having then $900. How much had he at first?
24. A, B, and C do a piece of work in 12 days. B can do it in 8 days, and C in 9 days; how long will it take A?
25. A and B earned $25 and divided it so that A had $3 more than B. How much had each?
26. What is the relation of 5¼ to 6⅜?
27. A company reduced the pay of their men 20%; but owing to dissatisfaction, increased their pay 20%. The men then received 8 cts. per day less than at first. What did they then receive?
28. A man buys goods at a discount of 20 and 10 from the list price, and sells making 25% profit. How much does he discount the list price to his customers?
29. A bicyclist rides 12 miles an hour and walks 4. His wheel breaks and he is obliged to walk to his home, which he reaches 8 hrs. after starting. How far did he go?
30. A sells goods at a certain loss per cent; B buys the same goods, but discounts the list 20% off for cash and sells at the same price as A, losing 15% less. What does A lose?

## VI. QUESTIONS PREPARED BY THE SUPERINTENDENT OF PUBLIC INSTRUCTION FOR THE REGULAR EXAMINATION, OCTOBER, 1899.

### ALGEBRA.

#### Second Grade.

1. General excellence, including neatness, will count for this number.
2. (a) Distinguish between demonstration and rule.
   (b) Between axiom and corollary.

3. How would you explain algebraic subtraction to a beginner?
4. Factor: $4a^2 - 3a - 1$; $4a^2 + 11ab + 6b^2$; $4a^2y^2 - 9b^2x^2$.
5. (a) Of what use is elimination and upon what principle founded?
   (b) Make and solve a problem to illustrate elimination by comparison.
6. Give the rule for finding H. C. D. of two polynomials without resolving them into prime factors.
7. Make and solve a problem to illustrate the use of Newton's Binomial Theorem.
8. Solve the problem below: (a) with one unknown quantity; (b) with two unknown quantities.
   A farmer purchased 100 acres of land for $2,450; for a part of the land he paid $20 an acre, for the rest $30. How many acres in each part?
9. How may any number be reduced to a radical of any given degree? Illustrate.
10. Solve: $\sqrt{\sqrt{x}+ 3} - \sqrt{\sqrt{x}-3} = \sqrt[3]{\sqrt{x}}$

## ARITHMETIC.

### Second Grade.

1. I buy hardware, receiving 30, 20, 10, and 5 off, and settle the bill with $957.60. What was the list price of the bill?
2. A note for 6 mos. at 6%, was discounted after 3 mos., without grace, at 9%, yielding $1217.46. What was its face?
3. Divide $1200 among A, B, C. and D, so that the difference between the amounts received by any two consecutive persons, will be $20.
4. From the formula, Area = $3.1416r^2$, deduce another formula for area.
5. A circular cistern has an upper diameter of 8 ft., a lower diameter of 6 ft., and a depth of 8 ft. Indicate the operations necessary to find its contents.

#### THIRD GRADE, CLASS B.

1. How do you teach the following:
   (a) To write large numbers?
   (b) To subtract in cases where the figures of the subtrahend are larger than the corresponding figures of the minuend? (Give explicit answers.)
2. 40 rds. 11 ft. is what part of a mile?
3. Paid cash for the following pieces of lumber at $12 per M.: 12 boards, 16 ft. long and 9 in. wide; eight 2x4 scantling, 16 ft. long; fifteen 8x10 joists, 14 ft. long; three 8x14 timbers, 24 ft. long.
   Make a receipted bill for the above, using some imaginary dealer's name.
4. Draw a $1200-note for 60 days at 6% and discount the same at a bank, 20 days after date, at 8%.
5. At $1.50 a perch, what will it cost to build the wall of a cellar 24 ft. long, 18 ft. wide, and 5 ft. deep, the wall to be 2 ft. thick and to extend 30 in. above the ground.

#### CLASS A.

1. How do you teach the following:
   (a) To write large numbers?
   (b) To subtract in cases where the figures of the subtrahend are larger than the corresponding figures of the minuend? (Give explicit answers.)
2. 40 rds. 11 ft. is what part of a mile?
3. Paid cash for the following pieces of lumber at $12 per M.: 12 boards, 16 ft. long and 9 in. wide; eight 2x4 scantling, 16 ft. long; fifteen 8x10 joists, 14 ft. long; three 8x14 timbers, 24 ft. long.
   Make a receipted bill for the above, using some imaginary dealer's name.
4. Give rules for "precedence of signs."
5. Explain standard time.

## MENTAL ARITHMETIC.

### All Grades.

NOTE.—A member of the Examining Board will examine candidates in classes of twenty-five or less, testing quickness to grasp the salient features of a problem, accuracy and rapidity of work, clearness and simplicity of analysis. In the right hand margin applicants will write *as many answers to the first twenty questions as possible in fifteen minutes*; one half per cent for each answer and one per cent additional for each *correct* one, is given in this part of the examination.

1. Add 25, 14, 35, 28, 18, 36, 24.
2. Add $2\frac{1}{2}$, $5\frac{3}{4}$, $6\frac{7}{8}$, $12\frac{1}{2}$.
3. $26^2 = ?$ $89^2 = ?$
4. $\sqrt{25 \times 16 \times 3 \times 12 \times 100} = ?$
5. What is the relation of $2\frac{1}{2}$ to $12\frac{1}{2}$?
6. What is the relation of $6\frac{1}{4}$ to 50?
7. If $\frac{1}{2}$ of a rod of side-walk cost $\$2\frac{1}{2}$, *how many times $\$2\frac{1}{2}$* will 55 feet cost?
8. $\frac{3}{4}$ of 24 is $\frac{1}{2}$ of $\frac{3}{4}$ of how many times $\frac{1}{3}$ of 24?
9. $36 \times 33\frac{1}{3} = ?$
10. $72 \times 75 = ?$
11. What cost 1,275 lbs. of hay at $12 a ton?
12. How many feet of lumber in a timber 10 in. by 15 in., and 30 ft. long?
13. If a metal ball 2 in. in diameter weighs 8 lbs., what will a 4 in. ball of the same metal weigh?
14. Paid 96c a gross for pens and sold them at one cent each. Give per cent of gain.
15. Four and one-half inches is what part of a yard?
16. $(85 \times 65 \times 12) + (17 \times 13 \times 60) = ?$ (According to good authority, the result of this problem would be the same if parentheses were omitted.)
17. Find the bank discount on $360 for 63 days at 5%.

N. B.—In making the following estimates, applicants are not expected to make calculations, but to *estimate* results from conditions.

18. Estimate the cost of $12\frac{3}{4}$ lbs of sugar at $5\frac{1}{4}$ cents a pound.
19. The cost of 120 acres of land at $49.85 an acre.
20. The value of a circular field 80 rds. in diameter, at $50 an acre.

N. B.—From the remaining problems third grade applicants write the *full analysis* of four selected by the examiner; second grade applicants write the *last* four, exact results are not expected.

21. Explain, as to a class, why we invert the divisor.
22. Lost $\frac{1}{4}$ my money, then earned $\frac{1}{4}$ as much as I lost, and with $\frac{1}{2}$ of what I then had, bought a watch which cost $3 less than the money lost. How much did I lose?
23. A and B owning 120 acres of land in the ratio of 5 to 3, sold a third interest to C for $300. How should A and B divide the money?
24. What number is that whose $\frac{1}{2}$ is $5\frac{1}{4}$ more than its $\frac{1}{12}$ divided by its $\frac{1}{3}$?
25. Bought a reader, a pencil, and three note-books for 30 cents. The reader cost as much as three pencils, and a pencil as much as a note-book. Required the price of each book.
26. How large is that square field which has as many square rods in its area as linear rods in the fence inclosing it?
27. A carries two purses, keeping twice as much money in one as in the other. From the larger he pays $50, and from the smaller $10. How will he restore the ratio with the money remaining?

## BOTANY.

### Second Grade.

1. Distinguish between nucleus, germ, and bud.
2. Define follicle, legume, capsule, nectary, frond.
3. What terms indicate the relative position of ovary and calyx?
4. (a) What are "double" flowers?
   (b) What are bacteria?

5. Describe five kinds of stems.
6. Mention some simple experiment to show the presence in plants of inorganic elements.
7. Describe some insectivorous plant.
8. In what part of the plant are the following found: sugar, starch, oil, gum?
9. Mention as many benefits as possible to be gained by the child from a study of plants and flowers.
10. If possible reproduce the outline for study of a fruit as given in the "Institute Outline." If not, give one of your own.

## CIVIL GOVERNMENT.

### Second Grade.

1. General excellence, including neatness, will count for this number.
2. In case of failure to elect a President, why should the House rather than the Senate choose one?
3. Name five men, exclusive of the cabinet, prominent in national politics.
4. (a) What is meant by the three-fifths compromise of the Constitution?
   (b) To what portions of the United States was it advantageous? Why?
5. (a) What is meant by the term "trust" as used in commercial circles?
   (b) Why is this question being so much discussed?
6. Mention several of the open political questions of the day.
7. State the origin of the terms strict constructionists and loose constructionists.
8. Briefly describe the government of the district of Columbia.
9. (a) From what position in Congress did Reed recently resign?
   (b) Why is this position so important?
10. (a) What do you understand by arbitration?
    (b) Mention some question that has been settled by arbitration.

### THIRD GRADE, CLASS B.

1. General excellence, including neatness, will count for this number.
2. Distinguish between ambassadors and consuls. Who appoints them?
3. (a) How are the presiding officers of the House and Senate chosen?
   (b) Briefly compare their duties.
4. (a) Enumerate five duties of the Auditor General.
   (b) For what length of term is he elected?
5. What argument can you give against the present method of electing United States senators?
6. Give the names of five good text-books on government.
7. Briefly describe the state judicial department.
8. Mention two state institutions in Michigan, locating and giving control of each.
9. Mention some of the exclusive powers of Congress.
10 (a) What do you understand by the following terms: protection, free trade, tariff for revenue only, and reciprocity?
    (b) Which of the above is the policy of the United States?

### CLASS A.

1. General excellence, including neatness, will count for this number.
2. Distinguish between ambassadors and consuls. Who appoints them?
3. (a) How are the presiding officers of the House and Senate chosen?
   (b) Briefly compare their duties.
4. Briefly explain the organization of city government.
5. What argument can you give against the present method of electing United States senators?
6. Give the names of five good text-books on government.
7. Who is the national Secretary of State? Secretary of War?
8. Mention two state institutions in Michigan, locating and designating control of each.

9. In case both the office of president and vice-president should be vacant, who would succeed to the presidency?
10. (a) What do you understand by the following terms: protection, free trade, tariff for revenue only, and reciprocity?
    (b) Which of the above is the policy of the United States?

## GENERAL HISTORY.

### Second Grade.

1. By what means is the kinship of the early nations traced?
2. Give some interesting fact in connection with each of the following: Pericles, Homer, Alexander, Darius, and Scipio.
3. What effect had the fall of Rome upon the history of the world?
4. Explain what is meant in English history by the following: Magna Charta, Doomsday Book, Petition of Rights, and Bill of Rights.
5. State some method, or device, for teaching current events.
6. Distinguish between the German and English Reformations.
7. Under what circumstances was Scotland united with England?
8. Briefly discuss the struggle in which Robespierre, Danton, and Marat figured.
9. What led to the union of the German states?
10. State the result of the Peace Conference at the Hague.

## GEOGRAPHY.

### Second Grade.

1. General excellence, including neatness, will count for this number.
2. Distinguish between physical geography and geology.
3. (a) What Spanish possessions were recently purchased by Germany? Locate them.
   (b) What are Spain's present colonial posessions?
4. Locate the Transvaal and tell what has recently brought it before the public.
5. Mention five topics on commercial geography given in the State Manual and Course of Study, with at least one subhead under each.
6. Make an itinerary of a trip including the St. Lawrence river, Niagara falls, and at least five of the eastern cities, mentioning one point of interest in connection with each.
7. Why was the isthmus of Panama selected as the site of a canal?
8. Locate five buildings or cities of historical interest, stating their importance.
9. What form of government has each of the following: Spain, Sweden, Greece, Switzerland, Mexico?
11. Designate five of the principal ocean routes.

### THIRD GRADE, CLASS B.

1. General excellence, including neatness, will count for this number.
2. Explain why the coast of Norway is free from ice, while that of Sweden is blocked with it.
3. Locate the important copper regions of the world, stating the value of copper to commerce.
4. Through what waters would you pass in taking the shortest route from Liverpool to Bombay?
5. Locate Samoa, the Ladrones, Ceylon, Madagascar, Guam.
6. Compare the industries of the eastern and southern sections of the United States, giving reasons for difference.
7. Write fifteen or twenty lines on Porto Rico, including surface, climate, and vegetation.
8. What border sea is separated from the ocean by (a) the Aleutian Islands, (b) West Indies, (c) Philippines, (d) Ireland.
9. Make an outline for a thorough study of Africa. (20 credits.)

### CLASS A.

1. General excellence, including neatness, will count for this number.
2. Mention several geographical topics which you would consider before taking up the formal study of geography.
3. Locate the important copper regions of the world, stating the value of copper to commerce.
4. Through what waters would you pass in taking the shortest route from Liverpool to Bombay?
5. Name five of the higher institutions of learning for women, locating each.
6. Mention the countries in which the rulers have the following titles: sultan, empress, khedive, czar, mikado.
7. Write fifteen or twenty lines on Porto Rico, including surface, climate, and vegetation.
8. What is the importance of Alaska to the United States?
9. Mention some devices for teaching the points of compass.
10. How would you develop the idea of latitude and longitude?

## GRAMMAR.

### Second Grade.

Note.—Capitalization, punctuation, paragraphing, diction, and grammatical construction should all be carefully noted by the examiner in marking the final question of each grade, as it counts for thirty credits.

1. General excellence, including neatness, will count for this number.
2. (a) With what authorities on grammar are you familiar?
   (b) What do you consider the best *reference* book on this subject?
3. Distinguish between the two uses of *that* in the following:
   (a) It is to the Union that we owe our safety.
   (b) It is the Union that must be preserved.
4. How does *shooting* differ in these two sentences:
   (a) He was arrested for the shooting of his son.
   (b) He was arrested for shooting his son.
5. Point out the advantages and disadvantages of the diagram.
6. Analyze without diagram:
   "Another time, being sent on a message to the vicarage and left for some minutes alone in the parlor with a piano standing open in the room, she could not resist the temptation to touch the keys."
7. Parse all the words in the following: "She laughed at the song she heard."
8. Write not less than 150, nor more than 250 words, on any one of the following topics:

   A Country Road.       A Nutting Party.
   The American Navy.     Value of Competition.
         Influence of Our Surroundings.

*N. B.—Take care that your essay reaches the required limit by the expression of thought, not by the addition of superfluous words.*

### THIRD GRADE, CLASS B.

1. General excellence, including neatness, will count for this number.
2. Explain the necessity of memorizing definitions.
3. Give sentences to illustrate:
   (a) *It* used as impersonal subject.
   (b) *It* used as anticipative subject.
4. How does the synopsis of a verb differ from its conjugation?
5. (a) Write a simple interrogative sentence containing an adjective phrase.
   (b) Write a complex declarative sentence containing an adverbial clause.
6. Name the only pure copulative verb, and several that may be used as copulas.
7. Illustrate the principal uses of punctuation marks.
8. (a) Write a letter to your County Commissioner asking for a copy of the State Manual and Course of Study.
   (b) Write a short letter of congratulation to some friend to whom great good fortune has come.

## CLASS A.

1. General excellence, including neatness, will count for this number.
2. With what authorities in grammar are you familiar?
3. By sentences show distinction between thankful and grateful, right and privilege, grand and sublime, interfere and interpose, like and love.
4. Name the things which the language work of the first three grades should try to accomplish.
5. (a) Write a simple interrogative sentence containing an adjective phrase.
   (b) Write a complex declarative sentence containing an adverbial clause.
6. What things are to be avoided during the first year of technical grammar?
7. How would you endeavor to overcome the common errors of speech to which children are liable, such as *be* for *am*, *came* for *come*, etc?
8. (a) Write a letter to your Commissioner asking for a copy of the State Manual and Course of Study.
   (b) Write a short letter of congratulation to some friend to whom great good fortune has come.

## ORTHOGRAPHY.

### All Grades.

NOTE.—These questions count 50 % and the list of words 50 %.

1. State your methods of teaching spelling in the first three grades. What errors of spelling do you aim to avoid in these grades?
2. Mark diacritically the following words: apparatus, spiritual, squarely, exit, determine.
3. Define and illustrate the use of each of the following: synonym, homonym, derivative.
4. Illustrate use of the following prefixes: de, ex, con, semi, re.
5. Should the spelling lesson be oral or written? Why?

## LIST OF WORDS.

| | |
|---|---|
| 1. chargeable | 13. habitable |
| 2. tangible | 14. cede (yield) |
| 3. tenable | 15. watchful |
| 4. susceptible | 16. evidences |
| 5. Aguinaldo | 17. pre-eminent |
| 6. legible | 18. defective |
| 7. fragile | 19. succumb |
| 8. Appalachian | 20. accept |
| 9. parallel | 21. leopard |
| 10. noticeable | 22. banyan |
| 11. preceding | 23. tropical |
| 12. proceeding | 24. maple |

25. walnut

## PENMANSHIP.

### All Grades.

(NOTE.—This should be written with a pen. 30 % for answers, 70 % for handwriting.)

1. What care should be exercised in selecting the following materials: pen-holders, ink, pens, copy-books?
2. Discuss the following with relation to penmanship: (a) height of seat, (b) height of desk, (c) firmness of seat and desk.
3. What time of day do you advise for the writing exercise? Give reason for answer.

13

## PHYSICS.

### Second Grade.

1. Describe an experiment by which you could show to pupils the expansibility of air.
2. (a) Why does it require more force to start a loaded wagon than to keep it moving?
   (b) What is momentum?
3. Illustrate the different classes of levers.
4. What is the length of a pendulum beating seconds? half-seconds? quarter-seconds?
5. (a) Discriminate between cohesion and adhesion.
   (b) Show their practical value.
6. The specific gravity of gold is 19.34. How large must a box be to hold a ton of gold, if a cu. ft. of water weighs 1000 oz.?
7. (a) Explain saturation as applied to the atmosphere.
   (b) Why is it often so oppressively warm after a summer shower?
8. (a) Why does swinging the arms warm the hands?
   (b) "A rainbow in the morning is a sailor's warning." Why?
9. (a) What changes the boiling point of water?
   (b) Why does the ear-trumpet aid in hearing?
10. Mention some of the recent scientific discoveries and inventions.

## PHYSIOLOGY.

### Second Grade.

1. General excellence, including neatness, will count for this number.
2. Define tissue and name the various kinds found in the body.
3. Briefly discuss kinds of food for summer and winter.
4. Name the three intestinal fluids and briefly state the work of each.
5. (a) Give the structure of the skin.
   (b) What is the function of the sebaceous glands.
6. Distinguish between flexor and extensor muscles. Illustrate.
7. Account for the fact that alcohol is no protection against cold, although there is a feeling of warmth after taking it.
8. Why is the liver regarded as such an important organ?
9. Explain how poisons on the surface of the body are often communicated to the blood.
10. Distinguish between secretion and excretion. Give examples to illustrate.

### THIRD GRADE, CLASS B.

1. General excellence, including neatness, will count for this number.
2. (a) What gives the red color to the blood?
   (b) What is the effect of alcohol upon the arteries?
3. How is the human voice produced?
4. What is the function of the perspiratory glands?
5. State the effect of tobacco upon the heart.
6. Give your opinion of the value of teaching physical culture in the schools.
7. What is the objection to eating much sweets?
8. Briefly discuss the importance of the spinal cord.
9. Name the divisions of the brain and briefly state the function of each.
10. Write an outline for the study of the lungs.

### CLASS A.

1. General excellence, including neatness, will count for this number.
2. Mention some hygienic rules to be observed in eating. Give reasons for same.
3. What topics on the ear would you present to pupils of the second grade?
4. What is the function of the perspiratory glands?
5. State the effect of tobacco upon the heart.

6. Give your opinion of the value of teaching physical culture in the schools.
7. What is the objection to eating much sweets?
8. (a) In what way are nerves a help to us?
   (b) What precautions should be observed to avoid becoming nervous?
9. What is the relation between circulation and respiration?
10. Mention five suggestions concerning the lungs, given in the State Manual and Course of Study.

## READING.

### All Grades.

(Answers to these four questions should be written and count for forty credits, sixty being given on the oral test.)

1. What is diction?
2. How may a fine selection be made "a mere corpse to be dissected?"
3. Which is of greater importance in good reading, quantity or quality of tone?
4. (a) Distinguish between stress and emphasis.
   (b) What can you say of radical stress?

### I.

Fading beneath our passing feet,
Strewn upon lawn and lane and street,
3.      Beautiful leaves!

Dyed with the hues of the sunset sky,
Falling in glory so silently,
6.      Beautiful leaves!

Never to freshen another spring,
Never to know what the summer may bring,
9.      Beautiful leaves!

Withered beneath the frost and cold,
Soon to decay in the common mould,
12.      Beautiful leaves!

So will the years that change your tint,
Mark upon us their autumnal print,
15.      Beautiful leaves!

So shall we fade from the tree of time,
Fade as ye fade in a wintry clime,
18.      Beautiful leaves!

But when the harvest of life is past,
And we wake in eternal spring at last,
21.      Beautiful leaves!

May be who paints your brilliant hue,
Form of our lives a chaplet new,
24.      Of beautiful leaves!

—*Anon.*

### II.

The school system of the future must have life in itself; no dead forms will suffice. It must be American, in its deepest significance, liberty loving, liberty promoting. As a friend to true liberty, it must encourage industry, sobriety, impartiality. It must inculcate love of order and respect for law. Its course
5.  must widen in the principles of government; the theory of politics; the resources of the people; questions of economy in industries and in finance; the responsibilities of office-holding, with more patriotic and less personal ends in

10. view; the sacredness of the ballot—the emblem of a freeman's power and the pledge of a freeman's honor. The school of the future must impress upon the pupil the value of American citizenship in all political and economic relations. "Intelligence is essential to good government," declared the Ordinance of 1787. Every day the words of John Stuart Mill will become more applicable to the American people: "The province of government is to increase to the utmost the pleasures, and to diminish to the utmost the pains, which men derive from
15. each other."—*Josiah Little Pickard.*

## SCHOOL LAW.

### All Grades.

1. What authority has the teacher as to the expulsion of pupils?
2. What authority has the director of schools in the matter of providing and maintaining decent outhouses?
3. Into how many classes does the school law divide voters at school meetings? What are the qualifications and rights of each class?
4. Give four items of the director's report that must be presented at the annual school meeting?
5. Why are school officers prohibited from acting as agents for any publishing house or manufacturer of school supplies?

## THEORY AND ART.

### All Grades.

1. (a) Why should a child never be held up to the school as a model of excellence?
   (b) As a subject of ridicule?
2. Name some ways in which the State Manual and Course of Study has been helpful to you in the work of teaching.
3. Which is the more important end of education, acquisition of knowledge or development of the intellect? Why?
4. What is the value of child study? Mention two important works on the subject.
5. Name five educational reformers.

## UNITED STATES HISTORY.

### Second Grade.

1. General excellence, including neatness, will count for this number.
2. Name five Indian tribes that have lived in the western portion of the United States.
3. Give a brief account of the settlement of Pennsylvania.
4. (a) What led to the confederation of the New England colonies?
   (b) What were some of the permanent effects of the confederation?
5. Give the names of five leading members, and the subjects discussed at the convention that framed the constitution.
6. What is the Monroe doctrine? Give two instances where it has been brought prominently to the attention of the world, and the outcome in each instance.
7. What were President Jackson's reasons for vetoing the law to renew the charter of the United States Bank?
8. Give a brief account of the territorial acquisitions made at different times by the United States. (20 credits.)
9. Make a definite statement about any five of the following:
   The International Yacht Race.
   Thomas B. Reed.
   San Domingo's Revolution.
   *John R. McLean.*

J. G. Schurman.
The Transvaal Troubles.
The Venezuelan Arbitration.
Hurricane in Porto Rico.
Dewey's Home-coming.
McKinley's Plan for the Permanent Government of our Colonies.

### THIRD GRADE, CLASS B.

1. General excellence, including neatness, will count for this number.
2. Give an account of the treatment of the Indians by the Spanish explorers.
3. From what country came the settlers of the following: Santa Fe, Jamestown, St. Augustine, Plymouth, New York.
4. Who and for what noted was each of the following: Cotton Mather, King Philip, Gen. Braddock, Israel Putnam, Anthony Wayne.
5. Briefly discuss the Missouri Compromise.
6. Discuss the capture and destruction of Washington in the War of 1812.
7. What perplexing questions called for settlement at the close of the Civil War?
8. For what events are the following places noted: Bemis Heights, Wyoming Valley, Yorktown, Havana.
9. What is the Homestead Law? Why did our government from the first sell the public lands at very low prices?
10. Make a definite statement about any five of the following:
    The International Yacht Race.
    Thomas B. Reed.
    San Domingo's Revolution.
    John R. McLean.
    J. G. Schurman.
    The Transvaal Troubles.
    The Venezuelan Arbitration.
    Hurricane in Porto Rico.
    Dewey's Home-coming.
    McKinley's Plan for the Permanent Government of our Colonies.

### CLASS A.

1. General excellence, including neatness, will count for this number.
2. Give an account of the treatment of the Indians by the Spanish explorers.
3. From what country came the settlers of the following: Santa Fe, Jamestown, St. Augustine, Plymouth, New York?
4. Give briefly the story of Braddock's defeat.
5. What were the three great inventions?
6. What national song was inspired by the attempted capture of Baltimore in the War of 1812? Relate the story.
7. What use would you make of historic story books in teaching history? Name several good ones.
8. For what events are the following places noted: Bemis Heights, Wyoming Valley, Yorktown, Havana.
9. What is the Homestead Law? What were some of the results achieved by the passage of this bill?
10. Make a definite statement about any five of the following:
    The International Yacht Race.
    Thomas B. Reed.
    San Domingo's Revolution.
    John R. McLean.
    J. G. Schurman.
    The Transvaal Troubles.
    The Venezuelan Arbitration.
    Hurricane in Porto Rico.
    Dewey's Home-coming.
    McKinley's Plan for the Permanent Government of our Colonies.

# SUPREME COURT DECISIONS

ON MATTERS OF

# EDUCATIONAL INTEREST

## FINANCIAL REPORT

OF

# UNIVERSITY OF MICHIGAN

# DECISIONS OF THE SUPREME COURT.

LANGSTON vs. SCHOOL DISTRICT NO. 3 OF SPRINGWELLS TOWNSHIP.

(Supreme Court of Michigan.   November 7, 1899.)

### EMPLOYMENT OF SCHOOL TEACHER—CONTRACT.

A school teacher brought an action to recover for a year's services, claiming that she had a contract with the school district, and was prevented from carrying it out. She had several conversations with different members of the school board prior to the commencement of the term, but no definite salary was agreed upon, nor was it expressly agreed that she should teach.   After teaching two days, she was informed that she had not been employed, and was forbidden to teach. The only action taken by the board appeared from a record of a meeting, in which the officers were ordered to hire certain teachers for the ensuing year, among whom was the plaintiff; but no salary was mentioned, or terms of contract fixed. The statute provides that the district board shall hire and contract with such qualified teachers as may be required, and that all contracts shall be in writing, and signed by a majority of the board; that said contract shall specify the wages agreed on, and shall require the teacher to keep a correct list of the pupils, etc.; and that said contract shall be filed with the director, and a duplicate copy furnished to the teacher.   *Held*, that plaintiff had no valid contract.

Error to circuit court, Wayne county; Robert E. Frazer, Judge.

Action by Isabella Langston against School District No. 3 of the township of Springwells.   There was a judgment for defendant and plaintiff brings error. Affirmed.

Plaintiff sued to recover for a year's services as a school teacher, claiming that she had a contract with the defendant, and was prevented from carrying it out.   She had been employed the year previous under a written contract.   She had some talk with two of the officers of the school district in February about employment for the next year.   This talk was with Mr. Collins and Mr. Frink, two of the trustees. She testified that they stated "that I would be given a school for the following year,—that is, the year beginning September, 1895,—and also that I would be made principal of the school at the time."   About the close of the school year, in the latter part of June, she had a conversation with another trustee, Mr. Roulo, in which she testified he asked her what wages she wanted; that she replied $50 per month; that he said he did not think the board would pay that, and that she then said to him that she would leave it with the board, and let them settle the matter; that in the subsequent conversation with Roulo he stated that they had decided to give her $45.   She also testified that Mr. Collins, who was the director of the school board, told her that she was engaged for the next year; that in August she saw Mr. Frink, who told her that they had decided to pay $45, and "wanted to know if I would accept the school for the year; I made no reply, because I knew he was going out of office;" that on Wednesday before the first day of September she saw Mr. Addison, who was a member of the school board, and asked him when the school would open; that she told him she would be there; that she "demanded the signature of the contract that day, and asked him to tell the other members of the board that she demanded the signature of the contract." She appeared at the school house, and, it appears, taught two days, after which she was informed that she had not been employed, and was forbidden to teach.

14

The only action of the board appears from the record of a meeting held July 23, in which it was "ordered the proper officers to hire Pardee, Miss Cummings, and Miss I. Langston as teachers for the ensuing year." The court directed a verdict for the defendant, upon the ground that the statute requires a contract in writing, that the resolution did not fix the rate of wages, and that there was not such action as would bind either Miss Langston or the defendant.

GRANT, C. J., (After stating the facts). The statute provides: "The district board shall hire and contract with such duly qualified teachers as may be required; and all contracts shall be in writing and signed by a majority of the board on behalf of the district. Said contract shall specify the wages agreed upon and shall require the teacher to keep a correct list of the pupils, and the age of each attending the school, and the number of days each pupil is present, and to furnish the director with a correct copy of the same at the close of the school. Said contract shall be filed with the director, and a duplicate copy of the contract shall be furnished to the teacher." How. Am. St., par. 5065.—If it be held that plaintiff had a valid contract with the defendant then this statute is of no force or effect. There was no contract in writing; and her version of the material conversation is contradicted by the members of the board. The case furnishes an apt illustration of the purpose of this statute. The resolution of the board did not constitute a hiring, or fix the terms of the contract, but simply delegated the authority to the proper officers to hire and execute the necessary written contract. As late as August, when asked if she would accept the school, she made no reply. Counsel cite and rely upon Holloway v. School Dist., 62 Mich., 153, 28 N. W., 764; Crane v. School Dist., 61 Mich., 229, 28 N. W., 105; Farrell v. School Dist., 98 Mich., 45, 56 N. W., 1053. In Holloway v. School Dist., plaintiff had taught the full term provided by the written contract, except the holidays, and the officers knew that the plaintiff was teaching. In Crane v. School Dist., plaintiff had taught ten weeks, —half the term. In Farrell v. School Dist., plaintiff was employed by a resolution of the school board. In all these cases contracts were made, and signed by the teachers and all the officers but one. It was held that an officer had not the power to defeat the action of the boards by refusing to sign contracts authorized by them. The judgment is affirmed. The other justices concurred.

### JOHNSTON et al. v. MITCHELL.

#### (Supreme Court of Michigan.  July 5, 1899.)

#### SCHOOL BOARD—VACANCIES—MANDAMUS—COSTS.

1. Comp. Laws, § 4668, provides that, in case of a vacancy among the trustees of a school district, not graded, the two remaining officers shall immediately fill such vacancy, and, in case of two vacancies, the remaining officer shall immediately call a meeting of the district to fill the vacancies. Section 4774 provides that all provisions of the act shall apply to every school district in the state. *Held*, that mandamus will not lie to compel a member of a graded district to meet with his colleagues to fill two vacancies in the board, where it does not appear that the vacancy could not have been filled by an election.

2. The minority of a board have no authority to commence an action in its name, and, if they do so, they will be individually responsible for the costs.

Certiorari to circuit court, Oakland county; George W. Smith, Judge.

Application for mandamus by Alfred Johnston and another against George H. Mitchell. To review an order awarding the writ, respondent brings certiorari. Reversed.

Jerome W. Robbins, for appellant.  A. & S. H. Perry, for relators.

HOOKER, J. Alfred Johnston is moderator, Warren D. Clizbe director, and George H. Mitchell assessor, of a graded school district. The other two trustees resigned as early as January 5, 1899. Johnston and Clizbe joined in an application for a mandamus to compel Mitchell to meet with them and fill the vacancies caused by such resignations. He having refused to do so, said application was sworn to on February 1, 1899. The circuit court granted the writ, and the case is before us on certiorari. Comp. Laws, § 4747, authorizes the board of trustees to fill vacancies in their number until the next annual meeting. A similar provision is found in section 4668, which provides for filling such vacancies in districts not graded. It provides that in case of such vacancy the two remaining officers shall immediately fill such vacancy, and in case of two vacancies, the remaining officer shall immediately call a meeting of the district to fill the vacancies, and in case the vacancy is not filled in one of these modes within 20 days the board of school inspectors shall fill them. It is contended by counsel for the respondent that section 4747 contains a similar provision as to school inspectors, but we think the language of that section restricts the power of school inspectors to the election of the officers of the board. Section 4774 provides: "All provisions of this act shall apply and be in force in every school district, township, city and village in this state, except such as may be inconsistent with the direct provisions of some special enactment of the legislature." This provision has the effect to make section 4668 applicable to graded school districts, and the provision of that section as to school inspectors would be applicable, unless it should be thought that section 4747 is inconsistent with section 4668. We do not so consider it, but, if it were, the other provisions of section 4668 are applicable, and the vacancies could have been filled by the trustees or at a special election called by the board for the purpose. People v. Board of Education of Detroit, 18 Mich. 401; Keweenaw Ass'n v. School Dist. No. 1 of Hancock Tp., 98 Mich. 442, 57 N. W. 404. If it be said that the meeting could not be called, because Mitchell refused to join in a meeting for the purpose, the exigency could have been met under sections 4659, 4660, and 4661. Thus, there is full power in the district to fill such vacancies, either by a special meeting, or by action of the school inspectors, if such provision is applicable to graded districts. The record indicates that the respondent may have carried out the wishes of the district in not participating in an election to fill the vacancies. We are not advised that there would have been any difficulty in obtaining the desired written request of five legal voters of the district for a special meeting to fill these vacancies, or of any reason why the selection by the board would be preferable. It would certainly have been a more expeditious and less expensive way than to attempt to coerce a member of the board. We are of the opinion that this is not a case where there is no other remedy. It appears to be thought that the petitioners could make the district a party to this proceeding, but the minority of the board had no such authority, and, notwithstanding the fact that they have petitioned as trustees, they have no standing here except as private litigants. It is as though any other voter of the district had instituted the proceeding, without showing that his personal rights were injured. See People v. Whipple, 41 Mich. 548, 49 N. W. 922. The order of the circuit court is reversed, and the writ is denied, with costs of both courts against the relators personally. This is not a proceeding by or against the district. The other justices concurred.

### FERRIS v. BOARD OF EDUCATION OF DETROIT.

(Supreme Court of Michigan. December 12, 1899.)

SCHOOL DISTRICT BOARD—LIABILITY FOR NEGLIGENCE—PROXIMATE CAUSE —ELECTION BETWEEN COUNTS.

1. A school-district board, which erects a school building in such a manner that ice and snow must inevitably slide from the roof, there being no barrier to prevent it, onto plaintiff's premises, and which has notice thereof, is liable for his injury from slipping thereon; it being guilty of a wrongful act causing, and the proximate cause of, a direct injury to plaintiff, while outside the limits of the board's premises.

2. The school-district board is not within Loc. Acts 1895, No. 463, requiring notice to be given before action for negligent injury can be brought against the city of D., or any of its boards, commissions, or officers; it being a separate entity from the city, under Loc. Acts 1869, No. 233, establishing the whole city as one school district, providing for such board, with powers, among which are the right to purchase lands for school purposes, erect school buildings, and appropriate money therefor; though such act makes the mayor of the city an ex-officio member of the board, without a vote, and Loc. Acts 1891, No. 397, provides that the city council shall cause a tax to be levied and paid to such board, and Loc. Acts 1893, No. 394, requires the board, to transmit to the city council an estimate of moneys deemed necessary, and provides that a resolution of it creating a liability or originating the disposal of property shall be presented to the mayor, and that he may disapprove thereof, but that it may, by a two-thirds vote, pass the same over his veto.

3. A count alleging failure to erect sufficient barriers to prevent the sliding of snow and ice from the roof, and one alleging failure to keep such barriers in repair, are not so inconsistent as to require an election.

Error to circuit court, Wayne county; Robert E. Frazer, Judge.

Action by William Ferris against the board of education of Detroit. Judgment for defendant. Plaintiff brings error. Reversed.

Henry B. Graves and George H. Carlisle, for appellant.    Arthur Webster (Charles Flowers, of counsel), for appellee.

LONG, J.  Plaintiff for a number of years has owned and occupied, with his family, a house and lot on Lysander street, in Detroit.  His house stands within three feet of the east line of his lot, and a sidewalk extends along that side, filling the space between his house and the lot line.  In 1896 the defendant erected what is called the "Poe School Building" on its lot on the east of plaintiff's lot.  This building stands within six feet six inches of the lot line next adjoining plaintiff's lot.  Its cornice projects four feet from the wall, bringing the edge of the cornice within two feet six inches of the plaintiff's lot.  The school building is much higher than the plaintiff's house, and has a large amount of slate roof sloping towards plaintiff's lot.  This roof, prior to the accident, had no projections or guards above the edge of the roof to interrupt the falling of snow and ice.  During the winter months large quantities of snow and ice, when melting, slid down from the roof onto plaintiff's house and lot, and upon the sidewalk and steps which lead into the back part of plaintiff's house, and on one occasion his roof was injured by this falling ice and snow.  Prior to the accident he notified different members of the school board of the injury to his premises by the snow and ice, and his wife also notified the secretary of the school board of the fact.  Nothing was done about the matter, however.  On February 22, 1898, snow fell during the day, but stopped in the afternoon, and plaintiff's wife cleaned it off this walk and back steps.  Subsequently, and before the accident, large quantities of snow and ice slid from the roof of the school building down upon these steps.  Plaintiff who is a fireman in the employ of the city, came home to his supper in the evening, when his wife informed him of the falling of the snow and ice.  He stepped out through the back door, and upon this snow and ice, and claims that by reason of that he fell heavily, breaking a rib and otherwise injuring himself.  This action is brought against the board of education to recover damages for such injuries.

The first count of the declaration charges the defendant with so constructing the building that the accumulations of rain, snow, and ice in the winter time, would inevitably be precipitated upon plaintiff's premises; that the defendant failed to keep the roof clear from such accumulations; and that the defendant failed to provide sufficient gutters, eave troughs, screens, and combings, which would have prevented such precipitations.  The second count charges the construction of the school building with gutters, eave troughs, screens, and combings, which were permitted to become and remain out of repair, and the falling of the snow and ice because of the lack of repair.  Before any evidence was introduced, on motion of defendant's counsel, plaintiff was compelled to elect which count to proceed under.  Plaintiff took an exception to the order, and elected to proceed under the first count.  All evidence under the second count was rejected.  The trial court held that the two counts were inconsistent.  There was but little, if any, controversy over the facts as above set forth.  The court below directed the verdict in favor of the defendant.

Apparently this direction of the verdict for defendant was based upon the fact that no written notice was given to the corporation counsel, or to his chief assistant, as provided by section 46, Act No. 463, Loc. Acts 1895; and also for the reason that the plaintiff had no right of action against the defendant, as it could not be held liable for the manner of the construction of the building.  It is contended by counsel for plaintiff that the court was in error (1) in holding that no sufficient notice was given, and also in holding that notice was required; (2) in compelling the plaintiff to elect under which count he would proceed; (3) in directing the verdict for the defendant.

The trial court was of the opinion that the defendant, being a municipal corporation, could not be held liable for negligent injuries under the common law, and, there being no liability created by statute, the plaintiff could not recover.  It is conceded by counsel for plaintiff that municipal corporations are not generally held liable, under the common law, for negligent injuries to individuals arising from defective plans for construction of public works or failure to keep the same in repair; but it is contended that, where the injury is the result of the direct act or trespass of the municipality, it is liable, no matter whether acting in a public or private capacity.  We are satisfied that counsel for plaintiff are right in this contention.  The plaintiff had the right to the exclusive use and enjoyment of his property, and the defendant had no more right to erect a building in such a manner that the ice and snow would inevitably slide from the roof, and be precipitated upon the plaintiff's premises, than it would have to accumulate water upon its own premises, and then permit it to flow in a body upon his premises. It has been many times held in this court that a city has no more right to invade, or cause the invasion of, private property than an individual. In Rice v. City of Flint, 67 Mich. 401, 34 N. W. 719, it was said: "For a direct act which causes water to flow upon the premises of another to his injury a municipality is responsible. A city has no more right to invade, or cause the invasion of, private property than an individual."—citing 2 Dill. Mun. Corp. §§ 1042, 1043; Byrnes v. City of Cohoes, 67 N. Y. 204; Nooman v. City of Albany, 21 Alb. Law J. 174; Inman v. Tripp, 11 R. I. 520; Ross v. City of Clinton, 46 Iowa, 606; Ashley v. Port Huron, 35 Mich. 296; Pennoyer v. City of Saginaw, 8 Mich. 534.

If this action had been commenced for damages to the plaintiff's freehold, had any resulted, there could arise no doubt of his right to recover. The declaration alleges the damages to have accrued to the plaintiff by his slipping upon the ice which fell from the roof of the defendant's building upon plaintiff's premises, and that the defendant had had notice of the fact that snow and ice had from time to time been so precipitated upon the premises, and defendant had neglected, and continued to neglect, to take the steps necessary to prevent the same. The declaration, therefore, counts upon an actionable wrong. The cause of action is not a neglect in the performance of a corporate duty rendering a public work unfit for the purposes for which it was intended, but the doing of a wrongful act, causing a direct injury to the person of the plaintiff, while outside the limits of the defendant's premises. We think it must be said that the erection of the building without these barriers was the proximate cause of the injury. An injury has happened by the defendant's wrongful act, and it cannot be set up as a defense that there was a more immediate cause of injury. To entitle a party to exemption, he must show, not only that such injury might have happened, but that it must have happened if the act complained of had not been done. Davis v. Garrett, 6 Bing. 716. Judge Cooley, in his work on Torts, at page 71, gives some illustrations from cases cited by him. He says: "We may pause here to give some illustrations of this proposition, beginning with the leading case of Scott v. Shepherd, 3 Wils., 403, 2 W. Bl. 892, where the facts were that the defendant threw a lighted squib into a crowd of people, one after another of whom, in self-protection, threw it from him, until it exploded near the plaintiff's eye, and blinded him. Here was a single wrong, the original act of throwing the dangerous missile; and, though the plaintiff would not have been harmed by it but for the subsequent act of others throwing it in his direction, yet, as these were instinctive and innocent, it is the same as if a cracker had been flung, which had bounded and rebounded again and again before it struck out the plaintiff's eye, and the injury is therefore a natural and proximate result of the original act. It is an injury that should have been foreseen by ordinary forecast, and, the circumstances conjoined with it to produce the injury being perfectly natural, these circumstances should have been anticipated." In the present case it appeared that snow and ice must inevitably slide from this slate roof, as there were no barriers to prevent it. The school board had notice of it. It should have anticipated that the plaintiff or his family might receive an injury by the falling of the snow and ice, or that, by attempting to travel or go over it, they might be injured in that way. The defendant cannot now say that the injury must have happened the plaintiff if the snow and ice had not been thrown upon these premises.

But it is contended by the defendant, and so held by the court below, that the plaintiff cannot maintain this action, because he has not complied with the provisions of Act No. 463, Loc. Acts 1895, which provides: "No action shall be brought against said city, nor any of its boards, commissions or officers for any negligent injury, unless it be commenced within one year from the time when the injury was received, nor unless notice shall be given in writing within three months from the time of such injury to the head of the law department, or to his chief assistant, of the time, place and cause of such injury and of the nature thereof." Plaintiff's counsel contend (1) that a sufficient notice was given; (2) that this statute has no reference to the board of education of Detroit.

We need not discuss the question of whether there was a proper notice, as we are satisfied that this statute has no reference to the defendant here.

By act No. 233, Loc. Acts 1869, free schools were established in the city of Detroit. The whole city was by the act established one school district. The act provided for a board of education, and clothed said board with certain powers, among which were the right to purchase lands for school purposes, erect school buildings, and appropriate moneys therefor. The recorder's court was given jurisdiction of all suits which the board might be a party to, and of all prosecutions for the violation of the ordinances and by-laws of the board. This act is no part of the city charter. While the act has been several times amended, the school district remains a distinct entity, and has no connection with the city government as such, except as the act provides, by the amendment of 1891, that the common council of the city shall cause to be levied a sum not exceeding in any one year five mills on the dollar of all the property of the city, and the moneys thus raised to be paid to the treasurer of the board of education. Act No. 397, Loc. Acts 1891. By the amendment of 1893, it is provided that the board of education shall transmit to the common council of the city an estimate of the amount of money it may deem necessary for the purchase of lots, etc. Act No. 394, Loc. Acts 1893. By Act No. 233 of the act of 1869, the mayor of the city was made ex officio member of the board, but given no vote therein; and in 1893 an amendment to the act provided that "every resolution or proceeding of said board of education, whereby any liability or debt may be created or originating the disposal or expenditure of property or money, shall before it takes effect be presented by the secretary of said board to the mayor of said city of Detroit. If the mayor approve thereof, he shall thereon write his approval; * * * and such as he shall not approve he shall return to the board, with his objections thereto," etc. The same section, however, provides that the board of education may, by a two-thirds vote of its members, pass the same over the mayor's veto. It is evident, from these provisions of the statute, that the school-district board is not one of the boards mentioned in the act referred to, and no notice to the corporation counsel was required before action could be commenced. In Pingree v. Board, 99 Mich. 404, 58 N. W. 333, the provision of the statute making the mayor of Detroit ex officio member of the board, and his right to veto certain measures of the board, were under discussion. It was not then intimated that the school district was not a separate entity from the city, but the question was whether the legislature might provide in a school district for such an officer with such powers, and it was held that the legislature had power to do so.

It is further contended that the court was in error in requiring counsel for plaintiff to elect which of the two counts of his declaration he would proceed under. We have stated that the substance of the two counts was—First, a failure to erect sufficient barriers to prevent the snow and ice from sliding from the roof; and, second, a failure to keep such barriers in repair. There is no such variance between these two counts as warranted the court in ruling that an election must be made. The judgment below must be reversed, and a new trial awarded. The other justices concurred.

# STATE INSTITUTIONS.

## BY ACT OF LEGISLATURE.

### EDUCATIONAL.

### STATE AGRICULTURAL COLLEGE.

#### LANSING—ESTABLISHED IN 1855.

It is the design of this institution to afford thorough instruction in agriculture and the natural sciences connected therewith. The curriculum also includes a literary course and instruction in household and industrial arts. The college farm, including 676 acres, is located three miles east of Michigan's Capital City, the buildings numbering 55 and total valuation of property being nearly $500,000. During the past year 469 students were enrolled with 38 instructors.

Controlled by the State Board of Agriculture.—Thos. F. Marston, President, Bay City; Franklin Wells, Constantine; Charles J. Monroe, South Haven; Edward P. Allen, Ypsilanti; Henry F. Marsh, Allegan; L. Whitney Watkins, Manchester.

JONATHAN L. SNYDER, A. M., Ph. D., President.
A. C. BIRD, Secretary, Agricultural College.

#### FACULTY AND OFFICERS.

ROBERT C. KEDZIE, M. A., M. D., D. Sc., Professor of Chemistry, and Curator of the Chemical Laboratory.
WILLIAM J. BEAL, A. M., M. S., Ph. D., Professor of Botany and Forestry, and Curator of the Botanical Museum.
LEVI R. TAFT, M. S., Professor of Horticulture and Landscape Gardening, and Superintendent of the Horticultural Department.
HOWARD EDWARDS, M. A., LL. D., Professor of English Literature and Modern Languages.
HERMAN K. VEDDER, C. E., Professor of Mathematics and Civil Engineering.
CLINTON D. SMITH, M. S., Dean of Special Courses and Superintendent of Farmers' Institutes.
CHAS. L. WEIL, S. B., Professor of Mechanical Engineering and Director of the Mechanical Department.
WALTER B. BARROWS, S. B., Professor Zoology and Physiology, and Curator of the General Museum.
GEORGE A. WATERMAN, B. S., V. S., Professor of Veterinary Science.
MAUD RYLAND KELLER, A. M., Dean of the Women's Department.
FRANK S. KEDZIE, M. S., Adjunct Professor of Chemistry.
WILLIAM S. HOLDSWORTH, M. S., Assistant Professor of Drawing.
MARTIN D. ATKINS, A. B., Assistant Professor of Physics.
WILBUR O. HEDRICK, M. S., Assistant Professor of History and Political Economy.
C. O. BEMIES, Director of Physical Culture.
WARREN BABCOCK, B. S., Assistant Professor of Mathematics.
CHARLES F. WHEELER, B. S., Assistant Professor of Botany.
HERBERT W. MUMFORD, B. S., Professor of Agriculture and Superintendent of Farm.
GEORGIANA BLUNT, Ph. M., Assistant Professor of English and Modern Languages.
U. P. HEDRICK, M. S., Assistant Professor of Horticulture.
J. A. JEFFERY, B. S., Assistant Professor of Agriculture.
MRS. LINDA E. LANDON, Librarian.

A. L. WESTCOTT, B. M. E., Instructor in Mechanical Engineering.
BURTON O. LONGYEAR, Instructor in Botany.
J. J. FERGUSON. B. S., Instructor in Dairying.
HARRY E. SMITH, B. S., Instructor in Mechanical Engineering.
RUFUS H. PETTIT, B. S. A., Instructor in Zoology.
MRS. MAUD A. MARSHALL, Instructor in Music.
MRS. JENNIE L. K. HAINER, Instructor in Sewing.
WILLIAM O. BEAL, B. S., M. A., Instructor in Mathematics.
CARRIE L. HOLT, Instructor in Drawing.
ELLEN R. RUSHMORE, Instructor in Domestic Science.
BERTHA M. RONAN, Instructor in Calisthenics.
THOMAS GUNSON, Foreman of Greenhouse.
W. S. LEONARD, Foreman of Machine Shop.
W. R. BRADFORD, Foreman of Wood Shop.
CHACE NEWMAN, Assistant Foreman of Wood Shop.
E. C. BAKER, Foreman of Foundry.
CHARLES A. WOOD, Foreman of Gardens.
FRED C. KENNEY, Cashier.
B. A. FAUNCE, Clerk to President.
F. L. NEWELL, Engineer.

## NORMAL SCHOOL SYSTEM OF MICHIGAN.

PRESIDENT OF SYSTEM, Dr. Albert Leonard, Ypsilanti.

Controlled by State Board of Education.—Perry F. Powers, President, Cadillac; Jason
E. Hammond, Secretary, Lansing; Elias F. Johnson, Ann Arbor; Frederick A. Platt, Flint.

### STATE NORMAL COLLEGE.

#### YPSILANTI—ESTABLISHED 1849.

##### FACULTY AND OFFICERS.

ELMER A. LYMAN, A. B., Principal, Professor of Mathematics.
DANIEL PUTNAM, A. M., LL. D., Professor of Psychology and Pedagogy.
CHAS. O. HOYT, A. B., Professor of Psychology and Pedagogy.
S. B. LAIRD, M. S., B. Pd., Associate Professor of Psychology and Pedagogy.
JULIA ANNE KING, A. M., M. Pd., Professor of History and Civics.
MARY B. PUTNAM, Ph. B., B. Pd., Assistant in Civics.
FLORENCE SHULTES, Assistant in History.
ELIZABETH YOST, Instructor in History.
EDITH M. TODD, Instructor in History.
BERTHA G. BUELL, B. L., Instructor in History.
FREDRIC H. PEASE, Director of Conservatory of Music.
CLYDE E. FOSTER, Assistant in Music.
JOHN WHITTAKER, Instructor in Music.
MYRA BYRD, Instructor in Music.
LAMBERT L. JACKSON, A. M., Assistant in Mathematics.
ADA A. NORTON, Ph. M., Assistant in Mathematics.
LETITIA THOMPSON, Ph. B., Instructor in Mathematics.
KATE R. THOMPSON, Instructor in Mathematics.
FLORUS A. BARBOUR, A. B., Professor of English.
ABBIE PEARCE, B. Pd., Ph. B., Assistant in English.
HELEN E. BACON, A. B., Assistant in English.
J. STUART LATHERS, B. L., Instructor in English.
ESTELLE DOWNING, Instructor in English.
AUGUST LODEMAN, A. M., Professor of French and German.
ALICE R. ROBSON, Ph. B., Assistant in French and German.
BENJAMIN L. D'OOGE, A. M., Professor of Greek and Latin. (Absent on leave.)
DUANE REED STUART, A. B., Acting Professor of Greek and Latin.
HELEN B. MUIR, Assistant in Greek and Latin.
SERENO B. CLARK, Instructor in Greek and Latin.
EDWIN A. STRONG, A. M., Professor of Physical Science.
FRED R. GORTON, Assistant in Physical Science.
B. W. PEET, M. S., Instructor in Physical Science.
WILL H. SHERZER, M. S., Professor of Natural Science.
ERNEST B. HOAG, Assistant in Natural Science.
ANNA A. SCHRYVER, Assistant in Botany.
JESSIE PHELPS, B. S., Instructor in Natural Sciences.
FOREST B. H. BROWN, Instructor in Natural Sciences.

For statistics of Normal Schools see tables in this report; also full write-up of the system.

C. T. McFARLANE. Ph. B., B. Pd., Professor of Drawing and Geography.
ISABELLA STICKNEY, Instructor in Drawing.
BERTHA C. HULL, Assistant in Drawing.
R. D. CALKINS, Assistant in Geography.
WILBUR P. BOWEN, Director of Physical Training.
MARY IDA MANN, Instructor in Physical Training.
FANNIE C. BURTON, Assistant in Physical Training.
GENEVIEVE M. WALTON, Librarian.
GERTRUDE E. WOODARD, Assistant Librarian.
FRANCIS L. D. GOODRICH, Assistant Librarian.
FRANCES L. STEWART, Clerk.
AGNES MORSE, Stenographer.

## TRAINING SCHOOL.

C. T. GRAWN, M. Pd., Superintendent.
HESTER P. STOWE, Kindergartner.
MARGARET E. WISE, Critic Teacher, 1st grade.
ADELLA JACKSON, Critic Teacher, 2d grade.
L. ZELLA STARKES, Critic Teacher, 3d grade.
HARRIET M. PLUNKETT, Critic Teacher, 4th grade.
MARY L. BERKEY, Critic Teacher, 5th grade.
ABBIE ROE, Critic Teacher, 6th grade.
CAROLYN W. NORTON, Critic Teacher, 7th and 8th grades.
JULIA MARTIN, Assistant Teacher, 7th and 8th grades.

## CENTRAL STATE NORMAL.

### MOUNT PLEASANT.—ESTABLISHED IN 1895.

#### FACULTY AND OFFICERS.

*CHARLES McKENNY, A. M., Principal, Professor of Psychology and Pedagogy.
LUCY ADELLA SLOAN, M. S., Professor of English Language and Literature.
RACHEL TATE, Assistant in English.
FRED L. KEELER, B. S., Professor of Physics and Chemistry.
WILLIAM BELLIS, Pd. B., Professor of Mathematics.
CHARLES T. TAMBLING, A. B., Assistant in Mathematics.
CARL E. PRAY, B. L., Professor of History and Civics.
ELIZABETH WIGHTMAN, Professor of Geography and Drawing.
ANNA M. BARNARD, A. B., Professor of Latin and German.
MAE WOLDT, Professor of Biology.
T. BATH GLASSON, Director of Conservatory.
EVELYN McALLASTER, Assistant in Music.
ALBERT J. ARCHER, Professor of Penmanship and Bookkeeping.

#### TRAINING SCHOOL.

GEORGE W. LOOMIS, M. S., Superintendent.
MARGARET WAKELEE, Kindergartner.
FRANCES BURT, Critic Teacher, 1st grade.
LOIS WILSON, Critic Teacher, 2nd grade.
IRENE GETTY, Critic Teacher, 3rd grade.
CARRIE SIMPSON, Critic Teacher, 4th grade.
MYRTA WILSEY, Critic Teacher, 5th grade.
GERTRUDE ROBINSON, Critic Teacher, 6th grade.
GERTRUDE DOBSON, Critic Teacher, 7th grade.
MARY J. JORDAN, Librarian.
ESTELLA D. WHITTEN, Stenographer.

## NORTHERN STATE NORMAL.

### MARQUETTE.—ESTABLISHED IN 1899.

#### FACULTY.

DWIGHT B. WALDO, A. M., Principal, Professor of History and Civics.
LEWIS F. ANDERSON, A. B., Professor of Pedagogy.
WILLIAM McCRACKEN, A. B., Professor of Natural Sciences.
EDWARD G. MAUL, B. S., Professor of Mathematics.
FLORA E. HILL, B. L., Professor of English.
MARTHA ACKERMAN, Professor of Geography and Drawing.

*Resigned.
15

## MICHIGAN COLLEGE OF MINES.

### HOUGHTON.—ESTABLISHED IN 1885.

The object of this institution is to turn out graduates who can take an active part in the development of the mineral wealth of the State. Besides being one of the foremost schools of mining engineering in the country, it enjoys the distinction of being the only one having a full and free elective system. Located at Houghton, Houghton county, in the vicinity of some of the largest mines in the world, operating the most powerful mining machinery known, its students enjoy many advantages of observation furnished through the liberality of these mining companies. Its five buildings and five acres, with the necessary equipment, have an estimated value of $252,655.56. During the last year 122 students were enrolled, with 19 instructors.

Board of Control
- Walter Fitch, President, Beacon.
- John Monroe Longyear, Marquette.
- Alfred Kidder, Marquette.
- William Kelley, Vulcan.
- Elbridge G. Brown, Calumet.
- Horatio Stewart Goodell, Houghton.

FRED WALTER McNAIR, B. S., President.
ALLEN F. REES, Secretary, Houghton.

### FACULTY AND OFFICERS.

FRED WALTER McNAIR, B. S., Professor of Mathematics and Physics.
GEORGE AUGUSTUS KOENIG, M. E., A. M., Ph. D., Professor of Chemistry and Metallurgy.
FREDERICK WILLIAM SPERR, E. M., Professor of Civil and Mining Engineering.
OZNI PORTER HOOD, M. S., M. E., Professor of Mechanical and Electrical Engineering.
ARTHUR EDMUND SEAMAN, S. B., Professor of Mineralogy and Geology.
MRS. FRANCES HANNA SCOTT, Librarian and Secretary.
JAMES FISHER, E. M., Instructor in Mathematics and Physics.
———————— Instructor in Civil and Mining Engineering.
GEORGE LUTHER CHRISTENSEN, B. S., Instructor in Mechanical Engineering.
NATHAN SANFORD OSBORNE, E. M., Instructor in Mathematics and Physics.
————————Instructor in Machine Shop.
EMIL ARTHUR FRANKE, S. B., Instructor in Chemistry and Metallurgy.
SAMUEL WALTER OSGOOD, S. B., Instructor in Petrography and Mineralogy.
HARRY TALLMAN MERCER, S. B., E. M., Assistant in Mineralogy, and Honorary Mineralogist, U. S. Commission to Paris Exposition.
WILLARD LAWSON CUMINGS, Instructor in Mineralogy.
FREDERICK WILLIAM O'NEIL, E. M., Assistant in Mechanical Engineering.
CHARLES WARD BOTSFORD, Assistant in Civil and Mining Engineering.
CHARLES DUVAL HOHL, Assistant in Physics.
RALPH CLARK WORKS, Assistant in Chemistry.
HENRY AUGUSTUS COLLIN, Assistant in Chemistry.
HENRY GIBBS, Purchasing Agent and Supply Clerk.
MISS MAY D. HOAR, Stenographer and Typewriter.
HENRY HOWES, Engineer and Janitor of Engineering Hall.
MAXIME MORIN, Carpenter.
FRANK DeMARCE, Janitor of Science Hall.
HOWARD GIBBS, Janitor of Chemical Laboratories.

## UNIVERSITY OF MICHIGAN.

### ANN ARBOR.—ESTABLISHED IN 1837.

A description of this great educational institution is scarcely necessary, since its reputation is world-wide. With its 64 acres, 21 buildings, and superior equipment in every department, its total valuation is somewhat more than two million dollars. The collegiate staff consists of 138 professors and instructors; and more than 700 graduates are annually sent out from a total enrollment of over 3,000.

*For statistics see tables in this report.*

Board of Regents
{
Henry S. Dean, Ann Arbor.
Herman Kiefer, Detroit.
Frank W. Fletcher, Alpena.
Roger W. Butterfield, Grand Rapids.
George A. Farr, Grand Haven.
William J. Cocker, Adrian.
Charles D. Lawton, Lawton.
Eli R. Sutton, Detroit.
}

JAMES B. ANGELL, LL. B., President.
JAMES H. WADE, Secretary.

#### FACULTIES AND OFFICERS.

The names of professors (including librarian), junior professors, assistant professors, and other officers, are placed in their appropriate divisions, according to term of appointment and length of continuous service with present rank.

PERMANENT APPOINTMENTS AND APPOINTMENTS FOR TERMS LONGER THAN ONE YEAR.

ALBERT B. PRESCOTT, M. D., LL. D., Director of the Chemical Laboratory, Professor of Organic Chemistry, and Dean of the School of Pharmacy.
*REV. MARTIN L. D'OOGE, LL. D., Professor of the Greek Language and Literature.
CHARLES E. GREENE, A. M., C. E., Professor of Civil Engineering and Dean of the Department of Engineering.
JONATHAN TAFT, M. D., D. D. S., Professor of the Principles and Practice of Oral Pathology and Surgery and Dean of the College of Dental Surgery.
WILLIAM H. PETTEE, A. M., Professor of Mineralogy, Economic Geology, and Mining Engineering.
JOHN A. WATLING, D. D. S., Professor of Operative and Clinical Dentistry.
ISAAC N. DEMMON, LL. D., Professor of English and Rhetoric.
WILLIAM H. DORRANCE, D. D. S., Professor of Prosthetic Dentistry and Dental Metallurgy.
ALBERT H. PATTENGILL, A. M., Professor of Greek.
MORTIMER E. COOLEY, M. E., Professor of Mechanical Engineering.
WILLIAM J. HERDMAN, M. D., LL. D., Professor of Diseases of the Mind and Nervous System, and Electrotherapeutics.
WOOSTER W. BEMAN, A. M., Professor of Mathematics.
VICTOR C. VAUGHAN, Ph. D., Sc. D., M. D., Professor of Hygiene and Physiological Chemistry, Director of the Hygienic Laboratory, and Dean of the Department of Medicine and Surgery.
CHARLES S. DENISON, M. S., C. E., Professor of Descriptive Geometry, Stereotomy, and Drawing.
*HENRY S. CARHART, LL. D., Professor of Physics and Director of the Physical Laboratory.
RAYMOND C. DAVIS, A. M., Librarian.
VOLNEY M. SPALDING, Ph. D., Professor of Botany.
HENRY C. ADAMS, LL. D., Professor of Political Economy and Finance.
BURKE A. HINSDALE, LL. D., Professor of the Science and the Art of Teaching.
RICHARD HUDSON, A. M., Professor of History and Dean of the Department of Literature, Science, and the Arts.
BRADLEY M. THOMPSON, M. S., LL. B., Jay Professor of Law.
ALBERT A. STANLEY, A. M., Professor of Music.
FRANCIS W. KELSEY, Ph. D., Professor of the Latin Language and Literature.
JEROME C. KNOWLTON, A. B., LL. B., Marshall Professor of Law.
CHARLES B. NANCREDE, M. D., LL. D., Professor of Surgery and Clinical Surgery in the Department of Medicine and Surgery.
FLEMMING CARROW, M. D., Professor of Ophthalmic and Aural Surgery and Clinical Ophthalmology in the Department of Medicine and Surgery.
OTIS C. JOHNSON, A. M., Professor of Applied Chemistry.
PAUL C. FREER, Ph. D., M. D., Professor of General Chemistry and Director of the Laboratory of General Chemistry.
JAMES N. MARTIN, Ph. M., M. D., Bates Professor of Diseases of Women and Children in the Department of Medicine and Surgery.
NELVILLE S. HOFF, D. D. S., Professor of Dental Materia Medica and Dental Mechanism.
GEORGE DOCK, A. M., M. D., Professor of the Theory and Practice of Medicine and Clinical Medicine, and of Pathology, in the Department of Medicine and Surgery.
ANDREW C. McLAUGHLIN, A. M., LL. B., Professor of American History.
JOSEPH B. DAVIS, C. E., Professor of Geodesy and Surveying.
ASAPH HALL, JR., Ph. D., Professor of Astronomy and Director of the Observatory.
ISRAEL C. RUSSELL, C. E., LL. D., Professor of Geology.
WARREN P. LOMBARD, A. B., M. D., Professor of Physiology.
FLOYD R. MECHEM, A. M., Tappan Professor of Law.

*Absent on leave.

116            DEPARTMENT OF PUBLIC INSTRUCTION.

JACOB E. REIGHARD, Ph. B., Professor of Zoology and Director of the Zoological Laboratory and the Zoological Museum.
THOMAS C. TRUEBLOOD, A. M., Professor of Elocution and Oratory.
JAMES A. CRAIG, Ph. D., Professor of Semitic Languages and Literatures and Hellenistic Greek.
OTTO KIRCHNER, A. M., Professor of Law.
ARTHUR R. CUSHNY, A. M., M. D., Professor of Materia Medica and Therapeutics in the Department of Medicine and Surgery.
JOHN C. ROLFE, Ph. D., Professor of Latin.
J. PLAYFAIR McMURRICH, Ph. D., Professor of Anatomy and Director of the Anatomical Laboratory.
HARRY B. HUTCHINS, LL. D., Professor of Law and Dean of the Department of Law.
THOMAS A. BOGLE, LL. B., Professor of Law in charge of the Practice Court.
WILBERT B. HINSDALE, A. M., M. D., Professor of the Theory and Practice of Medicine and Clinical Medicine, Dean of the Homœopthic Medical College, and Director of the University Hospital (Homœopathic).
OSCAR LESEURE, M. D., Professor of Surgery and Clinical Surgery in the Homœopathic Medical College.
ROYAL S. COPELAND, A. M., M. D., Professor of Ophthalmology, Otology, and Pædology in the Homœopathic Medical College.
ROBERT M. WENLEY, Sc. D., D. Phil., Professor of Philosophy.
ELIZA M. MOSHER, M. D., Professor of Hygiene, and Women's Dean in the Department of Literature, Science, and the Arts.
WILLIS A. DEWEY, M. D., Professor of Materia Medica and Therapeutics in the Homœopathic Medical College.
*GEORGE HEMPL, Ph. D., Professor of English Philology and General Linguistics.
VICTOR H. LANE, C. E., LL. B., Fletcher Professor of Law and Law Librarian.
JAMES H. BREWSTER, Ph. B., LL. B., Professor of Conveyancing.
HORACE L. WILGUS, M. S., Professor of Law.
ELIAS F. JOHNSON, B. S., LL. M., Professor of Law and Secretary of the Faculty of the Department of Law.
CLAUDIUS B. KINYON, M. D., Professor of Obstetrics and Gynæcology in the Homœopathic Medical College.
AARON V. McALVAY, A. B., LL. B., Professor of Law.
FREDERICK G. NOVY, Sc. D., M. D., Junior Professor of Hygiene and Physiological Chemistry.
EDWARD D. CAMPBELL, B. S., Junior Professor of Analytical Chemistry.
FRED M. TAYLOR, Ph. D., Junior Professor of Political Economy and Finance.
FRED N. SCOTT, Ph. D., Junior Professor of Rhetoric.
ALEXANDER ZIWET, C. E., Junior Professor of Mathematics.
GEORGE W. PATTERSON, JR., Ph. D., Junior Professor of Physics.
FREDERICK C. NEWCOMBE, Ph. D., Junior Professor of Botany.
ALLEN S. WHITNEY, A. B., Junior Professor of the Science and the Art of Teaching, and Inspector of Schools.
G. CARL HUBER, M. D., Junior Professor of Anatomy, Director of the Histological Laboratory, and Secretary of the Faculty of the Department of Medicine and Surgery.
JOHN O. REED, Ph. D., Junior Professor of Physics.
ALFRED H. LLOYD, Ph. D., Junior Professor of Philosophy.
PAUL R. DE PONT, A. B., B. S., Assistant Professor French, Registrar of the Department of Literature, Science, and the Arts, and Registrar of the Department of Engineering.
JOSEPH H. DRAKE, A. B., Assistant Professor of Latin.
ALVISO B. STEVENS, Ph. C., Assistant Professor of Pharmacy.
†DEAN C. WORCESTER, A. B., Assistant Professor of Zoology and Curator of the Zoological Museum.
JOSEPH L. MARKLEY, Ph. D., Assistant Professor of Mathematics.
MAX WINKLER, Ph. D., Assistant Professor of German.
MORITZ LEVI, A. B., Assistant Professor of French.
JULIUS O. SCHLOTTERBECK, Ph. C., Ph. D., Assistant Professor of Pharmacognosy and Botany.
ERNST H. MENSEL, Ph. D., Assistant Professor of German.
EARLE W. DOW, A. B., Assistant Professor of History.
CHARLES H. COOLEY, Ph. D., Assistant Professor of Sociology.
ALDRED S. WARTHIN, Ph. D., M. D., Assistant Professor of Pathology in the Department of Medicine and Surgery.
LOUIS P. HALL, D. D. S., Assistant Professor of Dental Anatomy, Operative Technique, and Clinical Operative Dentistry.
MOSES GOMBERG, Sc. D., Assistant Professor of Organic Chemistry.
WILLIAM F. BREAKEY, M. D., Lecturer on Dermatology.
GEORGE O. HIGLEY, M. S., Instructor in General Chemistry.
DAVID M. LICHTY, M. S., Instructor in General Chemistry.
JOHN R. EFFINGER, JR., Ph. D., Instructor in French.
CLARENCE G. WRENTMORE, M. S., Instructor in Descriptive Geometry and Drawing.
KARL E. GUTHE, Ph. D., Instructor in Physics.
TOBIAS DIEKHOFF, Ph. D., Instructor in German.
CLARENCE L. MEADER, A. B., Instructor in Latin.
ARTHUR G. HALL, B. S., Instructor in Mathematics.
GEORGE REBEC, Ph. D., Instructor in Philosophy.
JAMES W. GLOVER, Ph. D., Instructor in Mathematics.
LOUIS A. STRAUSS, Ph. M., Instructor in English.
EDWIN C. GODDARD, Ph. B., LL. B., Instructor in Mathematics.

*Professor Hempl is also temporarily in charge of the Department of German.
†Absent on leave.

HERBERT J. GOULDING, B. S., Instructor in Descriptive Geometry and Drawing.
*VICTOR E. FRANCOIS, Instructor in French.
PERRY F. TROWBRIDGE, Ph. B., Instructor in Organic Chemistry and Accountant in the Chemical Laboratory.
JOSEPH H. VANCE, LL. B., Assistant Law Librarian.
HAMILTON REEVE, Superintendent of Buildings and Grounds.

## OTHER APPOINTMENTS FOR 1899-1900.

KEENE FITZPATRICK, Director of the Gymnasium.
JOHN R. ALLEN, M. E., Assistant Professor of Mechanical Engineering.
BENJAMIN P. BOURLAND, Ph. D., Assistant Professor of French.
WILLIAM L. NIGGETT, B. S., Superintendent of Engineering Shops.
VICTOR C. VAUGHAN, Ph. D., Sc. D., M. D., Lecturer on Toxicology in its Legal Relations in the Department of Law.
HE R  C. ADAMS, LL. D., Lecturer on the Railroad Problem in the Department of Law, N Y
ANDREW C. McLAUGHLIN, A. M., LL. B., Lecturer on Constitutional Law and Constitutional History in the Department of Law.
RICHARD HUDSON, A. M., Lecturer on Comparative Constitutional Law in the Department of Law.
WILLIAM J. HERDMAN, M. D., LL. D., Lecturer on Neurology, Electrology, and Railway Injuries in the Department of Law.
JOSEPH H. DRAKE, A. B., Lecturer on Roman Law in the Department of Law.
SIMON M. YUTZY, M. D., Instructor in Anatomy and Demonstrator of Anatomy.
JOHN W. DWYER, LL. M., Instructor in Law.
WILLIAM H. WAIT, Ph. D., Instructor in Greek, Latin, and Sanskrit.
HERBERT H. WAITE, A. B., Instructor in Bacteriology, and Dispensing Clerk in the Hygienic Laboratory.
WARREN W. FLORER, Ph. D., Instructor in German.
WALTER B. PILLSBURY, Ph. D., Instructor in Psychology.
ALBERT J. FARRAH, LL. B., Instructor in Law.
EDWIN C. ROEDDER, Ph. D., Instructor in German.
ALFRED H. WHITE, A. B., Instructor in Chemical Technology.
CARROLL D. JONES, E. E., Instructor in Electrical Engineering.
JOHN S. P. TATLOCK, A. M., Instructor in English.
ALICE G. SNYDER, Instructor in the Women's Gymnasium.
S. LAWRENCE BIGELOW, Ph. D., Instructor in General Chemistry.
JAMES B. POLLOCK, Sc. D., Instructor in Botany.
EWALD BOUCKE, Ph. D., Instructor in German.
AUGUSTUS TROWBRIDGE, Ph. D., Instructor in Physics.
WILLIAM H. BUTTS, A. M., Instructor in Mathematics.
JULIA W. SNOW, Ph. D., Instructor in Botany.
JOHN R. ROOD, LL. B., Instructor in Law.
SHIRLEY W. SMITH, B. L., Instructor in English.
HUGO P. THIEME, Ph. D., Instructor in French.
GEORGE L GRIMES, B. S., Instructor in Mechanical Engineering.
CARL V. TOWER, Ph. D., Instructor in Philosophy.
HERBERT S. JENNINGS, Ph. D., Instructor in Zoology.
THOMAS E. OLIVER, Ph. D., Instructor in French.
HERBERT F. DE COU, A. M., Instructor in Greek.
CHRISTIAN F. GAUSS, A. M., Instructor in French.
JAMES R. ARNEILL, A. B., M. D., Instructor in Clinical Medicine in the Department of Medicine and Surgery.
HENRY A. SANDERS, Ph. D., Instructor in Latin.
BENJAMIN F. BAILEY, B. S., Instructor in Electrotherapeutics.
ROBERT C. BOURLAND, A. B., M. D., Instructor in Anatomy.
EUGENE C. SULLIVAN, Ph. D., Instructor in Analytical Chemistry.
HENRY C. ANDERSON, M. E., Instructor in Mechanical Engineering.
ARTHUR L CROSS, Ph. D., Instructor in History.
GEORGE A. HULETT, Ph. D., Instructor in General Chemistry.
SAMUEL J. HOLMES, Ph. D., Instructor in Zoology.
JONATHAN A. C. HILDNER, Ph. D., Instructor in German.
JOHN DIETERLE, A. B., Instructor in German.
CHARLES M WILLIAMS, Instructor in the Waterman Gymnasium.
KARL W. GENTHE, Ph. D., Instructor in Zoology.
ALICE L. HUNT, Instructor in Drawing.
CHARLES BAIRD, A. B., Director of Out-of-Door Athletics.
JAMES G. LYNDS, M. D., Demonstrator of Obstetrics and Diseases of Women.
FRED P. JORDAN, A. B., Assistant in the General Library in Charge of Catalogue.
CYRENUS G. DARLING, M. D., Lecturer on Genito-urinary and Minor Surgery and Demonstrator of Surgery in the Department of Medicine and Surgery, and Clinical Lecturer on Oral Pathology and Surgery in the College of Dental Surgery.
BYRON A. FINNEY, A. B., Assistant in the General Library in charge of Circulation.
JAMES P. BRIGGS, Ph. C., Pharmacist in the University Hospital.
JEANNE C. SOLIS, M. D., Demonstrator of Nervous Diseases in the Department of Medicine and Surgery.
NORMAN A. WOOD, Taxidermist.
D. MURRAY COWIE, M. D., Assistant in Internal Medicine in the Department of Medicine and Surgery.
AUGUSTUS E. GUENTHER, B. S., Assistant in Physiology.
CHARLES L. BLISS, B. S., Assistant in Physiological Chemistry.

*Absent on leave.

HARRY W. CLARK, B. S., Superintendent of the University Hospital.
GEORGE B. WALLACE, M. D., Assistant in Pharmacology in the Department of Medicine and Surgery.
WILLIAM A. SPITZLEY, A. B., M. D., First Assistant in Surgery in the Department of Medicine and Surgery.
HENRY O. SEVERANCE, A. M., Assistant in the General Library.
THEOPHIL KLINGMANN, Ph. C., M. D., Assistant to the Professor of Diseases of the Mind and Nervous System and Electrotherapeutics in the Department of Medicine and Surgery.
HERBERT F. SARGENT, B. S., Curator of the Museum.
HENRY H. PARKE, B. L., Assistant in Zoology.
THOMAS B. COOLEY, A. B., M. D., Assistant in Hygiene.
HAROLD M. DOOLITTLE, Assistant Demonstrator of Anatomy.
JAMES F. BREAKEY, M. D., Assistant in Dermatology.
LYDIA M. DeWITT, B. S., M. D., Assistant in Histology.
FRANK S. BACHELDER, Assistant in Zoology.
ROBERT B. HOWELL, D. D. S., Demonstrator of Mechanical Technique in the College of Dental Surgery.
NORMAN K. McINNIS, A. M., Assistant in English.
FREDERICK A. BALDWIN, M. D., Assistant in Pathology in the Department of Medicine and Surgery.
FREDERICK J. WILBUR, Assistant in Astronomy.
RAYMOND H. POND, M. S., Assistant in Plant Physiology.
HELEN BENDER, Assistant in the Women's Gymnasium.
ALFRED E. LINDAU, Assistant to the Dean of the Department of Engineering.
CHARLES W. JOHNSON, Ph. C., Assistant in Qualitative Chemistry.
LEON J. COLE, Assistant in Zoology.
ROBERT L. JOHNSON, M. D., Superintendent of the University Hospital (Homœopathic).
CORA J. BECKWITH, Assistant in Zoology.
ALPHONSO M. CLOVER, B. S., Assistant in General Chemistry.
GEORGE H. ALLEN, A. M., Assistant in Latin.
HENRY W. HARVEY, D. D. S., Assistant in Clinical, Operative, and Prosthetic Dentistry.
WILLARD H. HUTCHINGS, B. L., M. D., Second Assistant in Surgery in the Department of Medicine and Surgery.
JOHN J. MERSEN, A. M., M. D., Assistant to the Bates Professor of the Diseases of Women and Children in the Department of Medicine and Surgery.
ARTHUR E. GALE, M. D., Assistant in Internal Medicine in the Department of Medicine and Surgery.
EDWARD A. WILLIS, Assistant Demonstrator of Anatomy.
AUGUSTUS HOLM, Assistant Demonstrator of Anatomy.
GERTRUDE FELKER, A. B., Assistant Demonstrator of Anatomy.
CONRAD GEORG, A. B., M. D., Interne in the University Hospital.
ROY B. CANFIELD, A. B., M. D., Assistant to the Professor of Ophthalmic and Aural Surgery in the Department of Medicine and Surgery.
DEAN W. MYERS, M. D., Assistant to the Professor of the Theory and Practice of Medicine and to the Professor of Ophthalmology Otology, and Pædology in the Homœopathic Medical College.
HARVEY M. PIPER, M. D., House Physician in the University Hospital (Homœopathic).
FLOYD E. WESTFALL, M. D., House Physician in the University Hospital (Homœopathic).
OVIDUS A. GRIFFIN, B. S., M. D., Demonstrator of Ophthalmology and Otology in the Department of Medicine and Surgery.
JOHN W. SLAUGHTER, A. B., B. D., Assistant in Psychology.
CHARLES SIMONS, B. L., Assistant in Elocution.
HARRIE N. COLE, Assistant in Qualitative Chemistry.
FRED L. WOOD, Assistant in Quantitative Analysis.
GEORGE M. HEATH, Ph. C., Assistant in Pharmacy.
NORMAN F. HARRIMAN, Assistant in Chemical Technology.
HARRY M. GORDIN, Ph. D., Assistant in Chemical Research.
RAYMOND A. CLIFFORD, M. D., Assistant to the Professor of Surgery in the Homœopathic Medical College.
RAYMOND PEARL, A. B., Assistant in Zoology.
CHARLES M. BRIGGS, Assistant in Clinical, Operative, and Prosthetic Dentistry.
MARY A. GODDARD, Assistant in Botany.
ELMA CHANDLER, Assistant in Botany.
HOWARD S. REED, Assistant in the Botanical Laboratory.
HOWARD B. BISHOP, Laboratory Assistant in General Chemistry.
ARTHUR M. LINDAUER, Assistant in Organic Chemistry.
LOUALLEN F. MILLER, B. S., Dispensing Clerk in the Electrotherapeutical Laboratory.
ALICE S. HUSSEY, A. M., Assistant in English.
PAUL I. MURRILL, Ph. D., Assistant for Research in Pharmacognosy.
WALTER D. HADZEITS, A. M., Assistant in Latin.
RICHARD D. T. HOLLISTER, Assistant in the Museum.
WILLIAM D. MUELLER, M. D., Interne in the University Hospital.
GEORGE F. YOUNG, M. D., Interne in the University Hospital.
JAMES GOSTANIAN, M. D., Interne in the University Hospital.

## CHARITABLE.

### THE STATE INDUSTRIAL HOME FOR GIRLS.

#### ADRIAN.—ESTABLISHED IN 1879.

The object of this institution is the correction of juvenile female offenders; girls between the ages of ten and seventeen, convicted of disorderly conduct, are sent here till twenty-one years of age. The property, which is located near Adrian, Lenawee county, comprises 92 acres and 19 buildings, with a total valuation of $191,171.46. The number of pupils at present is about 300, with 33 teachers and officers. Instruction is given in common schools branches, also in cooking, sewing, knitting, dress-making, and all useful household duties.

Board of Guardians { Mrs. Allaseba M. Bliss, President, Saginaw.
Mrs. Alma M. Smith, Secretary, Flint.
Fred C. Bowerfind, Adrian.

OFFICERS AND TEACHERS.

*LUCY M. SICKELS, Superintendent.
S. HELEN KING, Asst. Superintendent
WINIFRED IVES, Book-keeper.
MINA L. FULLER, Physician.
JEAN S. HALL, Cottage Manager.
SARAH E. CREW, Cottage Manager.
IDA J. PLANK, Cottage Manager.
LENA L. FORREST, Cottage Manager.
CYNTHIA BRENNAN, Cottage Manager.
ANNA L. HELBING, Cottage Manager.
CLELLIE ANDERSON, Cottage Manager.
EMMA COWAN, Asst. Manager.
EMMA V. JONES, Asst. Manager.
DELLA SKAATS, Teacher.
MINNIE WIGGINS, Teacher.
ELLA B. MILLS, Teacher.

FRANC HUTCHINSON, Teacher.
ELIZABETH REYBURN, Teacher.
LESSIE TISDALE, Teacher.
JEANETTE McINNESS, Teacher.
CELIA BRANCH, Teacher.
CLARA ANGEVINE, House Keeper.
LAURA J. WING, House Keeper.
MARY BIDLEMAN, House Keeper.
MARY MARTIN, House Keeper.
BESSIE M. BOWLEY, House Keeper.
MARY B. STALKER, House Keeper.
KATHERINE THEILMAN, House Keeper.
MARY MACHALIS, Sewing Teacher.
MARY E. CURTISS, Laundry Teacher.
FRANCES ROSE, Relief Officer.
TINA GIPPERT, Relief Officer.
CLARA B. STALKER, Relief Officer.

*Resigned.
For statistics see tables in this report.

## INDUSTRIAL SCHOOL FOR BOYS.

### LANSING.—ESTABLISHED IN 1855.

The object of this school, formerly known as the State Reform School, is the correction of juvenile male offenders; boys between the ages of ten and sixteen, convicted of any offense punishable by fine or imprisonment (save life imprisonment), may be sentenced till the age of seventeen. In addition to common school branches, the following trades are taught; carpentry, printing, baking, shoe-making, tailoring, and farming. The property, which is located in the city of Lansing, Ingham county, consists of 260 acres of land and eight buildings, exclusive of shops and barns. Its estimated value is $260,812.08. In April, 1899, 648 pupils were enrolled, with 47 teachers and employes.

Board of Trustees {
Wm. McPherson, Jr., Chairman, Howell.
Frank P. Sayre, Secretary, Flushing.
Jacob Stahl, Lansing.

### OFFICERS AND TEACHERS.

J. E. ST. JOHN, Superintendent.
E. M. LAWSON, Asst. Superintendent.
A. E. ST. JOHN, Matron.
CLARA RUHL, Housekeeper.
R. L. GAGE, Superintendent's Clerk and Bookkeeper.
ALICE C. STANLEY, Stenographer.
J. H. WELLINGS, Physician.
P. A. GILLE, Cottage Manager and Overseer.
SARA J. GILLE, Teacher.
MARY McADAMS, Teacher.
JENNIE IRVING, Teacher.
ANNA R. BRYANT, Teacher.
MAGGIE ESLER, Teacher.
ANNA L. PINKERTON, Teacher.
ANNA DAVIS, Teacher.
MINNIE ROOT, Teacher.
NETTIE RELYEA, Teacher.
HANNAH C. LYON, Teacher.
PEARL NYE, Teacher.
LILLA D. STRONG, Teacher.
W. H. STRONG, Cottage Manager and Store Room Keeper.
GEO. G. IRVING, Cottage Manager and Farmer.
D. E. BRYANT, Cottage Manager and Instructor in Printing.
W. A. BOOS, Tailor.
W. N. RELYEA, Cottage Manager and Overseer.
A. I. DAVIS, Cottage Manager and Painter.
F. M. McAdams, Overseer.
ROBT. BURNS, Shoemaker.
W. L. BRUSH, Overseer and Instructor Carpentry Department.

J. M. NYE, Cottage Manager and Band Master.
F. M. ROOT, Cottage Manager and Musical Instructor.
A. J. PLUMBE, Baker.
DAVID COLLINS, Engineer.
J. C. CAMPBELL, Assistant Farmer.
H. F. DARLING, Herdsman.
D. S. CROSSMAN, Watchman.
B. C. HULING, Watchman.
NETTIE DARLING, Laundress.
PHOEBA WICKENS, Supervisor Boys' Dining Room.
HANNAH BAILEY, Supervisor Boys' Kitchen.
ALICE K. LARNED, Hospital Nurse.
SARAH WILLIAMS, Supervisor Mending Room.
C. R. PLUMBE, Supervisor Dormitory Work.
E. A. GOODHUE, Supervisor Dormitory Work.
SOPHIE HOWE, Supervisor Dormitory Work.
HATTIE CAMPBELL, Supervisor Dormitory Work.
LENA ALLEMENDINGER, Dining Room Girl.
MARIE BELLIS, Dining Room Girl.
BIRDIE DOWD, Domestic.
BELLE HAMS, Cook.
CHAS. JOHNSON, Florist.
C. CAHILL, Teamster.
W. D. FULLER, Overseer.
A. L. ROGERS, Dormitory.
ORIE CHANDLER, Asst. Nurse.

## MICHIGAN SCHOOL FOR THE BLIND.

### LANSING.—ESTABLISHED IN 1881.

In this institution pupils between the ages of 7 and 19 years whose defective vision prevents their education in the public school, receive instruction in common school branches (without charge for tuition or board), and in such useful arts and trades as they are best adapted

---

*For statistics see* tables in this report.

to pursue. Proper moral and physical training is also given. Located in the city of Lansing, the grounds contain 45 acres with four main buildings, the total valuation being $155,000. Last year the students numbered 109, teachers 10.

Board of Control { Theodoret W. Crissey, President, Midland.
Frank H. Rankin, Jr., Secretary, Flint.
G. Willis Bement, Lansing.

OFFICERS AND TEACHERS.

E. P. CHURCH, Superintendent and Steward.
ANNA E. POTTER, Clerk and Book-keeper.
MRS. ELIZABETH BUSH, Matron.
J. F. CAMPBELL, M. D., Physician.
CHRISTINE KEYES, Nurse.
CARRIE McKENNY, Junior Boys' Matron.

LITERARY DEPARTMENT.

EDWARD H. GOODRICH.
LOUIE M. CHURCH.
A. WINIFRED CHILDS.

EVA S. ANDREWS, Kindergartner.

MUSICAL DEPARTMENT.

AARON C. BLAKESLEE, Musical Director.
LEMMA M. VOORHEIS, Vocal Music.
GRACE A. BROWN, Assistant, Instrumental Music.

HANDICRAFT.

MISS E. A. FOOTE, Girls' Work.
RHA CONKLIN, Broom Making.
KATE WRIGHT, Cooking.
MRS. PAULINE TOOLAN, Hammock, Netting, etc.

## MICHIGAN SCHOOL FOR THE DEAF.

### FLINT.—ESTABLISHED IN 1854.

This institution furnishes instruction to all children of the State between 7 and 21 years of age who, by reason of defective hearing, cannot be taught in the common schools. The only charge is for clothing and traveling expenses, and even these are furnished to indigent children. The method of instruction pursued is what is known as the American or combined system of teaching the deaf. Its object is to give every pupil who enters the school a fair trial by regular instruction in teaching speech, and to discontinue such instruction only after it is shown that the attainment of a useful amount of speech and lip-reading is impossible. The course of study begins at the very first rudiments of the English language, with the teaching of the language idea by means of pictures, objects, actions, gestures, etc.; and the course for the thirteen years extends to about the same point as a class of the junior year in the Michigan high schools, with the exception that no language except English is taught save to those few pupils who are preparing themselves for the National College at Washington.

In the Art Department instruction is given in drawing, designing, wood-carving, etching, etc. The boys are also taught cabinet making, printing, and tailoring, while the girls are instructed in all kinds of sewing; and every pupil must at least attempt to master some trade.

The institution is located at Flint, Genesee county. In addition to the 160 acres owned by the State, the school rents 125 from private parties. The buildings occupy about 30 acres, the remainder being devoted to a large herd of cattle kept by the school. The present total valuation of the property is $434,496.36. Enrollment for the past year was 412 pupils, 34 teachers.

For statistics see tables in this report.

OFFICERS AND TEACHERS.

FRANCIS D. CLARKE, A. M., C. E., Superintendent.
EDWIN F. SWAN, Steward.
MARTHA E. DRURY, Matron.
MRS. EMILY TWIST, Assistant Matron.
RANSOM N. MURRAY, M. D., Physician.
MRS. ANNIE S. RUNDELL, Assistant Physician.
JOHN AUSTIN, Engineer.
E. C. TOWER, Farmer.
FRED M. KAUFMAN, Supervisor.
SARAH R. JONES, Supervisor.
MARK H. PIPER, Supervisor.
FLORENCE H. JONES, Supervisor.
CLARK DeLONG, Supervisor.
EDWIN P. BARTON, Instructor of Cabinet-making.
PARLEY P. PRATT, Instructor of Shoe-making.
E. MORRIS BRISTOL, Instructor of Printing.
ROBERT FORD, Instructor of Tailoring.
MRS. HULDA R. J. MERCER, Instructor of Art.
AGNES BALLANTYNE, Instructor of Dress-making.
ROBERT L. ERD, Teacher of Physical Culture.
NETTIE R. CROSBY, Teacher of Primary Drawing.

TEACHERS IN MANUAL DEPARTMENT.

THOMAS L. BROWN.
WILLIS HUBBARD.
THOMAS J. ALLEN.
THOMAS P. CLARKE.
ARTHUR D. BUCHANAN.
JAMES M. STEWART.
ARLINGTON EICKHOFF.
EMMA F. KNIGHT.
CARRIE W. EARLE.
GRACE M. BEATTIE.

MADGE M. TURNER.
CLARA B. SCOTT.
CAROLINE F. ELWOOD.
MARY KNICKERBOCKER.
HINDA M. LONG.
SARA FENNER.
LINDA DE MOTTE.
JOSEPHINE TITUS.
FANNIE THAYER.
MARY SPENCER.

TEACHERS IN ORAL DEPARTMENT.

MRS. L. K. CLARKE, Principal in Charge.

THOMAS P. CLARKE.
ELLA E. J. CRAWFORD.
CARRIE E. BILLINGS.
JESSIE S. BALLANTYNE.
GRACE R. LOCHHEAD.
MABEL GALBRAITH.
MARY BEAGLE.

GEORGIA E. ANDREWS.
ABIGAIL BUCKINGHAM.
MINNIE H. BRABYN.
IDA M. AUSTIN.
EMMA D. FARNUM.
INA GREAR.

## STATE PUBLIC SCHOOL.

### COLDWATER.—ESTABLISHED IN 1871.

Any child in the state between the ages of six months and twelve years who is of sound mind and body and dependent on the public for support, may be committed to the care of this institution. The average age of pupils is seven and one-half years, and the instruction is that of primary and grammar grades. Those who are old enough, are instructed in common daily labor. During the twenty-eight years since its establishment, 4,107 children have been received, most of whom were placed in good homes. The number of teachers is four, cottage matrons nine. The school owns 18 buildings occupying 160 acres; present valuation, $248,650.08.

For statistics see tables in this report.

Board of Control
{
Marshall E. Rumsey, President, Lansing.
Caleb D. Randall, Secretary, Coldwater.
Frank M. Stewart, Hillsdale.

### OFFICERS AND TEACHERS.

JOHN B. MONTGOMERY, Champion, Marquette Co., Superintendent.
STANLEY C. GRIFFIN, Albion, Calhoun Co., State Agent.
AGNES F. CHALMERS, Grand Rapids, Kent Co., Clerk.
N. BALDWIN, Coldwater, Branch Co., Physician.
FLORENCE L. BISHOP, Leslie, Ingham Co., Stenographer.
ANDREW J. BENNETT, Coldwater, Branch Co., Engineer and Superintendent of Buildings.
W. H. LOSSING, Coldwater, Branch Co., Farmer.

### COTTAGE MANAGERS.

MISS LUA FOX, Grand Rapids, Kent Co., Cottage No. 1.
MRS. IDA ANDERSON, Saginaw, Saginaw Co., Cottage No. 2.
MRS. JENNIE BROWN, Union City, Branch Co., Cottage No. 3.
MRS. FANNIE RUSSELL, Coldwater, Branch Co., Cottage No. 5.
MRS. HARRIETT WHEELER, Quincy, Branch Co., Cottage No. 6.
MRS. FANNIE BAYNE, Albion, Calhoun Co., Cottage No. 7.
MISS MATTIE BARBER, Coldwater, Branch Co., Cottage No. 8.
MRS. ANNA GILMAN, Union City, Branch Co., Cottage Supply.
MISS DORA WEBB, Paw Paw, Van Buren Co., Cottage Supply.

### TEACHERS.

MR. MARTIN SLINGER, Chicago, Ill.
MISS WINIFRED BARTLETT, Plymouth, Wayne Co.
MISS LOUISE HARDING, Hillsdale, Hillsdale Co.
MISS MARTHA E. NILES, Flushing, Genesee Co.

## INCORPORATED.

### *DENOMINATIONAL.

### ADRIAN COLLEGE.—ESTABLISHED IN 1859

At present four schools are included under the management of this college; viz., College of Literature and the Arts, School of Music, School of Theology, and Preparatory School. A Teachers' Course has also been added to meet the increasing demand for better qualified teachers in graded and district schools. The various courses lead to four degrees, B. A., B. S., Ph. D., B. L. The institution is controlled by thirty trustees, twenty-four of whom are elected by the General Conference of the Methodist Protestant Church, and six by the college alumni. It is located at the county seat of Lenawee county, a city of about 10,000.

Officers of the Board
{
President, W. N. Swift, Adrian.
Secretary, G. B. McElroy, Adrian.

### FACULTY AND OFFICERS.

DAVID JONES, D. D., President, and Dean of the School of Theology.
J. D. H. CORNELIUS, A. M., Secretary of Faculty, Greek and Latin.
W. H. HOWARD, Ph. D., Physics, Chemistry, and French.
ORREN L. PALMER, A. M., Mathematics.
EDSON G. WALKER, M. S., Literature, Economics, and Sociology.
SARAH J. KNOTT, Preceptress, History, and Pedagogy.
C. S. MORRISON, Instrumental Music.
CARRIE B. PHELPS, O. M., Elocution and Physiculture.
LILY SIHLER BOWERFIND, German.

*As the governing boards of these institutions vary in number (from five to forty members) only the president and secretary are given.
For statistics see tables in this report.

GRACE GIFFORD, Vocal Music.
BERTHA M. LAMBERT, Latin Teacher in Academic Department.
EMMA YARD, History Teacher in Academic Department.
P. W. JONES, Mathematics Teacher in Academic Department.
E. G. Palmer, Greek Teacher in Academic Department.
ELIZABETH GIBBS-PALMER, Registrar.
J. D. H. CORNELIUS, Secretary.
CARRIE GREGORY, Librarian.
JOSHUA P. TOLFORD, Steward.

## ALBION COLLEGE.—ESTABLISHED IN 1843.

This institution styles itself a "College of Liberal Arts," and three degrees are granted on completion of its courses—A. B., B. S. ,and B. L. The Board of Trustees comprises six members elected by the Detroit Conference, and six by the Michigan Conference of the Methodist Episcopal Church, together with three elected by the Alumni Society. It is a nonsectarian school, but aims to promote the interests of Christ's kingdom more fully than is usually done in educational institutions. Though the atmosphere is intensely religious and the course includes a few biblical studies, it is in no sense a theological school. In addition to the Literary Department, which includes a course in peadagogy approved by the State Board of Education, there is a Business Department, Department of Oratory, School of Painting, and a Preparatory School. It is located ,at Albion, a thriving city of 5,000 inhabitants, in Calhoun county.

Officers of the Board { President, Horace Hitchcock, Detroit. Secretary, Samuel Dickie, Albion.

### FACULTY AND OFFICERS.

JOHN P. ASHLEY, S. T. B., Ph. D., President, John Owen Professor of Philosophy.
LEWIS R. FISKE, D. D., LL. D., Emeritus Professor of Philosophy.
GEORGE AVANN, Instructor in Physics.
DELOS FALL, Sc. D., Senior Professor, David Preston Professor of Chemistry.
FREDERICK LUTZ, A. M., Professor of Latin, Romance Languages and Literature.
CHARLES ELISHA BARR, A. M., Samuel O. Knapp Professor of Geology and Biology, Registrar.
WILLIAM MAXWELL BURKE, Ph. D., Henry M. Loud Professor of History, Acting Professor of Economics.
FRERERICK SAMUEL GOODRICH, A. M., Professor of Greek Language and Literature.
HENRIETTA ASH BANCROFT, Ph. D., Preceptress, Professor of English Language and Literature.
HENRY BENNER, Ph. D., W. H. Brockway Professor of Mathematics, Acting Ezra Bostwick Professor of Astronomy.
WILLIS M. BLOUNT, A. M., Professor of Pedagogy.
GRANT STEWART, Ph. D., Professor of Elocution and Oratory.
RICHARD CLYDE FORD, Ph. M., Assistant Professor of German Language and Literature.
ELLEN JOSEPHINE CLARK, A. M., Instructor in English and Latin.
ELEANOR T. AVANN, A. M., Instructor in Latin, Librarian.
OWEN MOYER, A. B., Instructor in Latin.
ALTA M. ALLEN, A. B., Instructor in Greek.
SARAH M. BLAIR, Instructor in Art.
GUSTAVUS SYLVESTER KIMBALL, M. Accts., Principal of Commercial Department.
DORA HOUSTON PITTS, Teacher of Shorthand and Typewriting.
OTTO SAND, Professor of Violin, Harmony and Counterpoint, Director of Orchestra.
ZELLA BRIGHAM SAND, Teacher of Piano, Pipe Organ, Harmony and Voice.
ETHEL CALKINS, Teacher of Piano.
CLARISSA DICKIE, Teacher of Piano.
FRANK A. FALL, Assistant Librarian.
FREDERICK LUTZ, A. M., Secretary.

For statistics see tables in this report.

## ALMA COLLEGE.—ESTABLISHED IN 1886.

This college was established by the Michigan Synod of the Presbyterian Church, and its affairs are administered by a Board of Trustees numbering twenty. It embraces six divisions—College, Academy, School of Pedagogy (approved by State Board of Education), Commercial School, School of Music, and School of Art—with three courses leading to the degrees B. A., B. S., Ph. D. Located at Alma, Gratiot county, this college is very near the geographical center of Lower Michigan.

Officers of the Board { President, Nathan B. Bradley, Bay City.
                        { Secretary, Joseph W. Ewing, Alma.

### FACULTY AND OFFICERS.

AUGUST F. BRUSKE, M. S., D. D., President, and Wells Professor of Philosophy and Theism.
JOSEPH W. EWING, A. M., Folsom Professor of Pedagogy and Principal of the Academy.
MARY C. GELSTON, A. M., Professor of Latin.
CHARLES A. DAVIS, A. M., Wright-Davis Professor of Natural Sciences and Secretary of the Faculty.
JOHN T. EWING, A. M., Folsom Professor of Greek, and Registrar.
JAY CLIZBE, A. M., Professor of Biblical Literature. A. B.
JAMES MITCHELL, A., M., Ph. B., Wright Professor of History and Political Science.
MARY A. CLARKE, Principal, Stone Professor of English.
FRANK N. NOTESTEIN, Ph. D., Wright Professor of Mathematics and Physics.
KATHERINE M. INGLIS, Instructor in French and German.
FRED FULLERTON, M. S., Instructor in Mathematics.
KATE L. BOOTH, Principal of the School of Art.
MRS. MARY D. PLUM, Principal of Training School for Kindergartners.
ROBERT C. KING, Principal of Commercial School.
JENNIE E. WAGNER, Principal of School of Music.
JOSEPHINE ST. JOHN, Instructor in Voice.
EDWIN FAUVER, B. A., Instructor in Athletics and Director of Gymnasium.
EDGAR A. BAGLEY, M. D., Medical Examiner for Gymnasium Work.
LIZABETH B. CASE, Librarian.
HUGH McCOLL, M. D., Special Lecturer on Hygiene.
S. C. J. OSTRUM, M. D., Special Lecturer on Hygiene.

### BATTLE CREEK COLLEGE.—ESTABLISHED IN 1872.

This institution under control of twelve trustees elected by the Seventh-day Adventists, is called a "Training School for Christian Workers," and its first object is the training of missionaries who shall promulgate the truth as understood by this denomination. Accordingly there are no set courses or degrees, but each student is urged "prayerfully to decide upon a course of training best adapted to his natural ability and in accordance with the manifest guidance of the Spirit of God." Upon leaving the school students are granted certificates indicating the amount and character of work done. The departments of instruction are the following; Ministerial, Medical, Musical, Commercial, and Industrial.

The college is situated in Battle Creek, a most enterprising city of about 18,000 inhabitants.

Officers of the Board { President, A. T. Jones, Battle Creek.
                       { Secretary, Percy T. Magan, Battle Creek.

For statistics see tables in this report.

## FACULTY AND OFFICERS.

EDWARD A. SUTHERLAND, President, English Bible.
PERCY T. MAGAN, Dean.
ALVIN J. BREED, Supt. Ministerial Department.
ALONZO T. JONES, Mental, Moral, Political Science.
EDWIN BARNES, Supt. Musical Department.
EMORY D. KIRBY, Biblical Greek and Latin.
————————, English Language.
DR. S. S. EDWARDS and MRS. S. S. EDWARDS, M. D., Natural Sciences and Mathematics.
HOMER R. SALISBURY, Preceptor, Hebrew and History.
ELMER E. GARDNER, Bookkeeping and Phonography.
MISS M. BESSIE De GRAW, Pedagogy.
E. P. BOGGS, Canvassing.
J. H. HAUGHEY, Phonography.

C. M. CHRISTIANSEN, Industrial Department.
MRS. S. V. SUTHERLAND, Supt. Domestic Department.
JOHN P. CHRISTIANSEN, Mechanics.
ARTHUR HALLOCK, Carpentry.
MERRILL N. CROSS, Broom Making.
J. M. JONES, Tailoring.
MISS NELLIE V. DICE, Dressmaking.
MISS ROSMA M. WHALEN, Librarian. and Secretary of the Faculty.
MISS MARY LAMSON, Preceptress.
D. H. PINCKNEY, Instructor.
MRS. D. H. PINCKNEY, Instructor.
MRS. A. W. SPAULDING, Instructor.
CHAS. J. STONE, Instructor.
MISS MELINDA LAMSON, Instructor.
W. H. SMITH, Bookkeeper.
A. W. SPAULDING, Stenographer.
C. E. DUNLAP. Farm Superintendent.
F. M. WILSON, Cook.

## LECTURERS.

WM. COVERT.
R. S. DONNELL.
N. W. KAUBLE.
J. D. GOWELL.
G. A. IRWIN.

J. H. KELLOGG, M. D.
DAVID PAULSON, M. D.
ALFRED B. OLSEN, M. D.
ABBIE WINEGAR, M. D.
JUDGE JESSE ARTHUR.

## DETROIT COLLEGE.—ESTABLISHED IN 1877.

Under the care of the Fathers of the Society of Jesus, the purpose of this college is to impart instruction in the branches of a Christian and liberal education. The course includes religious instruction, mental and moral philosophy, astronomy and mathematics, history, literature,. and the natural sciences; it embraces two departments, Collegiate and Academic. The trustees are five in number, and the location is at Detroit, the metropolis of Michigan.

Officers of the Board { President, Rev. James D. Foley, S. J., Detroit.
Secretary, Rev. A. J. Burrows, S. J., Detroit.

## FACULTY AND OFFICERS.

REV. JAMES D. FOLEY, S. J., President.
REV. A. J. BURROWS, S. J., Vice President, Prefect of Studies.
REV. BENEDICT MASSELIS, S. J., Chaplain.
REV. JAMES MELOY, Mental and Moral Philosophy.
REV. THOS. TREACY, Astronomy, Geology, Physics.
VINCENT FUSZ, Mathematics, Chemistry, Special Classes.
REV. AUGUSTINE M. EFFINGER, S. J., Rhetoric, Evidences of Religion.
R. S. JOHNSTON, Poetry.
REV. P. BURKE, S. J., Humanities, A.
JOHN SYNNOTT, First Academic, A. Second Academic.
L. LEALEY, First Academic. B.
LEO J. LYONS, S. J., Third Academic, A.
REV. JOHN OTTEN, S. J., Third Academic, B.
PATRICK J. BURKE. S. J., and L. LEALEY, S. J., Prefects of Discipline.
REV. ROBT. HENNEMAN, Humanities, B.

## PRECEPTORS IN SPECIAL STUDIES.

REV. AUGUSTINE M. EFFINGER, S. J., and REV. JOHN OTTEN, S. J., German.
REV. P. BURKE, S. J., Bookkeeping.
ROBERT HENNEMAN, S. J., Music.

For statistics see tables in this report.

ELOCUTION.

JOHN LANE CONNOR, A. B.
REV. EDMUND S. MURPHY, S. J.
ROBERT S. JOHNSTON, S. J.
PATRICK J. BURKE, S. J.

JOHN F. SYNNOTT, S. J.
LEO J. LYONS, S. J.
L. LEALEY.

## HILLSDALE COLLEGE.—ESTABLISHED IN 1855.

The thirty-five trustees who administer the affairs of this college are controlled by the Free Baptist denomination, and the curriculum offers four courses—Classical, Philosophical, Literary, and Normal, the latter approved by State Board of Education. These lead respectively to the degrees of A. B., Ph. B., L. B., Pd. B. There is also a Department in Theology, Music, Art, Oratory, and a Preparatory School. Hillsdale, the seat of the college, is a flourishing city in Southern Michigan of about 3000 inhabitants.

Officers of the Board { President, George F. Mosher, Hillsdale.
{ Secretary, Samuel E. Kelley, Hillsdale.

### FACULTY AND OFFICERS.

GEORGE F. MOSHER, A. M., LL. D., President. Mental and Moral Philosophy.
KINGSBURY BACHELDER, A. M., Professor of the Greek Language and Literature.
CHARLES HENRY GURNEY, A. M., Alumni Professor of Logic, Rhetoric, and English Literature, and Principal of Normal Department.
DUNCAN McLAREN MARTIN, Ph. M., Hart Professor of Mathematics, Fowler Professor of Physics, Instructor in Gymnasium.
WILLIAM H. MUNSON, B. S., Professor of Chemistry, Biology, and Geology.
STEPHEN BENJAMIN HARVEY, A. M., Professor of German and Acting Waldron Professor of Latin.
ELLEN ADELAIDE COPP, A. B., B. D., Lady Principal and Instructor in Latin and English.
FRANCES STEWART MOSHER, A. M., Professor of French and History.
ELEANOR BARNUM JOHNSON, Instructor in English and Science.
MARY WARD, A. M., Instructor in Latin.
REV. RANSOM DUNN, D. D., Emeritus De Wolf Professor of Homiletics.
REV. ASHMUN THOMPSON SALLEY, A. M., D. D., Dunn Professor of Hebrew Language and Literature.
REV. DELAVAN BLOODGOOD REED, A. M., D. D., Marks Professor of Ecclesiastical History and History of Christian Doctrine.
REV. JOHN T. WARD, D. D., Burr Professor of Systematic Theology.
*——,Smith Professor Metaphysics and Theology.
*——,Aldrich Professor of Biblical and Pastoral Theology.
MELVILLE WARREN CHASE, Mus. Doc , Professor of the Pianoforte, Harmony, and Theory.
JOHN MURRAY MERRILL, Professor of Voice and Chorus Director.
CLARENCE MELVILLE CHASE, Teacher of Pianoforte.
S. MAY HEWES, Teacher of Violin.
MILLICENT ARLINE HILL, Accompanist.
GEORGE B. GARDNER, A. M., Professor of Painting and Drawing.
M. MYRTILLA DAVIS, Instructor in Elocution and Oratory.
PROF. K. BACHELDER, Librarian and Registrar.
ELBERT W. VAN AKEN and MISS ZOE N. SMITH, Assistant Librarians.
PROF. S. B. HARVEY, Secretary.

### HOPE COLLEGE.—ESTABLISHED IN 1851.

This college is the out come of immigration to this country of those sturdy Netherlanders who in 1847 began coming hither for larger religious liberty and greater material prosperity. In 1850 they united with the Reformed Church in America, and in 1851 established a "Pioneer School;" this in 1857 was merged in "Holland Academy" and in 1866 again changed

---

*The studies of these Professorships are taught by the professors already mentioned. For statistics see tables in this report.

its name to that at present employed.  Its council includes eight members elected by the general Synod, together with two from the Classis of
Wisconsin, Michigan, Pleasant Prairie, Grand River, Holland, Dakota,
Iowa, and Illinois, respectively. It is in no sense a local institution, but
represents a territory reaching from New York to the Dakotas.     Its
leading course is Literary, leading to the degree of A. B.   There is also
an Elective Course and a Preparatory Department.  A Theological
Department is conducted in a separate building near the college campus,
with the same college president, but under a different governing board of
eighteen members.  This department was established in 1869, and is
known as the "Western Theological Seminary of the Reformed Church
in America."   Hope College is located at Holland, a city of nearly 10,000
people, twenty-five miles south-west of Grand Rapids.

Officers of the Council { President, Rev. W. Moerdyke, Milwaukee, Wis.
                         { Secretary, G. J. Diekema, Holland.

### COLLEGE FACULTY.

GERRIT J. KOLLEN, LL. D., President, Political Economy.
CORNELIUS DOESBURG, A. M., Secretary and Registrar.
HENRY BOERS, A. M., Professor of History. Zoology.
JOHN H. KLEINHEKSEL, A. M., Vice President, Professor Mathematics, Biology.
JAMES G. SUTPHEN, A. M., Rodman Professor of the Latin Language and Literature.
JOHN B. NYKERK, A. M., Professor of the English Language and Literature, Vocal
Music.
DOUWE B. YNTEMA, A. M., Professor of Chemistry and Physics, Pedagogy.
REV. JOHN TALLMADGE BERGEN, A. M., Robert Schell Professor of Ethics and
Evidences of Christianity, Logic.
REV. PIETER SIEGERS, A. M., Professor of the Dutch Language and Literature.
HENRY VEGHTE, A. M., Professor of the French and German Languages, and
Literatures.
EDWARD D. DIMNENT, A. B., Ralph Voorhees Professor of the Greek Language and
Literature.
ADONIRAM J. LADD, A. B., Professor of Psychology and Pedagogy.
S. O. MAST, B. S., Instructor in Natural Sciences.
MRS. C. VAN RAALTE GILMORE, Lady Principal.
HON. G. J. DIEKEMA, A. M., LL. B., Lecturer on Political Economy.
GEO. E. KOLLEN, A. M., LL. B., Lecturer on Political Economy.

### SEMINARY FACULTY.

REV. JOHN W. BEARDSLEE, D. D., President, Professor of Biblical Languages
and Literature.
REV. HENRY E. DOSKER, D. D., Secretary of the Faculty and Professor of Historical
Theology, Hermeneutics and Harmony of the Gospels.
REV. EGBERT WINTER, D. D., Professor of Didactic and Polemic Theology, Practical
Theology.
REV. J. TALLMADGE BERGEN, Instructor in Elocution.

### KALAMAZOO COLLEGE.—ESTABLISHED IN 1833.

This college, known in its earliest days as "The Kalamazoo Literary
Institute," is Michigan's oldest classical educational institution, as also
one of the first co-educational colleges in America, having admitted
women as early as 1855, at which time a most liberal charter was
granted by the legislature, empowering the trustees (numbering 36) to
administer its affairs; it is controlled by the Baptist denomination.  In
1895-6 an agreement was entered into whereby the institution was
affiliated with Chicago University.  There are three courses of study leading respectively to the degrees B. A., Ph. B., B. S.  A course in pedagogy
approved by the State Board of Education, has also been added.  Kalamazoo is a beautiful city of about 25,000 inhabitants, in southwestern
Michigan.

*For statistics see tables in this report.*

Officers of the Board { President, C. C. Bowen, Detroit.
{ Secretary, H. B. Colman, Kalamazoo.

### FACULTY AND OFFICERS.

ARTHUR GAYLORD SLOCUM, LL. D., President, Professor of Mental and Moral Philosophy.
SAMUEL BROOKS, D. D., Professor of the Latin Language and Literature.
SETH JONES AXTELL, A. M., Professor of the Greek Language and Literature.
STILLMAN GEORGE JENKS, B. S., Professor of Natural Sciences, Librarian.
CLARKE BENEDICT WILLIAMS, A. M., Professor of Mathematics.
CLARK MILLS BRINK, Ph. D., Professor of English and History.
ELIPHALET ALLISON READ, Ph. D., Professor of Psychology and Pedagogy.
LUCY JOHNSON, Ph. B., Instructor in Latin and History.
CAROLINE HARDER SWARTOUT, A. B., Instructor in German.
CLARA P. ANDERSON, A. M., Instructor in English.
GEORGE HERBERT FAIRCLOUGH, Instructor in Piano, Organ and the Theory of Music.
PAULINE LATOURETTE, A. M., Instructor in the Preparatory Department and in Vocal Music.
ANDRE BE'ZIAT de B 'RDES. Ph. D.. Profess r of Romance Languages.
SETH JONES AXTELL, A. M., Steward.

### OLIVET COLLEGE.—ESTABLISHED IN 1844.

The devoted little colony that journeyed from Oberlin, Ohio, into the wilds of Michigan for the purpose of founding a college " for the education of young men and women, especially such as are not rich in this world's goods, but heirs of the Kingdom of God,"—for fifteen years worked under the name of Olivet Institute. But in 1859 a charter was granted and the Institute transformed into the College. The colony also established the First Congregational Church of Olivet, and the two have builded and worshiped together, the College being governed by twenty-four trustees chosen from that denomination. There is a Classical, Philosophical, and Scientific Course, besides the Musical, Art, and Preparatory Departments, the latter including a Normal Course approved by the State Board of Education. Olivet is a small village in Eaton county a little off from the railway line, whose quiet beauty at once attracts notice.

Officers of the Board { President, Rev. Willard G. Sperry, Olivet.
{ Secretary, Albert L. Lee, Olivet.

### FACULTY AND OFFICERS.

WILLIARD G. SPERRY, D. D., President, Drury Professor or Mental and Moral Philosophy.
JOSEPH L. DANIELS, D. D., Parsons Professor of Greek Language and Literature.
STEWART MONTGOMERY, A. M., Erwin Professor of Chemistry and Physiology.
WALTER E. C. WRIGHT, D. D., Professor of Evidences of Christianity and Applied Christianity.
GEORGE A. KNAPP, A. M., Stone Professor of Astronomy, Natural Philosophy, and Mathematics.
HUBERT LYMAN CLARK, Ph. D., Professor of Biology and Geology.
MISS FLORA BRIDGES, Principal of Young Women's Department.
MRS. LIZZIE E. BINTLIFF. Professor of Music.
MISS GRACE ANNETTE GEORGE, B. Pd., Instructor of French and German Languages and Literature.
THOMAS F. KANE, Ph. D., Professor of Latin Language and Literature. Principal of Preparatory Department.
THOMAS W. NADAL ,Instructor in English Literature and Oratory.
GEORGE N. ELLIS, A. M., Instructor in Latin.
MISS M. IDA SWINDT. M. L., L. C.. Instructor in Mathematics and History.
FREDERICK ARTHUR OSBORN, Ph. B., Instructor in Physics and Pedagogy.
EDWARD N. STONE, A. M., Instructor in Latin.
LUDWIG T. LARSEN, Instructor in Greek and English.
MRS. ESTELLA HALL READE, Teacher of Voice Culture and Singing.
JOHN B. MARTIN, Teacher of Violin and Orchestral Instruments.
MISS ANNIE E. TENNANT, Teacher of Piano, Organ and Theory.
MRS. ADA T. SMITH, Teacher of Piano and Voice Culture.

For statistics see tables in this report.
17

MRS. ANNE S. BATCHELLOR, Director of Art Department, Instructor in Painting and Drawing.
WILLIAM F. LYON, JR., Director of Gymnasium.
MARY AUGUSTA REEDER, Physical Instructor.
JOSEPH L. DANIELS, Librarian.
ALBERT L. LEE, Registrar and Clerk.

## ACADEMIES AND SEMINARIES.

### ACADEMY OF LADIES OF LORETTO OF THE INSTITUTE OF THE BLESSED VIRGIN MARY.—ESTABLISHED IN 1898.

This Roman Catholic institution was incorporated late in 1898, and no data is available.

### THE ACADEMIES OF THE SACRED HEART.

These two Academies were incorporated in 1888 and 1889, and are respectively located at Detroit and Grosse Point. As the name implies, they are conducted by the religion of the Sacred Heart, the instructors being strictly confined to members of this order. In compliance with a request, their names are not published.

### AKELEY INSTITUTE.—ESTABLISHED IN 1888.

This is a Diocesan School for Girls under the supervision of Rt. Rev. Geo. D. Gillespie, Bishop of Western Michigan, and the Board of Trustees includes fifteen members. The institute was founded by the generous gift to Bishop Gillespie, in 1887, of a block of land and large mansion in Grand Haven, presented by Hon. H. C. Akeley of Minneapolis. Besides grammar grade studies, the work includes a College Preparatory and a Literary Course, with Business and Music Departments additional. Grand Haven is an exceptionally healthy city on the eastern shore of Lake Michigan, directly across from Milwaukee.

#### FACULTY AND OFFICERS.

RT. REV. GEORGE D. GILLESPIE, D. D., Rector.
MRS. J. E. WILKINSON, Principal, History, English.
JANE K. ANKETELL, Associate Principal, Sacred Studies.
MRS. FRANCES C. NOURSE, French, Psychology, English.
LUMINA C. RIDDLE, Higher Mathematics, Science.
RUTH PEET SMITH, A. B., Greek, Latin, German.
MARGARETTA CHEYNEY, Preparatory Classes.
HENRY C. POST, Piano.
JOSEPHINE SMITH, Vocal.
CLARA V. TRAVIS, Dancing and Delsarte.
AGNES MACFIE, Lecturer on Art.
JULIA ALLEN, Art Teacher.
JOSEPHINE SMITH, Bookkeeping and Penmanship.
AREND VANDERVEEN, M. D., Physician.

### DETROIT FEMALE SEMINARY.—ESTABLISHED IN 1859.

This Seminary is under the control of two lady principals, and endeavors to meet the demand for a school more thorough than the usual boarding school, yet less severe than a woman's college. The course runs through kindergarten, primary, intermediate and grammar grades, with a Preparatory and Collegiate Department of three years each. Both Smith and Wellesley Colleges receive its graduates without examination. It is located on Jefferson Avenue, one of the most beautiful streets of Detroit, and is accessible from all parts of the city. Both home and day students are received.

## FACULTY.

ELIZA F. HAMMOND, Principal, History of Art, Botany, English Literature.
LAURA C. BROWNING, Principal, Psychology, Latin.
CLAIRE FORBES HAMMOND, B. A., Greek. Sciences, Mathematics.
RUTH WINIFRED LANE, B. A., Latin, History.
MINNIE EADE, English, Algebra.
SUZANNE GRENÉ French Language and Literature.
EMELIE MEINHARDT, German Language and Literature.
BLANCHE LOUISE STRICKLAND. Physical Training.
MARY NEWMAN, Arithmetic, Grammar and Intermediate Departments.
ETHEL A. MITTLEBERGER. Primary Department.
JEANNETTE FITCH. Drawing.

### KINDERGARTEN DEPARTMENT.

MAUDE M. GILLET; LUCY JOHNSON, Ass't.; ADA MERCER, Accompanist for Gymnastics;————————, Geography.

### DETROIT SCHOOL FOR BOYS.—ESTABLISHED IN 1890.

This school was founded by Mrs. Mary Ekin Whitton and Frederick Whitton, and has an advisory board of 16 members. Training is given in the essentials of a common school education, and special attention is paid to preparation for college, certificates admitting to several of the leading Universities. There is a primary, intermediate, and upper class, and a Manual Training Course is a regular part of the school work. It is located on Putnam Avenue, Detroit. Both day and home students are received.

### FACULTY.

FREDERICK DEXTER GREEN. A. B., Greek. Latin.
FREDERICK EDWARDS SEARLE, A. B., Science.
EMMA DOAN, Primary Studies.
MARION A. CAMPBELL. Clay Modelling, Wood Carving, Drawing.
EMILE J. FERMIER, B. S., M. E., Mathematics, Shop Work.
CARL COPELAND PARSONS, A. B., Latin, Mathematics.
JOSEPH M. KREWER, B. L., B. S., French, Geography.
FREDERICK HENRY WENG, Ph. B., German, English.
PERCY WALL JONES, B. L., History, English.
HARRIET WING LITTLE, Music, Primary Studies.
HOMER ERWIN SAFFORD, Ph. B., M. D., Medical Examinations.

### DETROIT HOME AND DAY SCHOOL.—ESTABLISHED IN 1878.

This school was opened by Rev. J. D. Liggett and daughters, but in 1882 a number of persons united with them in its incorporation and the erection of a suitable building. The Board of Trustees numbers six. The course ranges from kindergarten to academic inclusive, special attention being given to preparation for college. Vassar, Smith, and Cornell, admit graduates without examination, and Michigan University accredits upon an inspection every two years. The location is about a mile from the business center of Detroit, in a very pleasant part of the city.

### FACULTY AND OFFICERS.

ELLA M. LIGGETT, A. B., Principal. English Literature, Algebra.
JEANNETTE M. LIGGETT, Associate Principal, Beginning Latin, History of Art.
SARAH P. HAVEN, Principal's Assistant
EMMA CARHARTT, History, Mythology, Geography.
IDA F. SMITH (leave of absence for study in Europe), Geometry, Algebra, History of Art.
STUART A. COURTIS, Physics.
KATHERINE FLYNN, Botany, Physiology, Spelling, Penmanship.
HELEN CHURCH. French.
LOUISE M. BREITENBACH, Ph. B., German, Advanced Latin.
MARY R. MUMFORD, A. B., English.
FLORENCE A. BROWN, Connecting Class.

CLARA V. SMITH, Principal of Intermediate Department, Arithmetic, Geography, United States History.
JANE A. PERINE, English in Intermediate Department.
SARAH HITT MITCHELL, Principal of Primary Department
MRS. ANNIE DUNLAP, Assistant in Primary Department.
GRACE MARY AUSTIN, Assistant in Primary Department.
CLARA B. MERCER, French in Primary Department.
RUTH HOFFMAN, First and Second Grades in Primary Department.
IRENE C. FARQUHAR, Kindergartner.
MABLE RUTH BROADWELL, Assistant in Kindergarten.
SUSAN COREY, Music.
H. A. STRASSBURG, Dancing.
ELIZABETH MITCHELL FESSENDEN, Ph. B., Physical Training.
MARGARET M. SILL, Matron.
NELLIE A. McMILLAN, Accountant.

### DETROIT UNIVERSITY SCHOOL.—ESTABLISHED IN 1899.

This school having been organized in the summer of 1899, we glean facts concerning it from its "preliminary calendar." The furniture and equipment is entirely new. The Manual Training equipment was designed by Supt. Skinner, Director of that Department (formerly of the Toledo University Manual Training School), and is the best procurable. The school designs to furnish a thorough general and college preparatory education for boys, and special attention will be given to the primary grades, with a view to teaching right habits of study from the outset. As students will be prepared for any college or technical school in the country, the course of study is very flexible; it is conducted under three departments,—primary, intermediate, and secondary. A wholesome hot luncheon will be served daily, or students living near may go home at noon. The school grounds front on Elmwood Avenue, Detroit.

#### FACULTY.

FREDERICK LEROY BLISS, A. B., Principal, History, Geography.
HENRY GRAY SHERRARD, A. B., Associate-Principal, Greek, Latin.
WILLIAM CHARLES SKINNER, Director of Manual Training.
MYRA McPHERSON POST, B. L., English.
WALTER EDWARD SANDERS, A. B., Science, Mathematics.
JEANNETTE LAMBIE ELLIOTT, Mathematics, English.
ELLEN ANN KENNAN, A. M., Latin, History.
ANNETTE BERTHA COLBY, Primary Department, English.
ALFRED COESTER, A. B., French and German
WALTER DWIGHT HERRICK, A. B., Mathematics, History.
STEWART ALFRED McCOMBER, A. M., Director of the Gymnasium.
*————————, Drawing,Clay Modelling.
FLORENCE GERTRUDE TAYLOR, Vocal Music.
*————————, Piano.
*————————, Violin.
*————————, 'Cello.

### MICHIGAN FEMALE SEMINARY.—ESTABLISHED IN 1856.

This institution is under the auspices of the Presbyterian Synod of Michigan, and has a Board of 20 Trustees. Its course of study covers six years, two of seminary work and four of college preparatory. The work of the former is largely elective: the latter is based on the courses in the University of Michigan that lead to the degrees of B. A., Ph. B., B. S., and B. L. There is also a Music and Art Department. The Seminary stands on a high hill on the outskirts of Kalamazoo, and commands a fine view of this picturesque city and the fertile country surrounding it.

*Not yet filled.

## MICHIGAN MILITARY ACADEMY.—ESTABLISHED IN 1877.

The purpose of this school is three-fold,—the development of a manly character, a preparatory college training, and the best known physical culture attained both through military drill and the gymnasium. Besides receiving a military training such as develops the desirable qualities summed up in three words—obedience, responsibility, and honor—students are prepared for all colleges or other educational institutions, including West Point and Annapolis. The Academy is conducted by Col. J. Sumner Rogers, its Board of Trustees numbering six. It has an ideal location at Orchard Lake, little more than a mile from Pontiac, Oakland county.

A large number of graduates served with all theMichigan regiments, and all the recent army appointments from this State have been from the ranks of its alumni. In many other states, also, its former students have rendered distinguished services both in the volunteer and in the regular army.

## NAZARETH ACADEMY.—ESTABLISHED IN 1897.

This is a girl's school under the direction of the Sisters of St. Joseph of the Diocese of Detroit, and seven Sisters of this order compose the Board of Trustees. The course of study extends through Primary, Intermediate, Academy, and Collegiate Departments, with special attention paid to young ladies whose early education has been neglected. A business course is also provided. The school is pleasantly located on a farm of 160 acres on the highlands at Nazareth, about one mile from Kalamazoo city.

134     DEPARTMENT OF PUBLIC INSTRUCTION.

RAISIN VALLEY SEMINARY.—ESTABLISHED IN 1850.

This is one of Michigan's pioneer schools, and was established through the efforts of the Friends of Adrian Quarterly Meeting. Its Board of Trustees numbers sixteen. Its chief aim is "to develop strong, upright, cultured men and women, and intelligent citizens." There are four courses of study,—English, Latin, Scientific, and Latin-Scientific, with a recently added Commercial Course. This Seminary stands in one of the pleasantest rural districts of Southern Michigan, four miles northeast of Adrian, Lenawee county.

FACULTY.

E. T. ARMSTRONG, Principal, Mathematics, Science, Commercial Department.
CELIA B. JONES, Preceptress, Languages, Literature, and History.
ROBERT GLENN, Superintendent.
ELIZABETH GLENN, Matron.

ST. MARY'S ACADEMY.—ESTABLISHED IN 1890.

This institution is under the direction of the Sisters, Servants of the Immaculate Heart of Mary, and is governed by seven trustees. The Academic Department comprises seven courses, namely, Classical, Latin, Scientific, English, Commercial, Music, and Art, the courses being specially planned for those preparing for normal or commercial work. The first four degrees respectively lead to the degrees of A. B., Ph. B., B. S., and B. L. The Preparatory Department is divided in to primary, intermediate, and junior, little girls under twelve receiving special attention. Twenty-two unincorporated schools are conducted by this order in Michigan. This Academy is situated on the banks of the Raisin River, in the city of Monroe, Monroe county.

FACULTY.

MOTHER M. JUSTINA, President and Prefect of Studies.
SISTER M. AUGUSTINE, Directress of Young Ladies.
SISTER M. MARGARET, Directress of Juniors.
SISTER M. FIDELIA, Principal of Academic Department.
SISTER M. EVANGELISTA, Assistant Academic Department.
SISTER M. LEONILLA, Commercial Department.
SISTER M. ALPHONSINE, Preparatory Department.
SISTER M. ODILLA, Junior Department.
SISTER M. EUSEBIA, Intermediate Department.
SISTER M. PAULA, Primary Department
SISTER M. ANGELA, Music Department.
SISTER M. SCHOLASTICA, Music Department.
SISTER M. FLORENCE, Music Department.
SISTER M. GRACE, Music Department.
SISTER M. ANNETTA, Music Department.
SISTER M. CLEMENS, Music Department.
SISTER M. LOYOLA, Teacher of Elocution and Physical Culture.
SISTER M. BLANCHE, Teacher of Art and French.
SISTER M. ATHANASIA, Teacher of Art-needlework.

SEMINARY OF THE FELICIAN SISTERS.—ESTABLISHED IN 1882.

This school is under control of five trustees chosen by the Order of Felician Sisters, and is located at Detroit. The Mother Superior, Mother Brunona Pydynkowska, is assisted by a corps of eight teachers.

SISTERS OF THE ORDER OF ST. DOMINIC.

In 1892 articles of incorporation were taken out by this order for the purpose of establishing an institution of learning in or near Grand Rapids, as also in other parts of the State. As yet the only academy opened is at Essexville, a few miles from Bay City. It is known as The Academy of The Holy Rosary and is presided over by Mother M. Aquinta. There are *four instructors.*

This Seminary is controlled by the Free Methodist Church, and looks especially to the Conferences of Michigan, Indiana, Ohio, and Canada, for its support. The Board of Trustees numbers fifteen. There is an intermediate and an academic department, with a three-year English Course and Classical, Latin, and Scientific Courses, each requiring four years. A one-year course for Christian Workers is also presented, and the atmosphere of the school is decidedly religious. The location is at Spring Arbor, a small village about eight miles southwest of Jackson City.

FACULTY.

REV. DAVID S. WARNER, A. M., Principal, Latin and Greek.
REV. GEO. LAUBACH, A. B., Theology and Music.
MISS E. E. PRETTY, English and History.
MISS BERTHA KILGOUR, Science and Mathematics.
MISS BERTHA B. BASSETT, Intermediate.
MRS. M. S. BENN, Primary.

THEOLOGICAL SCHOOL OF THE HOLLAND CHRISTIAN CHURCH OF AMERICA.—
ESTABLISHED IN 1878.

This is a strictly theological school, and the work is confined absolutely to studies necessary for the ministry. The full course involves seven years, four in Preparatory and three in Theological Department. In the Literary Department a thorough classical and historical course is presented. The Board of Trustees includes eighteen members, representing the states of Michigan, New Jersey, Illinois, Iowa, and Minnesota. The school is pleasantly situated in Grand Rapids, the county seat of Kent county and second largest city in Michigan.

FACULTY.

REV. G. E. BOER, Professor of History, Logic and Psychology, Hermeneutics, Biblical History and Natural Theology.
REV. G. K. HEMKES, Rector, Professor of Greek and Hebrew Languages and Literature, Biblical Languages and Literature, Church History and Christian Ethics.
REV. H. BEUKER, D. D., In Charge of Biblical Instruction, Professor of Systematic and Practical Theology.
A. J. ROOKS, A. M., Professor of English, German and American History. In Charge of Geography and Greek.
K. SCHOOLLAND, Professor of Holland, Latin and Literature.

URSULINE ACADEMY OF ST. IGNACE.—ESTABLISHED IN 1898.

This is a recently established private Boarding and Day School under rule of the Roman Catholic Church, with six teachers and Mother Angela as its Superioress. It is located at St. Ignace, on the bluff over-looking the Island and Straits of Mackinac.

PROFESSIONAL SCHOOLS.

DETROIT COLLEGE OF LAW.—ESTABLISHED IN 1891.

Four trustees administer the affairs of this school whose aim is to turn out both scholarly and practical lawyers, and great advantage is claimed through its situation in Michigan's metropolis, giving access to the various courts and libraries. The instructors are all regularly engaged in the practice of law. The course of study for the degree of LL. B. covers three years and includes not only the regular text-book exposition, but also the study of illustrative cases, criticism of briefs, drafting of contracts and other legal papers, conduct of causes in practice courts, etc.

Officers of the Board $\left\{ \begin{array}{l} \text{President, William D. Atkinson, Detroit.} \\ \text{Secretary, Malcolm McGregor, Detroit.} \end{array} \right.$

### FACULTY.

HON. CHARLES D. LONG, Justice of the Supreme Court of Michigan, President.
PHILIP T. VAN ZILE, LL D., Dean of the Faculty; Elementary Law, Personal Property, Sales, Mortgages, Equity Pleading and Practice, Code Pleading, Bailments, and Common Carriers.
WILLIAM L. CARPENTER, LL. B., Judge, Third Judicial Circuit; the Law of Torts, Fraud and Damages.
ALFRED RUSSELL. LL. D., Jurisdiction and Practice of Federal Courts.
O'BRIEN J. ATKINSON, Judge Thirty-first Judicial Circuit; Law of Libel and Slander.
FRED A. BAKER, Constitutional Limitations.
GEORGE S. HOSMER, Judge. Third Judicial Circuit; Conduct of Law Suits.
R. A. PARKER. LL. B., Patents and Copyrights.
WILLARD M. LILLIBRIDGE, A. M., Judge of Third Judicial Circuit; Michigan Constitution and Statutes, and Legal Ethics.
JASPER C. GATES, A. M., LL. B., Domestic Relations, Evidence, Real Estate, Trusts, and Law of Landlord and Tenant.
ELISHA A. FRASER, A. M., Contracts.
FRANK E. ROBSON. B. S., LL. B., Partnership, Insurance, Private Corporations, and Common Law Pleading.
JOHN W. BEAUMONT, B. S., LL. B., Equity Jurisprudence.
JOHN G. HAWLEY. A. B., Criminal Law and Criminal Procedure.
EDGAR O. DURFEE, Judge of Probate Court for the County of Wayne; Estates of Deceased Persons, and Probate Practice.
JOHN C. SHAW. LL. B., Admiralty.
WILLIAM H. WETHERBEE. LL. B., Conveyancing and Practice Court.
JOHN LANE CONNOR, A. B., Oratory.

### DETROIT COLLEGE OF MEDICINE.—ESTABLISHED IN 1885.

The trustees of this College aim to furnish the best instruction and facilities for study in all branches of medical art. In addition to the regular Department of Medicine, there is a Department of Pharmacy and of Dental Surgery.   As in law, so in medicine, Detroit is a desirable location on account of the opportunities afforded for a practical illustration of the subjects taught.   Connected with this College are St. Mary's, Harper, and St. Luke's Hospitals, also the Free Dispensary of St. Mary's, The Children's Free Hospital, Harper Hospital Polyclinic, and the Contagious Disease Building of the latter institution.   Among other advantages afforded by these hospitals, is the fact that the ten interne and ten externe physicians employed by them are annually supplied from the graduates of Detroit College.

Officers of the Board $\left\{ \begin{array}{l} \text{President, Sidney D. Miller, Detroit.} \\ \text{Secretary, H. O. Walker, M. D., Detroit.} \end{array} \right.$

### FACULTY.

THEO. A. McGRAW. M. D., President, Professor of Principles and Practice of Surgery and Clinical Surgery.
H. O. WALKER. M. D.,Secretary.
N. W. WEBBER. M. D., Professor of Gynecology and Obstetrics.
H. O. WALKER. M. D., Professor of Rectal Surgery, Genito-Urinary Diseases and Clinical Surgery.
E. L. SHURLY. M. D., Professor of Laryngology and Clinical Medicine.
A IEL LA FERTE, M. D., Professor of Anatomy, Orthopaedic Surgery and Clinical Surgery.
J. H. CARSTENS. M. D., Professor of Obstetrics and Clinical Gynecology.
C. HENRI LEONARD, M. D., Professor of Medical and Surgical Diseases of Women and Clinical Gynecology.
EUGENE SMITH. M. D., Professor of Ophthalmology and Otology.
CHARLES DOUGLAS, M. D., Professor of Diseases of Children and Clinical Medicine.

DAVID INGLIS, M. D., Professor of Mental and Nervous Diseases.
J. E. CLARK, M. D., Professor of General Chemistry and Physics, Director of Chemical Laboratory.
ALBERT E. CARRIER, M. D., Professor of Dermatology and Clinical Medicine.
E. A. CHAPOTON, M. D., Professor of Principles and Practice of Medicine.
CHARLES G. JENNINGS, M. D., Professor of Practice of Medicine and Diseases of Children.
C. A. DEVENDORF, M. D., Professor of Obstetrics and Clinical Midwifery.
R. A. JAMIESON, M. D., Emeritus Professor of Materia Medica.
GEORGE DUFFIELD, M. D., Professor of Clinical Medicine.
F. L. NEWMAN, M. D., Professor of Materia Medica and Therapeutics.
A. W. IVES, M. D., Professor of Physiology and Clinical Assistant to Chair of Nervous Diseases.
S. G. MINER, M. D., Professor of Laryngology and Physical Diagnosis.
E. T. TAPPEY, M. D., Professor of Principles and Practice of Surgery and Clinical Surgery.
F. W. ROBBINS, M. D., Adjunct Professor of Genito-Urinary Diseases.
A. P. BIDDLE, M. D., Lecturer on Dermatology.
ANGUS McLEAN, M. D., Lecturer and Demonstrator of Anatomy.
W. P. MANTON, M. D., Professor Adjunct of Obstetrics.
A. H. STEINBRECHER, M. D., Adjunct Professor of Practice of Medicine.
W. M. DONALD, M. D., Lecturer on Practice of Medicine and Clinical Medicine.
DON M. CAMPBELL, M. D., Lecturer on Diseases of the Eye and Ear.
W. C. MARTIN, M. D., Lecturer on Histology and Assistant Demonstrator of Anatomy.
P. M. HICKEY, M. D., Lecturer on Pathology and Assistant in Physical Diagnosis and Laryngology.
C. A. LIGHTNER, M. A., Lecturer on Medical Jurisprudence.
JOHN LEE, M. D., Lecturer on Electricity and Clinical Assistant to Chair of Medicine.
C. W. HITCHCOCK, M. D., Assistant to Chair of Nervous Diseases.
GEO. E. CLARK, M. D., Instructor in Chemistry.
F. B. WALKER, M. D., Registrar, Demonstrator of Operative Surgery.
GEORGE L. FIELD, D. D. S., Professor of Clinical Operative Dentistry and Instructor in Continuous Gum Work.
F. W. CLAWSON, D. D. S., Professor of Operative Dentistry and Dental Therapeutics.
E. C. MOORE, D. D. S., Professor of Clinical Dentistry and Mechanical Technique.
G. S. SHATTUCK, M. D., D. D. S., Sec., Professor of Special Anatomy, Oral Pathology and Oral Surgery.
W. S. ANDERSON, M. D., Assistant to Chair of Laryngology.
G. L. KIEFER, M. D., Lecturer on Hygiene.
L. E. SCHELL, M. D., Assistant to Chair of Physiology.
E. G. KNILL, M. D., Lecturer on Pathology and Morbid Anatomy.
J. A. MacMILLAN, M. D., Lecturer on Materia Medica.
C. D. AARON, M. D., Lecturer on Materia Medica.
J. L. IRWIN, M. D., Instructor in Chemistry.
H. McEACHREN, M. D., Assistant Demonstrator of Anatomy.
J. N. BELL, M. D., Assistant Demonstrator of Anatomy.
A. C. LEE, M. D., Prosector of Anatomy.
DELOS L. PARKER, M. D., Lecturer on Materia Medica.
CHAS. T. McCLINTOCK, M. D., Ph. D., Lecturer on Bacteriology.
E. MARK HOUGHTON, Ph. C., M. D., Lecturer on Experimental Pharmacology.
E. H. TROY, M. D., Lecturer on Biology.
B. R. SHURLY, M. D., Lecturer on Physiology
W. A. WILSON, M. D., Lecturer on Hydrotherapeutics and Clinical Assistant in Practice of Medicine.
P. C. McEWEN, M. D., Instructor in Embryology.
R. E. MERCER, M. D., Instructor in Physical Diagnosis.
G. W. IRVINE, M. D., Instructor in Chemical Laboratory.
G. KEMPF, M. D., Instructor in Chemical Laboratory.
W. A. REPP, M. D., Assistant to Chair of Gynecology and Director of Clinic at St. Mary's Hospital.
H. R. VARNEY, M. D., Instructor in Dermatology.
J. A. ATTRIDGE, M. D., Instructor in Physical Diagnosis.
AUG. GORENFLO, M. D., Director of Harper Hospital Polyclinic and Instructor in Bacteriology.
W. G. HUTCHINSON, M. D., Children's Free Hospital, Prosector of Anatomy.
R. S. DUPONT, M. D., Prosector of Anatomy.
W. R. PARKER, M. D., Clinical Assistant in Ophthalmology.
I. L. POLOZKER, M. D., Clinical Assistant to the Chair of Diseases of Children.
J. E. EMERSON, M. D., Clinical Professor of Nervous Diseases.
J. K. GAILEY, M. D., Clinical Professor of Surgery.
H. W. LONGYEAR, M. D., Clinical Professor of Gynecology.
W. R. CHITTICK, M. D., Clinical Professor of Medicine.
R. W. GILLMAN, M. D., Clinical Professor of Ophthalmology and Otology.
G. E. FROTHINGHAM, JR., M. D., Clinical Professor of Ophthalmology and Otology.
F. W. MANN, M. D., Clinical Professor of Medicine.
CHAS. C. SHERRARD, Ph. C., B. S., Professor of Theoretical and Practical Pharmacy.
GEORGE SUTTIE, M. D., Ph. C., Professor of Botany.
FRANKLIN H. FRAZEE, Ph. C., Secretary, Professor of Materia Medica, and Instructor in Operative Pharmacy
W. G. RANKIN, Ph. C., Professor of Pharmacognosy and Microscopy.
W. H. ALLEN, Ph. G., Instructor in Applied, Quantitative, and Qualitative Chemistry.
J. W. T. KNOX, Ph. C., Assistant Professor of Organic Chemistry.

18

## DETROIT HOMEOPATHIC COLLEGE.—ESTABLISHED IN 1899.

Michigan homeopaths have located their college at Detroit on account of the facilities for clinical study afforded by that city; and its students have access to Grace Hospital, one of the finest and most completely equipped hospitals in America. The course requires four years, and senior students are given actual charge of patients. The five trustees are all physicians, and the Advisory Board comprises fourteen representative men of Michigan.

Officers of the Board { President, C. C. Miller, M. D., Detroit.
{ Secretary, S. H. Knight, M. D., Detroit.

### FACULTY.

D. A. MacLACHLAN, M. D., Dean, Professor of Ophthalmology, Otology and Laryngology.
H. P. MERA, M. D., Vice Dean, Professor of Materia Medica and Clinical Medicine.
R. C. RUDY, M. D., Registrar, Professor of Obstetrics.
E. J. KENDALL, M. D., Assistant Registrar.
CHRISTOPHER C. MILLER, M. D., Professor of Theory and Practice.
B. H. LAWSON, M. D., Professor of Theory and Practice.
OTTO LANG, M. D., Professor of Theory and Practice.
W. R. McLAREN, M. D., Professor of Diseases of the Chest.
E. J. KENDALL, M. D., Professor of the Organon and Institutes of Medicine, and of Chemistry.
H. L. OBETZ, M. D., Professor of Operative and Clinical Surgery.
STEPHEN H. KNIGHT, A. M., M. D., Professor of Principles and Practice of Surgery and Clinical Surgery.
A. E. GUE, M. D., Professor of Principles of Practice of Surgery and Clinical Surgery.
WILLIAM M. BAILEY, M. D., Professor of Gynecology.
C. G. CRUMRINE, M. D., Professor of Gynecology.
R. MILTON RICHARDS, M. D., Professor of Obstetrics.
ALFRED GRAHAM, A. M., M. D., Professor of Mental and Nervous Diseases and Electro-Theraputics.
GEORGE G. CARON, M. D., Professor of Paedology.
J. M. GRIFFIN, M. D., Professor of Dermatology.
C. G. CRUMRINE, M. D., Professor of Anatomy.
JAMES I. MURRAY, M. D., Instructor and Demonstrator of Anatomy.
JOHN VAN HEE, M. D., Instructor and Demonstrator of Anatomy.
ERNEST SPINNEY, M. D., Lecturer on Anatomy.
R. MILTON RICHARDS, M. D., Professor of Physiology.
H. MILLER-ROBERTSON, M. D., Instructor in Physiology.
EZRA WARE, Ph. D., Instructor in Chemistry and Director of the Laboratory.
E. J. KENDALL, M. D., Professor of Chemistry.
R. M. McKENNA, Ph. G., Instructor in Chemistry.
F. V. HORNE, M. D., Lecturer on Pathology, Bacteriology and Histology.
H. P. MERA, JR., M. D., Lecturer on Pathology, Bacteriology and Histology.
DOUGLAS LONG, M. D., Professor of Sanitary Science and Hygiene.
JONATHAN PALMER, JR., LL. B., Professor of Medical Jurisprudence.
J. M. THOMPSON, D. D. S., Lecturer on Dental Surgery.

### NON-RESIDENT LECTURERS.

O. E. PRATT, M. D., Ypsilanti, Mich.
A. B. ARMSBARY, M. D., Marine City, Mich.
A. W. SAXTON, M. D., Jackson, Mich.
D. J. SINCLAIR, M. D., Woodstock, Ont.
G. HENDERSON, M. D., Strathrcy, Ont.

## GRAND RAPIDS MEDICAL COLLEGE.—ESTABLISHED IN 1897.

This College offers a course consisting of three eight-month terms, with an optional fourth year, and the instruction is by means of recitations, didactic and clinical lectures, and practical work in the laboratory and dissecting room. This city with its 900 manufacturing establishments and five hospitals, affords many facilities for clinical teaching. The College is located on East St., and has a Veterinary Department on Cor. Butterworth Ave. and Indiana Street.

Officers of the Board { President, Clarence H. White, M. D., Grand Rapids.
Secretary, H. E. Locher, M. D., Grand Rapids.

### COLLEGE FACULTY.

JOHN E. BRADY, M. D., Emeritus Professor of Physical Diagnosis and Diseases of the Chest.

E. G. EDWARDS, M. D., C. M., L. C., P. & S., L. C., Dean, Professor of Physical Diagnosis and Clinical Medicine.

CLARENCE H. WHITE, M. D., Professor of the Principles and Practice of Medicine and Clinical Medicine.

WILLIAM FULLER, M. D., C. M., Professor of Surgery and Clinical Surgery.

LEONIDAS E. BEST, M. D., Treasurer, Professor of Fractures and Dislocations and Clinical Surgery.

JOHN W. RIECKE, M. D., Professor of Mental and Nervous Diseases and Clinical Medicine.

F. DUNBAR ROBERTSON, B. A., M. D., C. M., L. R. C. P. Edinburgh, L. R. C. S. Edinburgh, L. F. P. & S. Glasgow, Professor and Clinical Professor of the Principles and Practice of Ophthalmology, Otology and Laryngology.

JOHN L. BURKHART, M. D., Professor of Materia Medica and Therapeutics.

J. S. EDWARDS, M. D., C. M., M. C., P. and S. Ontario, Professor of Diseases of Children.

EARL BIGHAM, M. D., Professor of the Principles and Practice of Obstetrics and Clinical Obstetrics.

LOUIS A. CHAMBERLIN, M. D., Professor of Hygiene, Sanitary Science and Preventative Medicine.

THOMAS C. IRWIN, M. D., M. C. P. & S. Ontario, Professor of Physiology and Clinical Medicine.

FRANK J. LEE, M. D., C. M., Professor of Descriptive and Applied Anatomy.

J. A. McPHERSON, M. D., Professor of Principles and Practice of Gynaecology and Clinical Gynaecology.

GEO. L. McBRIDE, M. D., Professor of Surgical Pathology.

A. BLYTH THOMPSON, M. D., L. R. C. S. Edinburgh, L. R. C. P. Edinburgh, L. F. P. & S. Glasgow, Professor of General Pathology.

C. B. HERNAM, M. D., Professor of Bacteriology and Microscopy.

G. PARKER DILLON, M. D., Professor of Dermatology, Genito-Urinary Diseases and Osteology.

H. E. LOCHER, M. D., Professor of General and Medical Chemistry and Urinary Analysis.

C. M. KELLY, M. D., Professor of the Principles of Surgery and Clinical Surgery.

ELTON P. BILLINGS, A. B., Lecturer on Chemistry.

O. C. FLANEGAN, B. A., LL. D., Lecturer on Medical Jurisprudence.

### VETERINARY DEPARTMENT.

JOSEPH B. GRISWOLD, M. D., Professor of Surgical Pathology.

JOSEPH B. WHINERY, Ph. C., M. D., Professor of Bacteriology, Histology and Microscopy.

R. R. SMITH, M. D., Professor of Didactic and Clinical Surgery.

M. T. BANASAWITZ, M. D., D. V. S., Professor of Materia Medica and Therapeutics.

LEONARD L. CONKEY, D. V. S., M. F. Dean, Professor of the Principles and Practice of Veterinary Surgery, Surgical Anatomy, Obstetrics and Horse-shoeing.

WILLIAM ROSE, V. S., Professor of Anatomy and Clinical Equine Surgery.

D. P. YONKERMAN, V. S. Kalamazoo, Professor of Hygiene, Breeding and Management of Domestic Animals.

COLEMAN NOCKOLDS, V. S., M. D., Professor of the Principles and Practice of Veterinary Medicine and Lecturer on Anatomy, Materia Medica and Therapeutics.

E. W. WELLS, V. S., Professor of Comparative Physiology.

HUGH E. WILSON, LL. B., Lecturer on Veterinary Jurisprudence.

GEORGE HARE, D. V. S., Allegan, Demonstrator of Anatomy.

ALVA SHERWOOD, B. S., D. V. S., Three Oaks, Professor of Obstetrics and Assistant to the Chair of Surgery.

A. W. OLDS, Ph. C., Lecturer on Chemistry and Urinalysis.

### SAGINAW VALLEY MEDICAL COLLEGE.—ESTABLISHED IN 1895.

In response to a widely expressed desire for a Medical College at Saginaw, a number of progressive business men organized and established one, erecting a $40,000 building. Three hospitals—Saginaw, the Woman's and St. Mary's—furnish practical advantages to the students, and the magnificent Hoyt Library is of no little value to them. The Saginaw Free Dispensary is entirely under control of the College. The course of instruction is by means of quizzes, lectures, clinics, and practical work in the dissecting room, laboratory, and hospitals.

Officers of the Board { President. Harry T. Wickes, Grand Rapids.
{ Secretary, Wm. Heim, Ph. C., Grand Rapids.

### FACULTY.

L. W. BLISS, M. D., President of Faculty, Professor of Gynœcology.
B. B. ROWE, M. D., Vice President, Professor of Principles and Practice of Surgery and Clinical Surgery.
D. B. CORNELL, M. D., Secretary of Faculty, Professor of Diseases of the Eye, Ear, Nose and Throat.
EUGENE W. DAVIS, M. D., Professor of Surgery and Clinical Surgery.
F. W. EDELMANN, M. D., Professor of Diseases of Children, Materia Medica and Therapeutics.
SYLVESTER C. J. OSTROM. M. D., Professor of Mental and Nervous Diseases.
ROBERT McGREGOR, M. D., Professor of Electro-Therapeutics and Associate Professor of Mental and Nervous Diseases.
M. J. PURCELL, Attorney-at-Law, Professor of Medical Jurisprudence.
G. W. STEWART, M. D., Professor of Obstetrics.
O. P. BARBER, M. D., Professor of Principles and Practice of Surgery and Clinical Surgery.
R. W. ERWIN, M. D., Professor of the Principles and Practice of Medicine and Clinical Medicine.
M. C. L. KITCHEN, M. D., Professor of the Principles and Practice of Medicine and Clinical Medicine.
J. N. KEMP, M. D., Professor of Minor Surgery.
A. GRIGG. M. D., Professor of the Principles and Practice of Medicine.
HARRIET V. B. BROOKS, M. D., Professor of Bacteriology, Histology and Pathology.
C. W. TAYLOR GOODMAN, M. D., Professor of Sanitary Science and Preventive Medicine; and Adjunct to Chair of Gynœcology.
WILLIAM HEIM, Ph. C., Professor of Chemistry and Urinary Analysis.
W. B. CUBBAGE, M. D., Professor of Principles and Practice of Medicine.
J. W. BLISS, B. S., M. D., Professor and Demonstrator of Anatomy.
R. CAMPBELL MACGREGOR, M. A., M. D., C. M., Professor of Physiology.
ELMORE E. CURTIS, M. D., Professor of Diseases of Children, Materia Medica and Therapeutics.
J. M. CAMPBELL. M. D., Professor of Medical Jurisprudence.
HENRY J. MEYER, M. D., Professor of Anatomy.
H. C. WATKINS, M. D., Professor of Physical Diagnosis, and Clinical Medicine.
W. L. DICKINSON, M. D., Professor of Rectal Diseases.
J. W. McMEEKIN, M. D., Professor of Clinical Surgery, and Surgical Pathology.

### SPRAGUE CORRESPONDENCE SCHOOL OF LAW.—ESTABLISHED IN 1889.

This school, established by William C. Sprague, is by several years the oldest one of its kind in the country. It is in no sense a competitor of the University Law Schools, its sole purpose being to provide instruction for those who cannot afford the time or money to attend regular schools. The character of its instruction differs only in such particulars as are made necessary by the inability of the instructor to meet the student in person. The entire curriculum has been remodeled five times, and is now deemed permanent, offering three courses; Preparatory, Business Law, and College, besides special courses on different branches of the law. The school occupies twelve finely equipped rooms in the Majestic Building at Detroit. Twelve assistants are employed by the following.

### BOARD OF CONTROL.

WILLIAM C. SPRAGUE, Detroit. President.
JUNIUS E. BEAL. A. B., Ann Arbor. Vice President.
GRIFFITH OGDEN ELLIS, LL. B., Vice Principal.
EMIL WILLIAM SYNDER, LL. B., Chief Examiner.
J. COTNER, JR., Financial Manager.

### SCHOOLS WITH NORMAL AND BUSINESS COURSES.

### BAY CITY BUSINESS COLLEGE.—ESTABLISHED IN 1890.

This college was first established at Bay City as the "International Business College." by Messrs. Lane & Bowles, and conducted for seven years with Mr. Lane as Principal. In 1897 it absorbed two other schools —the J. G. Lamson Private School and Devlin's Business College—and was incorporated as the "Bay City Business College." Its motto is "Learn to do by doing;" and students are taught by carrying on business operations, such as buying, selling, meeting liabilities, etc. The instructors are R. R. Lane, F. W. Bowles, Mrs. C. E. McCausland.

### BENTON HARBOR COLLEGE.—ESTABLISHED IN 1886.

This institution, which was at first conducted by Prof. Edgcumbe as a Collegiate Institute, was incorporated in 1892 under a board of seven trustees. Its aim is to prepare for both a business life and a collegiate course. The curriculum includes Collegiate, Academic, Preparatory, Teacher's Training, Business, Kindergarten, Elocution, Art, and Musical Departments. Physical culture receives much attention, both the Swedish and Delsarte systems being taught. Military drill is also a prominent feature, the cadets being uniformed after the West Point pattern and armed with Springfield rifles.

#### FACULTY.

G. J. EDGCUMBE, A. M., Ph. D., Principal Pedagogy and Science.
MRS. V. C. EDGCUMBE, Lady Principal, Kindergartner.
J. H. NIZ, French and German.
MISS ALICE M. DONNELLY, Latin and Greek.
MISS MARTHA BARBOUR, School of Elocution and Physical Culture.
MISS CARRIE BILLINGHURST, English and Mathematics.
W. B. PARKER, Principal Business Department.
MISS LILLIAN HITTELL, Musical Director, Piano and Organ.
MISS SADIE HESS, Art.
LIEUT. H. POUND, Military Drill.
MISS MILLIE EARLE, Assistant in Preparatory.
WM. WOODLEY, Assistant in Mathematics and English.
MILLARD SEITZ, English.
JAMES ADAMS, Librarian.

#### CLEARY BUSINESS COLLEGE.—ESTABLISHED IN 1883.

A beautiful and finely equipped building in the heart of Ypsilanti, Washtenaw county, is devoted to the work of this College, and it contains three large business rooms, representing as many cities, each having offices for wholesaling, jobbing, banking, etc., so that the most business like methods are employed for giving students a practical education. The courses are two, business and shorthand. The school was incorporated in 1891, with a board of five directors of which P. Roger Cleary is president.

#### *FACULTY.

P. ROGER CLEARY, President, Business Practice, Correspondence, Commercial Law, Penmanship.
H. B. SMELLIE, Bookkeeping, Penmanship, Mathematics.
FRED R. SALWAY, Bookkeeping.
M. E. BENEDICT, English Grammar and Spelling.
ELIZABETH HATTON, Shorthand, Dictation.
MARGARET E. BENEDICT, Shorthand, Dictation, Office Practice, Typewriting.
FRANCES B. HILL, Clerk.

#### FENTON NORMAL AND COMMERCIAL COLLEGE.—ESTABLISHED IN 1883.

The courses of this school are very flexible, its avowed aim being the development of the pupil, whatever his degree of advancement. It is divided into Normal and Business Departments. The school was first incorporated in 1883 as the "Fenton Normal School," but was reorganized in 1898 by its present principal, at which time the Commercial Course was added.

---

*Assistant teachers are employed as requered.

### FACULTY.

W. A. STEVENSON, A. M., Ph. D., Principal, Pedagogy and Common Branches.
MRS. W. A. STEVENSON, B. L., Algebra, Orthography.
F. A. CHAPIN, B. A., History, Latin.
GEORGIANA BILBY, Latin, Arithmetic.
T. M. SHERMAN, B. S., Sciences, Higher Mathematics.
H. L. HOLMES, Business Branches.
NORA SHIPLEY, B. L., Greek, German and Literature.
D. S. FRACKELTON, LL. B., Commercial Law.
JENNIE TOWNSEND, Stenography.
W. H. KING, Telegraphy.
CARRIE RAMSDELL, Music.

### FERRIS INDUSTRIAL SCHOOL.—ESTABLISHED IN 1884.

This school is a monument to the pluck and perseverance of its organizer, after whom it is named. In 1893, after nearly a decade of untiring labor, its fine new building was erected; and the following year the school was incorporated. It is called "The People's College" and according to the catalog its mission is "to make the world better." Its courses are now arranged under the following heads: College Preparatory, Normal, Kindergarten, Elocution, Common English, Pharmacy, Commercial, Shorthand, Civil Service, Telegraphy, Typewriting. It is located at Big Rapids, a city of about 5,000 inhabitants in Mecosta county.

### FACULTY.

W. N. FERRIS, Methods, Rhetoric, Literature, Teachers' Arithmetic.
W. D. HENDERSON, Science.
C. A. WESSEL, Bookkeeping, Business Arithmetic, Commercial Law, Penmanship.
CHARLES CARLISLE, Elocution, Physical Culture, Vocal Music, Orthography.
W. R. SMITH, Shorthand, Typewriting, Telegraphy.
H. H. BARROWS, History, Geography, Geology, Drawing.
B. S. TRAVIS, Civics, Grammar, Spelling.
ROSE ANDERSON, Greek, Latin, Algebra.
GERRIT MASSELINK, Geometry, Trigonometry, German.
MRS. MARY BREEN, French.
S. B. NORCROSS, Arithmetic, Correspondence, Penmanship.
GERTRUDE TREIBER, Kindergarten.

### GRAND RAPIDS BUSINESS UNIVERSITY.—ESTABLISHED IN 1866..

This is one of the few pioneer schools still existing. Established over thirty years ago by Prof. C. G. Swensburg as the "Grand Rapids Business College," in 1897 it was incorporated and the word College changed to University. It came under its present control ten years ago, A. S. Parish being its president and manager. The science of accounts receives especial attention, and the work of the school is all directed along lines in harmony with that of business offices. The location in the Norris building in Grand Rapids city is an admirable one, being in the heart of commercial activity.

### INTERNATIONAL BUSINESS COLLEGE.

This school, established some fourteen or fifteen years ago, was incorporated under its present management in 1896. It occupies commodious and finely equipped quarters in the building originally erected for the general offices of the F. & P. M. railroad, in Saginaw city. The courses are all modeled after some business institution; and banking, railroading, and other lines of business are conducted as in actual life. The institution is under the management of Fred H. Harper, who is president of the Board of Directors and also of the Faculty.

### LANSING BUSINESS UNIVERSITY.—ESTABLISHED IN 1897.

This institution located in the Capital City, offers the usual Commercial and Shorthand Courses. H. J. Beck is President and Treasurer, and the instructors are C. L. Beck, P. A. Johnson, H. J. Beck, with such other assistants as are necessary.

### LUDINGTON BUSINESS COLLEGE.—ETABLISHED IN 1895.

This is another of those institutions designed to furnish a practical business education. It was incorporated in 1898 by Messrs. Martindill & Rose, and is located at Ludington, Manistee county. Its courses are known as Commercial, English, and Amanuensis.

### THE MICHIGAN BUSINESS AND NORMAL COLLEGE.—ESTABLISHED IN 1882.

This school claims to be "one of attainment, not of time." It occupies one entire floor of the fine Tacoma Block in Battle Creek, and is equipped with banking department, shipping offices, wholesale department, commission house, etc. The "Cabinet Method of Actual Business Training" is employed, and its students are busily engaged with face to face transactions of the business world. It was incorporated in 1896, and reorganized in 1896. C. J. Argurbright is president and manager; D. Sillers secretary and treasurer.

### THREE RIVERS BUSINESS ACADEMY AND NORMAL SCHOOL.—ESTABLISHED IN 1883.

This school, as its name implies, furnishes both a Business and Normal Course. It was incorporated in 1899 by Chas. H. Sage, its present principal. It is located at Three Rivers, a city of about 4,000, at the junction of the St. Joe, Rocky, and Portage Rivers in St. Joseph county.

# ABSTRACT OF REPORTS

FROM

# COUNTY COMMISSIONERS OF SCHOOLS

## FOR THE YEAR 1898-99

19

# REPORTS OF COUNTY COMMISSIONERS OF SCHOOLS.

---

Owing to lack of space, these reports do not appear in full; but from them we have gleaned the salient features, so as to present a birds-eye view of the entire field.

## TEACHERS' MEETINGS.

Most of the counties report regular meetings of the county association, while some maintain both township and county organizations. Various plans are pursued. Van Buren county tells of sixteen local meetings, with an aggregate enrollment of 560. Jackson county reports two large teachers' associations, eight teachers and patrons' meetings, and two officers' meetings attended by all three officers and the teacher of each district in the county. Commr. Harlow says these latter meetings are a potent factor for good. Bay county has been trying a combination of teachers' association and institute of one day's duration four times during the year, with part of the program taken by state instructors, the rest by "home talent." Commr. Smith says he thinks this plan worthy of continuance, but that there should also be a summer institute of not less than two weeks, in which academic and professional instruction should be happily united.

## INSTITUTES.

The long term institute with academic instruction, seems to be very generally favored. Especially has it proven valuable in the northern counties and parts of the State remote from Normal schools. At the last institute in Alger county, all but two of the teachers were on hand; and both Schoolcraft and Iron counties speak enthusiastically of the good thus accomplished. In the latter county 97 per cent of the teachers had little or no experience. The commissioners as a whole seem to agree with the following from Commr. Tuttle of Gratiot county:

"The plan of holding long-term institutes is a marked improvement over the old plan. Our institute last summer was the best of the many excellent ones it has been our good fortune to have. The academic training was just what the teachers most needed and desired. The good results of the work done in the institute, have been seen during the y in the better work done and the more enthusiastic, progressive, and fessional spirit manifested by those who were in attendance. T term is all right."

## READING CIRCLE.

Quite a goodly number of counties are carrying on the work of the State Reading Circle; in some counties it is correlated with the work of the county association. The plan in Eaton county is outlined by Commr. Wagner as follows:

"Beginning on the first Saturday in September, the teachers with the county commissioner held each Saturday thereafter a meeting in which the Teachers' Reading Circle work of the State was taken up, after which general topics were brought out and considered; teachers who attended these meetings declare them to be very helpful and among the most profitable of the meetings held in the county. They are desirous of continuing them."

In Calhoun county, where there is an unusually large membership, the following plan has been successfully followed:

The county was organized into fifteen circles with a conductor appointed for each. Five meetings were held in each circle, and the Reading Circle books were carefully reviewed; a short general program usually followed. Besides the Reading Circle certificates issued to those completing this year's work, a large number of diplomas were given to teachers who had completed the three years' course.

Perhaps the largest membership in proportion to the number of teachers is found in Gladwin county, where thirty of the thirty-five teachers are pursuing the course. In Hillsdale county 166 are faithfully doing the work, and 100 in Kalamazoo county. Newaygo county has a membership of 60, with six local circles; and Iosco county has three reading circle centers, with a good percentage of teachers interested. Presque Isle and Tuscola counties also emphasize work along this line, and quite a large number of commissioners count this work a valuable factor in the general education of their teachers.

## PROGRESS OF TEACHERS.

Almost every county reports the teachers better prepared for their work and manifesting a good professional spirit. We quote a few typical remarks:

Commr. Chew of Charlevoix county:

"Improvement in teaching methods of the past few years, is very noticeable. A number of teachers have attended training schools."

Commr. Swanson of Lake county:

"Our teachers have progressed more in the last two years than the majority did in six years before."

Commr. Borden of Gladwin county:

"Nearly every teacher takes up some new study during the year, either by correspondence or by Saturday class."

Commr. Bath of Houghton county:

"Better preparation for the work and an increasing desire for higher attainments in their field of labor, are manifested by a large majority of those teaching in our schools."

Commr. Warner of Midland county:

"Our teachers are anxious to improve, and many secure second grade certificates as soon as possible after teaching the required number of months."

Commr. Stillson of Newaygo county:

"Better instruction is demanded, and many teachers attend the Ferris School in summer. Better wages are paid and longer contracts are the rule."

Commr. Snowdon of Oakland county:

"We have found the teachers much better prepared for examination and manifesting more of a professional spirit. The year's work has been marked by improvement in all lines of work."

Commr. Spencer of Huron county:

"We have nearly as many teachers holding second grade certificates as third. They are making noble efforts to keep abreast of the times."

Commr. Campbell of Iosco county:

"Our teachers are progressive and turn out almost to a unit at all educational gatherings."

Commr. Payne of Roscommon county:

"The teachers of this county are progressive, and those who are able attend the Ferris Institute, while others are taking correspondence courses."

Commr. Crawford of Macomb county:

"We have more second grade teachers than third grade, and there are thirty-four state, college, and first grade certificates held in the county. Nearly a hundred teachers attended the long-term institute held at Richmond, and other teachers were in summer schools at Chicago University, Normal College, and the Big Rapids Industrial School. A few teachers take the correspondence course from the Fenton Normal, while nearly all are readers of one or more educational journals."

Commr. Thompson of Osceola county:

"Many of our young teachers entered the Normal at Ypsilanti or Mt. Pleasant during the past year, and more will go this coming year."

Commr. Davis of Tuscola county:

"Many of our teachers make a careful study of all the publications sent out by the Department of Public Instruction and of the Reading Circle books. Others are taking work in correspondence courses."

Commr. Cooke of Wayne county submits some encouraging figures to show the progress in his county. Number of applicants that received *third* grade certificates:

Last year ..................................... 103
This year ..................................... 70

Number of applicants receiving certificates who had no experience teaching:

Last year ..................................... 32
This year ..................................... 16

Number receiving certificates who had Normal school instruction:

Last year .................................... 25

This year .................................... 28

Number teachers holding State Normal certificates:

Last year .................................... 48

This year .................................... 55

Commr. Willitts of Calhoun county seems to sum up the matter as follows:

"A strong desire for higher qualifications and more thorough preparation for the profession of teaching, is manifested by our teachers throughout the county. Among the encouraging signs of professional zeal and a progressive spirit, may be noted the number of those who are pursuing a course of study in training school or college after teaching a few terms; the increasing number of teachers whose work is of such excellent quality that their services are retained term after term in the same school; the large percentage of second and first grade certificates held by our teachers; and the extent to which educational periodicals are taken and utilized in the school room."

The good effects of the Mt. Pleasant Normal are very evident in that portion of the state, and Isabella county reports that nearly 75 per cent of the teachers have had professional training. The encouraging condition of affairs shown by the preceding reports, is by most commissioners largely ascribed to the operation of the law regarding third grade certificates. On this point we quote Commr. Smith of Bay county, who says:

"Further experience with the law limiting the number of third grade certificates to three, impresses me with its wisdom. It may be true that some very good teachers have been forced to seek other occupations because their means would not permit them to avail themselves of the instruction required to enable them to obtain a second grade certificate, but this number is comparatively few, while the elevating influence upon the remainder is unquestioned. The efficiency of the teaching force has steadily advanced; and while the necessity of licensing a sufficient number of teachers to fill the schools has forced the board of examiners to grant licenses which it might not otherwise have done, yet some of these teachers have caught the spirit of progress and have made a creditable record."

### CO-OPERATION OF PATRONS.

An equally encouraging sign of the times is the hearty co-operation of patrons and teachers so frequently mentioned in these reports, numerous counties sending a statement similar to the following from Berrien county:

"Many of our districts this year voted for longer terms of school and higher wages for teachers. This indicates an improved school sentiment. We can report less trouble and friction between parents and teachers than in any previous year."

In some cases this co-operation has been secured through the medium of "Parent's Meetings," in others by special day exercises; but in one way or another, teachers are getting more in touch with their patrons than ever before.

## SPECIAL DAY OBSERVANCE.

The reports would seem to indicate an increasing interest in these exercises. Arbor Day and Memorial Day are especially emphasized, and the former is utilized in getting the "District Fathers" to assist in beautifying the grounds,—a work in which the pupils take great interest.

Commr. Aldrich writes from Clare county: "It would do your heart good to see how our boys and girls take hold of this work." And Tuscola county alone reports 746 trees planted on Arbor Day.

In this connection we note many appreciative words like the following from Commr. Winston of Clinton county:

"The publication of Suggestive Programs for special days by the Department of Public Instruction, has been an inspiration in that it has given our teachers great aid in providing suitable programs for these days."

In some districts Mother's Day and Library Day are added to the list, the latter being specially devoted to awakening an interest in good literature and the increase of libraries. A small admittance is usually charged, the proceeds going to the purchase of new books.

## INCREASE OF LIBRARIES.

There has been a very gratifying increase in this direction, as may be seen from such reports as the following:

In Branch county there are two new libraries and new books added to the majority of old ones, besides a Student's Cyclopedia in every district. Eaton county reports more districts putting in new libraries, and adds the suggestive comment, "The best teachers are found where are the best libraries." Gladwin county boasts of nine new $10 libraries, Isabella county eight new ones, and Hillsdale reports a large increase, with 102 libraries now in that county. In Midland county about one-third the districts have enlarged their libraries during the year, and added several new ones, nearly all the money being raised by entertainments.

Ingham county has libraries in nearly all the schools, with the number of books increasing yearly; St. Joseph county has four-fifths of its schools provided with a library; and in Otsego county libraries have been established, Pioneer collections secured, and a respectable reading table established in an encouraging number of schools. Indeed, the reading table is coming to be an indispensable adjunct of every up-to-date school.

Many other counties tell a story similar to the above, but Berrien county is perhaps the banner one in this respect, as there is a library in every school and all receive additions each year, in some instances even going beyond the hundred mark in this regard. There are about twenty-five districts that appropriate a ten dollar library fund each year.

## STATE MANUAL AND COURSE OF STUDY.

The warm words of commendation regarding this little book and the good resulting from its use, are especially gratifying to the department. On this point we again quote:—

Commr. Straight of Montcalm county:

"The Manual is on all teachers' desks in the county. The teachers follow it closely. I feel it is doing splendid work in our school."

Commr. Renkes of Barry county:

"The large majority of our teachers have used the State Manual and Course of Study as a guide. As a result of its use, this year's work has been more systematic and thorough, pupils better graded and more punctual and regular in attendance."

Commr. Cone of Cass county:

"The value of the State Manual and Course of Study is becoming more and more apparent."

Commr. Smith of Bay county:

"The publication of the State Manual and Course of Study has done much to unify, classify, and simplify the work in the rural schools. Although the actual grading is not close in all the school, yet it is a distinct advantage to have the plan for grading in the hands of every teacher, and the plan furnished by the State department has in all cases been followed to a greater or less extent."

Commr. Tuttle of Gratiot county:

"The course of study has been carefully studied and used by the teachers. It has enabled them to greatly systematize their work. I consider it one of the best and most helpful books that can be put into the hands of a teacher. I have invariably found that the more familiar a teacher is with this invaluable book, the better work she is capable of doing."

Commr. Spencer of Huron county:

"On all questions of school practice the State Manual and Course of Study is taken as authority. It is the rule and guide of all our actions. No teacher cares, much less dares, to deviate from it. It has done more for the rural school than any other one thing in all its history."

Commr. Clarke of St. Joseph county:

"The random work of the past is being done away with through use of the Manual, which is leading to more thorough work and more symmetrical intellectual development."

### GENERAL.

A review of the whole field impresses one with the improved conditions everywhere. The number of new school houses and the many reseated and repaired; the new apparatus; the increasing number of teachers hired by the year,—all these tell a tale of growing interest in school matters, and, in the words of one commissioner, "show a sentiment that will not tolerate poor schools."

# STATISTICAL TABLES.

# STATISTICAL TABLES.

## TABLE I.

*Comparative summary of statistics for the years 1898 and 1899.*

| Items. | 1898. | 1899 | Increase. | Decrease. |
|---|---|---|---|---|
| *Districts and schools.* | | | | |
| Number of townships and independent districts reporting................................ | 1,284 | 1,280 | ............ | 4 |
| Number of graded school districts................ | 672 | 692 | 20 | ............ |
| Number of ungraded school districts........... | 6,485 | 6,469 | ............ | 16 |
| Total....................................... | 7,157 | 7,161 | 4 | ............ |
| Number of township unit districts.............. | 111 | 115 | 4 | ............ |
| School census of graded school districts....... | 402,715 | 416,169 | 13,454 | ............ |
| School census of ungraded school districts .... | 301,015 | 297,521 | ............ | 3,494 |
| Total....................................... | 703,730 | 713,690 | 9,960 | ............ |
| Enrollment in graded schools................... | 287,274 | 293,942 | 6,668 | ............ |
| Enrollment in ungraded schools................. | 208,751 | 204,723 | ............ | 4,028 |
| Total....................................... | 496,025 | 498,665 | 2,640 | ............ |
| Percentage of attendance in graded schools.... | 71.3 | 70.6 | ............ | .7 |
| Percentage of attendance in ungraded schools.. | 69.3 | 68.8 | ............ | .5 |
| Percentage for the State.................... | 70.5 | 69.9 | ............ | .6 |
| Number of districts reporting having maintained school............................... | 7,083 | 7,091 | 8 | ............ |
| Average duration in months in graded schools | 9.24 | 9.26 | .02 | ............ |
| Average duration in months in ungraded schools | 8.01 | 8.05 | .04 | ............ |
| Average for the State....................... | 8.12 | 8.17 | .05 | ............ |

## TABLE I.—*Continued.*

| Items. | 1898. | 1899. | Increase. | Decrease. |
|---|---|---|---|---|
| Number of districts furnishing free text-books. | 741 | 685 | ............ | 56 |
| Number of private and select schools reported.. | 403 | 397 | ......... .... | 6 |
| Number of men teachers in such schools........ | 406 | 395 | ............ | 11 |
| Number of women teachers in such schools..... | 737 | 802 | 65 | ............ |
| Estimated number of pupils attending such schools ................................... | 45,465 | 45,568 | 103 | ............ |
| *Teachers and their employments.* | | | | |
| Number of teachers necessary to supply graded schools................... | 6,255 | 6,530 | 275 | |
| Number of teachers necessary to supply ungraded schools................... | 6,485 | 6,469 | ............ | 16 |
| Total...................... .......... | 12,740 | 12,999 | 259 | |
| Number of men teachers employed in graded schools........................ | 988 | 1,051 | 63 | |
| Number of men teachers employed in ungraded schools........................ ............. | 2,637 | 2,420 | ............ | 217 |
| Total....................... | 3,625 | 3,471 | ............ | 154 |
| Number of women teachers employed in graded schools................... | 5,430 | 5,631 | 201 | ... ....... |
| Number of women teachers employed in ungraded schools................... | 6,618 | 6,462 | ............ | 156 |
| Total........................ | 12,048 | 12,093 | 45 | ............ |
| Whole number of teachers employed in graded schools....... | 6,418 | 6,682 | 264 | |
| Whole number of teachers employed in ungraded schools....................... | 9,255 | 8,882 | ............ | 373 |
| Total. ..................... | 15,673 | 15,564 | 109 | ............ |
| Average number of months taught by men in graded schools................... | 9.10 | 9.02 | ............ | .08 |
| Average number of months taught by men in ungraded schools ......... ..... | 6.06 | 6.33 | .27 | ............ |
| General average . ................... | 6.89 | 7.14 | .25 | ............ |
| Average number of months taught by women in graded schools ..... | 9.44 | 9.46 | .02 | ... ....... |
| Average number of months taught by women in ungraded schools ..... ...... . | 5.41 | 5.82 | .41 | ........... |
| General average............................. | 7.22 | 7.52 | .30 | |
| Total wages of men teachers in graded schools | $625,326 44 | $665,527 28 | $40,200 84 | ............ |
| Total wages of men teachers in ungraded schools. ..... ..... | 450,432 82 | 437,559 17 | ............ | $12,873 65 |
| Total ...... ........ ....... ..... | $1,075,759 26 | $1,103,086 45 | $27,327 19 | ............ |

## TABLE I.—*Continued.*

| Items. | 1898. | 1899. | Increase. | Decrease. |
|---|---|---|---|---|
| Total wages of women teachers in graded schools.................................... | $2,201.008 87 | $2,301,472 91 | $100,464 04 | .......... |
| Total wages of women teachers in ungraded schools........................................ | 869,681 45 | 911,476 75 | 41,795 30 | .......... |
| Total....................... ...... | $3,070,690 32 | $3,212,949 66 | $142,259 34 | .......... |
| Aggregate wages of all teachers in graded schools..................................... | $2,826,335 31 | $2,967,000 19 | $140,664 88 | .......... |
| Aggregate wages of all teachers in ungraded schools ...................................... | 1,320,114 27 | 1,349,035 92 | 28,921 65 | .......... |
| Total........................................ | $4,146,449 58 | $4,316,036 11 | $169,586 53 | .......... |
| Average monthly wages of men teachers in graded schools................................ | $69 56 | $70 17 | $0 61 | .......... |
| Average monthly wages of men teachers in ungraded schools................................ | 28 15 | 28 57 | 0 42 | .......... |
| Average monthly wages of men teachers in all schools............................... | $43 05 | $44 48 | $1 43 | .......... |
| Average monthly wages of women teachers in graded schools............................... | $42 96 | $43 20 | $0 24 | .......... |
| Average monthly wages of women teachers in ungraded schools........................... | 24 29 | 24 23 | .......... | $0 06 |
| Average monthly wages of women teachers in all schools........................... | $35 28 | $35 35 | $0 07 | .......... |
| *Examination and certification of teachers.* | | | | |
| Number of public examinations held............ | 321 | 320 | ............ | 1 |
| Number of applicants for regular certificates... | 15,646 | 14,233 | ............ | 1,413 |
| Number of first grade certificates granted..... | 133 | 158 | 25 | .......... |
| Number of second grade certificates granted.. | 2,073 | 2,075 | 2 | .......... |
| Number of third grade certificates granted.... | 5,507 | 5,185 | ............ | 322 |
| Whole number regular certificates granted.. | 7,713 | 7,418 | ............ | 295 |
| Number of applicants for special certificates.. | 1,276 | 1,006 | ............ | 270 |
| Number of special certificates granted......... | 803 | 624 | ............ | 179 |
| Number of teachers who held State or Normal school certificates ...................... | 692 | 945 | 253 | .......... |
| Whole number of legally qualified teachers.... | 11,720 | 11,988 | 268 | .......... |
| Number licensed without previous experience in teaching............................... | 1,146 | 2,132 | 986 | .......... |
| Number of applicants who had attended State Normal school............................. | 665 | 604 | ............ | 61 |
| Number of applicants who had attended institutes during the year...................... | 4,311 | 4,249 | ............ | 62 |
| Number making teaching a permanent profession................................... | 6,678 | 6,803 | 125 | .......... |

## TABLE I.—*Continued.*

| Items. | 1898. | 1899. | Increase. | Decrease. |
|---|---|---|---|---|
| *School property.* | | | | |
| Number of frame school houses................ | 6,059 | 6,121 | 62 | ............ |
| Number of brick school houses................. | 1,471 | 1,510 | 39 | ............ |
| Number of stone school houses................. | 74 | 71 | ............ | 3 |
| Number of log school houses ................... | 281 | 271 | ............ | 10 |
| Total......................................... | 7,885 | 7,973 | 88 | ............ |
| Whole number of sittings in school houses..... | 614,043 | 621,319 | 7,276 | ............ |
| Estimated value of property in graded school districts....................................... | $13,946,524 00 | $14,486,124 00 | $539,600 00 | ............ |
| Estimated value of property in ungraded school districts ............................. | 4,192,065 00 | 5,260,319 00 | 1,068,254 00 | ............ |
| Total......................................... | $18,138,589 00 | $19,746,443 00 | $1,607,854 00 | ............ |
| Number of districts reporting dictionaries in schools...... | 6,409 | 6,617 | 208 | ............ |
| Number of districts reporting globes in schools.. | 5,495 | 5,698 | 203 | ............ |
| Number of districts reporting maps in schools... | 6,191 | 6,378 | 187 | ............ |
| Total number of U. S. flags in school districts... | 6,318 | 6,451 | 133 | ............ |
| *Financial.* | | | | |
| Amount of one-mill tax received............... | $650,973 68 | $641,897 65 | ............ | $9,076 03 |
| Amount of primary school interest fund received...................................... | 950,080 79 | 1,020,283 12 | $70,202 33 | ............ |
| Amount received from non-resident tuition.... | 86,538 63 | 86,949 47 | 410 84 | ............ |
| Amount received from district taxes........... | 4,524,995 08 | 4,549,062 36 | 24,067 28 | ............ |
| Amount received from all other sources........ | 331,884 75 | 362,607 46 | 30,722 71 | ............ |
| Total net receipts........................... | $6,544,472 93 | $6,660,800 06 | $116,327 13 | ............ |
| Amount received from loans.................. | 404,276 61 | 519,243 11 | 114,966 50 | ............ |
| Balance on hand from preceding year.......... | 918,897 41 | 1,176,578 06 | 257,680 65 | ............ |
| Total resources, including amount on hand from preceding year...................... | $7,867,646 95 | $8,356,621 23 | $488,974 28 | ............ |
| Amount paid men teachers...................... | $1,075,621 56 | $1,102,778 47 | $27,156 91 | ............ |
| Amount paid women teachers.................. | 3,077,257 04 | 3,209,466 75 | 132,209 71 | ............ |
| Amount paid for building and repairs........... | 621,194 86 | 760,097 74 | 138,902 88 | ............ |
| Amount paid for interest on loans .............. | 118,996 94 | 117,338 60 | ............ | $1,658 34 |
| Amount paid for all other purposes............ | 1,387,932 30 | 1,466,803 48 | 78,871 18 | ............ |
| Total net expenditures........................ | $6,281,002 70 | $6,655,485 04 | $375,482 34 | ............ |
| Amount paid on bonded indebtedness.......... | 402,021 80 | 656,536 04 | ............ | $23,485 78 |
| Balance carried to next year................... | 1,184,622 45 | 1,322,600 62 | 136,977 72 | ............ |
| Total expenditures, including balance on hand........................................ | $7,867,646 95 | $8,356,621 23 | $488,974 28 | ............ |
| Total expenditures in graded school districts... | $4,519,090 84 | $4,829,519 03 | $310,428 19 | ............ |
| Total expenditures in ungraded school districts. | 1,761,911 86 | 1,826,966 01 | 65,054 15 | ............ |
| Total net expenditures......................... | $6,281,002 70 | $6,656,485 04 | $375,482 34 | ............ |

## TABLE I.—*Continued.*

| Items. | 1898. | 1899. | Increase. | Decrease. |
|---|---|---|---|---|
| Total bonded indebtedness of districts......... | $1,826,955 55 | $1,964,616 94 | $137,661 39 | ............ |
| Total floating indebtedness of districts......... | 180,918 55 | 212,738 31 | 31,819 76 | ............ |
| Total indebtedness.......................... | $2,007,874 10 | $2,177,355 25 | $169,481 15 | ............ |
| Total indebtedness in graded school districts.. | $1,794,957 92 | $1,978,861 86 | $183,903 94 | ............ |
| Total indebtedness in ungraded school districts. | 212,916 18 | 198,493 39 | ............ | $14,422 79 |
| Total indebtedness............ ............... | $2,007,874 10 | $2,177,355 25 | $169,481 15 | ............ |
| Total amount due the districts............ ...... | $357,105 90 | $327,538 59 | ............ | $29,567 31 |
| *School libraries.* | | | | |
| Number of townships reporting libraries........ | 445 | 431 | ............ | 14 |
| Number of districts reporting libraries.......... | 2,937 | 3,292 | 355 | ............ |
| Total number of libraries..................... | 3,382 | 3,723 | 341 | ............ |
| Number of volumes in township libraries....... | 158,033 | 158,000 | ............ | 33 |
| Number of volumes in district libraries......... | 664,377 | 723,813 | 59,436 | ............ |
| Total number of volumes in all libraries.... | 822,410 | 881,813 | 59,403 | ............ |
| Amount of taxes voted for township libraries. | $2,592 86 | $2,852 16 | $259 30 | ............ |
| Amount received from county treasurers for township libraries............................. | 8,034 48 | 11,015 45 | 2,980 97 | ............ |
| Number of townships diverting money to general school purposes............................. | 384 | 388 | 4 | ............ |
| Number of townships forfeiting library moneys. | 404 | 413 | 9 | ............ |
| Amount paid for support of township libraries. | $12,829 60 | $11,474 74 | ............ | $1,354 86 |
| Amount paid for support of district libraries.. | 86,350 20 | 98,920 06 | $12,569 86 | ............ |
| *Teachers' Institutes.* | | | | |
| Number of State institutes held................ | 72 | 67 | ............ | 5 |
| Number of men enrolled at such institutes..... | 1,533 | 1,317 | ............ | 216 |
| Number of women enrolled at such institutes.. | 5,509 | 5,097 | ............ | 412 |
| Total enrollment......................... .... | 7,042 | 6,414 | ............ | 628 |
| Amount received from State Treasurer for such institutes......................... | $1,735 56 | $2,974 85 | $1,239 29 | ............ |
| Amount received from county treasurers for such institutes................................ | 12,569 28 | 11,257 36 | ............ | $1,311 92 |
| Total amount expended ..................... | $14,304 84 | $14,222 21 | ............ | $72 63 |

## TABLE I.—*Concluded.*

| Items. | 1898. | 1899. | Increase. | Decrease. |
|---|---|---|---|---|
| *Miscellaneous.* | | | | |
| Number of counties reporting county teachers' associations.. ............................... | 68 | 68 | ............ | ............ |
| Amount of per diem received by examiners... | $16,349 70 | $15,873 90 | ............ | $475 80 |
| Amount paid commissioners of schools......... | 66,505 00 | 66,785 00 | $280 00 | ............ |
| Total compensation........................... | $82,854 70 | $82,658 90 | ............ | $195 80 |
| Amount allowed by supervisors for expenses of county boards................. .... ....... | $9,133 81 | $9,581 09 | $447 28 | ............ |
| Amount paid and due township inspectors for services....................................... | 15,440 88 | 15,121 32 | ............ | $319 56 |
| Amount paid chairmen of board of inspectors. | 31,061 35 | 31,280 99 | 219 64 | ............ |
| Total amount of primary school interest fund apportioned.................................. .. | $1,048,354 50 | $1.052,871 50 | $4,517 00 | ............ |
| Rate per capita, May apportionment............ | $0 50 | $0 50 | ............ | ............ |
| Rate per capita, November apportionment .... | 1 00 | 1 00 | ............ | ............ |
| Rate per capita for year...................... | $1 50 | $1 50 | ............ | ............ |

TABLE II.—*Twenty-eighth and twenty-ninth semi-annual apportionment of the primary school interest fund.*

| Counties. | Apportionment made May 10, 1899, rate per capita, 50 cents. | | | Apportionment made November 10, 1899, rate per capita, 100 cents. | | |
|---|---|---|---|---|---|---|
| | Whole number of children. | Number included in apportionment. | Amount apportioned. | Whole number of children. | Number included in apportionment. | Amount apportioned. |
| Totals.................... | 703,730 | 701,871 | $350,935 50 | 703,686 | 701,936 | $701,936 00 |
| Alcona...................... | 2,032 | 2,032 | $1,016 00 | 2,032 | 2,032 | $2,032 00 |
| Alger....................... | 1,411 | 1,392 | 696 00 | 1,411 | 1,392 | 1,392 00 |
| Allegan..................... | 12,220 | 12,220 | 6,110 00 | 12,220 | 12,220 | 12,220 00 |
| Alpena..................... | 6,798 | 6,766 | a 3,585 50 | 6,798 | 6,766 | 6,766 00 |
| Antrim..................... | 4,368 | 4,353 | 2,176 50 | 4,368 | 4,353 | 4,353 00 |
| Arenac..................... | 3,132 | 3,071 | 1,535 50 | 3,132 | 3,071 | 3,071 00 |
| Baraga..................... | 1,453 | 1,424 | 712 00 | 1,453 | 1,424 | 1,424 00 |
| Barry...................... | 6,553 | 6,553 | 3,276 50 | 6,553 | 6,553 | 6,553 00 |
| Bay........................ | 20,894 | 20,894 | 10,447 00 | 20,894 | 20,894 | 20,894 00 |
| Benzie..................... | 2,633 | 2,625 | 1,312 50 | 2,633 | 2,625 | 2,625 00 |
| Berrien.................... | 13,897 | 13,897 | 6,948 50 | 13,897 | 13,897 | 13,897 00 |
| Branch.................... | 6,553 | 6,518 | 3,259 00 | 6,553 | 6,518 | 6,518 00 |
| Calhoun................... | 11,714 | 11,694 | 5,847 00 | 11,714 | 11,694 | 11,694 00 |
| Cass....................... | 5,798 | 5,774 | 2,887 00 | 5,798 | 5,774 | 5,774 00 |
| Charlevoix................ | 4,034 | 3,982 | 1,991 00 | 4,034 | 3,982 | 3,982 00 |
| Cheboygan................ | 5,103 | 5,081 | 2,540 50 | 5,103 | 5,081 | 5,081 00 |
| Chippewa.................. | 5,044 | 4,952 | 2,476 00 | 5,044 | 4,952 | 4,952 00 |
| Clare...................... | 2,514 | 2,467 | 1,233 50 | 2,514 | 2,467 | 2,467 00 |
| Clinton.................... | 7,403 | 7,403 | 3,701 50 | 7,403 | 7,403 | 7,403 00 |
| Crawford.................. | 685 | 635 | 317 50 | 685 | 635 | 635 00 |
| Delta ..................... | 6,174 | 6,164 | 3,082 00 | 6,174 | 6,164 | 6,164 00 |
| Dickinson................. | 5,098 | 5,098 | 2,549 00 | 5,098 | 5,098 | 5,098 00 |
| Eaton...... ... | 8,441 | 8,441 | 4,220 50 | 8,441 | 8,441 | 8,441 00 |
| Emmet...... ........... | 3,469 | 3,424 | 1,712 00 | 3,469 | 3,424 | 3,424 00 |
| Genesee.................... | 11,041 | 11,018 | 5,509 00 | 11,041 | 11,018 | 11,018 00 |
| Gladwin................... | 1,991 | 1,987 | 993 50 | 1,991 | 1,987 | 1,987 00 |
| Gogebic.................... | 3,851 | 3,851 | 1,925 50 | 3,851 | 3,851 | 3,851 00 |
| Grand Traverse........... | 5,397 | 5,390 | 2,695 00 | 5,397 | 5,390 | 5,390 00 |
| Gratiot.................... | 9,234 | 9,234 | 4,617 00 | 9,234 | 9,234 | 9,234 00 |
| Hillsdale.............. ..... | 7,792 | 7,749 | 3,874 50 | 7,792 | 7,749 | 7,749 00 |
| Houghton.................. | 17,135 | 17,135 | 8,567 50 | 17,135 | 17,135 | 17,135 00 |
| Huron..................... | 12,617 | 12,617 | 6,308 50 | 12,617 | 12,617 | 12,617 00 |
| Ingham.................... | 10,820 | 10,820 | 5,410 00 | 10,820 | 10,820 | 10,820 00 |
| Ionia...................... | 9,356 | 9,356 | 4,678 00 | 9,356 | 9,356 | 9,356 00 |
| Iosco...................... | 3,570 | 3,542 | 1,771 00 | 3,570 | 3,542 | 3,542 00 |
| Iron........... ... | 1,873 | 1,856 | 928 00 | 1,873 | 1,856 | 1,856 00 |
| Isabella................... | 7,390 | 7,390 | 3,695 00 | 7,390 | 7,390 | 7,390 00 |
| Jackson.................... | 11,888 | 11,852 | 5,926 00 | 11,888 | 11,852 | 11,852 00 |
| Kalamazoo................ | 10,907 | 10,907 | 5,453 50 | 10,907 | 10,907 | 10,907 00 |
| Kalkaska.................. | 1,739 | 1,739 | 869 50 | 1,739 | 1,739 | 1,739 00 |
| Kent....................... | 38,803 | 38,803 | 19,401 50 | 38,803 | 38,803 | 38,803 00 |
| Keweenaw................ | 674 | 674 | 337 00 | 674 | 674 | 674 00 |
| Lake....................... | 1,689 | 1,675 | 837 50 | 1,689 | 1,675 | 1,675 00 |
| Lapeer..................... | 9,062 | 9,062 | 4,531 00 | 9,062 | 9,062 | 9,062 00 |
| Leelanau................... | 3,456 | 3,424 | 1,712 00 | 3,456 | 3,424 | 3,424 00 |
| Lenawee................... | 12,968 | 12,921 | 6,460 50 | 12,968 | 12,921 | 12,921 00 |
| Livingston................ | 5,517 | 5,494 | 2,747 00 | 5,517 | 5,494 | 5,494 00 |
| Luce....................... | 594 | 582 | 291 00 | 594 | 582 | 582 00 |
| Mackinac.................. | 2,319 | 2,255 | 1,127 50 | 2,319 | 2,255 | 2,255 00 |

a Includes $302.50 deficiency May and November, 1898.

## TABLE II.—*Concluded.*

| Counties. | Apportionment made May 10, 1899, rate per capita, 50 cents. | | | Apportionment made November 10, 1899, rate per capita, 100 cents. | | |
|---|---|---|---|---|---|---|
| | Whole number of children. | Number included in apportion-ment. | Amount apportioned. | Whole number of children. | Number included in apportion-ment. | Amount apportioned. |
| Macomb...................... | 10,728 | 10,706 | $5,353 00 | 10,728 | 10,706 | $10,706 00 |
| Manistee.................... | 9,381 | 9,374 | 4,687 00 | 9,381 | 9,374 | 9,374 00 |
| Marquette.................. | 12,223 | 12,214 | 6,107 00 | 12,223 | 12,214 | 12,214 00 |
| Mason...................... | 6,439 | 6,439 | 3,219 50 | 6,439 | 6,439 | 6,439 00 |
| Mecosta.................... | 7,081 | 7,081 | 3,540 50 | 7,081 | 7,081 | 7,081 00 |
| Menominee................. | 8,424 | 8,356 | 4,178 00 | 8,424 | 8,424 | b 8,458 00 |
| Midland.................... | 5,023 | 4,887 | 2,443 50 | 5,023 | 4,887 | c 4,917 24 |
| Missaukee.................. | 2,462 | 2,429 | 1,214 50 | 2,462 | 2,429 | 2,429 00 |
| Monroe .................... | 10,925 | 10,884 | 5,442 00 | 10,881 | 10,881 | d e 10,879 50 |
| Montcalm.................. | 10,718 | 10,718 | 5,359 00 | 10,718 | 10,718 | 10,718 00 |
| Montmorency............... | 849 | 828 | 414 00 | 849 | 828 | 828 00 |
| Muskegon.................. | 12,315 | 12,292 | 6,146 00 | 12,315 | 12,292 | 12,292 00 |
| Newaygo............ ...... | 6,042 | 5,957 | 2,978 50 | 6,042 | 5,957 | 5,957 00 |
| Oakland.................... | 11,131 | 11,121 | 5,560 50 | 11,131 | 11,121 | 11,121 00 |
| Oceana..................... | 5,600 | 5,520 | 2,760 00 | 5,600 | 5,520 | 5,520 00 |
| Ogemaw..... ............. | 2,203 | 2,168 | 1,084 00 | 2,203 | 2,168 | 2,168 00 |
| Ontonagon.. . ........... | 1,129 | 1,109 | 554 50 | 1,129 | 1,109 | 1,109 00 |
| Osceola..................... | 5,937 | 5,921 | 2,960 50 | 5,937 | 5,921 | 5,921 00 |
| Oscoda..................... | 359 | 339 | 169 50 | 359 | 339 | 339 00 |
| Otsego............. ........ | 1,520 | 1,519 | 759 50 | 1,520 | 1,519 | 1,519 00 |
| Ottawa..................... | 13,991 | 13,991 | 6,995 50 | 13,991 | 13,991 | 13,991 00 |
| Presque Isle................ | 2,312 | 2,289 | 1,144 50 | 2,312 | 2,289 | 2,289 00 • |
| Roscommon................. | 440 | 323 | 161 50 | 440 | 323 | 323 00 |
| Saginaw ..............•...... | 25,952 | 25,952 | 12,976 00 | 25,952 | 25,952 | 25,952 00 |
| St. Clair................... | 17,629 | 17,605 | 8,802 50 | 17,629 | 17,605 | 17,605 00 |
| St. Joseph.................. | 6,602 | 6,602 | 3,301 00 | 6,602 | 6,602 | 6,602 00 |
| Sanilac..................... | 12,703 | 12,703 | 6,351 50 | 12,703 | 12,703 | 12,703 00 |
| Schoolcraft................. | 1,939 | 1,887 | 943 50 | 1,939 | 1,887 | 1,887 00 |
| Shiawassee................. | 9,038 | 9,027 | 4,513 50 | 9,038 | 9,027 | 9,027 00 |
| Tuscola..................... | 11,431 | 11,389 | 5,694 50 | 11,431 | 11,389 | 11,389 00 |
| Van Buren.................. | 9,519 | 9,519 | 4,759 50 | 9,519 | 9,519 | 9,519 00 |
| Washtenaw................. | 11,847 | 11,830 | 5,915 00 | 11,847 | 11,830 | 11,830 00 |
| Wayne..................... | 95,990 | 95,963 | 47,981 50 | 95,990 | 95,963 | 95,963 00 |
| Wexford............. ..... | 4,744 | 4,736 | 2,368 00 | 4,744 | 4,736 | 4,736 00 |

b Includes $34.00 deficiency May, 1899.
c Includes $30.24 deficiency May and November, 1897.
d Includes $20.50 deficiency May, 1899.
e Less $22.00 overpaid May, 1899.

21

## TABLE III.

### General school statistics as reported by the school inspectors for the year ending September 4, 1899.

| Counties | Number of townships and cities reporting | Whole number of school districts | Number of districts that maintained school | Number of Graded school districts | Number of township unit districts | Number of children between 5 and 20 years of age | Number of children between 5 and 20 years of age that attended school | Whole number of days of school | Stone | Brick | Frame | Log | Whole number of sittings provided for in school houses | Estimated value of school property | Average number months of school |
|---|---|---|---|---|---|---|---|---|---|---|---|---|---|---|---|
| Totals | 1,280 | 7,161 | 7,091 | 602 | 115 | 713,690 | 496,665 | 1,158,868 | 71 | 1,510 | 6,121 | 271 | 621,319 | $19,746,443 | 8.2 |
| Alcona | 11 | 27 | 27 | 1 | 1 | 1,996 | 1,420 | 4,042 |  |  | 25 | 4 | 1,632 | 816,575 | 7.4 |
| Alger | 7 | 7 | 7 | 6 | 7 | 1,360 | 1,001 | 1,141 |  | 1 | 13 | 8 | 1,506 | 17,350 | 8.1 |
| Allegan | 24 | 184 | 184 | 19 | 5 | 12,078 | 9,020 | 30,220 |  | 30 | 161 |  | 12,995 | 214,882 | 8.2 |
| Alpena | 8 | 28 | 26 | 4 |  | 6,807 | 3,153 | 3,501 |  | 2 | 50 | 8 | 3,640 | 101,376 | 6.7 |
| Antrim | 16 | 72 | 72 | 6 |  | 4,619 | 3,536 | 11,469 |  | 6 | 65 | 7 | 4,418 | 96,349 | 7.9 |
| Arenac | 11 | 39 | 36 | 6 | 5 | 3,345 | 2,318 | 5,522 |  | 1 | 33 | 5 | 3,048 | 39,344 | 7.6 |
| Baraga | 5 | 6 | 5 | 5 |  | 1,397 | 660 | 918 |  |  | 16 | 1 | 1,158 | 23,100 | 9.1 |
| Barry | 17 | 146 | 146 | 6 |  | 6,407 | 6,194 | 24,224 |  | 16 | 134 |  | 8,684 | 175,085 | 8.2 |
| Bay | 16 | 65 | 65 | 5 |  | 21,634 | 12,146 | 10,944 |  | 15 | 67 |  | 12,141 | 552,275 | 8.4 |
| Benzie | 12 | 49 | 49 | 6 |  | 2,773 | 2,285 | 7,145 |  | 1 | 49 | 1 | 3,069 | 70,412 | 7.2 |
| Berrien | 23 | 147 | 147 | 19 |  | 13,810 | 10,879 | 28,543 |  | 54 | 108 |  | 13,470 | 381,213 | 8.0 |
| Branch | 17 | 129 | 129 | 9 |  | 6,821 | 5,159 | 21,796 |  | 43 | 78 | 13 | 8,352 | 229,035 | 8.5 |
| Calhoun | 23 | 164 | 164 | 9 | 3 | 11,944 | 9,155 | 27,881 | 11 | 37 | 136 | 20 | 13,011 | 553,525 | 8.4 |
| Cass | 16 | 114 | 112 | 5 | 5 | 5,754 | 4,546 | 18,996 | 6 | 27 | 87 | 7 | 7,273 | 170,075 | 8.4 |
| Charlevoix | 14 | 65 | 65 | 6 |  | 4,213 | 3,205 | 9,542 |  | 3 | 60 |  | 4,454 | 98,006 | 7.3 |
| Cheboygan | 15 | 61 | 54 | 4 |  | 5,167 | 3,292 | 8,333 |  | 2 | 51 | 13 | 3,798 | 85,430 | 7.7 |
| Clare | 13 | 44 | 43 | 3 | 3 | 5,233 | 3,536 | 6,122 |  | 3 | 38 | 20 | 4,004 | 116,080 | 7.1 |
| Clinton | 16 | 50 | 49 | 3 | 5 | 2,703 | 1,930 | 6,743 |  | 2 | 94 | 7 | 2,918 | 66,388 | 6.8 |
| Crawford | 6 | 24 | 24 | 1 | 1 | 702 | 566 | 1,595 | 38 |  | 32 | 1 | 1,083 | 23,425 | 4.9 |
| Delta | 14 | 27 | 27 | 7 | 6 | 6,471 | 4,237 | 4,117 |  | 3 | 42 | 9 | 3,905 | 138,185 | 7.6 |
| Dickinson | 8 | 8 | 8 | 5 |  | 5,414 | 4,069 | 1,460 |  |  | 22 | 1 | 4,294 | 146,809 | 9.1 |
| Eaton | 18 | 146 | 146 | 11 | 6 | 8,215 | 6,581 | 24,445 |  | 47 | 108 |  | 9,967 | 188,715 | 8.3 |
| Emmet | 16 | 70 | 66 | 8 |  | 3,857 | 2,581 | 8,910 |  | 2 | 61 | 6 | 3,445 | 71,915 | 6.7 |
| Genesee | 30 | 160 | 160 | 12 | 1 | 11,012 | 8,685 | 27,274 |  | 27 | 143 |  | 12,419 | 370,445 | 8.5 |
| Gladwin | 13 | 37 | 35 | 2 | 4 | 2,125 | 1,509 | 5,397 |  | 3 | 24 | 15 | 1,962 | 29,390 | 7.7 |
| Gogebic | 7 | 7 | 7 | 4 |  | 4,148 | 3,027 | 1,360 |  |  | 18 | 1 | 3,885 | 193,480 | 9.7 |
| Grand Traverse | 14 | 67 | 67 | 9 | 1 | 4,807 | 4,440 | 9,705 |  | 4 | 69 |  | 5,211 | 201,850 | 7.2 |
| Gratiot | 18 | 132 | 132 | 12 |  | 9,176 | 7,353 | 21,590 |  | 14 | 118 | 1 | 9,537 | 165,450 | 8.1 |

| | | | | | | | | | | | | | | | | | | | | | |
|---|---|---|---|---|---|---|---|---|---|---|---|---|---|---|---|---|---|---|---|---|---|
| Hillsdale | 12 | 166 | 166 | 14 | | 7,664 | 5,673 | 27,600 | 9 | | 57 | 105 | 2 | 9,345 | 220,337 | 8.3 |
| Houghton | 12 | 29 | 29 | 12 | | 18,510 | 11,986 | 6,253 | 1 | | 3 | 55 | | 11,651 | 233,188 | 9.3 |
| Huron | 26 | 113 | 113 | 16 | | 90,870 | 7,982 | 90,180 | | | 21 | 89 | | 8,540 | 119,983 | 8.9 |
| Ingham | 17 | 136 | 136 | 10 | | 10,508 | 7,384 | 23,966 | | | 48 | 102 | | 10,504 | 303,975 | 8.5 |
| Ionia | 18 | 142 | 143 | 12 | | 9,508 | 2,570 | 4,035 | 1 | | 33 | 118 | 2 | 3,151 | 221,535 | 8.4 |
| Iosco | 13 | 25 | | 5 | | 3,567 | | | | | | 30 | | | 39,250 | 8.0 |
| Iron | 8 | | | 5 | 8 | 1,974 | 1,629 | 1,351 | | | 12 | 22 | 6 | 2,016 | 39,165 | 8.4 |
| Isabella | 17 | 101 | 101 | 9 | | 7,482 | 5,298 | 16,158 | | | 59 | 89 | 3 | 7,196 | 96,900 | 7.9 |
| Jackson | 20 | 157 | 157 | 11 | | 11,904 | 8,217 | 29,614 | | | 39 | 113 | | 11,704 | 399,805 | 8.4 |
| Kalamazoo | 17 | 138 | 138 | 2 | | 10,800 | 9,221 | 22,698 | | 1 | 1 | 47 | 2 | 11,947 | 557,253 | 9.6 |
| Kalkaska | 12 | 50 | 50 | | | 1,846 | 1,397 | 7,007 | | | | | | 2,409 | 38,840 | 7.0 |
| Kent | 25 | 307 | 307 | 19 | | 38,684 | 25,049 | 36,227 | | | 64 | 190 | 1 | 28,982 | 1,504,986 | 8.6 |
| Keweenaw | 5 | 5 | 5 | 4 | 5 | 783 | 533 | 990 | | | | 7 | 2 | 1,170 | 14,900 | 8.6 |
| Lake | 11 | 34 | 42 | 4 | | 1,604 | 1,160 | 5,344 | | | 2 | 40 | 1 | 2,028 | 29,875 | 8.7 |
| Lapeer | 11 | 135 | 134 | 13 | | 8,831 | 6,164 | 23,354 | 1 | | 10 | 120 | | 9,777 | 193,440 | 7.5 |
| Leelanau | 11 | 57 | 57 | 5 | | 3,554 | 2,381 | 7,843 | | | 30 | 53 | | 3,080 | 44,500 | 8.6 |
| Lenawee | 24 | 197 | 195 | 13 | 16 | 12,999 | 9,671 | 34,140 | 8 | | 2 | 104 | 2 | 7,172 | 178,700 | 7.8 |
| Livingston | 16 | 135 | 135 | 19 | | 5,483 | 4,302 | 22,878 | 2 | | 5 | 120 | 5 | 8,986 | 351,200 | 9.1 |
| Luce | 4 | 4 | 4 | 11 | | 655 | 597 | 700 | | | 6 | 9 | | 5,246 | 151,029 | 7.8 |
| Mackinac | 13 | 16 | 16 | 3 | | 2,373 | 1,449 | 2,425 | | | 5 | 24 | 3 | 6,999 | 115,643 | 7.6 |
| Macomb | 15 | 114 | 114 | 5 | | 10,757 | 6,514 | 19,687 | | | 7 | 100 | 11 | 6,347 | 200,880 | 7.7 |
| Manistee | 13 | 57 | 58 | 8 | 16 | 9,491 | 6,367 | 8,965 | | | 2 | 59 | 13 | 4,502 | 85,397 | 7.2 |
| Marquette | 19 | 19 | 19 | 15 | | 12,422 | 6,996 | 3,449 | | | 5 | 48 | 3 | 2,761 | 42,545 | 9.1 |
| Mason | 14 | 92 | 92 | 6 | | 6,595 | 4,028 | 9,687 | 2 | | 6 | 84 | 9 | 9,215 | 171,040 | 8.0 |
| Mecosta | 17 | 103 | 104 | 7 | | 7,307 | 5,481 | 15,748 | | | 5 | 86 | 8 | 10,352 | 150,665 | 8.2 |
| Menominee | 10 | 31 | 34 | 7 | 5 | 8,866 | 6,315 | 4,817 | | | 7 | 62 | 6 | 905 | 16,500 | 7.0 |
| Midland | 17 | 71 | 73 | 5 | | 5,049 | 3,402 | 10,392 | | | | 54 | 13 | 10,402 | 532,301 | 7.2 |
| Milwaukee | 13 | 50 | 50 | 4 | | 2,684 | 1,978 | 7,249 | | 1 | 70 | 50 | 3 | 6,614 | 94,200 | 7.3 |
| Monroe | 16 | 40 | 140 | 9 | 9 | 10,721 | 6,744 | 23,123 | | 2 | 13 | 71 | 8 | 13,243 | 330,416 | 8.2 |
| Montcalm | 22 | 139 | 139 | 12 | | 10,786 | 7,941 | 23,246 | | | | 128 | 8 | 5,498 | 93,580 | 8.2 |
| Montmorency | 4 | 7 | 7 | 5 | | 10,897 | 7,648 | 986 | | | | 15 | | 2,385 | 31,498 | 7.0 |
| Muskegon | 19 | 92 | 92 | 9 | | 12,484 | 9,216 | 13,321 | 1 | | 21 | 88 | 6 | 10,493 | 582,301 | 7.2 |
| Newaygo | 22 | 115 | 117 | 5 | | 6,160 | 4,520 | 14,738 | | | 7 | 100 | 4 | 6,614 | 94,200 | 7.3 |
| Oakland | 25 | 296 | 207 | 19 | | 11,100 | 8,300 | 34,400 | | | 36 | 188 | 2 | 13,243 | 330,416 | 7.6 |
| Oceana | 11 | 30 | 44 | 3 | | 5,500 | 4,256 | 13,145 | | 12 | 9 | 77 | | 5,498 | 93,580 | 7.6 |
| Ogemaw | 17 | 122 | 42 | 9 | | 2,335 | 1,647 | 5,823 | | | 3 | 38 | | 2,385 | 31,498 | 7.1 |
| Ontonagon | 9 | 8 | 9 | 2 | | 1,392 | 967 | 1,396 | | | | 88 | 6 | 1,377 | 28,378 | 8.0 |
| Osceola | 9 | 82 | 94 | 9 | | 5,146 | 4,493 | 14,045 | 1 | | 3 | 90 | 6 | 5,999 | 101,700 | 7.5 |
| Oscoda | 4 | 12 | 12 | 9 | | 339 | 282 | 1,450 | | | | 16 | | 526 | 6,950 | 6.0 |
| Otsego | 3 | 40 | 40 | 17 | | 1,677 | 1,080 | 5,390 | | | | 39 | | 710 | 31,600 | 6.7 |
| Ottawa | 28 | 122 | 122 | | | 13,676 | 10,375 | 21,000 | | 1 | 26 | 108 | | 1,945 | 248,300 | 8.6 |
| Presque Isle | 11 | 31 | 55 | 11 | | 2,535 | 970 | 3,508 | | | | 18 | 19 | 12,462 | 16,310 | 5.6 |
| Roscommon | 8 | 10 | 10 | 8 | | 526 | 374 | 526 | | | | 7 | 6 | 2,037 | 5,885 | 4.8 |
| Saginaw | 30 | 156 | 157 | 30 | | 26,714 | 16,975 | 26,566 | | | 45 | 135 | 1 | 20,100 | 784,738 | 8.5 |
| St. Clair | 25 | 162 | 154 | 25 | 2 | 17,449 | 11,586 | 25,761 | | | 82 | 141 | | 14,564 | 482,580 | 8.4 |
| St. Joseph | 18 | 124 | 124 | 9 | | 12,828 | 5,007 | 20,648 | | | 55 | 98 | | 8,325 | 235,382 | 8.3 |

## TABLE III.—CONCLUDED.

| Counties. | Number of townships and cities reporting. | Whole number of school districts. | Number of districts that maintained school. | Number of graded school districts. | Number of township unit districts. | Number of children between 5 and 20 years of age. | Number of children between 5 and 20 years of age that attended school. | Whole number of days of school. | Stone. | Brick. | Frame. | Log. | Whole number of sittings provided for in school houses. | Estimated value of school property. | Average number of months of school. |
|---|---|---|---|---|---|---|---|---|---|---|---|---|---|---|---|
| Sanilac | 26 | 146 | 146 | 24 | .... | 12,562 | 9,460 | 26,187 | 2 | 28 | 115 | .. | 11,487 | $148,980 | 8.9 |
| Schoolcraft | 8 | 14 | 14 | 3 | 4 | 2,011 | 1,584 | 2,148 | .. | 3 | 17 | 7 | 2,008 | 36,818 | 7.6 |
| Shiawassee | 18 | 155 | 154 | 10 | .... | 9,050 | 7,316 | 21,635 | .. | 27 | 108 | .. | 10,335 | 283,700 | 8.7 |
| Tuscola | 23 | 149 | 148 | 13 | .... | 11,606 | 8,046 | 25,338 | .. | 36 | 124 | 2 | 10,746 | 171,175 | 8.5 |
| Van Buren | 18 | 152 | 152 | 17 | .... | 9,475 | 7,493 | 24,925 | .. | 30 | 125 | .. | 10,896 | 230,405 | 8.2 |
| Washtenaw | 22 | 107 | 107 | 9 | .... | 11,695 | 8,441 | 28,291 | .. | 62 | 110 | .. | 11,455 | 490,605 | 8.4 |
| Wayne | 22 | 155 | 155 | 28 | .... | 99,199 | 61,145 | 27,238 | 6 | 125 | 103 | .. | 50,488 | 4,371,740 | 8.7 |
| Wexford | 17 | 77 | 75 | 6 | .... | 5,040 | 3,856 | 11,307 | .. | 3 | 74 | 4 | 5,186 | 121,715 | 7.5 |

## TABLE IV.

*Employment of teachers as reported by school inspectors for the year ending September 4, 1899.*

| Counties | Number of teachers required. Graded schools | Ungraded schools | Number of teachers employed. Men | Women | Aggregate number of months taught. Men | Women | Total wages of teachers. Men | Women | Total | Average monthly wages. Men | Women |
|---|---|---|---|---|---|---|---|---|---|---|---|
| Totals | 6,530 | 6,499 | 3,471 | 12,068 | 24,798 | 90,900 | $1,103,066 45 | $3,212,949 66 | $4,316,036 11 | $44 48 | $35 35 |
| Alcona | 4 | 26 | 13 | 23 | 104 | 154 | $4,117 50 | $4,625 68 | $8,743 18 | $39 59 | $30 04 |
| Alger | 30 | 1 | 8 | 29 | 68 | 235 | 4,206 22 | 9,949 50 | 14,155 72 | 61 83 | 44 02 |
| Allegan | 83 | 165 | 75 | 267 | 501 | 1,627 | 19,569 00 | 43,855 61 | 63,414 61 | 39 04 | 28 95 |
| Alpena | 53 | 24 | 9 | 90 | 62 | 650 | 5,785 00 | 21,403 60 | 25,188 60 | 61 05 | 33 31 |
| Antrim | 38 | 66 | 30 | 99 | 220 | 665 | 8,485 08 | 20,817 82 | 29,302 88 | 43 84 | 31 32 |
| Arenac | 18 | 63 | 15 | 45 | 94 | 383 | 3,520 50 | 8,014 46 | 11,534 96 | 37 45 | ... |
| Baraga | 25 | 140 | 7 | 19 | 68 | 173 | 4,890 00 | 7,576 50 | 12,466 50 | 71 91 | 43 70 |
| Barry | 43 | 50 | 70 | 207 | 499 | 1,106 | 16,399 24 | 26,647 89 | 43,047 13 | 32 86 | 24 09 |
| Bay | 190 | 43 | 30 | 221 | 539 | 2,078 | 20,033 62 | 78,066 43 | 98,100 05 | 59 10 | 37 57 |
| Benzie | 50 | 43 | 23 | 65 | 128 | 46 | 5,807 50 | 13,380 60 | 18,688 10 | 41 46 | 30 02 |
| Berrien | 145 | 128 | 68 | 208 | 665 | 1,96 | 30,613 77 | 56,980 82 | 89, | 44 69 | 32 25 |
| Branch | 55 | 123 | 65 | 86 | 80 | 1,79 | 15,063 53 | 31,365 60 | 46,428 13 | 36 83 | 28 60 |
| Calhoun | 151 | 155 | 78 | 301 | 96 | 2,284 | 20,679 14 | 73,887 96 | 94,567 10 | 43 44 | 33 63 |
| Cass | 47 | 109 | 63 | 38 | 53 | 990 | 16,140 96 | 27,277 53 | 43,418 49 | 37 87 | 29 47 |
| Charlevoix | 32 | 59 | 55 | 93 | 43 | 61 | 5,740 08 | 16,534 25 | 22,274 33 | 37 32 | 29 47 |
| Cheboygan | 38 | 57 | 26 | 78 | 96 | 546 | 99 | 18,073 75 | 26,577 74 | 43 30 | 33 10 |
| Chippewa | 52 | 41 | 99 | 77 | 208 | 601 | 9,145 90 | 22,837 65 | 31,983 55 | 43 97 | 37 90 |
| Clare | 17 | 47 | 18 | 64 | 91 | 382 | 3,754 46 | 10,028 00 | 13,782 46 | 37 17 | 27 07 |
| Clinton | 50 | 130 | 57 | 76 | 80 | 1,63 | 13,895 60 | 28,505 10 | 42,401 70 | 35 02 | 31 53 |
| Crawford | 2 | 23 | 4 | 23 | 17 | 44 | 1,071 25 | 4,540 00 | 5,611 25 | 63 02 | 31 53 |
| Delta | 66 | 30 | 13 | 81 | 10 | 606 | 7,254 25 | 28,146 25 | 35,400 50 | 65 96 | 40 59 |
| Dickinson | 72 | 3 | 9 | 73 | 82 | 650 | 7,553 72 | 31,754 86 | 39,307 58 | 92 10 | 48 85 |
| Eaton | 80 | 125 | 68 | 239 | 430 | 1,66 | 16,801 66 | 42,126 82 | 58,927 90 | 39 07 | 28 71 |
| Emmet | 12 | 67 | 23 | 102 | 37 | 81 | 5,815 25 | 17,421 15 | 23,236 40 | 42 44 | 29 98 |
| Genesee | 109 | 148 | 26 | 81 | 60 | 1,097 | 24,341 25 | 50,771 62 | 75,112 87 | 38 03 | 29 92 |
| Gladwin | 7 | 26 | 18 | 34 | 53 | 97 | 3,923 50 | 5,497 25 | 9,420 75 | 31 99 | 27 90 |
| Gogebic | 77 | 2 | 5 | 74 | 49 | 731 | 5,303 75 | 32,450 61 | 37,754 36 | 108 24 | 44 98 |
| Grand Traverse | 56 | 61 | 24 | 19 | 168 | 790 | 8,673 00 | 28,128 25 | 36,801 25 | 53 89 | 34 82 |
| Gratiot | 58 | 130 | 91 | 66 | 485 | 1,041 | 16,182 00 | 28,003 50 | 44,185 90 | 33 57 | 25 90 |
| Hillsdale | 66 | 152 | 88 | 97 | 553 | 1,356 | 17,895 90 | 34,047 90 | 51,943 80 | 33 58 | 25 11 |
| Houghton | 246 | 10 | 34 | 225 | 327 | 2,202 | 29,442 50 | 108,542 72 | 137,985 22 | 90 04 | 49 21 |

## TABLE IV.—CONCLUDED.

| Counties. | Number of teachers required. | | Number of teachers employed. | | Aggregate number of months taught. | | Total wages of teachers. | | | Average monthly wages. | |
|---|---|---|---|---|---|---|---|---|---|---|---|
| | Graded schools. | Ungraded schools. | Men. | Women. | Men. | Women. | Men. | Women. | Total. | Men. | Women. |
| Huron | 68 | 97 | 65 | 98 | 555 | 820 | $20,909 80 | $23,453 50 | $44,363 30 | $37 65 | $28 60 |
| Ingham | 120 | 125 | 81 | 280 | 470 | 1,807 | 18,695 00 | 59,300 00 | 77,995 77 | 39 77 | 32 82 |
| Ionia | 91 | 131 | 60 | 217 | 440 | 1,513 | 16,686 00 | 42,103 69 | 58,788 69 | 37 92 | 27 88 |
| Iosco | 35 | 21 | 8 | 51 | 60 | 430 | 3,250 00 | 13,571 75 | 16,831 75 | 54 33 | 32 31 |
| Iron | 37 | 3 | 11 | 38 | 74 | 322 | 4,050 00 | 14,455 00 | 18,505 00 | 54 73 | 44 86 |
| Isabella | 32 | 96 | 46 | 113 | 817 | 761 | 11,230 59 | 22,446 15 | 33,676 74 | 35 43 | 29 49 |
| Jackson | 122 | 148 | 96 | 257 | 614 | 1,887 | 26,442 98 | 63,393 09 | 89,835 70 | 43 07 | 33 33 |
| Kalamazoo | 72 | 127 | 56 | 259 | 376 | 1,923 | 16,844 98 | 64,204 06 | 81,049 04 | 44 80 | 33 39 |
| Kalkaska | 9 | 48 | 19 | 62 | 96 | 323 | 3,546 50 | 9,110 70 | 12,656 20 | 36 93 | 28 21 |
| Kent | 433 | 188 | 119 | 514 | 927 | 4,964 | 46,810 58 | 213,599 42 | 260,410 00 | 50 49 | 42 86 |
| Keweenaw | 9 | 1 | 3 | 8 | 28 | 67 | 1,905 00 | 2,625 00 | 4,530 00 | 68 04 | 39 18 |
| Lake | 17 | 38 | 11 | 60 | 72 | 262 | 2,525 25 | 6,653 60 | 9,178 75 | 35 07 | 29 51 |
| Lapeer | 112 | 121 | 47 | 160 | 379 | 1,213 | 14,296 25 | 31,049 60 | 45,335 85 | 37 60 | 25 59 |
| Leelanau | 18 | 82 | 21 | 55 | 140 | 331 | 5,151 80 | 9,601 00 | 14,752 80 | 36 70 | 29 01 |
| Lenawee | 119 | 179 | 96 | 279 | 666 | 1,998 | 27,160 29 | 56,715 40 | 83,875 69 | 40 79 | 28 38 |
| Livingston | 57 | 129 | 75 | 200 | 389 | 1,071 | 12,848 20 | 23,698 60 | 36,546 80 | 33 03 | 22 13 |
| Luce | 12 | 2 | 3 | 18 | 24 | 154 | 2,070 00 | 5,130 00 | 7,200 00 | 86 25 | 33 31 |
| Mackinac | 14 | 13 | 10 | 42 | 66 | 279 | 3,246 00 | 9,696 50 | 12,942 50 | 49 18 | 34 75 |
| Macomb | 67 | 103 | 53 | 123 | 460 | 1,061 | 18,445 00 | 31,854 50 | 50,299 50 | 40 09 | 29 44 |
| Manistee | 165 | 50 | 36 | 61 | 290 | 1,127 | 15,023 87 | 41,568 88 | 56,592 75 | 53 65 | 36 88 |
| Marquette | 188 | 4 | 98 | 171 | 251 | 1,639 | 19,335 00 | 76,700 00 | 96,035 00 | 95 85 | 46 90 |
| Mason | 45 | 58 | 27 | 97 | 195 | 726 | 8,067 60 | 24,610 75 | 32,668 25 | 41 82 | 38 80 |
| Mecosta | 38 | 97 | 82 | 143 | 212 | 884 | 7,502 00 | 24,591 50 | 32,093 50 | 56 89 | 27 82 |
| Menominee | 93 | 57 | 80 | 116 | 178 | 1,004 | 10,840 10 | 38,977 50 | 49,817 60 | 58 89 | 38 82 |
| Midland | 25 | 68 | 13 | 100 | 105 | 612 | 3,932 50 | 16,662 96 | 20,595 45 | 57 46 | 27 23 |
| Missaukee | 14 | 47 | 21 | 54 | 149 | 320 | 5,296 15 | 9,551 33 | 14,849 48 | 35 56 | 39 85 |
| Monroe | 46 | 131 | 62 | 163 | 462 | 1,062 | 16,300 19 | 27,929 38 | 44,229 57 | 38 88 | 26 65 |
| Montcalm | 72 | 127 | 70 | 200 | 444 | 1,884 | 16,358 00 | 35,643 00 | 52,001 00 | 38 21 | 26 76 |
| Montmorency | 23 | 2 | 9 | 21 | 58 | 144 | 2,100 00 | 4,597 68 | 6,697 68 | 36 21 | 31 93 |
| Muskegon | 151 | 88 | 39 | 218 | 290 | 1,693 | 16,611 50 | 56,854 87 | 73,466 37 | 77 66 | 57 29 |
| Newaygo | 26 | 112 | 33 | 165 | 218 | 814 | 7,416 50 | 21,301 84 | 28,717 84 | 34 02 | 28 18 |
| Oakland | 98 | 188 | 70 | 249 | 616 | 1,995 | 25,872 77 | 52,126 76 | 77,999 53 | 42 07 | 28 53 |
| Oceana | 28 | 83 | 34 | 111 | 222 | 661 | 7,781 67 | 19,245 24 | 27,026 91 | 35 05 | 29 11 |
| Ogemaw | 10 | 39 | 12 | 88 | 94 | 357 | 3,434 00 | 7,567 30 | 11,001 70 | 36 54 | 28 67 |
| Ontonagon | 25 | 4 | 3 | 40 | 29 | 282 | 2,180 00 | 12,315 00 | 14,495 00 | 75 16 | 44 88 |
| Osceola | 39 | 98 | 31 | 130 | 207 | 731 | 8,271 70 | 24,218 50 | 32,490 20 | 30 96 | 33 12 |
| Oscoda | 4 | 11 | 5 | 13 | 40 | 56 | 1,201 00 | 1,553 00 | 2,754 00 | 30 03 | 25 05 |

| | | | | | | | | | | | | |
|---|---|---|---|---|---|---|---|---|---|---|---|---|
| Otsego | 13 | 57 | 57 | 38 | 140 | 212 | 5,156 15 | 6,530 00 | 11,695 15 | 34 80 | 30 80 |
| Ottawa | 129 | 85 | 69 | 188 | 504 | 1,568 | 21,213 00 | 44,629 81 | 66,842 81 | 33 31 | 28 63 |
| Presque Isle | 5 | 31 | 22 | 20 | 129 | 77 | 3,975 00 | 2,262 00 | 6,237 00 | 42 31 | 30 68 |
| Roscommon | 3 | 16 | 2 | 13 | 9 | 67 | 262 00 | 1,670 80 | 1,932 80 | 29 21 | 29 31 |
| Saginaw | 272 | 140 | 79 | 387 | 621 | 8,247 | 34,514 90 | 119,678 88 | 154,193 73 | 55 58 | 35 86 |
| | | | | | | | | | | | |
| St. Clair | 119 | 144 | 58 | 229 | 53 | 1,94 | 19,069 93 | 60,165 05 | 79,834 99 | 41 58 | 51 77 |
| St. Joseph | 72 | 116 | 68 | 177 | 48 | 1,04 | 17,260 42 | 32,850 65 | 50,111 07 | 67 51 | 38 53 |
| Sanilac | 55 | 132 | 47 | 101 | 35 | 82 | 25,485 82 | 21,576 00 | 47,061 82 | 33 00 | 25 84 |
| Schoolcraft | 27 | 11 | 22 | 42 | 74 | 325 | 4,580 50 | 13,176 07 | 17,606 57 | 61 08 | 40 54 |
| Shiawassee | 90 | 116 | 68 | 198 | 31 | 1,42 | 18,356 62 | 40,880 96 | 59,077 98 | 40 48 | 28 91 |
| | | | | | | | | | | | |
| Tuscola | 56 | 135 | 56 | 78 | 447 | 1,253 | 15,807 84 | 31,834 10 | 47,641 98 | 35 36 | 25 41 |
| Van Buren | 81 | 135 | 78 | 73 | 64 | 1,54 | 22,708 72 | 34,738 35 | 57,527 07 | 37 74 | 27 37 |
| Washtenaw | 140 | 159 | 127 | 289 | 67 | 2,33 | 26,385 82 | 70,561 81 | 96,937 63 | 64 83 | 30 50 |
| Wayne | 990 | 119 | 90 | 1,00 | 1,45 | 9,747 | 88,230 80 | 574,566 04 | 663,178 84 | 78 99 | 38 98 |
| Wexford | 57 | 71 | 30 | 24 | 70 | 785 | 7,338 00 | 27,323 54 | 34,061 54 | 40 99 | 34 81 |

## TABLE V.

Resources of school districts as reported by school inspectors for year ending September 4, 1899.

| Counties. | One-mill tax. | Primary school interest fund. | Library moneys. | Tuition of non-resident pupils. | District taxes for all purposes. | Raised from all other sources. | Total net receipts. | Received from loans. | Money on hand Sept. 5, 1899. | Total resources including amount on hand and loans. |
|---|---|---|---|---|---|---|---|---|---|---|
| | | | | Ordinary receipts. | | | | | | |
| Totals | $641,897 65 | $1,020,283 12 | $107,171 41 | $86,949 47 | $4,549,062 36 | $255,436 05 | $6,660,800 06 | $519,243 11 | $1,176,578 06 | $8,356,621 23 |
| Alcona | $201 93 | $2,990 50 | $88 23 | | $7,781 66 | $1,104 58 | $12,101 20 | $111 00 | $2,407 23 | $14,619 43 |
| Alger | 306 73 | 2,389 09 | | | 24,414 36 | 229 85 | 27,430 03 | 740 00 | 1,068 65 | 29,228 68 |
| Allegan | 12,736 63 | 17,838 87 | 1,941 38 | 2,158 35 | 69,540 84 | 2,505 11 | 106,721 38 | 12,995 51 | 18,111 02 | 137,827 91 |
| Alpena | 217 39 | 10,116 36 | 1,182 27 | 7 50 | 26,277 89 | 1,560 57 | 39,361 98 | | 6,822 35 | 46,184 33 |
| Antrim | 2,215 12 | 6,324 83 | 307 09 | 171 09 | 36,968 63 | 1,864 96 | 47,851 72 | 3,867 06 | 8,500 12 | 60,324 92 |
| Arenac | 356 67 | 4,173 41 | 236 56 | 1 75 | 11,032 28 | 6,535 94 | 22,336 61 | 5,839 92 | 4,262 98 | 32,439 46 |
| Baraga | 147 15 | 2,196 25 | 70 50 | | 15,668 27 | 409 25 | 18,491 42 | 500 00 | 5,774 03 | 24,765 45 |
| Barry | 10,096 80 | 9,722 40 | 834 88 | 1,401 90 | 38,103 89 | 1,306 82 | 56,527 99 | 3,560 51 | 9,744 25 | 69,862 75 |
| Bay | 4,057 04 | 31,640 19 | 342 97 | 1,020 40 | 113,388 40 | 4,698 42 | 154,516 32 | 1,470 93 | 33,578 12 | 199,574 37 |
| Benzie | 841 76 | 3,329 08 | 264 35 | 104 35 | 25,805 59 | 2,443 68 | 32,789 98 | 4,765 78 | 3,380 97 | 40,985 61 |
| Berrien | 13,768 40 | 20,660 34 | 1,922 06 | 2,459 70 | 84,685 62 | 12,048 50 | 135,488 62 | 6,249 34 | 24,532 83 | 166,270 79 |
| Branch | 11,002 92 | 9,687 12 | 1,411 22 | 1,674 05 | 43,579 00 | 908 77 | 66,203 09 | 1,091 17 | 18,877 16 | 88,171 42 |
| Calhoun | 19,861 75 | 13,812 25 | 1,462 60 | 2,443 05 | 104,667 52 | 2,612 16 | 144,879 33 | 6,322 64 | 16,066 45 | 167,290 42 |
| Cass | 11,667 16 | 8,649 21 | 674 46 | 1,081 36 | 34,329 15 | 1,225 24 | 59,230 58 | 6,295 40 | 10,372 67 | 74,889 65 |
| Charlevoix | 1,607 71 | 5,671 04 | 163 18 | 271 98 | 25,275 82 | 2,099 06 | 35,069 63 | 16,354 63 | 6,286 10 | 57,710 36 |
| Cheboygan | 2,244 19 | 7,216 77 | 153 69 | 197 12 | 27,044 04 | 3,867 42 | 40,723 23 | 3,568 70 | 7,440 00 | 51,731 93 |
| Chippewa | 4,150 35 | 7,071 47 | 28 50 | 17 50 | 47,024 45 | 2,138 59 | 60,430 87 | 40,238 77 | 3,126 65 | 103,796 29 |
| Clare | 462 24 | 3,566 60 | 106 47 | 136 05 | 18,075 87 | 2,463 89 | 24,844 12 | 674 47 | 4,734 38 | 30,248 97 |
| Clinton | 11,423 13 | 11,110 65 | 1,251 66 | 1,995 34 | 27,887 65 | 5,061 70 | 58,900 08 | 1,499 05 | 15,912 39 | 75,611 47 |
| Crawford | 64 96 | 884 12 | 7 88 | 24 76 | 5,124 76 | 1,270 90 | 7,377 37 | | 4,097 35 | 11,674 72 |
| Delta | 766 93 | 8,700 99 | 54 79 | 51 58 | 42,359 95 | 4,278 57 | 56,303 41 | 6,401 31 | 10,634 69 | 73,339 41 |
| Dickinson | 348 96 | 6,982 75 | 477 64 | 87 07 | 62,703 25 | 907 54 | 71,587 10 | 29,505 05 | 4,968 76 | 106,010 91 |
| Eaton | 15,004 98 | 12,882 50 | 1,106 52 | 2,945 62 | 46,664 22 | 1,679 80 | 78,786 73 | 2,988 52 | 13,471 22 | 95,215 47 |
| Emmet | 705 66 | 5,046 16 | 39 12 | 186 41 | 29,256 87 | 2,184 63 | 37,510 57 | 564 41 | 8,978 45 | 47,053 43 |
| Genesee | 19,935 66 | 16,050 86 | 1,973 44 | 3,219 53 | 73,913 06 | 1,845 02 | 116,938 58 | 27,109 60 | 13,687 77 | 157,735 95 |
| Gladwin | 356 77 | 2,702 84 | | 104 05 | 9,800 86 | 837 81 | 13,892 43 | 1,001 41 | 3,580 77 | 18,474 61 |
| Gogebic | 573 73 | 5,963 34 | 222 30 | 1,095 19 | 59,792 94 | 5,318 20 | 71,600 51 | 27,100 00 | 18,211 57 | 116,912 08 |
| Grand Traverse | 4,908 22 | 7,400 02 | 399 52 | 950 18 | 43,441 64 | 1,216 78 | 58,431 37 | 11,203 66 | 21,270 08 | 90,905 11 |
| Gratiot | 8,666 78 | 13,183 49 | 1,023 19 | | 43,792 91 | 4,037 44 | 71,655 99 | 1,348 96 | 1,561 66 | 86,556 60 |
| Hillsdale | 15,554 89 | 11,384 82 | 1,676 95 | 2,524 20 | 40,615 28 | 535 14 | 72,290 58 | 4,184 17 | 10,865 15 | 87,339 90 |
| Houghton | 38,391 10 | 22,802 77 | 1,399 60 | 1,376 15 | 158,717 21 | 2,588 76 | 225,777 59 | 7,630 69 | 12,907 40 | 306,315 68 |
| Huron | 6,927 21 | 18,271 62 | 643 06 | 284 36 | 57,364 27 | 1,331 12 | 64,821 63 | 2,728 72 | 12,706 90 | 80,346 65 |

Ingham

Ionia

Iosco

Iron

Isabella

Jackson

Kalamazoo

Kalkaska

Kent

Keweenaw

Lake

Lapeer

Leelanau

Lenawee

Livingston

Luce

Mackinac

Macomb

Manistee

Marquette

Mason

Mecosta

Menominee

Midland

Missaukee

Monroe

Montcalm

Montmorency

Muskegon

Newaygo

Oakland

Oceana

Ogemaw

Ontonagon

Osceola

Oscoda

Otsego

Ottawa

Presque Isle

Roscommon

Saginaw

St. Clair

St. Joseph

Sanilac

Schoolcraft

Shiawassee

TABLE V.—CONCLUDED.

| Counties. | Ordinary receipts. | | | | | | Total net receipts. | Received from loans. | Money on hand Sept 5, 1898. | Total resources including amount on hand and loans. |
|---|---|---|---|---|---|---|---|---|---|---|
| | One-mill tax. | Primary school interest fund. | Library moneys. | Tuition of non-resident pupils. | District taxes for all purposes. | Raised from all other sources. | | | | |
| Tuscola | $8,059 99 | $16,710 11 | $811 35 | $1,270 88 | $42,887 23 | $2,186 83 | $71,875 84 | $3,552 51 | $16,173 40 | $91,601 75 |
| Van Buren | 11,914 74 | 14,143 28 | 1,596 67 | 3,191 88 | 50,456 46 | 2,552 86 | 83,854 74 | 10,013 34 | 16,336 28 | 110,204 36 |
| Washtenaw | 21,098 61 | 17,737 40 | 1,586 85 | 9,172 22 | 84,869 51 | 1,068 57 | 135,531 16 | 25,702 84 | 11,985 40 | 173,209 40 |
| Wayne | 43,673 05 | 142,086 43 | 45,151 00 | 3,704 72 | 822,105 04 | 21,669 31 | 1,078,360 55 | 17,549 71 | 148,319 25 | 1,244,259 51 |
| Wexford | 2,507 50 | 6,822 43 | 169 02 | 195 48 | 46,966 49 | 2,892 51 | 59,243 43 | 10,861 71 | 13,478 70 | 82,573 84 |

## TABLE VI.

*Expenditures of school districts as reported by school inspectors for the year ending September 4, 1899.*

| Counties | Paid male teachers. | Paid female teachers. | Ordinary expenditures for maintaining the schools. Paid for books and care of library. | Paid interest on loans. | Paid for building and repairs. | Paid for all other purposes. | Total net expenses. | Paid on indebtedness (principal). | Amount on hand Sept. 4, 1899. | Total expenditures, including amoun on hand and paid on indebtedness. |
|---|---|---|---|---|---|---|---|---|---|---|
| Totals | $1,168. 47 | $3,209,466. 75 | $98,980. 06 | $117,338. 80 | $760,097. 74 | $1,367,863. 42 | $6,056,485. 04 | $378,536. 02 | $1,321,600. 17 | $8,356,021. 23 |
| Alcona | 4,062.95 | 4,710.76 | 82.65 | 834.88 | 908.12 | 2,091.16 | 11,240.52 | 342.67 | 3,036.24 | 14,619.43 |
| Alger | 4,305.22 | 9,949.50 | 309.75 | 701.07 | 2,333.12 | 8,985.44 | 26,495.10 | 1,331.41 | 1,401.17 | 29,228.68 |
| Allegan | 19,559.00 | 43,865.00 | 337.30 | 1,782.19 | 10,297.39 | 17,837.00 | 93,058.49 | 8,672.18 | 35,487.24 | 137,827.91 |
| Alpena | 3,785.00 | 20,055.02 | 538.13 | 1,129.00 | 1,297.71 | 8,985.45 | 34,950.31 | 1,278.03 | 10,245.99 | 46,184.33 |
| Antrim | 8,960.05 | 20,793.92 | 38.95 | 1,119.53 | 3,076.02 | 8,502.11 | 42,487.59 | 5,947.81 | 11,889.52 | 60,324.92 |
| Arenac | 3,520.50 | 8,011.45 | 139.33 | 216.09 | 4,573.84 | 5,884.61 | 22,348.82 | 602.50 | 9,488.14 | 32,439.40 |
| Barsa | 4,190.00 | 7,576.00 | 190.51 | 77.81 | 1,351.78 | 4,414.34 | 18,400.04 | 1,500.00 | 4,864.51 | 24,765.45 |
| Barry | 16,399.24 | 26,647.80 | 168.90 | 155.50 | 3,763.72 | 8,765.53 | 55,900.07 | 3,180.02 | 10,783.06 | 69,802.76 |
| Bay | 20,032.62 | 78,066.43 | 155.59 | 5,800.09 | 12,812.89 | 28,906.04 | 145,864.36 | 10,017.45 | 33,692.56 | 189,574.87 |
| Benzie | 5,307.50 | 13,316.60 | 133.92 | 2,017.02 | 1,634.01 | 4,444.75 | 29,854.30 | 9,247.31 | 4,834.00 | 40,985.61 |
| Berrien | 30,613.77 | 56,960.82 | 1,134.09 | 1,357.73 | 14,165.26 | 27,119.81 | 131,841.50 | 4,806.43 | 29,532.86 | 166,270.79 |
| Branch | 15,082.53 | 31,935.60 | 176.43 | 880.26 | 4,671.95 | 12,091.93 | 64,248.70 | 4,539.48 | 19,383.24 | 89,171.42 |
| Calhoun | 20,679.14 | 78,112.95 | 1,245.70 | 1,042.86 | 8,022.85 | 22,049.14 | 125,152.05 | 22,778.70 | 18,354.67 | 167,290.42 |
| Cass | 16,140.06 | 27,277.53 | 735.93 | 521.23 | 1,780.42 | 9,750.46 | 56,197.51 | 7,360.84 | 11,381.30 | 74,939.65 |
| Charlevoix | 5,740.04 | 16,397.30 | 143.40 | 1,466.64 | 5,860.10 | 5,843.64 | 35,540.50 | 14,267.95 | 7,901.91 | 57,710.36 |
| Cheboygan | 8,823.90 | 18,047.50 | 374.35 | 2,176.10 | 2,012.87 | 11,653.55 | 42,588.36 | 2,199.36 | 6,944.21 | 51,731.93 |
| Chippewa | 9,145.90 | 22,957.45 | 222.31 | 3,049.70 | 30,125.95 | 19,868.69 | 85,340.53 | 1,363.14 | 17,102.62 | 103,796.99 |
| Clare | 3,669.46 | 9,938.50 | 187.18 | 746.55 | 945.65 | 3,677.86 | 19,034.40 | 2,684.18 | 8,630.39 | 30,349.97 |
| Clinton | 13,490.60 | 28,506.10 | 444.04 | 136.96 | 6,451.35 | 9,209.25 | 59,643.29 | 1,429.89 | 15,638.29 | 75,611.47 |
| Crawford | 1,041.25 | 4,547.00 | 70.75 | | 173.00 | 1,531.44 | 7,369.44 | 68.25 | 4,087.03 | 11,474.72 |
| Delta | 7,254.25 | 28,356.25 | 239.10 | 2,497.98 | 7,903.17 | 17,485.30 | 63,735.96 | 1,512.90 | 8,060.58 | 73,539.41 |
| Dickinson | 7,552.72 | 31,704.86 | 854.58 | 3,205.21 | 11,781.70 | 28,479.76 | 83,026.83 | 5,875.00 | 16,507.08 | 106,010.91 |
| Eaton | 16,801.08 | 42,116.61 | 565.12 | 155.33 | 4,883.34 | 14,681.84 | 79,144.56 | 3,136.41 | 12,934.51 | 95,215.47 |
| Emmet | 5,810.35 | 17,421.15 | 190.96 | 1,471.00 | 1,649.18 | 5,214.74 | 31,757.98 | 6,359.40 | 8,898.16 | 47,053.43 |
| Genesee | 24,341.25 | 50,796.62 | 1,233.95 | 1,406.99 | 21,481.64 | 39,135.87 | 138,387.22 | 4,358.48 | 14,995.25 | 157,735.96 |
| Gladwin | 3,754.50 | 5,367.17 | 6.00 | 180.62 | 2,256.99 | 2,907.49 | 14,494.57 | 596.71 | 3,383.33 | 18,474.61 |
| Gogebic | 5,303.75 | 32,450.61 | 538.04 | 1,937.01 | 10,433.07 | 16,121.18 | 66,773.68 | 6,780.00 | 43,365.46 | 116,912.08 |
| Grand Traverse | 8,673.00 | 28,128.25 | 272.22 | 1,335.08 | 13,810.07 | 11,712.28 | 63,920.88 | 1,249.89 | 25,724.34 | 90,905.11 |
| Gratiot | 16,182.30 | 28,003.50 | 657.48 | 1,711.13 | 4,904.94 | 14,003.16 | 65,402.61 | 3,685.55 | 17,508.44 | 86,586.60 |
| Hillsdale | 17,636.90 | 34,047.90 | 571.75 | 397.89 | 4,823.49 | 13,963.33 | 71,511.26 | 4,192.36 | 11,636.28 | 87,339.90 |

TABLE VI.—CONCLUDED.

| Counties. | Ordinary expenditures for maintaining the schools. | | | | | | | Paid on indebtedness (principal). | Amount on hand Sept. 4, 1899. | Total expenditures, including amount on hand and paid on indebtedness. |
|---|---|---|---|---|---|---|---|---|---|---|
| | Paid male teachers. | Paid female teachers. | Paid for books and care of library. | Paid interest on loans. | Paid for building and repairs. | Paid for all other purposes. | Total net expenses. | | | |
| Houghton | $29,442 50 | $108,187 92 | $1,511 27 | $1,544 26 | $25,724 40 | $63,904 61 | $219,964 86 | $5,295 09 | $81,055 73 | $306,315 66 |
| Huron | 20,884 50 | 23,460 50 | 87 24 | 1,880 06 | 3,451 92 | 13,818 05 | 63,582 57 | 3,719 41 | 13,044 67 | 90,346 65 |
| Ingham | 18,708 00 | 59,500 68 | 1,359 40 | 1,963 22 | 4,886 85 | 22,490 66 | 108,708 89 | 9,632 68 | 34,506 35 | 152,837 92 |
| Ionia | 16,665 95 | 42,091 99 | 567 98 | 550 65 | 3,827 81 | 17,224 56 | 80,947 99 | 3,064 36 | 22,761 12 | 106,773 17 |
| Iosco | 3,298 65 | 13,051 89 | 42 09 | 49 66 | 1,056 72 | 4,404 66 | 22,475 67 | 162 77 | 6,213 71 | 29,862 15 |
| Iron | 4,050 00 | 14,455 00 | 398 25 | 892 24 | 5,418 94 | 6,831 56 | 32,015 99 | 1,200 00 | 2,888 06 | 36,104 05 |
| Isabella | 11,230 62 | 22,384 21 | 94 81 | 1,426 00 | 2,530 57 | 11,786 15 | 49,432 16 | 3,004 18 | 7,907 07 | 60,343 41 |
| Jackson | 25,412 72 | 63,376 99 | 349 75 | 2,361 60 | 21,802 44 | 23,070 75 | 138,294 25 | 8,529 50 | 16,456 38 | 163,042 13 |
| Kalamazoo | 16,844 98 | 64,231 30 | 4,064 80 | 1,180 76 | 17,342 41 | 23,903 41 | 127,367 66 | 6,948 42 | 15,582 10 | 149,908 17 |
| Kalkaska | 3,545 50 | 9,064 70 | 55 70 | 153 00 | 1,700 60 | 3,799 97 | 18,318 56 | 2,200 37 | 5,884 13 | 26,412 06 |
| Kent | 46,810 58 | 213,549 42 | 10,884 13 | 14,606 55 | 26,378 43 | 69,741 18 | 381,924 59 | 19,770 01 | 108,372 96 | 506,067 26 |
| Keweenaw | 1,905 00 | 2,625 00 | | | 88 85 | 1,104 46 | 5,723 31 | | 6,019 52 | 11,742 83 |
| Lake | 2,985 25 | 6,986 50 | | 72 02 | 775 55 | 2,084 80 | 12,934 12 | 606 35 | 5,340 26 | 18,339 73 |
| Lapeer | 14,996 25 | 30,966 60 | 384 96 | 464 37 | 12,407 16 | 9,996 66 | 68,476 02 | 6,221 15 | 13,345 09 | 88,042 26 |
| Leelanau | 5,151 50 | 9,601 00 | | 230 83 | 4,883 08 | 2,906 68 | 22,365 54 | 3,010 30 | 4,029 24 | 29,405 08 |
| Lenawee | 27,160 29 | 56,715 40 | 3,142 00 | 305 53 | 7,909 07 | 19,232 18 | 114,524 47 | 3,740 54 | 22,122 35 | 140,387 36 |
| Livingston | 12,848 20 | 23,694 60 | 181 23 | 22 47 | 2,105 64 | 7,812 23 | 46,066 87 | 402 28 | 10,209 17 | 57,279 82 |
| Luce | 2,070 00 | 5,130 00 | 101 00 | 10 00 | 1,097 51 | 4,281 86 | 13,090 97 | 65 10 | 3,566 55 | 16,924 62 |
| Mackinac | 3,994 50 | 9,696 50 | 53 00 | 1,187 15 | 1,135 57 | 3,590 18 | 19,060 90 | 3,164 84 | 4,135 86 | 26,242 60 |
| Macomb | 18,446 00 | 31,824 50 | 1,303 50 | 580 06 | 9,966 38 | 9,441 49 | 71,561 91 | 4,923 35 | 17,525 82 | 94,010 08 |
| Manistee | 14,968 59 | 41,566 88 | 1,086 00 | 1,722 45 | 3,965 92 | 17,826 46 | 82,163 30 | 3,903 38 | 10,236 44 | 96,303 12 |
| Marquette | 19,335 80 | 76,700 60 | 1,000 17 | 6,380 58 | 10,739 48 | 46,757 70 | 159,913 63 | 8,996 70 | 17,416 29 | 186,326 62 |
| Mason | 8,057 50 | 24,545 76 | 315 78 | 1,641 46 | 3,612 24 | 8,187 61 | 46,400 61 | 3,404 00 | 10,030 37 | 59,834 98 |
| Mecosta | 7,802 00 | 24,574 07 | 84 04 | 274 17 | 6,497 91 | 8,302 63 | 46,305 12 | 1,295 25 | 10,297 93 | 60,517 30 |
| Menominee | 10,840 10 | 38,962 50 | 545 57 | 4,721 88 | 10,614 38 | 17,191 87 | 82,876 30 | 6,065 06 | 9,619 89 | 98,551 87 |
| Midland | 3,968 78 | 16,576 14 | 15 14 | 743 03 | 2,530 45 | 6,430 09 | 30,063 63 | 5,683 29 | 11,518 84 | 47,205 76 |
| Missaukee | 5,598 15 | 9,561 87 | 295 17 | 511 97 | 1,504 90 | 4,000 35 | 21,792 41 | 1,267 66 | 9,463 23 | 32,523 32 |
| Monroe | 16,300 19 | 27,929 38 | 974 93 | 149 66 | 11,682 25 | 18,445 85 | 75,481 76 | 1,738 95 | 9,045 99 | 86,266 10 |
| Montcalm | 16,384 60 | 35,643 40 | 333 76 | 940 14 | 6,288 80 | 18,496 64 | 78,046 94 | 972 86 | 22,131 53 | 101,161 83 |
| Montmorency | 2,100 00 | 4,597 63 | 76 00 | 148 90 | 95 45 | 2,448 64 | 9,466 62 | 1,247 41 | 2,741 12 | 11,454 15 |
| Muskegon | 16,611 50 | 56,684 66 | 7,006 47 | 4,534 52 | 3,500 52 | 39,631 35 | 128,059 04 | 2,036 84 | 17,632 73 | 147,628 61 |
| Newaygo | 7,408 50 | 21,199 84 | 84 00 | 1,272 84 | 5,339 81 | 7,195 20 | 41,500 19 | 1,419 60 | 12,259 66 | 55,179 45 |
| Oakland | 25,254 27 | 62,139 76 | 621 87 | 1,213 04 | 6,728 00 | 17,968 81 | 104,325 86 | 6,021 17 | 16,596 12 | 127,183 14 |
| Oceana | 7,673 47 | 19,238 90 | 23 23 | 474 46 | 2,277 92 | 6,507 36 | 36,195 43 | 2,462 03 | 13,709 36 | 52,366 82 |
| Ogemaw | 3,316 50 | 7,630 20 | 11 00 | 712 02 | 3,119 39 | 2,686 36 | 17,359 87 | 6,324 46 | 6,521 84 | 30,206 17 |
| Ontonagon | 2,180 00 | 12,315 00 | | 310 05 | 3,218 45 | 7,249 13 | 25,273 28 | 9,550 00 | 2,867 40 | 37,410 63 |

| | | | | | | | | | | | | | |
|---|---|---|---|---|---|---|---|---|---|---|---|---|---|
| Oscoda | 8,271 70 | 24,184 32 | 73 16 | | | 1,391 57 | 1,358 66 | 7,476 65 | 42,591 06 | 4,925 65 | 10,184 13 | 57,700 84 |
| Otsego | 1,301 00 | 1,469 00 | 16 32 | | | | 42 30 | 596 82 | 3,336 44 | 383 18 | 591 48 | 4,311 10 |
| Ottawa | 5,155 15 | 6,515 00 | 7 00 | | | 60 84 | 1,357 13 | 3,105 93 | 16,781 86 | 516 11 | 6,259 43 | 123,557 00 |
| Ottawa | 21,213 00 | 44,659 81 | 389 34 | | | 1,707 12 | 5,425 50 | 21,499 64 | 64,874 41 | 5,884 86 | 17,834 95 | 118,604 22 |
| Presque Isle | 3,895 75 | 2,404 53 | 156 99 | | | 18 14 | 864 28 | 2,584 46 | 10,055 15 | 2,028 77 | 2,908 99 | 14,963 91 |
| Roscommon | 132 00 | 1,604 02 | | | | 187 50 | 226 67 | 596 39 | 2,745 58 | 74 37 | 1,073 09 | 3,983 04 |
| Saginaw | 34,674 90 | 119,078 83 | 1,726 07 | | | 2,506 00 | 28,870 98 | 46,396 44 | 228,843 30 | 7,060 90 | 23,229 53 | 250,743 33 |
| St. Clair | 19,099 93 | 60,165 08 | 4,024 69 | | | 1,515 88 | 6,870 27 | 28,275 10 | 130,821 93 | 7,841 95 | 16,616 57 | 144,940 95 |
| St. Joseph | 17,290 42 | 32,850 65 | 312 74 | | | 164 98 | 2,700 80 | 14,221 44 | 67,570 43 | 2,582 99 | 8,621 41 | 78,774 73 |
| Sanilac | 25,480 92 | 21,876 00 | 139 08 | | | 2,089 40 | 12,379 96 | 12,973 00 | 74,608 80 | 6,159 44 | 16,514 97 | 97,283 21 |
| Schoolcraft | 4,505 96 | 12,903 57 | 195 61 | | | 790 50 | 3,664 82 | 5,747 46 | 27,963 91 | 4,654 74 | 12,917 24 | 45,535 99 |
| Shiawassee | 18,556 82 | 40,842 01 | 674 88 | | | 1,219 67 | 11,535 49 | 30,596 54 | 93,124 12 | 3,976 97 | 19,449 08 | 110,560 15 |
| Tuscola | 15,827 44 | 31,834 10 | 124 99 | | | 1,082 88 | 5,066 03 | 12,634 74 | 66,514 60 | 6,779 80 | 1X,307 28 | 91,801 75 |
| Van Buren | 22,703 72 | 34,733 85 | 1,018 63 | | | 33 91 | 13,749 99 | 16,078 04 | 88,747 24 | 5,989 02 | 15,468 10 | 110,204 98 |
| Washtenaw | 35,346 82 | 70,562 96 | 1,776 53 | | | 2,416 03 | 25,150 36 | 27,241 49 | 153,823 09 | 7,231 23 | 12,455 08 | 173,909 40 |
| Wayne | 99,475 80 | 574,958 04 | 30,258 32 | | | 9,210 74 | 200,701 14 | 205,102 22 | 1,117,706 30 | 16,541 36 | 110,004 85 | 1,244,259 51 |
| Wexford | 7,334 00 | 27,259 04 | 216 14 | | | 562 23 | 10,387 10 | 15,896 96 | 61,069 56 | 6,439 65 | 14,474 73 | 82,573 84 |

DEPARTMENT OF PUBLIC INSTRUCTION.

## TABLE VII.

*Miscellaneous statistics as reported by school inspectors for the year ending September 4, 1899.*

| Counties. | Bonded indebtedness of the districts. | Total indebtedness of the districts. | Amount due the districts. | Amount paid and due inspectors and members of school boards for services. | Amount paid and due township chairmen and other officers for services. |
|---|---|---|---|---|---|
| Totals.................. | $1,964,616 94 | $2,177,355 25 | $327,537 54 | $15,121 32 | $31,280 99 |
| Alcona.................... | $296 00 | $441 65 | $1,584 93 | $90 50 | $24 75 |
| Alger..................... | 8,675 00 | 10,115 96 | 744 68 | 221 00 | 650 00 |
| Allegan................... | 38,611 92 | 39,479 55 | 3,319 17 | 189 05 | 96 80 |
| Alpena.................... | 2,150 00 | 5,988 09 | 3,782 28 | 416 50 | 527 83 |
| Antrim................... | 17,540 00 | 18,407 04 | 2,253 57 | 120 50 | 21 00 |
| Arenac.................... | 12,648 91 | 13,575 08 | 1,609 72 | 121 50 | 35 00 |
| Baraga.................... |  |  |  | 181 50 | 317 00 |
| Barry..................... | 2,774 51 | 3,514 42 | 1,045 16 | 119 00 | 82 50 |
| Bay....................... | 92,066 00 | 92,905 13 | 9,188 26 | 492 75 | 65 23 |
| Benzie.................... | 23,873 00 | 27,183 21 | 2,426 31 | 64 50 | 9 00 |
| Berrien................... | 37,412 80 | 39,856 83 | 3,163 02 | 195 10 | 210 67 |
| Branch.................... | 10,550 00 | 10,992 27 | 1,113 95 | 189 00 | 217 00 |
| Calhoun................... | 9,765 00 | 14,718 58 | 978 37 | 125 50 | 332 50 |
| Cass...................... | 7,425 00 | 7,515 44 | 787 85 | 159 75 | 74 00 |
| Charlevoix................ | 25,225 00 | 30,573 15 | 2,471 35 | 124 25 | 36 50 |
| Cheboygan................. | 40,807 25 | 43,527 75 | 3,046 51 | 115 50 | 159 50 |
| Chippewa.................. | 75,190 00 | 82,159 07 | 13,746 92 | 159 75 | 383 50 |
| Clare..................... | 12,150 00 | 12,954 97 | 1,769 79 | 100 00 | 108 15 |
| Clinton................... | 935 50 | 2,529 86 | 960 50 | 111 75 | 4 50 |
| Crawford.................. | 222 00 | 358 50 | 747 36 | 39 70 | 16 25 |
| Delta..................... | 51,000 00 | 51,358 56 | 1,121 76 | 297 33 | 720 50 |
| Dickinson................. | 13,751 50 | 69,731 03 | | 278 00 | 1,179 41 |
| Eaton..................... | 714 92 | 3,047 32 | 1,054 41 | 110 25 | 348 25 |
| Emmet..................... | 19,717 83 | 20,837 36 | 6,420 71 | 115 50 | 38 25 |
| Genesee................... | 28,993 15 | 29,490 48 | 1,666 10 | 232 00 | 330 75 |
| Gladwin................... | 2,925 00 | 4,190 50 | 2,516 02 | 132 90 | 51 25 |
| Gogebic................... | 55,000 00 | 57,000 00 | 2,304 68 | 449 50 | 1,119 99 |
| Grand Traverse.... ...... | 27,875 00 | 28,589 76 | 1,540 79 | 104 96 | 39 13 |
| Gratiot................... | 30,589 50 | 33,108 96 | 2,515 74 | 127 25 | 108 00 |
| Hillsdale................. | 2,855 00 | 5,350 32 | 711 53 | 94 00 | 121 00 |
| Houghton.................. | 22,600 00 | 24,439 77 | 9,052 60 | 254 50 | 257 50 |
| Huron..................... | 29,501 00 | 30,486 59 | 2,662 30 | 216 25 | 48 50 |
| Ingham.................... | 32,152 78 | 33,364 32 | 950 55 | 98 50 | 809 75 |
| Ionia..................... | 5,600 00 | 5,864 27 | 777 31 | 92 25 | 30 25 |
| Iosco..................... | 300 00 | 1,089 03 | 1,672 24 | 227 75 | 217 75 |
| Iron...................... | 13,000 00 | 17,601 77 | 1,285 33 | 411 00 | 934 59 |
| Isabella.................. | 19,912 50 | 21,332 62 | 5,108 16 | 169 75 | 147 25 |
| Jackson................... | 47,592 50 | 48,575 96 | 1,096 63 | 139 25 | 915 00 |
| Kalamazoo................. | 19,085 00 | 19,352 57 | 781 81 | 97 25 | 416 25 |
| Kalkaska.................. | 1,850 00 | 3,005 90 | 1,689 41 | 65 20 | 12 75 |
| Kent...................... | 303,033 33 | 304,341 77 | 29,600 23 | 231 85 | 952 50 |
| Keweenaw.................. | ............. | ............. | 71 50 | 77 00 | 97 50 |
| Lake...................... | 400 00 | 604 05 | 4,161 58 | 93 85 | 26 25 |
| Lapeer.................... | 11,015 00 | 11,327 94 | 1,048 01 | 134 50 | 99 26 |
| Leelanau ................. | 3,878 00 | 5,138 00 | 1,578 48 | 93 00 | 14 50 |
| Lenawee ..... ........... | 1,464 00 | 3,359 26 | 1,188 57 | 174 24 | 214 00 |
| Livingston................ | 760 00 | 1,336 24 | 1,356 51 | 102 25 | 13 75 |
| Luce...................... | ............. | 918 80 | 344 87 | 112 50 | 170 00 |
| Mackinac.................. | 16,725 00 | 18,195 07 | 2,114 95 | 242 15 | 509 50 |
| Macomb.................... | 6,310 00 | 9,659 72 | 1,288 37 | 255 75 | 116 75 |

## TABLE VII.—CONCLUDED.

| Counties. | Bonded indebtedness of the districts. | Total indebtedness of the districts. | Amount due the districts. | Amount paid and due inspectors and members of school boards for services. | Amount paid and due township chairmen and other officers for services. |
|---|---|---|---|---|---|
| Manistee................................ | $27,403 | $33,582 | $10,143 55 | $140 00 | $42 75 |
| Marquette............................ | 85,000 | 96,360 | 26,704 93 | 937 34 | 2,283 50 |
| Mason.................................. | 20,256 | 20,646 | 4,834 12 | 107 00 | 117 00 |
| Mecosta................................ | 4,775 40 | 5,419 87 | 3,081 11 | 168 50 | 184 40 |
| Menominee............................ | 73,475 00 | 74,796 98 | 1,340 85 | 234 16 | 735 00 |
| Midland................................ | 7,875 00 | 9,230 42 | 10,923 60 | 142 00 | 102 00 |
| Missaukee............................. | 5,400 00 | 6,299 18 | 4,766 65 | 117 00 | 35 50 |
| Monroe................................. | 12,850 00 | 13,449 00 | 756 26 | 256 25 | 29 50 |
| Montcalm.............................. | 15,040 00 | 15,925 50 | 2,609 78 | 189 00 | 67 25 |
| Montmorency......................... | 300 00 | 1,614 36 | 240 00 | 246 30 | 253 82 |
| Muskegon.............................. | 39,587 69 | 53,245 98 | 57,333 72 | 175 00 | 56 25 |
| Newaygo.............................. | 6,289 13 | 7,231 79 | 9,718 14 | 215 30 | 41 75 |
| Oakland................................ | 17,019 61 | 17,742 52 | 1,754 13 | 189 85 | 73 25 |
| Oceana................................. | 6,514 00 | 7,448 72 | 2,303 45 | 188 72 | 83 77 |
| Ogemaw............................... | 12,465 00 | 13,840 40 | 2,359 84 | 148 00 | 22 00 |
| Ontonagon. ......................... | 9,818 31 | 12,612 22 | 2,951 35 | 339 00 | 671 00 |
| Osceola................................ | 15,850 00 | 16,253 46 | 5,049 90 | 210 55 | 53 00 |
| Oscoda................................. | ............... | 497 82 | 437 50 | 79 50 | 62 50 |
| Otsego.................................. | 8,754 07 | 9,212 80 | 1,643 49 | 90 75 | 29 25 |
| Ottawa................................. | 27,904 00 | 30,237 32 | 1,466 13 | 172 75 | 307 15 |
| Presque Isle.......................... | 1,267 50 | 3,308 44 | 1,958 68 | 105 75 | 37 50 |
| Roscommon........................... | 3,000 00 | 3,968 53 | 749 97 | 47 00 | 4 50 |
| Saginaw............................... | 34,952 50 | 36,506 03 | 3,063 97 | 304 63 | 2,583 60 |
| St. Clair.............................. | 21,459 00 | 21,983 95 | 1,441 44 | 181 50 | 170 00 |
| St. Joseph............................ | 2,116 50 | 3,091 23 | 406 85 | 132 50 | 138 75 |
| Sanilac ............................... | 35,612 00 | 36,976 99 | 1,947 78 | 187 25 | 50 00 |
| Schoolcraft........................... | 17,250 00 | 18,991 89 | 1,287 39 | 150 50 | 250 35 |
| Shiawassee............................ | 37,750 60 | 39,732 39 | 1,447 52 | 105 50 | 285 50 |
| Tuscola................................ | 17,093 83 | 17,211 56 | 2,923 07 | 194 51 | 37 50 |
| Van Buren ............................ | 2,507 00 | 10,533 25 | 2,929 89 | 119 85 | 26 72 |
| Washtenaw............................ | 41,500 00 | 46,067 98 | 315 97 | 192 45 | 525 00 |
| Wayne.................................. | 158,457.50 | 164,038 13 | 13,272 49 | 384 75 | 8,549 00 |
| Wexford............................... | 8,655 00 | 9,393 01 | 3,004 17 | 151 48 | 40 12 |

## TABLE VIII.

*Cost per capita of public schools of the State for the school year ending September 4, 1899.*

| Counties. | Number of pupils included in school census in— | | Number of pupils enrolled in— | | Cost per capita for instruction based on school census in— | | | Cost per capita for instruction based on enrollment in— | | | Total expenses per capita during year based on enrollment in— | | |
|---|---|---|---|---|---|---|---|---|---|---|---|---|---|
| | Graded school dists. | Ungraded school districts. | Graded school dists. | Ungraded school districts. | Graded school districts. | Ungraded school districts. | All school districts. | Graded school districts. | Ungraded school districts. | All school districts. | Graded school districts. | Ungraded school districts. | All school districts. |
| Totals...... | 416,169 | 297,521 | 293,942 | 204,723 | $7 13 | $4 52 | $6 04 | $10 09 | $6 57 | $8 65 | $16 43 | $8 92 | $13 35 |
| Alcona......... | 227 | 1,768 | 183 | 1,237 | $5 80 | $4 24 | $4 51 | $7 13 | $6 06 | $6 20 | $9 53 | $7 68 | $7 92 |
| Alger.......... | 1,316 | 44 | 966 | 35 | 10 16 | 17 90 | 10 41 | 13 84 | 22 50 | 14 14 | 25 77 | 45 80 | 26 47 |
| Allegan........ | 3,991 | 8,087 | 3,165 | 5,855 | 7 36 | 4 21 | 5 25 | 9 28 | 5 81 | 7 30 | 15 22 | 7 77 | 10 38 |
| Alpena......... | 5,165 | 2,642 | 2,303 | 850 | 3 38 | 3 87 | 3 50 | 7 50 | 7 48 | 7 56 | 11 39 | 9 91 | 10 99 |
| Antrim......... | 1,993 | 625 | 1,614 | 1,922 | 6 43 | 6 45 | 6 74 | 7 94 | 8 81 | 8 42 | 11 99 | 12 05 | 12 02 |
| Arenac......... | 1,458 | 1,857 | 1,077 | 1,241 | 3 80 | 3 19 | 3 45 | 5 12 | 4 85 | 4 98 | 10 36 | 9 02 | 9 64 |
| Baraga......... | 1,397 | ... | 869 | ...... | 8 99 | ...... | 8 99 | 14 35 | ...... | 14 35 | 21 20 | ...... | 21 20 |
| Barry.......... | 1,663 | 4,744 | 1,427 | 3,767 | 9 47 | 5 88 | 6 72 | 10 80 | 7 33 | 8 27 | 14 69 | 9 27 | 10 76 |
| Bay............ | 15,011 | 6,513 | 8,600 | 3,546 | 5 40 | 2 62 | 4 56 | 9 42 | 4 59 | 8 08 | 14 11 | 6 92 | 12 01 |
| Benzie......... | 1,496 | 1,7 | 1,263 | 1,002 | 6 95 | 6 45 | 6 72 | 8 23 | 8 22 | 8 22 | 12 46 | 11 09 | 11 86 |
| Berrien........ | 7,400 | 6,410 | 6,351 | 4,528 | 7 74 | 4 73 | 6 33 | 9 02 | 6 70 | 8 05 | 14 68 | 8 53 | 12 12 |
| Branch......... | 2,597 | 4,224 | 2,043 | 3,116 | 8 61 | 5 72 | 6 81 | 10 89 | 7 76 | 8 99 | 16 37 | 9 88 | 12 45 |
| Calhoun........ | 7,032 | 4,912 | 5,599 | 3,556 | 8 92 | 5 56 | 8 68 | 11 19 | 8 75 | 10 24 | 15 52 | 11 08 | 13 77 |
| Cass........... | 2,031 | 3,723 | 1,764 | 2,782 | 9 40 | 6 53 | 7 55 | 10 88 | 8 67 | 9 55 | 14 43 | 11 39 | 12 32 |
| Charlevoix..... | 1,755 | 2,458 | 1,517 | 1,688 | 5 94 | 4 76 | 5 25 | 6 87 | 6 93 | 6 91 | 13 23 | 9 17 | 11 08 |
| Cheboygan..... | 2,911 | 2,246 | 1,886 | 1,396 | 8 48 | 5 43 | 5 11 | 7 48 | 8 78 | 8 03 | 12 96 | 12 78 | 12 98 |
| Chippewa...... | 3,225 | 1,569 | 2,207 | 1,329 | 6 76 | 5 12 | 6 13 | 9 80 | 7 73 | 9 07 | 32 61 | 10 06 | 24 13 |
| Clare......... | 1,042 | 1 | 743 | 1,187 | 5 52 | 4 74 | 5 05 | 7 75 | 6 63 | 7 96 | 11 63 | 8 75 | 9 86 |
| Clinton....... | 1,145 | 1,095 | 1,882 | 3,287 | 8 69 | 4 66 | 5 86 | 9 90 | 7 23 | 8 20 | 13 23 | 9 92 | 11 34 |
| Crawford...... | 427 | 275 | 387 | 171 | 8 74 | 6 76 | 7 96 | 9 87 | 10 87 | 10 02 | 13 19 | 13 23 | 13 21 |
| Delta.......... | 5,085 | 1,386 | 3,343 | 894 | 5 78 | 4 70 | 5 50 | 8 79 | 6 97 | 8 40 | 16 52 | 9 51 | 15 05 |
| Dickinson...... | 5,062 | 352 | 3,754 | 335 | 6 99 | 11 19 | 7 29 | 9 42 | 11 75 | 9 61 | 20 71 | 17 50 | 20 45 |
| Eaton.......... | 232 | 4,963 | 2,786 | 3,795 | 9 90 | 5 40 | 7 17 | 11 50 | 9 31 | 9 46 | 16 25 | 8 93 | 12 03 |
| Emmet......... | 801 | 2,056 | 1,298 | 1,283 | 6 82 | 5 33 | 6 03 | 9 46 | 8 54 | 9 12 | 13 12 | 11 49 | 12 30 |
| Genesee....... | 083 | 5,929 | 4,127 | 4,458 | 9 07 | 4 89 | 6 82 | 11 17 | 6 51 | 8 25 | 23 84 | 8 08 | 16 12 |
| Gladwin....... | 534 | 1,591 | 407 | 1,102 | 4 58 | 4 21 | 4 30 | 5 77 | 6 07 | 6 06 | 8 06 | 10 18 | 9 61 |
| Gogebic....... | 4,048 | 100 | 3,542 | 85 | 9 13 | 8 00 | 9 10 | 10 40 | 9 00 | 10 41 | 18 42 | 18 06 | 18 41 |
| G'd Traverse.. | 3,119 | 2,688 | 2,653 | 1,827 | 7 59 | 4 88 | 6 34 | 8 93 | 7 17 | 8 21 | 17 20 | 10 01 | 14 28 |
| Gratiot....... | 2,966 | 6,210 | 2,617 | 4,736 | 6 71 | 3 92 | 4 82 | 7 57 | 5 15 | 6 01 | 12 88 | 6 72 | 8 95 |
| Hillsdale...... | 2,885 | 4,799 | 2,304 | 3,565 | 8 32 | 5 81 | 6 76 | 10 39 | 7 82 | 8 83 | 15 39 | 10 09 | 12 18 |
| Houghton...... | 17,879 | 631 | 11,657 | 331 | 7 49 | 5 94 | 7 43 | 11 48 | 11 31 | 11 48 | 18 44 | 15 18 | 18 35 |
| Huron......... | 3,956 | 8,789 | 2,716 | 5,216 | 4 69 | 2 95 | 3 48 | 6 82 | 4 91 | 5 59 | 9 53 | 7 23 | 8 13 |
| Ingham........ | 6,377 | 4 | 4,715 | 3,284 | 8 19 | 5 74 | 7 15 | 11 08 | 7 85 | 9 75 | 15 87 | 10 33 | 13 60 |
| Ionia......... | 4,363 | 5,1 | 3,739 | 3,625 | 7 82 | 4 79 | 6 18 | 9 13 | 6 80 | 7 95 | 13 23 | 8 68 | 10 99 |
| Iosco......... | 2,400 | 1,167 | 1,875 | 704 | 5 24 | 3 73 | 4 75 | 6 70 | 6 18 | 6 56 | 8 73 | 8 66 | 8 71 |
| Iron.......... | 1,784 | 190 | 1,489 | 140 | 9 00 | 12 97 | 9 37 | 10 77 | 17 61 | 11 36 | 18 04 | 33 31 | 19 66 |
| Isabella...... | 1,675 | 5,777 | 1,400 | 3,886 | 7 44 | 3 66 | 4 51 | 8 90 | 5 44 | 6 36 | 15 49 | 7 11 | 9 39 |
| Jackson....... | 001 | 4,903 | 4,676 | 3,541 | 8 63 | 5 98 | 7 55 | 12 93 | 8 29 | 10 92 | 21 57 | 10 58 | 16 83 |
| Kalamazoo..... | 039 | 3,761 | 6,519 | 2,702 | 8 11 | 6 39 | 7 51 | 8 76 | 8 88 | 8 79 | 14 60 | 11 91 | 13 81 |
| Kalkaska...... | 502 | 1,344 | 435 | 962 | 6 74 | 6 86 | 6 83 | 8 93 | 9 58 | 9 02 | 10 65 | 14 23 | 13 11 |
| Kent.......... | 29,460 | 9,224 | 18,711 | 6,338 | 7 41 | 4 47 | 6 70 | 11 71 | 6 51 | 10 39 | 17 58 | 8 35 | 15 24 |
| Keweenaw..... | 627 | 156 | 414 | 119 | 5 72 | 6 06 | 5 73 | 8 66 | 7 77 | 8 50 | 10 25 | 10 69 | 10 74 |
| Lake.......... | 742 | 862 | 503 | 657 | 4 92 | 6 80 | 5 93 | 7 25 | 8 77 | 8 20 | 9 21 | 11 66 | 10 69 |
| Lapeer........ | 2,806 | 6,025 | 2,255 | 4,339 | 7 75 | 3 73 | 5 12 | 9 64 | 5 46 | 6 86 | 16 89 | 6 77 | 10 39 |
| Leelanau...... | 895 | 2,669 | 633 | 1,748 | 4 93 | 3 91 | 4 14 | 6 81 | 5 85 | 6 19 | 11 16 | 8 75 | 9 04 |
| Lenawee....... | 5,974 | 7,025 | 4,597 | 5,074 | 7 79 | 5 31 | 6 45 | 10 13 | 7 35 | 8 67 | 14 25 | 9 66 | 11 84 |
| Livingston.... | 1,440 | 4,023 | 1,268 | 3,034 | 9 83 | 5 32 | 6 69 | 11 17 | 7 37 | 8 73 | 14 97 | 9 12 | 10 85 |
| Luce.......... | 508 | 147 | 487 | 110 | 10 87 | 11 48 | 10 99 | 11 33 | 15 27 | 12 07 | 21 79 | 24 32 | 22 36 |
| Mackinac...... | 973 | 1,400 | 594 | 855 | 5 90 | 5 26 | 5 47 | 9 44 | 8 61 | 8 61 | 14 28 | 12 26 | 13 06 |
| Macomb........ | 4,362 | 6,495 | 2,860 | 3,654 | 6 42 | 3 53 | 4 67 | 9 51 | 6 27 | 7 72 | 10 21 | 8 86 | 10 98 |

## TABLE VIII.—Concluded.

| Counties. | Number of pupils included in school census in— | | Number of pupils enrolled in— | | Cost per capita for instruction based on school census in— | | | Cost per capita for instruction based on enrollment in— | | | Total expenses per capita during year based on enrollment in— | | |
|---|---|---|---|---|---|---|---|---|---|---|---|---|---|
| | Graded school districts. | Ungraded school districts. | Graded school districts. | Ungraded school districts. | Graded school districts. | Ungraded school districts. | All school districts. | Graded school districts. | Ungraded school districts. | All school districts. | Graded school districts. | Ungraded school districts. | All school districts. |
| Manistee........ | 6,914 | 2,577 | 4,711 | 1,656 | $6 48 | $4 55 | $5 96 | $9 52 | $7 09 | $8 88 | $13 86 | $6 17 | $12 75 |
| Marquette...... | 12,056 | 366 | 8,680 | 256 | 7 72 | 7 88 | 7 74 | 10 74 | 11 27 | 10 75 | 17 83 | 20 14 | 17 84 |
| Mason .......... | 2,979 | 3,297 | 2,214 | 2,414 | 6 33 | 4 19 | 5 21 | 8 51 | 5 71 | 7 05 | 11 69 | 8 49 | 10 02 |
| Mecosta........ | 2,356 | 4,951 | 1,891 | 3,530 | 5 73 | 3 76 | 4 39 | 7 13 | 5 27 | 5 92 | 10 06 | 7 70 | 8 52 |
| Menominee.... | 7,089 | 1,777 | 5,265 | 1,050 | 5 90 | 4 11 | 5 62 | 8 07 | 6 95 | 7 88 | 13 13 | 13 10 | 13 12 |
| Midland......... | 1,605 | 3,444 | 1,344 | 2,058 | 5 42 | 3 44 | 4 06 | 6 47 | 5 75 | 6 04 | 9 32 | 8 51 | 8 83 |
| Missaukee...... | 880 | 1,804 | 668 | 1,310 | 5 26 | 5 66 | 5 53 | 8 93 | 7 80 | 7 50 | 9 88 | 11 60 | 11 02 |
| Monroe......... | 3,217 | 7,504 | 1,623 | 5,121 | 5 04 | 3 73 | 4 13 | 9 99 | 5 47 | 6 56 | 22 91 | 7 16 | 11 20 |
| Montcalm....... | 3,705 | 7,081 | 2,947 | 4,994 | 7 14 | 3 61 | 4 82 | 8 97 | 5 12 | 6 55 | 13 93 | 7 99 | 9 83 |
| Montmorency.. | 791 | 106 | 595 | 53 | 8 04 | 4 06 | 7 47 | 10 54 | 8 11 | 10 33 | 15 03 | 10 09 | 14 61 |
| Muskegon ...... | 8,559 | 3,925 | 6,460 | 2,756 | 6 82 | 5 40 | 5 87 | 9 07 | 5 40 | 7 95 | 16 54 | 7 34 | 13 89 |
| Newaygo........ | 1,349 | 4,731 | 1,111 | 3,409 | 6 37 | 4 23 | 4 71 | 7 76 | 5 87 | 6 33 | 12 15 | 8 21 | 9 18 |
| Oakland........ | 5,228 | 5,962 | 3,999 | 4,201 | 8 10 | 6 05 | 7 00 | 10 59 | 8 58 | 9 56 | 4 96 | 10 73 | 12 77 |
| Oceana......... | 1,308 | 4,192 | 1,137 | 3,119 | 7 60 | 4 05 | 4 90 | 8 71 | 5 45 | 6 32 | 11 01 | 7 59 | 8 50 |
| Ogemaw........ | 764 | 1,571 | 619 | 1,028 | 4 95 | 4 49 | 4 64 | 6 11 | 6 85 | 6 57 | 11 70 | 9 84 | 10 54 |
| Ontonagon..... | 1,088 | 204 | 777 | 180 | 10 96 | 16 54 | 11 20 | 14 31 | 16 70 | 15 16 | 25 57 | 30 23 | 26 41 |
| Osceola........ | 1,863 | 3,983 | 1,651 | 2,842 | 7 97 | 4 43 | 5 55 | 8 97 | 6 21 | 7 22 | 11 82 | 8 12 | 9 48 |
| Oscoda......... | 135 | 194 | 107 | 155 | 6 96 | 8 92 | 8 12 | 8 79 | 11 16 | 10 19 | 12 44 | 12 94 | 12 74 |
| Otsego......... | 696 | 981 | 560 | 520 | 6 46 | 7 32 | 6 96 | 8 03 | 13 80 | 10 81 | 11 40 | 19 51 | 15 54 |
| Ottawa......... | 7,919 | 5,757 | 6,391 | 3,984 | 5 62 | 3 68 | 4 82 | 6 02 | 5 35 | 6 34 | 10 29 | 7 29 | 9 14 |
| Presque Isle.... | 547 | 1,988 | 208 | 768 | 2 66 | 2 43 | 2 48 | 7 02 | 6 30 | 6 45 | 10 95 | 10 13 | 10 30 |
| Roscommon.... | 235 | 306 | 139 | 135 | 4 00 | 3 86 | 3 94 | 6 76 | 5 89 | 6 34 | 11 57 | 8 43 | 10 02 |
| Saginaw........ | 17,407 | 9,307 | 11,173 | 5,802 | 7 14 | 3 22 | 5 78 | 11 12 | 5 16 | 9 09 | 16 77 | 7 19 | 13 47 |
| St. Clair....... | 9,246 | 8,223 | 5,965 | 5,621 | 5 24 | 3 81 | 4 57 | 8 13 | 5 58 | 6 98 | 12 84 | 7 82 | 10 40 |
| St. Joseph..... | 2,869 | 3,459 | 2,445 | 2,562 | 10 22 | 6 01 | 7 92 | 11 99 | 8 11 | 10 01 | 16 55 | 10 58 | 13 49 |
| Sanilac......... | 3,870 | 8,692 | 3,001 | 6,459 | 4 74 | 3 32 | 3 75 | 6 08 | 4 46 | 4 97 | 11 78 | 6 07 | 7 88 |
| Schoolcraft.... | 1,481 | 530 | 1,164 | 420 | 8 32 | 9 71 | 8 68 | 10 60 | 12 25 | 11 02 | 17 86 | 16 85 | 17 76 |
| Shiawassee.... | 4,241 | 4,828 | 3,840 | 3,476 | 8 49 | 4 78 | 6 52 | 9 38 | 6 64 | 8 08 | 16 41 | 8 84 | 12 73 |
| Tuscola......... | 3,363 | 8,243 | 2,471 | 5,575 | 5 99 | 3 33 | 4 11 | 8 16 | 4 94 | 5 92 | 10 91 | 7 09 | 8 26 |
| Van Buren..... | 3,967 | 5,508 | 3,475 | 4,018 | 7 51 | 5 04 | 6 07 | 8 58 | 6 90 | 7 66 | 14 52 | 9 53 | 11 84 |
| Washtenaw.... | 6,154 | 5,541 | 4,684 | 3,757 | 11 04 | 5 24 | 8 29 | 14 49 | 7 46 | 11 48 | 25 02 | 9 96 | 18 19 |
| Wayne... ...... | 90,946 | 8,253 | 56,279 | 4,866 | 6 93 | 3 96 | 6 69 | 11 21 | 6 71 | 10 85 | 18 89 | 9 14 | 18 28 |
| Wexford........ | 2,582 | 2,458 | 2,194 | 1,734 | 7 78 | 5 92 | 6 87 | 9 46 | 8 38 | 8 97 | 19 35 | 11 85 | 16 59 |

23

## TABLE IX.

Statistics of township and district libraries as reported by school inspectors for the year ending September 4, 1899.

| Counties. | No. of townships using library money for general school purposes. | No. of townships forfeiting library money. | No. of townships maintaining libraries. | Number of volumes added to township libraries during the year. | Whole number of volumes in township libraries. | Amount of taxes voted for township libraries. | Amount of fines, etc. received from county treasurer for township libraries. | Amount paid for books and care of township libraries. | Amount of township library money on hand Sept. 4, 1899. | Number of districts maintaining libraries. | Number of volumes added to district libraries during the year. | Whole number of volumes in district libraries. | Amount paid for the support of such libraries. | Amount of fines, etc. received from county treasurer for such libraries. |
|---|---|---|---|---|---|---|---|---|---|---|---|---|---|---|
| Totals....... | 396 | 413 | 431 | 7,770 | 188,000 | $2,882 16 | $11,015 45 | $11,574 74 | $15,068 18 | 3,292 | 62,006 | 723,813 | $96,920 06 | $107,171 41 |
| Alcona........ | 3 | 3 | 4 | 19 | 963 | .... | 81 42 | 827 15 | 830 75 | 8 | 13 | 382 | 82 65 | 963 23 |
| Alger......... | 2 | .... | .... | .... | .... | .... | 29 38 | .... | .... | 1 | .... | .... | 309 75 | 1,941 38 |
| Allegan....... | 11 | 4 | 9 | 490 | 4,410 | .... | 155 52 | 404 76 | 145 50 | 121 | 457 | 8,280 | 337 30 | 1,182 27 |
| Alpena........ | 4 | 3 | 2 | 58 | 399 | .... | 118 22 | 92 23 | 30 97 | 6 | 185 | 3,606 | 538 13 | 307 09 |
| Antrim........ | 3 | 3 | 12 | 296 | 3,213 | $75 00 | 93 44 | 428 59 | 520 58 | 18 | 225 | 1,404 | 36 96 | .... |
| Arenac........ | 9 | .... | .... | .... | .... | .... | .... | .... | .... | .... | .... | .... | .... | .... |
| Baraga........ | .... | 9 | 5 | 30 | 464 | .... | 18 84 | 41 84 | 46 27 | 8 | 151 | 730 | 139 33 | 296 56 |
| Barry......... | 9 | 6 | 4 | 590 | 2,983 | 180 00 | 3,209 61 | 389 45 | 28 43 | 3 | 290 | 1,170 | 190 51 | 70 50 |
| Bay........... | 6 | 5 | 3 | 171 | 2,005 | 175 00 | 108 50 | 240 88 | 435 88 | 67 | 606 | 5,802 | 166 90 | 834 86 |
| Benzie........ | 7 | 5 | 6 | .... | .... | .... | .... | 92 88 | 141 98 | 28 | 1,515 | 22,906 | 155 99 | 342 97 |
| Berrien....... | 6 | 7 | 5 | 124 | 4,761 | .... | 202 83 | 321 56 | 219 08 | 24 | 170 | 1,916 | 138 82 | 284 36 |
| Branch........ | 3 | 6 | 4 | 55 | 3,274 | .... | 40 52 | 275 34 | 164 04 | 138 | 3,357 | 17,804 | 1,134 09 | 1,962 08 |
| Calhoun....... | 4 | 8 | 3 | .... | 1,186 | .... | 90 32 | 10 00 | 98 48 | 43 | 319 | 2,904 | 176 43 | 1,411 22 |
| Cass.......... | 9 | 6 | 4 | 56 | 2,126 | 150 00 | .... | 44 86 | 92 88 | 82 | 706 | 23,054 | 1,345 70 | 1,462 60 |
| Charlevoix.... | 1 | 2 | 6 | 295 | 1,836 | .... | 113 96 | 286 88 | 204 07 | 60 | 987 | 5,048 | 725 93 | 674 46 |
| Cheboygan..... | 5 | 5 | 6 | 19 | 915 | 46 48 | .... | 34 48 | 46 05 | 15 | 196 | 1,150 | 143 80 | 163 18 |
| Chippewa...... | 3 | 2 | 2 | 38 | 276 | .... | 12 98 | 8 00 | 7 00 | 9 | 448 | 4,559 | 371 35 | 153 90 |
| Clare......... | 4 | 5 | 5 | 117 | 948 | 50 00 | .... | 30 41 | 196 17 | 7 | 384 | 2,350 | 222 84 | 29 50 |
| Clinton....... | 9 | 7 | 7 | 114 | 1,755 | 100 00 | 204 50 | 96 38 | 397 31 | 74 | 172 | 708 | 137 18 | 105 47 |
| Crawford...... | 1 | 2 | 4 | .... | 1,680 | .... | 53 55 | 120 92 | 78 41 | 9 | 546 | 3,605 | 444 04 | 1,251 88 |
| Delta......... | 8 | 8 | 1 | 83 | 375 | .... | .... | .... | .... | 10 | 40 | 437 | 76 75 | 7 |
| Dickinson..... | 5 | 4 | .... | .... | 5,553 | .... | .... | 25 00 | 108 33 | 7 | 220 | 2,430 | 239 10 | 54 70 |
| Eaton......... | 2 | 5 | 8 | 145 | 4,964 | .... | 201 71 | 396 57 | 573 60 | 70 | 394 | 1,964 | 854 58 | 477 64 |
| Emmet......... | 6 | 1 | 1 | 370 | 2,005 | 50 00 | 82 73 | 844 66 | 348 46 | 34 | 797 | 6,990 | 555 12 | 1,108 02 |
| Genesee....... | .... | 1 | .... | 40 | 400 | .... | .... | 47 73 | 163 22 | 102 | 531 | 2,465 | 190 96 | 30 12 |
| Gladwin....... | 2 | 6 | 3 | 71 | 481 | 75 00 | .... | 77 00 | 31 70 | 8 | 131 | 434 | 1,338 95 | 1,973 44 |
| Gogebic....... | 2 | 4 | 9 | .... | .... | .... | 29 44 | .... | 75 00 | 4 | 1,665 | 5,371 | 6 00 | 222 30 |
| Grand Traverse | 2 | 3 | .... | .... | 250 | .... | .... | .... | 534 00 | 98 | 327 | 3,051 | 528 04 | 369 22 |
| Gratiot....... | 6 | 10 | .... | 200 | 4,250 | .... | 119 76 | 259 14 | .... | 111 | 1,194 | 9,451 | 272 22 | 1,023 19 |
| | | | | | | | | | | | | | 657 44 | |

| | | | | | | | | | | | | | | | |
|---|---|---|---|---|---|---|---|---|---|---|---|---|---|---|---|
| Hillsdale | | | | | | | | | | | | | | | |
| Houghton | | | | | | | | | | | | | | | |
| Huron | | | | | | | | | | | | | | | |
| Ingham | | | | | | | | | | | | | | | |
| Ionia | | | | | | | | | | | | | | | |
| Iosco | | | | | | | | | | | | | | | |
| Iron | | | | | | | | | | | | | | | |
| Isabella | | | | | | | | | | | | | | | |
| Jackson | | | | | | | | | | | | | | | |
| Kalamazoo | | | | | | | | | | | | | | | |
| Kalkaska | | | | | | | | | | | | | | | |
| Kent | | | | | | | | | | | | | | | |
| Keweenaw | | | | | | | | | | | | | | | |
| Lake | | | | | | | | | | | | | | | |
| Lapeer | | | | | | | | | | | | | | | |
| Leelanau | | | | | | | | | | | | | | | |
| Lenawee | | | | | | | | | | | | | | | |
| Livingston | | | | | | | | | | | | | | | |
| Luce | | | | | | | | | | | | | | | |
| Mackinac | | | | | | | | | | | | | | | |
| Macomb | | | | | | | | | | | | | | | |
| Manistee | | | | | | | | | | | | | | | |
| Marquette | | | | | | | | | | | | | | | |
| Mason | | | | | | | | | | | | | | | |
| Mecosta | | | | | | | | | | | | | | | |
| Menominee | | | | | | | | | | | | | | | |
| Midland | | | | | | | | | | | | | | | |
| Missaukee | | | | | | | | | | | | | | | |
| Monroe | | | | | | | | | | | | | | | |
| Montcalm | | | | | | | | | | | | | | | |
| Mon morency | | | | | | | | | | | | | | | |
| Muskegon | | | | | | | | | | | | | | | |
| Newaygo | | | | | | | | | | | | | | | |
| Oakland | | | | | | | | | | | | | | | |
| Oceana | | | | | | | | | | | | | | | |
| Ogemaw | | | | | | | | | | | | | | | |
| Ontonagon | | | | | | | | | | | | | | | |
| Osceola | | | | | | | | | | | | | | | |
| Oscoda | | | | | | | | | | | | | | | |
| O sego | | | | | | | | | | | | | | | |
| Ottawa | | | | | | | | | | | | | | | |
| Presque Isle | | | | | | | | | | | | | | | |
| Roscommon | | | | | | | | | | | | | | | |
| Saginaw | | | | | | | | | | | | | | | |
| St. Clair | | | | | | | | | | | | | | | |
| St. Joseph | | | | | | | | | | | | | | | |

## TABLE IX.—CONCLUDED.

| Counties | No. of townships using library money for general school purposes. | No. of townships forfeiting library money. | No. of townships maintaining libraries. | Number of volumes added to township libraries during the year. | Whole number of volumes in township libraries. | Amount of taxes voted for township libraries. | Amount of fines, etc., received from county treasurer for township libraries. | Amount paid for books and care of township libraries. | Amount of township library money on hand Sept. 4, 1895. | Number of districts maintaining libraries. | Number of volumes added to district libraries during the year. | Whole number of volumes in district libraries. | Amount paid for the support of such libraries. | Amount of fines, etc., received from county treasurer for such libraries. |
|---|---|---|---|---|---|---|---|---|---|---|---|---|---|---|
| Sanilac | 11 | 6 | 10 | 155 | 2,367 | | $165 96 | $172 08 | $241 08 | 7 | 337 | 2,181 | $139 03 | $1,239 73 |
| Schoolcraft | 3 | 4 | 1 | | 305 | $20 00 | 31 45 | 52 00 | 281 41 | 57 | 6 | 1,771 | 195 61 | 1,198 18 |
| Shiawassee | 5 | 9 | 1 | | 650 | | 64 23 | 15 00 | 69 46 | 97 | 802 | 4,568 | 674 88 | 811 35 |
| Tuscola | | 6 | 10 | 176 | 3,476 | | | 181 89 | 206 14 | | 174 | 5,354 | 128 99 | |
| Van Buren | 4 | 7 | 7 | 464 | 5,039 | 200 00 | 223 89 | 536 31 | 680 90 | 62 | 1,642 | 7,401 | 1,018 63 | 1,505 57 |
| Washtenaw | 6 | 8 | 5 | 109 | 2,431 | | 37 04 | 109 08 | 13 92 | 128 | 2,708 | 15,255 | 1,775 53 | 1,596 80 |
| Wayne | 4 | | 12 | 21 | 3,725 | | 135 23 | | 178 17 | 21 | 9,375 | 183,905 | 39,258 82 | 45,151 00 |
| Wexford | | 4 | | 91 | 3,740 | 50 00 | 50 04 | 217 08 | 170 17 | | 136 | 2,527 | 216 18 | 159 02 |

## TABLE X.

*Branches of instruction as reported by school inspectors for the year ending Sept. 4, 1899.*

| Counties. | Algebra. | Arithmetic. | Botany. | Civil Government. | Geography. | Geometry. | Grammar. | Physics. | Orthography. | Physiology. | Reading. | U. S. History. | Writing. |
|---|---|---|---|---|---|---|---|---|---|---|---|---|---|
| Totals ............ | 2,028 | 7,041 | 881 | 5,673 | 6,795 | 727 | 6,707 | 746 | 4,340 | 6,523 | 6,874 | 6,648 | 5,654 |
| Alcona ................ | 9 | 25 | 3 | 19 | 23 | 5 | 23 | ...... | 16 | 20 | 22 | 21 | 20 |
| Alger ................. | 4 | 7 | 2 | 7 | 7 | 1 | 7 | 2 | 7 | 7 | 7 | 7 | 6 |
| Allegan ............... | 51 | 178 | 10 | 167 | 170 | 9 | 76 | 13 | 109 | 174 | 173 | 176 | 158 |
| Alpena ................ | 1 | 27 | 1 | 20 | 26 | 1 | 26 | 1 | 22 | 22 | 26 | 25 | 26 |
| Antrim ................ | 17 | 71 | 6 | 52 | 71 | 5 | 71 | 3 | 48 | 67 | 70 | 70 | 44 |
| Arenac ................ | 3 | 22 | 1 | 19 | 23 | 3 | 22 | ...... | 15 | 20 | 21 | 21 | 19 |
| Baraga ................ | 3 | 5 | 2 | 5 | 5 | 2 | 5 | 2 | 4 | 5 | 5 | 5 | 5 |
| Barry ................. | 40 | 144 | 19 | 132 | 144 | 15 | 144 | 17 | 82 | 141 | 144 | 146 | 108 |
| Bay ................... | 15 | 64 | 4 | 56 | 64 | 12 | 62 | 2 | 32 | 62 | 62 | 63 | 55 |
| Benzie ................ | 24 | 48 | 20 | 52 | 56 | 20 | 43 | 18 | 36 | 43 | 43 | 41 | 34 |
| Berrien ............... | 53 | 140 | 30 | 117 | 141 | 23 | 142 | 19 | 109 | 134 | 142 | 146 | 118 |
| Branch ................ | 40 | 128 | 7 | 106 | 127 | 6 | 129 | 13 | 64 | 121 | 126 | 122 | 101 |
| Calhoun ............... | 65 | 162 | 19 | 128 | 162 | 9 | 156 | 10 | 81 | 150 | 158 | 155 | 135 |
| Cass .................. | 40 | 112 | 10 | 96 | 111 | 8 | 111 | 7 | 73 | 108 | 110 | 116 | 74 |
| Charlevoix ............ | 17 | 64 | 5 | 52 | 64 | 6 | 63 | 4 | 39 | 60 | 64 | 63 | 49 |
| Cheboygan ............. | 7 | 58 | 2 | 36 | 58 | 3 | 53 | 2 | 36 | 54 | 57 | 54 | 51 |
| Chippewa .............. | 6 | 41 | 2 | 31 | 40 | 2 | 40 | 1 | 20 | 39 | 41 | 39 | 36 |
| Clare ................. | 5 | 49 | 3 | 35 | 45 | 5 | 49 | 4 | 37 | 45 | 49 | 42 | 41 |
| Clinton ............... | 24 | 129 | 12 | 115 | 129 | 7 | 129 | 6 | 83 | 113 | 127 | 128 | 108 |
| Crawford .............. | 2 | 16 | 9 | 12 | 20 | 1 | 20 | 1 | 14 | 20 | 21 | 13 | 19 |
| Delta ................. | 7 | 27 | 3 | 19 | 25 | 3 | 25 | 3 | 20 | 27 | 27 | 25 | 27 |
| Dickinson ............. | 5 | 8 | 3 | 6 | 8 | 4 | 8 | 3 | 7 | 8 | 8 | 8 | 8 |
| Eaton ................. | 36 | 148 | 25 | 112 | 145 | 22 | 136 | 22 | 70 | 134 | 145 | 141 | 116 |
| Emmet ................. | 19 | 64 | 7 | 42 | 65 | 7 | 62 | 18 | 39 | 49 | 64 | 60 | 54 |
| Genesee ............... | 74 | 157 | 45 | 136 | 155 | 34 | 154 | 35 | 105 | 145 | 155 | 153 | 119 |
| Gladwin .............. | 12 | 44 | 7 | 34 | 42 | 7 | 43 | 8 | 30 | 41 | 43 | 42 | 35 |
| Gogebic ............... | 3 | 7 | 2 | 4 | 7 | 2 | 7 | 3 | 6 | 6 | 7 | 7 | 6 |
| Grand Traverse ........ | 15 | 67 | 6 | 54 | 66 | 3 | 66 | 2 | 52 | 66 | 67 | 64 | 57 |
| Gratiot ............... | 38 | 128 | 17 | 107 | 126 | 16 | 126 | 15 | 94 | 119 | 126 | 117 | 108 |
| Hillsdale ............. | 48 | 163 | 18 | 117 | 162 | 11 | 158 | 11 | 75 | 154 | 163 | 156 | 137 |
| Houghton .............. | 22 | 29 | 15 | 26 | 28 | 12 | 29 | 11 | 25 | 27 | 27 | 27 | 25 |
| Huron ................. | 30 | 113 | 15 | 91 | 109 | 9 | 106 | 7 | 79 | 98 | 111 | 106 | 83 |
| Ingham ................ | 34 | 134 | 16 | 101 | 128 | 15 | 130 | 12 | 74 | 126 | 129 | 129 | 95 |
| Ionia ................. | 37 | 141 | 24 | 122 | 136 | 29 | 125 | 25 | 84 | 126 | 135 | 132 | 100 |
| Iosco ................. | 11 | 24 | 8 | 17 | 25 | 5 | 23 | 6 | 16 | 21 | 25 | 22 | 20 |
| Iron .................. | 3 | 8 | 2 | 6 | 8 | 2 | 8 | 2 | 6 | 8 | 8 | 7 | 7 |
| Isabella .............. | 24 | 96 | 7 | 80 | 92 | 3 | 91 | 7 | 55 | 88 | 94 | 88 | 72 |
| Jackson ............... | 55 | 156 | 13 | 135 | 150 | 10 | 153 | 8 | 81 | 149 | 153 | 152 | 135 |
| Kalamazoo ............. | 41 | 136 | 14 | 102 | 131 | 9 | 131 | 10 | 79 | 119 | 131 | 125 | 101 |
| Kalkaska .............. | 13 | 50 | 3 | 35 | 50 | 1 | 47 | 1 | 38 | 45 | 50 | 49 | 37 |
| Kent .................. | 52 | 207 | 18 | 181 | 202 | 10 | 208 | 14 | 116 | 197 | 197 | 193 | 175 |
| Keweenaw .............. | 3 | 5 | ...... | 4 | 5 | 2 | 5 | 1 | 5 | 5 | 5 | 5 | 4 |
| Lake .................. | 3 | 41 | 2 | 32 | 40 | 2 | 37 | 1 | 33 | 39 | 40 | 35 | 31 |
| Lapeer ................ | 43 | 134 | 23 | 120 | 129 | 18 | 132 | 29 | 76 | 120 | 130 | 128 | 109 |
| Leelanau .............. | 7 | 57 | 7 | 40 | 55 | 3 | 55 | 1 | 44 | 53 | 53 | 53 | 49 |
| Lenawee ............... | 70 | 197 | 17 | 164 | 195 | 15 | 197 | 9 | 119 | 186 | 194 | 191 | 167 |
| Livingston ............ | 61 | 129 | 6 | 106 | 126 | 6 | 128 | 10 | 81 | 117 | 125 | 120 | 111 |
| Luce .................. | 3 | 3 | 2 | 4 | 4 | 2 | 4 | 1 | 4 | 4 | 4 | 4 | 4 |
| Mackinac .............. | 4 | 15 | 1 | 6 | 15 | 1 | 14 | 3 | 11 | 14 | 16 | 15 | 16 |
| Macomb ................ | 37 | 114 | 24 | 91 | 114 | 15 | 114 | 24 | 79 | 100 | 115 | 103 | 99 |

## TABLE VIII.

*Cost per capita of public schools of the State for the school year ending September 4, 1899.*

| Counties. | Number of pupils included in school census in— | | Number of pupils enrolled in— | | Cost per capita for instruction based on school census in— | | | Cost per capita for instruction based on enrollment in— | | | Total expenses per capita during year based on enrollment in— | | |
|---|---|---|---|---|---|---|---|---|---|---|---|---|---|
| | Graded school districts. | Ungraded school districts. | Graded school districts. | Ungraded school districts. | Graded school districts. | Ungraded school districts. | All school districts. | Graded school districts. | Ungraded school districts. | All school districts. | Graded school districts. | Ungraded school districts. | All school districts. |
| Totals ...... | 416,169 | 297,521 | 293,942 | 204,723 | $7 13 | $4 52 | $6 04 | $10 09 | $6 57 | $8 65 | $16 43 | $8 92 | $13 35 |
| Alcona.......... | 227 | 1,768 | 183 | 1,237 | $5 80 | $4 24 | $4 51 | $7 13 | $6 06 | $6 20 | $9 53 | $7 68 | $7 92 |
| Alger........... | 1,316 | 44 | 966 | 35 | 10 16 | 17 90 | 10 41 | 13 84 | 22 50 | 14 14 | 25 77 | 45 80 | 26 47 |
| Allegan......... | 3,991 | 8,087 | 3,165 | 5,855 | 7 36 | 4 21 | 5 25 | 9 28 | 5 81 | 7 30 | 15 22 | 7 77 | 10 38 |
| Alpena......... | 5,165 | 1,642 | 2,303 | 850 | 3 38 | 3 87 | 3 50 | 7 59 | 7 48 | 7 56 | 11 39 | 9 91 | 10 99 |
| Antrim......... | 1,993 | 2,626 | 1,614 | 1,922 | 6 43 | 6 45 | 6 74 | 7 94 | 8 81 | 8 42 | 11 99 | 12 05 | 12 02 |
| Arenac......... | 1,458 | 1,887 | 1,077 | 1,241 | 3 80 | 3 19 | 3 45 | 5 12 | 1 85 | 4 98 | 10 36 | 9 02 | 9 64 |
| Baraga......... | 1,397 | ........ | 869 | ........ | 8 99 | ...... | 8 99 | 14 35 | ...... | 14 35 | 21 20 | ...... | 21 20 |
| Barry.......... | 1,663 | 4,744 | 1,427 | 3,767 | 9 47 | 5 88 | 6 72 | 10 80 | 7 33 | 8 27 | 14 69 | 9 27 | 10 76 |
| Bay............ | 15,011 | 6,513 | 8,600 | 3,546 | 5 40 | 2 62 | 4 56 | 9 42 | 4 59 | 8 08 | 14 11 | 6 92 | 12 01 |
| Benzie......... | 1,496 | 1,277 | 1,263 | 1,002 | 6 95 | 6 45 | 6 72 | 8 23 | 8 22 | 8 22 | 12 46 | 11 09 | 11 86 |
| Berrien........ | 7,400 | 6,410 | 6,351 | 4,528 | 7 74 | 4 73 | 6 35 | 9 02 | 6 70 | 8 05 | 14 68 | 8 53 | 12 12 |
| Branch......... | 2,507 | 4,224 | 2,043 | 3,116 | 8 61 | 5 72 | 6 81 | 10 89 | 7 76 | 8 99 | 16 37 | 9 88 | 12 45 |
| Calhoun ........ | 7,032 | 4,912 | 5,599 | 3,556 | 8 92 | 5 56 | 8 68 | 11 19 | 8 75 | 10 24 | 15 52 | 11 08 | 13 77 |
| Cass .......... | 2,031 | 3,723 | 1,764 | 2,782 | 9 40 | 6 53 | 7 55 | 10 88 | 8 67 | 9 55 | 14 43 | 11 39 | 12 32 |
| Charlevoix...... | 1,755 | 2,458 | 1,517 | 1,688 | 5 94 | 4 76 | 5 25 | 6 87 | 6 93 | 6 91 | 13 22 | 9 17 | 11 08 |
| Cheboygan..... | 2,911 | 2,246 | 1,886 | 1,396 | 8 48 | 5 43 | 5 11 | 7 48 | 8 78 | 8 03 | 12 96 | 12 78 | 12 98 |
| Chippewa ..... | 3,225 | 2,008 | 2,207 | 1,329 | 6 76 | 5 12 | 6 13 | 9 89 | 7 73 | 9 07 | 32 61 | 10 06 | 24 13 |
| Clare.......... | 1,042 | 1,661 | 743 | 474 | 8 61 | 5 52 | 5 05 | 7 75 | 6 63 | 7 96 | 11 63 | 8 75 | 9 86 |
| Clinton ........ | 2,145 | 5,095 | 1,882 | 3,287 | 8 69 | 4 66 | 5 86 | 9 90 | 7 23 | 8 20 | 13 83 | 9 92 | 11 34 |
| Crawford....... | 427 | 275 | 387 | 171 | 8 74 | 6 76 | 7 96 | 9 87 | 10 87 | 10 02 | 13 19 | 13 23 | 13 21 |
| Delta.......... | 5,085 | 1,386 | 3,343 | 894 | 5 78 | 4 59 | 5 50 | 8 79 | 6 97 | 8 40 | 16 52 | 9 51 | 15 05 |
| Dickinson...... | 5,062 | 352 | 3,754 | 335 | 6 99 | 11 19 | 7 29 | 9 42 | 11 75 | 9 61 | 20 71 | 17 50 | 20 45 |
| Eaton.......... | 3,232 | 4,983 | 2,786 | 3,795 | 9 90 | 5 40 | 7 17 | 11 50 | 9 31 | 8 95 | 16 25 | 8 93 | 12 03 |
| Emmet......... | 1,801 | 2,056 | 1,298 | 1,283 | 6 82 | 5 33 | 6 03 | 9 46 | 8 54 | 9 12 | 13 12 | 11 49 | 12 30 |
| Genesee....... | 5,083 | 5,929 | 4,127 | 4,458 | 9 07 | 4 89 | 6 82 | 11 17 | 6 51 | 8 75 | 23 84 | 8 08 | 16 12 |
| Gladwin ........ | 534 | 1,591 | 407 | 1,102 | 4 58 | 4 21 | 4 30 | 5 77 | 6 07 | 6 06 | 8 06 | 10 18 | 9 61 |
| Gogebic ........ | 4,048 | 100 | 3,542 | 85 | 9 13 | 8 00 | 9 10 | 10 40 | 9 00 | 10 41 | 18 42 | 18 06 | 18 41 |
| G'd Traverse.. | 3,119 | 2,688 | 2,653 | 1,827 | 7 59 | 4 88 | 6 34 | 8 93 | 7 17 | 8 21 | 17 20 | 10 01 | 14 28 |
| Gratiot........ | 2,968 | 6,210 | 2,617 | 4,736 | 6 71 | 3 92 | 4 82 | 7 57 | 5 15 | 6 01 | 12 88 | 6 72 | 8 95 |
| Hillsdale....... | 2,885 | 4,799 | 2,308 | 3,565 | 8 32 | 5 81 | 6 76 | 10 39 | 7 82 | 8 83 | 15 39 | 10 09 | 12 18 |
| Houghton ...... | 17,879 | 691 | 11,657 | 331 | 7 49 | 5 94 | 7 43 | 11 48 | 11 31 | 11 48 | 18 44 | 15 18 | 18 35 |
| Huron ......... | 3,956 | 8,757 | 2,716 | 5,216 | 4 69 | 2 95 | 3 48 | 6 82 | 4 91 | 5 59 | 9 53 | 7 23 | 8 13 |
| Ingham........ | 6,377 | 4,493 | 4,715 | 3,284 | 8 19 | 5 74 | 7 18 | 11 08 | 7 85 | 9 75 | 15 87 | 10 33 | 13 60 |
| Ionia.......... | 4,363 | 5,145 | 3,739 | 3,625 | 7 82 | 4 79 | 6 18 | 9 13 | 6 80 | 7 95 | 13 23 | 8 68 | 10 99 |
| Iosco.......... | 2,400 | 1,167 | 1,875 | 704 | 5 24 | 3 73 | 4 75 | 6 70 | 6 18 | 6 56 | 8 73 | 8 66 | 8 71 |
| Iron.......... | 1,784 | 190 | 1,489 | 140 | 9 00 | 12 97 | 9 37 | 10 77 | 17 61 | 11 36 | 18 04 | 33 31 | 19 68 |
| Isabella........ | 1,675 | 5,777 | 1,400 | 3,886 | 7 44 | 3 66 | 4 51 | 8 90 | 5 44 | 6 36 | 15 49 | 7 11 | 9 39 |
| Jackson........ | 7,001 | 4,903 | 4,676 | 3,541 | 8 63 | 5 38 | 7 55 | 12 93 | 8 29 | 10 92 | 21 57 | 10 58 | 16 83 |
| Kalamazoo..... | 7,039 | 3,761 | 6,519 | 2,702 | 8 11 | 6 39 | 7 51 | 8 76 | 8 88 | 8 79 | 14 60 | 11 91 | 13 81 |
| Kalkaska....... | 502 | 1,344 | 435 | 962 | 6 74 | 6 86 | 6 83 | 8 93 | 9 58 | 9 02 | 10 65 | 14 23 | 13 11 |
| Kent.......... | 29,460 | 9,224 | 18,711 | 6,338 | 7 41 | 4 47 | 6 70 | 11 71 | 6 51 | 10 39 | 17 58 | 8 35 | 15 24 |
| Keweenaw..... | 627 | 156 | 414 | 119 | 5 72 | 6 06 | 5 78 | 8 66 | 7 77 | 8 50 | 10 75 | 10 69 | 10 74 |
| Lake.......... | 742 | 862 | 503 | 657 | 4 92 | 6 80 | 5 93 | 7 25 | 8 77 | 8 20 | 9 21 | 11 66 | 10 69 |
| Lapeer......... | 2,808 | 6,025 | 2,255 | 4,339 | 7 75 | 3 73 | 5 12 | 9 64 | 5 46 | 6 86 | 16 89 | 6 77 | 10 39 |
| Leelanau....... | 895 | 2,669 | 633 | 1,748 | 4 93 | 3 91 | 4 14 | 6 81 | 5 85 | 6 19 | 11 16 | 8 75 | 9 04 |
| Lennwee....... | 5,974 | 7,025 | 4,597 | 5,074 | 7 79 | 5 31 | 6 45 | 10 13 | 7 35 | 8 67 | 14 25 | 9 66 | 11 84 |
| Livingston...... | 1,440 | 4,023 | 1,268 | 3,034 | 9 83 | 5 32 | 6 89 | 11 17 | 7 37 | 8 73 | 14 97 | 9 12 | 10 85 |
| Luce.......... | 508 | 147 | 487 | 110 | 10 87 | 11 43 | 10 99 | 11 33 | 15 27 | 12 07 | 21 79 | 24 32 | 22 26 |
| Mackinac...... | 973 | 1,400 | 594 | 855 | 5 90 | 5 26 | 5 47 | 9 44 | 8 61 | 8 92 | 14 28 | 12 26 | 13 08 |
| Macomb........ | 4,262 | 6,495 | 2,860 | 3,654 | 6 42 | 3 53 | 4 67 | 9 51 | 6 27 | 7 72 | 10 21 | 8 86 | 10 98 |

## TABLE VIII.—CONCLUDED.

| Counties. | Number of pupils included in school census in— | | Number of pupils enrolled in— | | Cost per capita for instruction based on school census in— | | | Cost per capita for instruction based on enrollment in— | | | Total expenses per capita during year based on enrollment in— | | |
|---|---|---|---|---|---|---|---|---|---|---|---|---|---|
| | Graded school districts. | Ungraded school districts. | Graded school districts. | Ungraded school districts. | Graded school districts. | Ungraded school districts. | All school districts. | Graded school districts. | Ungraded school districts. | All school districts. | Graded school districts. | Ungraded school districts. | All school districts. |
| Manistee........ | 6,914 | 2,577 | 4,711 | 1,656 | $6 48 | $4 55 | $5 96 | $9 52 | $7 09 | $8 88 | $13 86 | $6 17 | $12 75 |
| Marquette........ | 12,056 | 366 | 8,680 | 356 | 7 72 | 7 88 | 7 74 | 10 74 | 11 27 | 10 75 | 17 83 | 20 14 | 17 84 |
| Mason ......... | 2,979 | 3,287 | 2,214 | 2,414 | 6 33 | 4 19 | 5 21 | 8 51 | 5 71 | 7 05 | 11 60 | 8 49 | 10 02 |
| Mecosta........ | 2,356 | 4,951 | 1,891 | 3,530 | 5 73 | 3 76 | 4 39 | 7 13 | 5 27 | 5 92 | 10 06 | 7 70 | 8 52 |
| Menominee..... | 7,089 | 1,777 | 5,265 | 1,059 | 5 99 | 4 11 | 5 02 | 8 07 | 6 05 | 7 88 | 13 13 | 13 10 | 13 12 |
| Midland........ | 1,605 | 3,444 | 1,344 | 2,058 | 5 42 | 3 44 | 4 06 | 6 47 | 5 75 | 6 04 | 9 93 | 8 51 | 8 83 |
| Missaukee..... | 880 | 1,804 | 668 | 1,310 | 5 36 | 5 66 | 5 53 | 6 93 | 7 80 | 7 50 | 9 88 | 11 60 | 11 02 |
| Monroe........ | 3,217 | 7,504 | 1,623 | 5,121 | 5 04 | 3 73 | 4 13 | 9 99 | 5 47 | 6 56 | 23 91 | 7 16 | 11 20 |
| Montcalm..... | 3,705 | 7,081 | 2,947 | 4,994 | 7 14 | 3 61 | 4 82 | 8 97 | 5 12 | 6 55 | 13 93 | 7 99 | 9 83 |
| Montmorency.. | 791 | 106 | 595 | 53 | 8 04 | 4 06 | 7 47 | 10 54 | 8 11 | 10 33 | 15 03 | 10 09 | 14 61 |
| Muskegon...... | 8,559 | 3,925 | 6,460 | 2,756 | 6 82 | 5 40 | 5 87 | 9 07 | 5 40 | 7 95 | 16 54 | 7 34 | 13 89 |
| Newaygo...... | 1,349 | 4,731 | 1,111 | 3,409 | 6 37 | 4 23 | 4 71 | 7 76 | 5 87 | 6 33 | 12 15 | 8 21 | 9 18 |
| Oakland ...... | 5,228 | 5,962 | 3,999 | 4,201 | 8 10 | 6 05 | 7 00 | 10 59 | 8 58 | 9 56 | 14 96 | 10 73 | 12 77 |
| Oceana........ | 1,308 | 4,192 | 1,137 | 3,119 | 7 60 | 4 05 | 4 90 | 8 71 | 5 45 | 6 32 | 11 01 | 7 59 | 8 50 |
| Ogemaw........ | 764 | 1,571 | 619 | 1,028 | 4 95 | 4 49 | 4 64 | 6 11 | 6 85 | 6 57 | 11 70 | 9 84 | 10 54 |
| Ontonagon...... | 1,088 | 204 | 777 | 180 | 10 96 | 16 54 | 11 20 | 14 31 | 18 70 | 15 16 | 25 57 | 30 23 | 26 41 |
| Osceola........ | 1,863 | 3,983 | 1,651 | 2,842 | 7 97 | 4 43 | 5 55 | 8 97 | 6 21 | 7 22 | 11 82 | 8 12 | 9 48 |
| Oscoda......... | 135 | 194 | 107 | 155 | 6 96 | 8 92 | 8 12 | 8 79 | 11 16 | 10 19 | 12 44 | 12 94 | 12 74 |
| Otsego......... | 696 | 981 | 560 | 520 | 6 46 | 7 32 | 6 96 | 8 03 | 13 80 | 10 81 | 11 40 | 19 51 | 15 54 |
| Ottawa......... | 7,919 | 5,757 | 6,391 | 3,984 | 5 62 | 3 68 | 4 82 | 6 02 | 5 35 | 6 34 | 10 29 | 7 29 | 9 14 |
| Presque Isle.... | 547 | 1,988 | 208 | 768 | 2 66 | 2 43 | 2 48 | 7 02 | 6 30 | 6 45 | 10 95 | 10 13 | 10 30 |
| Roscommon.... | 236 | 206 | 139 | 135 | 4 00 | 3 86 | 3 94 | 6 76 | 5 89 | 6 34 | 11 57 | 8 43 | 10 02 |
| Saginaw........ | 17,407 | 9,307 | 11,173 | 5,802 | 7 14 | 3 92 | 5 78 | 11 12 | 5 16 | 9 09 | 16 77 | 7 19 | 13 47 |
| St. Clair....... | 9,246 | 8,223 | 5,965 | 5,621 | 5 24 | 3 81 | 4 57 | 8 13 | 5 58 | 6 98 | 12 84 | 7 82 | 10 40 |
| St. Joseph...... | 2,869 | 3,459 | 2,445 | 2,592 | 10 22 | 6 01 | 7 92 | 11 99 | 8 11 | 10 01 | 16 55 | 10 58 | 13 49 |
| Sanilac........ | 3,870 | 8,692 | 3,001 | 6,459 | 4 74 | 3 82 | 3 75 | 6 08 | 4 46 | 4 97 | 11 78 | 6 07 | 7 86 |
| Schoolcraft.... | 1,481 | 530 | 1,164 | 420 | 8 32 | 9 71 | 8 68 | 10 60 | 12 25 | 11 02 | 17 86 | 16 85 | 17 76 |
| Shiawassee.... | 4,241 | 4,828 | 3,840 | 3,476 | 8 49 | 4 78 | 6 52 | 9 38 | 6 64 | 8 08 | 16 41 | 8 84 | 12 73 |
| Tuscola........ | 3,863 | 8,243 | 2,471 | 5,575 | 5 99 | 3 33 | 4 11 | 8 16 | 4 94 | 5 92 | 10 91 | 7 09 | 8 26 |
| Van Buren.... | 3,967 | 5,508 | 3,475 | 4,018 | 7 51 | 5 04 | 6 07 | 8 54 | 6 90 | 7 66 | 14 52 | 9 53 | 11 84 |
| Washtenaw.... | 6,154 | 5,541 | 4,684 | 3,757 | 11 04 | 5 24 | 8 29 | 14 49 | 7 46 | 11 48 | 25 02 | 9 96 | 18 19 |
| Wayne ....... | 90,946 | 8,253 | 56,279 | 4,866 | 6 93 | 3 96 | 6 69 | 11 21 | 6 71 | 10 85 | 18 89 | 9 14 | 18 28 |
| Wexford....... | 2,582 | 2,458 | 2,124 | 1,734 | 7 78 | 5 92 | 6 87 | 9 46 | 8 28 | 8 97 | 19 35 | 11 85 | 16 59 |

23

## TABLE IX.

*Statistics of township and district libraries as reported by school inspectors for the year ending September 4, 1899.*

| Counties. | No. of townships using library money for general school purposes. | No. of townships forfeiting library money. | No. of townships maintaining libraries. | Number of volumes added to township libraries during the year. | Whole number of volumes in township libraries. | Amount of taxes voted for township libraries. | Amount of fines, etc., received from county treasurer for township libraries. | Amount paid for books and care of township libraries. | Amount of township library money on hand Sept. 4, 1899. | Number of districts maintaining libraries. | Number of volumes added to district libraries during the year. | Whole number of volumes in district libraries. | Amount paid for the support of such libraries. | Amount of fines, etc., received from county treasurer for such libraries. |
|---|---|---|---|---|---|---|---|---|---|---|---|---|---|---|
| Totals | 396 | 113 | 431 | 7,770 | 156,000 | $2,852 16 | $11,015 45 | $11,474 74 | $15,968 18 | 3,292 | 62,096 | 723,813 | $99,920 06 | $107,171 41 |
| Alcona | 3 | 3 | 4 | 19 | 983 | | 81 42 | 827 15 | 30 75 | 8 | 13 | 388 | 82 65 | 983 23 |
| Alger | | 2 | | | | | 29 38 | 404 76 | | 1 | | 106 | 369 75 | 1,941 38 |
| Allegan | 11 | 5 | 9 | 450 | 4,410 | 875 00 | 156 88 | 82 25 | 145 50 | 121 | 457 | 8,280 | 337 30 | 1,182 27 |
| Alpena | 4 | 5 | 8 | 56 | 598 | | 113 22 | 428 50 | 30 97 | 6 | 185 | 3,005 | 538 13 | 307 09 |
| Antrim | 3 | 3 | 12 | 296 | 3,213 | | 93 44 | | 350 28 | 18 | 225 | 1,404 | 38 96 | |
| Arenac | | | | | | | | | | 8 | 151 | 730 | 139 33 | 226 56 |
| Baraga | 9 | | | | | | | | 46 87 | 3 | | 1,170 | 190 51 | 70 80 |
| Barry | 6 | 5 | 10 | 30 | 464 | | 13 84 | 41 84 | 23 43 | 67 | 696 | 5,802 | 164 90 | 834 88 |
| Bay | 9 | 5 | 9 | 290 | 2,983 | | 3,299 61 | 389 45 | 435 86 | 28 | 1,515 | 2,996 | 156 89 | 342 97 |
| Benzie | 6 | 3 | 5 | 171 | 2,005 | | 106 50 | 240 85 | 141 95 | 24 | 179 | 1,916 | 133 82 | 354 38 |
| Berrien | 9 | 7 | 4 | 124 | 4,761 | 180 00 | 202 62 | 321 56 | 219 08 | 138 | 3,367 | 17,804 | 1,184 09 | 1,922 06 |
| Branch | 6 | 6 | 3 | 55 | 3,274 | 175 00 | 40 62 | 275 34 | 164 78 | 43 | 319 | 2,904 | 176 43 | 1,411 22 |
| Calhoun | 14 | 3 | 6 | 56 | 2,128 | | 90 32 | 10 00 | 98 48 | 86 | 705 | 23,624 | 1,245 70 | 1,462 60 |
| Cass | 7 | 5 | 5 | 285 | 1,836 | | 113 96 | 44 85 | 92 86 | 60 | 887 | 5,048 | 725 93 | 674 46 |
| Charlevoix | | 2 | 2 | | | 150 00 | | 286 98 | 204 07 | 20 | 195 | 1,130 | 143 80 | 153 18 |
| Cheboygan | 5 | 5 | 5 | 19 | 915 | 46 48 | 12 98 | 34 48 | 46 05 | 15 | 448 | 4,590 | 371 35 | 153 00 |
| Chippewa | 3 | 3 | 7 | | 276 | | | 8 00 | 7 00 | 9 | 384 | 2,280 | 222 84 | 208 50 |
| Clare | 4 | 5 | 4 | 385 | 948 | | | 30 41 | 195 17 | 7 | 172 | 3,606 | 137 18 | 108 47 |
| Clinton | 9 | 1 | 1 | 117 | 1,756 | 50 00 | 204 59 | 86 38 | 397 31 | 74 | 546 | 657 | 441 04 | 1,251 56 |
| Crawford | | 8 | | 114 | 1,680 | 100 00 | 53 35 | 120 92 | 78 41 | 9 | 40 | | 76 76 | 7 88 |
| Delta | 3 | 6 | 8 | 83 | 375 | | 201 71 | 25 00 | 108 33 | 10 | 220 | 2,430 | 329 10 | 54 70 |
| Dickinson | 5 | 4 | | 145 | 5,685 | | 82 08 | 386 57 | 573 62 | 7 | 584 | 5,964 | 384 58 | 477 64 |
| Eaton | 6 | 2 | 11 | 370 | 2,000 | | | 244 64 | 348 46 | 70 | 797 | 6,960 | 565 12 | 1,106 52 |
| Emmet | | 11 | 1 | 40 | 400 | 75 00 | 32 73 | 47 73 | 163 22 | 34 | 531 | 2,488 | 100 95 | 30 12 |
| Genesee | 6 | 6 | | | | | | | | 102 | 1,409 | 15,566 | 1,233 95 | 1,973 44 |
| Gladwin | 3 | 6 | 3 | 71 | | | 29 44 | | 31 70 | 8 | 131 | 424 | 6 00 | |
| Gogebic | | 2 | 9 | | | | | | 75 00 | 4 | | 5,374 | 529 04 | 222 20 |
| Grand Traverse | 3 | 3 | | | 461 | | | 77 00 | 288 00 | 28 | 1,566 | 3,051 | 272 22 | 369 52 |
| Gratiot | | 10 | 9 | 200 | 4,250 | | 119 70 | 299 14 | | 111 | 1,194 | 9,551 | 657 48 | 1,023 19 |

| County |
|---|
| Hillsdale |
| Houghton |
| Huron |
| Ingham |
| Ionia |
| Iosco |
| Iron |
| Isabella |
| Jackson |
| Kalamazoo |
| Kalkaska |
| Kent |
| Keweenaw |
| Lake |
| Lapeer |
| Leelanau |
| Lenawee |
| Livingston |
| Luce |
| Mackinac |
| Macomb |
| Manistee |
| Marquette |
| Mason |
| Mecosta |
| Menominee |
| Midland |
| Missaukee |
| Monroe |
| Montcalm |
| Montmorency |
| Muskegon |
| Newaygo |
| Oakland |
| Oceana |
| Ogemaw |
| Ontonagon |
| Osceola |
| Oscoda |
| Otsego |
| Ottawa |
| Presque Isle |
| Roscommon |
| Saginaw |
| St. Clair |
| St. Joseph |

TABLE IX.—CONCLUDED.

| Counties | No. of townships using library money for general school purposes. | No. of townships forfeiting library money. | No. of townships maintaining libraries. | Number of volumes added to township libraries during the year. | Whole number of volumes in township libraries. | Amount of taxes voted for township libraries. | Amount of fines, etc., received from county treasurer for township libraries. | Amount paid for books and care of township libraries. | Amount of township library money on hand Sept. 4, 1899. | Number of districts maintaining libraries. | Number of volumes added to district libraries during the year. | Whole number of volumes in district libraries. | Amount paid for the support of such libraries. | Amount of fines, etc., received from county treasurer for such libraries. |
|---|---|---|---|---|---|---|---|---|---|---|---|---|---|---|
| Sanilac | 11 | 6 | 10 | 155 | 2,367 | | $165 96 | $172 06 | $241 08 | 7 | 337 | 2,181 | $139 08 | $1,239 73 |
| Schoolcraft | 3 | 4 | 1 | | 805 | $20 00 | | 82 00 | 281 41 | 57 | 6 | 1,771 | 195 61 | |
| Shiawassee | 6 | 9 | 1 | | 650 | | 31 45 | 16 00 | 69 45 | 57 | 802 | 4,558 | 674 88 | 1,506 57 |
| Mia. | 7 | 6 | 10 | 176 | 3,476 | | 64 23 | 181 89 | 205 14 | 97 | 174 | 5,354 | 128 90 | 1,598 85 |
| Van Buren | 4 | 1 | 7 | 464 | 5,989 | 200 00 | 223 89 | 595 31 | 680 90 | 62 | 1,042 | 7,401 | 1,018 63 | 811 35 |
| Waw. | 6 | 8 | 5 | 109 | 2,431 | | 37 04 | 109 06 | 18 92 | 122 | 2,708 | 15,386 | 1,776 32 | 45,151 00 |
| Wexford | 4 | 11 | 12 | 91 | 3,725 | 50 00 | 135 88 | 96 90 | 173 17 | 21 | 9,375 | 183,906 | 39,258 82 | |
| | | | | | 8,740 | | 59 64 | 217 06 | 170 17 | | 196 | 2,527 | 216 18 | 169 02 |

## TABLE X.

*Branches of instruction as reported by school inspectors for the year ending Sept. 4, 1899.*

| Counties | Algebra | Arithmetic | Botany | Civil Government | Geography | Geometry | Grammar | Physics | Orthography | Physiology | Reading | U. S. History | Writing |
|---|---|---|---|---|---|---|---|---|---|---|---|---|---|
| **Totals** | 2,028 | 7,041 | 881 | 5,673 | 6,795 | 727 | 6,707 | 746 | 4,340 | 6,523 | 6,874 | 6,648 | 5,654 |
| Alcona | 9 | 25 | 3 | 19 | 23 | 5 | 23 | | 16 | 20 | 22 | 21 | 20 |
| Alger | 4 | 7 | 2 | 7 | 7 | 1 | 7 | 2 | 7 | 7 | 7 | 7 | 6 |
| Allegan | 51 | 178 | 10 | 167 | 170 | 9 | 76 | 13 | 109 | 174 | 173 | 176 | 158 |
| Alpena | 1 | 27 | 1 | 20 | 26 | 1 | 26 | 1 | 22 | 22 | 26 | 25 | 26 |
| Antrim | 17 | 71 | 6 | 52 | 71 | 5 | 71 | 3 | 48 | 67 | 70 | 70 | 44 |
| Arenac | 3 | 22 | 1 | 19 | 23 | 3 | 22 | | 15 | 20 | 21 | 21 | 19 |
| Baraga | 3 | 5 | 2 | 5 | 5 | 2 | 5 | 2 | 4 | 5 | 5 | 5 | 5 |
| Barry | 40 | 144 | 19 | 132 | 144 | 15 | 144 | 17 | 82 | 141 | 144 | 146 | 108 |
| Bay | 15 | 64 | 4 | 56 | 64 | 12 | 62 | 2 | 32 | 62 | 62 | 63 | 55 |
| Benzie | 24 | 48 | 20 | 52 | 56 | 20 | 43 | 18 | 36 | 43 | 43 | 41 | 34 |
| Berrien | 53 | 140 | 30 | 117 | 141 | 23 | 142 | 19 | 109 | 134 | 142 | 146 | 118 |
| Branch | 40 | 128 | 7 | 106 | 127 | 6 | 129 | 13 | 64 | 121 | 126 | 122 | 101 |
| Calhoun | 65 | 162 | 19 | 128 | 162 | 9 | 156 | 10 | 81 | 150 | 158 | 155 | 135 |
| Cass | 40 | 112 | 10 | 96 | 111 | 8 | 111 | 7 | 73 | 108 | 110 | 116 | 74 |
| Charlevoix | 17 | 64 | 5 | 52 | 64 | 6 | 63 | 4 | 39 | 60 | 64 | 63 | 49 |
| Cheboygan | 7 | 58 | 2 | 36 | 58 | 3 | 53 | 2 | 36 | 54 | 57 | 54 | 51 |
| Chippewa | 6 | 41 | 2 | 31 | 40 | 2 | 40 | 1 | 20 | 39 | 41 | 39 | 36 |
| Clare | 5 | 49 | 3 | 35 | 45 | 5 | 49 | 4 | 37 | 45 | 49 | 42 | 41 |
| Clinton | 24 | 129 | 12 | 115 | 129 | 7 | 129 | 6 | 83 | 113 | 127 | 128 | 108 |
| Crawford | 2 | 16 | 9 | 12 | 30 | 1 | 20 | 1 | 14 | 20 | 21 | 13 | 19 |
| Delta | 7 | 27 | 3 | 19 | 25 | 3 | 25 | 3 | 20 | 27 | 27 | 25 | 27 |
| Dickinson | 5 | 8 | 3 | 6 | 8 | 4 | 8 | 3 | 7 | 8 | 8 | 8 | 8 |
| Eaton | 36 | 148 | 25 | 112 | 145 | 22 | 136 | 22 | 70 | 134 | 145 | 141 | 116 |
| Emmet | 19 | 64 | 7 | 42 | 65 | 7 | 62 | 18 | 39 | 49 | 64 | 60 | 54 |
| Genesee | 74 | 157 | 45 | 136 | 155 | 34 | 154 | 35 | 105 | 145 | 155 | 153 | 119 |
| Gladwin | 12 | 44 | 7 | 34 | 42 | 7 | 43 | 8 | 30 | 41 | 43 | 42 | 35 |
| Gogebic | 3 | 7 | 2 | 4 | 7 | 2 | 7 | 3 | 6 | 6 | 7 | 7 | 6 |
| Grand Traverse | 15 | 67 | 6 | 54 | 66 | 3 | 66 | 2 | 52 | 66 | 67 | 64 | 57 |
| Gratiot | 38 | 128 | 17 | 107 | 126 | 16 | 125 | 15 | 94 | 119 | 126 | 117 | 103 |
| Hillsdale | 48 | 163 | 18 | 117 | 162 | 11 | 158 | 11 | 75 | 154 | 163 | 156 | 137 |
| Houghton | 22 | 29 | 15 | 26 | 28 | 12 | 29 | 11 | 25 | 27 | 27 | 27 | 25 |
| Huron | 30 | 113 | 15 | 91 | 109 | 9 | 106 | 7 | 79 | 98 | 111 | 105 | 83 |
| Ingham | 34 | 134 | 16 | 101 | 124 | 15 | 130 | 12 | 74 | 126 | 129 | 129 | 95 |
| Ionia | 37 | 141 | 24 | 122 | 136 | 29 | 125 | 25 | 84 | 126 | 135 | 132 | 100 |
| Iosco | 11 | 24 | 8 | 17 | 25 | 5 | 23 | 6 | 16 | 21 | 25 | 22 | 20 |
| Iron | 3 | 8 | 2 | 6 | 8 | 2 | 8 | 2 | 6 | 8 | 8 | 7 | 7 |
| Isabella | 24 | 96 | 7 | 80 | 92 | 3 | 91 | 7 | 55 | 88 | 94 | 88 | 72 |
| Jackson | 55 | 156 | 13 | 135 | 150 | 10 | 158 | 8 | 81 | 149 | 153 | 152 | 136 |
| Kalamazoo | 41 | 126 | 14 | 102 | 131 | 9 | 131 | 10 | 79 | 119 | 131 | 125 | 101 |
| Kalkaska | 13 | 50 | 3 | 38 | 50 | 1 | 47 | 1 | 34 | 45 | 50 | 49 | 37 |
| Kent | 52 | 207 | 18 | 181 | 202 | 10 | 208 | 14 | 116 | 197 | 197 | 193 | 175 |
| Keweenaw | 3 | 5 | | 4 | 5 | 2 | 5 | 1 | 5 | 5 | 5 | 5 | 4 |
| Lake | 3 | 41 | 2 | 32 | 40 | 2 | 37 | 1 | 33 | 39 | 40 | 35 | 31 |
| Lapeer | 43 | 134 | 23 | 120 | 129 | 18 | 132 | 29 | 76 | 120 | 130 | 128 | 109 |
| Leelanau | 7 | 57 | 7 | 40 | 55 | 3 | 55 | 1 | 44 | 53 | 53 | 53 | 49 |
| Lenawee | 70 | 197 | 17 | 164 | 195 | 15 | 197 | 9 | 119 | 186 | 194 | 191 | 167 |
| Livingston | 61 | 129 | 6 | 104 | 126 | 6 | 128 | 10 | 81 | 117 | 125 | 120 | 111 |
| Luce | 3 | 3 | 2 | 4 | 4 | 2 | 4 | 1 | 4 | 4 | 4 | 4 | 4 |
| Mackinac | 4 | 15 | 1 | 6 | 15 | 1 | 14 | 3 | 11 | 14 | 16 | 15 | 16 |
| Macomb | 37 | 114 | 24 | 91 | 114 | 15 | 114 | 24 | 79 | 100 | 115 | 103 | 99 |

## TABLE X.—CONCLUDED.

| Counties. | Algebra. | Arithmetic. | Botany. | Civil Government. | Geography. | Geometry. | Grammar. | Physics. | Orthography. | Physiology. | Reading. | U. S. History. | Writing. |
|---|---|---|---|---|---|---|---|---|---|---|---|---|---|
| Manistee | 31 | 57 | 20 | 49 | 57 | 9 | 55 | 18 | 47 | 53 | 57 | 53 | 47 |
| Marquette | 10 | 19 | 6 | 16 | 18 | 6 | 19 | 6 | 15 | 19 | 19 | 19 | 19 |
| Mason | 5 | 60 | 2 | 50 | 60 | 2 | 60 | 3 | 34 | 59 | 60 | 49 | 49 |
| Mecosta | 21 | 99 | 10 | 80 | 93 | 10 | 89 | 6 | 65 | 85 | 92 | 87 | 69 |
| Menominee | 6 | 29 | 7 | 20 | 31 | 4 | 31 | 2 | 22 | 30 | 31 | 29 | 26 |
| Midland | 16 | 70 | 13 | 50 | 70 | 11 | 66 | 9 | 39 | 66 | 71 | 59 | 66 |
| Missaukee | 8 | 49 | 4 | 33 | 49 | 6 | 49 | 5 | 33 | 49 | 49 | 48 | 33 |
| Monroe | 21 | 132 | 7 | 112 | 131 | 6 | 130 | 5 | 90 | 124 | 131 | 125 | 112 |
| Montcalm | 25 | 139 | 14 | 109 | 136 | 9 | 129 | 10 | 58 | 131 | 136 | 139 | 92 |
| Montmorency | 4 | 7 | 1 | 7 | 7 | 1 | 7 | 2 | 6 | 7 | 7 | 5 | 7 |
| Muskegon | 39 | 89 | 16 | 70 | 88 | 13 | 79 | 26 | 56 | 84 | 89 | 87 | 69 |
| Newaygo | 25 | 113 | 8 | 83 | 113 | 10 | 106 | 14 | 62 | 103 | 112 | 107 | 90 |
| Oakland | 76 | 201 | 21 | 136 | 96 | 22 | 196 | 13 | 100 | 171 | 187 | 183 | 158 |
| Oceana | 13 | 87 | 9 | 72 | 83 | 4 | 85 | 5 | 53 | 77 | 84 | 82 | 65 |
| Ogemaw | 6 | 39 | 8 | 24 | 39 | 3 | 38 | 7 | 26 | 37 | 39 | 32 | 32 |
| Ontonagon | 5 | 9 | 4 | 8 | 9 | 4 | 9 | 2 | 8 | 9 | 9 | 9 | 7 |
| Osceola | 15 | 91 | 10 | 67 | 90 | 7 | 91 | 4 | 62 | 87 | 89 | 82 | 64 |
| Oscoda | 5 | 12 | 2 | 9 | 12 | 2 | 11 | 1 | 8 | 12 | 12 | 11 | 11 |
| Otsego | 5 | 40 | 2 | 28 | 40 | 4 | 39 | 1 | 22 | 39 | 40 | 37 | 37 |
| Ottawa | 38 | 121 | 13 | 113 | 121 | 6 | 122 | 14 | 91 | 121 | 122 | 122 | 117 |
| Presque Isle | 8 | 33 | 2 | 27 | 33 | 6 | 33 | 5 | 18 | 32 | 32 | 33 | 28 |
| Roscommon | 1 | 13 | 1 | 8 | 13 | 1 | 12 | 1 | 12 | 12 | 13 | 12 | 13 |
| Saginaw | 50 | 153 | 28 | 137 | 157 | 25 | 150 | 16 | 98 | 154 | 153 | 152 | 142 |
| St. Clair | 38 | 152 | 14 | 131 | 153 | 11 | 150 | 9 | 106 | 145 | 152 | 148 | 121 |
| St. Joseph | 38 | 117 | 13 | 97 | 119 | 12 | 119 | 14 | 77 | 111 | 118 | 113 | 92 |
| Sanilac | 63 | 147 | 25 | 134 | 139 | 22 | 144 | 29 | 113 | 145 | 145 | 143 | 114 |
| Schoolcraft | 2 | 14 | 1 | 10 | 14 | 1 | 14 | 1 | 10 | 10 | 14 | 13 | 11 |
| Shiawassee | 26 | 119 | 23 | 100 | 119 | 13 | 110 | 9 | 67 | 126 | 122 | 121 | 104 |
| Tuscola | 49 | 146 | 18 | 129 | 144 | 23 | 142 | 20 | 107 | 140 | 143 | 140 | 119 |
| Van Buren | 46 | 150 | 14 | 124 | 150 | 12 | 150 | 12 | 91 | 140 | 150 | 148 | 123 |
| Washtenaw | 41 | 165 | 21 | 123 | 158 | 19 | 159 | 15 | 72 | 145 | 157 | 142 | 114 |
| Wayne | 47 | 155 | 20 | 110 | 153 | 17 | 152 | 21 | 87 | 142 | 149 | 148 | 133 |
| Wexford | 9 | 76 | 7 | 46 | 71 | 5 | 74 | 14 | 55 | 67 | 75 | 70 | 60 |

Number of districts in which instruction is given in—

## TABLE XI.

*Private and select schools for the year ending September 4, 1899.*

| Counties. | No. of schools. | No. of teachers. Men. | No. of teachers. Women. | Estimated No. of pupils. | Counties. | No. of schools. | No. of teachers. Men. | No. of teachers. Women. | Estimated No. of pupils. |
|---|---|---|---|---|---|---|---|---|---|
| Totals............... | 397 | 395 | 802 | 45,568 | Kent.................... | 31 | 24 | 53 | 3,199 |
| | | | | | Keweenaw............. | .... | .... | .... | ...... |
| | | | | | Lake................... | .... | .... | .... | ...... |
| Alcona................. | .... | .... | .... | ...... | Lapeer................ | 1 | 1 | .... | 12 |
| Alger.................. | .... | .... | .... | ...... | Leelanau ............. | 3 | 2 | 3 | 270 |
| Allegan................ | 4 | 1 | 4 | 195 | Lenawee ............. | 10 | 13 | 10 | 503 |
| Alpena................. | .... | .... | .... | ...... | | | | | |
| Antrim................ | .... | .... | .... | ...... | Livingston............ | .... | .... | .... | ...... |
| | | | | | Luce.................. | .... | .... | .... | ...... |
| Arenac................ | .... | .... | .... | ...... | Mackinac.............. | 1 | .... | 1 | 18 |
| Baraga................ | .... | .... | .... | ...... | Macomb ............. | 21 | 21 | 11 | 1,448 |
| Barry ................ | .... | .... | .... | ...... | Manistee............. | 7 | 7 | 5 | 582 |
| Bay .................. | 19 | 14 | 43 | 3,445 | Marquette............ | 6 | 1 | 18 | 1,250 |
| Benzie... ........ | .... | .... | .... | ...... | | | | | |
| | | | | | Mason................. | 5 | 6 | 6 | 315 |
| Berrien ............... | 6 | 8 | 15 | 601 | Mecosta .............. | 5 | 12 | 6 | 1,320 |
| Branch................ | 1 | 1 | .... | 25 | Menominee............ | 3 | 1 | 7 | 350 |
| Calhoun............... | 5 | 2 | 16 | 640 | Midland.............. | 1 | .... | 1 | 20 |
| Cass.................. | .... | .... | .... | ...... | Missaukee............. | .... | .... | .... | ...... |
| Charlevoix............ | .... | .... | .... | ...... | Monroe............... | 13 | 7 | 31 | 897 |
| Cheboygan............ | 4 | .... | .... | 309 | Montcalm............. | 1 | 1 | .... | 30 |
| Chippewa............. | 3 | 2 | 6 | 280 | Montmorency . ....... | 1 | 1 | .... | 20 |
| Clare................. | .... | .... | .... | ...... | Muskegon............. | 9 | 6 | 13 | 853 |
| Clinton............... | 5 | 1 | 10 | 483 | Newaygo.............. | 1 | 1 | .... | 25 |
| Crawford............. | .... | .... | .... | ...... | Oakland.............. | 1 | .... | 5 | 160 |
| Delta................. | 2 | .... | 16 | 800 | Oceana................ | 1 | 1 | .... | 50 |
| Dickinson............. | 1 | .... | 3 | 150 | Ogemaw............... | .... | .... | .... | .... |
| Eaton................. | 1 | 14 | 9 | 257 | Ontonagon............ | .... | .... | .... | .... |
| Emmet................ | 3 | 1 | 7 | 230 | Osceola............... | 3 | 2 | 1 | 102 |
| Genesee .............. | 4 | 4 | 7 | 160 | Oscoda................ | .... | .... | .... | .... |
| Gladwin............... | .... | .... | .... | ...... | Otsego................ | .... | .... | .... | .... |
| Gogebic............... | 1 | .... | 12 | 500 | Ottawa................ | 4 | 3 | 8 | 320 |
| Grand Traverse........ | 2 | 2 | 5 | 350 | Presque Isle.......... | 2 | 2 | .... | 60 |
| Gratiot................ | 2 | 3 | 3 | 120 | Roscommon .......... | .... | .... | .... | .... |
| Hillsdale.............. | 1 | 1 | .... | 15 | Saginaw.............. | 27 | 53 | 22 | 2,085 |
| Houghton.............. | 10 | 10 | 32 | 1,970 | St. Clair.............. | 19 | 10 | 34 | 1,705 |
| Huron................. | 11 | 10 | 5 | 952 | St. Joseph............ | 4 | 4 | 1 | 136 |
| Ingham ............... | 8 | 6 | 7 | 500 | Sanilac............... | 3 | 2 | 1 | 105 |
| Ionia................. | 4 | 3 | 6 | 210 | Schoolcraft........... | .... | .... | .... | .... |
| Iosco................. | 2 | 2 | .... | 160 | Shiawassee............ | 3 | 1 | 5 | 50 |
| Iron.................. | .... | .... | .... | ...... | Tuscola............... | 7 | 6 | 2 | 268 |
| Isabella............... | 2 | .... | 6 | 265 | Van Buren ........... | 1 | 1 | .... | 75 |
| Jackson............... | .... | .... | .... | ....... | Washtenaw ........... | 10 | 10 | 16 | 780 |
| Kalamazoo........... | 16 | 12 | 50 | 881 | Wayne................ | 76 | 99 | 280 | 15,071 |
| Kalkaska .............. | .... | .... | .... | ........ | Wexford.............. | .... | .... | .... | ...... |

## TABLE XII.

Examination and certification of teachers as reported by the county commissioner for the year ending July 1, 1899.

| Counties | Number of public examinations. | Number of applicants for regular certificates. | Number of applicants for special certificates. | Number of applicants receiving certificates. First grade. | Second grade. | Third grade. | Special. | Number licensed without experience in teaching. | Number of applicants having received Normal School instruction. | Number of applicants having attended Institute during the year. | Number of teachers having State certificates. | Number of teachers holding Normal School certificates. | Number of legally qualified teachers in the county. | Number making a permanent profession. | Number of certificates suspended. | Number of certificates revoked. | Average per cent required for certificates. First grade. | Second grade. | Third grade. |
|---|---|---|---|---|---|---|---|---|---|---|---|---|---|---|---|---|---|---|---|
| Totals | 880 | 14,233 | 1,006 | 158 | 2,075 | 5,185 | 624 | 2,182 | 604 | 4,249 | 214 | 731 | 11,268 | 6,803 | 4 | 1 | | | |
| Alcona | 4 | 59 | 5 | | | 13 | 5 | 9 | | 12 | 1 | 2 | 29 | 28 | 3 | | 85 | 80 | 75 |
| Alger | 3 | 35 | | 2 | 6 | 22 | | 9 | | 20 | | 6 | 42 | 35 | | | 90 | 85 | 80 |
| Allegan | 6 | 374 | 6 | 7 | 53 | 188 | 6 | 42 | 38 | 78 | 8 | 9 | 311 | 140 | | | 85 | 80 | 80 |
| Alpena | 3 | 77 | 8 | 1 | 9 | 21 | 8 | 42 | 5 | 28 | 1 | 1 | 40 | 30 | | | 85 | 85 | 80 |
| Antrim | 4 | 119 | 3 | | 28 | 46 | 3 | 14 | | 54 | 1 | 9 | 130 | 60 | | | 90 | 85 | 80 |
| Arenac | 4 | 90 | | | 10 | 38 | 2 | 18 | | 42 | | 2 | 60 | 16 | | | 85 | 75 | 75 |
| Baraga | 3 | 18 | 4 | | 6 | 5 | 4 | 3 | 36 | 10 | | | 23 | 22 | | | 90 | 80 | 80 |
| Barry | 4 | 199 | 12 | 1 | 22 | 97 | 5 | 47 | 5 | 125 | 5 | 13 | 210 | 15 | | | 85 | 85 | 85 |
| Bay | 4 | 143 | 5 | | 18 | 44 | 4 | 19 | 7 | 44 | | 4 | 152 | 15 | | | 80 | 75 | 75 |
| Benzie | 4 | 107 | 4 | 2 | 28 | 30 | 3 | 16 | 11 | 30 | 5 | 5 | 104 | 60 | | | 90 | 80 | 75 |
| Berrien | 4 | 306 | | 4 | 44 | 124 | 3 | 61 | 6 | 70 | 8 | 10 | 235 | 150 | | | 90 | 85 | 80 |
| Branch | 4 | 175 | | 3 | 31 | 79 | 18 | 31 | 3 | 70 | | 8 | 175 | | | | 85 | 85 | 75 |
| Calhoun | 4 | 417 | 12 | 5 | 75 | 124 | 20 | 70 | 19 | 185 | 2 | 8 | 374 | 388 | | | 85 | 85 | 80 |
| Cass | 4 | 194 | 50 | 5 | 23 | 57 | 12 | 16 | 4 | 53 | 3 | 13 | 162 | 100 | | | 90 | 85 | 80 |
| Charlevoix | 4 | 100 | 14 | | 22 | 39 | | 17 | 1 | 25 | | 6 | 118 | 78 | | | 90 | 85 | 80 |
| Cheboygan | 4 | 80 | 16 | | 16 | 30 | 9 | 8 | 2 | 31 | 2 | 5 | 80 | 50 | | | 95 | 85 | 80 |
| Chippewa | 4 | 60 | 8 | 2 | 9 | 34 | 7 | 11 | 9 | 51 | 1 | 5 | 61 | 45 | | | 90 | 90 | 70 |
| Clare | 4 | 64 | 6 | 4 | 11 | 22 | 6 | 13 | 9 | 9 | | 12 | 66 | 66 | | | 85 | 85 | 75 |
| Clinton | 4 | 295 | 12 | | 36 | 82 | 11 | 23 | 2 | 182 | 5 | | 204 | 200 | | | 85 | 85 | 75 |
| Crawford | 3 | 17 | 2 | | 5 | 11 | 12 | 2 | | | 2 | 2 | 23 | 30 | | | 90 | 90 | 75 |
| Delta | 4 | 51 | 15 | 1 | 13 | 22 | 10 | 7 | 5 | 3 | 1 | 1 | 68 | 25 | | | 85 | 85 | 80 |
| Dickinson | 2 | 37 | 6 | | 3 | 18 | 3 | 6 | 6 | 16 | | 1 | 38 | 17 | | | 85 | 75 | 70 |
| Eaton | 3 | 266 | 5 | | 25 | 107 | 4 | 88 | 10 | 200 | 2 | 2 | 290 | 80 | | | 90 | 80 | 75 |
| Emmet | 4 | 198 | 9 | | 23 | 44 | 5 | 21 | 9 | 31 | 2 | 7 | 100 | 40 | | | 85 | 80 | 75 |
| Genesee | 5 | 270 | 15 | | 49 | 115 | 4 | 56 | 21 | 75 | 6 | 5 | 290 | 140 | | | 85 | 80 | 75 |
| Gladwin | 2 | 95 | 6 | 7 | 10 | 13 | | 6 | 2 | 23 | 1 | 2 | 38 | 38 | | | 80 | 80 | 75 |
| Gogebic | 3 | 29 | | | 1 | 10 | | 2 | | | 1 | 1 | 14 | 14 | | | 80 | 80 | 70 |

Grand Traverse  
Gratiot  
Hillsdale  
Houghton  
Huron  

Ingham  
Ionia  
Iosco  
Iron  
Isabella  

Jackson  
Kalamazoo  
Kalkaska  
Kent  
Keweenaw  

Lake  
Lapeer  
Leelanau  
Lenawee  
Livingston  

Luce  
Mackinac  
Macomb  
Manistee  
Marquette  

Mason  
Mecosta  
Menominee  
Midland  
Milwaukee  

Monroe  
Montcalm  
Montmorency  
Muskegon  
Newaygo  

Oakland  
Oceana  
Ogemaw  
Ontonagon  
Osceola  

Oscoda  
Otsego  
Ottawa  
Presque Isle  
Roscommon  
Saginaw

TABLE XII.—CONCLUDED.

| Counties. | Number of public examinations. | Number of applicants for regular certificates. | Number of applicants for special certificates. | Number of applicants receiving certificates. | | | | Number licensed without experience in teaching. | Number of applicants having received Normal School instruction. | Number of applicants having attended institute during the year. | Number of teachers having State certificates. | Number of teachers holding Normal School certificates. | Number of legally qualified teachers in the county. | Number making a permanent profession. | | Number of certificates suspended. | Number of certificates revoked. | Average per cent required for certificates. | | |
|---|---|---|---|---|---|---|---|---|---|---|---|---|---|---|---|---|---|---|---|---|
| | | | | First grade. | Second grade. | Third grade. | Special. | | | | | | | | | | | First grade. | Second grade. | Third grade. |
| St. Clair, | 4 | 311 | 1 | 1 | 45 | 90 | 1 | 38 | 5 | 104 | .. | 1 | 217 | 65 | 0 | .. | .. | 85 | 80 | 75 |
| St. Joseph, | 3 | 223 | 27 | 4 | 48 | 82 | 25 | 24 | .. | 50 | 5 | 7 | 215 | 140 | 0 | .. | .. | 85 | 85 | 75 |
| Sanilac, | 4 | 378 | 5 | 2 | 37 | 122 | 3 | 31 | 10 | .. | 4 | 8 | 162 | 118 | | .. | .. | 90 | 85 | 80 |
| Schoolcraft, | 4 | 27 | 2 | .. | 9 | 16 | 2 | 9 | 2 | 6 | 1 | 6 | 47 | 44 | 0 | .. | .. | 90 | 80 | 75 |
| Shiawassee, | 4 | 275 | 30 e | .. | 34 | 114 | 13 | 43 | 20 | 125 | 3 | 10 | 225 | 100 | 0 | .. | .. | 85 | 75 | 70 |
| Tuscola, | 4 | 312 | 16 | 1 | 47 | 130 | 5 | 46 | 8 | 82 | 2 | 7 | 217 | 100 | 0 | .. | .. | 90 | 85 | 80 |
| Van Buren, | 4 | 273 | 37 | 4 | 48 | 106 | 2 | 57 | 9 | 72 | 6 | 11 | 250 | 210 | 0 | .. | .. | 90 | 80 | 75 |
| Washtenaw, | 4 | 264 | 19 | 5 | 67 | 118 | 9 | 42 | 17 | 74 | 1 | 19 | 305 | 100 | 0 | .. | .. | 85 | 80 | 75 |
| Wayne, | 5 | 298 | 41 | .. | 48 | 70 | 29 | 16 | 38 | 73 | 3 | 15 | 292 | 100 | 0 | .. | .. | 90 | 75 | 75 |
| Wexford, | 4 | 121 | 6 | 5 | 38 | 66 | 6 | 45 | 3 | 45 | 3 | 2 | 113 | 68 | 0 | .. | .. | 90 | 85 | 75 |

e. estimated.

## TABLE XIII.

*Condition of schools and school houses as reported by the county commissioners of schools for the school year ending July 1, 1899.*

| Counties. | Number of districts visited by the commissioner during the year. | Number of schools supplied with dictionaries. | Number of schools supplied with maps. | Number of schools supplied with globes. | Number of school houses properly heated and ventilated. | Number of schools having uniform text-books in each branch. | Number of schools having a prescribed course of study. | Number of schools properly classified. | Number of schools in which physiology, etc. is taught. | Number of districts that have adopted text-books in physiology. |
|---|---|---|---|---|---|---|---|---|---|---|
| Totals | 7,556 | 6,617 | 6,378 | 5,698 | 2,890 | 6,160 | 5,304 | 6,326 | 7,204 | 6,145 |
| Alcona | 27 | 26 | 27 | 27 | 1 | 27 | 27 | 25 | 27 | 27 |
| Alger | 23 | 15 | 15 | 14 | 20 | 24 | 24 | 20 | 20 | 20 |
| Allegan | 168 | e 175 | e 180 | e 160 | 175 | 170 | 184 | 168 | e 180 | 180 |
| Alpena | 44 | 20 | 25 | 25 | ...... | | 35 | 35 | 49 | 50 |
| Antrim | 73 | 70 | 70 | 71 | 3 | e 60 | 4 | 69 | 73 | 71 |
| Arenac | 29 | 24 | 27 | 12 | 24 | 27 | 31 | 28 | 30 | 27 |
| Baraga | 16 | 16 | 14 | 14 | 16 | 16 | 16 | 16 | 16 | 16 |
| Barry | 145 | 140 | 122 | e 90 | e 75 | 145 | 5 | 145 | 145 | e 128 |
| Bay | 63 | 63 | 63 | 63 | 5 | 63 | 63 | 63 | 63 | 63 |
| Benzie | 49 | 40 | 45 | 42 | 12 | 48 | 15 | 48 | 49 | e 48 |
| Berrien | 148 | 147 | 146 | 145 | 145 | 148 | 148 | 148 | 148 | 148 |
| Branch | 127 | 122 | 112 | 109 | e 12 | e 115 | 127 | 128 | 127 | 127 |
| Calhoun | 168 | 150 | 150 | 135 | e 100 | 160 | 161 | 150 | 155 | 161 |
| Cass | 109 | 106 | 97 | 84 | e 10 | 70 | 112 | 112 | 112 | 112 |
| Charlevoix | 63 | 64 | 65 | 64 | 5 | 60 | 65 | 65 | 66 | 66 |
| Cheboygan | 60 | 50 | 51 | 40 | e 20 | 50 | 6 | 58 | 58 | e 50 |
| Chippewa | 57 | 35 | 45 | 30 | ...... | 15 | 64 | 45 | 64 | 45 |
| Clare | 38 | 36 | 33 | 33 | | 31 | 3 | 51 | 51 | 51 |
| Clinton | 129 | 129 | e 100 | 60 | e 100 | 129 | 129 | 129 | 129 | 129 |
| Crawford | 34 | 19 | 19 | 19 | e 19 | e 14 | 19 | 10 | 19 | 19 |
| Delta | 20 | 31 | 35 | 30 | e 20 | 35 | e 25 | 28 | 30 | 30 |
| Dickinson | 6 | 20 | 24 | 22 | 20 | 24 | 24 | 24 | 24 | 34 |
| Eaton | 137 | 130 | 109 | 100 | | 137 | 137 | 137 | 137 | ...... |
| Emmet | 64 | 56 | 47 | 34 | | 21 | 4 | ...... | 67 | ...... |
| Genesee | 158 | e 150 | e 180 | e 125 | e 12 | e 140 | 158 | 150 | 140 | 130 |
| Gladwin | 28 | 30 | 30 | 25 | ...... | 30 | 34 | 34 | 34 | 34 |
| Gogebic | 5 | 12 | 12 | 12 | 5 | 14 | 2 | 2 | 3 | ...... |
| Grand Traverse | 66 | 66 | 60 | 60 | 3 | 63 | 5 | 5 | 66 | 66 |
| Gratiot | 131 | 123 | 93 | 96 | 13 | 125 | 132 | 115 | 132 | ...... |
| Hillsdale | 250 | 163 | 145 | 148 | 100 | 165 | 165 | 165 | 166 | 166 |
| Houghton | 27 | 27 | 27 | 36 | 32 | 20 | 18 | 27 | 25 | 16 |
| Huron | 113 | 96 | 107 | 97 | 11 | 113 | 113 | 113 | 113 | 113 |
| Inghum | 134 | 123 | 96 | 81 | 19 | 44 | e 115 | e 36 | ·127 | e 110 |
| Ionia | 140 | 124 | 120 | 128 | 20 | ...... | 130 | 130 | 140 | 140 |
| Iosco | 30 | 30 | 30 | 29 | ·1 | 26 | 4 | 2 | 30 | 30 |
| Iron | 8 | 12 | 12 | 8 | 7 | 25 | 25 | 21 | 25 | 25 |
| Isabella | 224 | 66 | 86 | 40 | e 80 | 100 | 102 | 102 | 102 | 102 |
| Jackson | 195 | 138 | 142 | 120 | e 84 | 136 | 152 | 120 | 150 | 156 |
| Kalamazoo | 137 | 130 | 119 | 98 | 25 | 125 | 130 | 125 | 135 | 130 |
| Kalkaska | 19 | 50 | 50 | 28 | 5 | e 5 | e 3 | e 12 | 52 | 52 |
| Kent | 185 | 240 | 236 | 234 | 146 | 200 | 12 | 175 | 206 | 206 |
| Keweenaw | 9 | 10 | 9 | 9 | 10 | 10 | 10 | 10 | 10 | 10 |
| Lake | 42 | 40 | 40 | 40 | 10 | 17 | 3 | 3 | 42 | ...... |
| Lapeer | 133 | 128 | 99 | 99 | 20 | 110 | 15 | 100 | 110 | e 75 |
| Leelanau | 57 | e 50 | e 50 | e 30 | 5 | e 55 | e 45 | 60 | 57 | 57 |
| Lenawee | 162 | 185 | 172 | 168 | 90 | 190 | 192 | 180 | 190 | 192 |

# DEPARTMENT OF PUBLIC INSTRUCTION.

## TABLE XIII.--CONCLUDED.

| Counties. | Number of districts visited by the commissioner during the year. | Number of schools supplied with dictionaries. | Number of schools supplied with maps. | Number of schools supplied with globes. | Number of school houses properly heated and ventilated. | Number of schools having uniform text-books in each branch. | Number of schools having a prescribed course of study. | Number of schools properly classified. | Number of schools in which physiology, etc., is taught. | Number of districts that have adopted text-books in physiology. |
|---|---|---|---|---|---|---|---|---|---|---|
| Livingston | 135 | 115 | 80 | 85 | 20 | 80 | 25 | 135 | 135 | 135 |
| Luce | 13 | 8 | 11 | 7 | 11 | 10 | 3 | 8 | 13 | 10 |
| Mackinac | 37 | .... | .... | .... | .... | e 18 | 3 | 3 | e 37 | e 25 |
| Macomb | 113 | 113 | 113 | 113 | e 80 | 113 | 113 | 113 | 113 | 113 |
| Manistee | 56 | 56 | 55 | 57 | 57 | 57 | 57 | 57 | 5 | 57 |
| Marquette | 100 | 36 | 36 | e 20 | 36 | 36 | 36 | 36 | 36 | 36 |
| Mason | 65 | 70 | 63 | 60 | .... | 62 | 71 | 60 | 71 | 71 |
| Mecosta | 103 | e 85 | e 93 | e 75 | 14 | 97 | 4 | 50 | 103 | 105 |
| Menominee | 58 | 57 | 55 | 50 | 2 | 60 | 61 | 61 | 61 | 61 |
| Midland | 59 | e 60 | e 60 | e 50 | 65 | 60 | .... | 62 | e 68 | 70 |
| Missaukee | 53 | 49 | 50 | 50 | .... | 44 | 53 | e 40 | 52 | .... |
| Monroe | 140 | 137 | 135 | e 127 | 4 | 135 | 140 | 135 | 140 | 140 |
| Montcalm | 137 | 130 | 130 | 125 | 75 | e 125 | 95 | 95 | 130 | 130 |
| Montmorency | 7 | 13 | 18 | 18 | 1 | 21 | 27 | 27 | 27 | .... |
| Muskegon | 94 | e 75 | e 75 | e 75 | e 75 | e 80 | 94 | 94 | 94 | 25 |
| Newaygo | 112 | 86 | 85 | 84 | e 20 | 106 | 110 | 100 | 116 | 116 |
| Oakland | 160 | 175 | 150 | 100 | 50 | 75 | 207 | 207 | 207 | 207 |
| Oceana | 85 | 83 | 79 | 74 | 14 | 84 | 3 | 80 | e 85 | e 75 |
| Ogemaw | 41 | 40 | 33 | 32 | .... | 26 | 5 | 38 | 41 | 36 |
| Ontonagon | 31 | 26 | 23 | 19 | 4 | 19 | 22 | 20 | 23 | 30 |
| Osceola | 87 | 87 | 83 | 80 | 4 | 90 | 86 | 88 | 98 | 87 |
| Oscoda | 12 | 16 | 15 | 15 | 8 | 8 | 19 | 19 | 19 | 19 |
| Otsego | 40 | 40 | 38 | 34 | 20 | 35 | 40 | 40 | 40 | 40 |
| Ottawa | 121 | 118 | 108 | 92 | 90 | 121 | 90 | 90 | 110 | e 30 |
| Presque Isle | 40 | 34 | 38 | 25 | 37 | 1 | 39 | 40 | 41 | .... |
| Roscommon | 6 | 6 | 10 | 7 | 1 | 6 | 1 | 8 | 21 | e 9 |
| Saginaw | 153 | 139 | 143 | 129 | 153 | 176 | 5 | 176 | 176 | 153 |
| St. Clair | 152 | 140 | e 125 | e 125 | e 75 | e 140 | 153 | 150 | 153 | e 15 |
| St. Joseph | 240 | 117 | 115 | 83 | e 50 | e 100 | 124 | 120 | 124 | .... |
| Sanilac | 144 | 98 | 124 | 78 | 79 | 129 | 52 | 52 | 141 | 141 |
| Schoolcraft | 25 | 21 | 19 | 12 | 4 | 26 | 1 | 26 | 26 | 26 |
| Shiawassee | 125 | 100 | 80 | 65 | e 10 | 120 | 8 | 100 | 125 | 125 |
| Tuscola | 139 | 129 | 134 | 132 | e 135 | 143 | 147 | 147 | 147 | 146 |
| Van Buren | 235 | 151 | 115 | 141 | 125 | 140 | 151 | 151 | 151 | 151 |
| Washtenaw | 164 | 127 | 138 | 135 | e 50 | e 100 | e 150 | 100 | 164 | 164 |
| Wayne | 153 | 136 | 143 | 125 | 26 | 145 | 40 | 139 | 145 | e 130 |
| Wexford | 76 | 75 | 76 | 76 | 70 | 70 | 76 | 70 | 75 | e 75 |

e. estimated.

## TABLE XIV.

*Miscellaneous statistics as reported by the county commissioner of schools for the year ending July 1, 1899.*

| Counties. | Number of meetings of county teachers' associations. | Number of meetings of township teachers' associations. | Number of days devoted to meetings of county board. | Amount allowed by board of supervisors for stationery, etc. | Amount of compensation received by members of the board other than the commissioner. | Salary of the commissioner. | Amount of institute fees collected. | Number of townships organized as township districts. | Number of districts furnishing free text-books. |
|---|---|---|---|---|---|---|---|---|---|
| Totals | 207 | 654 | 903 | $9,581 09 | $15,873 90 | $66,785 00 | $10,293 00 | 129 | 685 |
| Alcona | 3 | | 4 | $21 00 | $60 00 | $300 00 | e $12 00 | 1 | 5 |
| Alger | | 2 | 9 | 200 00 | 84 00 | 300 00 | 29 00 | 7 | 7 |
| Allegan | 6 | 13 | 22 | | 286 00 | 1,350 00 | 295 00 | ..... | ..... |
| Alpena | | | 30 | 100 00 | 240 00 | 550 00 | 50 50 | 5 | ..... |
| Antrim | 2 | | 16 | 118 00 | 144 00 | 600 00 | 41 00 | | |
| Arenac | 1 | | 12 | e 50 00 | 96 00 | 250 00 | 53 50 | ..... | 3 |
| Baraga | | | 3 | 48 60 | 121 40 | 500 00 | 25 00 | 5 | 5 |
| Barry | 4 | 16 | 4 | 158 70 | 288 00 | 1,200 00 | 169 50 | ..... | 4 |
| Bay | 4 | | 12 | 300 00 | 262 00 | 1,000 00 | 135 50 | 1 | 25 |
| Benzie | 2 | 5 | 10 | 47 38 | 122 00 | 500 00 | 67 50 | ..... | 3 |
| Berrien | 2 | 62 | 12 | 175 29 | 247 50 | 1,200 00 | 219 50 | ..... | 10 |
| Branch | 3 | | 4 | 84 39 | 236 00 | 1,200 00 | 187 50 | ..... | ..... |
| Calhoun | 4 | 46 | 12 | 187 25 | 229 00 | 1,200 00 | 285 00 | | 3 |
| Cass | 2 | | 12 | 187 39 | 392 50 | 1,000 00 | 136 00 | | |
| Charlevoix | 4 | | 4 | e 100 00 | e 96 00 | 600 00 | 62 50 | | 13 |
| Cheboygan | 3 | | 13 | 89 50 | 208 00 | 500 00 | 57 50 | 2 | 20 |
| Chippewa | 1 | | 4 | 400 00 | 188 00 | 800 00 | ..... | 6 | 20 |
| Clare | 1 | | 12 | e 20 00 | 96 00 | 500 00 | 39 00 | ..... | e 10 |
| Clinton | 2 | 3 | 28 | ..... | 228 00 | 1,200 00 | 139 00 | | 4 |
| Crawford | | | 3 | 5 00 | 24 00 | 200 00 | 14 00 | 1 | e 12 |
| Delta | | | 12 | e 50 00 | 156 00 | 500 00 | 41 50 | 6 | ..... |
| Dickinson | 1 | 3 | ..... | e 50 00 | 48 00 | 300 00 | 48 50 | 6 | 4 |
| Eaton | 3 | 26 | 4 | 200 00 | 212 00 | 1,200 00 | 184 50 | ..... | 12 |
| Emmet | 1 | | 4 | 93 00 | 168 00 | 600 00 | 87 00 | ..... | 11 |
| Genesee | 2 | 10 | 6 | 143 64 | 425 00 | 1,200 00 | 247 00 | ..... | 1 |
| Gladwin | 2 | | 2 | e 40 00 | 80 00 | 300 00 | 44 50 | ..... | 6 |
| Gogebic | | 10 | 3 | 22 00 | 12 00 | 450 00 | ..... | 5 | 4 |
| Grand Traverse | 1 | 6 | 4 | 50 00 | 180 00 | 600 00 | 108 50 | 1 | 6 |
| Gratiot | 2 | 7 | 12 | e 140 00 | 290 00 | 1,300 00 | 176 00 | ..... | 2 |
| Hillsdale | 3 | 24 | 4 | 250 00 | ..... | 1,200 00 | 216 50 | ..... | |
| Houghton | 1 | | 5 | 54 00 | 128 00 | 800 00 | 145 50 | 2 | e 10 |
| Huron | 4 | 2 | 3 | 200 00 | ..... | 1,000 00 | ..... | ..... | 35 |
| Ingham | 3 | | 35 | 139 42 | 308 00 | 1,350 00 | 228 50 | ..... | |
| Ionia | 3 | 12 | 8 | 200 00 | 150 00 | 1,200 00 | 174 50 | ..... | |
| Iosco | 2 | | 13 | 40 70 | 52 00 | 300 00 | 31 00 | ..... | 9 |
| Iron | | 3 | 3 | 75 00 | 64 00 | 300 00 | 12 50 | 8 | 3 |
| Isabella | 1 | 3 | 4 | 116 00 | 108 00 | 1,100 00 | 76 00 | ..... | 7 |
| Jackson | 2 | 6 | 32 | ..... | 350 00 | 1,200 00 | 200 00 | ..... | |
| Kalamazoo | 2 | 20 | 6 | 206 00 | 340 00 | 1,200 00 | 228 00 | ..... | 8 |
| Kalkaska | 3 | | 3 | 73 00 | ..... | 500 00 | 28 00 | ..... | e 3 |
| Kent | 9 | 49 | 46 | 200 00 | 844 00 | 1,500 00 | 392 50 | ..... | 4 |
| Keweenaw | | | 4 | e 6 00 | e 24 00 | 125 00 | 6 50 | 3 | |
| Luke | 1 | | 4 | 32 15 | 192 00 | 400 00 | 40 00 | ..... | 6 |
| Lapeer | 2 | 20 | 12 | 115 00 | 250 00 | 1,200 00 | 222 00 | ..... | 1 |
| Leelanau | 2 | | 12 | e 15 00 | ..... | 550 00 | 47 50 | ..... | 7 |
| Lenawee | 2 | 19 | 8 | 194 58 | 245 00 | 1,200 00 | 292 00 | ..... | 4 |

# DEPARTMENT OF PUBLIC INSTRUCTION.

## TABLE XIV.—Concluded.

| Counties. | Number of meetings of county teachers' associations. | Number of meetings of township teachers' associations. | Number of days devoted to meetings of county board. | Amount allowed by board of supervisors for stationery, etc. | Amount of compensation received by members of the board other than the commissioner. | Salary of the commissioner. | Amount of institute fees collected. | Number of townships organized as township districts. | Number of districts furnishing free text-books. |
|---|---|---|---|---|---|---|---|---|---|
| Livingston | 3 | | 4 | $90 00 | $92 00 | $1,200 00 | $164 00 | | |
| Luce | | | 16 | 24 00 | 104 00 | 250 00 | 20 00 | 13 | 13 |
| Mackinac | | | 20 | 20 00 | 160 00 | 400 00 | 35 00 | 10 | e 6 |
| Macomb | 1 | 42 | 4 | 200 00 | 328 00 | 1,100 00 | 223 50 | | 2 |
| Manistee | 3 | 2 | 6 | 20 00 | 140 00 | 600 00 | 108 50 | 1 | 3 |
| Marquette | | 6 | 4 | 200 00 | 224 00 | 1,000 00 | 156 00 | 16 | 10 |
| Mason | 1 | 18 | 15 | 200 00 | 212 00 | 550 00 | 101 00 | | 18 |
| Mecosta | | 12 | 4 | 200 00 | e 140 00 | 1,000 00 | 167 50 | | e 14 |
| Menominee | 4 | | 20 | 35 00 | e 63 00 | 500 00 | 122 50 | 5 | 34 |
| Midland | 2 | | 13 | e 60 00 | e 100 00 | 500 00 | 86 50 | | e 16 |
| Missaukee | 3 | | 11 | 40 00 | 40 00 | 550 00 | 46 00 | | 42 |
| Monroe | 4 | 20 | 37 | 200 00 | 150 00 | 1,200 00 | 152 50 | | |
| Montcalm | 2 | | 12 | 200 00 | 267 00 | 1,300 00 | 133 50 | | 2 |
| Montmorency | 1 | | 16 | 50 00 | 128 00 | 300 00 | | 5 | 6 |
| Muskegon | 2 | 30 | 4 | e 75 00 | e 280 00 | 1,200 00 | 158 00 | | e 15 |
| Newaygo | 4 | 7 | 55 | e 300 00 | e 500 00 | 1,000 00 | 112 00 | | |
| Oakland | 1 | 25 | 9 | 200 00 | 238 50 | 1,200 00 | 236 50 | | |
| Oceana | 3 | e 25 | 5 | 118 89 | e 144 00 | 750 00 | 94 00 | 1 | 3 |
| Ogemaw | 3 | | 4 | | 80 00 | 300 00 | 32 50 | 1 | 8 |
| Ontonagon | 3 | | 12 | 14 27 | 96 00 | 300 00 | 19 50 | 7 | 1 |
| Osceola | 1 | 6 | 4 | 168 40 | 208 00 | 750 00 | 101 50 | | 25 |
| Oscoda | | 5 | 8 | e 25 00 | 64 00 | 200 00 | 3 50 | 8 | |
| Otsego | 5 | | 8 | 35 00 | 160 00 | 500 00 | 53 50 | | 17 |
| Ottawa | 18 | | 4 | 29 64 | 180 00 | 1,000 00 | 134 50 | | 21 |
| Presque Isle | 2 | | 12 | 80 00 | 48 00 | 360 00 | 29 00 | | |
| Roscommon | | | 12 | 10 00 | 72 00 | 200 00 | 13 50 | | 1 |
| Saginaw | 4 | | 11 | 162 81 | 568 00 | 1,200 00 | 299 50 | | 38 |
| St. Clair | 2 | 8 | 13 | 200 00 | 376 00 | 1,200 00 | 220 50 | | 5 |
| St. Joseph | 1 | 36 | 3 | e 200 00 | 150 00 | 1,200 00 | 182 50 | | 1 |
| Sanilac | 22 | 10 | 4 | 152 00 | 300 00 | 1,200 00 | 244 00 | | 8 |
| Schoolcraft | | | 12 | e 120 00 | 104 00 | 500 00 | 30 50 | 4 | 17 |
| Shiawassee | 2 | 8 | 4 | 200 00 | 265 00 | 1,200 00 | 233 00 | | 1 |
| Tuscola | 3 | 10 | 4 | 178 00 | 272 00 | 1,200 00 | 165 50 | | 6 |
| Van Buren | 1 | 16 | 4 | e 175 00 | 232 00 | 1,200 00 | 197 50 | | 2 |
| Washtenaw | 5 | | 4 | e 200 00 | 258 00 | 1,200 00 | 143 50 | | 3 |
| Wayne | 3 | | 24 | 200 00 | 612 00 | 1,500 00 | 682 50 | | 3 |
| Wexford | 2 | 6 | 26 | 200 00 | 208 00 | 750 00 | 111 50 | | 52 |

e. estimated.

## TABLE XV.

*Showing the extent to which physiology was taught in the schools of the State during the year ending September 4, 1899, as compiled from director's reports.*

| Counties. | Number of districts in county. | Number of districts reporting physiology taught. | Number of districts reporting physiology not taught. | Number of districts not reporting. | Counties. | Number of districts in county. | Number of districts reporting physiology taught. | Number of districts reporting physiology not taught. | Number of districts not reporting. |
|---|---|---|---|---|---|---|---|---|---|
| Totals......... | 7,161 | 5,962 | 266 | 1,033 | Kent............ | 207 | 168 | 5 | 34 |
| | | | | | Keweenaw....... | 5 | 3 | 1 | 1 |
| | | | | | Lake............ | 42 | 34 | 1 | 7 |
| | | | | | Lapeer.......... | 134 | 95 | 11 | 28 |
| Alcona.......... | 27 | 22 | ...... | 5 | Leelanau ........ | 57 | 57 | ...... | ...... |
| Alger .......... | 7 | 7 | | | | | | | |
| Allegan.......... | 184 | 154 | 7 | 23 | Lenawee ........ | 197 | 190 | 7 | ...... |
| Alpena.......... | 29 | 20 | 3 | 5 | Livingston....... | 135 | 96 | 13 | 26 |
| Antrim.......... | 72 | 54 | 1 | 17 | Luce............ | 4 | 3 | 1 | ...... |
| | | | | | Mackinac........ | 16 | 14 | 1 | 1 |
| Arenac ......... | 39 | 26 | ...... | 13 | Macomb ......... | 114 | 103 | 3 | 8 |
| Baraga.......... | 5 | 5 | | | | | | | |
| Barry........... | 146 | 117 | 6 | 23 | Manistee........ | 58 | 48 | 3 | 7 |
| Bay............ | 65 | 48 | 3 | 14 | Marquette....... | 19 | 19 | ...... | ...... |
| Benzie.......... | 49 | 46 | | 3 | Mason.......... | 62 | 54 | 1 | 7 |
| | | | | | Mecosta......... | 104 | 80 | | 24 |
| Berrien ........ | 147 | 122 | 2 | 23 | Menominee...... | 34 | 21 | ...... | 13 |
| Branch......... | 129 | 102 | 5 | 22 | | | | | |
| Calhoun......... | 164 | 130 | 4 | 30 | Midland......... | 73 | 55 | 5 | 13 |
| Cass........... | 114 | 88 | 2 | 24 | Missaukee ...... | 51 | 39 | 1 | 11 |
| Charlevoix....... | 65 | 52 | 4 | 9 | Monroe ......... | 140 | 103 | 7 | 30 |
| | | | | | Montcalm........ | 139 | 118 | 6 | 15 |
| Cheboygan ...... | 61 | 51 | 2 | 8 | Montmorency .... | 7 | 5 | | 2 |
| Chippewa....... | 44 | 32 | 5 | 7 | | | | | |
| Clare........... | 50 | 39 | 2 | 9 | Muskegon....... | 92 | 77 | 2 | 13 |
| Clinton......... | 129 | 129 | | | Newaygo........ | 117 | 88 | 4 | 25 |
| Crawford........ | 24 | 17 | 5 | 2 | Oakland......... | 207 | 138 | 26 | 43 |
| | | | | | Oceana......... | 88 | 74 | 1 | 13 |
| Delta........... | 27 | 27 | | | Ogemaw......... | 42 | 31 | 2 | 9 |
| Dickinson....... | 8 | 8 | | | | | | | |
| Eaton .......... | 146 | 115 | 9 | 22 | Ontonagon....... | 9 | 9 | | |
| Emmet.......... | 70 | 59 | 1 | 10 | Osceola......... | 94 | 79 | 3 | 12 |
| Genesee........ | 160 | 120 | 8 | 32 | Oscoda......... | 12 | 9 | 1 | 2 |
| | | | | | Otsego.......... | 40 | 35 | 2 | 3 |
| Gladwin........ | 37 | 21 | 2 | 14 | Ottawa......... | 122 | 118 | 4 | ...... |
| Gogebic......... | 7 | 7 | ...... | ...... | | | | | |
| Grand Traverse... | 67 | 56 | 2 | 9 | Presque Isle..... | 33 | 27 | | 6 |
| Gratiot......... | 132 | 100 | 6 | 26 | Roscommon...... | 16 | 9 | | 7 |
| Hillsdale........ | 166 | 162 | ...... | 4 | Saginaw........ | 157 | 144 | 4 | 9 |
| | | | | | St. Clair........ | 154 | 135 | 8 | 11 |
| Houghton........ | 29 | 24 | ...... | 5 | St. Joseph....... | 124 | 95 | 5 | 24 |
| Huron.......... | 113 | 89 | | 24 | | | | | |
| Ingham ........ | 136 | 109 | 5 | 22 | Sanilac ...... | 146 | 127 | 4 | 15 |
| Ionia ........... | 143 | 107 | 6 | 30 | Schoolcraft...... | 14 | 9 | ...... | 5 |
| Iosco........... | 26 | 21 | 2 | 3 | Shiawassee...... | 126 | 115 | 1 | 10 |
| | | | | | Tuscola......... | 149 | 129 | 3 | 17 |
| Iron............ | 8 | 6 | ...... | 2 | | | | | |
| Isabella......... | 101 | 77 | 7 | 17 | Van Buren ...... | 152 | 132 | 1 | 19 |
| Jackson........ | 187 | 135 | 5 | 17 | Washtenaw...... | 167 | 132 | 7 | 28 |
| Kalamazoo ...... | 138 | 109 | 7 | 22 | Wayne......... | 155 | 127 | 9 | 19 |
| Kalkaska........ | 50 | 43 | 1 | 6 | Wexford......... | 77 | 62 | 1 | 14 |

## TABLE XVI.

Graded school statistics compiled from inspectors' reports for the year ending September 4, 1899.

| Districts. | Counties. | Number of children between 5 and 20 years. | Number of children that attended school during the year. | Number of days' school. | Estimated value of school property. | Total indebtedness. | Number of teachers employed. Men. | Number of teachers employed. Women. | Aggregate number of months taught by all teachers. Men. | Aggregate number of months taught by all teachers. Women. | Total wages of teachers for the year. Men. | Total wages of teachers for the year. Women. | Average monthly wages of teachers. Men. | Average monthly wages of teachers. Women. | Amount paid for superintendence and instruction. | Total cost of school. |
|---|---|---|---|---|---|---|---|---|---|---|---|---|---|---|---|---|
| Totals | | 416,169 | 358,942 | 128,145 | $14,486,124 | $1,978,861 96 | 1,051 | 5,681 | 9,484 | 53,276 | $265,827 28 | $2,301,472 91 | $70 17 | $43 30 | $2,905,286 84 | $4,829,519 03 |
| Acme | 3d Traverse | 92 | 76 | 180 | $1,000 | $89 04 | | 3 | 9 | 18 | | $665 | | $32 50 | $665 00 | $633 41 |
| Ada | Kent | 152 | 121 | 180 | 5,500 | | | 3 | 9 | 18 | $946 00 | 477 | $45 00 | 26 50 | 888 00 | 1,177 22 |
| Addison | Lenawee | 189 | 197 | 180 | 22,500 | | 1 | 2 | 18 | 18 | 671 00 | 465 | 46 88 | 27 50 | 1,386 00 | 1,788 98 |
| Adrian | Lenawee | 2,509 | 1,888 | 191 | 147,000 | | 6 | 36 | 30 | 360 | 8,550 00 | 14,405 00 | 121 66 | 40 29 | 18,155 00 | 27,575 92 |
| Akron | Tuscola | 135 | 107 | 200 | 1,500 | | 1 | 1 | 10 | 10 | 400 00 | 300 | 40 00 | 30 00 | 700 00 | 807 40 |
| Alaska | Kent | 103 | 67 | 180 | 2,000 | | 1 | 1 | 9 | 7 | 315 00 | 90 | 35 00 | 13 84 | 405 00 | 686 14 |
| Alanson | | 115 | 86 | 180 | 2,500 | 1,500 | | 2 | 4 | 12 | 130 00 | 280 | 30 00 | 30 00 | 480 00 | 874 55 |
| Alba | Antrim | 136 | 98 | 180 | 5,000 | | 1 | 2 | 9 | 18 | 450 00 | 540 | 50 00 | 37 00 | 490 00 | 1,207 90 |
| Albion | | 1,160 | 1,041 | 190 | 70,000 | 6,700 00 | 4 | 24 | 19 | 225 | 1,687 50 | 8,643 | 88 65 | 38 40 | 10,270 00 | 14,015 57 |
| Algonac | St. Clair | 432 | 327 | 180 | 11,500 | 2,300 00 | 1 | 6 | 9 | 54 | 590 00 | 1,800 | 64 44 | 33 33 | 2,050 00 | 3,519 90 |
| Allegan | Allegan | 637 | 524 | 190 | 20,000 | 18,000 00 | 2 | 16 | 20 | 160 | 1,300 00 | 6,037 | 130 84 | 36 86 | 7,387 70 | 16,185 17 |
| Allen | Hillsdale | 80 | 64 | 180 | 8,000 | 150 00 | | 1 | | 18 | 576 00 | 405 | 69 86 | 22 50 | 980 00 | 1,387 90 |
| Allouez | Keweenaw | 434 | 284 | 180 | 1,000 | | | 4 | | 36 | | 1,675 | 43 75 | 43 75 | 1,675 00 | 2,069 25 |
| Alma | Gratiot | 554 | 546 | 200 | 20,000 | 8,000 00 | 2 | 10 | 20 | 100 | 1,300 00 | 3,125 | 65 00 | 33 55 | 4,425 00 | 6,901 88 |
| Almont | Lapeer | 265 | 199 | 198 | 18,500 | | 1 | 5 | 10 | 50 | 750 00 | 1,675 | 75 00 | 32 50 | 2,425 00 | 3,312 14 |
| Alpena | Alpena | 4,368 | 1,839 | 194 | 80,000 | 2,086 44 | 8 | 34 | 30 | 340 | 3,000 00 | 13,112 10 | 96 66 | 37 46 | 14,571 75 | 21,843 35 |
| Ann Arbor | Washtenaw | 2,922 | 2,131 | 190 | 240,000 | 28,425 00 | 9 | 58 | 90 | 580 | 11,988 00 | 28,511 28 | 131 66 | 43 98 | 37,378 28 | 75,207 00 |
| Applegate | Sanilac | 157 | 135 | 175 | 700 | | 1 | 1 | 9 | 9 | 450 00 | 138 | 45 00 | 17 00 | 400 00 | 644 54 |
| Arcadian Mine | Houghton | 308 | 254 | 190 | | 360 00 | | 6 | 6 | 60 | | 550 | 50 00 | 50 00 | 600 00 | 1,275 24 |
| Armada | Macomb | 214 | 174 | 180 | 10,000 | | 3 | 3 | 18 | 27 | 389 00 | 840 | 47 33 | 31 11 | 1,092 00 | 2,436 23 |
| Ashley | Gratiot | 195 | 145 | 180 | 2,000 | | 1 | 2 | 9 | 18 | 405 00 | 450 | 45 00 | 25 00 | 585 00 | 1,149 17 |
| A tbams | Calhoun | 182 | 178 | 180 | 4,000 | | 2 | 2 | 18 | 18 | 450 00 | 540 | 50 00 | 30 55 | 1,440 00 | 1,205 07 |
| A sdc Mine | Houghton | 776 | 521 | 200 | 11,000 | 250 00 | 4 | 13 | 30 | 59 | 8,255 50 | 2,565 | 61 66 | 55 00 | 5,237 00 | 7,161 64 |
| Attica | Lapeer | 124 | 75 | 200 | 1,200 | | 1 | 1 | 10 | 9 | | 00 | 50 00 | 50 00 | 00 | 78 76 |
| Auburn | Bay | 163 | 131 | 180 | 1,300 | 550 00 | 2 | 1 | 10 | 18 | | 340 | 40 00 | 30 00 | 540 00 | 754 51 |

| | County |
|---|---|
| Audires | Arenac |
| Augusta | Kalamazoo |
| Ausable | Iosco |
| AuTrain | Alger |
| Bad Axe | Huron |
| Baldwin | Lake |
| Baldwin Tp. | Delta |
| Bancroft | Shiawassee |
| Bangor | Van Buren |
| Hamister | Gratiot |
| Baraga | Baraga |
| Haroda | Berrien |
| Harryton | Mecosta |
| Hates Tp | Iron |
| Bath | Clinton |
| Battle Creek | Calhoun |
| Bay City | Bay |
| Beacon | Marquette |
| Bear Lake | Manistee |
| Beaver Dam | Ottawa |
| Beaverton | Gladwin |
| Bedford Tp. & | Calhoun |
| Bellaire | Antrim |
| Belding | Ionia |
| Belleville | Wayne |
| Bellevue | Eaton |
| Benton Tp. & ft | Berrien |
| Benton Harbor | Berrien |
| Benzonia | Benzie |
| Berlamont | Van Buren |
| Berlin | Ottawa |
| Berne | Huron |
| Berrien Springs | Berrien |
| Bessemer | Gogebic |
| Bessemer Tp | Gogebic |
| Leelanau | Leelanau |
| Big Creek and Mentor Tp | Oscoda |
| Big Rapids | Mecosta |
| Big Rock | Montmor'ney |
| Bingham | Oakland |
| Blanchard | Isabella |
| Blissfield Tp. 1 ft | Lenawee |
| Blissfield Tp. 2 ft | Lenawee |
| Bloomingdale | Van Buren |

TABLE XVI.—CONTINUED.

| Districts | Counties | Number of children between 5 and 20 years. | Number of children that attended school during the year. | Number of days school. | Estimated value of school property. | Total indebtedness. | Number of teachers employed. Men. | Women. | Aggregate number of months taught by all teachers. Men. | Women. | Total wages of teachers for the year. Men. | Women. | Average monthly wages of teachers. Men. | Women. | Amount paid for superintendence and instruction. | Total cost of school. |
|---|---|---|---|---|---|---|---|---|---|---|---|---|---|---|---|---|
| Bo...thia Tp. | Ontonagon | 33 | 28 | 180 | $300 | | 1 | | 9 | 9 | $450 00 | $360 00 | $40 00 | $40 00 | $360 00 | $560 93 |
| Boyne Falls | Charlevoix | 173 | 142 | 180 | 1,500 | | | 13 | 9 | 18 | | 680 00 | 35 00 | 35 00 | 1,080 00 | 1,341 50 |
| Bo...ne City | Charlevoix | 387 | 252 | 180 | 4,000 | $2,500 00 | 2 | 57 | 18 | 57 | 900 00 | 888 60 | 50 00 | 32 88 | 1,788 00 | 2,653 36 |
| Breckenridge | ...dot. | 165 | 149 | 180 | 3,500 | | 1 | 8 | 9 | 18 | 427 50 | 495 00 | 47 50 | 27 50 | 922 50 | 1,208 19 |
| Breedsville | Van Buren | 111 | 95 | 180 | 1,000 | | 1 | 9 | 9 | 9 | 360 00 | 252 50 | 40 00 | 28 00 | 612 00 | 709 70 |
| Breen Tp. | | 118 | 97 | 180 | 2,500 | | 1 | 3 | 9 | 18 | 405 00 | 810 00 | 45 00 | 45 00 | 1,215 00 | 1,782 26 |
| Borculo | Ottawa | 142 | 98 | 197 | 600 | | 1 | | 10 | | 397 00 | | 36 70 | | 397 00 | 444 81 |
| Bridgeh'pion Tp. 1 | Sanilac | 97 | 64 | 140 | 500 | | 1 | | 9 | | 270 00 | | 30 00 | | 270 00 | 316 30 |
| Bridgeh'pion Tp. 2 | Sanilac | 118 | 91 | 200 | 600 | | 1 | | 10 | | 380 00 | | 38 00 | 18 00 | 462 00 | 605 91 |
| ...gon Tp. 5 fl. | Sanilac | 59 | 48 | 176 | 800 | | 2 | 1 | 9 | 4 | 225 00 | 72 00 | 25 00 | 18 00 | 225 00 | 288 01 |
| ...th | Berrien | 135 | 79 | 160 | 750 | | 1 | 1 | 7 | 9 | 245 00 | 350 00 | 35 00 | 37 77 | 405 00 | 550 16 |
| Bridgeport | Saginaw | 124 | 103 | 175 | 2,000 | | 1 | 2 | 9 | 9 | 360 00 | 270 00 | 40 00 | 30 00 | 630 00 | 722 83 |
| Brighton | ...ton | 367 | 265 | 200 | 16,000 | | 1 | 4 | 10 | 40 | 800 00 | 1,200 00 | 80 00 | 30 00 | 2,000 00 | 2,610 33 |
| Britton | Lenawee | 190 | 95 | 180 | 3,000 | | 1 | 1 | 9 | 6 | 405 00 | 270 00 | 45 10 | 30 00 | 675 00 | 764 56 |
| ...bson | Branch | 298 | 230 | 190 | 3,000 | | 2 | 3 | 10 | 23 | 1,472 50 | 788 75 | 51 66 | 35 42 | 2,261 25 | 3,097 03 |
| Brooklyn | Jackson | 166 | 156 | 200 | 5,500 | 7,000 00 | 3 | 2 | 30 | 20 | 1,500 00 | 700 00 | 50 00 | 35 00 | 2,300 00 | 2,894 14 |
| Brown City | Sanilac | 238 | 201 | 200 | 7,000 | | 1 | 3 | 10 | 20 | 540 00 | 580 00 | 54 00 | 29 00 | 1,080 00 | 5,643 54 |
| Buchanan | Berrien | 446 | 425 | 190 | 25,000 | 300 00 | 2 | 12 | 18 | 114 | 900 00 | 4,148 75 | 94 73 | 27 36 | 5,048 75 | 6,873 94 |
| Buena Vista Tp. 1 | Saginaw | 163 | 103 | 200 | 2,500 | 36 00 | 1 | 1 | 10 | 10 | | 580 00 | | 37 50 | 520 00 | 1,516 47 |
| Buena Vista Tp. 5 | Saginaw | 134 | 78 | 200 | 1,000 | | 2 | | | 10 | | 400 00 | | 40 00 | 400 00 | 672 60 |
| ...ena Vista Tp. 6 | Saginaw | 501 | 321 | 200 | 4,500 | 640 00 | 1 | 3 | 10 | 30 | 450 00 | 900 00 | 45 00 | 30 00 | 1,050 00 | 1,650 46 |
| Burlington | Calhoun | 132 | 76 | 175 | 1,300 | | 1 | 1 | 9 | 18 | 350 00 | 423 50 | 40 00 | 23 50 | 773 50 | 832 76 |
| Burnips Corners | Allegan | 90 | 80 | 180 | 2,000 | | 1 | 1 | 9 | 9 | 405 00 | 225 00 | 45 00 | 25 00 | 680 00 | 768 41 |
| Burnside | Lapeer | 110 | 70 | 130 | 1,000 | | 1 | 1 | 6 | 9 | 240 00 | 132 00 | 40 00 | 22 00 | 372 00 | 476 47 |
| Burr Oak | St. Joseph | 501 | 192 | 177 | 25,000 | | 2 | 4 | 18 | 45 | 900 00 | 1,232 50 | 50 00 | 27 38 | 2,132 50 | 3,394 53 |
| Byron | Shiawassee | 134 | 119 | 190 | 6,000 | 5,500 00 | 1 | 2 | 10 | 20 | 575 00 | 625 00 | 57 50 | 31 25 | 1,200 00 | 1,444 11 |
| Byron Center | Kent | 108 | 78 | 190 | 2,000 | | 1 | 3 | 9 | 9 | 405 00 | 252 00 | 45 00 | 46 00 | 657 00 | 741 87 |
| Cadillac | | 1,730 | 1,372 | 190 | 60,000 | 7,340 00 | 27 | 279 | 166 | 279 | 1,500 00 | 13,196 70 | 166 00 | 47 00 | 14,696 70 | 31,933 86 |
| Caledonia | Kent | 182 | 109 | 200 | 6,500 | | 1 | 20 | 30 | 30 | 730 00 | 580 00 | 36 50 | 29 00 | 1,310 00 | 1,725 26 |
| ... | Houghton | 6,750 | 4,371 | 200 | 17,000 | | 27 | 830 | 70 | 830 | 8,100 00 | 45,704 85 | 114 28 | 55 73 | 53,804 85 | 77,239 13 |

| | | | | | | | | | | | | | | | | |
|---|---|---|---|---|---|---|---|---|---|---|---|---|---|---|---|---|
| Calumet Tp. 2 | Houghton | | | | | | | | | | | | | | | |
| Cambria | Hillsdale | | | | | | | | | | | | | | | |
| Cannonsburg | Kent | | | | | | | | | | | | | | | |
| Capac | St. Clair | | | | | | | | | | | | | | | |
| Carleton | Monroe | | | | | | | | | | | | | | | |
| Carney | Menominee | | | | | | | | | | | | | | | |
| Caro | Tuscola | | | | | | | | | | | | | | | |
| Carrollton Tp. 1 | Saginaw | | | | | | | | | | | | | | | |
| Carrollton Tp. 2 | Saginaw | | | | | | | | | | | | | | | |
| Carson City | Montcalm | | | | | | | | | | | | | | | |
| Carsonville | Sanilac | | | | | | | | | | | | | | | |
| Caseville | Huron | | | | | | | | | | | | | | | |
| Casnovia | Muskegon | | | | | | | | | | | | | | | |
| Cass City | Tuscola | | | | | | | | | | | | | | | |
| Cassopolis | Cass | | | | | | | | | | | | | | | |
| Cedar River | Menominee | | | | | | | | | | | | | | | |
| Cedar Springs | Kent | | | | | | | | | | | | | | | |
| Central Lake | Antrim | | | | | | | | | | | | | | | |
| Central Mine | Keweenaw | | | | | | | | | | | | | | | |
| Centreville | St. Joseph | | | | | | | | | | | | | | | |
| Ceresco | Calhoun | | | | | | | | | | | | | | | |
| Charlevoix | Charlevoix | | | | | | | | | | | | | | | |
| Charlotte | Eaton | | | | | | | | | | | | | | | |
| Chassell | Houghton | | | | | | | | | | | | | | | |
| Chase | Lake | | | | | | | | | | | | | | | |
| Cheboygan | Cheboygan | | | | | | | | | | | | | | | |
| Chelsea | Washtenaw | | | | | | | | | | | | | | | |
| Chesaning | Saginaw | | | | | | | | | | | | | | | |
| Chester Tp 7 R. | Ottawa | | | | | | | | | | | | | | | |
| Chickaming Tp. 3 | Berrien | | | | | | | | | | | | | | | |
| China Tp. 4 | St. Clair | | | | | | | | | | | | | | | |
| Clare | Clare | | | | | | | | | | | | | | | |
| Clarkston | Oakland | | | | | | | | | | | | | | | |
| Clarksville | Ionia | | | | | | | | | | | | | | | |
| Charlevoix | Charlevoix | | | | | | | | | | | | | | | |
| Clayton | Lenawee | | | | | | | | | | | | | | | |
| Clifford | Lapeer | | | | | | | | | | | | | | | |
| Climax | Kalamazoo | | | | | | | | | | | | | | | |
| Clinton | Lenawee | | | | | | | | | | | | | | | |
| Clio | Genesee | | | | | | | | | | | | | | | |
| Coldwater | Branch | | | | | | | | | | | | | | | |
| Coleman | Midland | | | | | | | | | | | | | | | |
| Coloma | Berrien | | | | | | | | | | | | | | | |
| Colon | St. Joseph | | | | | | | | | | | | | | | |
| Columbiaville | Lapeer | | | | | | | | | | | | | | | |

TABLE XVI.—CONTINUED.

| Districts. | Counties. | Number of children between 5 and 20 years. | Number of children that attended school during the year. | Number of days school. | Estimated value of school property. | Total indebtedness. | Number of teachers employed. Men. | Number of teachers employed. Women. | Aggregate number of months taught. Men. | Aggregate number of months taught. Women. | Total wages of teachers for the year. Men. | Total wages of teachers for the year. Women. | Average monthly wages. Men. | Average monthly wages. Women. | Amount paid for superintendence and instruction. | Total cost of school. |
|---|---|---|---|---|---|---|---|---|---|---|---|---|---|---|---|---|
| ... Tp | Luce | 95 | 92 | 180 | $2,000 | $918 80 | | 3 | | 18 | | $370 00 | | $30 55 | $370 00 | $630 00 |
| do | Oakland | 66 | 63 | 174 | 600 | | | 2 | | 14 | | 323 75 | | 23 12 | 323 75 | 386 69 |
| do | Kalamazoo | 114 | 85 | 180 | 3,000 | 1,000 00 | 1 | 3 | | 18 | | 545 00 | | 32 50 | 585 00 | 2,079 12 |
| Concord | Jackson | 155 | 118 | 190 | 7,000 | | 1 | 2 | 19 | 18 | $1,032 50 | 997 50 | $54 34 | 35 50 | 2,030 00 | 2,674 53 |
| Conklin | Ottawa | 103 | 67 | 190 | 1,000 | | 1 | 1 | 9 | 9 | 315 00 | 225 00 | 35 00 | 25 00 | 540 00 | 592 80 |
| ... | St. Joseph | 908 | 217 | 200 | 25,000 | 100 00 | | 6 | | 60 | 1,350 00 | 2,300 00 | 67 50 | 38 66 | 3,550 00 | 4,625 78 |
| Coopersville | Ottawa | 227 | 197 | 180 | 5,000 | | 1 | 5 | 9 | 36 | 540 00 | 1,080 00 | 60 00 | 30 00 | 1,620 00 | 1,991 54 |
| ...ish | Manistee | 144 | 143 | 200 | 1,800 | | 1 | 2 | 10 | 20 | 400 00 | 550 00 | 40 00 | 30 00 | 960 00 | 1,205 61 |
| Coral | Montcalm | 167 | 124 | 168 | 3,000 | 200 00 | 1 | 2 | 9 | 9 | 405 00 | 270 00 | 45 00 | 27 50 | 676 00 | 903 05 |
| Corunna | Shiawassee | 380 | 313 | 200 | 28,000 | | 1 | 8 | 10 | 80 | 1,000 00 | 3,300 00 | 100 00 | 38 66 | 4,300 00 | 6,337 46 |
| Covert | Van Buren | 162 | 139 | 180 | 9,180 | | | 2 | | 18 | | 495 00 | | 27 50 | 972 00 | 1,253 79 |
| Covington Tp | Baraga | 49 | 9 | 200 | 800 | | 1 | 1 | 9 | 10 | 477 00 | 400 00 | 53 00 | 40 00 | 400 00 | 672 41 |
| Croswell | Sanilac | 325 | 279 | 200 | 6,000 | 4,000 00 | 1 | 6 | 10 | 50 | 700 00 | 1,620 00 | 70 00 | 30 00 | 2,220 00 | 3,351 47 |
| ... | | 101 | 88 | 180 | 4,000 | | 1 | 1 | 3 | 9 | 280 00 | 165 00 | 35 00 | 20 55 | 465 00 | 596 34 |
| Crystal Falls | Iron | 817 | 727 | 200 | 21,000 | 12,000 00 | 1 | 14 | 10 | 140 | 1,200 00 | 7,100 00 | 120 00 | 50 71 | 8,300 00 | 16,349 78 |
| Custer | Mason | 165 | 141 | 180 | 2,250 | 700 00 | 1 | 1 | 9 | 9 | 388 50 | 270 00 | 42 50 | 30 00 | 652 50 | 772 74 |
| Dansville | | 123 | 101 | 200 | 4,000 | | 1 | 3 | 10 | 20 | 600 00 | 840 00 | 60 00 | 28 00 | 1,440 00 | 2,069 21 |
| Genesee | Genesee | 241 | 195 | 200 | 10,000 | 4,000 00 | 1 | 4 | 10 | 40 | 375 00 | 1,000 00 | 37 50 | 25 00 | 1,375 00 | 2,325 81 |
| Dearborn | | 346 | 258 | 180 | 20,000 | 5,000 00 | 1 | 4 | 10 | 36 | 540 00 | 1,000 00 | 60 00 | 30 00 | 1,480 00 | |
| Decatur | Van Buren | 372 | 357 | 165 | 15,000 | 100 00 | 1 | 7 | 10 | 68 | 1,000 00 | 2,281 50 | 102 70 | 33 55 | 3,281 50 | 4,309 74 |
| Deckerville | Sanilac | 254 | 143 | 200 | 2,500 | | 1 | 2 | 3 | 30 | 450 00 | 500 00 | 50 00 | 25 00 | 960 00 | 1,852 71 |
| Deerfield | | 207 | 179 | 180 | 6,000 | | 1 | 4 | 9 | 36 | 600 00 | 928 25 | 66 66 | 25 78 | 1,528 25 | 1,876 75 |
| Delaware Mines | | 55 | 57 | 160 | 1,700 | | | 1 | | 16 | | 480 00 | | 30 00 | 480 00 | 540 28 |
| ...ton | Harry | 44 | 48 | 125 | | | 1 | 1 | 9 | 9 | 405 00 | 135 00 | 45 00 | 15 00 | 540 00 | 638 85 |
| Detour | | 302 | 208 | 200 | 4,000 | 1,400 00 | 1 | 3 | 10 | 28 | 500 00 | 565 00 | 50 00 | 30 00 | 565 00 | 3,085 82 |
| Detroit | Wayne | 70,646 | 48,836 | 200 | 2,875,385 | | 5 | 280 | 510 | 7,800 | 58,524 00 | 512,520 84 | 114 75 | 65 70 | 571,045 44 | 905,297 21 |
| DeWitt | | 114 | 81 | 180 | 4,500 | 10,000 00 | 1 | 2 | 9 | 18 | 450 00 | 582 00 | 50 00 | 29 00 | 972 00 | 1,145 07 |
| Dexter | Washtenaw | 290 | 214 | 200 | 17,000 | | 1 | 2 | 9 | 18 | 900 00 | 1,860 00 | 90 00 | 31 00 | 2,760 00 | 4,327 00 |
| Dimondale | Eaton | 162 | 65 | 180 | 2,000 | | 1 | 2 | 9 | 18 | 450 00 | 540 00 | 50 00 | 30 00 | 990 00 | 1,166 38 |
| Dollar Bay | Houghton | 570 | 180 | 200 | 8,000 | | 2 | 7 | 20 | 54 | 1,450 00 | 2,219 62 | 72 50 | 44 39 | 3,669 62 | 6,623 65 |
| Dorr | Allegan | 135 | 94 | 177 | | | 1 | 2 | 9 | 9 | 380 00 | 225 00 | 40 00 | 25 00 | 585 00 | 662 95 |
| Douglas | Allegan | 194 | 147 | 180 | 3,000 | | 1 | 2 | 9 | 18 | 500 00 | 570 00 | 55 00 | 32 00 | 1,076 00 | 1,549 98 |

| | County | | | | | | | | | | | | | | | | | |
|---|---|---|---|---|---|---|---|---|---|---|---|---|---|---|---|---|---|---|
| Dxc | | | | | | | | | | | | | | | | | | 14,545 52 |
| Drenthe | | | | | | | | | | | | | | | | | | 695 42 |
| Dryden | | | | | | | | | | | | | | | | | | 1,394 68 |
| Dundee | Monroe | | | | | | | | | | | | | | | | | 3,000 99 |
| Durand | Shiawassee | | | | | | | | | | | | | | | | | 12,196 77 |
| Eagle | | | | | | | | | | | | | | | | | | 970 38 |
| East Jordan | Charlevoix | | | | | | | | | | | | | | | | | 7,330 81 |
| East Lake | | | | | | | | | | | | | | | | | | 4,396 38 |
| Eaton | Iosco | | | | | | | | | | | | | | | | | 4,935 81 |
| Eaton Rapids | Eaton | | | | | | | | | | | | | | | | | 7,752 93 |
| Eau Claire | Berrien | | | | | | | | | | | | | | | | | 913 91 |
| Ecorse Tp. 1 | Wayne | | | | | | | | | | | | | | | | | 2,755 72 |
| Ecorse Tp. 3 | Wayne | | | | | | | | | | | | | | | | | 2,598 79 |
| Edenville | | | | | | | | | | | | | | | | | | 10,423 93 |
| | | | | | | | | | | | | | | | | | | 163 96 |
| Edmore | Montcalm | | | | | | | | | | | | | | | | | 2,339 64 |
| Edwardsburg | Cass | | | | | | | | | | | | | | | | | 1,980 65 |
| Elk Rapids | Antrim | | | | | | | | | | | | | | | | | 6,885 07 |
| Elkton | Huron | | | | | | | | | | | | | | | | | 1,706 74 |
| Elk Tp. 2 | Lake | | | | | | | | | | | | | | | | | 430 61 |
| Elk Tp. 4 tl | Sanilac | | | | | | | | | | | | | | | | | 441 95 |
| Elk Tp. b | Sanilac | | | | | | | | | | | | | | | | | 512 85 |
| Ellsworth | Antrim | | | | | | | | | | | | | | | | | 725 29 |
| Elm Hall | Gratiot | | | | | | | | | | | | | | | | | 807 30 |
| Elmira | Otsego | | | | | | | | | | | | | | | | | 1,298 61 |
| Emle | | | | | | | | | | | | | | | | | | 1,689 16 |
| Empire | Leelanau | | | | | | | | | | | | | | | | | 1,211 86 |
| Erie | Monroe | | | | | | | | | | | | | | | | | 1,029 85 |
| Escanaba | Delta | | | | | | | | | | | | | | | | | 30,345 38 |
| Essexville | Bay | | | | | | | | | | | | | | | | | 4,179 51 |
| Eureka | Clinton | | | | | | | | | | | | | | | | | 513 52 |
| Evart | Osola | | | | | | | | | | | | | | | | | 5,413 03 |
| Farmington | Oakland | | | | | | | | | | | | | | | | | 1,407 65 |
| Farwell | | | | | | | | | | | | | | | | | | 1,648 76 |
| Fennville | Allegan | | | | | | | | | | | | | | | | | 2,197 00 |
| Fenton | Genesee | | | | | | | | | | | | | | | | | 9,072 80 |
| Ferrysburg | Ottawa | | | | | | | | | | | | | | | | | 1,091 22 |
| Fife Lake | G'd Traverse | | | | | | | | | | | | | | | | | 1,165 82 |
| Filer Cty | Manistee | | | | | | | | | | | | | | | | | 2,014 12 |
| Filer Tp. 4 | Manistee | | | | | | | | | | | | | | | | | 2,037 62 |
| Fillmore Tp. 1 | Allegan | | | | | | | | | | | | | | | | | 588 24 |
| Fillmore Tp. 2 | Allegan | | | | | | | | | | | | | | | | | 609 49 |
| Fillmore Tp. 3 | Allegan | | | | | | | | | | | | | | | | | 583 67 |
| Fillmore Tp. 4 | Allegan | | | | | | | | | | | | | | | | | 637 52 |
| Fillmore Tp. 5 n | Allegan | | | | | | | | | | | | | | | | | 462 60 |
| Flat Rock | Wayne | | | | | | | | | | | | | | | | | 2,199 06 |

TABLE XVI.— CONTINUED.

| Districts. | Counties. | Number of children between 5 and 20 years. | Number of children that attended school during the year. | Number of days school. | Estimated value of school property. | Total indebtedness. | Number of teachers employed. Men | Women | Aggregate number of months taught by all teachers. Men | Women | Total wages of teachers for the year. Men | Women | Average monthly wages of teachers. Men | Women | Amount paid for superintendence and instruction. | Total cost of school. |
|---|---|---|---|---|---|---|---|---|---|---|---|---|---|---|---|---|
| Flint | Genesee | 2,990 | 2,384 | 200 | $175,000 | $19,000 00 | 7 | 53 | 70 | 530 | $5,600 00 | $22,703 00 | $60 00 | $42 83 | $29,303 00 | $72,116 04 |
| F l  k | Genesee | 285 | 157 | 200 | 5,000 | 52 69 | 1 | 5 | 10 | 550 | 825 00 | 1,596 70 | 82 50 | 31 93 | 2,421 70 | 3,677 59 |
| Ford River | Delta | 255 | 169 | 197 | 3,000 | | 1 | 2 | | 20 | | 950 00 | | 47 50 | 950 00 | 1,420 20 |
| Forester | Sanilac | 119 | 49 | 200 | 1,250 | | 1 | | 10 | | 375 00 | | 37 50 | | 375 00 | 483 25 |
| Forest Grove | Ottawa | 109 | 84 | 180 | 1,500 | | 1 | 1 | 9 | 9 | 450 00 | 180 | 50 00 | 20 00 | 630 00 | 713 04 |
| Forestville | Sanilac | 141 | 85 | 160 | 1,200 | | 1 | 1 | 8 | 4 | 320 00 | 112 | 40 00 | 28 00 | 432 00 | 681 09 |
| Fostoria | Gin. | 124 | 98 | 198 | 3,500 | | 1 | 2 | 10 | 20 | 400 00 | 425 00 | 40 00 | 21 25 | 925 00 | 988 33 |
| Fowler | | 124 | 49 | 200 | 1,500 | | 1 | 1 | 10 | 10 | 460 00 | 275 00 | 46 00 | 27 50 | 725 00 | 982 44 |
| Fowlerville | Ia Men | 271 | 237 | 200 | 10,000 | | 1 | 7 | 10 | 60 | 800 00 | 1,840 00 | 80 00 | 30 66 | 2,640 00 | 2,963 51 |
| Frankenmuth | Saginaw | 380 | 156 | 220 | 250 | | 2 | | 21 | | 1,025 00 | | 49 19 | | 1,025 00 | 1,108 74 |
| Frankfort | Benzie | 535 | 470 | 200 | 25,000 | 21,000 00 | 1 | 10 | 10 | 100 | 800 00 | 3,555 00 | 80 00 | 35 55 | 4,356 00 | 7,241 20 |
| Franklin Tp. 1 | Houghton | 352 | 171 | 200 | 3,000 | | 1 | 2 | 10 | 20 | 800 00 | 950 00 | 80 00 | 47 50 | 1,750 00 | 2,334 94 |
| Franklin Tp. 2 | Houghton | 295 | 166 | 200 | 6,000 | | 1 | 3 | 10 | 30 | 850 00 | 1,150 00 | 85 00 | 38 33 | 2,000 00 | 3,770 55 |
| Franklin Tp. 3 | Houghton | 255 | 123 | 200 | 2,000 | | 1 | 1 | 10 | 10 | 550 00 | 400 00 | 55 00 | | 930 00 | 1,627 00 |
| Franklin Tp. 5 | Houghton | 208 | 157 | 200 | 3,000 | | 1 | 3 | 10 | 30 | 750 00 | 1,100 00 | 75 00 | 36 66 | 1,850 00 | 2,370 91 |
| Freeland | Saginaw | 130 | 123 | 200 | 1,500 | | 1 | 1 | 10 | 10 | 450 00 | 248 13 | 45 00 | 34 81 | 668 13 | 813 01 |
| Freeport | Barry | 174 | 149 | 180 | 3,000 | 900 00 | 1 | 3 | 10 | 27 | 405 00 | 605 25 | 45 00 | 22 41 | 1,010 25 | 1,208 57 |
| Freesoil | Mason | 156 | 102 | 180 | 2,500 | | | 2 | | 18 | | 540 00 | | 31 00 | 540 00 | 661 43 |
| Freemont | o | 417 | 330 | 200 | 7,000 | | | 3 | | 70 | | 2,300 00 | | 31 44 | 2,900 00 | 3,891 78 |
| Fro tier | le | 94 | 72 | 179 | 3,500 | 500 00 | 2 | 2 | 10 | 9 | 700 00 | 207 00 | 70 00 | 23 00 | 927 00 | 1,166 57 |
| Fruitport | Muskegon | 121 | 88 | 200 | 7,600 | | | 2 | 18 | 20 | 720 00 | 800 00 | 40 00 | 40 00 | 800 00 | 1,014 19 |
| Fulton | Kalamazoo | 100 | 65 | 178 | 900 | | 1 | 1 | 8 | 9 | 291 59 | 200 00 | 38 44 | 22 22 | 491 59 | 534 99 |
| Gagetown | Tuscola | 208 | 68 | 200 | 3,500 | | | 3 | 10 | 30 | 500 00 | | 50 00 | 20 70 | 500 00 | 738 56 |
| Gaines | Genesee | 112 | 95 | 200 | 5,000 | 2,500 00 | 1 | 3 | 10 | 27 | 512 66 | 617 00 | 51 28 | 33 00 | 1,129 64 | 2,458 25 |
| Galesburg | o | 160 | 144 | 180 | 10,000 | | 1 | 3 | 18 | 18 | 1,038 00 | 891 00 | 57 66 | 33 00 | 1,929 00 | 1,760 61 |
| Gallen | Berrien | 176 | 176 | 180 | 4,000 | | 2 | 2 | 18 | 18 | 815 00 | 540 00 | 45 27 | 30 00 | 1,355 00 | 3,919 94 |
| Garden | Delta | 418 | 327 | 170 | 4,200 | | 3 | 2 | 25 | 18 | 1,065 00 | 730 00 | 42 25 | 40 00 | 1,775 00 | 4,162 26 |
| Gaylord | Otsego | 352 | 270 | 180 | 10,000 | 8,000 00 | 2 | 5 | 18 | 45 | 855 00 | 1,530 00 | 47 50 | 34 00 | 2,386 00 | 708 17 |
| 6 | Branch | 54 | 48 | 190 | 3,000 | | | 9 | 9 | 9 | 315 00 | 1,225 00 | 35 00 | | 540 00 | 10,215 56 |
| G stone | Delta | 729 | 636 | 200 | 20,000 | 15,000 00 | | 2 | | 130 | | 5,645 00 | | 43 42 | 5,645 00 | 1,820 05 |
| Gl h | | 272 | 227 | 200 | 8,000 | | 2 | 3 | 10 | 10 | 500 00 | 960 00 | 50 00 | 31 66 | 1,450 00 | 1,882 03 |
| Gobleville | Van Buren | 181 | 177 | 190 | 4,000 | | 2 | 2 | 10 | 19 | 435 00 | 570 00 | 43 94 | 30 00 | 1,405 00 | 865 36 |
| Goodrich | Genesee | 77 | 59 | 186 | 2,000 | | 1 | 1 | 10 | 10 | 445 00 | 273 00 | 45 64 | 28 00 | 718 00 | |

| Place | County |
|---|---|
| Gore Tp. | Huron |
| Graafschap. | Allegan |
| ... Blanc | Genesee |
| Grand ... van | Ottawa |
| ... d J t ... | Van Buren |
| Grand , ... le 9 ft. | Eaton |
| ... Ledge 11 ft | Eaton |
| Grand Marais | Alger |
| Grand ... ds | Kent |
| ... ale | Kent |
| Grant Tp. 6 ft | Oceana |
| G ... Lake | Jackson |
| Grattan | Kent |
| Grayling | Crawford |
| Greenland Tp. | Ontonagon |
| Greenville | Montcalm |
| Grindstone City | Huron |
| Grosse Isle | Wayne |
| Grosse Pointe Tp. 1 | Wayne |
| Grosse Pointe Tp. 2 | Wayne |
| Hadley | Lapeer |
| Hamilton | Allegan |
| Hamtramck Tp. ... | Wayne |
| Hancock | ... |
| Hanover | Jackson |
| Harbor Beach | Huron |
| Harbor Springs | Emmet |
| Harrietta | Wexford |
| Harrison | Clare |
| Harrisville | Alcona |
| Hart | Oceana |
| Hartford | Van Buren |
| Hartland | Livingston |
| Harvey | Marquette |
| Hastings | Barry |
| ... ville | Osceola |
| Hesperia | ...co |
| Highland Park | Wayne |
| Hig ... nd Station | Oakland |
| Hillman | Montmorency |
| Hillsdale | Hillsdale |
| Hobart | Wexford |
| Holland | Ottawa |
| ... d Tp. 3 | Ottawa |
| ... d Tp. 4 | Ottawa |
| ... d Tp. 6 ft | Ottawa |

TABLE XVI.—CONTINUED.

| Districts. | Counties. | Number of children between 5 and 20 years. | Number of children that attended school during the year. | Number of days school. | Estimated value of school property. | Total indebtedness. | Number of teachers employed. Men. | Women. | Aggregate number of months taught by all teachers. Men. | Women. | Total wages of teachers for the year. Men. | Women. | Average monthly wages of teachers. Men. | Women. | Amount paid for superintendence and instruction. | Total cost of school. |
|---|---|---|---|---|---|---|---|---|---|---|---|---|---|---|---|---|
| Holland Tp. 9 | Ottawa | 137 | 101 | 200 | $2,000 | $250 00 | 1 | 2 | | 20 | $200 00 | $625 00 | | $31 25 | $625 00 | $627 91 |
| Holland Tp. 11 fl. | Ottawa | 87 | 64 | 200 | 950 | | 1 | | 10 | | | | | | 200 00 | 281 10 |
| Holly | Oakland | 396 | 335 | 200 | 15,000 | 400 00 | 1 | 7 | 10 | 70 | 1,000 00 | 2,450 00 | $20 00 | 35 00 | 3,450 00 | 4,357 84 |
| Hollywood | Berrien | 131 | 96 | 160 | 2,500 | | | 3 | 8 | 8 | 320 00 | 240 00 | 40 00 | 30 00 | 560 00 | 716 07 |
| Hd | Ingham | 116 | 101 | 180 | 2,000 | | 1 | 2 | 10 | 18 | 360 00 | 450 00 | 40 00 | 25 00 | 810 00 | 930 91 |
| Holton | Muskegon | 97 | 84 | 180 | 2,000 | | | 4 | | 18 | | 495 00 | | 27 50 | 496 00 | 667 88 |
| Homer | Calhoun | 292 | 234 | 180 | 15,000 | 2,000 00 | 1 | 6 | 10 | 70 | 700 00 | 2,110 75 | 70 00 | 30 15 | 2,810 75 | 3,021 61 |
| Honor | Benzie | 106 | 112 | 180 | 3,000 | 1,800 00 | 1 | 2 | 9 | 18 | 360 00 | 436 00 | 40 00 | 24 22 | 796 00 | 1,064 68 |
| Hope | Midland | 125 | 86 | 180 | 1,800 | 400 00 | 1 | 1 | 9 | 9 | 315 00 | 225 00 | 35 00 | 25 00 | 540 00 | 815 27 |
| Hopkins Station | Allegan | 123 | 99 | 180 | 2,000 | | | 2 | 9 | 18 | 500 00 | 450 00 | 55 00 | 25 00 | 950 00 | 1,166 90 |
| Horton | Jackson | 93 | 80 | 180 | 3,000 | | 1 | 1 | 10 | 10 | 766 00 | 266 00 | 40 33 | 28 00 | 1,032 00 | 1,387 00 |
| Houghton | Houghton | 1,008 | 897 | 200 | 43,000 | | 3 | 15 | 30 | 135 | 2,320 00 | 6,259 75 | 100 89 | 44 47 | 8,589 75 | 12,676 30 |
| Howard City | Montcalm | 418 | 356 | 190 | 4,860 | | 1 | 7 | 10 | 67 | 700 00 | 2,292 50 | 73 66 | 34 22 | 2,992 50 | 4,247 00 |
| Howell | Livingston | 605 | 543 | 200 | 35,000 | | 3 | 8 | 30 | 140 | 2,150 00 | 4,606 00 | 71 66 | 32 88 | 6,756 00 | 10,046 84 |
| Humboldt | Marquette | 126 | 80 | 200 | 2,500 | 1,113 50 | | 5 | | 40 | | 1,425 00 | | 36 30 | 1,425 00 | 2,313 34 |
| Hubbardston | Ionia | 159 | 99 | 195 | 4,500 | | 2 | 2 | 19 | 19 | 500 00 | 475 00 | 42 63 | 25 00 | 975 00 | 1,389 64 |
| Hudson | Lenawee | 377 | 340 | 100 | 17,000 | | 1 | 7 | 10 | 89 | 1,100 00 | 3,496 00 | 105 26 | 40 88 | 4,596 00 | 6,300 82 |
| Hudsonville | Ottawa | 124 | 124 | 180 | 2,000 | | | 1 | | 9 | | 270 00 | | 30 00 | 630 00 | 907 47 |
| Hudson Tp. 5 | Lenawee | 290 | 345 | 180 | 6,000 | 360 00 | 1 | 5 | 9 | 45 | 1,000 00 | 1,431 00 | 111 11 | 31 80 | 2,431 00 | 2,948 95 |
| Ida | Monroe | 129 | 93 | 175 | 1,500 | 3,700 00 | 1 | 3 | 9 | 27 | 360 00 | 270 00 | 40 00 | 30 00 | 630 00 | 787 88 |
| Imlay City | Lapeer | 490 | 419 | 200 | 15,000 | | 3 | 7 | 10 | 70 | 800 00 | 1,900 00 | 80 00 | 27 12 | 2,700 00 | 3,689 96 |
| Inverness Tp. 6 | Cheboygan | 153 | 131 | 180 | 1,400 | | | 5 | | 18 | 360 00 | 540 00 | 40 00 | 30 00 | 900 00 | 1,072 75 |
| Inwood Tp. | Schoolcraft | 101 | 149 | 140 | 2,950 | 302 00 | 1 | 5 | 10 | 85 | | 1,156 00 | | 43 65 | 1,155 00 | 1,862 40 |
| Ionia | Ionia | 1,439 | 1,599 | 190 | 65,000 | 60,360 65 | 3 | 27 | 30 | 320 | 1,000 00 | 11,001 86 | 330 00 | 43 91 | 12,901 86 | 18,298 39 |
| Iron Mountain | Dickinson | 2,256 | 2,201 | 180 | 100,000 | 3,700 00 | 10 | 40 | 100 | 390 | 3,722 75 | 18,004 00 | 103 40 | 46 08 | 21,732 61 | 57,776 26 |
| Iron River | Iron | 421 | 376 | 170 | 5,000 | | 1 | 7 | 18 | 66 | 1,060 00 | 2,910 00 | 60 00 | 44 00 | 3,990 00 | 4,096 49 |
| Ironwood | Gogebic | 1,635 | 2,291 | 200 | 150,000 | 41,000 00 | 3 | 47 | 30 | 470 | 3,500 00 | 20,075 61 | 116 66 | 42 71 | 23,575 61 | 44,299 26 |
| Ishpeming | Marquette | 4,022 | 3,207 | 200 | 120,000 | 25,000 00 | 5 | 56 | 50 | 500 | 5,075 00 | 27,045 00 | 101 50 | 49 30 | 32,120 00 | 50,431 01 |
| Ishpeming Tp. | Marquette | 123 | 85 | 200 | 2,000 | 4,330 00 | 2 | | 30 | 20 | 1,100 00 | 400 00 | 55 00 | 20 00 | 1,500 00 | 2,672 24 |
| Ithaca | Gratiot | 581 | 478 | 197 | 55,000 | | 1 | 12 | 10 | 110 | 1,100 00 | 3,875 00 | 110 00 | 43 18 | 4,975 00 | 6,687 24 |
| Jackson | Jackson | 5,460 | 3 742 | 200 | 250,000 | 46,000 00 | 10 | 78 | 100 | 780 | 9,325 00 | 38,029 54 | 103 61 | 48 75 | 47,354 54 | 82,386 88 |
| Jamestown | Ottawa | 147 | 133 | 180 | 2,000 | | 1 | 1 | | | 360 00 | 235 00 | 40 00 | 55 00 | 585 00 | 809 43 |

| | | | | | | | | | | | | | | | | | | |
|---|---|---|---|---|---|---|---|---|---|---|---|---|---|---|---|---|---|---|

Jasper
Jennings
Jonesville
&c, Tp. 6 ft

Kalkaska
Kawkawlin
Kendall
Kent City
Kenton

G'd Traverse.
Kilmanagh
Kingston
Kochville
Lacota

Laingsburg
Lake Ann
Lake City
Lake Linden
Lake Odessa

Lakeview
Lambertville
Lamont
Lansing

Lapeer
Laporte
Lawrence
Lawton
Leaton

Leland
Lenox
Leonard
Le Roy
Leslie

Lexington
Linden
Litchfield
Long Rapids

Lowell
Ludington
Luther
Lyons
McBride

TABLE XVI.—CONTINUED.

| Districts. | Counties. | Number of children between 5 and 20 years. | Number of children that attended school during the year. | Number of days school. | Estimated value of school property. | Total indebtedness. | Number of teachers employed. Men. | Women. | Aggregate number of months taught by all teachers. Men. | Women. | Total wages of teachers for the year. Men. | Women. | Average monthly wages of teachers. Men. | Women. | Amount paid for superintendence and instruction. | Total cost of school. |
|---|---|---|---|---|---|---|---|---|---|---|---|---|---|---|---|---|
| McMillan Tp. | Ontonagon | 204 | 175 | 144 | 9,278 | 4,109 41 | 1 | 8 | 9 | 54 | 630 00 | 2,400 00 | 70 00 | 44 44 | 3,030 00 | 3,925 76 |
| Mackinac Island. | Mackinac | 229 | 144 | 160 | 3,500 | 500 00 | 1 | 2 | 9 | 16 | 640 00 | 640 00 | 80 00 | 40 00 | 1,280 00 | 1,865 05 |
| Mackinaw City. | Cheboygan | 174 | 118 | 180 | 5,000 | ........ | 1 | 2 | 9 | 25 | 585 00 | 840 00 | 65 00 | 33 66 | 1,425 00 | 1,837 12 |
| Mancelona. | Antrim | 539 | 406 | 180 | 9,445 | ........ | 1 | 5 | 9 | 81 | 765 00 | 2,565 00 | 85 00 | 31 31 | 3,330 00 | 4,846 10 |
| Manchester. | Washtenaw | 404 | 382 | 195 | 20,000 | ........ | 1 | 7 | 9 | 70 | 950 00 | 2,190 00 | 95 00 | 31 25 | 3,140 00 | 4,240 16 |
| Manistee. | Manistee | 4,780 | 3,199 | 200 | 121,000 | 29,300 00 | 6 | 74 | 60 | 734 | 6,545 00 | 29,310 72 | 109 26 | 39 9- | 35,855 72 | 51,832 06 |
| Manistique. | Schoolcraft. | 1,174 | 910 | 200 | 24,318 | 17,000 00 | 2 | 19 | 20 | 198 | 1,900 00 | 8,450 00 | 70 00 | 45 18 | 10,350 00 | 17,686 43 |
| Manton. | Wexford. | 325 | 325 | 180 | 10,000 | 1,000 00 | | 6 | 9 | 64 | 630 00 | 1,665 00 | 70 00 | 30 83 | 2,295 00 | 4,003 52 |
| Mansfield. | Iron. | 65 | 50 | 198 | 1,300 | ........ | | 1 | | 10 | ....... | 500 00 | ....... | 50 00 | 1,530 00 | 888 00 |
| Me Rapids. | Clinton. | 196 | 144 | 200 | 8,000 | ........ | 2 | 2 | 20 | 20 | 950 00 | 580 00 | 47 50 | 29 00 | ........ | 2,005 11 |
| Me Ridge Tp. | Delta. | 147 | 118 | 150 | 2,300 | 170 75 | 1 | 4 | 9 | 30 | 650 00 | 869 25 | 72 22 | 29 97 | 899 25 | 1,524 16 |
| Marcellus. | Cass. | 237 | 234 | 180 | 15,000 | ........ | 1 | 6 | 9 | 54 | 650 00 | 1,775 00 | 72 22 | 32 87 | 2,425 00 | 3,412 73 |
| Marine City. | St. Clair. | 1,259 | 618 | 200 | 30,000 | 7,000 00 | 2 | 11 | 20 | 110 | 1,500 00 | 3,710 50 | 75 00 | 33 73 | 5,210 50 | 3,979 18 |
| Marion. | Osceola. | 201 | 161 | 200 | 3,500 | 2,000 00 | 1 | 3 | 10 | 30 | 1,500 00 | 825 00 | 50 00 | 27 50 | 1,325 00 | 2,069 85 |
| Me Tp. | Marquette | 70 | 99 | 145 | 1,500 | ........ | | 1 | | 7 | ....... | 315 00 | ....... | 45 00 | 315 00 | 451 18 |
| Me. | Marquette | 2,882 | 1,970 | 197 | 125,000 | 30,000 00 | 5 | 35 | 50 | 350 | 4,025 00 | 17,945 00 | 80 50 | 51 27 | 21,970 00 | 32,863 75 |
| Marlette. | Sanilac. | 363 | 270 | 195 | 15,000 | 11,000 00 | | 6 | 10 | 80 | 850 00 | 1,900 00 | 85 00 | 31 68 | 2,750 00 | 4,222 63 |
| Marshall. | Calhoun. | 1,103 | 815 | 195 | 100,000 | ........ | 4 | 23 | 30 | 230 | 3,250 00 | 7,550 00 | 108 33 | 34 00 | 10,738 00 | 14,721 01 |
| Min... | Allegan. | 115 | 130 | 180 | 5,500 | ........ | | 2 | 9 | 18 | 630 00 | 550 00 | 70 00 | 30 55 | 1,180 00 | 1,362 76 |
| Marysville. | St. Clair. | 125 | 91 | 180 | 2,075 | ........ | | 1 | 9 | 9 | 380 00 | 225 00 | 40 00 | 25 00 | 585 00 | 644 47 |
| Mason. | Ingham. | 417 | 366 | 200 | 18,000 | ........ | 1 | 11 | 10 | 100 | 1,000 00 | 3,700 00 | 100 00 | 37 00 | 4,700 00 | 5,902 67 |
| Masonville Tp. | Delta. | 643 | 528 | 180 | 6,030 | ........ | 4 | 7 | 37 | 65 | 2,215 00 | 2,435 00 | 59 86 | 37 46 | 4,650 00 | 5,925 61 |
| Mattawan. | Van Buren | 101 | 47 | 175 | 4,000 | ........ | 1 | 1 | 9 | 9 | 300 00 | 225 00 | 33 33 | 25 00 | 525 00 | 544 31 |
| Me. | Monroe | 202 | 71 | 190 | 1,800 | ........ | 2 | | 14 | | 510 00 | ........ | 38 66 | ....... | 510 00 | 627 02 |
| Mayville. | Tuscola | 303 | 243 | 200 | 10,000 | 6,700 00 | 2 | 3 | 30 | 50 | 1,100 00 | 600 00 | 36 66 | 30 00 | 1,700 00 | 2,814 11 |
| Mears. | Oceana. | 98 | 64 | 180 | 1,000 | ........ | 3 | 2 | | 18 | ........ | 540 00 | ....... | 30 00 | 540 00 | 607 00 |
| Mia... | Mecosta | 196 | 126 | 180 | 2,500 | ........ | 1 | 2 | 9 | 18 | 450 00 | 472 50 | 50 00 | 26 25 | 922 50 | 1,539 77 |
| Memphis. | Macomb. | 282 | 182 | 195 | 5,000 | ........ | 1 | 3 | 10 | 30 | 650 00 | 880 00 | 65 00 | 29 33 | 1,530 00 | 2,468 86 |
| Mendon. | St. Joseph. | 217 | 306 | 180 | 8,000 | ........ | 2 | 4 | 18 | 36 | 1,260 00 | 1,242 00 | 70 00 | 24 50 | 2,502 00 | 3,461 25 |
| Menominee. | Menominee. | 4,185 | ?,966 | 188 | 156,000 | 60,000 00 | 6 | 50 | 57 | 476 | 5,820 10 | 21,813 00 | 93 03 | 45 92 | 27,133 10 | 42,294 70 |
| Saginaw. | Saginaw | 176 | 146 | 200 | 4,000 | 350 00 | 1 | 2 | 10 | 30 | 420 00 | 630 00 | 45 00 | 28 50 | 980 00 | 1,439 08 |
| Merrill. | Wexford. | 128 | 107 | 180 | 1,800 | 850 00 | 1 | 2 | 9 | 14 | 315 00 | 410 00 | 35 00 | 29 32 | 725 00 | 1,455 78 |

| Place | County | | | | | | | | | | | | | | | | | | | |
|---|---|---|---|---|---|---|---|---|---|---|---|---|---|---|---|---|---|---|---|---|
| Metamora | Lapeer | | | | | | | | | | | | | | | | | | | |
| Michigamme | | | | | | | | | | | | | | | | | | | | |
| Middleton | Gratiot | | | | | | | | | | | | | | | | | | | |
| Middleville | Barry | | | | | | | | | | | | | | | | | | | |
| Midland | Midland | | | | | | | | | | | | | | | | | | | |
| Milan | Washtenaw | | | | | | | | | | | | | | | | | | | |
| Millburg | Berrien | | | | | | | | | | | | | | | | | | | |
| Mill Creek | Kent | | | | | | | | | | | | | | | | | | | |
| Milford | Oakland | | | | | | | | | | | | | | | | | | | |
| Millington | Tuscola | | | | | | | | | | | | | | | | | | | |
| Min Jen City | Manistee | | | | | | | | | | | | | | | | | | | |
| Monroe | Monroe | | | | | | | | | | | | | | | | | | | |
| Montague | Muskegon | | | | | | | | | | | | | | | | | | | |
| Montgomery | Hillsdale | | | | | | | | | | | | | | | | | | | |
| Morenci | Lenawee | | | | | | | | | | | | | | | | | | | |
| Morley | Mecosta | | | | | | | | | | | | | | | | | | | |
| Morrice | Shiawassee | | | | | | | | | | | | | | | | | | | |
| Moscow | Hillsdale | | | | | | | | | | | | | | | | | | | |
| Mt. Clemens | Macomb | | | | | | | | | | | | | | | | | | | |
| Mt. Morris | Genesee | | | | | | | | | | | | | | | | | | | |
| Mt. Pleasant | Isabella | | | | | | | | | | | | | | | | | | | |
| Muir | Ionia | | | | | | | | | | | | | | | | | | | |
| Mulliken | Eaton | | | | | | | | | | | | | | | | | | | |
| Munising | Alger | | | | | | | | | | | | | | | | | | | |
| Muskegon | Muskegon | | | | | | | | | | | | | | | | | | | |
| Muskegon Heights | Muskegon | | | | | | | | | | | | | | | | | | | |
| Nadeau | Menominee | | | | | | | | | | | | | | | | | | | |
| Napoleon | Jackson | | | | | | | | | | | | | | | | | | | |
| Nashville | Barry | | | | | | | | | | | | | | | | | | | |
| National Mine | Marquette | | | | | | | | | | | | | | | | | | | |
| Negaunee | Marquette | | | | | | | | | | | | | | | | | | | |
| Negaunee Tp | Marquette | | | | | | | | | | | | | | | | | | | |
| Newaygo | Newaygo | | | | | | | | | | | | | | | | | | | |
| New Baltimore | Macomb | | | | | | | | | | | | | | | | | | | |
| Newberry | Luce | | | | | | | | | | | | | | | | | | | |
| New Boston | Wayne | | | | | | | | | | | | | | | | | | | |
| New Buffalo | Berrien | | | | | | | | | | | | | | | | | | | |
| New Salem | Berrien | | | | | | | | | | | | | | | | | | | |
| New Holland | Ottawa | | | | | | | | | | | | | | | | | | | |
| New Hudson | Oakland | | | | | | | | | | | | | | | | | | | |
| New Lathrop | Shiawassee | | | | | | | | | | | | | | | | | | | |
| New Troy | Berrien | | | | | | | | | | | | | | | | | | | |
| Niles | Berrien | | | | | | | | | | | | | | | | | | | |
| North Adams | Hillsdale | | | | | | | | | | | | | | | | | | | |
| North Branch | Lapeer | | | | | | | | | | | | | | | | | | | |

TABLE XVI.—CONTINUED.

| Districts. | Counties. | Number of children between 5 and 20 years. | Number of children attended school during the year. | Number of days school. | Estimated value of school property | Total indebtedness. | Number of teachers employed. Men | Women | Aggregate number of months taught by all teachers. Men | Women | Total wages of teachers for the year. Men | Women | Average monthly wages of teachers. Men | Women | Amount paid for superintendence and instruction. | Total cost of school. |
|---|---|---|---|---|---|---|---|---|---|---|---|---|---|---|---|---|
| North Muskegon | Muskegon | 157 | 175 | 140 | $12,000 | $6,127 69 | 1 | 1 2 | 5 | 16 | $187 50 | $405 00 | $37 50 | $25 31 | $592 50 | $1,021 40 |
| Northport | Leelanau | 265 | 218 | 158 | 3,600 | | 1 | 3 | 16 | 16 | 760 00 | 560 00 | 46 00 | 35 00 | 1,320 00 | 1,765 58 |
| North Star | Gratiot | 131 | 90 | 180 | 3,000 | 3,224 00 | 1 | 1 | 9 | 9 | 592 50 | 225 00 | 32 50 | 25 00 | 517 50 | 1,171 69 |
| Norway | Dickinson | 1,322 | 870 | 180 | 25,000 | | 1 | 12 | 10 | 108 | 1,299 97 | 5,315 00 | 144 44 | 49 21 | 6,614 97 | 9,474 08 |
| Northville | Wayne | 430 | 313 | 200 | 20,000 | | 1 | 3 | 10 | 90 | 850 00 | 2,776 00 | 85 00 | 30 83 | 3,625 00 | 4,724 73 |
| Nottawa | St. Joseph | 78 | 66 | 180 | 2,000 | | 1 | 1 | 7 | 7 | 298 67 | 235 00 | 41 13 | 25 00 | 513 67 | 681 10 |
| Nunica | Ottawa | 111 | 98 | 180 | 500 | | 1 | 1 | 9 | 9 | 375 00 | 246 00 | 41 66 | 27 32 | 620 00 | 453 70 |
| Oak Grove | Livingston | 70 | 71 | 170 | 1,140 | | 1 | 1 | 9 | 9 | 382 00 | 214 00 | 28 00 | 23 77 | 466 00 | 584 23 |
| Oakley | Saginaw | 82 | 74 | 175 | 1,600 | | 1 | 1 | 9 | 9 | 373 80 | 180 00 | 41 33 | 20 00 | 553 80 | 553 80 |
| Ogden Center | Lenawee | 91 | 63 | 180 | 4,400 | | 1 | 1 | 8 | 8 | 240 00 | 300 00 | 30 00 | 25 00 | 440 00 | 510 67 |
| Okemos | Ingham | 116 | 132 | 180 | 2,500 | 1,025 00 | 1 | 2 | 9 | 18 | 405 00 | 450 00 | 45 00 | 25 00 | 855 00 | 1,031 64 |
| Old Mission | G'd Traverse | 112 | 87 | 160 | 3,000 | | 1 | 1 | 8 | 8 | 320 00 | 200 00 | 40 00 | 25 00 | 520 00 | 1,056 49 |
| Olivet | Eaton | 250 | 210 | 200 | 9,600 | 200 00 | 1 | 6 | 10 | 60 | 650 00 | 1,350 00 | 65 00 | 22 50 | 4,000 00 | 2,728 92 |
| Onaway | Presque Isle | 245 | 115 | 160 | 300 | | 1 | 1 | 8 | 8 | 320 00 | 240 00 | 40 00 | 30 00 | 560 00 | 805 05 |
| Omer | Arenac | 208 | 166 | 180 | 1,000 | | 1 | 1 | 9 | 9 | 450 00 | 270 00 | 50 00 | 30 00 | 720 00 | 901 00 |
| Onekama | Manistee | 156 | 112 | 180 | 2,000 | | 1 | 2 | 9 | 18 | 477 00 | 576 00 | 53 00 | 32 00 | 1,053 00 | 1,285 62 |
| Onondaga | Ingham | 100 | 74 | 175 | 400 | | 1 | 1 | 8 | 8 | 366 00 | 225 00 | 40 00 | 35 00 | 565 00 | 730 56 |
| Ontonagon | Ontonagon | 422 | 460 | 120 | 7,000 | 5,000 00 | | 14 | | | | 4,980 00 | 47 63 | 47 48 | 4,080 00 | 9,179 04 |
| Onota | Alger | 46 | 31 | 140 | 1,400 | | 1 | 1 | 11 | 3 | 821 00 | 150 00 | 83 73 | 50 00 | 674 00 | 840 22 |
| Ot__ | Houghton | 1,841 | 1,127 | 200 | 1,400 | | 4 | 23 | | 250 | 3,350 00 | 10,356 00 | 88 00 | 47 00 | 13,706 00 | 21,733 50 |
| Orion | Oakland | 234 | 174 | 200 | 10,000 | 2,000 00 | 1 | 3 | 10 | 20 | 533 50 | 819 15 | 84 71 | 32 34 | 1,352 65 | 1,916 18 |
| Ortonville | Oakland | 129 | 83 | 200 | 3,000 | | 1 | 2 | 10 | 20 | 625 00 | 507 50 | 62 50 | 25 37 | 1,132 50 | 1,337 12 |
| Oscoda | Iosco | 446 | 396 | 176 | 1,500 | 61 11 | 1 | 7 | | 63 | | 2,438 37 | | 28 70 | 2,438 37 | 2,500 39 |
| Osseo | Hillsdale | 76 | 66 | 180 | 1,600 | | 1 | 1 | 9 | 9 | 360 00 | 234 00 | 40 00 | 26 00 | 600 00 | 788 79 |
| Owineke Tp | Alpena | 168 | 70 | 100 | 2,000 | 639 24 | 1 | 1 | 1 | | 30 00 | 570 00 | 30 00 | 30 00 | 600 00 | 814 53 |
| ... | Genesee | 167 | 80 | 200 | 2,000 | | 1 | 2 | 10 | 20 | 450 00 | 560 00 | 45 00 | 25 00 | 960 00 | 1,204 34 |
| Osego | Allegan | 639 | 474 | 180 | 22,000 | 11,000 00 | 2 | 12 | 9 | 108 | 1,150 00 | 4,191 00 | 127 77 | 38 81 | 5,341 50 | 7,030 89 |
| Oster Lake | Lapeer | 96 | 76 | 180 | 1,700 | | 1 | 1 | 9 | 9 | 360 00 | 234 00 | 40 00 | 26 00 | 594 00 | 665 04 |
| Overisel | Allegan | 127 | 91 | 180 | 1,100 | | 1 | 1 | 8 | 8 | 335 00 | 225 00 | 41 25 | 30 00 | 545 00 | 563 35 |
| Ovid | Clinton | 367 | 398 | 200 | 15,000 | 19,500 00 | 2 | 8 | 16 | 73 | 1,218 00 | 2,615 00 | 76 12 | 35 82 | 3,833 00 | 5,734 14 |
| ... | Shiawassee | 2,339 | 2,150 | 100 | 125,000 | | 5 | 38 | 48 | 361 | 3,912 50 | 14,928 88 | 82 34 | 41 38 | 18,841 38 | 30,425 08 |
| Oxford | Oakland | 319 | 285 | 200 | 8,000 | | 1 | 7 | 10 | 60 | 900 00 | 2,005 00 | 90 00 | 33 41 | 2,905 00 | 3,687 80 |

| | | | | | | | | | | | | | | | | | | |
|---|---|---|---|---|---|---|---|---|---|---|---|---|---|---|---|---|---|---|
| Palmer. | Marquette | 153 | 58 | 50 | 900 | 2,000 | 115 00 | | 550 00 | | 550 00 | | | 10 | 15 00 | 30 00 | | 944 10 |
| Palms | Sanilac | 97 | 65 | 96 | 164 | 1,000 | | | 400 00 | | 400 00 | | | 10 | 40 00 | | | 476 65 |
| Palmyra | Lenawee | 90 | 62 | 82 | 166 | 2,500 | | | 540 00 | 30 00 | | | | | | | | 699 63 |
| Palo | Ionia | 107 | 82 | 67 | 166 | 4,000 | | 30 00 | 930 00 | 35 00 | 350 00 | 680 00 | 1X | 31 00 | | 540 00 | | 1,310 85 |
| Paris | Mecosta | 95 | 72 | 72 | 180 | 2,000 | | 30 00 | 540 00 | 30 00 | 540 00 | | 1X | | | | | 881 84 |
| Paris Tp. 1 | Kent | 113 | 60 | 60 | 200 | 1,000 | | | 400 00 | 40 00 | 667 50 | 400 00 | 10 | 10 | | | | 572 81 |
| Parma | Jackson | 135 | 125 | 180 | 10,000 | | 30 00 | 1,537 50 | 71 00 | 370 00 | 870 00 | 1X | 22 | | 10 00 | | | 2,419 33 |
| Paul | Kent | 110 | 92 | 197 | 3,500 | | 40 00 | 520 00 | 40 68 | 1,920 00 | 390 00 | 30 | 9 | | | | | 1,082 14 |
| Paw Paw | Van Buren | 380 | 368 | 365 | 3,920 00 | 40,000 | 38 40 | 3,920 00 | 66 68 | | 2,000 00 | 50 | 19 | | 40,000 | | 18,540 00 | | 5,802 33 |
| Peck | Sanilac | 155 | 159 | 159 | 200 | 1,000 | 35 27 | 650 00 | 31 00 | 250 00 | 400 00 | 10 | 10 | | | | | 898 49 |
| Pentwater | Oceana | 386 | 370 | 194 | 8,000 | | 33 54 | 3,587 00 | 90 00 | 2,687 50 | 900 00 | 80 | 9 | | | | | 4,493 81 |
| Perrinton | Gratiot | 112 | 149 | 177 | 1,500 | | 31 | 520 00 | 35 00 | 305 00 | 315 00 | 9 | 20 | | | | | 683 84 |
| Perry | Shiawassee | 181 | 174 | 300 | 4,000 | | 30 90 | 1,000 00 | 50 00 | 600 00 | 1,000 00 | 20 | 19 | | | 2,700 00 | | 1,978 74 |
| Petersburg | Monroe | 225 | 167 | 195 | 9,000 | | 27 96 | 1,577 60 | 65 56 | 1,020 50 | 567 19 | 35 | 9 | | | | | 2,013 31 |
| Petoskey | Emmet | 1,188 | 445 | 1,281 | 32,000 | | 35 27 | 8,673 40 | 88 31 | 7,036 00 | 1,640 00 | 200 | 30 | | | | | 12,186 63 |
| Pewamo | Ionia | 134 | 103 | 180 | 1,200 | | 30 00 | 945 00 | 45 00 | 540 00 | 405 00 | 18 | 9 | | | | | 1,157 31 |
| Pierson | Montcalm | 119 | 108 | 175 | 2,000 | | 30 00 | 630 00 | 40 00 | 270 00 | 380 00 | 9 | 9 | | | | | 705 67 |
| Pigeon | Huron | 270 | 175 | 300 | 4,000 | | 33 38 | 1,065 00 | 50 00 | 615 00 | 450 00 | 19 | 20 | | | | | 1,746 00 |
| Pinckney | Livingston | 144 | 127 | 300 | 8,000 | | 27 63 | 1,650 00 | 52 50 | 600 00 | 1,050 00 | 30 | 30 | | | 18,540 00 | | 2,015 04 |
| Pinconning | Bay | 430 | 335 | 197 | 3,000 | | 35 27 | 1,750 00 | 45 10 | 850 00 | 1,640 00 | 34 | 30 | | | 564 00 | | 2,422 19 |
| Pinnebog | Huron | 153 | 101 | 200 | 3,000 | | 27 93 | 711 00 | 38 56 | 628 73 | 711 00 | 20 | 20 | | | 150 00 | | 847 70 |
| Pittsford | Hillsdale | 143 | 125 | 188 | 3,500 | | 37 29 | 990 44 | 48 75 | 2,834 50 | 461 75 | 10 | 10 | | | | | 1,389 07 |
| Plainwell | Allegan | 356 | 340 | 190 | 13,000 | | 37 63 | 3,934 50 | 115 78 | | 1,100 00 | 80 | 10 | | | 1,000 00 | | 5,122 99 |
| Plymouth | Wayne | 431 | 386 | 195 | 12,000 | | 39 66 | 3,365 00 | 86 37 | 2,515 00 | 850 00 | 290 | 50 | | | | | 4,582 12 |
| Pontiac | Oakland | 1,810 | 1,291 | 197 | 110,000 | | | 15,375 40 | | 11,106 87 | 4,398 53 | | | | | 11,000 00 | | 25,021 79 |
| Portage Tp. 2 | Houghton | 201 | 119 | 193 | 10,000 | 10,000 | 52 50 | 2,100 00 | 84 21 | 2,100 00 | 711 00 | 40 | | | | | | 3,227 27 |
| Port Austin | Huron | 391 | 177 | 188 | 3,500 | 1,400 | 30 00 | 900 00 | 61 22 | 900 00 | 650 00 | 30 | 10 | | | 100 00 | | 2,113 56 |
| Port Hope | Huron | 239 | 132 | 140 | 225,000 | | 25 00 | 1,087 50 | 35 00 | 315 00 | 487 50 | 630 | 57 | | | | | 1,405 35 |
| Port Huron | St. Clair | 3,824 | 3,563 | 180 | 225,000 | | 40 50 | 25,553 40 | 111 66 | | 3,015 00 | 1X | 70 | | | | | 45,170 17 |
| Port Sanilac | Sanilac | 145 | 141 | 180 | 2,000 | | 43 00 | 918 00 | 50 00 | 400 00 | 450 00 | 1X | 2 | | | | | 1,038 09 |
| Portland | Ionia | 542 | 458 | 187 | 16,000 | | 31 03 | 4,001 77 | 84 21 | 3,801 77 | 800 00 | 122 | 15 | | | 16,000 00 | | 6,106 15 |
| Potterville | Eaton | 169 | 159 | 180 | 2,300 | | 30 00 | 1,081 00 | 61 22 | 540 00 | 551 00 | 1X | 5 | | | | | 1,477 22 |
| Prattville | Hillsdale | 112 | 98 | 180 | 1,000 | | 25 00 | 540 00 | 35 00 | 225 00 | 315 00 | 9 | 1 | | | | | 607 80 |
| Prescott | Ogemaw | 121 | 60 | 140 | 1,000 | | 25 00 | 540 00 | 25 00 | 315 00 | 225 00 | 10 | 1 | | | 352 92 | | 623 76 |
| Quincy | Branch | 317 | 294 | 200 | 10,000 | | 34 62 | 2,900 00 | 64 37 | 1,870 00 | 1,080 00 | 54 | 2 | | | | | 4,447 87 |
| Quincy Tp. | Houghton | 491 | 300 | 200 | 7,700 | | 42 50 | 3,700 00 | 115 00 | 2,550 00 | 1,150 00 | 60 | 6 | | | 5,748 88 | | 4,935 63 |
| Quinnesec | Dickinson | 295 | 201 | 180 | 8,560 | | 43 75 | 2,250 00 | 75 00 | 1,575 00 | 675 00 | 30 | 4 | | | | | 3,721 08 |
| Ravenna | Muskegon | 177 | 143 | 200 | 3,000 | | 28 00 | 1,077 75 | 44 77 | 560 00 | 447 76 | 30 | 2 | | | | | 1,290 73 |
| Reading | Hillsdale | 259 | 210 | 190 | 8,500 | | 34 69 | 2,374 00 | 77 77 | 1,024 50 | 750 00 | 47 | 6 | | | 1,000 00 | | 3,472 03 |
| Reed City | Osceola | 745 | 596 | 195 | 25,000 | | 38 50 | 5,730 00 | 83 78 | 4,390 00 | 1,340 00 | 114 | 13 | | | 7,627 83 | | 7,438 14 |
| Reese | Tuscola | 191 | 116 | 192 | 1,800 | | 45 22 | 800 00 | 45 00 | 850 00 | 800 00 | 10 | 1 | | | 1 85 | | 1,024 57 |
| Republic Tp | Marquette | 807 | 667 | 200 | 16,000 | | 33 13 | 5,860 00 | 80 00 | 1,250 00 | 1,600 00 | 90 | 3 | | | | | 8,421 15 |
| Richland | Kalamazoo | 102 | 84 | 180 | 4,300 | | 33 00 | 1,250 00 | 25 00 | | | 38 | 4 | | | | | 1,867 59 |
| Richland Tp. 4 | Saginaw | 134 | 101 | 140 | 2,000 | | 31 38 | 340 00 | 46 74 | 315 00 | 315 00 | 18 | 2 | | | | | 733 72 |
| Richmond | Macomb | 217 | 293 | 180 | 8,000 | | 31 38 | 1,809 00 | 40 73 | 567 00 | 1,242 00 | 9 | 1 | | | | | 2,305 85 |
| Ridgeway | Lenawee | 78 | 55 | 180 | 2,900 | | 30 00 | 675 00 | 45 00 | 270 00 | 405 00 | 9 | | | | | | 723 41 |

TABLE XVI.—CONTINUED.

| Districts. | Counties. | Number of children between 5 and 20 years. | Number of children that attended school during the year. | Number of days school. | Estimated value of school property. | Total indebtedness. | Number of teachers employed. Men | Women | Aggregate number of months taught by all teachers. Men | Women | Total wages of teachers for the year. Men | Women | Average monthly wages of teachers. Men | Women | Amount paid for superintendence and instruction. | Total cost of school. |
|---|---|---|---|---|---|---|---|---|---|---|---|---|---|---|---|---|
| ...th Muskegon | Muskegon | 157 | 175 | 140 | $12,000 | $6,127 69 | 1 | 2 | 5 | 16 | $187 50 | $405 00 | $37 50 | $25 50 | $592 50 | $1,021 64 |
| ...port | Leelanau | 265 | 218 | 158 | 3,500 | ........ | 3 | 2 | 16 | 16 | 780 00 | 560 00 | 46 00 | 35 00 | 1,320 00 | 1,765 56 |
| North Star | Gratiot | 131 | 90 | 180 | 2,000 | 3,224 00 | 1 | 1 | 9 | 9 | 292 50 | 225 00 | 32 00 | 25 00 | 517 50 | 1,171 69 |
| Norway | Dickinson | 1,322 | 870 | 189 | 22,000 | ........ | 12 | 12 | 108 | 108 | 1,290 97 | 5,315 00 | 144 00 | 49 21 | 6,614 97 | 9,474 05 |
| Northville | Wayne | 430 | 313 | 200 | 20,000 | ........ | 3 | 8 | 90 | 90 | 850 00 | 2,775 00 | 88 00 | 30 83 | 3,625 00 | 4,724 73 |
| ...th | St. Joseph | 78 | 66 | 180 | 2,000 | ........ | 1 | 1 | 7 | 9 | 298 67 | 225 00 | 41 53 | 25 00 | 513 67 | 684 10 |
| Nunica | Ottawa | 111 | 98 | 180 | 500 | ........ | 1 | 1 | 9 | 9 | 375 00 | 245 00 | 41 66 | 27 77 | 620 00 | 483 70 |
| Oak ridge | Livingston | 82 | 71 | 180 | 1,140 | ........ | 1 | 1 | 9 | 9 | 252 00 | 214 00 | 28 00 | 23 77 | 466 00 | 524 33 |
| Oakley | Saginaw | 91 | 74 | 175 | 1,000 | ........ | 1 | 1 | 9 | 9 | 373 80 | 180 00 | 41 53 | 20 00 | 553 80 | 553 80 |
| Ogden ...ter | Lenawee | ... | 63 | 160 | 4,400 | ........ | 1 | 1 | 8 | 8 | 240 00 | 200 00 | 30 00 | 25 00 | 440 00 | 510 67 |
| Okemos | Ingham | 116 | 182 | 180 | 2,570 | 1,025 00 | 1 | 2 | 9 | 18 | 405 00 | 450 00 | 45 00 | 25 00 | 855 00 | 1,031 64 |
| Old Mission | G'd Traverse | 112 | 87 | 160 | 3,000 | ........ | 1 | 1 | 8 | 8 | 320 00 | 200 00 | 40 00 | 22 50 | 520 00 | 2,056 49 |
| Olivet | Eaton | 259 | 210 | 200 | 9,000 | 200 00 | 1 | 4 | 10 | 69 | 650 00 | 1,350 00 | 65 00 | 22 00 | 2,000 00 | 2,726 02 |
| Onaway | Presque Isle | 245 | 116 | 160 | 1,000 | ........ | 1 | 3 | 8 | 8 | 320 00 | 240 00 | 40 00 | 30 00 | 560 00 | 846 05 |
| Omer | Arenac | 208 | 166 | 180 | 1,000 | ........ | 1 | 1 | 9 | 9 | 450 00 | 270 00 | 50 00 | 30 00 | 720 00 | 901 00 |
| Onekama | Manistee | 155 | 112 | 180 | 2,000 | ........ | 1 | 2 | 9 | 18 | 477 00 | 578 00 | 53 00 | 32 00 | 1,055 00 | 1,286 62 |
| ...tham | Ingham | 160 | 74 | 176 | 400 | ........ | 1 | 1 | 9 | 9 | 308 00 | 225 00 | 40 00 | 47 42 | 685 00 | 1,720 56 |
| Ontonagon | Ontonagon | 432 | 400 | 120 | 7,000 | 5,000 00 | ... | 14 | 11 | 105 | ........ | 4,960 00 | 47 42 | 50 00 | 1,640 00 | 9,179 04 |
| Alger | Alger | 46 | 31 | 140 | 1,400 | ........ | 1 | 1 | 11 | 3 | 324 00 | 150 00 | 88 75 | 50 00 | 674 00 | 840 22 |
| O...se | Houghton | 1,841 | 1,157 | 200 | ........ | ........ | 4 | 32 | 40 | 350 | 3,350 00 | 10,355 00 | 88 75 | 47 00 | 13,705 00 | 21,733 50 |
| Orion | Oakland | 234 | 174 | 200 | 10,000 | 2,000 00 | 1 | 2 | 10 | 29 | 533 50 | 819 15 | 54 71 | 28 24 | 1,352 00 | 1,016 18 |
| Ortonville | Oakland | 130 | 83 | 180 | 3,000 | ........ | 1 | 2 | 10 | 30 | 625 00 | 507 50 | 62 50 | 38 70 | 1,132 50 | 1,337 12 |
| Oscoda | Iosco | 446 | 394 | 176 | 1,500 | 61 11 | 1 | 2 | 9 | 63 | ........ | 2,434 37 | ........ | 38 70 | 2,438 37 | 2,400 30 |
| Osseo | Hillsdale | 76 | 66 | 100 | 2,500 | 659 24 | 1 | 1 | 1 | 9 | 360 00 | 234 00 | 40 00 | 26 00 | 594 00 | 788 70 |
| Oswineke Tp | Alpena | 108 | 70 | 100 | 2,000 | ........ | 1 | 1 | 10 | 19 | 30 00 | 570 00 | 30 00 | 30 00 | 600 00 | 814 53 |
| Otisville | Genesee | 167 | 80 | 200 | 2,000 | ........ | 1 | 3 | 10 | 20 | 450 00 | 500 00 | 45 00 | 25 00 | 950 00 | 1,204 34 |
| Otsego | Allegan | 695 | 474 | 180 | 22,000 | 11,000 00 | 1 | 12 | 9 | 108 | 1,150 00 | 4,191 50 | 127 77 | 28 81 | 5,341 50 | 7,080 89 |
| Otter Lake | Lapeer | 96 | 76 | 180 | 1,300 | ........ | 1 | 1 | 9 | 9 | 380 00 | 234 00 | 40 00 | 26 00 | 564 00 | 968 04 |
| Overisel | Allegan | 127 | 91 | 180 | 2,000 | ........ | 1 | 1 | 8 | 9 | ........ | 225 00 | 33 00 | 25 00 | 545 00 | 983 35 |
| Ovid | Clinton | 367 | 366 | 200 | 15,000 | 19,500 00 | 2 | 8 | 16 | 73 | 1,218 50 | 2,615 00 | 76 13 | 35 50 | 3,833 50 | 5,704 14 |
| Owosso | Shiawassee | 2,339 | 2,150 | 100 | 155,000 | ........ | 5 | 38 | 48 | 361 | 3,912 50 | 14,928 88 | 82 34 | 41 38 | 18,841 38 | 30,425 05 |
| Oxford | Oakland | 319 | 235 | 200 | 8,000 | ........ | 1 | 7 | 16 | 60 | 900 00 | 2,006 00 | 90 00 | 33 41 | 2,906 00 | 3,687 80 |

TABLE XVI.— CONTINUED.

| Districts. | Counties. | Number of children between 5 and 20 years. | Number of children that attended school during the year. | Number of days school. | Estimated value of school property. | Total indebtedness. | Number of teachers employed. Men | Women | Aggregate number of months taught by all teachers. Men | Women | Total wages of teachers for the year. Men | Women | Average monthly wages of teachers. Men | Women | Amount paid for superintendence and instruction. | Total cost of school. |
|---|---|---|---|---|---|---|---|---|---|---|---|---|---|---|---|---|
| Rica | Lenawee | 185 | 97 | 180 | 4,000 | 31 25 | 1 | 1 | 6 | 6 | 270 00 | 234 00 | 45 00 | 26 00 | 804 88 | 910 88 |
| Riverside Tp. 1 it | Mi-ssukee | 293 | 183 | 180 | 4,000 | 1,700 00 | 1 | 4 | 6 | 26 | 432 50 | 794 25 | 46 44 | 30 64 | 1,216 75 | 1,015 66 |
| Rochester | Oakland | 356 | 271 | 220 | 12,000 | 200 00 | 1 | 6 | 10 | 54 | 750 00 | 1,380 00 | 60 83 | 45 35 | 2,140 22 | 2,916 92 |
| Rock River | Alger | 53 | 29 | 180 | 3,500 | | 1 | | 10 | 9 | 402 50 | 405 00 | 80 00 | 44 45 | 807 50 | 1,077 07 |
| Rockford | Kent | 246 | 160 | 200 | 30,000 | 5,000 00 | 1 | 6 | 10 | 50 | 800 00 | 1,582 50 | 60 14 | 45 15 | 2,332 50 | 8,221 69 |
| Rockland Tp. | Ontonagon | 346 | 141 | 200 | 6,500 | 1,200 00 | 1 | 2 | 10 | 30 | 900 00 | 900 00 | 90 00 | 46 00 | 1,700 00 | 2,749 00 |
| Rockwood | Wayne | 107 | 53 | 180 | 3,000 | 800 00 | 1 | 1 | 9 | 9 | 315 00 | 260 00 | 35 00 | 28 88 | 575 00 | 755 08 |
| Rogers City | Presque Isle | 302 | 82 | 160 | 2,000 | | 4 | 7 | 34 | 7 | 900 00 | 900 00 | 37 50 | 29 50 | 900 00 | 1,382 43 |
| Romeo | Macomb | 444 | 425 | 200 | 20,000 | 1,500 00 | 3 | | 30 | 70 | 2,190 00 | 2,075 00 | 71 66 | 22 22 | 4,225 00 | 5,638 03 |
| Romulus | Wayne | 133 | 68 | 180 | 4,000 | | 1 | 1 | 9 | 9 | 405 00 | 500 00 | 45 00 | | 605 00 | 778 19 |
| Roscommon | Roscommon | 295 | 139 | 180 | 3,500 | 3,000 00 | 1 | 4 | 9 | 27 | 406 00 | 940 00 | 45 00 | 33 33 | 940 00 | 1,608 88 |
| Rose City | Ogemaw | 180 | 187 | 180 | 2,500 | 2,500 00 | 1 | 3 | 9 | 24 | 475 00 | 273 50 | 50 00 | 30 34 | 673 50 | 906 16 |
| Royal Oak | Oakland | 225 | 176 | 196 | 2,000 | | 2 | 3 | 12 | 24 | 475 00 | 688 75 | 40 00 | 28 69 | 1,163 75 | 1,473 47 |
| Rust Tp. | Montmorency | 135 | 89 | 160 | 1,050 | 307 50 | 1 | 1 | 10 | 15 | 380 00 | 420 00 | 38 00 | 43 80 | 420 00 | 912 31 |
| Saginaw | Saginaw | 8,344 | 5,220 | 189 | 404,982 | | 11 | 133 | 110 | 1,330 | 12,325 00 | 56,383 18 | 112 04 | 43 80 | 70,588 18 | 110,256 30 |
| Saginaw W. S. | Saginaw | 5,273 | 3,816 | 200 | 297,868 | 30,000 00 | 9 | 73 | 90 | 790 | 7,300 00 | 31,438 75 | 80 00 | 43 00 | 38,638 75 | 55,292 82 |
| Saganing | Arenac | 212 | 127 | 200 | 2,600 | 21 00 | 1 | 1 | 10 | 10 | 100 00 | 449 75 | 40 00 | 35 41 | 589 75 | 840 46 |
| St. Charles | Saginaw | 446 | 314 | 200 | 7,000 | 4,000 00 | 1 | 3 | 10 | 30 | 500 00 | 980 00 | 50 00 | 30 85 | 1,450 30 | 1,856 20 |
| St. Clair | St. Clair | 731 | 567 | 203 | 35,000 | 2,000 00 | 1 | 3 | 10 | 30 | 1,000 00 | 4,925 00 | 100 00 | 37 88 | 5,925 00 | 8,498 74 |
| St. Clair Heights | Wayne | 178 | 99 | 194 | 1,000 | | 2 | 12 | 20 | 130 | 840 00 | | 42 00 | | 840 00 | 1,143 76 |
| St. Ignace | Mackinac | 708 | 435 | 175 | 20,000 | 15,875 00 | 2 | 8 | 18 | 72 | 1,125 00 | 2,980 00 | 62 50 | 40 00 | 4,005 00 | 6,001 42 |
| St. Ignace Tp. | Mackinac | 36 | 55 | 100 | 400 | 650 00 | | 1 | | 10 | | 320 00 | | 32 00 | 320 00 | 572 19 |
| St. Ems | Clinton | 841 | 791 | 185 | 40,000 | 10,000 00 | 3 | 15 | 27 | 135 | 2,550 00 | 5,002 00 | 94 44 | 33 70 | 8,452 00 | 12,226 11 |
| St. Joseph | Berrien | 1,234 | 1,019 | 196 | 65,000 | 10,000 00 | 1 | 25 | 15 | 231 | 1,000 00 | 9,165 75 | 172 97 | 39 67 | 10,765 75 | 26,196 16 |
| St. Louis | Gratiot | 680 | 650 | 198 | 30,000 | 13,000 00 | 2 | 12 | 15 | 120 | 1,200 00 | 3,882 50 | 80 00 | 32 63 | 5,082 50 | 10,458 57 |
| Salem | Washtenaw | 75 | 47 | 180 | 1,000 | | 1 | 1 | 9 | 6 | 297 | 125 00 | 33 00 | 19 00 | 422 00 | 491 09 |
| Saline | Washtenaw | 307 | 165 | 200 | 25,000 | 2,000 00 | 1 | 5 | 10 | 50 | 900 00 | 1,640 00 | 90 00 | 32 80 | 2,540 00 | 3,525 80 |
| Sanborn Tp. | Alpena | 172 | 105 | 160 | 2,493 | 50 00 | 1 | 4 | 10 | 19 | 450 00 | 513 00 | 50 00 | 27 77 | 513 00 | 1,158 42 |
| Sand ... | Kent | 130 | 82 | 170 | 10,000 | | 1 | 2 | 10 | 18 | 495 00 | 500 00 | 50 00 | 27 00 | 900 00 | 1,082 50 |
| Sanilac ... | Sanilac | 241 | 215 | 200 | 1,500 | 7,000 00 | 1 | 1 | 10 | 18 | 400 00 | 486 00 | 40 00 | | 981 00 | 7,329 00 |
| Sanilac Tp. 2 | Sanilac | 108 | 69 | 180 | 900 | | 1 | | 10 | | 400 00 | | 40 00 | | 461 00 | 461 00 |
| Sanilac Tp. 3 | Sanilac | 75 | 66 | 178 | | | 1 | | 10 | | 270 00 | | 30 00 | | 270 00 | 299 04 |

| | |
|---|---|
| Sanilac Tp. 8 tl | Sanilac |
| Sands Tp | Marquette |
| Saranac | Ionia |
| Saugatuck | Allegan |
| Sault Ste. Marie | Chippewa |
| Schoolcraft | Kalamazoo |
| Scotts | Kalamazoo |
| Scottville | Mason |
| Sebewaing | Huron |
| Shelby | Oceana |
| Shepherd | Isabella |
| Sheridan | Montcalm |
| Sheridan Tp. 1 | Newaygo |
| Sherman Tp. | Wexford |
| Sherwood | Branch |
| Saginaw | Houghton |
| Skandia | Marquette |
| Skanee | Baraga |
| Smith's Creek | St. Clair |
| Smyrna | Ionia |
| Soule | Huron |
| South Arm | Charlevoix |
| South Blendon | Ottawa |
| South Boardman | Kalkaska |
| South Frankfort | Benzie |
| Van Buren | Van Buren |
| South Haven | Oakland |
| South Lyon | Monroe |
| South Rockwood | Menominee |
| Sparta | Kent |
| Spring Lake | Ottawa |
| Springport | Jackson |
| Springwells Tp. 1 | Wayne |
| Springwells Tp. 2 | Wayne |
| Springwells Tp. 3 | Wayne |
| Springwells Tp. 4 | Wayne |
| Springwells Tp. 7 | Wayne |
| Spurr Tp. | Baraga |
| Stambaugh | Iron |
| Standish | Arenac |
| Stanton | Montcalm |
| Stanwood | Menominee |
| Stephenson Tp | Arenac |
| Sterling | Berrien |
| Stevensville | Berrien |
| Stockbridge | Ingham |

TABLE XVI.—CONCLUDED.

| Districts. | Counties. | Number of children between 5 and 20 years. | Number of children that attended school during the year. | Number of days school. | Estimated value of school property. | Total indebtedness. | Number of teachers employed. Men. | Number of teachers employed. Women. | Aggregate number of months taught by all teachers. Men. | Aggregate number of months taught by all teachers. Women. | Total wages of teachers for the year. Men. | Total wages of teachers for the year. Women. | Average monthly wages of teachers. Men. | Average monthly wages of teachers. Women. | Amount paid for superintendence and instruction. | Total cost of school. |
|---|---|---|---|---|---|---|---|---|---|---|---|---|---|---|---|---|
| Stronach | Manistee | 180 | 150 | 210 | $2,700 | | 1 | 1 | 10 | 10 | $450 00 | $350 00 | $45 00 | $35 00 | $800 00 | $1,198 72 |
| Sturgis | St. Joseph | 615 | 472 | 177 | 50,000 | $1,000 00 | 1 | 11 | 9 | 99 | 1,100 00 | 3,934 00 | 122 22 | 35 09 | 5,034 00 | 7,968 74 |
| Sumner | | 116 | 107 | 180 | 5,000 | | 1 | 2 | 10 | 9 | 320 00 | 234 00 | 35 55 | 26 00 | 554 00 | 757 96 |
| Sinfield | | 137 | 110 | 195 | 4,000 | 2,000 00 | 1 | 3 | 10 | 23 | | 530 00 | 40 00 | 23 04 | 930 00 | 1,122 90 |
| Superior Tp. | | 540 | 385 | 163 | 2,975 | | 6 | 8 | 32 | 55 | 1,197 50 | 1,650 00 | 37 42 | 30 00 | 2,847 50 | 4,305 87 |
| Sutton's I Bay | Inham | 239 | 139 | 200 | 6,000 | 925 00 | 1 | 2 | 10 | 20 | 500 00 | 650 00 | 50 00 | 32 50 | 1,150 00 | 2,704 62 |
| Swartz Creek | Genesee | 65 | 50 | 190 | 2,000 | 200 00 | 1 | | 10 | 9 | 370 00 | 225 00 | 42 00 | 25 00 | 603 00 | 677 92 |
| Was City | Ioscoe | 536 | 349 | 200 | 4,000 | | 1 | 14 | 10 | 133 | 650 00 | 1,846 00 | 65 00 | 34 81 | 2,495 00 | 3,560 54 |
| Lenawee | Lenawee | 567 | 525 | 187 | 26,000 | | 1 | 3 | 9 | | 1,226 00 | 4,750 00 | 126 21 | 30 00 | 5,950 00 | 8,510 55 |
| Tekonsha | Calhoun | 180 | 106 | 180 | 5,000 | | 1 | 3 | 9 | 27 | 600 01 | 810 00 | 66 08 | 30 00 | 1,410 01 | 1,905 04 |
| Thompson | Schoolcraft | 146 | 103 | 180 | 1,000 | | 1 | 3 | 9 | 9 | 449 50 | 360 00 | 49 00 | 40 00 | 809 50 | 1,039 72 |
| Thornsonville | Dale | 342 | 202 | 181 | 3,000 | 800 00 | 1 | | 9 | 27 | 450 00 | 945 00 | 50 00 | 35 00 | 1,395 00 | 1,867 70 |
| Thornville | Lapeer | 96 | 70 | 180 | 2,500 | | 1 | 6 | 9 | 9 | 315 00 | 242 50 | 61 94 | 36 50 | 557 00 | 661 55 |
| Three Oaks | Berrien | 403 | 348 | 180 | 6,500 | | 2 | 4 | 18 | 45 | 1,115 50 | 1,642 50 | 62 71 | 40 89 | 2,787 50 | 3,372 81 |
| Three Rivers | St. Joseph | 804 | 787 | 190 | 25,000 | 300 00 | 3 | 20 | 40 | 174 | 2,708 75 | 7,099 50 | | | 9,808 25 | 12,790 53 |
| Torch Lake Tp. 6 | Houghton | 178 | 137 | 174 | 3,500 | 804 03 | 1 | 4 | 8 | 27 | 300 00 | 1,125 00 | 37 50 | 41 62 | 1,125 00 | 1,636 02 |
| Toquin | Van Buren | 97 | 73 | 163 | 1,000 | | 1 | 40 | 36 | 357 | 4,180 00 | 15,856 00 | 116 11 | 44 12 | 20,036 50 | 391 57 |
| Traverse City | G'd Traverse | 2,410 | 2,022 | 180 | 166,000 | 25,000 00 | 2 | 5 | 10 | 39 | 500 00 | 1,080 00 | 50 00 | 26 18 | 1,620 50 | 38,400 10 |
| Trenton | Wayne | 496 | 276 | 200 | 2,000 | | 1 | 1 | 9 | 9 | 286 00 | 250 00 | 32 00 | 27 77 | 538 00 | 2,022 94 |
| Trufant | Gain | 188 | 128 | 162 | 1,200 | | | | | | | | | | | 641 81 |
| Turner | Arenac | 239 | 135 | 176 | 1,800 | 1,550 00 | 1 | 1 | 9 | 10 | 350 00 | 400 00 | 40 00 | 40 00 | 400 00 | 1,398 55 |
| Tustin | Tuscola | 127 | 97 | 180 | 1,000 | | 1 | 1 | 10 | 9 | 500 00 | 140 00 | 50 00 | 20 00 | 540 00 | 648 51 |
| Ubly | Osceola | 133 | 130 | 300 | 3,500 | | 3 | 2 | 10 | 10 | 450 00 | 350 00 | 49 00 | 35 00 | 860 00 | 1,139 27 |
| Union City | Huron | 416 | 361 | 200 | 1,200 | 2,000 00 | 2 | 3 | 30 | 91 | 1,450 00 | 3,140 00 | 72 50 | 34 50 | 4,680 00 | 1,076 30 |
| Unionville | Branch | 193 | 140 | 200 | 25,000 | | 1 | 2 | 10 | 30 | 500 00 | 530 00 | 50 00 | 28 00 | 1,030 00 | 6,167 96 |
| Upton | Tuscola | | | | 2,500 | | | | | | | | | | | 1,105 16 |
| Utica | St. Clair | 90 | 62 | 200 | 1,000 | | 1 | 4 | 10 | 40 | 497 50 | 1,200 00 | 49 75 | 30 00 | 497 50 | 663 60 |
| Vandalia | Macomb | 257 | 167 | 190 | 6,000 | | 1 | 3 | 9 | 27 | 900 00 | 756 00 | 90 00 | 28 00 | 2,100 00 | 3,113 55 |
| Vanderbilt | Oaks | 164 | 129 | 180 | 5,000 | | 1 | 1 | 9 | 9 | 450 00 | 292 50 | 50 00 | 32 50 | 1,206 00 | 1,564 21 |
| Vassar | Otsego | 157 | 99 | 200 | 1,800 | | 3 | 10 | 18 | 100 | 742 50 | 3,037 00 | 41 25 | 30 37 | 1,035 00 | 1,187 55 |
| Tuscola | Tuscola | 883 | 435 | 200 | 29,000 | | 2 | 6 | 10 | 47 | 1,000 00 | | 100 10 | 30 15 | 4,037 20 | 5,435 19 |
| Vermontville | Eaton | 197 | 197 | 190 | 10,000 | | 1 | | 10 | | 600 00 | 1,567 50 | 103 15 | 33 00 | 2,167 50 | 2,693 92 |

| | | Shiawassee | Vernon | |
| --- | --- | --- | --- | --- |
| | | Montmor'ncy | Vienna Tp. | |
| | | Kalamazoo | Vicksburg | |
| | | Ottawa | Vrieland | |
| | | ...n | V...lsm | |
| | | Cli'tone | W...set | |
| | | Gogebic | Wakefield Tp. | |
| | | Hi'i..dale | Waldron | |
| | | Oakland | Walled Lake | |
| | | Macomb | Warren | |
| | | Macomb | Washington | |
| | | Sanilac | Washington Tp. 1 | |
| | | Sanilac | Washington Tp. 4 | |
| | | ...oland | Waterford | |
| | | Gogebic | Watersmeet | |
| | | Berrien | Watervliet | |
| | | Tuscola | Wayland, ...lle | |
| | | Allegan | Wayne | |
| | | Wayne | Webberville | |
| | | Ingham | | |
| | | Isabella | West Hay City | |
| | | Bay | West Branch | |
| | | Oxemaw | West Millbrook | |
| | | Mecosta | Weston | |
| | | Lenawee | | |
| | | Gratiot | Wheeler | |
| | | Newaygo | West Cloud | |
| | | Muskegon | Whitehall | |
| | | St. Joseph | White Pigeon | |
| | | ...in | White Lick | |
| | | I oeco | Whittemore | |
| | | G'd Traverse | Williamsburg | |
| | | Ingham | ...son | |
| | | Alger | W...m | |
| | | Oakland | Wixom | |
| | | Cheboygan | Wolverine | |
| | | Barry | Woodland | |
| | | Wayne | W...dte | |
| | | Kent | Wyoming Tp. 7 | |
| | | Kent | W...r Tp. 9 H | |
| | | St. Clair | Yale | |
| | | Washtenaw | York Tp. 1 | |
| | | Washtenaw | Ypsilanti | |
| | | Ottawa | Zeeland | |
| | | Saginaw | Zilwaukie | |
| | | Ottawa | Zutphen | |

27

TABLE

*Miscellaneous statistics of city schools as reported*

| Line number | Cities having a population over 4,000, census 1894. | School population from inspectors' report. | Enrollment. | | | | Average number belonging. | | | | Average daily attendance. | | | | No. of em- | |
|---|---|---|---|---|---|---|---|---|---|---|---|---|---|---|---|---|
| | | | High school department. | Grammar department. | Primary department. | Whole school. | High school department. | Grammar department. | Primary department. | Whole school. | High school department. | Grammar department. | Primary department. | Whole school. | H. S. dept. | |
| | | | | | | | | | | | | | | | M. | F. |
| 1 | Adrian.......... | 2,509 | 274 | 602 | 1,049 | 1,925 | 224 | 462 | 737 | 1,423 | 216 | 431 | 678 | 1,325 | 3 | 4 |
| 2 | Albion.......... | 1,160 | 246 | 363 | 505 | 1,114 | 206 | 293 | 354 | 855 | 202 | 280 | 340 | 822 | 1.3 | 5 |
| 3 | Alpena.......... | 4,358 | 144 | 487 | 1,468 | 2,009 | 109 | 395 | 1,049 | 1,553 | 106 | 381 | 984 | 1,471 | 1.2 | 2.5 |
| 4 | Ann Arbor...... | 2,922 | | | | | | | | | | | | | | |
| 5 | Battle Creek.... | 3,826 | 358 | 907 | 1,786 | 3,051 | 287 | 860 | 1,366 | 2,513 | 273 | 786 | 1,354 | 2,413 | 3 | 9 |
| 6 | Bay City........ | 9,536 | 591 | 2,169 | 4,855 | 7,615 | 386 | 1,143 | 2,383 | 3,912 | 377 | 1,114 | 2,308 | 3,799 | 6 | 8 |
| 7 | Benton Harbor.. | 1,553 | 160 | 548 | 822 | 1,530 | 135 | 340 | 510 | 985 | 127 | 375 | 558 | 1,060 | .2 | 5 |
| 8 | Big Rapids...... | 1,485 | 153 | 420 | 591 | 1,164 | 141 | 326 | 430 | 897 | 138 | 314 | 404 | 856 | .2 | 4 |
| 9 | Cadillac........ | 1,720 | 163 | 543 | 773 | 1,479 | 138 | 429 | 640 | 1,207 | 130 | 387 | 596 | 1,113 | .1 | 5 |
| 10 | Calumet........ | 6,760 | 214 | 807 | 3,250 | 4,271 | 182 | 677 | 2,709 | 3,568 | 178 | 630 | 2,640 | 3,448 | 5 | 3 |
| 11 | Charlotte....... | 965 | 168 | 326 | 551 | 1,045 | 135 | 271 | 357 | 763 | 130 | 259 | 335 | 724 | 1.3 | 4 |
| 12 | Cheboygan...... | 2,384 | 87 | 406 | 951 | 1,444 | 75 | 319 | 645 | 1,039 | 70 | 296 | 600 | 966 | 1.5 | 2 |
| 13 | Coldwater...... | 1,795 | 167 | 350 | 560 | 1,077 | 140 | 291 | 474 | 905 | 138 | 283 | 463 | 884 | 2.3 | 2 |
| 14 | Detroit ........ | 79,646 | 2,684 | 16,300 | 38,995 | 57,979 | 2,128 | 8,685 | 19,800 | 30,613 | 2,048 | 8,309 | 18,621 | 28,978 | 29 | 60 |
| 15 | Escanaba....... | 2,697 | 60 | 360 | 1,024 | 1,444 | 54 | 292 | 712 | 1,058 | 53 | 273 | 675 | 1,001 | 2.4 | 1 |
| 16 | Flint........... | 2,990 | 353 | 832 | 1,128 | 2,313 | 315 | 637 | 956 | 1,968 | 312 | 628 | 930 | 1,870 | 7 | 6 |
| 17 | Grand Haven.... | 1,685 | 145 | 541 | 639 | 1,325 | 128 | 339 | 557 | 1,024 | 129 | 333 | 518 | 980 | 2.5 | 2 |
| 18 | Grand Rapids.... | 25,854 | 1,616 | 7,481 | 13,724 | 22,821 | 1,141 | 4,987 | 7,972 | 14,100 | 1,049 | 3,647 | 7,518 | 12,214 | 13.7 | 22 |
| 19 | Hillsdale....... | 1,071 | 229 | 325 | 418 | 972 | 208 | 275 | 278 | 761 | 202 | 262 | 266 | 730 | 1.2 | 4 |
| 20 | Holland......... | 2,284 | 140 | 621 | 1,206 | 1,967 | 126 | 485 | 894 | 1,505 | 122 | 440 | 811 | 1,373 | 1 | 4 |
| 21 | Ionia........... | 1,430 | | | | | | | | | | | | | | |
| 22 | Iron Mountain.. | 2,957 | 110 | 1,161 | 1,940 | 3,211 | 97 | 664 | 1,231 | 1,992 | 92 | 613 | 1,131 | 1,836 | 2 | 2 |
| 23 | Ironwood....... | 2,656 | 120 | 358 | 1,813 | 2,291 | 105 | 290 | 1,495 | 1,890 | ..... | ..... | ..... | 1,785 | 3 | 2 |
| 24 | Ishpeming...... | 4,022 | 205 | 840 | 2,162 | 3,207 | 178 | 742 | 1,611 | 2,531 | 176 | 702 | 1,493 | 2,371 | 3 | 6 |
| 25 | Jackson........ | 5,860 | 371 | 1,176 | 2,544 | 4,091 | 309 | 963 | 1,881 | 3,153 | 298 | 914 | 1,777 | 2,989 | 4 | 7 |
| 26 | Kalamazoo...... | 5,596 | 388 | 1,850 | 3,049 | 5,287 | 311 | 1,152 | 1,915 | 3,378 | 307 | 1,092 | 1,821 | 3,220 | 3 | 10 |
| 27 | Lansing......... | 4,508 | 463 | 1,150 | 1,617 | 3,230 | 411 | 947 | 1,247 | 2,605 | 397 | 901 | 1,174 | 2,472 | 3 | 9 |
| 28 | Ludington...... | 2,431 | 172 | 491 | 1,145 | 1,808 | 152 | 405 | 935 | 1,492 | 146 | 387 | 897 | 1,430 | 2.3 | 3 |
| 29 | Manistee....... | 4,780 | 273 | 684 | 2,632 | 3,589 | 230 | 580 | 2,245 | 3,055 | 225 | 548 | 1,846 | 2,619 | 5 | 6 |
| 30 | Marquette...... | 2,832 | 141 | 531 | 1,298 | 1,970 | 128 | 411 | 891 | 1,430 | 125 | 388 | 843 | 1,356 | 2 | 4 |
| 31 | Marshall........ | 1,103 | 171 | 275 | 429 | 875 | 143 | 239 | 343 | 725 | 139 | 232 | 333 | 704 | 2.4 | 3 |
| 32 | Menominee...... | 4,135 | 174 | 812 | 2,009 | 2,995 | 127 | 615 | 1,772 | 2,514 | 122 | 583 | 1,622 | 2,327 | 3 | 3 |
| 33 | Monroe......... | 1,790 | 146 | 288 | 655 | 1,089 | 126 | 209 | 329 | 664 | 122 | 195 | 299 | 616 | 3.2 | 2 |
| 34 | Mt. Clemens.... | 2,069 | 100 | 286 | 756 | 1,142 | 88 | 245 | 578 | 911 | 86 | 236 | 562 | 884 | 2 | 3 |
| 35 | Muskegon....... | 6,735 | 426 | 1,311 | 3,256 | 4,993 | 366 | 1,080 | 2,292 | 3,738 | 361 | 1,017 | 2,076 | 3,543 | 3 | 9 |
| 36 | Negaunee....... | 2,037 | 93 | 425 | 1,040 | 1,558 | 82 | 304 | 684 | 1,070 | 79 | 294 | 657 | 1,030 | 1.1 | 3 |
| 37 | Niles........... | 1,156 | 138 | 280 | 595 | 1,013 | 114 | 246 | 468 | 828 | 113 | 235 | 443 | 791 | 1.2 | 3 |
| 38 | Owosso......... | 2,339 | 246 | 698 | 1,265 | 2,209 | 223 | 558 | 935 | 1,716 | 215 | 530 | 858 | 1,603 | .... | 6 |
| 39 | Pontiac......... | 1,810 | 214 | 448 | 763 | 1,425 | 185 | 367 | 569 | 1,121 | 178 | 349 | 530 | 1,057 | 3 | 3 |
| 40 | Port Huron..... | 5,824 | 272 | 1,223 | 2,394 | 3,889 | 243 | 971 | 1,599 | 2,813 | 232 | 898 | 1,524 | 2,654 | 2 | 8 |
| 41 | Saginaw........ | 8,244 | 582 | 1,734 | 2,910 | 5,226 | 490 | 1,518 | 2,378 | 4,386 | 469 | 1,442 | 2,250 | 4,161 | 6 | 14 |
| 42 | Saginaw, W.S... | 5,273 | | | | 3,702 | | | | 2,769 | | | | 2,650 | | |
| 43 | St. Joseph...... | 1,234 | 142 | 306 | 569 | 1,017 | 134 | 270 | 481 | 885 | 127 | 256 | 473 | 859 | .... | 5 |
| 44 | Sault St. Marie.. | 2,343 | 157 | 712 | 911 | 1,780 | 146 | 680 | 690 | 1,516 | 135 | 640 | 638 | 1,413 | 1 | 4 |
| 45 | Traverse City... | 2,410 | 328 | 580 | 1,107 | 2,015 | 239 | 501 | 769 | 1,509 | 220 | 480 | 695 | 1,395 | 3.2 | 5 |
| 46 | West Bay City... | 4,076 | | | | | 115 | 580 | 1,428 | 2,123 | 109 | 545 | 1,345 | 1,999 | 1 | 4 |
| 47 | Wyandotte...... | 1,541 | 71 | 350 | 698 | 1,119 | 65 | 250 | 490 | 805 | 61 | 246 | 450 | 737 | .5 | 2 |
| 48 | Ypsilanti ....... | 1,484 | 262 | 321 | 563 | 1,146 | 225 | 275 | 454 | 954 | 217 | 263 | 424 | 904 | 2.4 | 5 |

* Where a blank occurs, item was not reported.
† Superintendent included.

XVII.

*by superintendents for the school year 1898-9.*

| Gram. dept. M | Gram. dept. F | Prim. dept. M | Prim. dept. F | Whole school M | Whole school F | Portion of superintendent's time devoted to supervision | No. of special teachers | No. of graduates | Av. No. H.S. dept. | Av. No. Gram. dept. | Av. No. Prim. dept. | Av. No. Whole school | Non-res. H.S. dept. | Non-res. Gram. dept. | Non-res. Prim. dept. | Non-res. Whole school | Age Graduated | Age Promoted to high school | Age Promoted to gram. dept. | Latin | Greek | French | German | Vocal music? | Drawing? | Penmanship? | Has kindergarten below primary grade? | Portion time in 1st prim. devoted to kindergarten | No. of U.S. flags | Line number |
|---|---|---|---|---|---|---|---|---|---|---|---|---|---|---|---|---|---|---|---|---|---|---|---|---|---|---|---|---|---|---|
|  | 12 |  | 18 | 4 | 34 | all | 2 |  | 35 | 32 | 38 | 41 | 38 | 56 | 11 | 1 | 68 | 18.5 | 14.5 | 10 | 98 |  | 23 | 52 | yes | yes | no | no | 1-4 | 2 | 1 |
|  | 7 |  | 10 | 2 | 22 | 2 3 | 2 |  | 29 | 31 | 42 | 35 | 40 | 45 |  |  | 45 | 17.5 | 14 | 10 | 67 |  |  | 34 | yes | yes | no | no | 1-2 | 1 | 2 |
| .3 | 11 | .5 | 23.5 | 3 | 37 | all |  |  | 14 | 23 | 35 | 48 | 39 |  |  |  | 46 | 18 | 14.8 | 11.2 | 38 |  |  | 42 | no | no | no | no | 1-10 | 8 | 3 |
| 1 | 28 |  | 34 | 5 | 71 | all | 2 |  | 40 | 24 | 29 | 40 | 33 | 44 | 8 | 6 | 58 |  |  |  |  |  |  |  | yes | yes | no | no | 1-5 |  | 4 |
|  | 35 |  | 67 | 7 | 110 | all | .5 |  | 43 | 28 | 32 | 36 | 33 | 34 | 25 | 13 | 72 | 19 | 15 | 11.5 | 205 | 9 | 86 | 86 | no | no | no |  |  |  | 5 |
|  |  |  |  |  |  |  |  |  |  |  |  |  |  |  |  |  |  |  |  |  |  |  |  |  |  |  |  |  |  | 6 |
| 1 | 14 |  | 10 | 2 | 29 | 5-6 | 1 |  | 16 | 27 | 23 | 51 | 32 | 24 | 3 | 2 | 29 | 17 | 13 | 9 | 40 | 7 |  | 23 | yes | yes | yes | no | 1-5 | 3 | 7 |
|  | 9 |  | 10 | 1 | 23 | 3-4 |  |  | 17 | 33 | 36 | 43 | 40 |  |  |  | 12 | 18 |  |  | 40 |  |  | 45 | no | no | no | no | 1-2 | 4 | 8 |
|  | 10 |  | 15 | 1 | 30 | 6-7 | 1 |  | 20 | 27 | 43 | 42 | 41 |  |  |  | 17 |  |  |  | 70 | 4 |  | 24 | yes | yes | yes | yes | 1-2 | 3 | 9 |
| 1 | 14 |  | 54 | 7 | 71 | all | 4 |  | 16 | 22 | 45 | 50 | 47 |  |  |  | 28 | 18 | 14.5 |  | 60 |  |  | 45 | yes | yes | yes | yes | 1-2 | 12 | 10 |
|  | 7 |  | 11 | 2 | 22 | 5-7 | 1 |  | 12 | 25 | 39 | 52 | 37 | 41 | 9 |  | 50 | 19 | 15.5 | 10 | 60 | 12 |  | 35 | yes | no | no | yes | 1-3 | 6 | 11 |
| 1.4 | 6 | .6 | 13 | 4 | 21 | 1-2 |  |  | 11 | 21 | 43 | 47 | 42 | 9 | 8 | 1 | 18 | 18 |  |  | 25 |  |  | 10 | no | no | no | no |  | 6 | 12 |
|  | 8 |  | 11 | 4 | 21 | 5-7 |  |  | 15 | 28 | 36 | 43 | 37 | 31 | 12 | 6 | 49 | 18.5 | 15 | 11 | 50 | 5 |  | 29 | no | no | yes | no | 1-10 | 4 | 13 |
| 17 | 263.4 |  | 454 | 51 | 777 | all | 4 |  | 24 | 31 | 43 | 42 |  |  |  |  | 100 |  |  |  | 1,100 | 109 | 321 | 518 | yes | yes | yes | yes | 1-2 | 66 | 14 |
|  | 7.1 | 1 | 15 | 4 | 23 | 4-7 |  |  | 16 | 41 | 44 | 40 |  |  |  |  | 25 |  |  |  | 25 |  |  | 15 | no | no | no | no | 1-3 |  | 15 |
|  | 20 |  | 24 | 7 | 50 | all | 3 |  | 46 | 24 | 31 | 40 | 33 | 55 | 28 | 2 | 85 | 18 | 14 | 9 |  |  |  |  | yes | yes | yes | no |  | 8 | 16 |
|  | 8.1 |  | 15 | 4 | 25 | 1-2 | 1 |  | 20 | 32 | 42 | 35 | 36 | 18 |  |  | 18 | 17.1 | 14.5 | 10.5 |  |  |  |  | yes | yes | yes | yes |  | 4 | 17 |
| 6.7 | 106 | 2.6 | 215 | 23 | 343 | all | 2 |  | 137 | 32 | 44 | 37 | 39 | 85 | 12 | 10 | 107 | 18.5 | 14.7 | 10.9 | 522 | 47 | 58 | 287 | yes | yes | no | yes |  | 34 | 18 |
|  | 6 |  | 8 | 2 | 18 | 3-4 | 1 |  | 24 | 40 | 46 | 35 | 40 | 42 | 7 | 3 | 52 | 18.7 | 14.6 | 11.1 | 85 |  |  | 67 | yes | no | no | no | 1-12 | 1 | 19 |
|  | 10 |  | 21 | 2 | 37 | all | 1 |  | 14 | 25 | 48 | 42 | 40 |  |  |  | 25 | 18 | 13 | 9 | 66 |  |  |  | yes | yes | yes | no | 1-2 | 5 | 20 |
|  |  |  |  |  |  |  |  |  |  |  |  |  |  |  |  |  |  |  |  |  |  |  |  |  |  |  |  |  |  |  | 21 |
| 1 | 13 |  | 25 | 4 | 40 | all |  |  | 24 | 47 | 49 | 46 |  |  |  |  | 19 | 14.5 | 10.5 |  | 34 |  |  | 21 | no | no | no | no | 1-4 |  | 22 |
|  | 10 |  | 33 | 4 | 45 | all | 2 |  | 16 | 21 | 29 | 45 | 39 |  |  |  | 18 | 13 | 10 |  | 28 |  |  | 20 | yes | yes | no | no |  | 7 | 23 |
|  | 15 |  | 38 | 4 | 59 | all | 1 |  | 35 | 20 | 49 | 42 | 41 |  |  |  | 19.1 | 12.8 | 7.8 |  | 64 |  |  | 55 | yes | no | yes | yes |  | 6 | 24 |
| 5 | 22 |  | 49 | 10 | 78 | all | 2 |  | 37 | 29 | 36 | 38 | 36 | 29 | 11 | 5 | 45 | 18.7 | 15.6 | 11.3 | 214 | 15 | 27 | 52 | yes | no | no | no | 1-3 |  | 25 |
|  | 29 |  | 44 | 4 | 83 | all | 1 |  | 45 | 24 | 40 | 43 | 39 |  |  |  | 57 | 19 |  |  |  |  |  |  | yes | no | no | yes |  | 10 | 26 |
| 1 | 26 |  | 35 | 5 | 70 | all | 2 |  | 60 | 31 | 35 | 36 | 35 | 30 | 22 | 8 | 60 | 17.2 | 13 | 10 | 240 | 20 |  | 125 | yes | yes |  | no | 1-4 | 12 | 27 |
|  | 11 |  | 25 | 3 | 39 | 2-3 |  |  | 28 | 29 | 37 | 37 | 35 | 19 |  |  | 19 | 18.7 | 14 | 10 | 98 | 16 |  | 59 | no | no | no | no | 1-3 | 5 | 28 |
|  | 15 |  | 52 | 6 | 73 | all | 2 |  | 31 | 21 | 38 | 43 | 39 | 22 | 9 | 12 | 43 |  |  |  | 133 | 3 | 27 | 28 | yes | yes | no | no |  | 6 | 29 |
|  | 8 |  | 21 | 3 | 58 | all | 2 |  | 22 | 21 | 41 | 42 | 38 |  |  |  | 18 | 14 | 9 |  | 75 | 5 | 15 | 10 | yes | yes | no | no |  | 5 | 30 |
| 1 | 8 |  | 9 | 4 | 20 | 3-5 | 2 |  | 18 | 27 | 26 | 38 | 31 | 40 | 2 | 1 | 43 | 18 |  |  | 135 | 14 |  | 20 | yes | yes | no | no | 1-5 | 2 | 31 |
| 1 | 13 |  | 36 | 5 | 52 | all | 1 |  | 20 | 21 | 44 | 49 | 45 | 4 | 1 |  | 5 | 17 |  |  | 95 | 5 |  | 36 | yes | yes | no | yes |  | 8 | 32 |
|  | 5 |  | 7 | 4 | 14 | 5 6 | 1 |  | 10 | 24 | 42 | 47 | 37 | 17 | 18 | 5 | 70 | 18.2 | 14.3 | 10 | 30 |  |  | 40 | no | no | yes | no |  | 4 | 33 |
|  | 7 |  | 14 | 3 | 23 | all | 1 |  | 14 | 17 | 41 | 41 | 38 | 18 | 12 | 2 | 32 |  |  |  | 41 |  |  | 41 | yes | no | no | yes |  | 4 | 34 |
|  | 28 |  | 58 | 4 | 96 | all | 2 |  | 65 | 30 | 39 | 39 | 38 | 7 | 3 | 11 | 21 |  |  |  | 195 | 9 | 21 | 57 | yes | no | no | yes |  | 22 | 35 |
|  | 7 |  | 17 | 2 | 27 | 6 7 | 1 |  | 13 | 23 | 43 | 40 | 38 |  |  |  |  |  |  |  | 19 |  | 12 | 11 | no | no | no | yes | 1-5 | 2 | 36 |
|  | 6 |  | 11 | 2 | 20 | 3-4 | 1 |  | 20 | 27 | 41 | 42 | 39 | 33 | 8 | 6 | 47 | 18 |  |  | 86 |  |  | 39 | yes | no | no | no | 1 4 | 5 | 37 |
| 3 | 11 |  | 21 | 4 | 38 | all | 1 |  | 35 | 37 | 39 | 44 | 42 |  |  |  | 23 | 17.5 | 15.6 | 11.2 | 105 |  |  | 41 | yes | no | no | no | 1-6 | 4 | 38 |
| .3 | 9 | .5 | 15 | 5 | 27 | all | 1 |  | 20 | 29 | 37 | 36 | 36 | 49 | 14 | 3 | 66 | 18.5 | 15.8 | 11.5 | 148 | 15 | 21 | 30 | yes | yes | no | no |  | 7 | 39 |
|  | 26.1 | 1 | 36 | 4 | 70 | all |  |  | 23 | 24 | 38 | 43 | 38 | 13 | 4 |  | 17 | 18 | 14 | 9 | 121 | 7 | 29 | 36 | no | no | no | no |  | 14 | 40 |
| 5 | 40 |  | 59 | 12 | 123 | all | 2 |  | 65 | 24 | 33 | 40 | 33 |  |  |  | 65 | 18 |  |  | 275 | 12 | 45 | 159 | yes | yes | yes | no |  | 14 | 41 |
|  |  |  |  | 7 | 74 | all | 2 |  | 24 |  | 35 |  |  |  |  |  | 25 | 18 |  |  | 137 | 8 | 35 | 137 | yes | yes | no | no |  | 10 | 42 |
|  | 7 |  | 11 | 3 | 23 | all | 2 |  | 29 | 27 | 40 | 44 | 39 | 10 | 6 | 2 | 18 | 18.5 | 14 | 10.5 | 65 | 9 |  | 45 | yes | yes | no | yes | 1-5 | 2 | 43 |
| 3 | 13 |  | 15 | 5 | 32 | all | 2 |  | 12 | 29 | 42 | 46 | 45 |  |  |  | 18 | 18 | 14 | 9 | 38 |  |  | 21 | yes | yes | yes | no | 1-2 | 5 | 44 |
|  | 11 |  | 22 | 4 | 38 | 5-6 | 2 |  | 26 | 29 | 46 | 35 | 36 | 74 | 10 | 9 | 40 |  |  |  | 80 |  |  | 40 | yes | yes | yes | no | 1 2 | 4 | 45 |
| 4 | 15 |  | 36 | 6 | 55 | all | 2 |  | 10 | 25 | 30 | 40 | 35 | 4 | 4 | 3 | 11 |  |  |  | 55 |  |  | 25 | yes | yes | no | no |  | 8 | 46 |
|  | 6 |  | 9 | 1 | 17 | 1-2 | 2 |  | 11 | 33 | 41 | 55 | 46 | 10 | 4 | 2 | 16 | 18 | 13.5 | 10.2 | 15 |  |  | 16 | no | no | no | no | 1-2 | 3 | 47 |
|  | 7 |  | 11 | 3 | 23 | 2-3 | 2 |  | 29 | 30 | 39 | 41 | 37 | 63 | 7 | 4 | 74 | 19.3 | 15 | 11.5 | 125 | 13 |  | 44 | yes | no | no | no | 1 3 | 4 | 48 |

*TABLE XVII.—

| Line number. | Cities having a population between 1,000 and 4,000, census 1894. | School population from inspector's report. | Enrollment. | | | | Average number belonging. | | | | Average daily attendance. | | | | Number of teachers. | | | |
|---|---|---|---|---|---|---|---|---|---|---|---|---|---|---|---|---|---|---|
| | | | High school department. | Grammar department. | Primary department. | Whole school. | High school department. | Grammar department. | Primary department. | Whole school. | High school department. | Grammar department. | Primary department. | Whole school. | H. S. dept. M | H. S. dept. F | Gram. dept. M | Gram. dept. F |
| 1 | Algonac | 432 | 45 | 40 | 115 | 200 | 45 | 40 | 115 | 200 | 40 | 38 | 100 | 178 | .6 | 3 | .... | 6 |
| 2 | Allegan | 637 | 131 | 250 | 290 | 671 | 108 | 235 | 278 | 621 | 103 | 228 | 256 | 587 | .6 | 3 | .... | 6 |
| 3 | Alma | 554 | 88 | 200 | 215 | 503 | 77 | 185 | 210 | 472 | 66 | 175 | 205 | 446 | 1.8 | 1 | .... | 4 |
| 4 | Atlantic Mine | 776 | 57 | 90 | 374 | 521 | 53 | 69 | 252 | 374 | 50 | 60 | 223 | 333 | 2 | 1 | .... | 2 |
| 5 | Au Sable | 648 | 74 | 200 | 274 | 548 | 57 | 164 | 238 | 459 | 52 | 150 | 203 | 405 | .8 | 1 | .... | 3 |
| 6 | Bad Axe | 534 | 56 | 144 | 261 | 461 | 49 | 131 | 235 | 415 | 46 | 128 | 213 | 387 | .8 | 1 | .... | 3 |
| 7 | Baraga | 698 | | | | | | | | | | | | | | | | |
| 8 | Belding | 760 | 98 | 187 | 282 | 537 | 88 | 146 | 222 | 456 | 85 | 131 | 203 | 419 | .5 | 4 | .... | 5 |
| 9 | Bessemer | 856 | 55 | 162 | 610 | 827 | 48 | 149 | 503 | 700 | 46 | 142 | 439 | 627 | 1.2 | 1 | .... | 4 |
| 10 | Blissfield | 227 | 35 | 64 | 104 | 203 | 32 | 51 | 74 | 157 | 31 | 49 | 69 | 149 | 1 | .3 | .... | 1.3 |
| 11 | Buchanan | 448 | 107 | 162 | 211 | 480 | 96 | 145 | 190 | 431 | 94 | 140 | 170 | 404 | .7 | 3 | .... | 4 |
| 12 | Caro | 583 | 117 | 167 | 241 | 525 | 94 | 133 | 173 | 400 | 89 | 129 | 165 | 383 | .5 | 3 | .... | 4 |
| 13 | Carson City | 338 | 65 | 93 | 162 | 320 | 48 | 76 | 132 | 256 | 46 | 66 | 120 | 232 | .5 | 1.5 | .... | 2 |
| 14 | Cassopolis | 370 | 95 | 118 | 139 | 352 | 67 | 73 | 108 | 250 | 64 | 74 | 99 | 237 | .8 | 2 | 1 | 2 |
| 15 | Cedar Springs | 314 | 47 | 84 | 138 | 269 | 44 | 79 | 121 | 244 | 40 | 71 | 116 | 227 | 1 | 1 | .... | 2 |
| 16 | Champion | 582 | 29 | 90 | 309 | 428 | 26 | 83 | 270 | 379 | 23 | 80 | 250 | 353 | .5 | 2 | .... | 2 |
| 17 | Charlevoix | 650 | 90 | 186 | 355 | 631 | 80 | 173 | 322 | 575 | 60 | 139 | 245 | 453 | .... | 2.3 | .... | 4 |
| 18 | Chelsea | 403 | | | | | | | | | | | | | | | | |
| 19 | Chessaning | 341 | 82 | 85 | 164 | 331 | 65 | 73 | 131 | 269 | 62 | 67 | 119 | 248 | .8 | 1.6 | .... | 2.5 |
| 20 | Clare | 572 | 42 | 163 | 202 | 407 | 38 | 145 | 184 | 367 | 32 | 132 | 170 | 334 | 1 | 1 | 1 | 2 |
| 21 | Clinton | 276 | 58 | 78 | 114 | 250 | 42 | 69 | 108 | 219 | 38 | 67 | 102 | 207 | .7 | 1 | .... | 2 |
| 22 | Coleman | 460 | 53 | 49 | 265 | 367 | 48 | 40 | 231 | 319 | .... | | | | 2 | | .... | 1 |
| 23 | Constantine | 266 | 98 | 58 | 154 | 310 | 88 | 50 | 119 | 257 | 85 | 45 | 102 | 232 | .8 | 2 | 1 | 1 |
| 24 | Corunna | 380 | 78 | 90 | 200 | 368 | 70 | 79 | 143 | 292 | 68 | 74 | 135 | 277 | .7 | 2 | .... | 3 |
| 25 | Crystal Falls | 817 | 40 | 170 | 517 | 727 | 35 | 147 | 333 | 515 | 34 | 136 | 292 | 462 | .4 | 1.6 | .... | 3.4 |
| 26 | Decatur | 372 | 93 | 98 | 202 | 393 | 83 | 68 | 165 | 316 | 79 | 69 | 158 | 306 | .8 | 2 | .... | 2 |
| 27 | Dowagiac | 1 144 | 140 | 296 | 716 | 1, 152 | 122 | 248 | 495 | 865 | 120 | 245 | 465 | 830 | 2.3 | 2 | .... | 6 |
| 28 | Dundee | 317 | 68 | 115 | 159 | 342 | 59 | 118 | 146 | 323 | 52 | 111 | 142 | 305 | 1 | 1 | 1 | 1 |
| 29 | East Lake | 773 | | | | | | | | | | | | | | | | |
| 30 | East Tawas | 616 | 68 | 128 | 344 | 540 | 56 | 120 | 325 | 501 | 51 | 99 | 297 | 447 | .7 | 1 | 1 | 1 |
| 31 | Eaton Rapids | 503 | 131 | 220 | 251 | 602 | 113 | 137 | 173 | 423 | 110 | 133 | 170 | 413 | 1.3 | 3 | .... | 4 |
| 32 | Elk Rapids | 492 | 49 | 126 | 230 | 405 | 43 | 104 | 192 | 339 | 41 | 95 | 180 | 316 | .8 | 2 | .... | 3.5 |
| 33 | Essexville | 645 | 14 | 73 | 132 | 219 | 10 | 55 | 121 | 186 | 10 | 49 | 100 | 159 | .... | | 1 | 1 |
| 34 | Evart | 481 | 74 | 164 | 247 | 485 | 72 | 158 | 245 | 475 | 70 | 151 | 240 | 461 | .4 | 2 | .... | 3 |
| 35 | Fenton | 596 | 94 | 172 | 304 | 570 | 78 | 142 | 213 | 433 | 77 | 135 | 198 | 410 | 1.6 | 1 | 1 | 3 |
| 36 | Flushing | 235 | 60 | 65 | 100 | 225 | 48 | 50 | 90 | 188 | 46 | 46 | 85 | 179 | 1 | 1 | .... | 1 |
| 37 | Frankfort | 535 | 51 | 175 | 225 | 451 | 40 | 128 | 165 | 333 | 38 | 127 | 151 | 316 | .5 | 1 | .... | 4 |
| 38 | Fremont | 417 | 59 | 154 | 193 | 406 | 36 | 121 | 145 | 302 | 35 | 105 | 127 | 267 | 1 | 1 | .... | 3 |
| 39 | Gladstone | 729 | 44 | 295 | 297 | 636 | 40 | 201 | 198 | 439 | 38 | 205 | 238 | 481 | .... | 2.5 | .... | 3 |
| 40 | Grand Ledge, No. 9 | 284 | 94 | 106 | 96 | 296 | 85 | 80 | 78 | 243 | 75 | 92 | 70 | 237 | 1 | 2 | .... | 2 |
| 41 | Greenville | 812 | 131 | 234 | 483 | 848 | 112 | 194 | 353 | 659 | 108 | 182 | 326 | 616 | 2 | 3 | .... | 5 |
| 42 | Hancock | 1,589 | 110 | 412 | 777 | 1, 299 | 82 | 181 | 435 | 698 | 78 | 176 | 405 | 659 | 1.3 | 3 | .... | 5 |
| 43 | Harbor Beach | 420 | | | | 373 | | | | | | | | | .7 | 1 | .... | 2 |
| 44 | Hartford | 353 | 72 | 79 | 204 | 355 | 68 | 74 | 183 | 325 | 58 | 59 | 150 | 237 | 1 | 1 | 1 | 1 |
| 45 | Hastings | 757 | 160 | 241 | 340 | 741 | 130 | 207 | 255 | 592 | 129 | 204 | 248 | 581 | 3.5 | .... | 1 | 6 |
| 46 | Holly | 396 | 117 | 159 | 222 | 498 | | | | | | | | 331 | .... | | .... | |
| 47 | Homer | 292 | 49 | 89 | 112 | 250 | 48 | 88 | 112 | 248 | 47 | 86 | 102 | 235 | 1 | 2 | .... | 2 |
| 48 | Houghton, No. 1 | 1,093 | 58 | 124 | 405 | 587 | 47 | 96 | 292 | 435 | 44 | 89 | 279 | 412 | 1.7 | 1 | .... | 4 |
| 49 | Howard City | 418 | 91 | 209 | 228 | 528 | 44 | 111 | 127 | 282 | 43 | 100 | 112 | 255 | .8 | 1 | .... | 2 |
| 50 | Howell | 605 | 169 | 201 | 238 | 608 | 139 | 186 | 192 | 517 | 134 | 169 | 179 | 482 | 2.6 | 2 | .... | 4 |
| 51 | Hudson | 377 | 97 | 128 | 237 | 462 | 73 | 76 | 162 | 311 | 68 | 79 | 145 | 292 | 1 | 3 | .... | 3 |
| 52 | Imlay City | 499 | 85 | 134 | 200 | 419 | 78 | 122 | 193 | 393 | 81 | 115 | 175 | 371 | 1 | 1 | .... | 3 |
| 53 | Ithaca | 581 | 105 | 174 | 240 | 519 | 93 | 134 | 201 | 428 | 89 | 126 | 187 | 402 | .8 | 2 | .... | 3.4 |
| 54 | Jonesville | 364 | 84 | 156 | 125 | 365 | 59 | 79 | 95 | 233 | 53 | 78 | 89 | 220 | 1.5 | 1 | .... | 2 |
| 55 | Kalkaska | 384 | 45 | 102 | 164 | 311 | 37 | 86 | 133 | 256 | 35 | 82 | 122 | 239 | .2 | 1 | 1 | 1 |
| 56 | Lake City | 280 | 30 | 42 | 150 | 222 | 28 | 39 | 147 | 214 | 26 | 37 | 145 | 208 | .... | 1 | .... | 1 |
| 57 | Lake Linden | 2, 104 | 112 | 317 | 609 | 1, 038 | 98 | 266 | 548 | 912 | 98 | 257 | 445 | 800 | .3 | 4 | .... | 9 |
| 58 | Lakeview | 402 | 60 | 100 | 181 | 341 | 55 | 94 | 170 | 319 | 52 | 90 | 170 | 312 | 1 | .5 | 1 | .5 |
| 59 | Lapeer | 746 | 153 | 130 | 302 | 585 | 172 | 141 | 221 | 534 | 165 | 135 | 182 | 482 | 1.7 | 4 | .... | 4 |
| 60 | Leslie | 300 | 95 | 85 | 95 | 275 | 80 | 65 | 75 | 220 | 75 | 61 | 70 | 206 | 1 | 1 | .... | 2 |
| 61 | Lowell | 680 | 85 | 190 | 280 | 555 | 75 | 175 | 225 | 475 | .... | | | | .5 | 1 | 1 | 5 |

*Where a blank occurs the item was not reported.
†Superintendent included.

CONTINUED.

| regular employed. | | | | Portion of superintendent's time devoted to supervision | No. of special teachers. | No. of graduates. | Av. No. pupils to each teacher. | | | | No. of non-resident pupils. | | | | Average age of class. | | | Number studying— | | | | Does school give special instruction in— | | | Has school kindergarten below primary grade? | Portion of time in 1st prim. devoted to kindergarten work. | Number of U.S. flags. | Line number. |
|---|---|---|---|---|---|---|---|---|---|---|---|---|---|---|---|---|---|---|---|---|---|---|---|---|---|---|---|---|
| Prim. dept. | | †Whole school. | | | | | H. S. dept. | Gram. dept. | Prim. dept. | Whole school. | H. S. dept. | Gram. dept. | Prim. dept. | Whole school. | Graduated. | Promoted to high school. | Promoted to gram. dept. | Latin. | Greek. | French. | German. | Vocal music? | Drawing? | Penmanship? | | | | |
| M. | F. | M. | F. | | | | | | | | | | | | | | | | | | | | | | | | | |
| .... | 8 | .... | 7 | 1-10 | .... | 6 | .. | .. | 30 | 10 | .. | .. | 10 | .. | .. | .. | .. | .. | .. | .. | 10 | yes | yes | .... | .... | | 1 | 1 |
| .... | 8 | 1 | 17 | 3-8 | 1 | 24 | 30 | 39 | 34 | 35 | .. | .. | 25 | 17.2 | .. | .. | 70 | .. | .. | 48 | yes | no | yes | no | 1-5 | 4 | 2 |
| .... | 5 | 2 | 10 | 1-4 | 1 | 13 | 27 | 46 | 42 | 40 | .. | .. | .. | 18. | .. | .. | 40 | .. | .. | 25 | yes | no | no | .... | 1-4 | 4 | 3 |
| 2 | 8 | 4 | 6 | 1-15 | .. | 5 | 17 | 34 | 50 | 37 | 3 | 2 | 10 | 15 | 17. | 12. | 8.5 | .. | .. | .. | no | no | no | no | .... | 2 | 4 |
| .... | 4 | 1 | 8 | 1-4 | .. | 11 | 28 | 55 | 59 | 51 | 1 | 3 | 4 | 17. | .. | .. | 50 | .. | .. | 18 | .... | no | .. | yes | 1-4 | 2 | 5 |
| .... | 5 | 1 | 9 | 1-4 | .. | 4 | 29 | 44 | 47 | 42 | 9 | 11 | 1 | 21 | 18. | 12. | 8. | 24 | .. | .. | 17 | no | no | no | yes | 1-3 | 1 | 6 |
| | | | | | | | | | | | | | | | | | | | | | | | | | | | 7 |
| .... | 6 | 1 | 15 | 1-2 | 1 | 15 | 18 | 25 | 37 | 35 | 20 | .. | 18. | 14. | 11. | 31 | .. | .. | 42 | yes | no | yes | no | .... | 1 | 8 |
| .... | 8 | 1 | 13 | 1-4 | .. | 8 | 21 | 37 | 63 | 49 | 2 | 4 | 6 | 17.7 | 13.8 | 10.7 | 10 | .. | .. | 13 | yes | yes | no | no | 1-10 | 3 | 9 |
| 1.4 | .. | 1 | 3 | .. | .. | 3 | 24 | 30 | 56 | 39 | 16 | 6 | 1 | 26 | 17. | 14. | 10. | 5 | .. | .. | .. | no | no | no | no | 1-2 | 1 | 10 |
| .... | 5 | 1 | 12 | 2-7 | .. | 11 | 27 | 36 | 28 | 34 | .. | .. | .. | 60 | 18. | .. | .. | 23 | .. | .. | 11 | no | no | no | no | 3-4 | 2 | 11 |
| .... | 4 | 1 | 11 | 1-2 | .. | 13 | 27 | 33 | 43 | 34 | 41 | 6 | 3 | 50 | 18.6 | 13.5 | 11. | 32 | .. | .. | 27 | no | no | no | no | 1-2 | 2 | 12 |
| .... | 2.5 | 1 | 6 | 1-2 | .. | 14 | 24 | 46 | 53 | 40 | 16 | 6 | 1 | 23 | 17.5 | 14.5 | 10. | 20 | .. | .. | .. | no | yes | yes | no | 1-5 | 1 | 13 |
| .... | 3 | 1 | 7 | 1-4 | .. | 17 | 24 | 25 | 39 | 28 | 17 | 5 | 1 | 23 | 17.5 | .. | .. | 47 | .. | .. | 24 | yes | yes | yes | no | 1-2 | 1 | 14 |
| .... | 3 | 1 | 6 | 1-8 | .. | 9 | 22 | 39 | 40 | 35 | 18 | 5 | 1 | 24 | 19. | 15. | 12. | 8 | .. | .. | 6 | no | no | no | no | 1-6 | 1 | 15 |
| .... | 4 | 1 | 8 | 1-2 | .. | 8 | 9 | 40 | 68 | 44 | .. | .. | .. | 17. | 15. | 11. | .. | .. | .. | .. | yes | no | no | yes | .... | 1 | 16 |
| .... | 6 | .. | 13 | 1-3 | .. | 11 | 35 | 43 | 54 | 47 | 12 | 2 | .. | 14 | 19. | 14.5 | 10.5 | 22 | .. | .. | .. | no | no | no | no | 1-2 | 1 | 17 |
| | | | | | | | | | | | | | | | | | | | | | | | | | | | 18 |
| .... | 2.5 | 1 | 6.5 | 1-4 | .2 | 6 | 27 | 28 | 50 | 34 | 28 | 3 | .. | 31 | 17. | 13. | 9. | 20 | .. | .. | 14 | yes | no | yes | no | 1-2 | 1 | 19 |
| .... | 4 | 2 | 7 | 1-4 | .. | 2 | 19 | 48 | 46 | 41 | 6 | 2 | .. | 8 | 17. | 13. | 10. | 15 | .. | .. | 8 | no | no | no | no | 1-4 | 1 | 20 |
| .... | 2 | 1 | 5 | 1-3 | .. | 5 | 25 | 35 | 54 | 36 | 12 | .. | .. | 12 | 17.2 | .. | .. | 15 | .. | .. | 15 | no | yes | yes | no | 1-3 | 1 | 21 |
| .... | 4 | 2 | 5 | 1-6 | .. | 6 | 24 | 40 | 56 | 45 | 2 | .. | .. | 6 | 16. | 14. | 10. | .. | .. | .. | .. | yes | yes | yes | no | 1-2 | 1 | 22 |
| .... | 3 | 2 | 6 | 1-4 | 1 | 10 | 31 | 25 | 39 | 32 | 37 | .. | .. | 18. | 13. | 8.5 | 43 | .. | .. | 20 | yes | yes | no | no | 1-5 | 1 | 23 |
| .... | 4 | 1 | 9 | 1-3 | .. | 10 | 36 | 26 | 35 | 29 | 22 | 7 | 1 | 30 | 18. | 14. | 10. | 30 | .. | .. | 16 | yes | no | no | no | 1-4 | 1 | 24 |
| .... | 8 | 1 | 13 | 2-3 | 1 | 6 | 17 | 44 | 42 | 38 | .. | 2 | .. | 2 | 18. | 14. | 11. | 12 | .. | .. | .. | yes | yes | yes | yes | .... | 4 | 25 |
| .... | 3 | 1 | 7 | 1-4 | .. | 15 | 30 | 34 | 55 | 40 | .. | .. | .. | 38 | 18. | .. | .. | 50 | .. | .. | 24 | no | no | no | no | 1-4 | 1 | 26 |
| .... | 10 | 3 | 18 | 5-7 | 2 | 20 | 28 | 41 | 49 | 42 | 55 | 15 | 5 | 75 | 18.5 | .. | .. | 42 | 6 | .. | 18 | yes | yes | yes | yes | .... | 4 | 27 |
| .... | 4 | 2 | 6 | .. | .. | 5 | 28 | 59 | 36 | 40 | 16 | .. | .. | 2 | 18. | 18. | 14.5 | 10.7 | 18 | .. | .. | no | no | no | no | .... | 1 | 28 |
| | | | | | | | | | | | | | | | | | | | | | | | | | | | 29 |
| .... | 6 | 2 | 9 | 1-3 | .. | 5 | 33 | 60 | 54 | 52 | .. | .. | .. | 17. | 12. | 8. | .. | .. | .. | .. | no | no | yes | 1-3 | 1 | 30 |
| .... | 5 | 2 | 12 | 5-7 | .. | 22 | 26 | 34 | 35 | 32 | 66 | 4 | .. | 70 | 17.5 | 14. | 10. | .. | .. | .. | no | no | no | no | 1-10 | 2 | 31 |
| .... | 5.5 | 1 | 11 | 1-4 | .. | 3 | 16 | 30 | 35 | 28 | 8 | 4 | 1 | 13 | 18. | 13.5 | 10. | 4 | .. | .. | .. | no | no | no | yes | 1-2 | 1 | 32 |
| .... | 3 | 1 | 3 | .. | .. | 2 | 28 | 60 | 47 | 42 | 2 | 2 | 4 | 18. | 15. | 10. | .. | .. | .. | .. | no | no | no | no | .... | 1 | 33 |
| .... | 5 | 1 | 10 | 4-7 | .. | 3 | 30 | 52 | 49 | 45 | 12 | 13 | 6 | 31 | 17. | .. | .. | .. | .. | .. | .. | yes | yes | yes | no | .... | 1 | 34 |
| .... | 6 | 3 | 10 | 3-7 | 1 | 10 | 30 | 36 | 35 | 35 | .. | .. | .. | 18. | 14. | 10. | 45 | .. | .. | 38 | yes | yes | no | no | 1-4 | 3 | 35 |
| .... | 3 | 1 | .. | .. | .. | 5 | 24 | 50 | 30 | 31 | .. | .. | .. | 25 | 18. | .. | .. | 10 | .. | .. | .. | no | no | no | no | .... | 1 | 36 |
| .... | 5 | 1 | 10 | 1-2 | .. | 1 | 36 | 32 | 33 | 31 | 5 | 2 | 2 | 9 | 16. | 14. | 10. | .. | .. | .. | .. | no | no | no | no | 1-5 | 2 | 37 |
| .... | 3 | 1 | 7 | 1-7 | .. | 1 | 18 | 40 | 48 | 38 | 9 | 2 | .. | 11 | 16. | .. | .. | .. | .. | .. | .. | no | no | no | yes | all | 1 | 38 |
| .... | 6 | 1 | 12 | 1-4 | .. | 5 | 16 | 67 | 33 | 34 | .. | .. | .. | 16. | .. | .. | 24 | .. | 10 | .. | no | no | no | no | 1-3 | 1 | 39 |
| .... | 3 | 1 | 6 | 1-12 | .. | .. | 25 | 40 | 39 | 35 | 30 | 3 | 3 | 26 | 18. | 13 | 9. | 12 | .. | .. | 8 | no | no | no | yes | 1-4 | 1 | 40 |
| .... | 9 | 3 | 17 | 3-4 | 2 | 35 | 35 | 39 | 39 | 38 | 42 | 8 | 3 | 53 | 19. | 15. | .. | 39 | .. | 8 | 25 | yes | yes | no | yes | .... | 4 | 41 |
| .... | 12 | 3 | 20 | 1-2 | .. | 7 | 19 | 36 | 36 | 32 | 22 | 4 | 8 | 34 | .. | .. | .. | 33 | .. | .. | 25 | no | no | no | no | 1-36 | 3 | 42 |
| .... | 4 | 1 | 7 | 1-3 | .. | 5 | .. | .. | .. | .. | .. | .. | .. | .. | .. | .. | 10 | .. | .. | .. | yes | no | no | no | .... | 1 | 43 |
| .... | 3 | 1 | 8 | .. | .. | .. | 34 | 37 | 61 | 46 | .. | .. | .. | 29 | .. | .. | 17 | .. | .. | .. | .... | .... | .... | .... | .... | 1 | 44 |
| .... | 7 | 2 | 13 | 1-2 | .. | 16 | 37 | 30 | 36 | 41 | 60 | 2 | 1 | 63 | 20. | 15. | 11. | 70 | .. | .. | 28 | no | yes | yes | no | .... | 1 | 45 |
| .... | .... | 1 | 7 | 1-3 | .. | 12 | .. | .. | .. | .. | .. | .. | .. | 50 | .. | .. | 30 | .. | .. | 18 | no | yes | yes | no | .... | 1 | 46 |
| .... | 3 | 1 | 7 | 1-6 | 1 | 11 | 16 | 44 | 37 | 31 | .. | .. | .. | 14 | 17.4 | 14 | 12. | 8 | .. | .. | .. | no | yes | yes | no | 1-2 | 1 | 47 |
| .... | 9 | 2 | 14 | .. | .. | 9 | 15 | 24 | 32 | 27 | 9 | 3 | 1 | 13 | 18.3 | 14. | 11. | 27 | .. | 4 | 15 | no | no | no | no | 1-2 | 1 | 48 |
| .... | 4 | 1 | 7 | 1-4 | .. | 5 | 24 | 56 | 32 | 35 | 21 | .. | .. | 17. | .. | .. | 20 | .. | 5 | .. | yes | yes | no | no | 1-2 | 1 | 49 |
| .... | 7 | 3 | 13 | 3-7 | 1 | 16 | 30 | 47 | 37 | 33 | 57 | 7 | .. | 64 | 18.6 | 14 | 9.10 | 30 | 16 | .. | 50 | yes | yes | no | no | 1-8 | 2 | 50 |
| .... | 4 | 1 | 10 | 1-6 | 1 | 11 | 18 | 35 | 40 | 28 | .. | .. | .. | 18. | 14 | 11. | 30 | .. | .. | 18 | .... | .... | .... | yes | 1-5 | 1 | 51 |
| .... | 5 | 1 | 7 | 1-12 | .. | 11 | 39 | 41 | 67 | 49 | 30 | 2 | 2 | 34 | 18. | .. | .. | 23 | .. | .. | 10 | no | no | yes | no | 1-10 | 1 | 52 |
| .... | 5 | 1 | 10.4 | 1-4 | .6 | 10 | 33 | 39 | 40 | 40 | 26 | 9 | 4 | 39 | 18. | 14. | 10. | 49 | .. | .. | 29 | yes | no | no | yes | 1-8 | 1 | 53 |
| .... | 1.8 | 1 | 5 | .. | .5 | 14 | 24 | 36 | 48 | 36 | 13 | 7 | 3 | 22 | 18. | 14.5 | 8. | 10 | .. | .. | 12 | yes | yes | no | no | 1-4 | 1 | 54 |
| .... | 3 | 2 | 5 | 3-4 | .. | 4 | 19 | 43 | 44 | 36 | .. | .. | .. | 15 | 17. | .. | .. | 13 | .. | .. | .. | .... | .... | .... | yes | 1-4 | 1 | 55 |
| .... | 3 | 1 | 5 | .. | .. | 3 | 28 | 30 | 49 | 42 | .. | .. | .. | 10 | .. | .. | .. | .. | .. | .. | .. | yes | yes | yes | no | .... | 1 | 56 |
| .... | 13 | 1 | 30 | 2-3 | 1 | 18 | 23 | 29 | 42 | 32 | 1 | 4 | .. | 5 | 17. | 13 | 9.5 | 60 | 3 | 24 | 35 | yes | yes | yes | no | 1-3 | 3 | 57 |
| .... | 3.5 | 2 | 4.5 | .. | .5 | 3 | 37 | 62 | 49 | 49 | 14 | .. | .. | 14 | 18.5 | 14.2 | 9.3 | 4 | .. | .. | .. | yes | yes | yes | no | 1-2 | 1 | 58 |
| .... | 9 | 2 | 17 | 1-3 | .. | 22 | 29 | 35 | 35 | 42 | 65 | .. | .. | 65 | .. | .. | .. | 88 | 7 | 8 | 36 | yes | no | no | yes | .... | 1 | 59 |
| .... | 2 | 1 | 5 | .. | .. | 13 | 40 | 33 | 34 | 37 | 42 | .. | .. | 35 | 18. | 14. | 10. | 41 | .. | .. | 30 | no | no | no | no | 1-3 | 1 | 60 |
| .... | 4 | 2 | 10 | 1-2 | .. | 4 | 50 | 29 | 55 | 41 | 18 | 15 | 3 | 36 | 18. | .. | .. | 33 | .. | .. | 8 | .. | .. | .. | yes | .... | 4 | 61 |

*TABLE XVII.—

| Line number. | Cities having a population between 1,000 and 4,000 census of 1894. | School population from inspectors' report. | Enrollment. | | | | Average number belonging. | | | | Average daily attendance. | | | | No. of teachers | | | |
|---|---|---|---|---|---|---|---|---|---|---|---|---|---|---|---|---|---|---|
| | | | High school department. | Grammar department. | Primary department. | Whole school. | High school department. | Grammar department. | Primary department. | Whole school. | High school department. | Grammar department. | Primary department. | Whole school. | H. S. dept. M | H. S. dept. F | Gram. dept. M | Gram. dept. F |
| 62 | Mancelona......... | 539 | 43 | 115 | 358 | 516 | 32 | 86 | 249 | 367 | 29 | 74 | 212 | 315 | .5 | 1 | .... | 2 |
| 63 | Manchester....... | 404 | 68 | 114 | 200 | 382 | 58 | 95 | 166 | 319 | 56 | 91 | 161 | 308 | 1 | 1.4 | .. | 2.2 |
| 64 | Manistique........ | 1,174 | 42 | 250 | 734 | 1,026 | 37 | 193 | 512 | 742 | 36 | 176 | 477 | 689 | 1.4 | 1.4 | .. | 5 |
| 65 | Marcellus......... | 237 | 76 | 78 | 127 | 281 | 66 | 66 | 103 | 235 | 60 | 59 | 95 | 214 | 1 | 2 | .. | 2 |
| 66 | Marine City....... | 1,229 | 56 | 174 | 399 | 629 | 49 | 139 | 292 | 4*0 | 46 | 130 | 269 | 445 | .7 | 2 | 1 | 2.5 |
| 67 | Mason............. | 417 | 132 | 98 | 215 | 445 | 110 | 85 | 150 | 345 | 99 | 79 | 147 | 325 | .5 | 3 | .... | 2.8 |
| 68 | Midland .......... | 724 | 81 | 280 | 329 | 690 | 74 | 142 | 312 | 528 | 69 | 145 | 302 | 512 | .7 | 2 | .... | 3 |
| 69 | Milford ........... | 301 | 72 | 110 | 110 | 292 | 63 | 103 | 96 | 262 | 60 | 95 | 84 | 239 | 1.8 | .. | 1 | 1 |
| 70 | Montague.......... | 364 | 50 | 102 | 167 | 319 | 47 | 90 | 140 | 277 | 42 | 78 | 121 | 241 | 1 | 1 | 1 | 1 |
| 71 | Morenci........... | 276 | 52 | 75 | 123 | 250 | 47 | 70 | 110 | 227 | 40 | 65 | 100 | 205 | .7 | 1.5 | .. | 2 |
| 72 | Mount Pleasant.... | 1,058 | 134 | 313 | 466 | 913 | 115 | 301 | 452 | 868 | 110 | 294 | 436 | 840 | 2.3 | 2 | 2 | 4 |
| 73 | Nashville.......... | 315 | 77 | 125 | 140 | 342 | 76 | 99 | 138 | 313 | 73 | 96 | 136 | 305 | 1.5 | 2 | .. | 2 |
| 74 | Newaygo.......... | 402 | 59 | 84 | 178 | 321 | 46 | 68 | 132 | 246 | 45 | 64 | 109 | 218 | 1 | .. | 1 | 1 |
| 75 | Newberry.......... | 483 | | | | | | | | | | | | | | | | |
| 76 | Northville......... | 430 | 67 | 128 | 225 | 420 | 59 | 118 | 187 | 364 | 55 | 106 | 149 | 310 | 1 | 2 | .. | 3 |
| 77 | Norway........... | 1,322 | 75 | 275 | 520 | 870 | 70 | 251 | 410 | 731 | 64 | 240 | 340 | 644 | .8 | 2 | .. | 4 |
| 78 | Ontonagon........ | 422 | 26 | 52 | 263 | 341 | 22 | 40 | 185 | 247 | 20 | 36 | 180 | 236 | .. | 1.5 | .. | 2 |
| 79 | Oscoda........... | 446 | 36 | 130 | 232 | 398 | 34 | 116 | 205 | 355 | 32 | 105 | 182 | 319 | .. | 1.8 | .. | 2 |
| 80 | Otsego............ | 620 | 120 | 250 | 242 | 612 | 108 | 238 | 221 | 567 | 103 | 229 | 210 | 542 | .5 | 2 | .. | 4 |
| 81 | Ovid.............. | 367 | 91 | 127 | 198 | 416 | 75 | 134 | 119 | 328 | 72 | 124 | 109 | 305 | 1.8 | 1 | .. | 3 |
| 82 | Oxford............ | 319 | 59 | 75 | 116 | 250 | 46 | 65 | 89 | 200 | 43 | 50 | 80 | 182 | .8 | 1 | .. | 2 |
| 83 | Paw Paw......... | 360 | 124 | 90 | 136 | 350 | 118 | 82 | 110 | 310 | 112 | 80 | 113 | 305 | 1.5 | 1 | .. | 3 |
| 84 | Pentwater........ | 395 | 73 | 136 | 209 | 408 | 66 | 118 | 171 | 355 | 62 | 105 | 135 | 302 | .8 | 2 | 1 | 2 |
| 85 | Petoskey......... | 1,185 | 96 | 380 | 758 | 1,234 | 80 | 251 | 412 | 743 | 73 | 249 | 375 | 697 | 1.3 | 2 | .. | 7 |
| 86 | Pinconning........ | 430 | 45 | 85 | 170 | 300 | 35 | 70 | 160 | 265 | 33 | 70 | 150 | 253 | 2 | .. | .. | 1 |
| 87 | Plainwell......... | 355 | 128 | 124 | 163 | 415 | 110 | 135 | 82 | 327 | 100 | 116 | 69 | 285 | .8 | 2 | .. | 4 |
| 88 | Plymouth......... | 431 | 65 | 113 | 229 | 407 | 58 | 106 | 203 | 367 | 56 | 91 | 161 | 308 | .8 | 1 | .. | 3 |
| 89 | Portland.......... | 542 | 180 | 154 | 173 | 507 | 134 | 128 | 143 | 405 | 127 | 120 | 123 | 370 | .4 | 4 | .. | 4 |
| 90 | Quincy............ | 317 | 90 | 94 | 120 | 304 | 72 | 76 | 87 | 235 | 66 | 71 | 83 | 220 | .8 | 2 | 1 | 1 |
| 91 | Reading........... | 268 | | | | | | | | | | | | | | | | |
| 92 | Reed City......... | 745 | 102 | 181 | 350 | 633 | 85 | 145 | 250 | 480 | 82 | 138 | 226 | 446 | 1.8 | 1 | .. | 4 |
| 93 | Republic .......... | 807 | 19 | 134 | 515 | 668 | 18 | 118 | 415 | 551 | 17 | 110 | 393 | 520 | .9 | 1 | 1 | 2 |
| 94 | Richmond......... | 217 | 61 | 74 | 101 | 236 | 55 | 65 | 89 | 209 | 48 | 60 | 78 | 186 | 2 | .. | 1 | 1 |
| 95 | Rochester......... | 359 | 45 | 79 | 147 | 271 | 36 | 71 | 115 | 222 | 33 | 67 | 106 | 206 | 1 | .5 | .. | 2 |
| 96 | Romeo............ | 444 | 97 | 202 | 272 | 571 | 81 | 131 | 132 | 344 | 84 | 121 | 123 | 324 | 1.5 | 1.5 | 1 | 1.5 |
| 97 | Sebewaing........ | 501 | 48 | 63 | 256 | 367 | | | | 256 | | | | 250 | | | | |
| 98 | South Haven...... | 937 | 161 | 286 | 516 | 963 | 137 | 202 | 330 | 669 | 133 | 189 | 310 | 632 | .6 | 3 | .. | 5 |
| 99 | St. Clair.......... | 731 | | | | | | | | | | | | | | | | |
| 100 | St. Ignace........ | 708 | 36 | 157 | 366 | 559 | 35 | 149 | 340 | 524 | 34 | 143 | 316 | 493 | .8 | 1 | 1 | 2 |
| 101 | St. Johns......... | 841 | 195 | 275 | 406 | 876 | 174 | 233 | 336 | 743 | 170 | 220 | 302 | 692 | 2.5 | 2 | 1 | 4 |
| 102 | St. Louis......... | 640 | 91 | 191 | 373 | 655 | 74 | 154 | 248 | 476 | 69 | 137 | 221 | 427 | 1.8 | 2 | .. | 4 |
| 103 | Stanton........... | 417 | 66 | 98 | 209 | 373 | 55 | 82 | 179 | 316 | 51 | 49 | 155 | 255 | 1 | 1 | .. | 3 |
| 104 | Sturgis........... | 645 | 74 | 151 | 258 | 483 | 63 | 113 | 185 | 361 | 61 | 110 | 176 | 347 | .5 | 2 | .. | 4 |
| 105 | Tawas City....... | 536 | 54 | 114 | 226 | 394 | 43 | 90 | 157 | 290 | 39 | 82 | 155 | 276 | 1 | .. | .. | 2 |
| 106 | Tecumseh......... | 597 | 151 | 219 | 253 | 623 | 136 | 188 | 193 | 517 | 132 | 181 | 184 | 497 | .5 | 4 | .. | 4 |
| 107 | Three Rivers...... | 804 | 144 | 260 | 386 | 790 | 126 | 225 | 350 | 701 | 120 | 211 | 299 | 630 | 2.8 | 2 | .5 | 6 |
| 108 | Union City........ | 416 | 99 | 98 | 171 | 368 | | | | 310 | | | | 306 | 1.7 | 2 | .. | 3 |
| 109 | Vassar............ | 583 | 82 | 139 | 295 | 516 | 64 | 98 | 192 | 354 | 59 | 92 | 174 | 325 | .8 | 2 | .. | 3 |
| 110 | Vicksburg......... | 251 | 79 | 90 | 100 | 269 | | | | 225 | | | | 210 | 1 | 2 | .. | 2 |
| 111 | Wayne............ | 368 | 59 | 110 | 168 | 337 | 51 | 97 | 152 | 300 | 45 | 86 | 131 | 262 | .6 | 2 | .. | 3 |
| 112 | West Branch...... | 504 | | | | | | | | | | | | | | | | |
| 113 | Whitehall......... | 523 | 65 | 151 | 219 | 435 | 52 | 134 | 180 | 366 | 50 | 126 | 167 | 343 | 1 | 1 | 1 | 3 |
| 114 | Williamston....... | 359 | 115 | 117 | 140 | 372 | 105 | 106 | 120 | 331 | 95 | 100 | 110 | 305 | .7 | 2 | 1 | 2 |
| 115 | Yale.............. | 412 | 58 | 113 | 202 | 373 | 46 | 104 | 153 | 303 | 42 | 93 | 140 | 275 | 1 | 1 | .. | 2 |

* Where a blank occurs the item was not reported.
† Superintendent included.

CONCLUDED.

| regular employed — Prim. dept. M. | F. | + Whole school M. | F. | Portion of superintendent's time devoted to supervision. | No. of special teachers. | No. of graduates. | Av. No. pupils to each teacher — H. S. dept. | Gram. dept. | Prim. dept. | Whole school. | No. of non-resident pupils — H. S. dept. | Gram. dept. | Prim. dept. | Whole school. | Average age of class — Graduated. | Promoted to high school. | Promoted to gram. dept. | No. studying — Latin. | Greek. | French. | German. | Vocal music? | Drawing? | Penmanship? | Has school kindergarten below primary grade? | Portion of time in 1st prim. devoted to kindergarten work. | No. of U. S. flags. | Line number. |
|---|---|---|---|---|---|---|---|---|---|---|---|---|---|---|---|---|---|---|---|---|---|---|---|---|---|---|---|---|
| | 6 | 1 | 9 | 1-2 | | | 6 | 20 | 43 | 41 | 38 | 2 | 6 | 3 | 11 | 18 | 15 | 10 | | | 16 | no | no | no | yes | | 1 | 62 |
| 3 | 4 | 1 | 7 | 1-8 | | | 7 | 24 | 43 | 49 | 40 | 27 | 3 | 30 | 18 | 14 | 9 | 10 | | | 16 | | | | | | 1 | 63 |
| 12 | 2 | | 18 | 5-8 | 1 | | 6 | 15 | 38 | 43 | 38 | 2 | 2 | 4 | 18 | 14 | 11 | 15 | | 12 | | yes | | | no | 1-3 | 3 | 64 |
| 2 | 1 | | 6 | 1-7 | | | 22 | 33 | 51 | 33 | 28 | 4 | | 32 | 17 | 13 | 9 | 34 | | | 22 | | | | no | 1-5 | 1 | 65 |
| 6.5 | 2 | | 11 | 1-3 | | | 8 | 21 | 40 | 45 | 37 | 5 | 6 | 11 | 19 | 14 | 10 | 30 | | | 13 | no | no | no | no | 1-3 | 3 | 66 |
| 4.2 | 1 | | 10 | 1-2 | | 21 | 30 | 30 | 35 | 33 | 65 | 11 | 1 | 77 | 19 | 14.5 | 12 | 21 | | | 24 | | | | | 1-6 | 2 | 67 |
| 6 | 1 | | 11 | 2-7 | | 13 | 28 | 47 | 52 | 45 | 7 | | 7 | 17 | | | | 61 | | | 21 | no | no | no | no | | 4 | 68 |
| 3 | 3 | 4 | | 1 6 | | 12 | 32 | 56 | 32 | 37 | 26 | 4 | 2 | 32 | 18 | 15 | 9 | | | | | no | no | no | no | 1-8 | 6 | 69 |
| 4 | 2 | | 6 | 1-20 | 1 | | 24 | 43 | 35 | 35 | 7 | 2 | 1 | 10 | 15.5 | 13.9 | 7.9 | 8 | | | 9 | yes | no | no | yes | 1-3 | 1 | 70 |
| 2.5 | 1 | | 6 | 1-3 | | 8 | 21 | 35 | 44 | 32 | 13 | | 13 | 18 | 14 | 10 | 22 | | | 14 | | yes | no | yes | no | | 1 | 71 |
| 10 | 5 | | 16 | 2-3 | 1 | 19 | 27 | 50 | 45 | 43 | 5 | 2 | | 7 | 18 | | 10 | 42 | 1 | | 15 | yes | no | no | | 1-5 | 4 | 72 |
| 4 | 2 | | 8 | 1-2 | | 5 | 21 | 49 | 34 | 31 | 12 | 6 | | 18 | 17 | | | 20 | | | 14 | no | no | no | yes | 1-4 | 1 | 73 |
| 3 | 2 | | 4 | | | 9 | 16 | 34 | 44 | 41 | 10 | 2 | | 12 | 18 | | | | | | | no | no | no | no | | | 74 |
| | | | | | | | | | | | | | | | | | | | | | | | | | | | | 75 |
| 4 | 1 | | 9 | 1-6 | 1 | 11 | 20 | 39 | 47 | 36 | 21 | 4 | 2 | 27 | 18 | 15 | 11 | 31 | | | 21 | yes | | no | | | 1 | 76 |
| 6 | 1 | | 12 | 1-4 | | 3 | 25 | 62 | 66 | 57 | 2 | | 2 | 18 | | | 18 | | | 10 | no | yes | yes | no | 1-2 | 3 | 77 |
| 4 | 1 | | 8 | 1-2 | | | 15 | 20 | 46 | 31 | | | | 18 | 14 | 12 | | | | | no | no | no | | | | 78 |
| 3 | 1 | | 7 | 1-5 | | 8 | 17 | 58 | 68 | 51 | | | | 18 | 14 | 10 | | | | | no | no | no | yes | 1 3 | 2 | 79 |
| 7 | 1 | | 13 | 1-2 | 1 | 16 | 43 | 59 | 31 | 42 | 36 | | 1 | 37 | 18 | 14 | 11 | 31 | | | 28 | yes | no | no | no | 1-3 | 2 | 80 |
| 3 | 2 | | 7 | 1-6 | | 11 | 25 | 44 | 39 | 36 | 35 | 7 | 2 | 44 | 18.6 | 13.4 | 9.4 | 23 | | | | | no | | 1-5 | 1 | 81 |
| 3 | 1 | | 6 | 1-4 | | 18 | 26 | 33 | 29 | 30 | | | | 15 | | | 8 | | | | no | no | no | no | 1-4 | 1 | 82 |
| 2 | 3 | | 5 | 1-4 | | 26 | 42 | 27 | 55 | 40 | | | | 55 | 18 | | | 60 | 3 | | 30 | no | no | no | no | 1-3 | 1 | 83 |
| 4 | 1 | | 8 | 1-4 | | 4 | 24 | 59 | 42 | 40 | 9 | 4 | 1 | 13 | 19 | | | 12 | | | | no | no | yes | yes | | 1 | 84 |
| 19 | 2 | | 19 | 5-7 | 1 | 16 | 24 | 36 | 41 | 34 | | | | 12 | 18.6 | | | 30 | | | 14 | yes | no | no | no | 1-5 | 2 | 85 |
| 2 | 2 | | 3 | 1-8 | | 7 | 18 | 70 | 80 | 53 | 7 | | 7 | 16 | 13 | 9 | 5 | | | | | no | yes | yes | no | | 1 | 86 |
| 2 | 1 | | 8 | 1-6 | 1 | 19 | 36 | 33 | 41 | 36 | 53 | 17 | 5 | 75 | 19 | 14 | 9 | 55 | | | 23 | yes | yes | yes | no | 1-5 | 1 | 87 |
| 3 | 1 | | 7 | 1-4 | 1 | 9 | 32 | 35 | 67 | 46 | 33 | 2 | 1 | 36 | 19 | 15 | 11.5 | 11 | | | 8 | yes | no | no | no | 1-2 | 1 | 88 |
| 4 | 1 | | 12 | 4-7 | | 17 | 30 | 32 | 36 | 32 | 52 | 2 | | 54 | 18.8 | 13.8 | 10.1 | 52 | | | 21 | yes | no | no | no | | 2 | 89 |
| 2 | 2 | | 5 | 1-4 | | 12 | 26 | 38 | 44 | 34 | 20 | 4 | | 33 | 19 | | | 13 | | | 3 | no | | | no | 1-3 | 1 | 90 |
| | | | | | | | | | | | | | | | | | | | | | | | | | | | | 91 |
| 6 | 2 | | 11 | 1-4 | | 19 | 31 | 36 | 42 | 37 | 17 | 4 | 2 | 25 | 18.8 | 14 | 10.4 | 52 | | | 33 | no | no | no | yes | | | 92 |
| 6 | 2 | | 9 | 1-7 | | 4 | 9 | 39 | 69 | 60 | | | | 18.5 | 14.6 | 11 | 7 | | | 8 | no | no | no | no | 1-6 | 1 | 93 |
| 1 | 2 | | 2 | | | 14 | 28 | 33 | 59 | 42 | 20 | 9 | 2 | 31 | 17 | 14 | 10 | 20 | | | | no | no | no | no | 1-6 | 1 | 94 |
| 2.5 | 1 | | 5 | | | 11 | 24 | 36 | 46 | 37 | 12 | 2 | | 14 | 17.7 | 13 6 | | | | | 11 | no | no | no | yes | 1-6 | 1 | 95 |
| 3 | 3 | | 6 | 1 2 | | 15 | 26 | 52 | 44 | 38 | 30 | 2 | | 32 | 18 | 14.7 | 10 | 35 | 7 | | 16 | no | yes | no | no | 1-4 | 1 | 96 |
| 1 | 3 | | 2 | | | | | | 64 | | | | | 4 | | | | | | | no | no | no | | | | 97 |
| 7 | 1 | | 15 | 3 7 | | 18 | 38 | 40 | 47 | 42 | 65 | 20 | 9 | 94 | 19 | 13.9 | 9.5 | 82 | | | 16 | no | yes | yes | no | 1-4 | 2 | 98 |
| | | | | | | | | | | | | | | | | | | | | | | | | | | | | 99 |
| 5 | 2 | | 8 | 1-5 | | 5 | 20 | 49 | 68 | 54 | 1 | | 1 | 17 | | | 9 | | | | no | no | no | no | 1-2 | 3 | 100 |
| 8 | 4 | | 14 | 1-2 | | 19 | 40 | 46 | 42 | 72 | 11 | | 2 | 85 | 19 | 15.3 | 10.1 | 111 | | | 32 | no | no | no | no | | 3 | 101 |
| 6 | 2 | | 12 | 1-3 | | 10 | 20 | 39 | 41 | 25 | 20 | 4 | | 24 | 17 | 14 | 11 | 30 | | | 28 | | | | yes | | 2 | 102 |
| 5 | 1 | | 9 | 1-6 | | 11 | 28 | 37 | 36 | 31 | 22 | 3 | 1 | 20 | 19 | 15 | 12 | 20 | | | | no | no | no | yes | | 2 | 103 |
| 5 | 1 | | 11 | 1-2 | 1 | 12 | 25 | 28 | 37 | 31 | 15 | 7 | 5 | 27 | 18 | 14 | 9 | 30 | | | | yes | no | no | yes | 1-6 | 1 | 104 |
| 3 | 1 | | 5 | | | 4 | 43 | 45 | 52 | 48 | | | | 18 | | | | | | | no | no | yes | no | 1-6 | 2 | 105 |
| 5 | 1 | | 13 | 1 2 | 1 | 14 | 30 | 47 | 38 | 39 | 52 | 4 | | 56 | 19 | 14 | 9 | 57 | | | 20 | yes | no | no | no | 1-10 | 2 | 106 |
| 11 | 4 | | 19 | 3-4 | 1 | 13 | 29 | 35 | 32 | 31 | 15 | | 18 | 18.5 | 14 | 9 | 53 | | | | 9 | yes | yes | no | yes | 1-3 | 2 | 107 |
| 4 | 2 | | 9 | 1-3 | | 12 | | | 29 | | | | | 64 | 19 | | | | | | | no | no | no | yes | | 1 | 108 |
| 5 | 1 | | 10 | 1 4 | | 8 | 22 | 33 | 38 | 22 | 22 | 3 | 1 | 26 | 17.1 | 13.9 | 10.5 | 33 | | | 13 | no | no | no | no | 1-2 | 3 | 109 |
| 2 | 1 | | 6 | 1-8 | | 8 | | | 32 | 31 | 3 | | 1 | 35 | 18 | | | 15 | | | 10 | no | no | no | no | 1-8 | 1 | 110 |
| 4 | 1 | | 9 | 2-5 | 1 | 7 | 20 | 32 | 38 | 31 | 26 | 11 | 4 | 41 | 17.5 | 13.6 | 9.4 | 45 | 6 | | 10 | yes | no | no | no | 1-4 | 1 | 111 |
| | | | | | | | | | | | | | | | | | | | | | | | | | | | | 112 |
| 4 | | | 8 | 1 20 | | 8 | 26 | 33 | 45 | 36 | 4 | 2 | 3 | 9 | 17.5 | | | 5 | | | | no | yes | no | no | | 1 | 113 |
| 4 | 2 | | 8 | 1-3 | | 19 | 39 | 35 | 30 | 33 | 35 | 10 | 5 | 50 | 18 | 14 | 10 | 25 | | | 18 | no | no | no | yes | 1-2 | 1 | 114 |
| 3 | 1 | | 6 | 1-11 | | 9 | 23 | 52 | 51 | 43 | 11 | | 11 | 17.5 | 14 | | | | | | | no | yes | yes | no | | 1 | 115 |

## TABLE XVIII.

### Financial statistics of city schools as reported by superintendents for the year 1898-1899.

| Cities having population over 4,000, census 1894. | Amount paid superintendent. | Amount paid regular teachers. | Amount paid special teachers. | Total amount paid for instruction. | High school for— Instruction | High school for— Incidentals | High school for— Total | Grammar department for— Instruction | Grammar department for— Incidentals | Grammar department for— Total | Primary department for— Instruction | Primary department for— Incidentals | Primary department for— Total | Whole school for— Instruction | Whole school for— Incidentals | Whole school for— Total |
|---|---|---|---|---|---|---|---|---|---|---|---|---|---|---|---|---|
| Adrian | 1,500 00 | 15,345 00 | 300 00 | 18,155 00 | 21 44 | 4 88 | 26 32 | 12 67 | 4 88 | 17 55 | 9 76 | 4 88 | 14 63 | 12 76 | 4 88 | 17 64 |
| Albion | 1,300 00 | 6,634 90 | 435 00 | 10,270 90 | 16 26 | 4 29 | 20 55 | 10 97 | 4 29 | 15 26 | 10 40 | 4 29 | 14 69 | 9 38 | 4 29 | 16 30 |
| Alpena | 1,400 00 | 13,171 75 | | 14,571 75 | | | | | | | | | | 9 38 | 4 68 | 14 06 |
| Ann Arbor | 1,850 00 | 31,280 78 | 1,925 00 | 35,055 78 | 23 34 | 12 60 | 36 03 | 12 41 | 12 60 | 25 38 | 11 25 | 12 60 | 23 94 | 13 96 | 12 60 | 26 64 |
| Battle Creek | 2,000 00 | 48,745 42 | 400 00 | 51,145 42 | 26 83 | 4 92 | 31 75 | 12 41 | 4 92 | 17 33 | 10 00 | 4 92 | 14 92 | 13 07 | 4 92 | 17 99 |
| Bay City | 1,600 00 | 9,370 00 | 450 00 | 11,420 00 | 18 50 | 4 08 | 22 58 | 15 83 | 4 08 | 19 91 | 10 84 | 4 08 | 14 92 | 11 60 | 4 08 | 15 66 |
| Benton Harbor | 1,200 00 | 8,247 00 | | 9,447 00 | 17 37 | 3 66 | 21 03 | 9 00 | 3 66 | 12 66 | 8 70 | 3 66 | 12 86 | 10 53 | 3 66 | 14 19 |
| Big Rapids | 1,500 00 | 12,846 79 | 350 00 | 14,696 79 | | 3 28 | | | 3 28 | | | 3 28 | | 12 17 | 3 28 | 14 45 |
| Calumet | 3,000 00 | 47,454 85 | 3,350 00 | 53,804 85 | 38 45 | 3 67 | 42 12 | | 3 67 | | | 3 67 | | 15 06 | 3 67 | 18 76 |
| Charlotte | 1,200 00 | 9,678 64 | 250 00 | 11,328 64 | 22 48 | 4 74 | 27 22 | 13 20 | 4 74 | 17 94 | 12 70 | 4 74 | 17 44 | 14 85 | 4 74 | 19 59 |
| Cheboygan | 1,300 00 | 10,665 90 | | 11,755 90 | | 4 71 | | | 4 71 | | | 4 71 | | 11 34 | 4 71 | 16 05 |
| | | | | | | 4 90 | | | 4 90 | | | 4 90 | | 12 76 | 4 90 | 17 66 |
| Det. | 4,000 00 | 566,225 44 | 4,880 00 | 575,045 44 | 38 87 | 5 67 | 44 54 | 20 98 | 5 67 | 26 55 | 15 15 | 5 67 | 20 82 | 13 78 | 5 67 | 24 45 |
| Escanaba | 1,400 00 | 12,687 00 | 1,600 00 | 14,087 00 | 26 04 | 5 42 | | 9 22 | 5 42 | 25 06 | 10 88 | 5 42 | 25 42 | 13 27 | 5 42 | 18 83 |
| Flint | 1,500 00 | 25,303 00 | 450 00 | 28,303 00 | 26 04 | 15 84 | 41 90 | 9 22 | 15 84 | 25 06 | 10 88 | 15 84 | 25 42 | 14 83 | 15 84 | 30 67 |
| Grand Haven | 1,400 00 | 10,250 00 | 1,900 00 | 12,140 00 | 17 61 | 5 18 | 20 94 | 10 25 | 5 33 | 13 58 | 9 50 | 3 33 | 13 58 | 11 88 | 5 18 | 18 18 |
| Grand Rapids | 3,000 00 | 190,639 30 | | 195,729 30 | 23 56 | 4 44 | 28 00 | 12 24 | 4 44 | 16 68 | 11 45 | 4 44 | 15 99 | 13 88 | 4 44 | 18 32 |
| Hillsdale | 1,350 00 | 7,170 21 | 380 00 | 8,900 21 | 13 89 | 4 42 | 18 31 | 10 49 | 4 42 | 14 91 | 11 36 | 4 42 | 15 78 | 11 69 | 4 42 | 16 11 |
| Holland | 1,500 00 | 11,527 12 | 450 00 | 13,477 12 | | 5 12 | | | 5 12 | | | 5 12 | | 8 95 | 5 12 | 14 07 |
| Ionia | 1,700 00 | 19,965 17 | | 21,656 17 | 27 50 | 4 70 | 32 63 | 16 45 | 5 18 | 20 58 | 12 71 | 5 13 | 17 84 | 10 87 | 4 70 | 15 57 |
| Ironwood | 1,800 00 | 20,975 61 | 1,100 00 | 23,575 61 | 27 50 | 6 85 | 32 63 | 16 45 | 6 85 | 20 58 | 12 71 | 4 78 | 17 84 | 12 47 | 6 85 | 19 32 |
| Ishpeming | 2,700 00 | 28,920 00 | 1,700 00 | 32,120 00 | 32 00 | 5 64 | 36 78 | 15 33 | 5 64 | 16 11 | 11 66 | 6 02 | 14 44 | 12 69 | 5 64 | 18 33 |
| Jackson | 2,000 00 | 43,884 54 | 1,500 00 | 47,384 54 | 19 87 | 5 13 | 23 49 | 12 90 | 5 13 | 19 52 | 11 50 | 5 13 | 13 34 | 15 01 | 5 13 | 20 14 |
| Kalamazoo | 1,800 00 | 40,617 60 | 700 00 | 43,317 60 | | 4 78 | | | 4 78 | | | 4 78 | | 12 82 | 4 78 | 17 60 |
| Lansing | | 31,896 87 | 1,100 00 | 34,756 87 | | 3 62 | | | 3 62 | | | 3 62 | | 13 34 | 3 62 | 19 96 |
| Ludington | 1,170 00 | 15,164 55 | 597 50 | 16,334 55 | 21 85 | 3 32 | 25 17 | 9 81 | 3 32 | 13 13 | 9 56 | 3 32 | 12 88 | 10 95 | 3 32 | 14 27 |
| Manistee | 1,700 00 | 33,156 22 | 575 00 | 35,865 72 | 30 48 | 5 64 | 36 12 | 11 46 | 5 64 | 17 09 | 9 68 | 5 64 | 14 72 | 11 74 | 5 64 | 17 38 |
| | 1,400 00 | 8,763 00 | 950 00 | 10,738 00 | 22 48 | 5 47 | 27 96 | 11 70 | 5 47 | 19 14 | 11 19 | 5 47 | 14 10 | 14 81 | 5 47 | 20 28 |
| Marquette | 1,600 00 | 19,420 00 | 617 50 | 21,970 00 | 37 12 | 6 10 | 43 22 | 17 70 | 6 10 | 23 90 | 9 94 | 6 10 | 17 98 | 15 36 | 6 10 | 21 46 |
| Menominee | 2,250 00 | 24,315 00 | | 27,183 00 | 26 66 | 6 02 | 34 08 | 11 65 | 8 02 | 19 67 | 8 51 | 8 02 | 17 26 | 13 79 | 6 02 | 19 81 |
| Monroe | 1,200 00 | 6,500 00 | | 7,700 00 | 21 50 | 3 76 | 25 35 | 10 25 | 3 76 | 14 01 | | 3 76 | 12 27 | 11 59 | 3 76 | 15 36 |
| Mt. | 1,500 00 | 9,940 00 | 540 00 | 11,940 00 | 19 87 | 4 60 | | | 4 60 | | | 4 60 | | 13 10 | 4 60 | 17 70 |

| Office | | | | | | | | | | | | | | | | |
|---|---|---|---|---|---|---|---|---|---|---|---|---|---|---|---|---|
| Muskegon | | | | | | | | | | | | | | | | |
| Negaunee | | | | | | | | | | | | | | | | |
| Niles | | | | | | | | | | | | | | | | |
| Owosso | | | | | | | | | | | | | | | | |
| Pontiac | | | | | | | | | | | | | | | | |
| Port Huron | | | | | | | | | | | | | | | | |
| Saginaw | | | | | | | | | | | | | | | | |
| Saginaw, W. S. | | | | | | | | | | | | | | | | |
| St. Joseph | | | | | | | | | | | | | | | | |
| Sault Ste. Marie | | | | | | | | | | | | | | | | |
| Traverse City | | | | | | | | | | | | | | | | |
| West Bay City | | | | | | | | | | | | | | | | |
| Wyandotte | | | | | | | | | | | | | | | | |
| Ypsilanti | | | | | | | | | | | | | | | | |
| *Offices having a population between 1,000 and 4,000, census of 1884.* | | | | | | | | | | | | | | | | |
| Algonac | | | | | | | | | | | | | | | | |
| Allegan | | | | | | | | | | | | | | | | |
| Alma | | | | | | | | | | | | | | | | |
| Atlantic Mine | | | | | | | | | | | | | | | | |
| Au Sable | | | | | | | | | | | | | | | | |
| Bad Axe | | | | | | | | | | | | | | | | |
| Baraga | | | | | | | | | | | | | | | | |
| Belding | | | | | | | | | | | | | | | | |
| Bessemer | | | | | | | | | | | | | | | | |
| Blissfield | | | | | | | | | | | | | | | | |
| Buchanan | | | | | | | | | | | | | | | | |
| Caro | | | | | | | | | | | | | | | | |
| Carson City | | | | | | | | | | | | | | | | |
| Cassopolis | | | | | | | | | | | | | | | | |
| Cedar Springs | | | | | | | | | | | | | | | | |
| Champion | | | | | | | | | | | | | | | | |
| Charlevoix | | | | | | | | | | | | | | | | |
| Chelsea | | | | | | | | | | | | | | | | |
| Chesaning | | | | | | | | | | | | | | | | |
| Clare | | | | | | | | | | | | | | | | |
| Clinton | | | | | | | | | | | | | | | | |
| Coleman | | | | | | | | | | | | | | | | |
| Constantine | | | | | | | | | | | | | | | | |
| Corunna | | | | | | | | | | | | | | | | |
| Crystal Falls | | | | | | | | | | | | | | | | |
| Decatur | | | | | | | | | | | | | | | | |
| Dowagiac | | | | | | | | | | | | | | | | |
| Dundee | | | | | | | | | | | | | | | | |
| East Lake | | | | | | | | | | | | | | | | |
| East Tawas | | | | | | | | | | | | | | | | |
| Eaton Rapids | | | | | | | | | | | | | | | | |
| Elk Rapids | | | | | | | | | | | | | | | | |

TABLE XVIII.—CONCLUDED.

| Cities having a population between 1,000 and 4,000, census of 1894. | Amount paid superintendent. | Amount paid regular teachers. | Amount paid special teachers. | Total amount paid for instruction. | High school for— | | | Cost of education per capita in— Grammar department for— | | | Primary department for— | | | Whole school for— | | |
|---|---|---|---|---|---|---|---|---|---|---|---|---|---|---|---|---|
| | | | | | Instruction. | Incidentals. | Total. | Instruction. | Incidentals. | Total. | Instruction. | Incidentals. | Total. | Instruction. | Incidentals. | Total. |
| Essexville. | $700 00 | $1,200 00 | | $1,900 00 | $21 42 | $5 03 | $26 45 | $15 50 | $5 03 | $20 53 | $6 81 | $5 03 | $11 84 | $10 22 | $5 03 | $15 25 |
| Evart. | 700 00 | 3,763 18 | $175 00 | 4,463 18 | | | | | | | | | | 9 39 | 3 38 | 12 77 |
| Fenton. | 1,000 00 | 1,000 00 | | 6,075 00 | | | | | | | | | | 14 03 | 3 52 | 17 55 |
| Flushing. | 825 00 | | | 2,425 00 | | 3 00 | | | 3 00 | | | 3 00 | | 12 90 | 3 00 | 14 19 |
| Frankfort. | 800 00 | 3,566 00 | | 3,566 00 | 13 12 | 3 28 | 16 12 | 15 62 | | 18 62 | 11 18 | | 14 18 | 13 08 | 3 00 | 16 08 |
| Fremont. | 700 00 | 2,200 00 | | 2,900 00 | 7 25 | | 10 53 | | | | | | | 9 60 | 3 28 | 12 88 |
| Gladstone. | 900 00 | 4,600 00 | | 5,500 00 | 5 75 | 1 71 | 7 45 | 2 59 | 1 71 | 4 30 | 3 30 | 1 71 | 5 01 | 12 52 | 1 71 | 14 23 |
| r'nd Ledge, No. 9. | 850 00 | 2,900 00 | 550 00 | 3,050 00 | | | | 18 66 | | | 11 75 | | | 12 55 | 2 47 | 15 02 |
| Hancock. | 1,500 00 | 7,060 00 | | 8,300 00 | 17 86 | 3 79 | 21 65 | | 3 79 | 17 45 | | 3 79 | 15 54 | 13 98 | 3 79 | 17 16 |
| Harbor Beach. | 1,400 00 | 9,650 00 | | 11,420 00 | | | | | | | | | | 16 36 | 9 33 | 25 69 |
| Hartford. | 800 00 | 3,060 00 | | 3,050 00 | | | | | | | | | | | | |
| Hastings. | 1,000 00 | 1,945 00 | | 2,845 00 | 16 01 | 5 67 | 21 68 | 11 48 | 5 67 | 17 15 | 11 40 | 5 67 | 17 07 | 8 76 | 3 70 | 12 46 |
| | | 6,400 00 | | 7,400 00 | | | | | | | | | | 12 50 | 5 67 | 18 17 |
| Holly. | 1,000 00 | 2,450 00 | 60 00 | 3,450 00 | 16 10 | 3 14 | 19 24 | 9 56 | 3 14 | 12 70 | 10 54 | 3 14 | 13 68 | 10 42 | 2 74 | 13 16 |
| Homer. | 700 00 | 7,139 75 | 290 00 | 8,499 75 | 54 44 | 7 60 | 62 04 | 22 13 | 7 60 | 29 73 | 13 39 | 7 60 | 20 99 | 11 33 | 3 14 | 14 47 |
| Houghton, No. 1. | 1,350 00 | 2,232 50 | 500 00 | 2,992 50 | 21 40 | 3 18 | 24 58 | 9 36 | 3 18 | 12 54 | 7 90 | 3 18 | 11 08 | 19 61 | 7 12 | 27 12 |
| nd City. | 700 00 | 5,312 00 | | 6,702 00 | | | | | | | | | | 10 61 | 3 18 | 13 79 |
| Howell. | 1,200 00 | 2,996 00 | | 4,596 00 | | | | | | | | | | 13 14 | 6 09 | 19 43 |
| Hudson. | 1,100 00 | 1,900 00 | 210 00 | 2,900 00 | | | | | | | | | | 14 78 | 7 01 | 21 79 |
| Imlay City. | 800 00 | | | | | | | | | | | | | 7 38 | 2 75 | 10 13 |
| ia. | | 3,065 00 | 360 00 | 4,675 00 | 20 71 | 4 04 | 24 75 | 9 10 | 4 04 | 13 14 | 8 88 | 4 04 | 12 98 | 11 82 | 4 04 | 15 86 |
| Jonesville. | 1,100 00 | 1,860 00 | | 2,900 00 | 20 97 | 5 71 | 26 08 | 8 89 | 5 71 | 14 60 | 7 40 | 5 71 | 13 11 | 12 44 | 5 71 | 18 15 |
| Kalkaska. | 700 00 | 1,296 25 | | 2,680 00 | | | | | | | | | | 10 23 | 3 06 | 13 29 |
| Lake City. | 600 00 | | 400 00 | 1,746 25 | 28 90 | 6 30 | 35 20 | 19 43 | 6 30 | 25 73 | 14 56 | 6 30 | 20 88 | 8 16 | 3 59 | 11 75 |
| Lake Linden. | 430 00 | 14,208 75 | 160 00 | 16,498 75 | 11 25 | 1 14 | 12 39 | 6 65 | 1 14 | 7 79 | 4 24 | 1 14 | 5 38 | 18 00 | 6 30 | 24 39 |
| L'a'r. | 750 00 | 1,317 00 | | 2,217 00 | | | | | | | | | | 6 94 | 1 14 | 8 08 |
| Leslie. | 1,200 00 | 6,323 75 | | 7,523 75 | 16 90 | 85 | 17 75 | 10 90 | 85 | 11 65 | 9 33 | 85 | 10 18 | 14 00 | 2 59 | 16 68 |
| Lowell. | 950 00 | 1,900 00 | | 2,750 00 | | | | | | | | | | 12 50 | 85 | 13 35 |
| Ma. | 810 00 | 3,388 50 | | 4,198 50 | | | | | | | | | | 8 84 | 6 57 | 15 41 |
| M'n. | 705 00 | 2,290 00 | | 4,380 00 | 20 00 | 3 45 | 24 35 | 17 00 | 3 45 | 11 05 | 6 52 | 3 45 | 9 97 | 9 08 | 4 13 | 13 21 |
| Manchester. | 950 00 | 2,565 00 | 380 00 | 2,565 00 | 35 00 | 5 35 | 40 35 | 17 35 | 5 35 | 17 35 | 10 35 | 5 35 | 15 70 | 10 15 | 3 45 | 13 60 |
| Marcellus. | 1,200 00 | 3,340 00 | | 3,340 00 | 20 00 | | 20 00 | 12 00 | | 8 00 | 5 00 | | 5 00 | 15 13 | 5 35 | 20 48 |
| | 650 00 | 9,050 00 | | 11,280 00 | | | | | | | | | | 10 32 | | 10 32 |
| le City. | 1,100 00 | 1,775 00 | | 2,425 00 | | | | | | | | | | | | |
| | | 4,125 00 | | 5,225 50 | | | | | | | | | | 10 88 | 13 88 | 24 76 |

| Place | | | | | | | | | | | | | | | | | | | | |
|---|---|---|---|---|---|---|---|---|---|---|---|---|---|---|---|---|---|---|---|---|
| Mason | 1,000 00 | 3,300 00 | | 4,700 00 | 17 30 | 6 38 | 23 68 | 12 60 | 18 98 | 10 05 | 6 38 | 16 43 | 13 62 | 38 68 | 20 00 | | | | | |
| Midland | 400 00 | 4,030 00 | | 4,960 00 | 30 00 | 2 99 | 30 22 | 6 31 | 9 29 | 9 16 | 2 99 | 12 06 | 9 65 | 4 16 | 13 34 | | | | | |
| Milford | 560 00 | 1,630 00 | | 1,730 00 | 20 21 | 2 76 | 22 97 | 8 00 | 10 70 | 7 00 | 2 76 | 9 76 | 10 61 | 9 28 | 13 50 | | | | | |
| Montague | 540 00 | 1,380 51 | | 2,295 51 | | | | | | | | | 10 87 | 3 18 | 13 12 | | | | | |
| Moreuci | 700 00 | 1,36 75 | | 2,214 00 | | | | | | | | | 9 90 | 2 73 | 12 63 | | | | | |
| Mount Pleasant | 1,300 00 | 7,34 | 90 00 | 9,399 72 | | | | | | | | | 10 33 | 10 63 | 20 96 | | | | | |
| Nashville | 700 00 | 2,408 00 | 250 00 | 3,106 00 | | | | | | | | | 9 92 | 4 53 | 14 46 | | | | | |
| Newaygo | 90 00 | 68 | | 2,400 00 | | | | | | | | | 9 76 | 2 24 | 11 99 | | | | | |
| Newberry | 80 00 | 2,775 00 | | 3,635 00 | 21 18 | 2 96 | 24 14 | 9 11 | 12 07 | 9 90 | 2 96 | 12 16 | 9 96 | 2 98 | 12 92 | | | | | |
| Northville | 1,300 00 | 5,314 97 | | 6,614 97 | 34 00 | 3 33 | 37 33 | 8 00 | 11 33 | 9 05 | 3 33 | 10 33 | 9 05 | 3 93 | 12 34 | | | | | |
| Norway | 1,300 00 | 2,720 00 | 135 00 | 4,080 00 | | | | | | | | | 30 16 | 8 02 | 25 25 | | | | | |
| Ontonagon | 80 00 | 1,988 57 | | 2,438 57 | 15 00 | 1 02 | 16 02 | 5 68 | 6 70 | 5 08 | 1 02 | 6 10 | 6 87 | 1 21 | 7 92 | | | | | |
| Oscoda | 40 00 | 4,085 00 | | 1,900 00 | 21 13 | 2 11 | 23 15 | 5 75 | 7 86 | 5 22 | 2 11 | 10 33 | 9 56 | 2 11 | 11 67 | | | | | |
| Owosso | 1,320 10 | | | 5,430 00 | | | | | | | | | | | | | | | | |
| Ovid | 1,000 00 | 2,900 00 | | 3,000 00 | 22 45 | 5 94 | 28 40 | 8 45 | 14 44 | 9 15 | 5 94 | 15 08 | 11 92 | 5 98 | 17 98 | | | | | |
| Oxford | 940 00 | 2,005 00 | | 3,320 00 | 30 28 | 3 91 | 34 17 | 18 10 | 22 01 | 11 60 | 3 91 | 15 60 | 14 24 | 8 91 | 18 43 | | | | | |
| Paw Paw | 1,380 00 | 2,720 00 | | 3,347 00 | 21 17 | 2 56 | 24 78 | 6 66 | 9 12 | 7 87 | 2 56 | 10 43 | 12 64 | 3 56 | 19 16 | | | | | |
| Pentwater | 940 00 | 7,135 80 | 237 50 | 8,675 40 | | | | | | | | | 10 08 | 2 52 | 12 06 | | | | | |
| Petoskey | 1,300 00 | 600 00 | | 1,900 00 | 36 30 | 60 | 36 30 | 5 00 | 5 60 | 3 83 | 60 | 4 03 | 6 16 | 6 30 | 14 96 | | | | | |
| Pinconning | 600 00 | 2,725 50 | 104 00 | 3,031 50 | 18 68 | 2 33 | 18 68 | 10 70 | 13 12 | 8 28 | 2 33 | 10 49 | 12 03 | 2 33 | 14 36 | | | | | |
| Plainwell | 1,100 00 | | | | | | | | | | | | | | | | | | | |
| Plymouth | 950 00 | 2,535 00 | | 3,385 00 | 21 22 | 2 96 | 28 06 | 9 85 | 21 10 | 7 88 | 2 96 | 9 32 | 9 22 | 3 82 | 12 54 | | | | | |
| Portland | 300 00 | 3,801 77 | | 4,401 77 | 34 00 | 3 33 | 23 03 | 12 84 | 20 73 | 10 36 | 3 33 | | 11 36 | 3 06 | 14 43 | | | | | |
| Quincy | 850 00 | 2,070 00 | | 2,920 00 | 18 36 | | 17 34 | 8 46 | 10 12 | 7 37 | | | 12 42 | 6 50 | 18 92 | | | | | |
| Reading | | | | | | | | | | | | | | | | | | | | |
| Reed City | 1,100 00 | 4,630 00 | | 5,730 00 | 24 72 | 3 34 | 28 06 | 7 88 | 21 10 | 6 00 | 3 34 | 9 34 | 9 64 | 2 42 | 14 36 | | | | | |
| Republic | 1,100 00 | 4,750 00 | | 5,850 00 | 19 00 | 4 08 | 23 03 | 8 09 | 20 73 | 7 68 | 4 08 | 11 89 | 12 28 | 4 65 | 15 27 | | | | | |
| Richmond | 680 00 | 1,170 00 | | 1,809 00 | 14 30 | 2 96 | 17 34 | 7 17 | 10 12 | 7 37 | 2 96 | | 5 47 | 90 | 10 56 | | | | | |
| Rochester | 750 00 | 1,390 00 | 250 00 | 2,140 00 | 20 84 | 3 34 | 32 09 | 9 85 | 21 10 | 7 88 | 3 34 | 9 34 | 9 64 | 3 34 | 12 98 | | | | | |
| Romeo | 1,360 00 | 2,635 00 | | 4,225 00 | 33 12 | 4 08 | 31 01 | 12 84 | 20 73 | 7 80 | 4 08 | 18 25 | 12 28 | 4 16 | 16 21 | | | | | |
| Sebewaing | 500 00 | | | 1,400 00 | | | | | | | | | 5 47 | 7 10 | 7 11 | | | | | |
| South Haven | 1,100 00 | 4,705 00 | 380 00 | 5,865 00 | 18 36 | 3 97 | 22 32 | 8 46 | 12 43 | 9 64 | 3 97 | 13 51 | 8 77 | 3 72 | 12 48 | | | | | |
| St. Clair | 1,000 00 | 4,575 00 | | 5,925 00 | 17 96 | 4 | 25 66 | 13 61 | 17 96 | 14 54 | 4 | 18 79 | | 4 25 | 15 24 | | | | | |
| St. Ignace | 720 00 | 3,285 00 | | 4,005 00 | | | | | | | | | 7 64 | 1 49 | 9 13 | | | | | |
| St. Johns | 1,500 00 | 7,390 00 | | 8,490 00 | | | | | | | | | 11 42 | 9 56 | 20 98 | | | | | |
| St. Louis | 1,000 00 | 4,092 50 | | 5,092 50 | 21 01 | 4 48 | 25 49 | 7 56 | 12 04 | 6 00 | 4 48 | 19 13 | 10 70 | 11 25 | 21 96 | | | | | |
| Stanton | 768 50 | 2,765 00 | 298 00 | 3,625 50 | 19 80 | 2 13 | 21 93 | 14 40 | 16 53 | 9 00 | 2 13 | 18 25 | 11 15 | 3 07 | 14 22 | | | | | |
| Sturgis | 1,100 00 | 3,044 00 | | 3,034 10 | | | | | | | | | 13 94 | 3 72 | 21 32 | | | | | |
| Tawas City | 650 00 | 1,845 00 | 350 00 | 2,495 00 | 18 36 | 3 97 | 22 82 | 8 22 | 11 00 | 6 16 | 3 97 | 13 51 | 8 60 | 7 12 | 12 46 | | | | | |
| Tecumseh | 990 00 | 5,909 00 | 380 00 | 6,940 00 | 21 41 | 4 | 25 66 | 10 90 | 16 53 | 8 55 | 4 | 18 79 | 11 51 | 5 25 | 18 24 | | | | | |
| Three Rivers | 1,100 00 | 4,318 35 | | 6,808 25 | | | | 5 57 | 7 91 | 5 55 | | | 11 99 | 4 05 | 19 98 | | | | | |
| Union City | 850 00 | 3,740 00 | | 4,590 00 | | | | | | | | | 14 81 | | | | | | | |
| Vassar | 1,000 00 | 8,040 00 | | 4,040 00 | 24 04 | 4 34 | 26 72 | 7 50 | 12 04 | 6 00 | 4 34 | 10 48 | 11 41 | 4 34 | 15 65 | | | | | |
| Vicksburg | 950 00 | 1,839 44 | 150 00 | 2,959 50 | 16 40 | 4 44 | 19 95 | 14 | 16 53 | 9 00 | 4 44 | 11 13 | 11 95 | 4 11 | 16 43 | | | | | |
| Wayne | 850 00 | 2,850 00 | | 3,850 00 | 21 30 | 2 13 | 29 64 | 8 32 | 11 00 | 8 55 | 2 13 | 13 51 | 12 83 | 2 13 | 14 96 | | | | | |
| West Branch | 900 00 | 2,595 50 | | 3,496 50 | | | | | | | | | | | | | | | | |
| Whitehall | 1,000 00 | 2,140 00 | | 3,840 00 | 24 04 | 2 68 | 20 72 | 10 80 | 11 00 | 6 16 | 2 68 | 8 84 | 41 | 2 08 | 12 20 | | | | | |
| Williamston | 700 00 | 1,710 00 | | 2,410 00 | 21 30 | 2 34 | 23 64 | 5 57 | 7 91 | 5 55 | 2 34 | 7 89 | 11 88 | 2 34 | 15 16 | | | | | |
| Yale | | | | | | | | | | | | | 7 | | 10 29 | | | | | |

TABLE XIX.

*Special report of the superintendents of schools of cities and villages having a population over 1,200.*

| Line number. | Cities and villages having a population over 1,200, census of 1894. | No. of teachers in schools, not including the Supt. and special teachers. | No. of special teachers employed. | Are all regular teachers holders of legal certificates of qualification? | No. holding certificates granted or endorsed by State Board of Education. | No. holding State Normal certificates granted under provisions of Act 194, Laws of 1889. | No. holding University certificates granted according to Act 144, Laws of 1891. | No. holding college certificates granted according to Act 136, Laws of 1893. | No. holding county first grade certificates. | No. holding county second grade certificates. | No. holding county third grade certificates, class B. | No. holding county third grade certificates, class A. | No. holding county special certificates. | No. holding city certificates granted according to section 13, Act 66, Laws of 1895. | No. who have been teaching in the same school one year or less. | No. who have taught in the same school between 2 and 5 years. | No. between 5 and 10 years. | No. between 10 and 15 years. | No. between 15 and 20 years. | No. between 20 and 25 years. | No. over 25 years. | Greatest number of years service by any one teacher. | Line number. |
|---|---|---|---|---|---|---|---|---|---|---|---|---|---|---|---|---|---|---|---|---|---|---|---|
| 1 | Adrian | 38 | 1 | Yes | 1 | 3 | 3 | 6 | 32 | | | 2 | | 32 | 5 | 8 | 11 | 6 | 5 | | 2 | 30 | 1 |
| 2 | Albion | 24 | 2 | Yes | 2 | 10 | 1 | 2 | 6 | 5 | 1 | 2 | | 6 | 8 | 12 | 3 | 1 | 1 | | | 16 | 2 |
| 3 | Allegan | 18 | | Yes | | 2 | | | | 4 | | | | | 1 | 5 | 2 | 3 | | | | 9 | 3 |
| 4 | Alma | 10 | | Yes | | 2 | 1 | | | 4 | | 1 | | | 2 | 1 | 4 | | | | | 11 | 4 |
| 5 | Alpena | | | | | | | | | | | | | | | | | | | | | | 5 |
| 6 | Ann Arbor | 66 | 2 | Yes | | 1 | 2 | 3 | 65 | | | | 1 | 65 | 8 | 30 | 21 | 8 | 5 | | | 32 | 6 |
| 7 | Au Sable | 7 | 3 | Yes | 2 | 8 | 5 | 1 | 2 | 8 | 2 | 4 | | 2 | 8 | 21 | | 5 | | 4 | | 27 | 7 |
| 8 | Battle Creek | 78 | 2 | Yes | | 6 | | 1 | 28 | 30 | | | | 28 | 13 | 35 | 26 | 8 | 10 | | | 36 | 8 |
| 9 | Bay City | 118 | 3 | Yes | | 5 | 1 | 1 | 111 | | | | | 111 | 19 | 5 | 3 | 20 | | 5 | | | 7 | 9 |
| 10 | Belding | 14 | | Yes | | | | | 7 | 1 | | | | 7 | 6 | 5 | 3 | | | | | 7 | 10 |
| 11 | Benton Harbor | 31 | 1 | Yes | | | | | 2 | | | 7 | | 2 | 11 | 19 | 1 | | | | | 7 | 11 |
| 12 | Bauer | 15 | 3 | Yes | | 2 | | | | | | | | | 12 | 3 | | | | | | | 23 | 12 |
| 13 | Big Rapids | 24 | | Yes | | 4 | 1 | 1 | 16 | | | | | 16 | 1 | 2 | 4 | 8 | 10 | | | | 40 | 13 |
| 14 | Blissfield | 3 | | Yes | | 3 | | | | | | | | | 4 | 2 | | | | | | | 10 | 14 |
| 15 | Buchanan | | | | | | | | | | | | | | | | | | | | | | | 15 |
| 16 | Cadillac | 31 | 1 | Yes | | 14 | 3 | | 14 | | 18 | 1 | 2 | 14 | 5 | 16 | 8 | 2 | | | | 14 | 16 |
| 17 | Calumet | 84 | 3 | Yes | 1 | 44 | 5 | | | | | 21 | | | 17 | 56 | 18 | 3 | | | | 11 | 17 |
| 18 | Caro | 8 | | Yes | | 6 | | | | 6 | | 1 | | | 4 | 3 | 3 | | | | | | | 18 |
| 19 | Cass | 12 | | Yes | 1 | 4 | | | | 4 | | | | | 6 | 3 | | | | | | | | 19 |
| 20 | Charlevoix | | | Yes | | | | | | | | | | | | | | | | | | | 5 | 20 |
| 21 | Charlotte | 23 | 3 | Yes | | 10 | 2 | | 11 | 4 | | 2 | | 11 | 3 | 8 | 7 | | 1 | | | | 5 | 21 |
| 22 | Cheboygan | 24 | | Yes | | 3 | | | | 5 | | | | | 2 | 5 | | 1 | | | | | 22 | 22 |
| 23 | Chelsea | 11 | | Yes | 1 | 1 | 3 | 3 | | | | 1 | | | 7 | 1 | 2 | | | | | | 23 | 23 |
| 24 | Clare | 8 | | Yes | | 6 | | | | | | | | | 1 | 3 | 5 | | | | | | 23 | 24 |
| 25 | Coldwater | 24 | | Yes | | | | | 15 | | 6 | 2 | | 15 | 11 | 3 | 5 | 1 | 1 | | | | 22 | 25 |
| 26 | Corunna | 9 | | Yes | | | | | | | | | | | 1 | 5 | 3 | | | | | | | 26 |
| 27 | Crystal Falls | 1½ | 2 | Yes | | 3 | | | | 6 | | 3 | | | 2 | 1 | 3 | | | | | | | 27 |
| 28 | Decatur | 7 | | Yes | | 3 | | | | 2 | | 3 | | | 2 | 3 | | | | | | | 6 | 28 |
| 29 | Detroit | 1096 | 7 | Yes | | 73 | 59 | 55 | 687 | | 62 | 32 | | 687 | 103 | 218 | 242 | 150 | 59 | | 42 | 42 | 29 |

| No. | Place |
|---|---|
| 30 | Dowagiac |
| 31 | Dundee |
| 32 | East Tawas |
| 33 | Eaton Rapids |
| 34 | Escanaba |
| 35 | Essexville |
| 36 | Evart |
| 37 | Fenton |
| 38 | Flint |
| 39 | Frankfort |
| 40 | Fremont |
| 41 | Gladstone |
| 42 | Gladwin |
| 43 | Grand Haven |
| 44 | Gd. Lodge No. 9 |
| 45 | Grand Rapids |
| 46 | Greenville |
| 47 | Hancock |
| 48 | Harbor Beach |
| 49 | Harrison |
| 50 | Hastings |
| 51 | Hillsdale |
| 52 | Holland |
| 53 | Holly |
| 54 | Houghton |
| 55 | Howard City |
| 56 | Howell |
| 57 | Hudson |
| 58 | Ionia |
| 59 | Iron Mountain |
| 60 | Ironwood |
| 61 | Ishpeming |
| 62 | Ithaca |
| 63 | Jackson |
| 64 | Jonesville |
| 65 | Kalamazoo |
| 66 | Kalkaska |
| 67 | Lake Linden |
| 68 | Lansing |
| 69 | Lapeer |
| 70 | Lowell |
| 71 | Ludington |
| 72 | Mancelona |
| 73 | Manistee |
| 74 | Manistique |
| 75 | Marine City |

**TABLE XIX.—CONCLUDED.**

| Line number | Cities and villages having a population over 1,200, census of 1894. | No. of teachers in schools, not including the Supt. and special teachers. | No. of special teachers employed. | Are all regular teachers holders of legal certificates of qualification? | No. holding certificates granted or endorsed by State Board of Education. | No. holding State Normal certificates granted under provisions of Act 194, Laws of 1889. | No. holding University certificates granted according to Act 144, Laws of 1891. | No. holding college certificates granted according to Act 134, Laws of 1893. | No. holding county first grade certificates. | No. holding county second grade certificates. | No. holding county third grade certificates, class B. | No. holding county third grade certificates, class A. | No. holding county special certificates. | No. holding city certificates granted according to section 13, Act 66, Laws of 1895. | No. who have been teaching in the same school one year or less. | No. who have taught in the same school between 2 and 5 years. | No. between 5 and 10 years. | No. between 10 and 15 years. | No. between 15 and 20 years. | No. between 20 and 25 years. | No. over 25 years. | Greatest number of years service by any one teacher. | Line number |
|---|---|---|---|---|---|---|---|---|---|---|---|---|---|---|---|---|---|---|---|---|---|---|---|
| 76 | Marquette | 37 | 2 | Yes | | 3 | 9 | 8 | 6 | 1 | | | | 24 | 6 | 8 | 9 | 10 | 2 | | 1 | 16 | 76 |
| 77 | Marshall | 22 | 2 | Yes | | 15 | 3 | | | 2 | | | | 13 | 6 | 4 | 8 | 2 | 1 | | | 30 | 77 |
| 78 | Mason | 57 | 4 | Yes | | 1 | 1 | 1 | | | | | | 40 | 23 | 26 | 8 | | | | | | 78 |
| 79 | Menominee | 11 | | No | | 1 | 1 | 1 | 1 | 4 | | | | 3 | 3 | 5 | 3 | | | | | 10 | 79 |
| 80 | Midland | | | | | | | | | | | | | | | | | | | | | 7 | 80 |
| 81 | Milford | 17 | | Yes | | | | | | | | | | 13 | 7 | 11 | 4 | | | | | | 81 |
| 82 | Monroe | 6 | | | | 2 | 2 | 2 | | 3 | 1 | | | 19 | | 4 | 1 | 2 | | | | 11 | 82 |
| 83 | Montague | 24 | 1 | Yes | | | 1 | | | 3 | | | | | 1 | 10 | 6 | | | | | 10 | 83 |
| 84 | Morenci | | | | | | | | | | | | | | | | | 2 | | | | 13 | 84 |
| 85 | Mt. Clemens | | | | | | | | | | | | | | | | | | | | | | 85 |
| 86 | Mt. Pleasant | 21 | 1 | Yes | | 3 | 3 | 3 | | | | | | 11 | 8 | 13 | 42 | 10 | | | | 5 | 86 |
| 87 | Muskegon | 107 | 7 | Yes | 2 | 2 | | | 1 | 3 | 2 | 2 | | 102 | 12 | 37 | 3 | 2 | 5 | 1 | | 24 | 87 |
| 88 | Nashville | 9 | 2 | Yes | 1 | 4 | | | 1 | 3 | | | | | 4 | 7 | | | 1 | | | 5 | 88 |
| 89 | Negaunee | 28 | | Yes | | 4 | | | | 1 | | | | | 4 | 2 | | | | | | 17 | 89 |
| 90 | Newaygo | 5 | | Yes | | | | | | 3 | | | | | 2 | 1 | | | | | | 3 | 90 |
| 91 | Niles | 22 | 1 | Yes | | 2 | 2 | 2 | | 4 | 1 | | 1 | 10 | 7 | 6 | 6 | 1 | 2 | | | 7 | 91 |
| 92 | Northville | 9 | | Yes | 2 | 2 | 1 | | 1 | 8 | 6 | | | 6 | 4 | 4 | 1 | | | | | 12 | 92 |
| 93 | Norway | 13 | 1 | Yes | 1 | 2 | 1 | | | 3 | 1 | | | | 3 | 6 | 3 | 1 | | | | 11 | 93 |
| 94 | Ontonagon | 14 | 1 | Yes | | 2 | 1 | | | 6 | | | | 5 | 4 | 2 | 1 | 1 | | | | 11 | 94 |
| 95 | Oscoda | 6 | | Yes | | | | | | | | | | | 3 | 2 | | | | | | 6 | 95 |
| 96 | Otsego | 13 | 1 | Yes | | 4 | | | | 1 | | | | 2 | 3 | 1 | 2 | 2 | | | | | 96 |
| 97 | Ovid | 8 | | No | | 9 | | | 2 | 2 | | | | 3 | 10 | 8 | 9 | 5 | | | | 13 | 97 |
| 98 | Owosso | 42 | 1 | Yes | 2 | 2 | | | 1 | 2 | | 8 | | 3 | 3 | 2 | | | | | | 14 | 98 |
| 99 | Paw Paw | 8 | 1 | Yes | 1 | | | | | | | | | | | 4 | | | | | | 6 | 99 |
| 100 | Pentwater | 8 | | No | | | | | | | 1 | | | | | | | | | | | 9 | 100 |
| 101 | Petoskey | 22 | 1 | Yes | 12 | 6 | | 1 | 2 | 1 | | | | 13 | 7 | 8 | 6 | 1 | | | 2 | 12 | 101 |
| 102 | Plainwell | 8 | 1 | Yes | 1 | | | | | 2 | 2 | | | | 8 | 13 | | 1 | | | 2 | | 102 |
| 103 | Plymouth | 31 | 1 | Yes | | 10 | 3 | 1 | | 2 | | | | 16 | 12 | 5 | 1 | 1 | 1 | | | 26 | 103 |
| 104 | Pontiac | 31 | | Yes | | 4 | 3 | 1 | | 2 | | 2 | | 46 | 6 | 1 | 1 | 3 | 4 | | | 33 | 104 |
| 105 | Port Huron | 75 | 1 | Yes | 1 | 5 | 8 | | | 3 | | | | | 5 | 8 | 1 | 5 | | | | 30 | 105 |
| 106 | Portland | 12 | 1 | No | 1 | | | | | 6 | | | | | 2 | | 1 | 1 | 4 | | | 12 | 106 |

| | | | | | | | | | | | | | | | | | | |
|---|---|---|---|---|---|---|---|---|---|---|---|---|---|---|---|---|---|---|
| 107 | 1 | BdCity | 13 | | | | | | | | | | | | | | | Yes | | 107 |
| 104 | | Romeo | | | | | | | | | | | | | | | | | | 104 |
| 109 | | Saginaw | 130 | 2 | | | | | | | | | | | | | | Yes | | 109 |
| 110 | | Saginaw, W. S. | 82 | 2 | | | | | | | | | | | | | | Yes | | 110 |
| 111 | | St. Clair | 12 | 1 | | | | | | | | | | | | | | Yes | | 111 |
| 112 | | St. Ignace | 10 | | | | | | | | | | | | | | | Yes | | 112 |
| 113 | | St. Johns | 30 | 2 | | | | | | | | | | | | | | Yes | | 113 |
| 114 | | St. Jo ph | 25 | 2 | | | | | | | | | | | | | | Yes | | 114 |
| 115 | | St. Louis | 11 | 2 | | | | | | | | | | | | | | Yes | | 115 |
| 116 | | Sault Ste. Marie | 36 | | | | | | | | | | | | | | | Yes | | 116 |
| 117 | | Sebewaing | 3 | | | | | | | | | | | | | | | Yes | | 117 |
| 118 | | South Haven | 15 | | | | | | | | | | | | | | | Yes | | 118 |
| 119 | | Stanton | | | | | | | | | | | | | | | | | | 119 |
| 120 | | Sturgis | | | | | | | | | | | | | | | | | | 120 |
| 121 | | Tawas City | | | | | | | | | | | | | | | | | | 121 |
| 122 | | Tecumseh | 12 | 4 | | | | | | | | | | | | | | Yes | | 122 |
| 123 | | Three Rivers | 22 | 2 | | | | | | | | | | | | | | Yes | | 123 |
| 124 | | Traverse City | 44 | 2 | | | | | | | | | | | | | | Yes | | 124 |
| 125 | | Union City | 10 | | | | | | | | | | | | | | | Yes | | 125 |
| 126 | | Vassar | 10 | | | | | | | | | | | | | | | Yes | | 126 |
| 127 | | Vicksburg | 6 | | | | | | | | | | | | | | | Yes | | 127 |
| 128 | | Wayne | 9 | | | | | | | | | | | | | | | Yes | | 128 |
| 129 | | West Bay City | 62 | | | | | | | | | | | | | | | Yes | | 129 |
| 130 | | West Blksfield | | | | | | | | | | | | | | | | | | 130 |
| 131 | | Whitehall | 9 | | | | | | | | | | | | | | | Yes | | 131 |
| 132 | | W... | | | | | | | | | | | | | | | | | | 132 |
| 133 | | Ypsilanti | 36 | 2 | | | | | | | | | | | | | | Yes | | 133 |

## TABLE XX.

*Receipts and expenditures at teachers' institutes for the calendar year 1899.*

| Counties. | Location. | Date. | Receipts. County fund. | Receipts. State fund. | Disbursements. Compensation of instructors. | Disbursements. Expenses of instructors. | Disbursements. Other expenses. | Totals. |
|---|---|---|---|---|---|---|---|---|
| Totals.......... | .......... | .......... | $11,257 36 | $2,974 86 | $10,236 93 | $2,794 40 | $1,200 88 | $14,232 21 |
| Alcona.......... | Harrisville.... | February 18-17.... | $21 00 | $60 00 | $56 80 | $22 20 | .......... | 861 00 |
| ..er and ...be.. | Munising........ | ...ber 3-6........ | 20 50 / 20 00 | 95 35 | 64 00 | 55 05 | $16 20 | 135 85 |
| Alpena.......... | Alpena.......... | July 12?......... | 50 50 | 100 00 | 100 00 | 50 50 | .......... | 150 50 |
| Antrim.......... | Bellaire........ | July 17-28....... | 53 00 | 85 00 | 105 92 | 61 08 | .......... | 108 00 |
| Arenac.......... | Standish........ | July 5-28........ | 55 00 | 100 00 | 154 00 | 1 00 | .......... | 155 00 |
| Baraga.......... | L'Anse.......... | ...ber 9-13...... | 16 50 | 100 00 | 60 00 | 46 05 | 10 45 | 116 50 |
| Barry.......... | Hastings........ | July 5-28........ | 251 61 | .......... | 216 00 | 22 61 | 13 00 | 251 61 |
| Bay............ | Bay City........ | November 30-Dec. 2. | 173 16 | .......... | 110 00 | 43 81 | 19 35 | *173 16 |
| Benzie......... | Benzonia........ | July 5-21........ | 67 50 | 50 00 | 96 00 | 11 50 | 10 00 | 117 50 |
| Berrien........ | Benton Harbor... | July 5-21........ | 261 71 | .......... | 208 00 | 38 40 | 15 31 | 261 71 |
| Branch......... | Coldwater....... | July 31-August 16. | 183 25 | .......... | 130 00 | 48 40 | 4 85 | 183 25 |
| Calhoun........ | Marshall........ | July 5-28........ | 355 10 | .......... | 247 50 | 74 07 | 33 53 | 355 10 |
| Cass........... | Cassopolis...... | July 18-August 16. | 160 13 | .......... | 101 31 | 38 12 | 20 70 | 160 13 |
| Charlevoix..... | Charlevoix...... | August 21-25..... | 62 50 | 50 12 | 55 07 | 54 45 | 1 50 | 112 62 |
| Cheboygan...... | Cheboygan....... | July 31-August 16. | 57 50 | 100 00 | 137 21 | 20 29 | .......... | 157 50 |
| ..ac........... | Sault Ste. Marie. | ...ch 23-25...... | 72 00 | 60 00 | 60 00 | 70 00 | 12 00 | 132 00 |
| Clare.......... | Clare........... | July ...August 16. | 49 00 | 100 00 | 103 00 | 46 00 | .......... | 149 00 |
| Clinton........ | St. Johns....... | November 2-4..... | 117 37 | .......... | 85 00 | 27 37 | 5 00 | 117 37 |
| Delta.......... | Escanaba........ | August 7-16...... | 58 50 | 73 65 | 90 00 | 43 65 | 8 50 | 132 15 |
| Dickinson...... | Iron Mountain... | ...er 5-7........ | 56 00 | 100 00 | 64 00 | 65 86 | 26 14 | 156 00 |
| Eaton......... | Charlotte....... | July 31-August 11. | 184 50 | .......... | 120 00 | 24 50 | 40 00 | 184 50 |
| Emmet......... | Harbor Springs.. | July 10-21....... | 66 50 | 100 00 | 106 50 | 61 00 | .......... | 106 50 |
| Gl..c......... | Flint.......... | July 5-28........ | 355 61 | 77 10 | 288 00 | 39 51 | 28 10 | 355 61 |
| Gl...c........ | Gladwin........ | ...st 7-16....... | 28 50 | .......... | 74 00 | 28 60 | 3 00 | 106 60 |
| ...ac......... | Ironwood....... | ...st 5-7........ | 40 50 | 86 60 | 65 00 | 60 10 | 2 00 | 127 10 |
| G. Traverse and Leelanau | Traverse City.... | July 31-August 16. | 106 50 / 47 50 | 78 15 | 169 00 | 62 01 | 3 14 | 234 15 |
| Gratiot....... | Ithaca......... | July 31-August 16. | 187 00 | .......... | 156 00 | 24 50 | 6 50 | 187 00 |
| Hillsdale..... | Hillsdale...... | August 7-16..... | 58 30 | .......... | 5 00 | 25 95 | 27 25 | 58 20 |
| Huron......... | Bad Axe........ | ...ber 15-17.... | 100 70 | .......... | 70 00 | 27 20 | 3 50 | 100 70 |

| County | Location | Date | | | | | | |
|---|---|---|---|---|---|---|---|---|
| Ingham | Agricultural College | July 5-28 | *298 97 | 17 77 | 15 20 | 296 00 | | 298 97 |
| Ionia | Ionia | July 31 August 16 | *108 44 | 13 25 | 49 61 | 108 58 | | 108 44 |
| Iosco | Tawas City | August 28 September 1 | 75 55 | 1 02 | 19 55 | 55 00 | 44 25 | 31 00 |
| Isabella | Mt. Hasan | July 17-28 | 128 00 | 3 02 | 35 00 | 94 29 | 50 00 | 78 00 |
| Iron | Iron River | July 10-August 4 | 225 00 | | 74 00 | 151 00 | 100 00 | 125 00 |
| Kalamazoo | Kalamazoo | July 5-24 | 315 50 | 21 50 | 55 75 | 298 25 | | 315 50 |
| Kalkaska | | July 31-August 16 | 129 00 | 1 50 | 38 40 | 49 10 | 100 00 | 29 00 |
| Kent (circuit inst.) | Grand Rapids | Dec. 3, 1898-Feb. 27, 1899 | 105 00 | 2 00 | | 103 00 | 100 00 | 105 00 |
| Kent (see Osceola) | Grand Rapids | July 5-28 | 419 71 | 154 15 | 51 56 | 284 00 | | 419 71 |
| Lapeer | Imlay City | July 31-August 16 | *335 15 | 77 78 | 36 37 | 221 00 | | 335 15 |
| Leelanau (see G. Traverse) | | | | | | | | |
| Lenawee | Adrian | July 5-28 | 337 57 | 22 00 | 45 57 | 270 00 | | 337 57 |
| Livingston | Howell | August 21-September 1 | 203 95 | 38 00 | 38 95 | 127 00 | | 203 95 |
| Luce (see Alger) | | | | | | | | |
| Mackinac | St. Ignace | August 7-16 | 137 00 | 7 23 | 33 77 | 96 00 | 100 00 | 37 00 |
| Macomb | Richmond | July 31-August 11 | 215 97 | 43 64 | 36 33 | 136 00 | | 215 97 |
| Marquette | Negaunee | ...er 3-4 | 96 96 | 8 50 | 3 46 | 75 00 | | 96 96 |
| Mason | Ludington | July 5-28 | 201 00 | 10 80 | 47 86 | 142 34 | 100 00 | 101 00 |
| Mecosta | Big Rapids | ...er 30-Dec 2 | 138 65 | 9 75 | 43 90 | 85 00 | 100 10 | 138 65 |
| Menominee | Stephenson | August 7-16 | *189 50 | 10 62 | 70 62 | 108 25 | 100 00 | 59 50 |
| Midland | Midland | July 31-August 4 | 158 00 | 10 58 | 24 51 | 112 91 | 70 00 | 88 00 |
| Missaukee | Lake City | July 31-August 16 | 146 00 | 1 50 | 36 21 | 108 29 | 100 00 | 46 00 |
| Monroe | Monroe | July 5-21 | 202 50 | 24 00 | 22 50 | 156 00 | 50 00 | 152 50 |
| Montcalm | Greenville | July 5-21 | 139 61 | 28 75 | 12 40 | 100 46 | | 139 61 |
| Muskegon (circuit inst.) | Muskegon | Dec. 2, 1898-Mar. 4, 1899 | 66 50 | 15 00 | | 51 50 | | 66 50 |
| Muskegon and Oceana | Whitehall | July 5-28 | 349 29 | 10 00 | 68 69 | 270 00 | | 250 90 |
| Newaygo | Freemont | July 31-August 16 | 179 77 | 2 81 | 33 96 | 143 00 | 98 96 | 90 81 |
| Oakland | | August 7-16 | 168 25 | 19 75 | 31 50 | 117 00 | | 168 25 |
| Oceana (see Muskegon) | | | | | | | | |
| Ogemaw | West Branch | July 5-21 | 182 50 | | 21 66 | 110 84 | 100 00 | 82 50 |
| Ontonagon | Rockland | August 7-16 | 133 00 | 5 00 | 54 00 | 79 00 | 100 00 | 83 00 |
| Osceola and Lake | Reed City | July 5-28 | 247 45 | 19 50 | 47 50 | 180 45 | 100 00 | 101 50 / 46 95 |
| Otsego | Gaylord | July 5-28 | 140 29 | 5 00 | 18 29 | 117 00 | 86 79 | 53 50 |
| Ottawa | Grand Haven | July 31-August 16 | 171 87 | 5 00 | 36 87 | 130 00 | | 171 87 |
| Presque Isle | Rogers City | January 2-6 | 87 50 | | 27 50 | 60 00 | 60 00 | 27 50 |
| Roscommon | Roscommon | Dec. 5, 28-Jan. 16, 1899 | 113 50 | | 41 73 | 77 77 | 100 00 | 13 50 |
| Saginaw (circuit inst.) | Saginaw | | 105 00 | 2 00 | | 103 00 | | 105 00 |
| Saginaw | Saginaw | July 5-28 | 432 58 | 45 00 | 81 58 | 306 00 | | 432 58 |
| St. Clair | Port Huron | 31-August 16 | 255 55 | 15 00 | 68 55 | 182 00 | | 255 55 |
| St. Joseph | Sturgis | October 25-28 | *187 90 | 38 70 | 54 20 | 95 00 | | 187 90 |
| Sanilac | Sanilac | August 7-11 | 110 70 | 18 00 | 32 70 | 60 00 | | 110 70 |
| Shiawassee | | July 5-28 | *410 50 | 43 80 | 43 70 | 324 00 | | 410 50 |

* This amount includes expense of inspiration institute.

29

## TABLE XX.—CONCLUDED.

| Counties. | Location. | Date. | Receipts. | | Disbursements. | | | |
|---|---|---|---|---|---|---|---|---|
| | | | County fund. | State fund. | Compensation of instructors. | Expenses of instructors. | Other expenses. | Totals. |
| Tuscola | Caro | July 10-August 4 | $358 47 | .......... | $297 80 | $50 67 | $10 00 | $358 47 |
| Washtenaw | Ypsilanti | July 5 | 257 36 | .......... | 245 68 | .......... | 11 68 | 257 36 |
| Wayne (circuit inst.) | Detroit | Dec. 1, 1899-Jan. 12, 1890 | 305 50 | .......... | 257 50 | .......... | 48 00 | 305 50 |
| Wayne | Wayne | July 17-August 11 | 588 81 | .......... | 440 00 | 92 50 | 56 31 | 588 81 |
| Wexford | Manton | July 31-August 16 | 112 00 | 98 88 | 155 00 | 38 51 | 16 37 | 210 88 |

## TABLE XXI.

*Local committees, conductors, and instructors at teachers' institutes for the calendar year 1899.*

| Counties. | Term. | Local committees. | Conductors. | Instructors. | Instructors. | Instructors. |
|---|---|---|---|---|---|---|
| Alger | 1 week. | Lorenzo Frederick | A. Hamlin Smith | L. Frederick | F. D. Davis | Flora E. Hill. |
| La... | 3 days. | Mrs McLauchlin | W. N. Ferris | D. B. Waldo | | |
| Alpena | 2 weeks. | T. M. Sawyer / E. L. Little | J. D. Schiller / W. H. Shuart | W. H. Shuart | | |
| Antrim | 2 weeks. | J. R. Noogle | J. W. Simmons | Robt. Barbour | | |
| Arenac | 18 days. | F. D. Noogle | E. A. Carpenter | W. M. Gregory | J. C. Ketcham. | |
| Baga | 1 week. | M. J. McKanna | H. R. Pattengill | D. B. Waldo | | |
| Barry | 18 days. | J. C. | Delos Fall | Flora B. Renkes | | |
| Bay | 3 days. | C. W. | S. B. Laird | Alice Marsh | J. L. Hughes. | |
| Benzie | 13 days. | M. S. Gregory | C. H. Horn | M. S. Gregory | H. T. Blodgett. | |
| Berrien | 13 days. | E. P. Clarke | G. J. Edgcumbe | Eliz. Wightman | | |
| Branch | 13 days. | M. W. Mr. | W. J. McKone | F. J. Tooze | | |
| Calhoun | 18 days. | Ernest Burnham | O. I. Woodley | Harriet A. Marsh | Emma E. Hines. | E. F. Lohr. |
| Cass | 13 days. | C. E. Cone | C. L. ... | W. E. Conkling | | |
| Charlevoix | 1 week. | A. W. Chew | G. W. ... | A. Hamlin Smith | E. W. Baker. | |
| | 13 days. | E. W. Baker | W. C. Thompson | H. D. Nutt | | |
| Clare | 3 days. | T. R. Easterday | R. G. Boone | A. Hamlin Smith | Belle Waldo | |
| Clinton | 13 ... | A. H. Aldrich | L. M. Kellogg | Myra B. True | | |
| Delta | 3 days. | R. M. Winston | S. B. Laird | J. H. Kaye | | |
| | 8 days. | P. R. Legg | N. H. Hayden | E. O. Gillespie | | |
| | 3 days. | E. L. Parmenter | W. H. Sever | F. W. Parker | Lucretia Treat. | |
| Eaton | 2 weeks. | J. L. Warner | S. B. Laird | E. T. Austin | | |
| Emmet | 18 days. | H. S. Beck | E. T. Austin | C. E. Holmes | G. W. Peavy. | |
| Genesee | 13 days. | J. H. Tyler | A. Hamlin Smith | J. K. Oegerby | | |
| Gladwin | 8 days. | Kate Borden | O. D. Thompson | W. C. Hull | Lois B. Wilson. | |
| Gogebic | 3 ... | L. L. Wright | H. R. Pattengill | D. B. Waldo | | |
| Grand Traverse | 18 days. | Belle C. | A. P. Gk. | J. H. Hall | | |
| Gratiot | 13 days. | Retta Peet | H. C. Lott | O. G. Tuttle | | |
| Hillsdale | 8 days. | W. H. French | W. H. French | F. D. Harrington | A. M. Wallace. | |
| Huron | 3 ... | D. E. Spe or | Chas. Bemis / May | C. T. Grawn | P. B. Woodworth | O. T. Corson. |
| Ingham | 18 ... | M. Hanlon | S. B. Laird | C. F. Wheeler | | |
| Ionia | 2 weeks. | L. A. Burhans / E. B. Hale | J. G. Monroe / C. My. | P. A. Cowgill | G. J. Edgcumbe. | |
| Iosco | 1 week. | J. A. Chapbell | W. M. Gregory | N. H. Hayden | | |
| Iron | 4 weeks. | Thos. Conlin | C. W. Mickens | | | |

TABLE XXI.—(CONCLUDED.)

| Counties. | Term. | Local committees. | Conductors. | Instructors. | Instructors. | Instructors. |
|---|---|---|---|---|---|---|
| Ina... Jackson... Mo... | 2 weeks. 3 days. 18 days. | O. L. Burdick. F. M. Kw. J. W. Hazard. | W. E. Conkling. F. M. Harlow. D. B. Wo. | W. V. Sage. W. N. Ferris. E. N. Worth. | C. O. Hoyt. A. W. Bolt. | C. C. Rounds. Paul H. Haines. Arnold Tompkins. O. T. Corson. |
| Alka. Kent... ber... | 13 days. 18 days. 13 days. | E. L. Luther. G. T. Chapel. F. R. Hathaway. C. E. Pal m d. | L. B. Gilbert. F. L. Keeler. F. R. Hathaway. A. Hamlin I Shi C. E. Palmerlee | He B. My Berkey. Arnold Tompkins. Jsle Noyes. | A. R. Zimmer. C. H. Naylor. | |
| Iee... Kingston Akinac | 18 days. 2 weeks 8 days. | M. W. Hensel. J. H. Wallace. W. H. Lewis. | G. A. Me. W. N. Ferris. W. L. Shuart. | J. W. Wh. Chas. McKenny. Ella K. Sn. | Lucy Bettes. | Wm. McCracken. |
| Mb... Ne... Mn... | 2 weeks 3 days. 18 days. | R. J. Crawford. F. D. Davis. S. A. Louden. | G. A. Me. D. B. Waldo. C. E. Pray. | C. E. Pray. John P. Ashley. C. E. j dill. | L. F. Anderson. | |
| Ma... Me... Midl ad... | 3 days. 8 days. 2 weeks. | A. R. Not. O. L. Woodley. Jesse Hubbard. W. E. Culver. | C. O. Hoyt. H. R. Pattengill. R. D. Bailey. O. D. Sn. | Chas. McKenny. E. M. Plunkett. | C. T. McFarlane. | Jesse Hubbard. |
| Missaul ee Monroe... Mn... | 13 days. 13 days. 13 days. | Ezra Hall. S. H. kngdon. E. D. Straight. | W. V. Sage. H. C. Lott. F. D. Smith. | Wm Bellis. R. D. Briggs. E. D. Straight. | C. F. Straight. | |
| Ina... Ga... Newaygo... | 18 days. 13 days. | H. B. Carr. Cha B. Smith. F. C. Stillson. | David McKenzie. S. B. Laird. F. O. Still en. | Paul H. Haines. H. A. Lewis. Robt Barbour. | Arnold Tompkins. Vesta B. Smith. | C. C. Rounds. |
| Oakland... Ogemaw... agon... | 8 days. 13 days. 8 days. | H. S. Elliott. Ben. Be nt. J. D. Schiller | W. W. Coburn. W. J. McKone. J. D. Schiller | C. E. Holmes. Ben. Bst. W. D. Hill | A. L. Craft. | |
| Osceola... Be... Bo... | 18 days. 13 days. | E. G. Johnson. R. D. Bailey. | O. G. Tuttle. R. D. Bailey. | J. H. Tmpson. H. D. Nutt. | Albert Allen. | |
| Geo... Presque Isle Roscommon | 13 days. 1 week. 13 days. | L. P. Ernst. Ed. Erskine. E. G. Payne. | Delos Fall A. Hamlin Smith J. H. Sn. | Kath. McTavish. M. F. Scott. | | |
| Saginaw... St. Clair St. Joseph Sanilac | 18 days. 13 days. 3 days. 1 week. | A. S. Whitney. W. G. Ma. R. S. Campbell John Evert. H. A Sn. | E. C. Sn. J. G. Monroe. O. L. Way. Sa. McKenny Chas McKenny | Paul H. Haines. F. A. Osborn. A. L. Marvin. My E. Wise. Alice Sth. | Arnold Tompkins. Jessie Noyes. Lill'n McCutcheon L. D. Harvey. | C. C. Rounds. |

| | | | | | |
|---|---|---|---|---|---|
| Shiawassee | 18 days | O. L. Bristol | { O. L. Bristol... G. W. Loomis... } | C. I. Collins | W. G. Bauer | { Hattie Germaine. Cora D. Martin. |
| Tuscola | 4 weeks | P. G. Davis | R. L. Holloway | Jennie Tibbetts | J. W. Matthews | P. G. Davis. |
| Washtenaw | *18 days | W. N. Lister | | | | |
| Wayne | 4 weeks | E. W. Yost | { W. C. Martindale. J. H. Kaye. | Paul H. Haines. T. Dale Cooke. | Arnold Tompkins. | C. C. Rounds. |
| Wexford | 13 days | C. C. Siemons | F. D. Smith | E. F. Gee. | S. O. Wood | *Isabel N. Catlin. |

* Inspiration institute.
+ Summer school—Normal college.

## TABLE XXII.

*Enrollment at teachers' institutes for the calendar year 1899.*

| Counties. | Number of teachers required to supply schools. | No. enrolled. | | | Kinds and grades of certificates held by members. | | | | | | Number without experience in teaching. | Number having received normal instruction. | Average attendance each half day. | †Number of legally qualified teachers in county. | Percentage of teachers in county attending institutes. |
|---|---|---|---|---|---|---|---|---|---|---|---|---|---|---|---|
| | | Men. | Women. | Total. | State. | Normal. | First. | Second. | Third. | Special. | | | | | |
| Totals......... | 12,999 | 1,317 | 5,097 | 6,414 | 149 | 143 | 134 | 1,756 | 2,284 | 33 | 1,600 | 457 | 3,450 | 10,518 | 3,538 |
| Alcona............ | 30 | 14 | 37 | 51 | 2 | .... | 2 | 14 | 9 | 1 | 23 | 5 | 45 | 29 | 95. |
| Alger and Luce*.. | 31 | 8 | 50 | 58 | 3 | .... | 6 | 17 | 18 | .... | — | 5 | — | 42 | 104. |
| Allegan............ | 248 | | | | | | | | | | | | | | |
| Alpena............ | 77 | 3 | 84 | 87 | 46 | .... | 1 | 18 | 27 | .... | 46 | 1 | 66 | 40 | 230. |
| Antrim............ | 104 | 9 | 34 | 43 | 1 | .... | 3 | 19 | 14 | .... | 10 | ..... | 23 | 130 | 28. |
| Arenac............ | 51 | 11 | 35 | 46 | .... | .... | .... | .... | 15 | .... | 21 | 2 | 36 | 60 | 25. |
| Baraga............ | 25 | | | | | | | | | | | | | | |
| Barry............. | 185 | 26 | 87 | 113 | .... | .... | 2 | 19 | 45 | 1 | 40 | 6 | 82 | 210 | 32. |
| Bay*............. | 248 | 30 | 132 | 162 | 16 | 7 | 8 | 44 | 34 | .... | 2 | .... | 125 | 89 | 122. |
| Benzie............ | 72 | 7 | 38 | 45 | .... | 1 | 1 | 11 | 12 | .... | 21 | 2 | 29 | 104 | 24. |
| Berrien........... | 273 | 33 | 97 | 130 | 2 | 4 | 2 | 49 | 51 | .... | 39 | 8 | 101 | 235 | 46. |
| Branch.. ......... | 178 | 30 | 74 | 104 | .... | .... | .... | 18 | 54 | .... | 30 | 5 | 89 | 175 | 41. |
| Calhoun.......... | 306 | 25 | 80 | 105 | .... | .... | 2 | 39 | 37 | .... | 29 | 14 | 52 | 374 | 21. |
| Cass............. | 156 | 25 | 73 | 98 | .... | 3 | 1 | 43 | 30 | .... | 20 | 7 | 41 | 152 | 51. |
| Charlevoix........ | 91 | 10 | 54 | 64 | 1 | 1 | .... | 24 | 26 | .... | 12 | 8 | 50 | 118 | 44. |
| Cheboygan........ | 93 | 9 | 44 | 53 | .... | .... | 1 | 22 | 22 | .... | 9 | ..... | 44 | 80 | 56. |
| Chippewa*........ | 93 | 14 | 57 | 71 | .... | 20 | 8 | 16 | 22 | 3 | 3 | 31 | 66 | 61 | 113. |
| Clare............. | 64 | 9 | 40 | 49 | 1 | 1 | .... | 14 | 16 | 1 | 19 | 6 | 36 | 68 | 48. |
| Clinton*.......... | 170 | 40 | 121 | 161 | 3 | 8 | .... | 44 | 49 | 1 | 12 | 11 | 150 | 204 | 51. |
| Crawford.......... | 25 | | | | | | | | | | | | | | |
| Delta............. | 85 | 4 | 38 | 42 | .... | .... | 2 | 18 | 16 | .... | 9 | 5 | 20 | 60 | 60. |
| Dickinson......... | 75 | 14 | 88 | 102 | 16 | 6 | 6 | 23 | 18 | .... | — | — | — | 29 | 240. |
| Eaton............. | 215 | 31 | 109 | 140 | 1 | 2 | .... | 42 | 54 | .... | 43 | 10 | 85 | 299 | 33. |
| Emmet............ | 79 | 10 | 41 | 51 | 1 | 1 | .... | 24 | 19 | .... | 4 | .... | 20 | 109 | 41. |
| Genesee........... | 257 | 28 | 87 | 115 | .... | 2 | 3 | 32 | 51 | .... | 28 | 10 | 56 | 290 | 30. |
| Gladwin........... | 42 | 12 | 40 | 52 | .... | .... | 1 | 16 | 10 | 2 | 23 | 3 | 36 | 38 | 78. |
| Gogebic*.......... | 79 | 4 | 84 | 88 | 15 | 2 | 9 | 11 | 17 | .... | — | — | — | 14 | 384. |
| Grand Traverse.. | 117 | 13 | 96 | 109 | .... | .... | .... | 40 | 48 | .... | 25 | 5 | 73 | 160 | 55. |
| Gratiot........... | 178 | 20 | 72 | 92 | .... | ... | .... | 22 | 32 | 1 | 37 | 8 | 70 | 186 | 30. |
| Hillsdale......... | 217 | 40 | 133 | 173 | 2 | 1 | 2 | 46 | 82 | 3 | 46 | 6 | 135 | 240 | 64. |
| Houghton......... | 256 | | | | | | | | | | | | | | |
| Huron*........... | 150 | 48 | 95 | 143 | 4 | 7 | 6 | 55 | 34 | 3 | — | — | — | 187 | 58. |
| Ingham........... | 246 | 14 | 85 | 99 | 1 | .... | 2 | 26 | 39 | .... | 35 | 1 | 75 | 230 | 29. |
| Ionia............. | 222 | 17 | 68 | 85 | 1 | .... | .... | 33 | 34 | .... | 22 | ..... | 54 | 230 | 41. |
| Iosco............. | 56 | 5 | | 24 | .... | 2 | 1 | 18 | 7 | .... | 7 | 7 | 24 | 56 | 50. |
| Iron............. | 40 | 7 | 23 | 30 | .... | 1 | .... | 1 | 10 | .... | 17 | 2 | 25 | 47 | 25. |
| Isabella.......... | 128 | 29 | 92 | 121 | .... | 43 | .... | 33 | 11 | .... | 40 | 75 | 67 | ⊕ 240 | 36. |
| Jackson........... | 270 | | | | | | | | | | | | | | |
| Kalamazoo........ | 179 | 24 | 107 | 131 | .... | 2 | .... | 21 | 45 | .... | 60 | 6 | 93 | 205 | 33. |
| Kalkaska.......... | 57 | 19 | 45 | 64 | 1 | 1 | 2 | 21 | 16 | .... | 24 | 3 | 39 | 65 | 65. |
| Kent............. | 621 | 30 | 170 | 200 | 1 | .... | 5 | 48 | 91 | .... | 55 | 4 | 87 | 292 | 50. |
| Keweenaw......... | 10 | | | | | | | | | | | | | | |
| Lake............. | 55 | | | | | | | | | | | | | | |
| Lapeer...... .... | 233 | 30 | 89 | 119 | 1 | 3 | 3 | 40 | 51 | .... | 41 | 5 | 84 | 226 | 44 |
| Leelanau.......... | 65 | | | | | | | | | | | | | | |

## TABLE XXII.—CONCLUDED.

| Counties. | Number of teachers required to supply schools. | No. enrolled. | | | Kinds and grades of certificates held by members. | | | | | | Number without experience in teaching. | Number having received normal instruction. | Average attendance each half day. | †Number of legally qualified teachers in county. | Percentage of teachers in county attending institutes. |
|---|---|---|---|---|---|---|---|---|---|---|---|---|---|---|---|
| | | Men. | Women. | Total. | State. | Normal. | First. | Second. | Third. | Special. | | | | | |
| Lenawee.......... | 298 | 16 | 124 | 140 | .... | 1 | .... | 17 | 68 | .... | 53 | 6 | — | 346 | 25 |
| Livingston........ | 166 | 45 | 134 | 179 | 2 | 4 | 2 | 59 | 79 | .... | 33 | 21 | 129 | 275 | ...... |
| Luce.............. | 14 | ..... | | | | | | | | | | | | | |
| Mackinac.......... | 27 | 2 | 35 | 37 | .... | .... | 1 | 18 | 6 | 2 | 8 | 7 | 19 | 40 | 68 |
| Macomb......... . | 170 | 28 | 64 | 92 | 4 | 1 | 3 | 36 | 31 | .... | 17 | 2 | 54 | 205 | 37 |
| Manistee......... | 215 | ...... | | | | | | | | | | | | | |
| Marquette........ | 192 | 31 | 176 | 207 | — | — | — | — | — | — | — | — | — | 107 | — |
| Mason*........... | 103 | 7 | 78 | 85 | .... | 1 | .... | 13 | 36 | .... | 30 | 6 | .... | 78 | 64 |
| Mecosta*.......... | 136 | 60 | 147 | 207 | 2 | 1 | 5 | 67 | 74 | .... | 60 | 11 | — | 233 | 67 |
| Menominee........ | 120 | 5 | 50 | 55 | .... | .... | .... | 7 | 31 | 1 | 22 | 9 | 47 | 84 | 42 |
| Midland........... | 98 | 4 | 43 | 47 | .... | 1 | 1 | 11 | 19 | .... | 15 | 10 | 24 | 80 | 41 |
| Missaukee........ | 61 | 16 | 46 | 62 | .... | 1 | 3 | 11 | 24 | .... | 21 | 8 | 45 | 78 | 50 |
| Monroe........... | 177 | 29 | 83 | 112 | .... | .... | 1 | 47 | 41 | .... | 28 | 17 | 71 | 196 | 51 |
| Montcalm.......... | 199 | 12 | 84 | 96 | .... | .... | .... | 12 | 53 | .... | 31 | 6 | 78 | 241 | ...... |
| Montmorency..... | 25 | ...... | | | | | | | | | | | | | |
| Muskegon and Oceana........ | 234 | 18 | 89 | 107 | .... | 2 | .... | 37 | 34 | 2 | 31 | 8 | 69 | e 150 | 50 |
| Newaygo.......... | 137 | 19 | 77 | 96 | .... | .... | 1 | 23 | 47 | .... | 25 | — | 66 | 167 | 43 |
| Oakland.......... | 286 | 20 | 84 | 104 | 2 | 2 | 2 | 34 | 43 | .... | 21 | 11 | 67 | 300 | 28 |
| Oceana........... | 111 | ...... | | | | | | | | | | | | | |
| Ogemaw.......... | 49 | 6 | 28 | 34 | .... | .... | 2 | 10 | 11 | .... | 11 | ..... | 19 | 44 | 52 |
| Ontonagon........ | 29 | ..... | 22 | 22 | .... | .... | 1 | 5 | 11 | .... | 5 | ..... | 16 | 31 | 55 |
| Osceola and Lake | 127 | 4 | 45 | 49 | .... | .... | .... | 13 | ..... | ..... | ..... | ..... | .... | 164 | 8 |
| Oscoda............ | 15 | ..... | | | | | | | | | | | | | |
| Otsego............ | 50 | 9 | 35 | 44 | .... | .... | .... | 13 | 20 | .... | 16 | 1 | 34 | 63 | 52 |
| Ottawa........... | 224 | 16 | 69 | 85 | .... | .... | 1 | 24 | 42 | .... | 20 | 2 | 58 | 208 | 32 |
| Presque Isle...... | 36 | 29 | 17 | 46 | .... | .... | 2 | 7 | 24 | .... | 13 | 1 | 40 | 40 | 33 |
| Roscommon....... | 18 | 2 | 11 | 13 | .... | .... | .... | 2 | 4 | .... | 7 | .... | 10 | 14 | 43 |
| Saginaw.......... | 412 | 29 | 120 | 149 | .... | .... | 3 | 43 | 70 | .... | 46 | 7 | 57 | 263 | 45 |
| St. Clair.......... | 263 | 37 | 157 | 194 | .... | 1 | 4 | 45 | 79 | 6 | 59 | ..... | 130 | 217 | 62 |
| St. Joseph*....... | 187 | 32 | 112 | 144 | 15 | .... | 7 | 51 | 49 | .... | — | ..... | — | 215 | 57 |
| Sanilac.......... .. | 177 | 45 | 60 | 105 | 2 | 1 | 3 | 37 | 42 | .... | 15 | 11 | 91 | 162 | 52 |
| Schoolcraft...... | 38 | ...... | | | | | | | | | | | | | |
| Shiawassee...... | 205 | 33 | 123 | 156 | 3 | 4 | 4 | 41 | 64 | 5 | 54 | 12 | 88 | 225 | 54 |
| Tuscola........... | 192 | 21 | 75 | 96 | .... | .... | 3 | 31 | 43 | .... | 22 | 1 | 62 | 217 | 35 |
| Van Buren....... | 216 | ...... | | | | | | | | | | | | | |
| Washtenaw....... | 298 | 5 | 69 | 74 | .... | 3 | .... | 12 | 31 | 1 | 27 | 20 | .... | 306 | 15 |
| Wayne............. | 1,119 | 32 | 74 | 106 | .... | 2 | 3 | 36 | 29 | .... | 36 | 17 | 70 | 292 | 24 |
| Wexford.......... | 128 | 3 | 38 | 41 | .... | .... | 2 | 13 | 13 | .... | 13 | 2 | 28 | 113 | 25 |

— The blanks used indicate no data received.
* Inspiration institute.
† That this column is frequently less than the first, is due to the fact that some counties do not count city teachers.

## TABLE XXIII.

*County boards of school examiners for 1898-9.*

[The first named in each county is commissioner.]

| County. | Name. | Address. | Occupation. |
|---|---|---|---|
| Alcona. | L. Frederick | Gustin | Teacher. |
| | E. G. Holmes | Alcona | Teacher. |
| | W. H. Lanborn | Harrisville | Teacher. |
| Alger | Flora McLauchlin | Grand Marais | Ass't P. M. |
| | Wm. H. Fort | Munising | Teacher. |
| | S. H. Ostrander | Munising | Teacher. |
| Allegan | J. E. McDonald | Hopkins Station | Teacher |
| | Nellie M. Lewis | Martin | Teacher. |
| | Chas. F. Bacon | Fennville | Teacher. |
| Alpena | E. L. Little | Alpena | Clergyman. |
| | Jas. Cavanagh | Alpena | Lawyer. |
| | Egbert H. Fox | Long Rapids | Teacher. |
| Antrim | J. R. Jenkins | Mancelona | Teacher. |
| | F. J. Wheeler | Alba | Teacher. |
| | H. S. Roberts | Central Lake | Teacher. |
| Arenac | F. H. Noggle | Au Gres | Teacher. |
| | Julia A. Inglis | Au Gres | Teacher. |
| | Geo. H. Glasure | Sterling | Teacher. |
| Baraga | M. J. MaKanna | Baraga | Teacher. |
| | Kate Curry | L'Anse | Teacher. |
| | Helen O'Connor | L'Anse | Teacher. |
| Barry | J. C. Ketcham | Hastings | Teacher. |
| | Dorr N. Stowell | Woodland | Teacher. |
| | Wm E. Webb | Middleville | Teacher. |
| Bay | C. W. Hitchcock | Bay City | Lawyer. |
| | W. A. Collins | North Williams | Teacher. |
| | J. B. Laing | West Bay City | Teacher. |
| Benzie | M. S. Gregory | Benzonia | Teacher. |
| | W. E. Daines | Honor | Teacher. |
| | A. Gertrude Northrop | Thompsonville | Teacher. |
| Berrien | C. D. Jennings | St. Joseph | |
| | W. C. Stebbins | Colomo | Teacher. |
| | John Carmody | Berrien Springs | Teacher. |
| Branch | M. W. Wimer | Coldwater | Teacher. |
| | O. S. Bathrick | California | Teacher. |
| | J. B. Foote | Coldwater | |
| Calhoun | Ernest Burnham | Marshall | Teacher. |
| | Kassen Richardson | Burlington | Teacher. |
| | Frank D. Miller | Burlington | Teacher. |
| Cass | C. E. Cone | Cassopolis | |
| | S. E. Witwer | Pokagon | Teacher. |
| | John Finley | Dowagiac | Teacher. |
| Charlevoix | A. W. Chew | Bayshore | Farmer. |
| | H. M. Enos | Charlevoix | Miller. |
| | A. F. Melford | South Arm | Teacher. |
| Cheboygan | E. W. Baker | Cheboygan | Teacher. |
| | A. M. Galbraith | Cheboygan | Teacher. |
| | P. F. McCormick | Wolverine | Teacher. |
| Chippewa | T. R. Easterday | Sault Ste. Marie | Clergyman. |
| | C. E. Richmond | Sault Ste. Marie | Teacher. |
| | Thos. B. Aldrich | Pickford | Teacher. |
| Clare | A. H. Aldrich | Clare | Teacher. |
| | C. B. Chaffee | Farwell | Teacher. |
| | S. J. Skinner | Harrison | Teacher. |
| Clinton | R. M. Winston | St. Johns | Teacher. |
| | J. B. Stone | DeWitt | Teacher. |
| | E. M. Plunkett | Ovid | Teacher. |
| Crawford | Flora M. Marvin | Grayling | Teacher. |
| | Mrs. J. Cobb | Frederic | Farmer. |
| | A. J. Graham | Grayling | Teacher. |
| Delta | P. R. Legg | Gladstone | Teacher. |
| | Rose Headstine | Escanaba | Teacher. |
| Dickinson | Ed. L. Parmenter | Iron Mountain | Lumberman. |
| | E. P. Frost | Norway | Teacher. |
| | L. E. Amidon | Iron Mountain | Teacher. |

TABLE XXIII.—CONTINUED.

| County. | Name. | Address. | Occupation. |
|---|---|---|---|
| Eaton.................... | J. L. Wagner .............. | Charlotte............... | Teacher. |
| | C. G. Wade. ............. | Bellevue.................. | Teacher. |
| | J. W. Slaughter........... | Grand Ledge ........... | Teacher. |
| Emmet....... ........... | H. S. Babcock........... | Harbor Springs........... | Editor. |
| | H. N. Crandall.... | Cross Village ........... | Farmer. |
| | E. A Botsford............. | Petoskey................... | Teacher. |
| Genesee...... ............ | J. H. Tyler.............. | Davison................... | Teacher. |
| | Henry A. Luce.......... | Linden.................. | Teacher. |
| | Wm. E. Clark ............ | Montrose.................. | Teacher. |
| Gladwin.............. | Kate Borden............. | Gladwin................. | Teacher. |
| | Hugh A. Wagar.. ....... | Gladwin.................. | Teacher. |
| | Gertrude Reymore........ | Edenville................. | Teacher. |
| Gogebic................. | L. L. Wright..... .... | Ironwood.............. | Teacher. |
| | F. C. Chamberlain........ | Ironwood.............. | Lawyer. |
| | Wm. Prince............. | Bessemer............... | Banker. |
| Grand Traverse.............. | Nettie C. Gray.. ......... | Traverse City........... | Teacher. |
| | Wilkie A. White.......... | Fife Lake.. ......... | Editor. |
| | Jas. L. Gibbs............ | Mayfield.............. | Lumberman. |
| Gratiot.................. | Retta Peet............... | Ithaca.............. | Teacher. |
| | C. F. Pike.............. | Breckenridge............. | Teacher. |
| | J. M. Hoxie............. | Middleton............. | Teacher. |
| Hillsdale.............. | W. H. French.......... | Hillsdale........... | Teacher. |
| | Mrs. A. L Kinney........ | Reading............... | Teacher. |
| | D. L. Clark............. | Allen............. ...... | Teacher. |
| Houghton.............. .... | Wm. Bath............. | Houghton.............. | Accountant. |
| | Fred A. Jeffers............ | Atlantic Mine............ | Lawyer. |
| | Angus W. Kerr........... | Calumet............... | Teacher. |
| Huron.................... | D. E. Spencer............ | Bad Axe............... | Teacher. |
| | E. Baskin.............. | Ubly.................. | Farmer. |
| | D. Kearcher.............. | Sebewaing............. | Teacher. |
| Ingham................ | Martin Hanlon ......... | Williamston.............. | Druggist. |
| | G. W. Harvey............ | Okemos ............. | Teacher. |
| | F. E. Livrance............ | Williamston.............. | Farmer. |
| Ionia ................... | L. A. Burbans............. | Ionia ................... | Teacher. |
| | Geo. L. Jordan............ | Collins............... | Teacher. |
| | Chas. L. Bemis............ | Ionia................. | Teacher. |
| Iosco...... ...... | J. A. Campbell....... | Tawas City............. | Teacher. |
| | W. H. Price.............. | Whittemore ......... | Teacher. |
| | C. M. Jansky............ | Au Sable ............. | Teacher. |
| Iron...................... | Thos. Conlin............. | Crystal Falls............ | Editor. |
| | Geo. D. Crippen........ | Iron River...... ........ | Merchant. |
| | A. E. Farmer............ | Iron River.............. | Teacher. |
| Isabella.... ............ | O. L. Burdick............ | Mt. Pleasant............ | Teacher. |
| | F. L. Keeler............. | Mt. Pleasant............ | Teacher. |
| | Newman Smith.......... | Blanchard............. | Teacher. |
| Jackson.................. | F. M. Harlow........... | Springport.............. | Teacher. |
| | Wm. E. Videto.......... | Spring Arbor........... | Teacher. |
| | Frank H. Brown......... | Brooklyn............... | Teacher. |
| Kalamazoo ... .... | J. W. Hazard............ | Kalamazoo............. | Teacher. |
| | B. R. Platt............. | Vicksburg............. | Teacher. |
| | A. M. Nutten............ | Alamo ............. | Teacher. |
| Kalkaska .... | E. L. Luther............ | Kalkaska.............. | Teacher. |
| | E. L. Beebe............ | Kalkaska.............. | Teacher. |
| | Frank Leach............ | South Boardman .... | Teacher. |
| Kent . ............ | G. T. Chapel............ | Grand Rapids........... | Teacher. |
| | L. T. Herman ............ | Caledonia............. | Teacher. |
| | A. R. Zimmer............. | Kent City............. | Teacher. |
| Keweenaw ..... .. .... | F. M. Bradshaw ...... | Central Mine ........... | Teacher. |
| | Mary B. Richards........ | Allouez............... | Teacher. |
| | Philip Decker........... | Eagle River ........... | Teacher. |
| Lake ........... | E. G. Johnson ............ | Luther................. | .......... |
| | Homer Cutler ............ | Baldwin.............. | Co. Treas. |
| | Wm. P. Griffiths. ....... | Chase............... | Teacher. |
| Lapeer............. .... | C. E. Palmerlee.......... | Lapeer............... | Teacher. |
| | W. Frank Laughlin .... | Metamora.............. | Teacher. |
| | Orvice La Bounty.... ... | North Branch........... | Teacher. |
| Leelanau................ | G. W. Benjamin........ | Leland................. | .......... |
| | S. E. Blackwood......... | Leland............... | Teacher. |
| | J. O. Duncan............ | Sutton's Bay .. ...... | Teacher. |
| Lenawee..... ... ....... | M. W. Hensel ... ........ | Blissfield........ | Teacher. |
| | J. C. Howell ............ | Blissfield........ | Teacher. |
| | Carl Parsons............. | Jasper............... | Teacher. |
| Livingston ............. | J. H. Wallace........... | Fowlerville ............. | Teacher. |
| | N. Knoothuizen........... | Fowlerville ............. | Teacher. |
| | C. J. Gannon............ | Cohoctah............ | Teacher. |
| Luce ...... ..... | T. M. Sawyer ............ | Dollarville........... | Teacher. |
| | A. B. Chisholm........... | Newberry............. | Teacher. |
| | W. S. Hays.............. | Newberry................. | Clergyman. |

## TABLE XXIII.—CONTINUED.

| County. | Name. | Address. | Occupation. |
|---|---|---|---|
| Mackinac | W. H. Lewis | St. Ignace | Teacher. |
| | W. J. Feesant | Gould City | Clerk. |
| | John R. Bailey | Mackinac Island | Physician. |
| Macomb | R. J. Crawford | Mt. Clemens | Teacher. |
| | E. R. Wilcox | New Haven | Teacher. |
| | A. E. Millett | Utica | Teacher. |
| Manistee | Mrs. L. E. W. Hall | Manistee | Teacher. |
| | M. S. Hawes | Marilla | Farmer. |
| | Geo. Cook | Bear Lake | Clergyman. |
| Marquette | F. D. Davis | Negaunee | Teacher. |
| | D. B. Waldo | Marquette | Teacher. |
| | H. B. Krogman | Negaunee | Teacher. |
| Mason | S. A. Loudon | Ludington | Teacher. |
| | Iva Downing | Ludington | Teacher. |
| | C. A. Rinehart | Riverton | Teacher. |
| Mecosta | A. B. Lightfoot | Stanwood | Teacher. |
| | H. C. Ward | Chippewa Lake | Merchant. |
| | Jesse Hubbard | Menominee | |
| Menominee | C. M. Case | Hermansville | Accountant. |
| | Luman Burch | Stephenson | Teacher. |
| | W. E. Culver | Midland | Teacher. |
| Midland | T. W. Crissey | Midland | Editor. |
| | Wm. Buck | Coleman | Teacher. |
| | E. S. Hall | Lake City | Teacher. |
| Missaukee | Orville Dennis | Lake City | Editor. |
| | Fred Bartholomew | Lake City | Teacher. |
| Monroe | S. H. Langdon | Monroe | Student. |
| | P. H. Marron | Monroe | Teacher. |
| | J. E. Keeley | Steiner | Teacher. |
| | E. D. Straight | Stanton | Teacher. |
| Montcalm | A. L. Bemis | Carson City | Editor. |
| | F. D. Smith | Greenville | Teacher. |
| Montmorency | Jas. H. Briley | Hillman | Teacher. |
| | J. W. Farier | Hillman | Teacher. |
| | E. M. Hutchinson | Lewiston | Teacher. |
| Muskegon | H. B. Carr | Whitehall | Teacher. |
| | N. R. Dryer | Holton | Teacher. |
| | D. A. Seaman | Bailey | Teacher. |
| Newaygo | F. C. Stillson | Fremont | Teacher. |
| | John Howard | White Cloud | Lawyer. |
| | Jas. W. Alvord | Grant | Teacher. |
| Oakland | H. S. Elliott | Oxford | Teacher. |
| | H. N. McCracken | Farmington | Teacher. |
| | H. S. Gardner | Royal Oak | Teacher. |
| Oceana | Vesta B. Smith | Shelby | Teacher. |
| | H. A. Lewis | Pentwater | Teacher. |
| | L. G. Fairchild | Hesperia | Teacher. |
| Ogemaw | Ben Bennett | West Branch | Teacher. |
| | H. S. Karcher | Rose City | Teacher. |
| | E. H. Woughter | West Branch | Merchant. |
| Ontonagon | A. C. Adair | Rockland | Teacher. |
| | Clara Williams | Rockland | Teacher. |
| | A. E. Shuster | Ontonagon | Lawyer. |
| Osceola | Jas. H. Thompson | Evart | Teacher. |
| | Chas. A. Barnes | Tustin | Teacher. |
| | Geo. O. Roxburgh | Marion | Teacher. |
| Oscoda | S. J. Lewis | Mio | Teacher. |
| | Ethel Crawford | Red Oak | Housekeep'r. |
| | Eliza Dryarmond | Mio | Teacher. |
| Otsego | R. D. Bailey | Gaylord | Teacher. |
| | Vesta G. Lanning | Gaylord | Lawyer. |
| | Carrie G. Martindale | Gaylord | Teacher. |
| Ottawa | L. P. Ernst | Coopersville | Teacher. |
| | Leonard Rens | Zeeland | Teacher. |
| | Nelson Stanton | Forest Grove | Teacher. |
| Presque Isle | Ed. Erskine | Rogers City | Physician. |
| | W. Caldwell | Rogers City | Physician. |
| | C. W. Isanniger | Rogers City | Druggist. |
| Roscommon | E. G. Payne | Roscommon | Druggist. |
| | Jasper N. Greff | Roscommon | Teacher. |
| | H. H. Woodruff | Roscommon | Lawyer. |
| Saginaw | W. G. Graham | Saginaw, W. S. | Teacher. |
| | Jas. E. McDonald | Buena Vista | Teacher. |
| | Jas. B. Griffin | Carrollton | Teacher. |
| St. Clair | R. S. Campbell | Port Huron | Teacher. |
| | E. T. Blackney | Capac | Teacher. |
| | S. J. Gier | St. Clair | Teacher. |

## TABLE XXIII.—CONCLUDED.

| County. | Name. | Address. | Occupation. |
|---|---|---|---|
| St. Joseph | John Evert | Mendon | |
| | L. E. Miller | Colon | Teacher. |
| | Chas. Lockwood | Sturgis | Farmer. |
| Sanilac | H. A. Macklem | Marlette | |
| | Chas. G. Putney | Sanilac Centre | Teacher. |
| | John H. Hand | Port Sanilac | Teacher. |
| Schoolcraft | J. A. Chisholm | Seney | Teacher. |
| | C. W. Dunton | Manistique | Attorney. |
| | Mrs. E. B. Patterson | Manistique | Housekeep'r. |
| Shiawassee | O. L. Bristol | Corunna | Teacher. |
| | H. E. Slocum | Kirby | Teacher. |
| | A. N. Cody | Albion | Student. |
| Tuscola | P. G. Davis | Mayville | Teacher. |
| | H. Z. Wilber | Millington | Teacher. |
| | E. J. Darbee | Caro | Teacher. |
| Van Buren | W. G. Brown | Paw Paw | Teacher. |
| | C. B. Charles | Bangor | Teacher. |
| | Jas. Chamberlain | Decatur | Teacher. |
| Washtenaw | W. N. Lister | Ann Arbor | Teacher. |
| | A. D. DeWitt | Dexter | Teacher. |
| | Wirt I. Savery | Salem | Student. |
| Wayne | E. W. Yoat | Detroit | Teacher. |
| | Frank Cody | Delray | Teacher. |
| | Wm. Lightbody | Detroit | Teacher. |
| Wexford | C. C. Slemons | Sherman | Teacher. |
| | J. H. Kaye | Cadillac | Teacher. |
| | E. A. Carpenter | Harrietta | Teacher. |

TABLE XXIV.

*General statistics of educational institutions compiled from reports of officers for the academic year 1899–9.*

| Name of institution. | Location. | Name of president, superintendent, or principal. | Date of organization. | No. of instructors. | No. of students or inmates during the year. | No. of graduates at last commencement. | Whole number of graduates since founded. | No. of volumes in library. | No. of volumes added to library during year. |
|---|---|---|---|---|---|---|---|---|---|
| **ESTABLISHED BY ACTS OF LEGISLATURE.** | | | | | | | | | |
| *Educational:* | | | | | | | | | |
| Central State Normal School | Mt. Pleasant | Chas. McKenny | 1895 | 19 | 410 | 112 | 147 | 1,600 | 430 |
| Michigan Agricultural College | Lansing | J. L. Snyder | 1857 | 40 | 540 | 59 | 792 | 21,648 | 548 |
| Michigan College of Mines | Houghton | F. W. McNair | 1885 | 18 | 117 | 27 | 137 | 14,240 | 640 |
| Michigan State Normal College | Ypsilanti | E. A. Lyman | 1849 | 50 | 1,084 | 252 | 3,682 | 21,000 | 1,411 |
| Northern State Normal School | Marquette | D. B. Waldo | 1899 | 6 | 66 | | | | |
| University of Michigan | Ann Arbor | J. B. Angell | 1837 | 146 | 3,198 | 707 | 16,282 | 133,506 | 7,067 |
| *Charitable:* | | | | | | | | | |
| Industrial Home for Girls | Adrian | Lucy M. Sickels | 1879 | 28 | av. 309 | | | 800 | |
| Industrial School for Boys | Lansing | J. E. St. John | 1855 | 52 | av. 640 | 4 | | 3,000 | |
| School for the Blind | Lansing | E. P. Church | 1880 | 12 | 114 | | | 3,500 | |
| School for the Deaf | Flint | F. D. Clarke | 1854 | 41 | 423 | | 1,291 | 3,665 | 7 |
| State Public School | Coldwater | J. B. Montgomery | 1874 | | 489 | 315 | 4,666 | 1,650 | |
| **INCORPORATED UNDER ACT 39, LAWS OF 1855.** | | | | | | | | | |
| *Denominational Colleges:* | | | | | | | | | |
| Adrian College | Adrian | W. N. Swift | 1859 | 18 | 176 | 11 | 453 | 6,000 | 100 |
| Albion College | Albion | J. P. Ashley | 1861 | 58 | 452 | 32 | 800 | 15,000 | 1,000 |
| Alma College | Alma | A. F. Bruske | 1887 | 19 | 261 | 4 | 50 | 17,000 | 988 |
| Battle Creek College | Bat'le Creek | E. A. Sutherland | 1874 | 25 | 570 | | | 3,000 | 50 |
| Detroit College | Detroit | J. D. Foley | 1881 | 14 | 236 | 9 | 142 | 10,000 | 1,300 |
| Hillsdale College | Hillsdale | G. F. Mosher | 1855 | 21 | 383 | 39 | 950 | 10,000 | 75 |
| Hope College | Holland | G. J. Kollen | 1866 | 18 | 242 | 18 | 250 | 15,000 | 2,276 |
| Kalamazoo College | Kalamazoo | A. G. Slocum | 1855 | 18 | 344 | 20 | 259 | 6,735 | 346 |
| Olivet College | Olivet | W. G. Sperry | 1859 | 28 | 357 | 21 | 481 | 25,000 | |
| *Academies and Seminaries:* | | | | | | | | | |
| Academy of the Ladies of the Loretto | Sault Ste. Marie | | | | | | | | |
| Academy of the Sacred Heart | Grosse Pointe | | | | | | | | |
| Academy of the Sacred Heart | Detroit | Anna Hutton | 1850 | 12 | 60 | | | 2,200 | 10 |
| Akeley Institute | Grand Haven | Mrs. J. E. Wilkinson | 1858 | 8 | 40 | 6 | 39 | 4,000 | 25 |
| Benzonia College | Benzonia | G. R. Oaston | 1868 | 7 | 56 | 7 | 8 | 6,300 | |

| Institution | Location | Principal | Year | | | | | | |
|---|---|---|---|---|---|---|---|---|---|
| Detroit Female Seminary | Detroit | Mrs. E. F. Hammond, Miss L. C. Browning, Mrs Mary Whitton | 1890 | 11 | 126 | 7 | 206 | 2,000 | 100 |
| Detroit School for Boys | De rol t | F. D. Green, F. E. Searle | 90 | 10 | 90 | 4 | 46 | | |
| Detroit Home and Day School | De rol t | Ella M. Liggett | 82 | 23 | 282 | 12 | 192 | 1,000 | |
| Detroit University School | De rol t | F. L. Bliss | 1909 | 15 | 151 | | | | |
| Michigan Female Seminary | Kalamazoo | | | | | | | | |
| Michigan Military Academy | Orchard Lake | Sr. M. Anthony Nolan | 1887 | 11 | 32 | 1 | 1 | 3,528 | 2,100 |
| Nazareth Academy | Kalamazoo | L. A. Bailey | 85 | 5 | 51 | 4 | 153 | 700 | 10 |
| Raisin Valley Seminary | Adrian | Mother M. Justina | 1890 | 19 | 170 | 4 | 79 | 3,072 | 86 |
| St. Mary's Academy | Monroe | Mother Brunona Pydynkowska | 82 | 8 | 154 | 10 | 80 | 1,573 | 23 |
| Seminary of the Felician Sisters | Detroit | | | | | | | | |
| Sisters of the Order of St. Dominic | Emeryville | Mother M. Gonsalva | 1892 | 4 | 32 | 2 | 4 | 3?0 | 10 |
| Spring Arbor Seminary | Spring Arbor | D. S. Warner | 90 | 5 | 67 | 9 | 128 | 800 | 5 |
| St. Mary's School, Christian Reformed Church | Sault Ste. Marie | | 1898 | 5 | | | | | |
| Theological School, Christian Reformed Church | Grand Rapids | H. Beuker | 86 | 5 | 51 | 8 | 64 | 1,000 | 25 |
| Ursuline Academy | St. Ignace | Mother Angela | 89 | 6 | 76 | | | 500 | 80 |
| *Professional Schools:* | | | | | | | | | |
| Detroit College of Law | Detroit | P. T. Van Zile | 1863 | 16 | 150 | 150 | 193 | | |
| Detroit College of Medicine | Detroit | T. A. McGraw | 1867 | 90 | 305 | 68 | | | |
| Detroit Homeopathic College | Detroit | D. A. MacLachlen | 1872 | 34 | | 55 | | | |
| Grand Rapids Medical College | Grand Rapids | C. H. White | 1897 | | | | | | |
| Michigan College of Medicine and Surgery | Detroit | H. C. Wyman | 1888 | 18 | 145 | 12 | 295 | 5,000 | 300 |
| Saginaw Valley Medical College | Saginaw | L. W. Bliss | 1896 | 25 | 73 | 25 | 40 | | |
| Sprague Correspondence School of Law | Detroit | W. C. Sprague | 1891 | 3 | 855 | 44 | 231 | 400 | 100 |
| *Schools with Normal and Business Course:* | | | | | | | | | |
| Bay City Business College | Bay City | R. R. Lane | 1886 | 3 | 152 | | | | |
| Benton Harbor College | Benton Harbor | G. J. Edgecumbe | 1892 | 18 | 410 | 26 | 241 | 20 | |
| Cleary's Business College | Ypsilanti | P. R. Cleary | 1891 | | | | | 1,041 | |
| Fenton Normal School and Commercial College | Fenton | W. A. Stevenson | 1886 | 8 | 30 | 14 | | 1,100 | 100 |
| Ferris Industrial School | Big Rapids | W. N. Ferris | 1884 | 11 | e 1,300 | 72 | 291 | 650 | 50 |
| Grand Rapids Business University | Grand Rapids | A. S. Parish | 1899 | 3 | 149 | 4 | 11 | | |
| International Business College | Saginaw | F. H. Harper | 1896 | 5 | 84 | 5 | 8 | | |
| Lansing Business University | Lansing | H. J. Beck | 1897 | 3 | 68 | 3 | | | |
| Ludington Business College | Ludington | W. H. Martindill | 1898 | 3 | 132 | 55 | | 50 | 10 |
| Michigan Business and Normal College Company | Battle Creek | C. J. Argubright | 1896 | 3 | 214 | 6 | | 20 | |
| Three Rivers Business Academy and Normal School | Three Rivers | C. H. Sage | 1899 | 4 | 65 | 1 | | 200 | 8 |

\* As this college only trains for Christian workers, there are no graduating classes.
† Including employees.
‡ Placed in homes.
§ Exclusive of assistants and special lecturers.
e Estimated.

## TABLE XXV.

*Financial statistics of educational institutions compiled from reports of officers for the academic year 1898–9.*

| Name of institution. | Annual cost of tuition per student. | Average cost of board per week. | Total average annual cost to each student. | Total aver. annual cost of each student to the state. | Estimated value of grounds, buildings, library, apparatus, etc. | Amount of productive funds. | Income from productive funds. | Amount of legislative appropriation for 1899. | Receipts from tuition fees during the year. | Receipts from all other sources. | Current expenses for the year. | Expenses for permanent improvement. | Liabilities. |
|---|---|---|---|---|---|---|---|---|---|---|---|---|---|
| **ESTABLISHED BY ACTS OF LEGISLATURE** | | | | | | | | | | | | | |
| *Educational:* | | | | | | | | | | | | | |
| Central State Normal School.. | $10 00 | $2 50 | $125 00 | $30 00 | $29,602 90 | | | $12,000 00 | $567 50 | $96 25 | $12,613 00 | | |
| Mich. Agricultural College... | *150 00 | 1 98 | 125 50 | | 500,115 80 | $707,297 50 | $53,710 12 | 12,000 00 | 275 00 | 47,788 22 | 105,910 74 | $11,244 56 | $6,500 00 |
| Mich. College of Mines...... | 25 00 } | 4 50 | 762 00 } | 367 90 | 329,653 00 | 71,000 00 | 4,200 00 | 61,150 00 | 7,997 50 | 1,172 38 | 75,000 00 | | |
| Mich. State Normal College.. | 10 00 | 2 50 | 437 00 | 63 00 | | | | | | | | | |
| Northern State Normal School. | | 1 50 | 175 00 | | | | | | | | | | |
| University of Michigan...... | 65 00 | †4 50 | 312 00 | 60 00 | 2,050 00 | 540,946 00 | 38,500 00 | 163,133 33 | 178,252 30 | 118,176 30 | 440,697 53 | 68,304 40 | |
| *Charitable:* | | | | | | | | | | | | | |
| Industrial Home for Girls.. | | 49 | | 96 06 | 191,171 46 | 50,917 38 | 8,474 07 | 40,000 00 | 5,058 84 | 6,000 00 | 65,000 00 | | 1,594 59 |
| Industrial School for Boys. | | 50 | | 112 00 | 340,000 00 | 228,040 00 | 11,000 00 | 60,000 00 | 12,000 00 | 3,433 55 | 28,071 46 | 100 00 | 70,000 00 |
| School for the Blind ...... | 2 44 | 3 08 | | 246 24 | 185,305 00 | 219,000 00 | 8,000 00 | 28,000 00 | 3,000 00 | 79,953 17 | 76,518 62 | 6,389 67 | 8,000 00 |
| School for the Deaf ....... | 50 10 | 88 | | 274 61 | 250,000 00 | | | 70,000 00 | 21,000 00 | 2,300 00 | 31,000 00 | 1,276 33 | |
| State Public School........ | | 80 | | 25 99 | | | | 31,000 00 | | | | | |
| **INCORPORATED UNDER ACT 39, LAWS OF 1855.** | | | | | | | | | | | | | |
| *Denominational Colleges:* | | | | | | | | | | | | | |
| Adrian College............ | 45 00 | 2 50 | 171 00 | | 225,000 00 | 160,025 00 | 18,975 25 | | 7,394 42 | 11,030 44 | 19,553 35 | 345 53 | 43,000 00 |
| Albion College............ | 24 00 | 2 00 | 140 00 | | 100,025 00 | 225,386 00 | 13,000 00 | | 25 50 | 8,000 00 | 33,000 00 | 1,800 00 | |
| Alma College.............. | 24 00 | 2 25 | 143 00 | | 96,625 00 | 195,683 16 | 12,273 35 | | 2,250 00 | 2,300 00 | 13,325 00 | | |
| Battle Creek College....... | 45 00 | 1 25 | 135 00 | | 200,000 00 | 90,000 00 | 4,653 70 | | 4,983 90 | 5,539 94 | 18,000 00 | 1,000 00 | 8,000 00 |
| Detroit College............ | 40 00 | | 180 00 | | 160,000 00 | | | | 13,009 28 | 8,000 00 | 9,640 00 | | |
| Hillsdale College.......... | 22 00 | 1 75 | 140 00 | | 100,025 02 | | | | | 12,951 78 | 14,025 07 | | |
| Hope College.............. | 18 00 | 2 00 | 180 00 | | 80,000 00 | | | | | 1,600 00 | 16,000 00 | | |
| Kalamazoo College......... | 25 50 | 2 00 | 128 00 | | 64,500 00 | | | | | 5,539 94 | 22,805 19 | | |
| Olivet College............ | 45 00 | 2 25 | | | 46,253 00 | | | | | | 32,000 00 | | 1,465 66 |
| *Academies and Seminaries:* | | | | | | | | | | | | | |
| Academy of the Ladies of the Loretto | | | | | | | | | | | | | |
| Academy of the Sacred Heart. | 60 00 | 5 00 | 300 00 | | 75,000 00 | 5,000 00 | 225 00 | | 3,000 00 | 6,225 00 | 2,500 00 | | |
| Academy of the Sacred Heart. | 30 00 | 5 00 | | | | | | | | 6,225 00 | 6,225 00 | | 12,000 00 |
| Akeley Institute........... | | | | | | | | | | | | | |
| Benzonia College.......... | | | | | | | | | | | | | |

| | | | | | | | | | | | | | |
|---|---|---|---|---|---|---|---|---|---|---|---|---|---|
| Detroit Female Seminary | 75 00 | 10 00 | | 500 00 | 500 00 | 11,560 00 | | | | †1,000 00 | | 12,130 00 | 5,000 00 |
| Detroit School for Boys | 150 00 | 13 00 | | 450 00 | 312 05 | 11,382 37 | | | | 7,815 70 | | 16,344 42 | |
| Detroit Home and Day School | 90 00 | 12 00 | | 600 00 | 500 00 | 20,887 00 | | | | 50,000 00 | 18,148 00 | 31,946 00 | |
| Detroit University School | 120 00 | | | 120 00 | | | | | | | | | |
| Michigan Female Seminary | | | | | | | | | | | | | |
| Michigan Military Academy | 100 00 | 2 50 | | 85 00 | 5,000 00 | 3,200 00 | | | 15,300 00 | 50,000 00 | | 3,200 00 | 25,000 00 |
| Nazareth Academy | 15 00 | 2 00 | | 120 00 | | 730 90 | 171 58 | | 1,120 25 | 10,000 00 | | 2,050 05 | |
| Raisin Valley Seminary | 30 00 | 2 50 | | 90 | 185 50 | 3,400 00 | 14,974 70 | | | 94,570 00 | | 14,203 75 | |
| St. Mary's Academy | 60 00 | 1 20 | | | 52,000 00 | 3,600 00 | 52,000 00 | | | 52,000 00 | | 17,203 75 | |
| Seminary of the Felician Sisters | | | | | | | | | | | | 52,000 00 | |
| Sisters of the Order of St. Dominic | 100 00 | 2 00 | | 110 00 | 560 95 | 1,927 00 | 1,170 00 | | 5,000 00 | 12,000 00 | | 2,000 00 | 400 00 |
| Spring Arbor Seminary | 24 00 | 1 75 | | | | 1,200 00 | 400 00 | 250 00 | | 10,000 00 | | 1,500 00 | |
| St. Mary's School | | | | | | | | | | | | | |
| Theological School Christian Reformed Church | 25 00 | 3 00 | | 200 00 | 600 00 | 1,350 00 | 7,000 00 | 350 00 | 7,000 00 | 30,000 00 | 7,000 00 | 7,000 00 | 5,300 00 |
| Ursuline Academy | 5 00 | 3 00 | | 125 00 | 100 00 | 700 00 | 100 00 | | | 15,000 00 | | 600 00 | |
| *Professional Schools:* | | | | | | | | | | | | | |
| Detroit College of Law | 50 00 | 2 75 | | 90 00 | 1,000 00 | 7,193 46 | | | 27,000 00 | 105,336 61 | | 6,964 55 | 40,000 00 |
| Detroit College of Medicine | 100 00 | | | | 1,545 70 | 27,251 00 | 5,421 92 | | | 60,000 00 | | 31,571 59 | |
| Detroit Homeopathic College | 45 00 | 4 00 | | | 1,304 78 | 5,290 00 | 350 00 | | | 31,290 57 | | 2,000 00 | |
| Grand Rapids Medical College | | | | | | | | | | | | | |
| Michigan College of Medicine and Surgery | 80 00 | 4 50 | | 245 00 | 727 00 | 6,560 45 | 11,200 00 | 200 00 | 5,000 00 | 50,000 00 | | 10,200 00 | 10,500 00 |
| Saginaw Valley Medical College | 90 00 | 3 25 | | 210 00 | | | | | | 40,000 00 | | 4,584 00 | |
| Sprague Correspondence School of Law | 30 | | | 68 50 | | 22,985 50 | 14,065 39 | | | | | 32,419 00 | |
| *Schools with Normal and Business Courses:* | | | | | | | | | | | | | |
| Bay City Business College | 60 00 | 2 75 | | 200 00 | 500 00 | 3,180 87 | 494 34 | | | †3,300 00 | | 2,353 35 | |
| Benton Harbor College | 32 00 | 2 50 | | 125 00 | | 6,400 00 | | | | 60,000 00 | | 3,940 00 | |
| Cleary's Business College | | | | | | | | | | | | | |
| Fenton Normal School and Commercial College | 35 00 | 2 00 | | 150 00 | 1,000 00 | 6,083 38 | | | 6,000 00 | 6,000 00 | | 257 50 | 8,500 00 |
| Ferris Industrial School | 37 50 | 2 00 | | | 750 00 | 17,500 00 | | | 35,000 00 | 35,000 00 | | 13,000 00 | |
| Grand Rapids Business University | 60 00 | 3 50 | | 75 00 | 300 00 | 3,622 08 | 408 14 | | | 2,300 00 | | 3,580 73 | 1,000 00 |
| International Business College | 75 00 | 2 75 | | 275 00 | 152 50 | 3,514 00 | 347 41 | | | 1,150 00 | | 1,850 00 | |
| Lansing Business University | 85 50 | 2 50 | | 225 00 | 25 00 | 1,682 50 | 75 00 | | | 2,500 00 | | 1,500 00 | 500 00 |
| Ludington Business College | 98 00 | 2 50 | | | | 1,109 28 | | | | | | 600 00 | |
| Michigan Business and Normal College Company | 65 00 | 3 00 | | 223 50 | 565 00 | 4,463 96 | | | | 3,000 00 | | 3,525 40 | 1,000 00 |
| Three Rivers Business Academy and normal School | 24 00 | 2 50 | | 124 00 | 600 00 | 600 00 | 384 00 | | | 8,000 00 | | 1,000 00 | 1,800 00 |

* Non-resident students.
† Value of library and apparatus. Buildings ren ed.
‡ Including room.

# INDEX.

31